MINERVA SERIES OF STUDENTS' HANDBOOKS

No. 26

General Editor

BRIAN CHAPMAN

Professor of Government
University of Manchester

AN INTRODUCTION TO INDUSTRIAL ECONOMICS

Third Edition

The Minerva Series of Students' Handbooks

AN INTRODUCTION TO INDUSTRIAL ECONOMICS

BY

P. J. DEVINE
University of Manchester

N. LEE
University of Manchester

R. M. JONES
Polytechnic of Manchester

W. J. TYSON
University of Manchester

Third Edition

London
GEORGE ALLEN & UNWIN
Boston   Sydney

FIRST PUBLISHED IN 1979

George Allen & Unwin Ltd
40 Museum Street, London WC1A 1LU

British Library Cataloguing in Publication Data

An introduction to industrial economics. – 3rd ed.
– (Minerva series of students handbooks; no.26).
1. Industrial organization (Economic theory)
I. Devine, J II. Series
338   HD2326

ISBN 0-04-338086-7
ISBN 0-04-338087-5 Pbk

Photoset in 'Monophoto' Times by Northampton Phototypesetters Ltd
and printed in Great Britain by
McCorquodale (Newton) Ltd., Newton-le-Willows, Lancashire.

Preface to the First Edition

Industrial economics is commonly regarded as one of the more descriptive branches of economics, having a tenuous and uneasy relationship with neo-classical microeconomic theory. The false dichotomy between description and theory that is implicit in this kind of distinction has become more apparent with increased attention to new forms of theorising based upon behavioural and institutional assumptions borrowed from industrial economics and the increased use in both subject areas of econometric methods of hypothesis testing. It therefore seemed that a synthetic review of the economic analysis of industrial behaviour, which drew upon both these traditions, was needed.

The book is intended to serve this purpose. It is written for students who have previously studied economic theory at first-year university level or its equivalent, but it does not presume any prior knowledge of industrial economics as such. It is intended for the critical reader who wishes to know the present state of knowledge in the subject and to have its principal weaknesses exposed.

It starts with an historical and analytical review of the scope and method of industrial economics. This is followed by a chapter on the industrial and market environments within which firms operate. It contains a review of the methods that have been used to measure the structural features of these environments. Chapters 3–5 relate to the individual firm, the first examining the static concept of the firm and the second two analysing the firm in more dynamic terms as an organism growing by means of diversification, merger and innovative activities. Chapters 6 and 7 are concerned with two important areas of decision making – marketing and investment – and review both theoretical models and empirical studies to illuminate such behaviour. Chapter 8 provides an introduction to the remaining three chapters in the book by examining the theoretical and empirical problems arising in the measurement of business performance. Chapters 9 and 10 contain a survey and critique of government industrial policy and of its effect on private and publicly owned industry. The book ends with an examination of government locational and regional policy and its impact on industry.

The authorship of each of these chapters is shown in the Contents. While there has been a great deal of collaboration in the preparation of the book, each contributor's responsibility is limited to the particular chapters of which he is an author. In conclusion, we wish to express our appreciation to our colleagues in the Economics Department of the University of Manchester for their advice and encouragement although absolving them from responsibility for any errors that remain.

P. J. D.   N. L.   R. M. J.   W. J. T.

Preface to the Third Edition

The structure and purpose of this edition are the same as those of the two previous editions, but due to developments in the subject all chapters except the first have been extensively revised. In part this takes the form of new theoretical and empirical material, relating primarily to the UK situation, on topics already included in the earlier editions. However, a number of new topics have also been introduced, which include: structure–performance models (Chapter 2), the labour-managed firm (Chapter 3), the determinants of advertising activity (Chapter 6), growth accounting and X-efficiency (Chapter 8), governmental industrial policy (Chapter 9), industrial location and urban area problems (Chapter 11), and the impact of regional policies (Chapter 11). Each chapter now concludes with brief guidance on further reading, followed by more detailed notes and references that cross-refer to the text.

As in previous editions, there has been a great deal of collaboration in the preparation of this book, but each contributor's responsibility is limited to the particular chapters of which he is an author, as indicated in the Contents.

P. J. D.
N. L.
R. M. J.
W. J. T.

October 1978
University of Manchester

Contents

1 Scope and Method of Industrial Economics

1.1 INTRODUCTION

Although the study of industry by economists is as old as the study of economics itself,[1] the term 'industrial economics' is of quite recent origin. It appears to have crept into the literature in the early 1950s via the writings of Andrews.[2] Prior to this the economic analysis of industry was not recognised as a distinctive branch of economics in many quarters, and where it was, it was given a variety of different names, 'economics of industry', 'industry and trade', 'business economics', 'commerce' and 'industrial organisation' being the ones most frequently encountered. 'Industrial organisation' is still a commonly used term in the United States.

The absence of any generally accepted name for this area of economics is indicative of a lack of consensus not only as to the range of the subject but also as to its objectives and methodology. The editorial introduction to the American Economic Association's *Readings in Industrial Organisation and Public Policy,* published in 1958, indicates that at that time:

> . . . the field of industrial organisation and public policy has neither a well-defined content nor precise boundaries. Some [graduate] courses emphasize the organisation and characteristics of industrial markets in general and of some markets in particular. Others are designed to show the relationship between industrial markets and price theory and to modify and extend that theory in the light of the facts of industrial organisation. Still others are concerned primarily with public policy issues, with little attention given to an analysis of market organisation or price theory.[3]

A survey some ten years later of researchers and teachers in this field has drawn very similar conclusions: 'The diversity [of replies] supports the view that industrial organisation is not a clearly defined, homogeneous entity . . . The field continues to be broadly eclectic and evolving.'[4]

The reasons for this absence of a consensus lie in the historical development of the economic analysis of industrial and business behaviour and cannot be properly understood without reference to it. This is the subject of section 1.2. Arising from this historical account it is possible to identify a number of areas of current controversy in the subject of industrial economics, principally related to the objectives, units of analysis and methods of the subject. These are discussed in sections 1.3–1.5. In section 1.5 a basis is outlined for reaching a consensus on the objectives, scope and methodology of industrial economics that permits its closer integration into the mainstream of economic analysis. A short review of data sources, their methods of collection and their use in industrial economics is contained in an appendix to this chapter.

1.2 ANTECEDENTS OF INDUSTRIAL ECONOMICS

Central to the explanation of the historical development of the economic analysis of industrial activity is the methodological division that existed between the mainstreams of English economic thought and the Historical and Institutional Schools during the late nineteenth and early twentieth centuries.[5] The former is evident in the writings of J. S. Mill, Jevons and the mathematical economists at the turn of the century, finding its clearest exposition in Robbins's *An Essay on the Nature and Significance of Economic Science*.[6] It has been characterised by the acceptance of certain behavioural assumptions about individual consumers and firms, which were believed to be of widespread applicability, economic analysis taking the form of searching out the logical implications of these behaviour patterns when confronted by resource scarcity. This form of analysis readily lent itself to generalised theorising and to the use of mathematical tools in relatively long and complex chains of reasoning. It also necessarily involved a high degree of abstraction from the events of the real world to enable this degree of generalisation to be achieved.

The Historical School, which initially developed in Germany, questioned the assumed universality of the behavioural assumptions and the mode of operation of economic forces that was central to the economic analysis of the English School. Rather, its members argued, these differed significantly from one country to another and from one period of time to another because they were conditioned by the institutions that existed within a country at any given point in time.

Three important inferences for economic analysis were derived from this basic institutional premise:

(1) Economic analysis should be based upon empirical investigations designed to establish the nature of the existing institutional framework and the manner in which it conditions the operation of economic forces. In this sense theory and analysis are not absolute or universal but relative to the institutional framework through which they operate.
(2) Since institutions evolve over a period of time they are conditioned by environments that may no longer exist. Therefore, a proper understanding of their nature and the way in which they may subsequently alter involves a study of their historical development.
(3) Institutions should not be treated as given in economic analysis, i.e. as unchanging and unchangeable constraints; rather they should be treated as capable of modification where in their existing forms they hamper the operation of economic forces in achieving desired objectives.

Not all economists within the Historical School placed equal emphasis on each of these three inferences. For some the first of these three points was the most important, and when pushed to its logical limit this became a methodological plea for inductive empiricism. The second inference led to an emphasis upon the study of the operation of economic forces through economic history. In certain cases this developed further into an investigation for lessons or 'laws' in history concerning the evolution of institutions, which could then be regarded as fundamental forces operating on the nature and form of economic activity. The third inference introduced a new radical tone into economic analysis.

During the 1880s a number of German economists emigrated to the United States. Prior to that date American economics had mainly fallen under the influence of the English tradition; but thereafter, especially through the Institutional School, the influence of the Historical School became quite strong. Its main protagonists were Wesley Mitchell, Thorstein Veblen and, later, J. R. Commons. The movement was instrumental in the establishment of the American Economic Association and exercised a significant influence on its early history, especially in its advocacy of institutional change.[7, 8] The influence of this type of thinking subsequently reached Britain via both Germany and the United States, but its impact was considerably less than in those two countries. However, in one area of economics its influence was significant – the area subsequently called 'industrial economics'.

The methodological differences referred to above were taking place during the period while Marshall was at Cambridge. In tracing their influence on the work of English economists it is natural to start with their influence on his writings. The view has been expressed that Marshall's contribution to economic analysis was to reconcile divergent schools of thought. While limiting his contribution to that of a synthesiser is clearly a disservice to him, nonetheless a distinctive feature of his writings was his ability to draw upon and integrate methods of economic analysis that were apparently in open conflict with each other.[9] This is true both of his *Principles of Economics*[10] and even more so of his *Industry and Trade*,[65] which may be regarded as one of the early textbooks in industrial economics. In particular his ability to acknowledge the contributions of the Historical School and the institutionalists and to graft these on to the English tradition is very apparent in the following extracts from his writings:

> For the sake of simplicity of argument, Ricardo and his followers often spoke as though they regarded man as a constant quality, and they never gave themselves enough trouble to study his variations . . . They were aware that the inhabitants of other countries had peculiarities of their own that deserved study but they seemed to regard such differences as superficial and sure to be removed, as soon as other nations had got to know that better way which Englishmen were ready to teach them . . . But their most vital fault was that they did not see how liable to change are the habits and institutions of industry.[10]

The acceptance of this view led in turn to a considerable emphasis on empirical studies:

> . . . though no one life will reach out to a study in detail of the tactics of every fight which man has waged with his economic difficulties; yet no study of the broad problems of economic strategy is likely to be worth much unless it is combined with an intimate knowledge of the tactics as well as the strategy of man's struggles against his difficulties in some particular age and country . . .

the direct and formal study of facts, perhaps mainly those of his own age, will much exceed the study of mere analysis and 'theory', in its demands on the time of any serious economist.[11]

Marshall, however, was not an indiscriminate empiricist who believed in collecting factual information for its own sake. His methods provided for the interplay between induction and deduction, the one complementing and re-inforcing the other:

> Induction, aided by analysis and deduction, brings together appropriate classes of facts, arranges them, analyses them and infers from them general statements or laws. Then for a while deduction plays the chief role: it brings some of these generalisations into association with one another, works from them tentatively to new and broader generalisations or laws and then calls on induction again to do the main share of the work in collecting, sifting and arranging these facts so as to test and 'verify' the new law.[12]

While Marshall in his own work integrated the methods of analysis originating from divergent schools of thought, this was not equally true of many of his contemporaries or successors. The most important illustration of this has been the development of microeconomic theory within the received English tradition separate from, and often in conflict with, industrial economics with its strongly institutional antecedents. The reasons for this separate development are not fully known, but two possible explanations merit consideration apart from the obvious divisive influence of doctrinaire adherence to particular schools of economic thinking.

The first explanation is that the synthesised method of study outlined by Marshall demands a wide range of different *kinds* of skill that may not be easily mastered by one person. This point has been emphasised by Jevons[13] and more recently by Koopmans:

> The task of linking concepts with observations demands a great deal of detailed knowledge of the realities of economic life as well as of processes of measurement. On the other hand the reasoning from postulates to conclusions, and the appraisal of the postulates with regard to their suitability as a basis for reasoning, increasingly demands logical and mathematical skills not often found united in the persons most suited for the first category of tasks. The testing of conclusions, besides requiring the skills involved in aligning con-cepts and phenomena, also depends in many cases on the handling of subtle procedures of statistical inference.[14]

One 'solution' to this problem is to seek refuge in the division of labour, and this was certainly accepted by Jevons, who advocated the breakup of the science into separate branches or even separate sciences. The practice of specialisation, however, has its disadvantages, and these are most pronounced, as we shall see, where there is no effective provision for the co-ordination of the specialist activities and for sufficient interplay between them.

A second feature that may have contributed to the divorce of these two approaches concerns the relationship between the development of economics in the university curriculum and the vocational requirements of business education. During the 1960s and 1970s business schools and postgraduate courses in management education have been established at a number of universities with official encouragement, on the grounds that Britain's unsatisfactory economic performance has been partly attributable to inadequate senior-management education, especially in comparison with the United States and certain Western European countries. It is interesting to observe that precisely the same views were being expressed at the turn of the century and were to varying degrees responsible for the establishment of new economics faculties or degree courses at a large number of universities, including Birmingham, Cambridge, the London School of Economics and Manchester.[15-17] In each of these cases industrial firms contributed to their finances and expected there to be some vocational element in the courses provided. In most instances the universities concerned were careful to avoid any commitment to a narrowly defined form of vocational training, and as the years proceeded the strength of this particular influence tended to diminish. Nevertheless, it gave a significant impetus to the study of industrial and business behaviour within economic faculties, and in certain instances some degree of identification with vocational training may have contributed to its separation from the mainstream development in microeconomic theory.

One of the clearest examples of this development is shown in the work and writings of Sir William Ashley. While at Oxford as an undergraduate in the 1880s Ashley came under the influence of the Historical School through Leslie, Toynbee (his one-time tutor) and Ingram. In his inaugural lecture on his appointment to the Chair of Political Economy and Constitutional History at Toronto in 1888 he stated the methodological standpoint currently taken by many of the younger economists, including himself:

> . . . a Political Economy is possible which shall be of real value to society, in it the old doctrines will be shown to be not untrue, but to have only a relative truth, and to deserve a much less important place than has been assigned to them; and the direction for fruitful work is no longer in the pursuit of the abstractive deductive method which has done as much service as it is capable of but in following new methods of investigation – historical, statistical, inductive . . .[17]

After leaving Toronto he held a position at Harvard for ten years before being invited in 1901 to take the post of Professor at the newly created Faculty of Commerce at Birmingham University. He brought an institutional view of economics into a faculty established in the belief that it had a contribution to make in business education. His views were most clearly reflected in the emphasis that he gave to 'business economics' in contrast to the more firmly established 'political economy'.[18] Business economics, in his view, consisted of two elements. The first element was mainly descriptive and aimed to provide the businessman with a survey of the industrial and commercial organisations of his own country and of the other major countries with which he might come in contact. It would examine their natural resources, leading industries, lines of traffic, supplies of capital, labour forces, methods of trade and commercial policy. The second component of business economics related to business policy and decision making, covering such matters as pricing, location, finance, labour and commercial relations.

The longer term influence of Ashley on the advancement of the economic analysis of business and industrial behaviour is difficult to measure. In part his influence lay in the development of what would now be regarded as managerial economics – the multidisciplinary study of business decision making. On the other hand, a number of later industrial economists of prominence, such as Allen,[19] were ex-students of Ashley and to some degree were obviously influenced by his mode of thinking.

Quite separately other developments in the mainstream of microeconomic theory were taking place. With the systemisation of the perfect competition model based upon marginal analysis a fundamental inconsistency came to light. If increasing returns were prevalent in industry, how could an equilibrium position that satisfied the conditions of the perfect competition model be achieved at the individual firm level?[20] The answer, developed separately by Joan Robinson[21] and E. H. Chamberlin,[22] took the form of the downward-sloping individual firm's demand curve. While the initiative to this theoretical development was partially empirical, i.e. the observed phenomenon of increasing returns, the response to this initiative was essentially within the mainstream English tradition of economic analysis in general and of marginalism in particular.

The reaction of these developments on the 'institutional' analysis of industry is difficult to gauge. P. W. S. Andrews regarded them as retrograde influences, which deflected attention away from the industry to the individual firm.[23] Others believed that the publication of Chamberlin's work acted as a considerable stimulus to both empirical and theoretical work in the United States during the 1930s,[24] although this was almost certainly in part due to the contemporaneous publication of a related empirical study by Berle and Means.[25] The first courses in industrial organisation were started at Harvard in the early 1930s under Chamberlin and Mason. The influence of Chamberlin's work is evident in the early attention that these courses gave to the definition and classification of more realistic market structures. One of the early Harvard PhD students to work within this framework was J. S. Bain, who was later to play an important role in the development and popularisation of the market structure–conduct–performance paradigm in industrial economics.[4]

However, despite this the gulf between 'institutional' and 'mainstream' methods of economic analysis remained largely intact throughout the 1930s and 1940s. Its extent was made apparent by the furore following the publication of the results of an empirical inquiry into the pricing practices of business by the Oxford Economists' Research Group.[26] The details of this controversy so far as they relate to pricing theory are discussed in Chapter 6, and this section limits its attention to the controversy's historical and methodological significance. The controversy arose, not merely because the Oxford Economists *appeared* to be questioning the validity of the marginalist principles underlying received price theory, but because at a more fundamental level it was a debate about the validity of inductive empiricism and the particular methods of empirical investigation and interpretation used by them. These methodological issues are very evident in the writings of Machlup[27] – one of the principal defendants of marginalism. They remain as issues today, although probably in a more muted form than previously.

Nevertheless, there is some indication that during the 1960s and 1970s this gulf has been narrowing, due mainly to two factors. First, there has been a growing awareness among empirical researchers, partly arising from the Hall–Hitch controversy,[26] of the need to explore the wider implications of their findings for economic analysis and to become more explicitly involved in the process of theory formulation. This has been one of the formative influences on and through the *Journal of Industrial Economics*, established in 1952, as its editor, Andrews, has indicated:

> Economics needs a workable theory of the behaviour of the individual business. I venture to suggest that this approach will only be found through empirical work on actual businesses . . . If we wish to theorize fruitfully about individual businesses, we must find out what are the facts about their behaviour and then construct a general theory especially in order to take account of those facts.[28]

Bain has adopted a similar position:

> Although I have depended strongly upon received economic theory for concepts and hypotheses . . . the present work is definitely not one in *a priori* price theory. The emphasis is directly on empirical study concerning issues raised by such theory, or on the implementation, application and critical testing of such theory.[29]

Second, during the 1960s and 1970s there has been a new emphasis placed on the formal empirical testing of hypotheses as a means of establishing that theories are 'acceptable'. While there are dangers in the indiscriminate use of these testing techniques, which are discussed later, they do have the beneficial side effect of helping to bring these two divergent schools of thinking closer together. On the one hand, this new emphasis is leading economists working in the mainstream of microeconomic theory to enter certain of the traditional areas of empirical research within industrial economics. On the other, it is forcing the traditional industrial economist to clarify the *objectives* of his empirical research and to subject his *techniques* of investigation to more critical analysis.

The environment is therefore more favourable for an integration of industrial economics within a modified mainstream of microeconomic analysis. To indicate how this may be possible it is necessary to terminate this historical account and turn attention to the objectives and methods of industrial economics.

1.3 OBJECTIVES IN INDUSTRIAL ECONOMICS

Part of the confusion that has arisen over appropriate methods for the economic analysis of industry has occurred through a failure to specify clearly the objectives of the analysis. The specification of the objectives of a study is the logical starting point from which to derive the appropriate method of investigation to achieve that objective. Similarly, the use of differing and conflicting methodologies within a subject *may* arise from the implicit acceptance of differing and conflicting objectives of investigation.

THE BROAD OBJECTIVES OF INDUSTRIAL ECONOMICS AND TRADITIONAL MICROECONOMICS

The broad objective of industrial economics, as described in the previous section, is the development of satisfactory explanations of the ways in which economic forces operate within the industrial sector. This is really identical to the broad objective of microeconomic theory: an analysis of the manner in which the industrial sector responds to the conditions of scarcity. Differences between their more particularised objectives should not conceal the broad unity of purpose between these two types of study.[30]

A second popular misconception is that industrial economics forms part of applied economics, in contrast to received microeconomic theory, which is treated as a branch of theoretical economics. This confusion arises from identifying empirical investigation with applied economics and from identifying processes of logical deduction from generalised premises with economic theorising. As the references to Andrews[28] and Bain[29] have already indicated, empirical investigations in industrial economics now place the development and refinement of economic theory among their principal objectives. In addition the ultimate purpose of theorising, by whatever method it is undertaken, is to interpret and predict in actual situations in the real world. Applied economics is the logical extension of *any* theoretical economics and is the ultimate justification for it.

Although there may exist a unity of general purpose between industrial economics and general microeconomic theory, the recognition of this common objective has often been lost under pressure from the extreme use of particular methods of study. Examples of studies can be found where the 'institutional' form of economic investigation degenerated into a form of empiricism preoccupied with the collection of factual detail *per se* and where findings were largely devoid of any economic significance. This was particularly true of some of the early studies of individual industries and in some of the 'case' studies of individual businesses. Frequently, these were heavily historical in approach, with the narrative mainly centred on the technical processes of the firm or industry and the leading managerial personalities involved. Since the early 1950s newer-style individual industry and business history studies[31] that contain a greater proportion of economic analysis have appeared. Whether they have yet fully remedied the deficiencies of their forerunners, and indeed whether this is the most fruitful manner in which to extend economic analysis in the industrial sector, remains a matter of dispute. Similarly, examples can be found within microeconomic theory where a preoccupation with the elegance of long chains of reasoning has led to the neglect of the empirical relevance of theorising.

PARTICULAR OBJECTIVES IN INDUSTRIAL ECONOMICS AND THE
CONFLICT BETWEEN REALISM AND GENERALITY

In the process of examining these extremes in methods of study it has become appreciated that, whilst the two approaches (traditionally associated with industrial economics and microeconomic theory) may share the same *broad* objective, they may be pursuing different objectives at the *particularised* level. For example, it has been suggested that traditional microeconomic theory is aiming to make broader analyses and predictions than those with which industrial economists have been concerned.[32]

While this type of argument can easily be misused as an *ex post* rationalisation for a particular methodological standpoint, it does help to clarify a number of the disputes concerning realism and generality in theorising. In the first place the *type* of theory of the firm required depends upon the dimensions of business behaviour and the time period to which the analysis is to relate. Long-term price movements conceivably may be adequately analysed using a marginalist theory of the firm, but such a theoretical framework may be regarded as inadequate for analysing stockbuilding or innovatory activity. Second, the suitability of a particular theory also turns upon the degree of accuracy required from its predictions, one type of theory possibly being acceptable at one level of accuracy but being unsuitable at a more exacting level.

These two points can be illustrated from Machlup's defence of the marginalist theory of the firm. He has suggested that a theory of the firm may be required for a variety of different purposes but that, for the purpose for which (in his opinion) it is mainly intended, it is sufficient that the theory should accurately predict in *qualitative* terms the direction of price changes over a longish period of time. He would concede that the marginalist theory may be quite inappropriate for other purposes, for which a less general kind of theory may be more suitable.[33] Cyert and March have indicated four uses to which a theory of the firm may be put, suggesting that the potential contribution of their behavioural theory is much greater in respect to more specific objectives than the general objectives associated with the traditional theory of the firm.[34]

This, however, only touches half of the issue; it is a matter not only of how much realism is required to achieve a particular objective but also, as Baumol has indicated, of how much realism can be afforded in formulating objectives:

> . . . the perfectly general model, must abstract from everything or, what is very close to the same thing, take account of everything and so degenerate into a taxonomy . . . increased realism . . . usually involves a cost in decreased manipulatibility and insight into the working of our models . . . It is my plea that we follow our own good advice as economists and balance off costs against advantages in deciding on the level of generality at which we wish to operate our research.[35]

The degree of realism required in any economic analysis involves reference to the particular objective involved and the achievement of a suitable compromise between the desire to maintain reality and the desire to achieve the maximum generality in the findings. The ideal balance between the particular and the general in economic analysis will vary accordingly.

INDUSTRIAL ECONOMICS AND MANAGEMENT DISCIPLINES

The relationship between the objectives of industrial economics and those of business or managerial economics also requires clarification. Ashley used to argue that 'political economy' was principally geared to the requirements of civil servants and, therefore, placed the state in a central place in its analysis. He wished to see develop a corresponding 'business economy' approach that placed the individual firm in a similar position in the scheme of analysis and, therefore, was more closely related to the requirements of businessmen. The objective of using economic analysis, or those parts of it deemed relevant, for the vocational purpose of improving the quality of decision making in individual businesses led to the development of courses of study in business economics, later more generally called managerial economics. The following extracts from two earlier works in this field indicate the acceptance of this different type of objective:

> An attempt to extract from the general body of economic thought some parts that seem to be particularly relevant to taking decisions in business . . . In the process we have attempted to achieve a certain mixing of the ways of thought and techniques used by economists, econometricians and accountants.[36]

> The big gap between the problems of logic that intrigue economic theorists and the problems of policy that plague practical management needs to be bridged in order to give executives access to the practical contributions that economic thinking can make to top-management policies. In developing an economic approach to executive decisions, this book draws upon economic analysis for the concepts of demand, cost, profit, competition and so on, that are appropriate for the decision, and it draws upon modern methods of econometrics and market research for getting estimates of the relevant concepts.[37]

Managerial and business economics can be distinguished from industrial economics in two ways.[38] First, the majority of the writing on managerial economics starts from the assumption that the firm aims to maximise its profits, although in certain instances constrained by other objectives, and then proceeds to examine the manner in which the decision rules and procedures of the firm should be formulated in order to achieve its stated objective. The interests of industrial economics, however, are positive rather than normative. The main emphasis is placed upon understanding and explaining the working of existing systems and thereby being able to predict the effect of changes in variables within that system: 'Above all, as a branch of social science, industrial economics will be interested in what actually happens as distinct from what should happen in hypothetical or ideal circumstances.'[28] While there is this important difference in approach, these two types of study are related. If managerial economics is based upon untenable assumptions about the objectives of firms, the constraints built into their decision-making processes or the economic environment in which they operate, its findings will be likely in the long run to be as 'impractical' for businessmen as the traditional approach to economic analysis that it claims to supersede. The future development of managerial economics, therefore, partly depends upon further advances in industrial economics.

Second, managerial economics is interdisciplinary in a way and to a degree that does not apply to industrial economics, although other social science disciplines do have a contribution to make to the study of industrial economics. As the two quotations above indicate, disciplines additional to economic analysis may have a contribution to make in 'optimal' decision making within the firm. Accountancy, operations research and market research have most frequently been mentioned in this context. During the 1960s and 1970s there has been increasing recognition of the contribution that these other disciplines may make, and as a consequence the relative importance of economic analysis, as traditionally conceived, within managerial economics has tended to decline. Because of the multidisciplinary nature of the subject it is most usefully studied *after* a preliminary study of the main disciplines, including industrial economics, upon which it draws. The dangers of organising a study of business *immediately* around practical vocational interests have been expressed by Marshall as follows:

> . . . though we are bound, before entering on any study, to consider carefully what are its uses, we should not plan out our work with direct reference to them. For by so doing we are tempted to break off each line of thought as soon as it ceases to have an immediate bearing on that particular aim which we have in view at the time: the direct pursuit of practical aims leads us to group together bits of all sorts of knowledge, which have no connection with one another except for the immediate purposes of the moment; and which throw but little light on one another.[39]

1.4 FIRMS, INDUSTRIES AND MARKETS

In the one-product perfect-competition market model the relationship between firm, industry and market is relatively straightforward. Firms belonging to the same industry all produce a single identical product, which they sell in the same market. Therefore, the industry and the market are effectively identical since each contains the same group of small firms either as producers or sellers.

However, as described more fully in Chapter 2, this neat symmetry does not exist in more realistic market situations. Many firms are large and multiproduct and, therefore, produce in more than one industry and sell in more than one market. Each industry, as conventionally understood, produces a range of different products, many of which are not close substitutes and which are sold in a variety of different markets. Industry and market are therefore rarely coterminous.

A great deal of debate has taken place as to the most appropriate unit for analysis in an economic study of industry – industry, market or firm – and so far the controversy has not been finally resolved. The claims and limitations of each are therefore now examined.

The industry, as conventionally understood, is the longest established of these three units of analysis. The industry has always been a meaningful institutional unit to employers (in trade and employers' associations), to employees (in trade unions and collective-bargaining machinery) and to the government (in legislation and the publication of official statistics). Although the definitional boundaries of each industry may be disputed between the interested parties, it has served as a useful framework within which industrial problems can be identified, statistical data collected and analysed, and possible remedies proposed. On this basis many studies of individual industries, e.g. coal mining, steel and transport, have been undertaken. However, as previously mentioned, the early industry studies of the twentieth century were heavily descriptive in nature, including considerable attention to the nature of products produced, the techniques of production employed, the historical development of the industries and their institutional arrangements.[19, 31] Economic analysis played a relatively minor role in them.

The development of theories of imperfect competition by Chamberlin[22] and Robinson[21] in the early 1930s focused attention upon the structure of markets, rather than of industries, as determinants of business and industrial behaviour. This led, by analogy with the perfect-competition market model, to the notion that both the business conduct and the business performance of firms are dependent upon the structure of the markets in which they sell. This gave rise to the market structure–market conduct–market performance paradigm, which began to develop in the 1930s but probably reached its peak during the 1960s after the publication of Bain's major work on industrial organisation in 1959.[29] As a consequence the role of economic analysis greatly increased in industrial studies. Studies of individual industries were still made, but their relative importance diminished, and increasingly they came to incorporate the market structure–conduct–performance framework in their own investigations.[31]

The market-based studies, however, have also had their critics, and the volume of criticism has grown considerably during the late 1960s and 1970s. The main source of concern is that the structure–conduct–performance paradigm may provide a far less suitable analytical framework for large diversified enterprises, whose importance has greatly increased in the last forty years, than for small firms assumed to operate under perfect or near-perfect market conditions. The behaviour and performance of small firms may be strongly influenced by the exogenously determined structure of the market in which they operate, but in the case of the large multiproduct firm the extent of the influence of market structure on behaviour and performance is more questionable.

The atomistic market is now a rarity (see Chapter 2); in practice many firms do possess the power to alter significantly the level of output and prices in a market. Through technical innovation, product diversification or merger firms may transform the structure of a market, or indeed of many different markets. Similarly, consumer demand for particular goods and services is more malleable than was originally appreciated, and this enables large firms to exercise an initiatory role in influencing the size and structure of the markets that they serve. Finally, the existence of market imperfections confers upon individual firms a considerable measure of discretion in the goals that they are able to pursue; profit maximisation and technical efficiency are no longer the *sine qua non* for survival. Hence, the structure–conduct–performance framework is weakened at two important points:

(1) The conduct of large firms may change market structure; that is, the assumed chain of causality is reversed.
(2) Discretion in the formation of business goals further weakens the dependence of market performance upon market structure.

The issue has been summarised by Grether in the following terms:

The crux of the matter is whether the market structure framework can be used at all [in analysing the large diversified corporation]; in other words is it relevant? If such large corporations are free of the market, as some allege, it would seem futile to try to analyse their behaviour and performance results in a market structure framework. The focus of research then should be on internal organisation, policies and strategies, and their performance results. Orientation should then be from performance results back into internal organisation and decision-making. But if there is a significant amount of market determination and constraint, even if only for a period of time under given structural characteristics, it would seem reasonable to use the market structure framework of analysis.[4]

A second source of concern with market-based studies, which is related to the first concern, is that the market may provide too narrow a framework for the analysis of certain types of business behaviour. In studies of collusive behaviour, of innovatory activity and of responses to changes in government policy it may be that the broader 'industry' concept, based upon an institutional or statutory reality, is more helpful than a 'market' framework. Similarly, the influence of potential competition on longer-term business behaviour may be better analysed using the broader industrial framework:

... an individual business must be conceived as operating within an 'industry' which consists of all businesses which operate processes of a sufficiently similar kind ... and possessing sufficiently similar backgrounds of experience and knowledge so that each of them could produce the particular commodity under consideration, and would do so if sufficiently attractive.[66]

The general conclusion that suggests itself is that both 'market' and 'industry', and 'market' and 'firm', should be viewed as complementary rather than as competitive concepts in industrial analysis, as illustrated below:

The more interesting, more complex and important, and more exciting issues arise out of (1) the synergistic relations among the internal product lines, subsidiaries, and so forth, of the large diversified corporation and (2) the continuing interactions between internal firm organisation policies and practices and market structures. Careful detailed studies are needed of individual corporations, in which internal organisation and policies at a given time and over periods of time are related to market structures and structural changes with the clear awareness that the successful, well-managed corporation will use its discretionary power to optimise both synergistic effects and favourable market structure factors.[4]

At first, attention will be concentrated upon all commodities with very similar technical specifications, sold in circumstances entailing that similar services are rendered to the customer. Thus we may consider the producers of fractional horse-power motors or the producers of fitting shoes. This narrower definition of an industry will include all the businesses which are in most active competition with one another on any short-run analysis. But, studying the way in which competition actually emerges, we become aware of the significance of a much more widely drawn boundary to that industry – to include all those who possess such facilities, etc. that they could well turn over to the production of our narrowly-defined product in a rather longer run . . . Our analysis then runs in very broad terms: 'The boot and shoe industry,' 'electrical engineering,' even, on occasion, 'the leather and footwear industry' or 'engineering.'[66]

1.5 METHODOLOGY: THE SEARCH FOR A SYNTHESIS

At the conclusion to section 1.2 it is suggested that a reintegration of industrial economics within a modified mainstream of microeconomic analysis may be possible. In order to consider how this might take place the streams of thinking that would be involved in any such synthesis are first examined.

INDUCTIVE EMPIRICISM

This is the methodological approach with which industrial economics has had the greatest affinity in the past because of its previous links with the Historical and Institutional Schools. At the extreme the case for empiricism is based upon a denial of the existence of regularities in economic phenomena; in other words, the economic system can never be law abiding. Alternatively, where the existence of regularities is acknowledged it may be claimed that these can only be discerned by detailed empirical investigation. Using this approach data are collected in increasing quantity, within a prescribed area, until patterns of connection are observable and a generalisation can be established. In certain instances the empirical investigation is supposed to be undertaken without any particular hypothesis in mind since this might bias the process of collection and interpretation of the data. In other cases the investigation is viewed as an attempt to verify a hypothesis or the limits within which a relationship is supposed to hold.

The case study approach, which has been frequently used in industrial economics, has often been based upon the assumption either that it is impossible to generalise meaningfully about industrial behaviour or, in the less extreme cases, that it is only possible to generalise with any confidence *after* completing a detailed empirical investigation of the component elements to which the generalisation is supposed to apply. While this viewpoint has a good deal of intuitive appeal it also has its shortcomings. First, the gathering of data without any clear hypothesis in mind creates very great difficulties in determining which data to collect. Without such guidance one of two things is likely to happen; either an unmanageable quantity of data is acquired at great cost in time and effort, or some informal, i.e. unsystematic, selection procedure is used. The former is likely to yield no meaningful results at all; the latter may be (unjustifiably) used to confirm the implicit hypothesis accepted by the investigator. These dangers are magnified where the sample investigated is small relative to the size of the population and non-random in nature. Furthermore, where the phenomena under investigation are complex, i.e. where multicausal relationships exist, it is frequently difficult to establish the chains of causality, using the inductive approach, by observational or statistical means.

These limitations, it has been felt, preclude the exclusive use of inductive methods in the economic analysis of industrial behaviour, although induction has an important role to play in an enlarged methodology in industrial economics.

A PRIORI REASONING

For an *a posteriori* argument depending entirely upon the examination of concrete facts in all the complexity of their actual presentation is substituted an *a priori* argument depending upon knowledge of the general characteristics displayed by men in their economic dealings one with another.[40]

The nature of the *a priori* method has been expressed in the following terms by Robbins:

The analytic *(i.e. a priori)* method is simply a way of discovering the necessary consequences of complex collocations of facts – consequences whose counterpart in reality is not so immediately discernible as the counterpart of the original postulates. It is an instrument for 'shaking out' all the implications of given suppositions. Granted the correspondence of its original assumptions and the facts, its conclusions are inevitable and inescapable.[41]

In the extreme formulation of the *a priori* method the assumptions or postulates are regarded as self-evident and widely accepted truisms, which, therefore, do not require any form of empirical verification:

The propositions of economic theory, like all scientific theory, are obviously deductions from a series of postulates. And the chief of these postulates are all assumptions involving in some way simple and indisputable facts of experience relating to the way in which the scarcity of goods, which is the subject matter, actually shows itself in the world of reality . . . These are not postulates the existence of whose counterpart in reality admits of extensive dispute once their nature is fully realised. We do not need controlled experiments to establish their validity: they are so much the stuff of our everyday experience that they have only to be stated to be recognised as obvious.[42]

The emphasis on the *a priori* method and the self-evident nature of the postulates have had the effect of sharply delimiting the boundaries of economic analysis in a way that has been unacceptable to most empiricists, e.g. in Hutchison's following criticism of Robbins's standard definition of 'economics':

All facts . . . are excluded, for technical, social and psychological facts presumably comprise the entire possible factual material for the social scientist. Nor does Economics study economic conduct but begins just where the analysis of economic conduct leaves off, for this is 'Given' just as much as the social environment . . . What most scientists would regard as the problems they have to investigate, regularities in the facts of the world, are taken by the economist as assumptions.[43]

In fact Robbins, elsewhere in his essay, has adopted a considerably less extreme position towards empirical studies in economics.[44] Nevertheless, the extreme version of the *a priori* method has been sufficiently widely practised to tempt a number of empiricists to direct their attention towards:

(1) testing the realism of the 'self-evident' assumptions underlying received economic theory; and
(2) among the less wary, deducing that received theory is unacceptable where its assumptions can be demonstrated to be unrealistic.

At this particular point the gulf between the empiricists engaged in industrial economics and the advocates of the *a priori* method adhering to the marginalist theory of the firm is probably at its greatest:

The attempt to check the realism of the postulates led only to a methodological schism in economics: on the one hand we had those who paraded their 'Realism' – 'this is how businesses actually work' – and were indifferent to the arguments that their theory was indeterminate and therefore irrefutable; on the other hand we had those who stuck to 'rational' theory, and appeared more and more indifferent to reality (as understood by the first group).[45]

THE EMPIRICAL TESTING OF PREDICTIONS

More recently it has been contended, notably by Friedman, that the resolution of this conflict rests in the recognition that both methodologies are partially in error. On the one hand, empirical investigations have frequently been misdirected in their object; and on the other, the role of *a priori* reasoning in developing satisfactory theories has frequently been overstated:

> The ultimate goal of a positive science is the development of a 'theory' or 'hypothesis' that yields valid and meaningful (i.e. not truistic) predictions about phenomena not yet observed . . . the only relevant test of the validity of a hypothesis is a comparison of its predictions with experience. The hypothesis is rejected if its predictions are contradicted ('frequently' or more often than predictions from an alternative hypothesis); it is accepted if it has survived many opportunities for contradiction.[46]

The establishment of the validity of a hypothesis using this predictive test is not regarded as a sufficient criterion for adopting any particular hypothesis. Since more than one hypothesis may be consistent with the available data, the additional criteria of 'simplicity' and 'fruitfulness' should be applied:

> A theory is 'simpler' the less the initial knowledge needed to make a prediction within a given field of phenomena; it is more 'fruitful' the more precise the resulting prediction, the wider the area within which the theory yields prediction, and the more additional lines for further research it suggests.[46]

Whether or not the *ultimate* or only goal of economic science is prediction is discussed later in this section. Irrespective of this point the task of establishing the validity of a hypothesis by testing the empirical accuracy of its predictions can be extremely difficult. In Friedman's view this difficulty at least partly explains why erroneous methodologies have been widely adopted in place of the one that he has recommended.

On the other hand, it has fostered a misunderstanding of the role of empirical evidence in theoretical work. In particular it has led empiricists to contribution to make – in checking the correctness of reasoning, in discovering the implications of hypotheses and in determining whether supposedly different hypotheses may not really be equivalent – but in general its role has been exaggerated: 'Logical completeness and consistency are relevant but play a subsidiary role.'[46]

On the other hand, it has fostered a misunderstanding of the role of empirical evidence in theoretical work. In particular it has led empiricists to use the conformity of assumptions to reality as a test of the validity of an hypothesis different from or additional to the test of prediction. Friedman would argue that such a test is at best superfluous and at worst contrary to the development of valid hypotheses that are both simple and fruitful:

> Truly important and significant hypotheses will be found to have 'assumptions' that are wildly inaccurate descriptive representations of reality and, in general, the more significant the theory, the more unrealistic the assumptions . . . the relevant question to ask about the 'assumptions' of a theory is not whether they are descriptively 'realistic', for they never are, but whether they are sufficiently good approximations for the purpose in hand. And this question can be answered only by seeing whether the theory works,

which means whether it yields sufficiently accurate predictions. The two
supposedly independent tests thus reduce to one test.[47]

CRITICISMS OF AND REFINEMENTS TO EXISTING METHODS

The emphasis placed by Friedman on the importance of testing an hypothesis
according to the accuracy of its predictions has received considerable support
during recent years. As such it has restored the importance of empirical
investigation as an instrument of economic analysis, but in the process it has
changed its role. However, there are many who would argue that Friedman
has overstated his case. In particular, because he has not emphasised sufficiently
the difficulties that lie in the adequate empirical testing of the predictions of
hypotheses, he has failed to acknowledge sufficiently the supplementary role
that other tests, particularly as they relate to the postulates, have in the validating
of hypotheses. The major criticisms made are now considered, and these are
then taken into account in a summary of the methods of analysis believed to be
most appropriate for the type of purposes that industrial economics is expected
to serve.

First, Friedman has failed to indicate the criteria for a good test of predictions, especially where the conditions in which the hypothesis is supposed
to hold, i.e. the auxiliary assumptions,[48] are patently unrealistic. This is
substantially the issue raised by Archibald when posing the problem of how
the predictions of the received theory of the firm are to be tested: 'First, how
is any theory which is purely static to be tested at all? . . . Second, there is
the problem of the ubiquitous *ceteris paribus* clause. If the "other things" are
not specified in advance, there is an alibi for any refutation.'[49]

Second, given the difficulties that may exist in testing the predictions of an
hypothesis, Friedman's negative test of an hypothesis – that it has survived many
opportunities for refutation – is a dangerous criterion that is likely to create an
inbuilt bias in favour of long-accepted hypotheses. Klappolz and Agassi have
warned that 'the doctrine that the absence of refutation imposes a desirable degree
of confidence' in a hypothesis can be an impediment to critical argument'.[50]
Archibald has been much more explicit in accusing Friedman of discouraging
'that sceptical re-examination of the allegedly obvious that is the prerequisite of
progress':

> The age of a hypothesis and the absence of a 'widely accepted rival' are
> arguments that have been advanced in defence of practically every serious
> error ever made; hypotheses wrapped in the cotton wool and authority of
> 'tradition and folklore' most urgently require testing, the continued use of a
> hypothesis does not mean that there have been continuous tests to refute it.[51]

Third, recognition that the empirical testing of the predictions may not be as
satisfactory as may be desired has led to the suggestion that the test of the
realism of the postulates may be a useful or even necessary supplementary
test of an hypothesis:

> Before we can accept the view that obvious discrepancies between behaviour

postulates and directly observed behaviour do not affect the predictive power of specified implications of the postulates, we need to understand the reasons why these discrepancies do not matter . . . If, in comparison with some other sciences, economics is handicapped by severe and possibly insurmountable obstacles to meaningful experimentation, the opportunities for direct introspection by, and direct observation of, individual decision makers are a much needed source of evidence which in some degree offsets the handicap. We cannot really feel confident in acting upon our economic knowledge until its deductions reconcile directly observed patterns of individual behaviour with such implications for the economy as a whole as we find ourselves able to subject to test.[52]

A substantially similar point has been expressed by Rotwein: that validation of an hypothesis in the Friedman sense is not sufficient to place confidence in it. Additionally, it should satisfy the requirements of 'explanation':

Mere consistency of the formula with actual occurrences is not itself a sufficient basis for validating the theory or establishing confidence in it for purposes of further prediction. This is true because such consistency is not synonymous with 'explanation' by the assumption. 'Explanation' of an occurrence by any assumption is a function of the extent to which we may suppose that any entities denoted by the assumption are in reality associated with the event predicted so that 'unrealism' of the assumption and 'explanation' of the event are in fact mutually exclusive.[53]

Fourth, more detailed consideration of the role of assumptions in testing hypotheses has led to a number of refinements of Friedman's extreme view, based upon a classification of the types of assumption into different categories. Machlup[32] has drawn a distinction between 'fundamental' and 'other' assumptions, supporting the empirical testing of the latter but denying that 'fundamental' assumptions can be tested directly. Archibald[45] has distinguished between motivational assumptions (which he would claim cannot be tested in a reliable manner), 'empirical' assumptions relating to the existence and stability of functional relations (which should be tested and measured directly) and *ceteris paribus* assumptions (which merely delimit the area and type of analysis). This type of argument can, however, be turned upon itself: can the empirical test of the predictions of an hypothesis necessarily be undertaken more satisfactorily than the test of its behavioural assumptions? Using the following notation for three propositions:

X = Businessmen desire to maximise profits.
Y = Businessmen can and do make the calculations that identify the profit-maximising course of action.
Z = Prices and quantities are observed at those levels which maximise the profits of the firm in the market.

Simon has suggested that in the instance of the marginalist theory of the firm this is not the case:

Most critics have accepted Friedman's assumption that proposition Z is the empirically tested one, while X and Y are not directly observable. This, of course, is nonsense. No one has, in fact, observed whether the actual positions of business firms are the profit-maximising ones; nor has anyone proposed a method of testing this proposition by direct observation. I cannot imagine what such a test would be, since the tester would be as incapable as business firms are of discovering what the optimal position actually is . . . Now we do have a considerable body of evidence about X and Y, and the vast weight of evidence with respect of Y, at least, is that it is false . . . Let us make the observations necessary to discover and test true propositions, call them X^1 and Y^1, to replace the false X and Y. Then let us construct a new market theory on these firmer foundations.[54]

Possibly a more significant distinction is that made by Melitz between false and abstracted assumptions. Melitz would argue that Friedman's approval of inaccurate and unreal assumptions more properly relates to abstracted rather than false assumptions: 'abstraction facilitates the attainment of truth, and does not necessitate the acceptance of false assumptions, or immersion in "unrealism" of any sort'.[55] The distinction made is between an abridgement of the full catalogue of characteristics of the postulates and the acceptance of postulates known to be false, i.e. that do not correspond to any of the characteristics of the events to which the postulates relate. The acceptance of false 'generative' assumptions must lower the probability that any hypothesis derived from them will give rise to sufficiently accurate predictions. To this extent tests of the realism of assumptions may be important contributors in testing and appraising hypotheses and in indicating possible avenues of improvement upon them.

CONCLUSIONS ON METHODOLOGY

While an ultimate objective in economic analysis may be the formulation of hypotheses that are able to predict phenomena not yet observed, this is not the *only* important objective. To view it in this restrictive manner is likely to reinforce the inherent conservatism already noted in Friedman's methodology. The only hypotheses tested might be limited to those which have already been formulated or which can be most 'easily' formulated, taking the existing institutional framework as given. To counterbalance this tendency, at the crucial stage of identifying the significant issues for investigation and formulating hypotheses relating to them, inductive empiricism aided by *a priori* reasoning has an important role to play.

The end product of economic analysis is its application in practical situations, which are characterised by a great deal of complexity. Even though a theory, being an abstraction, may be simple in form, its successful application will frequently demand a fairly intimate knowledge of the actual situation in which it is being applied. Of the different methods of analysis considered, the inductive empirical approach is most likely to provide this intimate knowledge.

Given the importance of the ultimate objective, a hypothesis should ideally be formulated in a way that renders its predictions subject to empirical test. The criteria of a good test should be made explicit, and these will depend upon the purposes for which the tested hypothesis is to be used. In practice, however, the limitations of this method of testing give rise to the need for supplementary tests. In a number of instances, which are probably more numerous than is generally appreciated, difficulty is experienced in formulating suitable testable hypotheses, or the amount of testing that is practicable on account of data limitation is very limited. Where this type of situation exists it appears legitimate, as a supplementary test, to examine the degree of realism of the postulates of an hypothesis. The view that such a supplementary test is irrelevant to the predictive accuracy of an hypothesis is rejected.

The distinction between 'abstracted' and 'false' assumptions is useful in this connection. Abstraction is both necessary and desirable, the correct degree of abstraction being determined according to the purpose for which the hypothesis is to be used and to the 'indirect' test of the sensitivity of the quality of the predictions to abstraction in the postulates. False assumptions, however, both make the testing of predictions more difficult and increase the probability of inaccurate predictions. The test of the realism, i.e. the lack of falsity, of the assumptions, therefore, adds plausibility to the hypothesis. Such supplementary tests are also not without their difficulties. In certain circumstances the practical distinction between abstracted and false assumptions may be difficult to maintain while weaknesses can exist in the empirical derivation of postulates as well as in the empirical testing of hypotheses' predictions.

The main conclusion drawn from this review, therefore, is that an analytic method should draw upon all three approaches discussed – empirical, *a priori* and hypothesis testing – the precise blend varying according to the type of microeconomic problem being studied. Such a synthesis would draw upon the traditional methods of analysis used in both industrial economics and microeconomic theory, so that the division between these two branches of economics should cease to have relevance. It should also help to impart the unity of methodology and consensus on content that, as noted in the introduction to this chapter, has been largely missing in industrial economics.

FURTHER READING

A critical examination of Friedman's methodological position[64] should stimulate a further appreciation of the main methodological issues raised in industrial economics. An interesting short review, from an American standpoint, of the state of industrial economics is to be found in the paper by Grether[4] and the other papers and the discussion generated by them in *American Economic Review* (May 1970).[67] Readers who are insufficiently familiar with statistical sources and the methods of statistical analysis in industrial economics should consult the references contained in the following appendix on data collection and interpretation.

APPENDIX: DATA COLLECTION AND INTERPRETATION

A very important element in industrial analysis is the collection of statistical data and its use in measuring economic variables and testing economic relationships. The data requirements of industrial economics are considerable; but unfortunately, many of the types of data that are available in aggregate form at national level, for macroeconomic analysis, are for reasons of confidentiality not readily available at market or firm level, for industrial analysis. This may mean either that data that are not entirely appropriate to the type of analysis envisaged are used or that a special survey has to be undertaken to obtain the data required.

In certain cases, as illustrated in later chapters, the empirical findings on measures of particular economic variables and tests of particular economic relationships are conflicting. One possible explanation is that different sources of data have been used and that the quality of some or all of these sources is deficient. A discerning attitude towards the data sources used is therefore required. This can be developed through an appreciation of the more important sources of published statistics used in industrial economics,[56] e.g. Census of Production data[57] and accounting data relating to the performance of enterprises in the public and private sectors,[58] preferably by making use of the primary sources themselves. In addition it is advisable to have an understanding of the survey methods, e.g. questionnaires and interviews, by which additional data are acquired. Each of these methods has its own limitations, which should be appreciated in the interpretation of survey results.[59]

Industrial analysis also involves drawing inferences from the data collected, by using them to test hypotheses and to generalise the conclusions reached to a wider population. The latter draws upon sampling theory, and the former uses techniques of correlation analysis.[60-1] A second possible reason why empirical findings conflict lies in the choice or use of statistical techniques of inference. Therefore, it is advisable to have a basic understanding of the main techniques used and of the difficulties that arise in their application.

Ideally, any sample should be 'typical' of the population from which it is drawn, so that the results obtained from the sample also apply to its population. However, the sample cannot be fully typical; therefore, a method is needed to determine the margin of error where sample data are assumed to apply to a population. This margin of error can be estimated where the membership of the sample is determined on a *random* basis, i.e. where every member of the population has a calculable probability of being included in the sample.

Random sample methods, however, can be expensive to use, and less rigorous sampling techniques may be used in their place. Therefore, in evaluating any empirical study based upon sample data it is important to identify the size of the sample in relation to its population and the manner in which it was selected. Where the sample is relatively small and non-random and where observable sources of bias in its selection exist, the conclusions of the study should be limited to the sample and not extended to the population at large from which it was drawn.

A further role of statistical analysis is to infer relationships from observations of variables, to quantify the relationships wherever possible and to establish whether they are statistically significant or not. For example, statistical techniques may be used to 'test' the relationship between the number and size distribution of sellers in markets, i.e. the seller concentration, and the rates of profit that sellers obtain. Techniques of multiple regression analysis, using computer facilities, have been developed to perform this type of task.[62] Unfortunately, the complexity and sophistication of the statistical process used can result in an uncritical acceptance of its findings.

In order to counteract this tendency it is often advisable to subject regression results to examination, posing such questions as the following:

(1) Have all the plausible explanatory variables been included in the analysis? For example, profit levels may be dependent upon other factors in addition to seller concentration, and to ignore these may result in a misleading statistical relationship being established between profits and seller concentration.

(2) Have all the variables included in the analysis been defined in the most meaningful manner? Items such as 'seller concentration' and 'profit rate' can be defined in a number of different ways, and the results obtained may be sensitive to the particular definitions adopted.

(3) Can all variables be quantified? Where they cannot, less satisfactory proxy variables may be used. If this happens, care is required in the interpretation of results since the proxy variables may not adequately take account of the effects intended.

(4) Are sufficient data of the required quality available to enable a satisfactory statistical test to be made? Problems may arise because, for example, sample sizes are too small or time series data relate to too short a time period.

(5) Is the nature of the relationship between the explanatory variables and the dependent variable correctly specified? Sometimes, for the purposes of simplification, linear relationships are assumed in correlation analysis where non-linear relationships are more appropriate.

(6) Are the explanatory variables correlated with each other? Where there is a high degree of correlation between two explanatory variables included within the same regression equation, the coefficients attached to them cannot be treated as reliable.

(7) To what extent are the coefficients of the explanatory variables statistically significant, and how successful is the reported equation in explaining the observed variation in the dependent variable under examination? The value of the standard error attached to each explanatory variable's coefficient and of $\bar{R}^2$ for the reported equation as a whole is the statistical basis for making these assessments.

The emphasis up to this point has been placed upon the statistical measurement of variables and the quantification of economic relationships. Important as these are it is necessary to recognise their limits. Some variables, such as the inputs and outputs of innovative activity, cannot be measured in any direct sense, and difficulties arise in the use of indirect proxy measures. Similarly, the statistical data required to test hypotheses relating to long-term business behaviour, e.g: relating to the long term growth or decline of business enterprises, are frequently not available.

To restrict analysis to statistically measurable phenomena could impoverish studies in industrial economics by neglecting important dimensions of business behaviour and determinants of business performance. It might also inhibit the development of new and potentially richer hypotheses for empirical evaluation. Non-statistical or semi-statistical documentary sources should, therefore, not be neglected. Business histories[31] and case studies, together with official reports[63] – by such bodies as Royal Commissions, Committees of Inquiry and Select Committees and more specialised bodies like the Monopolies (and Mergers) Commission and the Restrictive Trade Practices Court – are important primary sources of data. As in the case of statistical sources, however, their quality and objectivity should be evaluated before they are used.

NOTES AND REFERENCES

1 A. Phillips and R. E. Stevenson, 'The historical development of industrial organisation', *History of Political Economy*, vol. 6, no. 3 (Fall 1974), pp. 324–42.

2 P. W. S. Andrews, 'Industrial analysis in economics', in T. Wilson and P. W. S. Andrews (eds), *Oxford Studies in the Price Mechanism* (Oxford, Clarendon Press, 1951); and P. W. S. Andrews, 'Industrial economics as a specialist subject', *Journal of Industrial Economics*, vol. 1 (1952).

3 R. B. Heflebower and G. W. Stocking (eds), *AEA Readings in Industrial Organisation and Public Policy* (Homewood, Ill., Irwin, 1958), p.v.

4 E. T. Grether, 'Industrial organisation: retrospect and prospect', *American Economic Review*, vol. 82 (May 1970), pp. 83–9.

5 The classification of economists into 'schools' or 'traditions' is a useful device when making broad comparisons of the content and method of economic analysis. However, differences in method can also exist within schools, and some economists have used methods drawn from more than one school.

6 L. C. Robbins, *An Essay on the Nature and Significance of Economic Science* (London, Macmillan, 1935).

7 J. Dorfman, 'The role of the German Historical School in American economic thought', *American Economic Association Papers and Proceedings*, vol. 67 (1955), pp. 17–28.

8 A. W. Coats, 'The first two decades of the American Economic Association', *American Economic Review*, vol. 50 (1960), pp. 555–74.

9 G. F. Shove, 'The place of Marshall's *Principles* in the development of economic theory', *Economic Journal*, vol. 52 (1942), pp. 294–329.

10 A. Marshall, *Principles of Economics*, 8th edn (London, Macmillan, 1938), pp. 762–3.

11 Marshall, op. cit. (n. 10), p. 778.

12 Marshall, op. cit. (n. 10), p. 781.

13 W. S. Jevons, *Principles of Economics and Other Papers* (London, Macmillan, 1905), pp. 195–6, 197–8, 200–1.

14 T. C. Koopmans, *Three Essays on the State of Economic Science* (New York, McGraw-Hill, 1957), p. 145.

15 A. Marshall, *The New Cambridge Curriculum in Economics and Associated Branches of Political Science* (London, Macmillan, 1903).

16 W. J. Ashley, *Commercial Education* (London, Williams & Norgate, 1926).

17 A. Ashley, *William J. Ashley* (London, King & Son, 1932), p. 50.

18 Ashley, op. cit. (n. 17), pp. 99–100.

19 G. C. Allen, *British Industries and their Organisation* (London, Longmans, 1959) which first appeared in 1933, had the stated aim 'to describe the structure of certain British industries against the background of their historical development, at the same

time considering some of the more significant trends in British industry as a whole' (preface to 1959 edn).

20 P. Sraffa, 'The law of returns under competitive conditions', *Economic Journal*, vol. 36 (1926), pp. 535–50.

21 J. Robinson, *The Economics of Imperfect Competition* (London, Macmillan, 1933).

22 E. H. Chamberlin, *The Theory of Monopolistic Competition*, 1st edn (Cambridge, Mass., Harvard UP, 1932).

23 P. W. S. Andrews, *On Competition in Economic Theory* (London, Macmillan, 1964), pp. 21*ff*.

24 J. S. Bain, 'The theory of monopolistic competition after thirty years', *American Economic Association Papers and Proceedings*, vol. 76 (1964), pp. 28–32.

25 A. A. Berle and G. C. Means, *The Modern Corporation and Private Property* (New York, Macmillan, reprinted 1948).

26 R. L. Hall and C. J. Hitch, 'Price theory and business behaviour', *Oxford Economic Papers*, vol. 49 (1939), pp. 12–45.

27 F. Machlup, 'Marginal analysis and empirical research', *American Economic Review*, vol. 36 (1946), pp. 518–53; and F. Machlup, 'Theories of the firm: marginal, behavioral, managerial', *American Economic Review*, vol. 57 (1967), pp. 1–33.

28 Andrews, op. cit. (n. 2, 1952).

29 J. S. Bain, *Industrial Organisation* (New York, Wiley, 1959).

30 M. J. Farrell, 'Deductive systems and empirical generalisations in the theory of the firm', *Oxford Economic Papers*, vol. 4 (1952), pp. 45–9.

31 An extensive annotated bibliography of earlier business histories is to be found in H. M. Larson, *Guide to Business History* (Cambridge, Mass., Harvard UP, 1964). For more recent studies, including articles on the methodology of business histories, see two periodicals: *Business History* (Liverpool UP); and *Business History Review* (Harvard UP). An extensive literature on individual industry studies exists; see, for example, W. Adams (ed.), *The Structure of American Industry*, 5th edn (New York, Macmillan, 1977).

32 Machlup, op. cit. (n. 27, 1946).

33 Machlup, op. cit. (n. 27, 1967).

34 R. M. Cyert and J. G. March, *A Behavioral Theory of the Firm* (Englewood Cliffs, Prentice-Hall, reprinted 1970).

35 W. J. Baumol, *Business Behavior, Value and Growth* (New York, Macmillan, 1959), pp. 3–5.

36 J. Bates and J. R. Parkinson, *Business Economics* (Oxford, Blackwell, 1963), preface.

37 J. Dean, *Managerial Economics* (New York, Prentice-Hall, 1951), p. viii.

38 W. W. Cooper, *et al.*, 'Managerial economics: a new frontier?', *American Economic Association Papers and Proceedings*, vol. 73 (1960), pp. 131–59.

39 Marshall, op cit. (n. 10), p. 39.

40 J. N. Keynes, *Scope and Method of Political Economy* (London, Macmillan, 1891), p. 216.

41 Robbins, op. cit. (n. 6), p. 122.

42 Robbins, op. cit. (n. 6), pp. 78–9.

43 T. Hutchison, *Significance and Basic Postulates of Economic Theory* (New York, Kelley, 1960), pp. 54–5.

44 Robbins, op. cit. (n. 6): 'business of discovery consists not merely in the elucidation of given premises but in the perception of the facts which are the basis of the premises' (p. 105); and 'Realistic studies may suggest the problem to be solved. They may test the range of applicability of the answer when it is forthcoming. They may suggest assumptions for further theoretical elaboration' (p. 120).

45 G. C. Archibald, 'The state of economic science', *British Journal for the Philosophy of Science*, vol. 10 (1959).

46 M. Friedman, *Essays in Positive Economics* (Chicago, Chicago UP, 1953), p. 10.
47 Friedman, op. cit. (n. 46), p. 15.
48 J. Melitz, 'Friedman and Machlup on testing economic assumptions', *Journal of Political Economy*, vol. 73 (1965), has discussed the distinction between auxiliary and generative assumptions.
49 Archibald, op. cit. (n. 45), p. 61.
50 K. Klappolz and J. Agassi, 'Methodological prescription in economics', *Economica*, vol. 26 (1959), pp. 60–75.
51 Archibald, op. cit. (n. 45), p. 62.
52 Koopmans, op. cit. (n. 14), p. 140.
53 E. Rotwein, 'On the methodology of positive economics', *Quarterly Journal of Economics*, vol. 73 (1959), pp. 561–2.
54 H. A. Simon, 'Problems of methodology: discussion', *American Economic Association Papers and Proceedings*, vol. 75 (1963), p. 230.
55 Melitz, op. cit. (n. 48), pp. 40–1.
56 See Central Statistical Office, *Guide to Official Statistics* (London, HMSO annual); or Central Statistical Office, *Government Statistics: A Brief Guide to Sources* (London, HMSO, annual).
57 Department of Industry, *Report on the Census of Production,* Business Monitor PA Series (London, HMSO, annual).
58 For example, Department of Industry, *Company Finance,* Business Monitor M5 (London, HMSO, annual); and Department of Industry, *Acquisitions and Mergers of Companies,* Business Monitor M7 (London, HMSO, annual).
59 C. A. Moser, *Survey Methods in Social Investigation* (London, Heinemann, 1971).
60 K. A. Yeomans, *Introducing Statistics* (Harmondsworth, Penguin Books, 1968), ch. 5.
61 K. A. Yeomans, *Applied Statistics* (Harmondsworth, Penguin Books, 1968), ch. 1.
62 J. Stewart, *Understanding Econometrics* (London, Hutchinson, 1976), ch. 3.
63 See Her Majesty's Stationery Office, *Sectional Lists* (London, HMSO, occasional).
64 Friedman, op. cit. (n. 46), ch. 1.
65 A. Marshall, *Industry and Trade* (London, Macmillan, 1921) second edition.
66 T. Wilson and P. W. S. Andrews, op. cit. (n. 2) p. 168.
67 E. T. Grether et al., 'Industrial Organisation: retrospect and prospect', *American Economic Review*, vol. 82 (1970) pp. 83–108.

2 Industrial and Market Structure

2.1 INTRODUCTION

'Structure' is a term frequently used, but rarely defined, in industrial economics. Where it is defined it is usually given a rather broad meaning covering a variety of different characteristics relating both to individual firms and to the relationships between firms.[1] For the purposes of this chapter two meanings of 'structure' are identified and distinguished. 'Industrial structure' refers to the relative importance of individual industries or groups of related industries within an economy and to the pattern of transactions between these industries. This is distinguished from 'market structure', which is a concept derived from the received theory of the firm. Used in this latter sense 'structure' refers to the levels of seller and buyer concentration, the height of entry barriers and the degree of product differentiation within individual markets.

The first part of this chapter (sections 2.2–2.6) is concerned with three main topics: the definition and measurement of industrial structure, patterns in industrial structure and the policy debate raised by changes in these patterns, and the measurement and analysis of industrial interdependence within economies. The second part of the chapter (sections 2.7–2.11) examines the definition and measurement of market structure, its determinants, and the relationship between market structure and market performance. The final section (2.12) contains guidance on further reading.

2.2 INDUSTRY: DEFINITIONAL PROBLEMS

In elementary economic analysis it is assumed that activities can be classified by grouping firms producing the same products into one industry, which are then distinguishable from groups of firms producing the same products belonging to different industries. In practice such neat distinctions are not possible. Apart from the complication that firms produce a variety of different products and, therefore, may belong to more than one industry, the line of demarcation between the products belonging to one industry and those belonging to another cannot be drawn in any absolute sense. In these circumstances it is not surprising to find that the boundaries of industries are defined differently both between countries and between different statistical sources within any single country.

Some definitional differences are not necessarily undesirable, since the suitability of an industry's boundaries must be related to the use to which the industry data are going to be put. Industrial earnings data used for wage negotiation purposes need to be collected according to the boundaries of jurisdiction of the main parties to the negotiation: wages council, employers' association, etc. A trade association or co-operative research association might find alternative definitions more appropriate.

At the same time definitional differences can occur unnecessarily. For this reason attempts have been made to establish standard definitions of industries, particularly to achieve comparability in the statistical data collected by government departments, which are usable for a variety of purposes, although not for all. Such *standard industrial classifications* (SICs) are now used in a large number of countries and are examined in detail below. However, the existence of an SIC system in a particular country is not a guarantee that complete standardisation in the presentation of official industrial statistics has been achieved there. All government departments may not rigidly apply the SIC system because it does not suit the particular uses that they have in mind or because they attach importance to maintaining the historical continuity of their statistical series. Alternatively, even where a standard definition has been generally adopted the classification of establishments and the choice of sample by which the data are obtained may differ between departments and so undermine the data's comparability.[2]

STANDARD INDUSTRIAL CLASSIFICATIONS

The British Standard Industrial Classification was first introduced in 1948 in order to promote uniformity and comparability in official statistics. It has been revised at ten-year intervals since then. The criteria used in determining the 1968 classification have been described in the following terms:

> The Classification has been prepared to conform with the organisation and structure of industry and trade as it exists within the UK. All relevant factors such as the commodity produced or services given, the raw materials used and the nature of the process or the work done, have been taken into consideration.[3]

Such criteria are far from being unambiguous. The definitions of 'raw material', 'process' and 'work done' may be broad or narrow. Also, there is no reason why these three criteria should coincide in their definition of an industry; therefore, an implicit (i.e. arbitrary) choice may have to be made between them. In the last resort common usage modified to take account of the more obvious inconsistencies has to be adopted.

This SIC system groups industrial activities at two levels: Orders and Minimum List Headings. Each Order consists of a group of related Minimum List industries. In the 1968 SIC there are twenty-seven Orders as follows:

Agriculture, forestry and fishing.	Clothing and footwear.
Mining and quarrying.	Bricks, pottery, glass, cement, etc.
Food, drink and tobacco.	Timber, furniture etc.
Coal and petroleum products.	Paper, printing and publishing.
Chemicals and allied industries.	Other manufacturing industries.
Metal manufacture.	Construction.
Mechanical engineering.	Gas, electricity and water.
Instrument engineering.	Transport and communication.
Electrical engineering.	Distributive trades.

Shipbuilding and marine engineering.	Insurance, banking, finance and
Vehicles.	business services.
Other metal goods.	Professional and scientific services.
Textiles	Miscellaneous services.
Leather, leather goods and fur.	Public administration and defence.

Minimum List Headings include the minimum degree of disaggregation within the Orders that is normally provided in published data. In the 1968 SIC there are 181 Minimum List Headings covering the twenty-seven Orders. For example, 'Food, drink and tobacco' (Order III) is divided into fifteen Minimum List Headings, and 'Vehicles' (Order XI) is divided into six as follows:

380   Wheeled tractor manufacturing.
381   Motor vehicle manufacturing.
382   Motorcycle, tricycle and pedal cycle manufacturing.
383   Aerospace equipment manufacturing and repairing.
384   Locomotives and railway track equipment.
385   Railway carriages and wagons and trains.

Certain of the Minimum List Headings are further subdivided; for example, '003 Fishing' is divided into 'Sea fishing' and 'Fishing in inland waters'. However, as already indicated, published data are not normally available to this degree of detail.

In assigning economic activities to particular industries the unit of account is the *establishment*. The establishment may be defined as a workplace with a separate single address and is allocated to a particular industry according to the nature of its principal activity. Since many firms consist of two or more establishments a firm may 'belong' to two or more industries if the principal activities of its establishments are attributable to different industries. In theory this is sound, although care has to be taken in the treatment of such establishments as head offices. In practice, however, firms can only supply information on separate workplaces if their accounting systems provide for this. Therefore, a compromise has to be reached. If a firm's activities at two establishments are integrated and separate accounts do not exist for each, the two will be treated as a single establishment. Alternatively, a factory may consist of two departments producing principal products belonging to different industries; in these circumstances, if separate accounting records exist, the two departments will be treated as separate establishments. The number of establishments within a particular industry and the size of that industry are, therefore, partly determined by the accounting procedures of firms with interests in that industry. Comparisons of industry data over time are therefore affected by changes in the definition of Orders and Minimum List Headings and by changes in firms' accounting systems.

Most other countries use the establishment as the statistical unit in allocating economic activities to particular industries. They also use similar principles in determining their SIC system. However, each country endeavours to construct an SIC that is appropriate to the composition and structure of its own economy and has the degree of sophistication that it considers to be administratively and financially feasible.[4] Because of this there are obvious difficulties in making international comparisons using individual country data based upon different SIC systems.

The United Nations has constructed an International Standard Industrial Classification (ISIC), first for 1948 and then revised at ten year intervals, which is:

> ... intended to meet the needs for comparably classified data and is in the nature of a reconciliation of [such] differing requirements and possibilities and hence not identical with the classification of any one country . . . the purpose of this ISIC is not to supersede national classifications but to provide an up-to-date framework for the international comparison of national statistics.[5]

The ISIC[6] categorises industrial activities at three levels: Division, Major Group and Group (one-, two- and three-digit categories respectively). The Divisions are:

1 Agriculture, hunting, forestry and fishing.
2 Mining and quarrying.
3 Manufacturing.
4 Electricity, gas and water.
5 Construction.
6 Wholesale and retail trade, restaurants and hotels.
7 Transport, storage and communication.
8 Financing, insurance, real estate and business services.
9 Community, social and personal services and other activities not adequately defined.

Then, for example, Division 1 ('Agriculture, hunting, forestry and fishing') is subdivided into three Major Groups:

11 Agriculture and hunting.
12 Forestry and logging.
13 Fishing.

In turn 'Agriculture and hunting' is divided into three Groups:

111 Agricultural and livestock production.
112 Agricultural services.
113 Hunting, trapping and game preparation.

The reliability of any data based upon the ISIC is determined by the quality of the original individual-country data and the success achieved in reconciling data collected on different bases. For the time being intercountry industrial comparisons based upon the ISIC have to be limited to rather broad industrial categories, and even then they have to be treated with a degree of caution.

2.3 INDUSTRIAL STRUCTURE IN BRITAIN

Industrial structure has been defined in terms of the relative importance of individual industries, or groups of related industries, within an economy. Once the boundaries of individual industries have been agreed the criteria for measuring their relative importance have to be determined. The most frequent measures of an industry's importance are based either upon its added value (or net output), expressed in monetary terms, or upon the quantity of one of its inputs (usually labour), expressed in physical terms. These two measures will give different results to the extent that the net output per unit of labour varies between industries and that industrial boundaries are defined differently. The trends in industrial structure recorded by these measures will also diverge if the rate of change in average productivity differs between industries.

Table 2.1 *Relative importance of different sectors in the British economy, 1976.*

Sectors	Contribution to gross domestic product[a] (%)	Working population employed[b] (%)
Agriculture, forestry and fishing	2·9	1·8
Mining and quarrying	2·3	1·5
Manufacturing	28·7	32·1
Construction	7·3	6·1
Gas, electricity and water	3·7	1·6
Transport and communication	9·7	6·6
Distributive trades	9·8	11·9
Other services (including insurance, banking, public administration, defence, health and education services)	35·6	38·4
Total	100·0	100·0

Source: Central Statistical Office, *Annual Abstract of Statistics* (London, HMSO, No. 114, 1978).

Notes:
(a) Contribution before adjustment for depreciation and financial services but after adjustment for ownership of dwellings.
(b) Percentage of total employees in employment.

Tables 2.1 and 2.2 summarise the industrial structure of the British economy in 1976, based upon net output and employment data. In Table 2.1 manufacturing activity is aggregated into a single sector, which is then divided into its fourteen constituent Orders in Table 2.2. Taken together the tables illustrate the well-known general characteristics of Britain's industrial structure: the minor importance of agriculture; a large and diversified industrial base with the emphasis on engineering products; and a substantial 'services' sector, which includes transport, distribution and a wide range of governmental, commercial and leisure activity services.

Table 2.2   *Relative importance of different manufacturing sectors, 1976 (% of working population engaged in manufacturing).*

Manufacturing sector	%
Food, drink and tobacco	9·8
Coal, petroleum and chemical products	6·3
Metal manufacture	6·5
Engineering	25·1
Shipbuilding	2·6
Vehicles	10·1
Other metal goods	7·2
Textiles	7·1
Leather and leather goods	0·5
Clothing and footwear	5·2
Bricks, pottery, glass and cement	3·7
Timber and furniture	3·7
Paper, printing and publishing	7·5
Other manufacturing	4·7
Total	100·0

Source: Central Statistical Office, *Annual Abstract of Statistics* (London, HMSO, No. 114, 1978).

The British industrial structure has changed considerably over time. This is illustrated in Figures 2.1 and 2.2, which highlight the Orders that have shown the biggest increases and decreases, measured in terms of both output and employment, over a fifteen-year period. There are a number of significant differences between the two diagrams, due in particular to the apparently slower rate of growth in labour productivity in service than in manufacturing and primary industries. The 'top five' in the output table include three manufacturing industries, one public-utility industry and a service industry, while

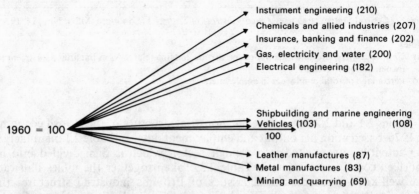

Fig. 2.1   Growth in output, at constant factor cost, of selected UK industries, 1960–75 (1960 output level = 100, 1975 output level shown in parentheses).
Source: Central Statistical Office, *Annual Abstract of Statistics* (London, HMSO, no. 114, 1978).

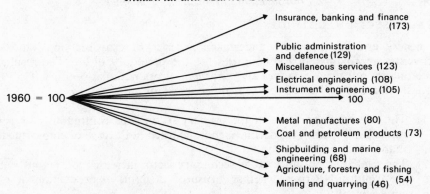

Fig. 2.2   Growth in employment of selected UK industries, 1960–75 (1960 employment level=100, 1975 employment level shown in parentheses).
Source: Central Statistical Office, *Annual Abstract of Statistics* (London, HMSO, no. 114, 1978).

the 'bottom five' consist of four manufacturing industries and one primary industry. By contrast, the 'top five' in the employment table include three service industries and two manufacturing industries, while the 'bottom five' consist of three manufacturing and two primary industries. This raises the issue of the relative importance in an economy of primary, secondary and tertiary activities, which is examined on a comparative basis in the next section and in greater detail in the British context in section 2.5.

2.4   PATTERNS OF INDUSTRIAL STRUCTURE

A number of studies have been undertaken into patterns of industrial structure in terms of a three-sector economy in which economic activity is classified as either *primary, secondary* or *tertiary*. The primary sector is frequently defined to include agriculture and the extractive industries, the secondary sector to include manufacturing and construction industries and the tertiary sector to include the service industries. However, departures from this classification system do occur. For example, mining activities are sometimes included in the secondary sector, and the generation of electricity and other public-sector manufacturing activities may be included in the tertiary sector. These discrepancies need to be taken into account when making comparisons between studies.

Such studies have been primarily concerned to establish a relationship between the pattern of industrial structure and different stages of economic development. They have derived such patterns either by comparing different economies at different stages of development but at the same point in time *(cross-sectional studies)*, or by examining the changes in industrial structure occurring over time within individual economies *(time series studies)*. The two types of study do not always yield the same results, and it is a matter of dispute which of the two approaches is likely to be the more useful in predicting future changes in industrial structure.

CROSS-SECTIONAL STUDIES

Chenery and Syrquin have undertaken a series of cross-sectional studies covering approximately 100 countries for the period 1950–70.[7] The results, relating to industrial structure and *per capita* gross national product (GNP), are summarised in Table 2.3. The main conclusions are as follows:

(1) The relative importance of the primary sector falls continuously as *per capita* GNP rises. This decline is more marked in the case of employment than in that of production.

(2) The relative importance of the secondary sector increases continuously as *per capita* GNP rises, whether measured in terms of production or of employment.

(3) The relative importance of the tertiary sector rises continuously as *per capita* GNP rises, when measured in terms of employment. However, when measured in terms of output there is some evidence that the share of services, after initially rising, falls slightly at higher *per capita* income levels.

Table 2.3 *Variation in industrial structure with level of development.*

Sector	Predicted values at different levels of per capita GNP			
	Under $100	$500	$1,000	Over $1,000
Production (% share)				
Primary	52	20	14	13
Secondary	13	29	35	38
Tertiary[a]	35	51	51	49
Total	100	100	100	100
Employment (% share)				
Primary	71	39	25	16
Secondary	8	26	33	37
Tertiary[a]	21	35	42	47
Total	100	100	100	100

Source: H. Chenery and M. Syrquin *Patterns of Development, 1950–1970* (London, Oxford UP, 1975).

Note:
(a) Includes public utilities.

Cross-sectional studies by Kuznets broadly support the above findings by Chenery and Syrquin. Kuznets also has examined the relationship between the importance of subdivisions of the secondary and tertiary sectors and different levels of economic development. In the case of the services sector, using employment data he has observed a positive correlation between each subsector (i.e. transport and communication, commerce, and other services) and *per capita* gross domestic product (GDP). However, using net output data, a clear positive correlation was only observable in the case of transport and communication. By contrast, a significant positive correlation was found between the relative importance of all the main manufacturing subsectors and *per capita* GDP, irrespective of whether the employment or output measure was used.[8]

Growth rates, however, do vary between manufacturing sectors. This has been illustrated in an earlier study by Chenery, who has established a relationship between net output *per capita* in each of six manufacturing subsectors and *per capita* GDP. The 'income elasticities' derived were: food, drink and tobacco, 1·10; metals, 1·68; metal products, 1·97; chemicals, 1·31; textiles, 0·93; and other manufacturing, 1·50. These indicate that, within the manufacturing sector of advanced economies as compared to more backward economies, food, drink and textiles industries were relatively less important while metals, metal products and chemicals were relatively more important.[9]

TIME SERIES STUDIES

While the cross-sectional studies shed light on the differences in industrial structure between different economies at different stages of economic development, it is an open question whether they can also be used to predict changes over time in the industrial structure of individual countries. The reason for this is that cross-sectional studies cannot directly take account of the variables affecting industrial structure that change over time and independently of *per capita* GNP, e.g. changes in the state of technical knowledge, in foreign trade restrictions and in relative factor prices.

Such influences should be reflected in time series data; but unfortunately, long-term time-series data extending over fifty years or more are in very limited supply, being mainly restricted to a small number of developed economies. In broad terms, Kuznets has found that such studies confirm the main findings of the cross-sectional studies, although the latter tend to underpredict the extent of the structural changes observed in the time series data. He has found that in all cases a relative decline in the importance of the agricultural sector occurred over time, when measured in terms of both employment and net output. Similarly, with only minor exceptions the relative importance of the secondary sector increased over time, whether measured in terms of employment or output, although the change recorded by the employment data was relatively less pronounced. In the case of the tertiary sector the pattern was more complex. Considerable increases in the relative share of the tertiary sector were recorded in all countries when using employment data, but stability or a decline in its relative share was recorded in a significant number of cases when using output data.[8] In a detailed study of the United States, which illustrates this situation, Fuchs has estimated that between 1929 and 1967 the service sector's share of total employment rose from 40 to over 55 per cent while its share of GDP at constant prices remained virtually unchanged.[10]

These cross-sectional and time series studies, although not reaching identical conclusions, appear to support the usefulness of the three-sector model in describing the broad pattern of the industrial structure of economies at different stages of economic development and in indicating the ways in which the structure of economies change as they become more developed. However, there are also sound theoretical reasons why economies at the same stage of development may have different industrial structures and why the pattern of development need not be the same in all countries. Such differences can arise due to differences between economies or over time in:

(1) the availability and cost of indigenous factors of production;
(2) the extent and cost of indigenous transport facilities;
(3) the general level and pattern of technical knowledge;
(4) the size of the domestic market and the pattern of demand within it;
(5) the extent and form of government intervention in economic affairs; or
(6) the nature and extent of barriers to international trade, which modify the influence of international specialisation on the industrial structure of individual economies.

The influence of these economic forces in causing deviations from the predicted patterns of industrial structure is evident in the above studies. These considerations, together with an appreciation of the limitations of the data used in the statistical investigations, have caused a number of writers to be cautious in using the conclusions drawn from such studies for policy and planning purposes:

> Cross-section or even comparative time series regression analysis of the pattern of industrial growth is an important tool of description. But it is a producer of useful yardsticks for classification rather than a guide to policy and planning . . . There is no reason from the statistical analysis to assume that normal patterns of growth are either desirable patterns of growth or possible patterns of growth for the future.[11]

Some of the pitfalls in the simplistic use of broad sectoral studies of this kind are illustrated in the next section.

2.5 GOODS *v.* SERVICES

The aspect of industrial structure that has most attracted public attention during the 1960s and 1970s has been the apparent growth in importance, in both absolute and relative terms, of employment in the services sector. In the case of Britain, this has been accompanied since 1961 by a decline in the relative importance of employment in the secondary sector. This trend has been officially projected to continue in the future (see Table 2.4), and some writers have feared that it may be symptomatic of a self-reinforcing process of 'de-industrialisation' in the UK economy.[12, 70]

While such a development may have some favourable effects – for example, employment in services exhibits greater stability than that in manufacturing[13] – it has been viewed with some concern, mainly for the following mixture of beliefs:

Table 2.4   *Distribution of employment between sectors* %

Year	Primary^a	Secondary^b	Tertiary^c	Total
1931	12	37	51	100
1951	9	44	47	100
1961	7	44	49	100
1971	4	43	53	100
1981 (forecast)	3	40	57	100

Source: *Department of Employment Gazette* (vol. 83, October 1975).

Notes:
(a) Agriculture, forestry and fishing; and Mining and quarrying.
(b) Manufacturing industries; Construction; and Gas, electricity and water.
(c) Service industries.

(1) that the supply of services is in some sense less 'productive' than the production of goods;
(2) that the expansion of the service sector at the expense of the production of goods could harm a country's balance of payments; and
(3) that labour productivity in the service sector is lower and rises more slowly than that in the secondary sector.

This concern led in 1966 to the introduction of a Selective Employment Tax (SET) in the United Kingdom in an attempt, later abandoned, to stem the relative growth of employment in tertiary activities and thereby make more labour available for the expansion of manufacturing industry.[14]

In view of their possible policy significance each of these beliefs will be examined in turn. Before this, however, the basic limitations of the distinction between goods and service sectors in the available statistics should be noted, since they are germane to each of these beliefs:

. . . the statistics for employment which are available are statistics for industrial groups, and one has to decide whether to label a particular industrial group 'goods' or 'services'. Thus, one classifies manufacturing as goods but distributive trades or transport as services . . . If a letter is typed by a person employed by a manufacturing enterprise, that work is counted as part of manufacturing, but if the typing were sent out to an agency, then in the statistics the typing would count as a service. In short, there is a goods/ service distinction within enterprises and within industries just as there is between industrial groups . . . Thus, the available statistics will be giving only a very blurred picture of the situation we are really after.[13]

The first of these beliefs – that the service sector is less 'productive' than the secondary – is based upon the misconception that work in the production of tangible goods yields benefits to society in a way that the production of services cannot. In fact employment in the production of goods and employment in that of services both yield benefits, which in a market economy may be measured as the marginal product of the labour used. Although the market is not always a satisfactory indicator of that benefit, it has rarely been suggested that the market overvalues all types of service produced. For example, those who consider that the market overvalues the services provided by pop stars and modern painters may also believe that the market undervalues the services provided by nurses and social workers. It seems, therefore, that the classification of employment in making goods as 'productive' and in making services as 'unproductive' is not a helpful foundation for an industrial policy.

In similar fashion the second belief – that employment in service rather than secondary activities harms a country's balance of payments – is also based upon a too simplistic view of the distinction between goods and services. Goods are generally more easily transported, and therefore exported, than many types of services, but against this must be set the following factors:

(1) Many 'invisible' exports are in the form of services to foreign buyers, e.g. services to foreign tourists.
(2) The production of services as well as of goods for domestic consumption indirectly benefits the balance of payments where they are substitutes for imported goods and services, e.g. home-based tourism as a substitute for overseas holidays.
(3) The impact of the increased production of goods and services on the balance of payments depends upon the import content of their inputs, e.g. raw materials and equipment, as well as on the ability to sell the finished product to overseas buyers.

The magnitude of each industry's potential contribution to the balance of payments can only be determined after examining its direct and indirect contribution to the external account at the margin of its production. The average proportion of its output currently sold to foreign buyers may be a misleading indicator of this contribution. In general it seems unlikely that goods industries are *uniformly* better average and marginal contributors to the external account than are service industries.[15]

The third belief – that labour productivity is lower and rises more slowly in the service sector than in the secondary – is lent initial support by the simple comparison of changes in output per employee in UK industries contained in Table 2.5, which shows that labour productivity increased more slowly

Table 2.5   *Increase in UK industrial output at constant factor cost per employee, 1960–75.*

Greatest increase	Least increase
Agriculture, forestry and fishing	Public administration and defence
Gas, electricity and water	Miscellaneous services
Chemicals and allied industries	Insurance, banking, finance,
Coal and petroleum products	professional and scientific services
Instrument engineering	Metal manufacture
	Other metal goods

Source: Central Statistical Office, *Annual Abstract of Statistics* (London, HMSO, No. 114, 1978).

in service than in goods industries over the period 1960–75. Of the five industries showing the greatest increase in this measure of labour productivity, none belonged to the service sector. By contrast, three of the five industries at the bottom of the productivity league were service industries. However, there are a number of reasons why such crude comparisons as these should be treated with caution.[16]

(1) Since the cyclical pattern of employment differs between goods and service industries, the results obtained are sensitive to the timing of the periods for which productivity changes are measured.
(2) The employment statistics used in the measurement of productivity exclude employers and other self-employed personnel. They also take no account of differences in the composition of the labour force between industries or within the same industry at different points of time. The practical significance of the second of these qualifications can be seen from the following quotation, relating to Table 2.4, from the *Department of Employment Gazette*:

> Between 1961 and 1971 almost all the growth in service employment was due to growth in the numbers of female workers, by nearly 1.2 million, and the indications are that almost all this growth has been in part-timers. Thus if the sectoral split was expressed in terms of equivalents to full-time men workers, the effective change in the proportion in services would be considerably reduced.[17]

(3) Difficulties also arise in measuring the levels of output in the service sector. For many types of service there is no satisfactory method of measuring in physical terms the quantity of output produced, and in particular cases such output cannot even be measured in money terms because it is not sold on an open market; certain public-sector services fall in this category. Where the market value of services output is known the level of output per employee can be compared over time, provided that the market values are first corrected for any price-inflationary influences. However, over time the price of a service may increase because the quality of the service rises as well as on account of general inflationary influences. It follows in this situation that, if market values are fully corrected for observed price increases, the true increase in service output and in employee productivity will be understated. Where such market values are not available the National Accounts statisticians may use employment data as an indicator of service output. When employment is used as a proxy for output then, by definition, labour productivity (i.e. output per unit of labour input) cannot change over time. For these two reasons it is likely that calculations of both output and productivity in the service sector, based upon uncorrected official statistics, are underestimates.[18]

A study by Briscoe of labour productivity estimates for UK service and manufacturing sectors over the period 1951–73 has attempted to make corrections for as many of the above factors as possible, and on this basis Briscoe has drawn the following tentative conclusions:

(1) The long term differential in productivity growth between these two sectors was appreciably reduced once these other factors were taken into account.
(2) Short-run productivity growth rates, over five-year periods, varied considerably between time periods. There was no firm evidence that the productivity differential was narrowing over time, but in a minority of time periods the adjusted productivity growth rate for services exceeded that for manufacturing.
(3) Considerable disparities occurred in the rates of growth in productivity *within* both the service and goods sectors. Over the period 1951–73 the growth in labour productivity within the service sector was greatest in the most capital-intensive industries, e.g. transport and communications.[19]

The 'goods *v.* services' debate provides a particular illustration of the limits of the three-sector model as a basis for formulating industrial plans and policies. On close examination the distinction between goods and services is not particularly meaningful in economic terms. However, even if it were, it would be too aggregative to form a reliable basis for policy action if it concealed the great disparities in output and productivity trends occuring within the service and manufacturing sectors.

2.6   INDUSTRIAL INTERDEPENDENCE

In the previous sections of this chapter industrial structure is examined in terms of the relative importance of different industries, and groups of industries, within an economy. 'Structure' is also concerned with industrial inter-dependence: the relationships between individual industries as buyers and sellers. These relationships are the subject of input–output analysis and are described in the industry input–output table.

INPUT-OUTPUT TABLES

An industry input-output table describes the inter-relationships between industries within an economy in terms of the value, or volume, of transactions that take place between individual industries, usually for a time period of one year. Therefore, it summarises the industrial origin of all the inputs and the destination of all the outputs of all industries within an economy. These relationships are shown in a matrix table, the output destinations being indicated in horizontal rows and the input origins in vertical columns.

Input-output tables have been constructed for a considerable number of economies, and some of these tables have as many as 200×200 sectors.[20, 21] Official input-output tables for the United Kingdom were initially prepared at intervals for 1954, 1963 and 1968 respectively, but they are now prepared on an annual basis. The latest tables divide the UK economy into sixty industrial sectors.[22]

Table 2.6 *Hypothetical input–output table (£ m.).*

Input from:	Output to: Agriculture	Manufactures	Services	Final use	Gross output
Agriculture	40	80	0	80	200
Manufactures	40	40	20	300	400
Services	0	80	20	100	200
Labour	120	200	160	20	500
Gross input	200	400	200	500	1,300

A simple hypothetical example of an input-output table, which relates to an economy consisting of three industries and one final-use sector, is given in Table 2.6 to illustrate the interpretation of input–output tables.[23] The gross output of the agricultural sector is 200 units, each unit in this table being £1 million. Of these, only 80 units are purchased in the 'final use' sector, 40 units are retained by the agricultural sector as an input for future agricultural production, and 80 units pass to the manufacturing sector for processing. Inputs to the agricultural sector consist of the 40 units of agricultural production already referred to, plus 40 units from the manufacturing sector (e.g. plant, buildings, processed fertiliser) and 120 units of labour. 'Labour', in fact, is the value added by the agricultural sector after the inputs from the other sectors, plus the agricultural output utilised within the agriculture sector, have been taken into account. Therefore, the value of the gross inputs of an industry is by definition equal to the value of the gross output. The input and output of the manufacturing and services sectors can be identified in the same manner.

The input–output table gives an indication of the nature and degree of interdependence between industries within an economy at a particular period of time. At one theoretical extreme is complete interdependence where each industry obtains inputs from all other industries and sells its product to all other industries. In such a situation transactions will occur between each pair of sectors so that changes affecting one industrial sector will necessarily react directly on all other sectors, which will further react among each other (see Table 2.7a). At the other theoretical extreme each industrial sector is completely self-sufficient and is not in a buyer or seller relationship with any other sector of the economy (Table 2.7b). Actual industrial structures are at various points between these two limits.

Statistical measures of inter-relatedness within actual economies are subject to a number of limitations, but in general they indicate that the degree of interdependence is higher among developed economies than among developing economies and that in the former the degree of interdependence may be increasing over time.[20, 21, 24, 25] Economies that are at broadly similar stages of development appear to have broadly similar transaction relationships between industries. The extent of the similarity recorded, however, is partially dependent upon the degree of disaggregation in the input–output tables compared.

Table 2.7   *Limits of industrial interdependence.*

(a) Complete inter-relatedness

Input from:	Output to industries:			
	1	2	3	4
Industry 1	*	*	*	*
Industry 2	*	*	*	*
Industry 3	*	*	*	*
Industry 4	*	*	*	*

(b) Sector self-sufficiency

Input from:	Output to industries:			
	1	2	3	4
Industry 1	*			
Industry 2		*		
Industry 3			*	
Industry 4				*

Key: * = transaction

Input–output tables can be used to identify 'key' industries in an economy, in the sense either of important suppliers to many other industries in the economy or of important buyers from a large number of supplying industries. In the British context, for example, steel may be regarded as 'key' in the former sense and motor vehicle assembly may be so regarded in the latter sense. Key industries are those whose performance indirectly affects the performance of many other industrial sectors in the economy. They are also the industries where strikes and wage increases[26] are likely to have extensive effects on the economy as a whole.

INPUT–OUTPUT ANALYSIS AND CHANGES IN INDUSTRIAL STRUCTURE

Input–output tables *describe* existing industrial structure; input–output analysis can be used to *explain* and, in certain circumstances, to *predict* changes in industrial structure. Industrial structure changes because of changes in either the composition of final use demand or the methods of production. Both of these sources of change can be examined through input–output analysis.

Changes in the composition of final demand

Exogenous changes in the composition of final demand can be very complex in their effects on industrial structure. For example, an increase in the general level of incomes may cause a more than proportionate increase in car purchases. Initially, this leads to an increase in the output of the motor-vehicle assembly industry, which generates increased purchases from the components industries. In turn this leads to increased purchases from a variety of industries supplying materials and machinery to the component manufacturers. The chain reactions thereafter become progressively more complex, involving increased numbers of industries, although the impact upon them at each stage becomes smaller. Input–output analysis identifies and quantifies this chain reaction and its cumulative effect on each industry. Where an increase in the final demand for one product is at the expense of that of the product of another industry, the chain reaction is even more complex, but the principles underlying the analysis are the same.

The use of input–output analysis requires data on the relationship *at the margin* between the factor inputs and outputs for each industry, i.e. *marginal technical coefficients*. In input–output analysis particularly restrictive assumptions are made about this relationship: namely, that factor inputs are combined in fixed proportions, and that constant returns to scale prevail. The simplest, but not the only, interpretation of this condition is to take the average input–output relationships observed in the existing input–output table and to assume that they will apply unchanged as *marginal* relationships in the foreseeable future. For example, if 40 units of manufacturing output are required as part of the input to produce 200 units of agricultural output at present, then in the future 80 units of manufacturing output will be needed in the production of 400 units of agricultural output.

This line of reasoning is open to a number of fairly obvious criticisms: it fails to allow for varying factor combinations, it fails to provide for scale effects, and it confuses present *average* relationships with future *marginal* relationships. The failure to allow for variations in factor combinations can be partially defended for short term predictions on the grounds that, with a given technology and production method in the short run, factor combination will be relatively fixed. The extent to which economies of scale are reaped in industry is still a matter of dispute, but where they are known to be important some steps can be taken to deal with them by selecting technical coefficients that are more appropriate to the equilibrium output level of the industry.

The existing average technical coefficients, derived from the input–output table, reflect an average of production functions established at different points of time in the past and not the production function based upon the latest technology. For example, electricity is currently generated in coal-fired plants, newer oil-fired generators and the latest nuclear generators. The construction of technical coefficients from the input–output table would imply, therefore, if used for prediction purposes, that additional electricity would require additional inputs of coal, oil and nuclear energy. For the purpose of short term prediction the technical coefficient should be based upon the marginal, not the average, technology in use. For longer periods the coefficients should take into account the likely effects of technical progress.

Using the data contained in Table 2.6 as a basis it is possible to illustrate the likely impact on industrial structure of a £40 million reduction in the purchase of agricultural products for final use and a compensating £40 million increase in the purchase of services for final use. This impact includes both *primary* or 'first-round' effects (i.e. the £40 million reduction in agricultural output and £40 million increase in service output) and *secondary* effects (e.g. the change in the intermediate demand for agricultural products resulting from the changes in the level of gross output in the three industrial sectors).

To calculate the combined primary and secondary impact it is necessary to determine the direct and indirect input requirements, by sector, for each unit of final use requirements. These are dependent upon the marginal technical coefficients, and in Table 2.8a the simplifying assumption has been made that these are equal to the average coefficients calculated from Table 2.6. Thus, a reduction of £40 million in the final use of agricultural products causes a combined (direct + indirect) reduction in the gross output of agricultural products of approximately £53 million (i.e. 1·3255×40 million). Similarly, an increase of £40 million in the final use of services causes a combined increase in the gross output of agricultural products of approximately £1·3 million (i.e. 0·0336×40 million). Therefore, the net combined impact of these two changes in final use is to reduce the output of agricultural products by approximately £51·7 million (i.e. £53 million−£1·3 million). The net combined impact on the services sector is to increase its output by £43 million, while in the manufactures sector, where final use purchases remain unaltered, output falls by £7 million (Table 2.8b.)

Table 2.8   *Effect on industrial structure of a change in final use demand.*

(*a*) *Direct and indirect requirements per £ of final demand*

Sector	Agriculture	Manufactures	Services
Agriculture	1·3255	0·3020	0·0336
Manufactures	0·3020	1·2081	0·1342
Services	0·0671	0·2685	1·1409

(*b*) *Impact on industrial structure of the specified change in final use consumption (£ m. rounded)*

Sector	Before		After	
	Final use	Gross output	Final use	Gross output
Agriculture	80	200	40	148
Manufactures	300	400	300	393
Services	100	200	140	243

The division of the economy into a larger number of industrial sectors would almost certainly reveal a greater change in industrial structure resulting from the specified change in the composition of final demand. For example, the manufacturing industries supplying the agricultural sector may not be the same as those supplying the services sector. Therefore, these two sections of the manufacturing sector would each be expected to experience greater changes in their levels of output than occurs in the aggregated manufacturing sector.

Changes in the methods of production
It is also possible to use input-output analysis to trace the effect on industrial structure of a change in technical coefficients, e.g. resulting from the substitution of electricity for solid fuels as a source of power in industry or the substitution of man-made fibres for natural fibres in the clothing industry.

For illustrative purposes the effect on industrial structure of increasing the ratio of manufacturing input to manufacturing output from 0·1 to 0·2 in Table 2.6, and of reducing the ratio of agricultural input to manufacturing

Table 2.9   *New input–output equilibrium after the specified change in technical coefficients (£ m. rounded).*

Input from:	Output to:			Final use	Gross output
	Agriculture	Manufactures	Services		
Agriculture	31	44	0	80	155
Manufactures	31	88	21	300	440
Services	0	88	21	100	209
Labour	93	220	167	20	500
Gross input	155	440	209	500	1,304

output from 0·2 to 0·1, is traced. The new equilibrium position is shown in Table 2.9, indicating a £45 million reduction in gross agricultural output, a £40 million increase in manufacturing output and, depite no change in its technical coefficients, a £9 million increase in gross services output. As in the previous illustration, no account is taken of the effect on final use demand of a change in aggregate output and income on the economy as a whole. Such feedback effects can be calculated using a more complex 'closed' input–output system.

CHANGES IN INDUSTRIAL STRUCTURE IN BRITAIN

With the assistance of input–output analysis it is possible to gain further insight into the causes of changes occurring in the relative importance of individual industries within an economy. One such study, of the changing structure of the UK economy over the period 1954–63, has grouped these possible causes into four main categories, the first two affecting final demand and the latter two affecting intermediate demand:

(1) changes in the structure of final demand due to differences in growth rates between private and public consumption, investment and the export sector;
(2) changes in the pattern of final demand within these sectors due to the differential impact of income, price and taste changes;
(3) changes in intermediate demand due to the indirect impact of changes in final demand; and
(4) changes in intermediate demand due to changes in technical coefficients.[27]

The findings of the study are illustrated in Table 2.10 by comparing the results obtained for four industries: coal, electricity, ships and motor vehicle assembly. Two of these industries, electricity and motor vehicles, benefited from an increase in purchases by the final use sector that greatly exceeded the average increase in the general level of final demand. This was predominantly due to favourable changes in the pattern of demand, which were in turn due to a mixture of favourable income, price and taste effects. These same industries also experienced a substantial increase in the level of their gross output. This was partly due to the combined direct and indirect impact of

Table 2.10　% Changes in the output of selected UK industries, 1954–63.

Type of change	Coal	Electricity	Ships	Motor vehicles
Change in final use	−15	+136	−15	+101
Change attributable to increase in general level of final demand	+30	+30	+30	+30
Change due to changes in the pattern of final demand	−43	+104	−41	+68
Change in gross output	−11	+102	−19	+89
Change (direct and indirect) due to changes in final use	+11	+82	−14	+89
Change due to changes in technical coefficients	−22	+20	−5	0

Source: R. Stone (ed.), 'Structural change in the British economy', in A Programme for Growth, 12 (Cambridge, Chapman & Hall, 1974), pp. 23 and 29.

changes in final use. However, in the case of electricity it was also due to a favourable change in technical coefficients whereby other industries used more electricity per unit of their output than previously – a consequence of such factors as changes in the relative price of fuels and advances in technology. By contrast the coal and shipbuilding industries experienced an unfavourable movement in the pattern of their final demand, whose impact on their gross output was reinforced by an unfavourable change in their technical coefficients.

This example again emphasises the complexity of the economic forces that determine the industrial structure of an economy. It also reinforces the caution, already expressed, in the use of statistically-derived industrial-structure 'patterns' for predictive and planning purposes. If common patterns of industrial structure apply to economies at similar stages of economic development, and if patterns of industrial change during the process of development are broadly identical, there must be:

(1) a basic similarity in the structure and pattern of final demand and in the input–output coefficients for the industries comprising economies at similar stages of development; and
(2) a basic similarity in the way in which these demand patterns and technical coefficients change at different stages of development.

Very restrictive assumptions relating to such matters as relative prices, tastes, income elasticities and the state of technical knowledge are required for these basic similarities to be guaranteed.

2.7　MARKETS AND MARKET STRUCTURE

The term 'market structure' refers to a selected number of organisational characteristics of a market that establish inter-relationships between the buyers and sellers of a particular product.[28] Market structure analysis is, therefore, a study of the organisational features of a market that are believed to have significance for the conduct and performance of firms comprising the market.

In simple theoretical analysis the concept of a *market* is unambiguous, and it has traditionally been defined as consisting of those buyers and sellers of a homogeneous product who are in sufficiently close contact with each other that a single price prevails. However, in practice the definition of a market presents many problems.

The basic difficulty is to distinguish between products that, although differentiated, belong to the same market and other products that, because they are more differentiated, belong to other markets. The distinction is essentially one of degree and is concerned with the extent of substitutability between products. In principle this is measurable as the price cross-elasticity of demand.[29] Where cross-elasticity is high and positive product substitutability should also be high, and such products may be regarded as belonging to the same market. However, the concept of cross-elasticity is unfortunately of limited help at a practical level. There are severe empirical difficulties with its computation, and there is no objective criterion to determine the critical level of the measure above which products are classified as differentiated and below which they are regarded as belonging to different markets. There are also difficulties in defining the spatial limits of markets. Normally, these are assumed to be coterminous with national boundaries; but in practice this may produce markets that (as in the case of internationally-traded raw materials) are too narrowly defined or that (as in the case of the retail trade) are too broadly delineated.

Statistical analyses of market structures are normally based upon industrial classifications at various levels of disaggregation, which do not necessarily equate to markets as defined above. In the United Kingdom a major source of data for the measurement of market structure is the Census of Production, in which data are classified according to the SIC (see section 2.2). Therefore, as an example, the examination of the degree of seller concentration in particular markets tends to proceed on the basis of production (not sales) data gathered for product-based census industries (not markets) at a national level. These basic weaknesses in market data necessarily limit the value of any market structure analysis based upon them.

The concept of market structure plays an important role in the received theory of the firm, where it is employed as an heuristic device describing the market circumstances under which the relevant theoretical models are believed to apply. It is also a central concept in industrial economics. Received price theory hypothesises certain relationships between market structure, firm behaviour and market performance; students of industrial economics attempt to verify or refute the existence and nature of these relationships. Caves has suggested that 'market structure is important because the structure determines the behaviour of firms . . . and that behaviour in turn determines the quality of the industry's performance'.[30] Therefore, if it is possible to demonstrate that particular types of market structure are consistently associated with particular types of performance, public policies may be framed to achieve predetermined performance targets through the manipulation of market structure. The remainder of this chapter is largely devoted to an examination of the nature of the structure–performance model, its empirical evaluation and its future role in industrial analysis.

2.8   STRUCTURE–PERFORMANCE MODELS

The structure–performance model hypothesises that particular types of market structure are associated with particular types of market behaviour and performance. The characteristics or dimensions of market structure traditionally identified in such a model are the degree of seller and buyer concentration, the extent of product differentiation and the height of barriers to entry into the market. In some cases other dimensions of market structure have also been investigated, such as the extent of product diversification and of vertical integration among sellers and buyers. In general it has been implicit to the model that relationships between structure and performance are unidirectional, namely, from structure via behaviour to performance. This assumption has been criticised and is reconsidered in section 2.11.

The most frequently used form of the structure–performance model has been one that relates various dimensions of market structure, as listed above, to one performance indicator: profits. However, the relationships between market structure and innovative activity (see section 5.4) and between market structure and advertising activity (see section 6.5) have also been investigated. In early empirical investigations the nature of the hypothesised relationship between each of the structural variables and the profit variable was not carefully specified, and where it was indicated it was normally assumed to be of a simple linear nature, as indicated in Table 2.11. However, the varying and sometimes conflicting results obtained from these empirical studies have, as described later in this chapter, prompted a number of respecifications of this model in terms of both:

(1) the definition and measurement of the variables to be included in the model; and
(2) the precise nature of the hypothesised relationships between these variables.

The definition and measurement of the structural variables are discussed in section 2.9 and of profit as a performance indicator in section 2.11 (also in

Table 2.11   *Relationships in the structure–performance model.*

Dimensions of market structure	*Performance indicator*	*Relationship*
Degree of seller concentration	Profit	Positive
Degree of buyer concentration	Profit	Negative
Degree of product differentiation	Profit	Positive
Height of entry barriers	Profit	Positive

greater detail in section 8.2). The relationships between the structural variables and profitability are reviewed in section 2.11. Therefore, it is sufficient at this stage to forewarn that these relationships are now recognised to be considerably more complex and ambiguous than was originally recognised. For example:

(1) Profit rates may increase only after a critical level of seller concentration has been exceeded rather than continuously as seller concentration increases. Alternatively, profit levels may stabilise or even decline at very high levels of seller concentration through fear of government intervention or because the market leaders are not pursuing profit-maximising objectives (see Figure 2.3).

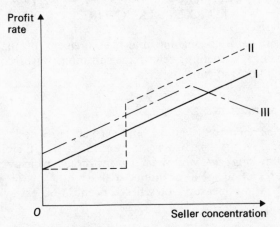

Fig. 2.3   Possible relationships between seller concentration and profit rates.

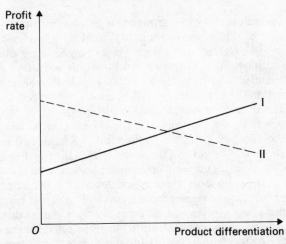

Fig. 2.4   Possible relationships between product differentiation and profit rates.

(2) High levels of product differentiation may enable individual firms to obtain considerable market protection for their products and thereby to earn high profit rates. On the other hand, a high level of product differentiation may reflect intense non-price competition and be associated with low profit rates (see Figure 2.4).

This situation underlines the importance of basing structure–performance models on clearly-articulated theoretical foundations. It also stresses the need for a willingness to re-examine both the foundations and the specification of these models where the empirical evidence highlights inadequacies.

2.9 DEFINITION AND MEASUREMENT OF MARKET STRUCTURES

This section examines the meaning and measurement of the four basic dimensions of market structure: seller concentration, buyer concentration, product differentiation and entry barriers.

SELLER CONCENTRATION

Seller concentration refers to the number and market shares of firms producing goods or services for a particular market.[31] It is, therefore, to be distinguished from *aggregate or overall concentration*, which relates to the number and shares of the total economic activity of firms in an economy (see section 3.3). Many measures of seller concentration exist, which differ according to:

(1) the concentration index used; and
(2) the size variable used in the construction of the concentration index.[32]

Concentration indices may be grouped into *absolute* and *relative* concentration measures. The most commonly used absolute measure is the *concentration ratio,* which records the percentage of an industry's size accounted for by a given number of the largest firms in that industry. As shown in Figure 2.5, this is indicated by the height of the cumulative concentration curve at a selected point on the horizontal axis. The choice of this point is a matter of judgement, which should be determined by the purpose for which the concentration ratio is to be used. In practice the choice may be restricted by the form in which the data are available. In the United Kingdom it has been most common to estimate the concentration ratio for the three or five largest firms, whereas in the United States the four-firm concentration ratio is more common.

The concentration ratio only records the level of seller concentration at one point on the cumulative concentration curve. Therefore, when comparing the level of seller concentration in different markets the rankings will alter according to the point on the concentration curves selected for the comparison, provided that the concentration curves for the different markets intersect. In practice this may not be a frequent occurrence, but this potential deficiency

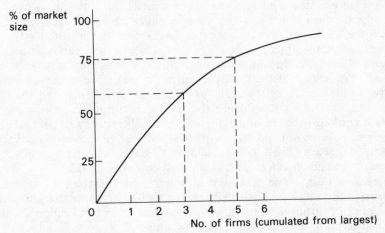

Fig. 2.5 Cumulative concentration curve showing three- and five-firm concentration ratios.

has encouraged the development of summary concentration indices that take into account the number and shares of *all* the firms producing for the market. One such index is the *Herfindahl index*, which is calculated by squaring and summating the share of market size accounted for by every firm producing for the market.

Measures of relative concentration record the degree of inequality in the share of firms producing for a given market. This inequality in share can be recorded in the form of a *Lorenz curve* (see Figure 2.6), which shows the cumulative percentage of market size accounted for by various percentages of the number of firms producing for the market, cumulated from the smallest. The diagonal line in Figure 2.6 indicates a distribution of complete equality in firm sizes, so that the extent to which the Lorenz curve deviates from this line is an indication of the relative seller concentration in a market. One

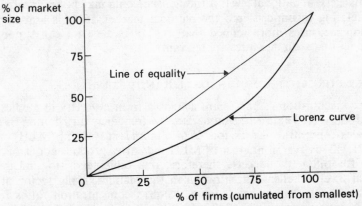

Fig. 2.6 The Lorenz curve as an indicator of relative seller concentration.

such measure is the *Gini concentration ratio*, which is defined as the area under the Lorenz curve divided by the area under the line of equality.

The size of the market and the producing firm's share of it have been measured in terms of sales, net output, employment and capital assets. The measure of seller concentration obtained will differ according to which of these size variables is used, if there are differences in the degree of capital intensity and vertical integration between firms of different sizes. However, the choice of size variable may not influence the seller-concentration ranking order of different markets if, for example, there is an equal tendency in all markets for large firms to be most capital intensive. In practice the choice of size variable is also restricted by the type and quality of data that are available, sales, net output and employment data being most commonly used.

There has been some tendency in the recent literature to search for mathematically more sophisticated measures of seller concentration without sufficient prior justification that these are needed. Such justification should be in similar terms to the following quotation, although it has to be admitted that at present *a priori* theory gives insufficient guidance on which measures of seller concentration are likely to be most helpful:

> Which measure of concentration is optimal depends on the intended use of the measure. If one is concerned with the relationship between seller concentration and industrial behaviour, the crucial issue is whether some aspect of the number and size distribution of firms in an industry influences the behaviour of firms in the industry. In other words, from a behavioural point of view, what is important is the weight accorded to the number and size distribution of rival firms by *decision-makers in an industry* in their decision-making.[33]

A further reason for caution in developing more sophisticated seller-concentration measures is the imperfect data from which these have to be calculated. As mentioned in section 2.7, seller concentration measures are usually calculated on the basis of Census of Production data, which relate to value of production (not sales) for census industries or groups of products (not markets) at national level. Although such data may be augmented, e.g. by data relating to imports into the national market, there is limited value in devising measures more refined than the available data can support, even assuming that such measures are relevant.

SELLER CONCENTRATION IN BRITISH INDUSTRY

Seller concentration estimates are available from a variety of studies for the period 1935–71. Table 2.12 summarises the frequency distribution of the five-firm sales-concentration ratio for 145 Minimum List Heading (MLH) industries in 1971.[34] However, a number of MLH industries produce goods of different kinds for different markets; therefore, this table tends to understate the general level of seller concentration in the manufacturing sector of British industry. Table 2.13 is based upon five-firm concentration ratios for more detailed product groups in 1968, which have been averaged according to the

Table 2.12 *Distribution of 145 MLH industries according to the level of five-firm sales-concentration ratio, 1971.*

Level of sales concentration ratio (% of net output of MLH industry of five largest enterprises)	No. of industries
0–19	15
20–39	35
40–59	43
60–79	28
80–99	24

Source: Department of Industry, *Report on the Census of Production, 1971: Summary Tables,* Business Monitor PA1002 (London, HMSO, 1976).

SIC Order to which they belong.[35] Taken together, these tables indicate the considerable variation in the level of seller concentration and the extensive nature of oligopolistic influences that exist in the manufacturing sector. Very little systematic evidence exists on the degree of seller concentration in the other sectors of the economy, but the data gathered by Aaronovitch and Sawyer lend support to the view that concentration levels are on average lower in these sectors than in the manufacturing sector.[36]

Estimates of changes in the general level of seller concentration over time are limited by the incomplete comparability of data, but the general trend is fairly clearly established. Evely and Little have compared the levels of the three-firm employment-concentration ratios for 1935 and 1951 for forty-one com-

Table 2.13 *Weighted five-firm sales-concentration ratios, 1968.*

Industry group	No. of products	Sales concentration ratio (%)
Food, drink, tobacco	42	82
Chemicals and allied industries	47	79
Metals manufactures	20	75
Plant, machinery and instrument engineering	40	54
Electrical engineering	27	76
Vehicles	9	93
Other metals	21	58
Textiles	28	53
Leather, clothing and footwear	19	32
Bricks, pottery, glass, cement	16	65
Timber, furniture	9	23
Paper, printing, publishing	10	52
Other manufacturing industries	14	61

Source: K. D. George, 'A note on changes in industrial concentration in the United Kingdom', *Economic Journal,* vol. 85 (1975), pp. 124–8.

parable trades, and have observed increases in twenty-seven cases and decreases in fourteen.[37] Armstrong and Silberston have compared concentration ratios for sixty-three trades in the Census of Production over the period 1951–8 and have observed thirty-six increases and sixteen decreases.[38] In a study of 209 product groups George has found 141 increases and 67 decreases in the five-firm seller-concentration ratio between 1958 and 1963.[39] Elliott, using data from the 1968 Census of Production, has concluded that seller concentration, as measured by the same ratio, increased between 1958 and 1968 and that the rate of increase accelerated after 1963.[40] In a parallel study based upon 157 products, George has calculated the unweighted five-firm average-concentration ratios in 1958, 1963 and 1968 to be 56·6, 59·6 and 65·4 per cent respectively, thus lending further support to the view that the rate of increase in seller concentration was accelerating during the period.[35] Therefore, it seems that the general level of seller concentration has been increasing since the late 1940s or earlier, moderately at first but then at an accelerated rate during the 1960s. A similar conclusion has been reached by Aaronovitch and Sawyer (see Table 2.14). However, this trend did not apply to all product groups because during each period there were a significant number of products for which the seller concentration ratio declined.

Table 2.14   *Changes in average concentration ratios, 1935–68.*

	1935–51	1951–8	1958–63	1963–8
Actual change (%)	+7·20	+5·21	+8·27	+8·66
Annual change (%)	+0·44	+0·73	+1·60	+1·67

Source: S. Aaronovitch and M. C. Sawyer, 'The concentration of British manufacturing industry', *Lloyds Bank Review,* No. 114, (October 1974), pp. 14–24.

SELLER CONCENTRATION IN OTHER COUNTRIES

A number of studies have shown that the ranking of manufacturing industries according to the level of seller concentration is similar in many developed economies.[41] However, this does not necessarily mean that the average level of concentration is the same in such countries or that the trends over time are identical. Comparisons of four-firm concentration ratios within the European Economic Community (EEC) suggest that a higher level of concentration exists in Britain than in West Germany, France or Italy (see Table 2.15). Also, compared with the situation in the United Kingdom, the increase in the average level of seller concentration in the United States appears to have been considerably more modest. In the United States the weighted four-firm average-concentration ratio rose by about 2 percentage points between 1947 and 1954, declined by about 1 percentage point in 1954–8 and then increased by less than 1 percentage point in 1958–70.[42] However, as in the United Kingdom, these average changes conceal much more substantial increases and decreases in the concentration ratio for individual product groups.

Table 2.15 *Four-firm employment-concentration ratios in EEC countries.*

	Weighted average-concentration ratio (%)			
	UK	*West Germany*	*France*	*Italy*
41 industries	30	19	22	19
All manufacturing industries	32	22	24	20

Source: K. D. George and T. S. Ward, *The Structure of Industry in the EEC* (Cambridge, Cambridge UP, 1975), table 3.2.

BUYER CONCENTRATION

Buyer concentration refers to the number and size distribution of firms purchasing a particular type of product, service or material. Therefore, it is analogous to seller concentration, and in principle a range of absolute and relative measures of buyer concentration corresponding to those already described for seller concentration could be constructed. However, such measures have not been constructed, due largely to the absence of data classifying the total purchases of each type of product etc. by purchasing firm.

Recently, attempts have been made to estimate buyer concentration ratios by using input–output statistics to identify flows of intermediate products from each seller industry to each of its purchasing industries.[43, 44] Provided that the intermediate-factor input–output ratio is the same for all firms within each purchasing industry, the buyer concentration curve in each such industry is identical to its seller concentration curve, which may be derived from Census of Production data. Therefore, given this simplifying assumption, buyer concentration ratios may be estimated using a combination of Census of Production and input–output data.

Guth *et al.* have used this approach on 1963 data relating to the US manufacturing sector and have drawn the following tentative conclusions:

(1) Overall, the general level of buyer concentration was substantially lower than the level of seller concentration.
(2) Substantial differences existed in the pattern of buyer concentration across industries.
(3) In general there was only a weak positive industry-by-industry relationship between buyer and seller concentration ratios, but in some industries concentration ratios were substantial for both buyers and sellers.

Therefore, in certain markets buyer power may have a significant influence on business behaviour and performance. If this is so, Guth *et al.* have suggested greater attention should be given to the development of models of oligopsony and bilateral oligopoly.[44]

PRODUCT DIFFERENTIATION AND BARRIERS TO ENTRY

Product differentiation exists where the products sold within the same market are not regarded by buyers as perfect substitutes. Although product differentiation has traditionally been regarded as one of the basic dimensions of market structure, there are a number of difficulties associated with its inclusion, particularly in empirical studies.

First, it is unsatisfactory to measure the degree of product differentiation within a market on the basis of the number of physical varieties of the product sold. This is a potentially misleading measure of the degree of product differentiation as perceived in the minds of buyers. Estimates of the price cross-elasticities of demand between products sold in the market provide a better basis for measurement, but these are generally unavailable.[29] Alternatively, proxy measures of product differentiation have been used, among which estimates of advertising intensity are the most common. However, the level of advertising intensity in a market is affected by a number of different factors, including the profit margins of sellers (see section 6.5); therefore, it may not accurately reflect the degree of product differentiation. Further, advertising intensity may be a determinant of other dimensions of market structure – notably entry barriers but also seller concentration (see section 6.5). Therefore, product differentiation is not separately included in many empirical studies of market structure but is subsumed under the entry barrier variable, most commonly by the inclusion of a measure of advertising intensity.

Entry barriers may be defined as obstacles that prevent new firms from engaging in the production and sale of products in a market. *Inter alia,* they may enable existing firms to obtain larger profit margins on their sales than would otherwise be the case without attracting competition from new entrants. These obstacles take four main forms:

(1) *legal obstacles,* such as patent rights or other forms of legal protection from new entry into a market;
(2) *buyer loyalty* to product brands of established firms, reinforced by the cumulative impact of advertising;
(3) *absolute cost advantages,* where the costs of established firms are lower than those of potential entrants at a comparable scale of output; and
(4) *economies of scale* in production, which discourage new entrants because of:
   (a) high initial capital requirements for an economic level of production; and
   (b) risk of substantial price reductions following entry, resulting from the increase in total supply on the market (see section 6.2, on the Sylos postulate).

Interview techniques have been used to obtain from businessmen direct estimates of the extent to which they believed that they could raise prices above basic average-cost levels without attracting. new firms into their market.[45] However, this is unlikely to provide a satisfactory objective measure. Instead, measures may be related to the particular forms that entry obstacles take. The two most common types of measure used relate to advertising intensity and economies of scale. The first of these, as previously stated, is examined in Chapter 6. The measurement of economies of scale is discussed in the next section.

2.10 DETERMINANTS OF MARKET STRUCTURE

Major differences exist between the structure of different markets, and over time the structure of many individual markets also changes considerably. The factors underlying these differences and changes have been explored in a number of studies, particularly in relation to seller concentration ratios.[35, 37 – 9, 42] It has been suggested that the main differences observed in market structures in an economy are due to the interplay of scale economies, market size and growth rate, government policies, merger activities by participating firms and chance factors.[42] Similarly, changes over time in the structure of particular markets are probably the product of the following factors:

(1) *Technical changes* resulting in product and process innovations. Product innovations alter the range of products sold in the market, and through this they may alter the number and size distribution of buyers and sellers as well as the ease of new entry into the market. Process innovations change the absolute cost advantages of some or all of the existing producers and may change the scale of production at which maximum economies are achieved.

(2) *Long term changes in demand and supply conditions.* Other things being equal, a secular rise in demand is expected to lead to a fall in seller concentration. Long term changes in the availability of resource inputs may change the absolute cost advantages of some or all of the existing firms within the market.

(3) *Government policy changes* on such matters as monopolies, mergers and restrictive practices, patent protection and import controls may be expected to bring about changes in seller and buyer concentration and in entry barriers.

(4) *Chance factors,* e.g. interruptions to supplies or markets during wartime periods, may temporarily or permanently alter market structures.

(5) *Corporate policies of established firms and new entrants.* If certain of these firms are large, in terms either of their absolute size or of their market share, they may possess sufficient influence to change the existing structure of markets through their own corporate policies relating to acquisition and merger, product differentiation and promotional advertising.

If the last of these factors is an important influence in changing market structures, it casts doubt upon the unidirectional relationship between market structure and market performance, as hypothesised in section 2.8. Therefore, it is considered further in section 2.11 as part of a general appraisal of the structure–performance model. First, however, the nature and measurement of scale economies and their relationship to market structures are examined further.

SCALE ECONOMIES

Economies, or diseconomies, of scale refer to 'the effect on average costs of production of different rates of output, per unit of time, of a given commodity, when all possible adaptations have been carried out to make production at each scale as efficient as possible'.[47] These economies may relate to the scale of a plant or firm and are reflected in the shape of its long-run average-cost function, which is constructed on the assumption of given factor prices and a given state of technical knowledge.

Traditionally, it has been assumed that long-run average-cost functions are U-shaped, but empirical studies indicate that they are more typically L-shaped. In other words, average costs initially fall as output increases, but above a certain level of output average costs remain relatively constant. The methods of estimation used in these empirical studies are briefly examined below, before some of their findings are presented and their significance in explaining market structures is discussed. For this purpose studies may be grouped into three categories[48] as:

(1) time series and cross-sectional statistical studies;[49]
(2) survivor technique studies;[50, 51] and
(3) engineering cost studies.[52]

Time series studies derive the shape of a cost function by comparing the costs of one or more firms, or plants, as their level of output changes over time; cross-sectional studies derive the cost function by comparing the costs of different-sized firms, or plants, in the same industry at the same point in time. Both approaches have the advantage that they are based on observed rather than hypothetical cost conditions. However, they encounter difficulties. First, the cost-accounting data may be incomplete or inconsistent between the different firms or periods of time to which the study relates. Second, the cost data may not satisfy the assumptions underlying the construction of cost functions concerning a homogeneous output, a given state of technology and factor prices, and efficiency in production. For example, time series observations may relate to a changing mix in the firm's products, and both the level of factor prices and the state of technical knowledge may alter over time. Similarly, in cross-sectional studies the firms included in the study may not be producing identical products or operating under the same cost conditions. The more-sophisticated statistical cost studies have attempted to take these elements of heterogeneity into account through multiple regression analysis, but it has rarely been possible to do so in a completely satisfactory manner.

An alternative approach, also based on observing actual market conditions, is the survivor technique:

The firms in an industry are grouped into size classes, and the share of industry output (or some other index of size) accounted for by each size class at two or more points in time is compared. The shape of the long-run costs. Size classes experiencing a declining share of industry output are assumed output of any size class are related to the average cost of producing and distributing the product in that size class. Size classes experiencing an increase in the share of industry output are assumed to have minimum average costs. Size classes experiencing a declining share of industry output are assumed to be relatively inefficient, that is, are assumed to have higher unit costs.[53]

The survivor technique is used to determine the general shape rather than the numerical values of the cost function, and it can only do this reliably if all the firms in the industry are operating in the same competitive market and under similar technical conditions. Otherwise, firms may grow at different rates because they face different market conditions or are pursuing different business objectives.

The third approach uses cost estimates for engineering-designed production facilities of different-sized capacities for a given product range. This method mainly avoids the problem of non-comparability in cost or other data encountered in the two previously-mentioned approaches. However, one important weakness is that the cost estimates are often based upon hypothetical production facilities, which may differ from the cost levels experienced under actual production conditions. Costing problems may arise, when using this approach, with complex production processes that involve balancing output at different stages of production for which the operating plant at each stage differs in its optimum size. Similarly, difficulties can arise in estimating non-production items such as distribution and general administration costs.

Because of the difficulties with each of the three approaches the costing results obtained by one method should be cross-checked with results obtained by the other methods, assuming that satisfactory data for this purpose are available. In practice this is rarely possible.

In the United Kingdom the most extensive studies of scale economies have been undertaken by Pratten and relate to the late 1960s.[52] They refer to economies of plant scale and are based upon the engineering cost approach, supplemented by cross-checking where this was possible. These have generally confirmed the L-shape of the typical long-run average-cost function and, therefore, focused attention on the scale of production where average costs first reach their minimum level: the *minimum efficient scale* (MES) of production. In Table 2.16 the MES is shown for a selection of products as a percentage of the total national

Table 2.16   *MES for selected products in the United Kingdom, 1969.*

Product	MES as % of UK market (% of submarket in parentheses)	% increase in total unit costs at 50% MES
Aircraft (one type)	>100	>20
Individual dye plants	100	22
Electronic capital goods	100	10
Detergents	20	2·5
Oil refineries	10 (40)	5
Cement	10 (40)	9
Beer	3 (6)	9
Bricks (non-Fletton)	0·5 (5)	25
Small engineering castings	0·2	5

Source: C. F. Pratten, *Economies of Scale in Manufacturing Industries* (Cambridge, Cambridge UP, 1971); quoted in A. Silberston, 'Economies of scale in theory and practice', *Economic Journal*, vol. 82 (1972), supplement, pp. 369–91.

market, and where relevant the subnational market, that it served. Thus, for this sample of products the MES varied between less than 5 per cent to over 100 per cent of the relevant national market. However, the significance of these percentages also depends upon the extent to which unit costs would rise if plant were operated at less than the MES. Table 2.16, therefore, also shows the extent to which unit costs would increase if plants had a capacity equal to half of the MES.

Other things being equal, it might be expected that trades producing goods that record high percentages in both columns in Table 2.16 would also have relatively high seller-concentration ratios and entry barriers. However, the relationship between the MES and these two dimensions of market structure is complicated by two other factors:

(1) The MES data relate to the optimum technical scale of plant constructed in 1969 whereas the seller concentration data for that year have been influenced by the sizes of existing plants, which because they were of different vintages may have had different MESs.
(2) Seller concentration ratios relate to the market shares of *enterprises* whereas the MES data relate to *plants*. A trade may have a high seller concentration ratio, even where the MES is a low percentage of the total market, if certain sellers each operate a sufficiently large number of plants. If the average cost function for individual plants is L-shaped, there will be no cost penalty in multiplant operation provided that each exceeds the MES and no diseconomies of large scale organisation are incurred. On the other hand, if there are financial, marketing or research-and-development advantages accruing to large organisations, multiplant operation may be encouraged. Similarly, if some large firms pursue growth rather than profit-maximising objectives, they may choose to grow beyond the scale where their unit costs are at a minimum.

For these reasons attempts have been made to relate differences in seller concentration ratios between industries to differences in their average plant size and plant–enterprise ratios. George, using 1958 data, has found a positive relationship between average plant size and the level of seller concentration in individual industries.[54] Sawyer, using 1963 data, has determined that over 72 per cent of the variation in seller concentration between trades could be explained by the combined effect of the plant size and plant–enterprise ratio variables.[55] In studies related to US industry Nelson and others have emphasised the importance of multiplant operation as a major contributor to high seller concentration.[56]

Table 2.17 contains a comparison, based upon 1971 data, of five high and five low seller-concentration industries in the United Kingdom. First, it shows that, of the five largest enterprises in the high seller-concentration industries, four had considerably larger establishments than the five largest enterprises in the low seller-concentration industries. Further, the relative difference in average establishment size between the largest and other enterprises was also greater in the high seller-concentration industries. The largest enterprises in the high seller-concentration industries also had a plant–

Table 2.17   Characteristics of selected high and low seller-concentration industries in the United Kingdom, 1971.

Industry	Five-firm[a] seller-concentration ratio (%)	Largest five[a] enterprises		Rest of industry		
		Average plant size (no. of employees)	Plant–enterprise ratio	Average plant size (no. of employees)	Plant–enterprise ratio	No. of enterprises
High seller concentration						
Tobacco	99	2,000	3·5	25	1·0	19
Coke ovens	98	350	5·7	16	1·6	11
Man-made fibres	98	2,000	3·5	200	1·0	5
Sugar	97	1,200	3·3	23	1·1	15
Cement	94	1,150	2·2	45	1·1	18
Low seller concentration						
Canvas goods	12	100	2·8	22	1·1	373
General printing and publishing	11	400	12·0	24	1·0	7,038
Furniture and upholstery	9	330	4·6	32	1·0	2,351
Miscellaneous metal manufacture	10	590	8·6	31	1·1	6,829
Shop and office fittings	9	300	1·8	23	1·1	1,154

Source: Department of Industry, *Report on the Census of Production, 1971: Summary Tables*, Business Monitor PA1002 (London, HMSO, 1976).
Note:
(a)   The number of firms included in the seller concentration ratio may differ slightly between industries due mainly to confidentiality in data.

enterprise ratio that was two to four times greater than that for other firms in the same industries. However, a similar, and in certain cases greater, difference in this ratio occurred in low seller-concentration industries; therefore, this cannot be a cause of the *relative* difference in seller concentration between these two groups of industries. Finally, the table draws attention to the important influence on the level of seller concentration of the size of the industry, given the plant size and plant–enterprise ratio of the five largest firms. In both the 'Coke ovens' and 'Furniture and upholstery' industries the five largest enterprises had broadly similar average plant sizes and plant–enterprise ratios. However, in the former case the market was only sufficiently large to support eleven other enterprises, whereas in the latter it could support over two thousand, three hundred.

Therefore, it seems that differences in average plant size, relative to market size, were the primary cause of *differences* in seller concentration between British industries, but the *absolute* seller-concentration level in most industries was substantially higher than would otherwise have been the case because large enterprises generally had relatively high plant–enterprise ratios. To what extent the general level of seller concentration, and its variation between individual industries, was due to interindustry differences in economies of scale cannot be confidently determined without more reliable and comprehensive MES data. The fact that the largest enterprises had larger average plant sizes and plant–enterprise ratios than other enterprises in the same industries has sometimes been taken as an indication that they had grown beyond their MES. However, the other enterprises may have been below the MES or may have belonged to a different section of the industry to which a lower MES applied.

A similar element of uncertainty arises when explaining the increase over time in the average level of seller concentration in the United Kingdom. Between 1935 and 1963 the percentage of total manufacturing employment in plants with over 1,500 employees rose from 15 to 28 per cent and had increased to 34 per cent by 1971.[34] The increase in the average size of establishments during this period would have resulted in an increase in the general level of seller concentration provided that it exceeded the increase in the average size of markets and provided that the plant–enterprise ratio remained constant or increased. However, it has been suggested that, particularly during the 1960s, increases in the seller concentration level have been closely associated with the level of merger and acquisition activity:

The average increase in concentration, and also the predominance of increases over decreases in concentration, are particularly noticeable in metals, electrical engineering, vehicles, textiles, leather, clothing and footwear, and bricks, etc. In the case of metals the major factor explaining the big increase was undoubtedly the nationalisation of the major steel companies in 1967. In other industries, however, mergers almost certainly played the dominant role. Certainly all of them, and especially electrical engineering, vehicles and textiles, experienced intensive merger activity in the second half of the 1960s.[35]

The reasons for merger activity are the subject of continuing debate (see section 5.3), involving the motives of reducing competition, reaping scale economies or achieving growth. Initially, whatever the motive the process of acquisition and merger may be expected to increase the seller concentration ratio by increasing the plant–enterprise ratio. However, depending upon the motivation of the merger it may eventually result in a process of plant rationalisation and closure, which will increase the average plant size of the new enterprise.

2.11 RELATIONSHIPS BETWEEN MARKET STRUCTURE AND PERFORMANCE

Many empirical studies have attempted to establish the relationships between the structure of markets and the performance of the firms operating within them, but these have been of limited scope in two senses. First, they have been mainly concerned with only one aspect of performance, namely, profits, although some studies have investigated the relationship between market structure and innovative activity (see section 5.4) and between market structure and advertising intensity (see section 6.5). Second, most studies have been restricted to the market impact of one or two dimensions of market structure, which have most frequently been seller concentration and various measures of entry barriers.

The North American literature on the market structure–profitability relationship is very extensive,[31] but there has been a shortage of comparable British studies. However, this has recently been partially remedied (see Table 2.18). The main features and findings of these British studies are described below. Although they differ from each other according to the detailed form of the structure–performance model and data used, most take the form of

$$P = P(S, B, C, D) \tag{2.1}$$

where P is a measure of profitability, S is one or more measures of seller concentration, B is one or more measures of entry barriers, C refers to the degree of capital intensity in production and D indicates the rate of change in the recent or current level of demand for the industry's (market's) products.

Profit has been measured most commonly as an average price-cost margin for the census-defined trade to which it refers or, less commonly through lack of data, as an average rate of return on capital employed in the trade. Because of data problems profits cannot normally be estimated according to the economist's definition of pure profit. Instead, for example, the price-cost margin may be measured as $(VA - W)/T$ where VA is the value added by the industry, W is wages and salaries and T is the value of sales (or value added) of the industry for a given time period.[57, 58] The price–cost margin will, therefore, include elements of depreciation, interest and rent as well as of profit – hence the significance of including a measure of the degree of capital intensity of an industry as one of the explanatory determinants of price–cost differences between industries.

Seller concentration was included as an explanatory variable in all eight studies reported in Table 2.18, but a number of different measures of this variable were used: five-firm sales-concentration ratio, five-firm employment-

Table 2.18   *The relationship between market structure and profitability in the United Kingdom.*

Study (period to which study relates in parentheses) [a]	Main explanatory variables [b] (hypothesised relationship with profitability in parentheses)					
	Seller concentration (+)	Imports (−)	Advertising intensity (+)	Plant or enterprise size (+)	Capital intensity (+)	Demand change (+)
Phillips (1951)[59]	√c	x	√c	√c	x	√
Shepherd (1958 and 1963)[60] (adjusted for imports)	√c	x	x	x	√	√c
Holtermann (1963)[61]	√	x	√c	√	√c	√c
Khalilzadeh-Shirazi (1963)[62]	√	√d	√c	√c	√c	√
Hart and Morgan (1968)[63]	√c	√	√c	√	√c	√
Hitiris (1968)[64]	√c	√c	√	x	√c	√c
Cowling and Waterson (1958–68)[65]	√c	x	x	x	x	√
Nickell and Metcalf (1974–6)[66]	√c	x	√c	√c	x	x

Key: √ Variable included in the study; x variable not included in the study.

Notes:
(a) Studies are given in detail in notes 59–66.
(b) The table does not include all the variables analysed in each of the studies. Additionally, the significance of a variable sometimes varies according to the other variables included in the model. Therefore, reference should be made to the original studies for full details.
(c) *t* value exceeded 1·65 (or standard error equivalent).
(d) Export variable significant.

concentration ratio, three-firm concentration ratio and the Hirfindahl measure. Additionally, in four cases imports were taken into account either as a separate variable or through a modification to the seller concentration ratio. Barriers to entry were mainly represented by two variables: advertising intensity (most commonly measured as an advertising expenditure–sales ratio) in six studies, and plant or enterprise size (most frequently calculated as average plant size) in five studies. The demand change and capital intensity variables were included in seven and five studies respectively.

In each study the significance of each variable as a determinant of profitability was tested using multiple regression analysis, usually on the assumption that the relationship was of a linear nature. The variables for which a statistically significant relationship was established are indicated in Table 2.18 ($t > 1.65$), and these findings are summarised below.

In six of the eight studies one or other of the measures of seller concentration was positively correlated with price–cost margins; and in two out of the four studies in which it was analysed, imports or import tariffs also had the expected relationship with profit levels. The advertising–sales ratio was positively correlated with price-cost margins in five out of six studies, as would be expected if it raises entry barriers. However, this is a suspect relationship because high advertising–sales ratios may in part be a response to, rather than a cause of, high price–cost margins (see section 6.5). The other entry barrier variable, namely, plant or enterprise size, was positively correlated with price–cost margins, as hypothesised, in three out of five studies. Capital intensity was also positively correlated, as expected, with price–cost margins in four studies, while demand changes were positively related to profit levels in three out of seven studies.

These results provide some support for the view that increased levels of seller concentration and entry barriers are associated with higher price–cost margins, but this is neither invariably nor unambiguously the case. The regression equations reported in these studies frequently accounted for less than 50 per cent of the variance in price–cost margins, and seller concentration and entry barriers combined invariably accounted for only a small proportion of the observed differences in these margins. The nature of these findings has led in turn to a more critical attitude towards the simple structure–performance model and its role in the analysis of industrial behaviour. In particular, the following possible deficiencies merit attention:

(1) *Omission of variables.* None of the studies reviewed include a buyer concentration variable, and only a minority of the studies have attempted to take the influence of imports into account. Similarly, price elasticity of demand, which affects the margin between price and marginal cost, is not taken into account in most of the studies.[65] Other writers have suggested that the degrees of vertical integration and of diversification among sellers and buyers in a market may be additional structural determinants of price–cost margins, but the nature of these relationships still needs to be clarified at the theoretical level.

(2) *Mis-specification of variables.* A number of variables, notably seller concentration and entry barriers, are defined in different ways in these

studies. The seller concentration ratio is favoured by some while the Hirfindahl measure is used by others. A variety of different measures of entry barriers are in use. The plant or enterprise size variable may, as indicated in section 2.10, be a determinant of seller concentration as well as of entry barriers. Similarly, the influence of advertising may be better represented by the absolute level of advertising expenditure than by the advertising–sales ratio.[58] In each case there is a need to clarify the theoretically preferred specification of the variable.

(3) *Mis-specification of relationships.* Although assumed in most studies, it is not yet clear that the relationship between the dimensions of market structure and price–cost margins is of a linear nature. A number of American studies, for example, have indicated a different kind of relationship whereby the price–cost margin increases when seller concentration and entry barriers exceed critical threshold levels.[67]

More fundamentally, the assumption in the simple market structure–performance model that structure–conduct–performance relationships are unidirectional is increasingly questioned. The assumption that market structure 'dictates' business behaviour and performance is most applicable to the small firm economy in which market structures are relatively stable over time. The growing importance in the national economy of the large diversified enterprise, which is analysed in Chapters 3–5, has seriously weakened the usefulness of this simple model. If large firms are unable to achieve a satisfactory performance in certain of their markets, they may use their economic power and influence to change the market's behaviour to provide them with a more acceptable performance. Alternatively, they may seek to change market structure from *within* the market by policies of merger and acquisition (to raise seller concentration), by product innovation (to increase product differentiation) or by intensified advertising campaigns (to raise entry barriers). These feedback effects may necessitate a simultaneous rather than a single equation approach in the construction of structure–performance models.

(4) *Measurement problems.* The omission and mis-specification of variables may arise because incomplete or unsatisfactory data are available. It is most frequently the case that published data relate to industries rather than markets, price–cost margins rather than profits, simple seller-concentration ratios (but not buyer concentration ratios) and relatively crude proxy measures for entry barriers. Substantial improvements in the data available for structure–performance studies will, therefore, probably require special investigations on an individual market, or product group, basis:

What do we know from the empirical studies of relations between structure and profitability? Very little, it appears. Market concentration may be the cause of high profits, or, conversely, market concentration and high profits may be the result of superior performance by a few firms. Similar observations apply to other variables used in the studies. Better theory, better data and above all, better econometrics are needed before policy can be based on anything other than in-depth institutional studies of particular markets.[68]

This conclusion concerns the relationship between structure and profitability, but from the standpoint of public policy there are other performance impacts due to market structures that require equally careful investigation: on technical progress and innovation (section 5.4), on the level of X-efficiency (section 8.6) and on promotional activities (section 6.5). In each of these cases also a more sophisticated structure–performance model may be needed, and the data required to use it will probably only be obtained by supplementing published data through more detailed investigations of particular product groups and markets.

2.12   FURTHER READING

A more detailed analysis of the industrial structure of economies at different stages of development can be found in Chenery and Syrquin[7] and Kuznets.[8] Production and productivity measurement in the UK services sector is examined in Briscoe,[19] and the basic issues raised by the 'de-industrialisation debate' are reviewed in Singh[12] and Blackaby.[70] Yan[23] contains an introductory explanation of input–output analysis. Its possible use in explaining the changing industrial structure of the UK economy can be studied in Stone.[27]

A review of the methods used in measuring the main dimensions of market structure is contained in Needham.[69] Seller concentration levels and trends in the United Kingdom are examined in George[35, 39] and George and Ward,[41] and more recent statistics are to be found in the Census of Production Summary Tables.[34] The determinants of market structure are analysed in Scherer[46] and the nature and extent of scale economies in Silberston.[47] Recent UK studies of the relationship between market structure and profitability are listed in Table 2.18,[59–66] while Phillips contains a useful critique of the simple structure–performance model.[58]

NOTES AND REFERENCES

1 D. Needham, *Economic Analysis and Industrial Structure* (New York, Holt, Reinhart & Winston, 1970) has defined these characteristics to include 'cost conditions, concentration, vertical integration, diversification and entry barriers'.

2 J. Stafford, 'The development of industrial statistics', *Statistical News* (May 1968).

3 Central Statistical Office (CSO), *Standard Industrial Classification* (London, HMSO, revised 1968), para. 4.

4 For example, Office of Management and Budget, *Standard Industrial Classification Manual* (Washington, DC, US Government Printing Office, 1972).

5 United Nations, *Indexes to the International Classification of All Economic Activities,* Statistical Papers Series M, No. 4 (New York, UN, 1959), p. 7.

6 United Nations, *International Standard Industrial Classification of All Economic Activities,* Statistical Papers Series M, No. 4, Rev. 2 (New York, UN, 1968).

7 H. Chenery and M. Syrquin, *Patterns of Development, 1950–1970* (London, Oxford UP, 1975).

8 S. Kuznets, *Economic Growth of Nations* (Cambridge, Mass., Harvard UP, 1971).

9 H. Chenery, 'Patterns of industrial growth', *American Economic Review,* vol. 50 (1960), pp. 624–54.

10 V. R. Fuchs, *The Service Economy* (New York, National Bureau of Economic Research, 1968).

11 R. B. Sutcliffe, *Industry and Underdevelopment* (London, Addison-Wesley, 1971), p. 62.

12 A. Singh 'UK industry and the world economy: case of de-industrialisation', *Cambridge Journal of Economics,* vol. 1 (1977), pp. 113–36.

13 G. D. N. Worswick and C. G. Fane, 'Goods and services once again', *District Bank Review,* vol. 161 (March 1967).

14 *The Selective Employment Tax,* Cmnd 2986 (London, HMSO, 1966).

15 An alternative and more meaningful distinction is made between tradable and non-tradable goods and services in W. Eltis, 'How public sector growth causes balance of payments deficits', *International Currency Review* (January–February 1975).

16 A fuller examination of the difficulties involved in estimating and interpreting productivity measures is contained in Chapter 8.

17 *Department of Employment Gazette,* vol. 83 (October 1975).

18 A. T. P. Hill and J. McGibbon, 'Growth of sector real product: measures and methods in selected OECD countries', *Review of Income and Wealth,* vol. 12 (March 1966), pp. 35–55.

19 G. Briscoe, 'Recent productivity trends in the UK service sector', *Oxford Bulletin of Economics and Statistics,* vol. 38 (November 1976), pp. 265–80.

20 H. B. Chenery and T. Watanabe, 'International comparisons of the structure of production', *Econometrica,* vol. 26 (October 1958), pp. 487–521.

21 United Nations Industrial Development Organisation, *International Comparisons of Inter-industry data,* Industrial Planning–Programming Series, No. 2 (New York, UN, 1969).

22 Department of Industry, *Input–Output Tables for the UK,* Business Monitor PA1004 (London, HMSO, annual).

23 The example illustrated in Tables 2.6–2.10 is based upon C. S. Yan, *Introduction to Input–Output Economics* (New York, Holt, Reinhart & Winston, 1969), pp. 20*ff.*

24 C. S. Yan and E. Ames, 'Economic inter-relatedness', *Review of Economic Studies,* vol. 32 (1965).

25 W. W. Leontief, *Input–Output Economics* (New York, Oxford UP, 1966), ch. 4.

26 S. Lerner, J. Cable and S. Gupta (eds), *Workshop Wage Determination* (Oxford, Pergamon, 1969), p. 155.

27 R. Stone (ed.), *Structural Change in the British Economy, 1948–1968,* University of Cambridge Department of Applied Economics, A Programme for Growth, No. 12 (Cambridge, Chapman & Hall, 1974), pp. 23 and 29.

28 Caves has defined market structure as 'the economically significant features of a market which affect the behaviour of firms . . . supplying the market' (R. Caves, *American Industry: Structure, Conduct and Performance,* 2nd edn, Englewood Cliffs, Prentice-Hall, 1967, p. 11).

29 Cross-elasticity of demand is measured as

$$\frac{\text{proportionate change in the quantity bought of product } \mathbf{B}}{\text{proportionate change in the price of } \mathbf{A}}$$

30 Caves, op. cit. (n. 28), p. 17.

31 A useful list of references on seller concentration is contained in D. Needham, *The Economics of Industrial Structure, Conduct and Performance* (Eastbourne, Holt, Reinhart & Winston, 1978), pp. 155–8.

32 Needham, op. cit. (n. 31), pp. 122–32.

33 Needham, op. cit. (n. 31), p. 128.

34 Department of Industry, *Report on the Census of Production, 1971: Summary Tables*, Business Monitor PA1002 (London, HMSO, 1976).

35 K. D. George, 'A note on changes in industrial concentration in the United Kingdom', *Economic Journal*, vol. 85 (1975), pp. 124–8.

36 S. Aaronovitch and M. C. Sawyer, *Big Business* (London, Macmillan, 1975), ch. 5.

37 R. Evely and I. M. D. Little, *Concentration in British Industry* (Cambridge, Cambridge UP, 1960).

38 A. Armstrong and A. Silberston, 'Size of plant, size of enterprise and concentration in British manufacturing industry, 1935–58', *Journal of the Royal Statistical Society*, series A, vol. 128 (1965), pp. 395–421.

39 K. D. George, 'The changing structure of competitive industry', *Economic Journal*, vol. 82 (1972), supplement, pp. 353–68.

40 D. Elliott, 'Concentration in UK manufacturing industry', *Trade and Industry*, vol. 16 (1974), pp. 240–50.

41 For example, K. D. George and T. S. Ward, *The Structure of Industry in the EEC* (Cambridge, Cambridge UP, 1975).

42 W. F. Mueller and L. G. Hamm, 'Trends in industrial concentration, 1947–70', *Review of Economics and Statistics*, vol. 56 (1974), pp. 511–20.

43 S. R. Lustgarten, 'The impact of buyer concentration in manufacturing industries', *Review of Economics and Statistics*, vol. 57 (1975), pp. 125–32. Also see L. A. Guth *et al.*, 'The use of buyer concentration ratios in tests of oligopoly models', *Review of Economics and Statistics*, vol. 58 (1976), pp. 488–92.

44 L. A. Guth *et al.*, 'Buyer concentration ratios', *Journal of Industrial Economics*, vol. 25 (1977), pp. 241–51.

45 J. S. Bain, *Barriers to New Competition* (Cambridge, Mass., Harvard UP, 1956).

46 F. M. Scherer, *Industrial Market Structure and Economic Performance* (Chicago, Rand McNally, 1970), ch. 4.

47 A. Silberston, 'Economies of scale in theory and practice', *Economic Journal*, vol. 82 (1972), supplement, pp. 369–91.

48 Needham, op. cit. (n. 31), pp. 48–52.

49 J. Johnston, *Statistical Cost Analysis* (New York, McGraw-Hill, 1960).

50 G. J. Stigler, 'The economies of scale', *Journal of Law and Economics*, vol. 1 (1958), pp. 54*ff.*

51 W. G. Shepherd, 'What does the survivor technique show about economies of scale?', *Southern Economic Journal*, vol. 34 (1967), pp. 113–22.

52 C. F. Pratten, *Economies of Scale in Manufacturing Industries* (Cambridge, Cambridge UP, 1971).

53 Needham, op. cit. (n. 31), p. 49.

54 K. D. George, 'Changes in British industrial concentration, 1951–58', *Journal of Industrial Economics*, vol. 15 (1967), pp. 200–12.

55 M. C. Sawyer, 'Concentration in British manufacturing industry', *Oxford Economic Papers*, vol. 23 (1971), pp. 352–84.

56 R. L. Nelson, *Concentration in the Manufacturing Industries of the United States* (New Haven, Yale UP, 1963).

57 S. I. Ornstein, 'Empirical uses of the price–cost margin', *Journal of Industrial Economics*, vol. 24 (1975), pp. 105–17.

58 A. Phillips, 'A critique of empirical studies of relations between market structure and profitability', *Journal of Industrial Economics*, vol. 24 (1976), pp. 241–9.

59 A. Phillips, 'An econometric study of price-fixing, market structure and performance in British industry in the early 1950s', in K. Cowling (ed.), *Market Structure and Corporate Behaviour* (London, Gray-Mills, 1972).
60 W. G. Shepherd, 'Structure and behaviour in British industry', *Journal of Industrial Economics*, vol. 21 (1972), pp. 35–54.
61 S. Holtermann, 'Market structure and economic performance in UK manufacturing industry', *Journal of Industrial Economics*, vol. 22 (1973), pp. 119–39.
62 J. Khalilzadeh-Shirazi, 'Market structure and price–cost margins in UK manufacturing industries', *Review of Economics and Statistics* (1974), pp. 67–76.
63 P. E. Hart and E. Morgan, 'Market structure and economic performance in the United Kingdom', *Journal of Industrial Economics*, vol. 25 (1977), pp. 177–93.
64 T. Hitiris, 'Effective protection and economic performance in UK manufacturing industry, 1963 and 1968', *Economic Journal*, vol. 88 (1978), pp. 107–21.
65 K. Cowling and M. Waterson, 'Price–cost margins and market structure', *Economica*, vol. 43 (1976), pp. 267–74.
66 S. Nickell and D. Metcalf, 'Monopolistic industries and monopoly profits', *Economic Journal*, vol. 88 (1978), pp. 254–68.
67 Needham, op. cit. (n. 31), pp. 172–4.
68 Phillips, op. cit. (n. 58), p. 249.
69 Needham, op. cit. (n. 31), chs 5–7.
70 F. Blackaby (ed.), *De-industrialisation* (London, Heinemann, 1978).

3 The Firm

3.1 INTRODUCTION

It is not easy to say just what role is played by the individual firm in economic theory. In the general equilibrium theory of value in perfect competition the basic units are not so much individual firms as processes of production of commodities. In the behavioural theory the object of study is not the firm in its environment but rather the firm's internal workings – its insides. Somewhere between perhaps comes the familiar partial-equilibrium theory of the firm, but the nature of the intended relationship between the firm of the theory and the actual firm in modern capitalist economies is not clear.

This chapter is concerned in a general way with the theory of the firm, the firm in the real world economy and the relationship between them. In section 3.2 the history of the traditional theory of the firm is briefly traced as a means of bringing out the assumptions and methods of analysis on which it is based, the objections that have been made to these and the alterations that have been proposed. What emerges is that ambiguity exists over the supposed purpose of a theory of the firm. Section 3.3 examines some of the characteristics of firms of which any theory must *prima facie* be expected to take account. One of these is the corporate institutional form of the modern firm, and section 3.4 analyses the relationship between ownership, control, objectives and behaviour – an issue that arises in the corporate context and also in the context of worker-managed enterprises. In section 3.5 the behavioural theory – perhaps the most radical break with the traditional theory to have gained currency – is outlined. Some conclusions on the present state of theory in relation to the firm are drawn in section 3.6.

3.2 THE FIRM I: THE THEORY OF THE FIRM

The 'theory of the firm' was created in the 1930s. It represented a sharp change of focus from the 'theory of value', which had dominated orthodox economics since its construction between 1870 and 1910. By the end of the 1930s the newly created theory of the firm was itself under attack, and ever since there has been an unending stream of proposals for its reformulation. None has so far won general acceptance. In this section these developments are briefly outlined as a convenient way of indicating some of the major approaches currently adopted by economists in the theoretical analysis of business behaviour.[1]

VALUE THEORY

What Shackle has called 'The Great Theory'[2] of the neoclassical economists was a general equilibrium theory, founded on perfect competition and perfect knowledge, which provided answers to 'all questions about prices, outputs and incomes'[3] throughout the economy. The answers were the logical implications of given preferences and technical production possibilities, a given initial distribution of resource ownership and maximising assumptions about motivation. It was the all-embracing general-equilibrium character of this theory, made possible by the assumptions of certainty and a perfectly competitive economy, that enabled it to fulfil the role of a universal unified theory of value, rendering determinate the structure of relative prices and the overall pattern of resource allocation and income distribution.

Marshall, despite the subtlety of his verbal discussion, adopted the method of static equilibrium analysis in his formal presentation. Coexisting within his analysis were both the general equilibrium approach of the 'Great Theory' and a partial equilibrium approach. Due to the assumption of perfect competition these two approaches appeared for a time to be quite consistent with one another. In 1926, however, this appearance was shattered by Sraffa's famous article[4] demonstrating that the conditions that are necessary to ensure static partial equilibrium in a perfectly competitive industry are incompatible with the requirements of static partial-equilibrium analysis. For a perfectly competitive industry to be in partial equilibrium the firms comprising the industry must also be in equilibrium. Since the demand curve of the individual firm is horizontal, if the firm is to have a determinate size, its long-run average-cost curve must eventually turn up; that is, it must be U-shaped. Now, given homogeneous inputs and the possibility of replication, unit costs will only rise if input prices rise. However, if input prices rise, the position of other industries making use of the inputs will be affected, and hence the partial equilibrium character of the analysis will be vitiated. In essence Sraffa argued that it is logically inconsistent to assume perfect competition while engaging in partial equilibrium analysis.

In retrospect it can be seen that two ways out of the crisis precipitated by Sraffa were tried. The first, adopted notably by Hicks,[5] was to retain the assumption of perfect competition, in order to retain general equilibrium analysis, and abandon the method of partial equilibrium analysis. Hick's reasons for choosing this course are well known but worth quoting:

> . . . it has to be recognised that a general abandonment of the assumption of perfect competition, a universal adoption of the assumption of monopoly, must have very destructive consequences for economic theory. Under monopoly the stability conditions become indeterminate; and the basis on which economic laws can be constructed is therefore shorn away . . . There must indeed be something to stop the indefinite expansion of the firm; but it can just as well be stopped by the limitation of the market as by rising marginal costs . . .
>
> It is, I believe, only possible to save anything from this wreck – and it must be remembered that the threatened wreckage is that of the greater part of general equilibrium theory – if we can assume that the markets confronting most of the firms with which we shall be dealing do not differ very greatly from perfectly competitive markets . . . At least, this get-away seems well worth trying. We must be aware, however, that we are taking a dangerous step, and probably limiting to a serious extent the problems with which our

subsequent analysis will be fitted to deal. Personally, however, I doubt if most of the problems we shall have to exclude for this reason are capable of much useful analysis by the methods of economic theory.[6]

The second way in which an attempt was made to escape from the crisis in value theory was to abandon perfect competition, and consequently general equilibrium analysis,[7] in order to retain partial equilibrium analysis. This course led to the development of the theory of imperfect or monopolistic competition associated with Joan Robinson and Chamberlin.[8] It was a course with far-reaching consequences, for, although by means of arbitrary and artificial assumptions the concept of an ostensible 'industry'[9] was for a time retained, the logic of the argument was to shift attention from the industry to the firm.

THE 'TRADITIONAL' THEORY OF THE FIRM

The transition from value theory to the theory of the firm has been superbly sketched by Shackle:

Mrs Robinson starts her first chapter with a strangely revealing sentence: 'The purpose of this book is to demonstrate that the analysis of the output and price of a single commodity can be conducted by a technique based upon the study of individual decisions.' The individual decisions were those of the entrepreneur or his firm, and each of the commodities whose prices and outputs were in question was defined, not as a stuff having given physical characteristics, but as the product of a particular firm. Primacy had passed from the autonomously self-subsisting technical commodity to the firm considered as a profit-maximising policy maker. The central theoretical concern was no longer with the means of life and how to produce and distribute it, but the actions and interactions of producers each with a product in some degree special to him. The *firm* was an entity which, being free to choose the character of its product, the means of producing it, and either the size of the output or else the price to be charged per unit, made all these choices as one, with the sole aim of making as large as possible the excess of sale-proceeds of product over outgoings necessitated by production. In making these choices each firm had to reckon with an environment composed of other firms as well as of demanders of its goods. And this environment of other firms was not constant in composition or conduct, but might press in upon a highly profitable firm and soak away some of its custom, or recede and leave breathing space for a firm which had been making losses. In the end, so long as demand, technology and the supply conditions of factors of production remained unchanged, everything would settle down and each firm would be making its best attainable unthreatened profit. But when this picture had taken shape, what importance was left to the *commodity?* Between the beginning and the end of Mrs Robinson's first sentence, the focus of interest has changed.[10]

The implications of this change in the focus of interest were not immediately apparent. Both Joan Robinson and Chamberlin had retained, however artificially, the concept of an 'atomistic' industry. Consequently, it was possible to analyse the profit-maximising firm's reaction to its environment on the assumption that this environment was beyond the firm's control. In such circumstances, however, it makes little sense to conceive of the firm as a 'decision maker'; there is nothing really to decide. The theory of imperfect competition is based not on real decisions but on 'the conditions of individual equilibrium'. [11]

The *'traditional'* or *'received'* theory of the firm, as it is called in this book, is in essence the static partial-equilibrium analysis, assuming certainty, of the profit-maximising firm in an exogenously given environment. Paradoxically, although the traditional theory of the firm was created for the analysis of imperfect or monopolistic competition, it has been most fully elaborated in the analysis of perfect competition. This is partly because the device of retaining the concept of the industry in imperfect competition has proved to be unconvincing,[12] but more importantly it is because of the 'elegance, simplicity and generality'[13] made possible by perfect competition. It is paradoxical because 'in perfect competition firms have so little to do, particularly in the absence of technical change and uncertainty, that there is nothing worthy of a separate title'.[14]

While imperfect or monopolistic competition gradually became a curio and the traditional theory of the firm soon came to focus primarily on perfectly competitive structures, the new theory was also able to embrace monopoly situations. Monopoly had long been recognised, but in effect it had been virtually ignored. Shackle has conjured up the delightful image of:

> . . . a smooth sea of perfectly competitive firms in equilibrium, interrupted here and there by a few monopolist whirlpools obeying a different law. The monopolist was a thing apart. He did not fit in with the rest of the system. He must be studied in isolation, then was best forgotten.[15]

Now, however, although the general equilibrium analysis of an economy comprising both perfectly competitive firms and monopolists remained as intractable as ever, at least the two types of firm could be studied in partial equilibrium by means of the same technique: marginal analysis. This is a technique for finding a maximum, and the standard marginal conditions that define the equilibrium position of an individual profit-maximising firm apply equally to perfectly competitive firms and to monopolists. Furthermore, there seemed for a time to be the possibility of using the new technique in the analysis of oligopoly. Indeed, the well-known 'kinked demand curve' was developed by Sweezy[16] to explain the observed price rigidities, not price levels, in oligopolistic industries in terms of marginal cost and revenue.

However, although the traditional theory of the firm appeared usable for the static partial-equilibrium analysis of all market structures, it flourished only when perfect competition was assumed. Monopoly can be handled formally, but the static analysis of firms enjoying market power invites questions about the rationale of assuming profit maximisation as the objective. Oligopoly cannot even be handled formally without additional highly-restrictive assumptions. It is the Achilles heel of the traditional theory of the firm, even on its own terms. As Shackle has noted in passing: 'Oligopoly is quite alien, in its essential demands upon theory, to the spirit of static or equilibrium analysis'.[17]

OBJECTIONS TO THE TRADITIONAL THEORY

Ironically, the first challenge presented to the traditional theory was probably only perceived as a challenge due to methodological confusion. In 1939 Hall and Hitch[18] published the results of an empirical study of the way in which businessmen actually set prices. They appeared to take no account of marginal cost or revenue and instead followed some sort of 'full-cost' principle. Loasby has argued that this empirical finding ought not to have been regarded as a threat to the traditional theory, at least as applied to atomistic structures, since 'both perfect and imperfect competition are empty of predictions about the ways in which firms actually fix prices'.[19] Nevertheless, the Hall and Hitch article was in fact the first of many attacks on the traditional theory based upon its lack of 'realism in process'. The ammunition for these attacks has been drawn from three major sources. First, there are further 'case studies' of particular categories of business decision.[20] Then there are the results of exercises in 'normative microeconomics' – studies by management scientists or consultants and by operations research workers of the decision-making processes of specific firms. Finally, there is the work on human behaviour in organisations that has been carried out under the umbrella of organisation theory.[21] The controversy has for the most part been not so much over the way in which firms actually take decisions as over the methodological question of the significance or relevance of this sort of empirical work for the theory of the firm.[22]

The second objection to the traditional theory relates to its assumption of profit maximisation as the firm's objective. In atomistic competition with free entry, profit maximisation is a sensible although largely redundant assumption. The long run behaviour of the firm is fully constrained, for in the long run profit maximisation is a survival condition. Once the elements of monopoly power are admitted, however, this ceases to be true. The firm can now survive in the static long run without maximising profits, and hence an area of discretion enters into its behaviour. The specification of an objective is no longer redundant but is essential if the area of discretion is to be narrowed to a determinate equilibrium solution. Profit maximisation will do, of course, but it is not mandatory and must be justified in competition with other possible objectives that meet the formal requirement equally well. The discussion of alternative objectives has been heavily influenced by the literature, initiated in 1932 by Berle and Means,[23] on the separation of ownership from control. It has been widely argued that, while shareholders may reasonably be assumed to be profit maximisers in some sense, managers are likely to have other objectives.[24] If so, they will use any area of discretion to pursue their own non-profit-maximising objectives. The relationship between ownership, control and objectives is considered in detail in section 3.4.

A more radical challenge to the traditional theory's assumption of profit maximisation as the firm's objective stems from organisation theory. The thesis of the separation of ownership from control is, of course, premised on the recognition of the firm as an institution and not merely as a theoretical construct. Yet this recognition has often not extended beyond discussion of the firm's objectives. In 'managerial' theories of the firm, once the objective to be assumed is settled the organisational characteristics of the firm are again abstracted from. The 'behavioural school',[25] however, has argued that it is illegitimate to abstract in this way since the behaviour of an organisation is not independent of its internal processes. In particular, it has been asserted, the firm cannot be conceived as an organisation acting consistently to maximise whatever objective it happens to be set. Rather, objectives must be seen as emerging from a process of internal bargaining between the individuals and groups comprising the firm, who will have conflicting interests. The outcome is likely to be a continuously shifting 'objective', consisting of a multiplicity of imperfectly articulated and integrated goals, which it probably does not make sense to think of in terms of maximising. This contrast between an 'holistic' and a 'behavioural' concept of the firm[26] is taken up again at several points in this chapter.

The third line of criticism of the traditional theory of the firm is concerned with its static equilibrium framework. Static equilibrium is a timeless state. Comparative statistics, of course, enables different timeless states to be compared, but the essence of the dynamic problem is that it is concerned not with comparing states but with 'a process in time'.[27] One important pressure for abandoning the static approach has been awakening interest in the growth of the firm. Accumulating evidence of constant or increasing returns[28] has steadily undermined the plausibility of assuming that there is an 'optimum' size for the firm in the static long run and suggested the need for a change of framework. In 1959 Penrose presented[29] an influential account of business behaviour in which the constraints to which the firm is subject relate not to absolute size but to the rate of growth. For the most part the study of the growth of firms through time has been thought to require a dynamic setting.

The critique of the static equilibrium framework of the traditional theory is reinforced by a fourth objection: the theory's inability to come to terms with oligopoly. Shackle's judgement that such a framework is inherently unsuitable for the analysis of oligopoly has already been noted. An essential requirement of the traditional theory is that the environment to which the firm adapts, including the behaviour of other firms, must be exogenously given. This formal requirement is satisfied for firms in atomistic competition and for monopolists, but by definition the problem of analysing oligopoly consists in the interdependence existing between the behaviour of the relevant set of firms. The action of each firm changes the environment confronting every other firm. Within the terms of the traditional theory of the firm the situation is indeterminate, and the formal requirements for a determinate equilibrium solution can only be satisfied by introducing additional assumptions about the nature of the interdependence. In fact within the framework of the traditional theory such assumptions as have been made have necessarily assumed away interdependence, thus avoiding rather than solving the problem.[30]

The inability of the traditional theory to deal convincingly with oligopoly is particularly damaging, since it has generally been agreed that the structure of manufacturing industry is predominantly oligopolistic.[31] Furthermore, the traditional theory's static framework is designed to handle primarily the determination of the price and output of individual products. Although it can be stretched to include some of the more obvious phenomena of contemporary business behaviour, it is not well equipped to deal with the problems of labour relations and investment – of marketing strategy, innovation, diversification, merger, overseas expansion and relations with governments. Such problems are not those of an atomistically competitive firm, nor of a monopolist, adapting to a perfectly known given environment; they are the problems of oligopolistic competitors pursuing strategies in a changing and uncertain world.[32]

The fifth and final major criticism of the traditional theory of the firm is directed at its assumption of perfect knowledge. In a sense this is the most fundamental criticism of all, with implications extending far beyond the bounds of the traditional theory alone. Although the four objections discussed so far are all more or less inter-related, the existence of uncertainty to some extent underlies them all and multiplies their force. As will become clear shortly, the traditional theory of the firm is a particular version of the constrained maximisation paradigm; its essence is the maximisation of an objective (profit) subject to constraints (given cost and demand conditions). For a determinate equilibrium to be specifiable everything must be clearcut. Uncertainty spoils the picture. In its presence the concept of maximisation becomes ambiguous, if not meaningless,[33] and with it the concept of equilibrium itself is brought into question. Not surprisingly, oligopoly stands out clearly as a catalyst. The relationship of interdependence and the associated uncertainty about rivals' behaviour preclude a determinate equilibrium solution without further assumptions. In the words of Andrews: 'What is at issue is the validity of that equilibrium concept which is at the root of the orthodox system of analysis.'[34] However, the point is of more general application. Shackle's attempt to capture the essence of Keynes's criticism of the 'Great Theory' retains its relevance for today:

> But our ignorance of the future was the one big thing which the refinements of equilibrium economics had allowed to slide into oblivion. The fatal defect of the older conception was its assumption that men possess adequate knowledge, that they can act in the light of reason fully supplied with its necessary data. But this assumption is contrary to all experience. It is the false analogy from celestial mechanics, the unconsciously wrong and misleading interpretation of the word 'equilibrium.'[35]

PROPOSALS FOR REFORMULATION

Objections to the traditional theory of the firm, by which has been meant 'the static partial-equilibrium analysis, assuming certainty, of the profit-maximising firm in an exogenously given environment', have been discussed under five interrelated headings: the relevance of lack of 'realism in process'; the rationale of assuming profit maximisation as the firm's objective; the adequacy of the static framework; the problem of oligopoly and the nature of the environment in which the firm is assumed to operate; and the assumption of perfect knowledge. Before considering proposed reformulations of the theory of the firm designed to take account of some of these objections, it may be helpful to clarify the terminology used in the subsequent discussion.

One essential distinction between different theories of the firm is between those which are within the constrained maximisation paradigm and those which are not. For a theory to fall within this paradigm it must be possible to present it as a problem of maximising a given objective subject to given con-constraints. The paradigm embraces all techniques[36] for 'solving' such problems, i.e. for specifying the conditions that must be satisfied if the extent to which the objective is realised cannot be increased without violating the constraints.

Marginal analysis is one technique for solving constrained maximisation problems. Hence, *'marginalist'* theories of the firm may be regarded as those in which the technique of marginal analysis is used for specifying the conditions under which the firm's objective will be maximised, given its environment. Of course: 'The concept of marginalism forms the core of the traditional theory of the firm,'[37] but marginal analysis is not confined to the traditional theory. It has also been used in *'managerial'* theories, in which the objective to be maximised is not profit and the firm's environment includes not only cost and demand conditions but also shareholders and may be dynamic rather than static.[38] Although marginal analysis has been the most common technique used in theories of the firm, in the discussion that follows no importance is attached to the use of different maximisation or optimisation techniques. Rather, emphasis is placed on the distinction between theories falling within the constrained maximisation paradigm and those using qualitatively different methods of analysis.

Reformulations within the paradigm

Reformulations within the constrained maximisation paradigm, which have constituted the bulk of recent work on the theory of the firm, have been concerned with the firm's objectives, the use of a dynamic framework, the nature of the environment in which the firm operates and the introduction of uncertainty in the sense of risk.

Objectives. Reformulations under this heading have adduced arguments and evidence in support of the replacement of profit as the maximand by some other variable. Sales, growth or more complex managerial 'objective functions', incorporating explicit trade-off relationships between the variables included, have been advocated.[39] Proposals have also been made to replace the notion of objective 'optimality' by that of subjectively 'rational' behaviour, i.e. behaviour seeking to maximise the variable selected in terms of the opportunities as perceived by the decision taker.[40] This has similarities with Simon's concept of 'bounded' or 'qualified' rationality,[41] although Simon has preferred to discard the concept of maximising in favour of that of 'satisficing', discussed below. The question of objectives is taken up again in section 3.4.

Dynamic approaches. When time is introduced into the analysis the traditional theory's adaptation to static timeless equilibrium becomes adaptation to dynamic equilibrium determined not just by the environment in the present period, but also by the environment of all future periods within the firm's time horizon: 'In other words, the firm is assumed to solve a T-period constrained maximisation problem and determine the optimal values of all components of all moves over the entire horizon. Solving this constrained maximisation problem requires knowing the specific form of every future constraint.'[42] Within this framework one approach has been merely to recast the traditional theory to take account of time. Profit maximisation in this context becomes the maximisation of the present value of the future stream of profits.[43] It is assumed that the relevant environment to the horizon is such that the firm's 'optimum' size is larger than its present size and that it wishes to adjust to the larger size but will not do so instantaneously because of adjustment costs.[44]

There are also theories specifically designed to analyse the process of and limits to growth, and these represent a much sharper break with the traditional theory. The theory of the growth of the firm, discussed in detail in Chapter 4, is based on the institutional framework of contemporary capitalism and is rooted in the organisational characteristics of the large corporation and the working of the stock market.

The nature of the environment. Associated with the development of the theory of the growth of the firm has been a redefinition of the nature of the environment within which the firm is assumed to operate. The traditional theory assumes that the firm is constrained by cost and demand structures defined by the characteristics of the market or industry within which it is situated; the firm is essentially passive. In the theory of the growth of the firm, however, the firm is conceived as an active agent, not confined to a single market or industry, but able to diversify into new fields whether by direct investment or merger. Thus, the firm is able to influence its environment rather than obliged to accept it passively as given. However, if the firm is free from the constraints of any given market or industry, it is not free from constraints altogether. The *'economic'* theory of the growth of the firm deriving from the work of Marris falls within the constrained maximisation paradigm, because in it the firm's environment-influencing ability is itself constrained by certain characteristics of the economy as a whole, which Marris has termed the 'super-environment'.[45] Diversification, merger and innovation, which are key aspects of environment-influencing activity, are the subject matter of Chapter 5.

Uncertainty. The concept of uncertainty can be interpreted broadly or narrowly. It may be taken to include all situations in which there is less than perfect knowledge, or it can be distinguished from risk – described by Knight as 'measurable uncertainty'[46] – and confined to situations in which the probabilities of alternative outcomes are not known or knowable.[47] Lintner, a pioneer in the field, has referred to a coming 'uncertainty revolution'.[48] However, the work so far has been largely limited to the areas of inventory and short-run pricing policy[49] and investment appraisal[50] and has been concerned with risk, not uncertainty in the second sense indicated above.

The reformulations so far outlined all fall within the constrained maximisation paradigm. The theories referred to have been framed to fulfil the requirements of the paradigm. These requirements are an unambiguously specified maximand and an exogenously given set of environmental constraints, both known with sufficient certainty for there to be a determinate maximum-equilibrium solution. For the requirements to be met any uncertainty must be reducible to a 'certainly equivalent', and this can only be done when uncertainty is interpreted to mean risk. In the presence of 'incalculable uncertainty' the paradigm breaks down.

Developments outside the paradigm
Developments outside the constrained maximisation paradigm have been mainly concerned with the problem of oligopoly and the application of a behavioural approach to the theory of the firm. There is also the work of Andrews, who has sought to resurrect the industry as an analytic tool by extending and generalising the 'cost-plus' approach.

Oligopoly and the theory of games.[51] Although there has been a good deal of empirical work over the years into aspects of behaviour and performance in oligopolistic industries,[52] progress in theoretical analysis has been meagre.[53] One promising development has been the theory of games, which has afforded insights into the essence of the oligopoly problem – that is, uncertainty about rivals' actions – which are not available within the constrained maximisation paradigm. These insights arise because 'the theory of games focuses attention upon the behaviour of other business players, as well as upon the firm itself. Opponents are vitally concerned not only with their own strategies but also with those of their competitors.'[54] The contrast between the two approaches has been sharply drawn by Morgenstern, who is joint author of the first analysis of business behaviour in terms of game theory:[55]

> The basic feature of the theory is to show that in economics one is not confronted with maximum problems but with a conceptually different and, *a fortiori*, more difficult situation. This stems from the fact that the outcome of the behaviour of firms and individuals does not depend on their own actions alone, nor on those combined with chance, but also on the actions of others . . . In such a case no maximum problem exists; indeed the notion of a maximum has no meaning.[56]

However, while insights have been gained, game theory has not fulfilled the initial hopes held out for it.[57] It has not so far been possible to develop general analytic solutions for oligopoly situations within a game-theoretic framework. There has been a tendency to argue that 'co-operative' outcomes will be likely. For instance, Marris has rehearsed the arguments for co-operative outcomes and has further suggested combining this approach with Shubik's concept of oligopoly as 'a game of economic survival' in order to develop a theory of relative bargaining strength.[58] Nevertheless, however plausible such reasoning may be in relation to price determination in oligopolistic markets, it is less convincing when the strategies involved concern not merely pricing but also the thrust and direction of the firm's overall policy, e.g. merger or the introduction of the new products.

The behavioural approach. The concept of the firm embodied in all the theories so far considered is essentially holistic. It abstracts from the internal organisation of the firm, with its processes of information gathering and decision making and the possibility of conflicting goals, and assumes that the firm is a unified entity acting rationally in pursuit of clearly defined objectives. By contrast, the behavioural theorists have adopted a concept of the firm as a coalition organisation attending, on the basis of limited information, to a set of more-or-less vaguely specified and often contradictory goals. They have argued that, in the absence of perfect knowledge, information gathering and processing are central aspects of the behaviour of the firm and that the ways in which these activities are undertaken will have an important influence on the decisions made.

In such circumstances, Simon has suggested, 'bounded' or 'qualified' rationality is the best attainable, and what rational firms do is not to maximise but to 'satisfice'. The firm is envisaged as attending to each of its several goals in turn, not simultaneously. With respect to each goal the objective is expressed in terms of attaining an acceptable (i.e. aspiration) level, not a maximum. If, but only if, attainment falls short of the minimum acceptable level, sequential search procedure is activated. Alternative courses of action are considered in turn, beginning with minor modifications and steadily encompassing ever more radical departures from existing practice, and the first to satisfy the aspiration level is adopted. Aspiration levels are altered upwards if they are too easily achieved and downwards if they cannot be satisfied after determined search. In a complex and rapidly changing environment, Simon has argued, there is no reason to suppose that a complex organisation will ever approach long run equilibrium; the constrained maximisation paradigm is inappropriate. Given uncertainty (not risk), satisficing is the rational thing to do.[59] The most fully developed application of this approach to the theory of the firm, the 'behavioural theory' of Cyert and March, is summarised in section 3.5.

Andrews and the industry. A somewhat neglected approach is that of Andrews, who has rejected the concept of individual firm equilibrium in favour of a 'steady state' in the industry. The essence of his position is that manufacturing industry is both oligopolistic and rather competitive in the long run and that actual or potential entry will set a definite limit to price in each industry.[60] Price is arrived at by adding a 'costing margin' to estimated average direct cost. The margin is calculated on the basis of estimates of 'normal' output and the profit that can be obtained without long run loss of custom due to competition. If there is an 'equilibrium', it is the equilibrium of industry price, not the equilibrium of individual firm output where marginal cost and revenue are equal.[61] The market share of each firm will depend on dynamic factors that determine the amount that the firm is able to sell at the going industry price. Thus, although large firms are thought likely in fact to be multiproduct,[62] each industry is analysable independently of the number of other industries in which a firm is active.

Although Andrews has widely been regarded as denying profit maximisation, he has rather raised 'the possibility that our existing method of theorizing may give wrong clues as to how profits may be maximised'.[63] In fact the main thrust of his argument is directed against 'the influence of atomistic methodology, which it is easy to argue *from* but difficult to argue *to*'.[64] It is this 'methodology' that, misleadingly in Andrews's view, focuses attention upon the equilibrium position of the firm. He has argued that for the long run it is 'possible to question the analytical independence of cost and demand functions, which marginal equilibrium theorists take for granted and which, indeed, is essential for the formal validity of their work'.[65] Finally, he has invoked Marshall's concept of the 'representative firm'[66] in support of his view that concentration on individual firm equilibrium rather than on the industry is likely to prove an unhelpful diversion.[67]

This brief survey of proposed reformulations of the theory of the firm may conveniently be drawn to a close by quoting Loasby's account of the 'paradigm crisis', which is still with us:

> For it is the concept of equilibrium which is at the heart of the crisis; and the abandonment of equilibrium is a much more fundamental change than that implied by the creation of the theory of the firm . . . Micro-economists need a theory of the firm; and for some purposes the marginalist equilibrium theory is the best theory we have.
>
> How, then, is the paradigm defended? . . . Expositions and explanations of business behaviour which conflict with microequilibrium theory . . . have met with vigorous onslaughts, in which the terms of the argument, as is usual in controversies over paradigms, have been defined in a way that comes near to ensuring success. Equilibrium theory is justified by assuming its validity. Rationality is equated with profit-maximisation, which in static equilibrium implies mathematically the equality of marginal cost and marginal revenue; therefore any business observed violating the theory is behaving irrationally, and any alternative theory must assume irrationality, which, as we all know, makes theorising impossible.[68]

Unfortunately, 'facts' are of no direct help:

> Neither party follows Beveridge's prescription, endorsed by Lipsey, to seek empirical verification. And on this issue they are right, and Beveridge and Lipsey are wrong. For the argument is not about hypotheses – concerning which Beveridge and Lipsey are of course quite correct – but about the kinds of hypotheses and the kinds of data that might be presented for verification; and here the empiricist's prescription is not only inappropriate but often impossible.[69]

CONCLUSION

The 'Great Theory' was a general equilibrium theory of value in perfect competition. The theory of the firm, as first developed in its traditional form, was a partial equilibrium theory of the firm in different market structures. Value theory is a theory of relative prices, income distribution and resource allocation throughout the economy. The theory of the firm is also supposed to be about resource allocation, but it is framed in terms of the partial equilibrium analysis of the firm.[70] The relationship between individual firm equilibrium (partial) and overall allocation of resources (general) is clear, if at all, only in the special case of perfect competition. This, together with its elegance and simplicity, largely accounts for the continuing attractive power of perfect competition. It also partly accounts for the tension and confusion that appear as soon as perfect competition is abandoned.

For forty years or more the traditional theory of the firm has been under attack, and alternative formulations have proliferated. As long as perfect competition and perfect knowledge or its equivalent are assumed the traditional theory, perhaps recast in dynamic form, is unassailable, and the analysis of the pattern and 'efficiency'[71] of overall resource allocation can proceed. Questions about 'realism in process' – the way in which 'actual' firms 'really' behave – are irrelevant.[72] However, this is in fact the old theory of value masquerading as the new theory of the firm. Once perfect competition is abandoned, an analysis of the partial equilibrium position of the firm can tell us little, if anything, about overall resource allocation; the theory of value is then really dead, and the theory of the firm comes into its own. However, what now is the purpose of the theory? If it is to explain the actual behaviour of a given specific firm, 'realism in process' probably ceases to be irrelevant, and a behaviourist approach may be called for.[73] Yet, the bulk of recent work on the theory of the firm has been within the constrained maximisation paradigm, based on an holistic, not a behavioural, concept of the firm. On the other hand, if the purpose of the theory is to throw light on the working of the economy as a whole, the partial equilibrium framework of the constrained maximisation paradigm when applied to firms in non-perfectly-competitive situations is called into question.

Much controversy within the general area of the theory of the firm appears to spring from a lack of clarity over the purpose of the analysis, from a lack of definition of the aspect of reality under investigation. However, while this may be a major source of confusion, agreement on purpose and definition is no guarantee of agreement on method of analysis. Perhaps the major issues that have emerged in this section concern the legitimacy of abstracting from uncertainty (not risk) and the relevance of the microequilibrium approach.

3.3 THE FIRM II: SOME INSTITUTIONAL CHARACTERISTICS

The reason for the creation of the theory of the firm in the 1930s was predominantly the crisis in value theory precipitated by Sraffa's 1926 article. There was also, however, a growing awareness of important aspects of industrial structure and business behaviour which appeared to pose problems for the existing theory. As argued in section 3.2, the first formulation of the theory of the firm – the 'traditional' theory – was most successful when applied to firms in 'atomistic', and especially in perfectly competitive, conditions. These are the conditions in which the concept of a firm passively adapting in terms of its objectives to an exogenously given environment is most plausible. Much of the controversy over the traditional theory has been about whether a theory premised on such a concept of the firm is relevant for the analysis of contemporary capitalist economies. Three inter-related considerations stand out: the prevalence of oligopoly, the large absolute size of the small group of dominant firms, and the active rather than passive behaviour of firms.

Later chapters examine different aspects of active business behaviour. In this section some characteristics of the firm as an institution that are not considered elsewhere are examined: legal status, size distribution, the phenomenon of the 'international' (or 'multinational' or 'transnational') firm, and relations between business and the state.

LEGAL STATUS

An important aspect of the institutional framework within which firms operate is the specification of the forms of business organisation legally recognised. The traditional theory of the firm abstracts from different types of business organisation and assumes an holistic firm defined essentially in terms of the characteristics of the single-person owner–manager entrepreneur.

In fact, however, the firm assumes several institutional forms in modern capitalist economies, namely, in the United Kingdom: sole proprietorship; partnership; limited partnership; private joint-stock company with or without limited liability; and public joint-stock company with limited liability. Whereas the sole proprietorship is the legal form assumed by the 'one-person' firm, an unincorporated firm consisting of more than one 'principal' becomes a partnership. Up to twenty partners are legally permitted, each being able to commit the others to any agreement entered into and all being liable without limit for any debts incurred. A rare variation is the limited partnership in which 'sleeping' partners, who play no part in the running of the firm, are limited in their liability for debts that the firm may incur to the extent of the capital that they have invested. Incorporated firms – private or public companies – are governed by their Memorandum and Articles of Association, which specify the objectives and inner constitution of the company. The shares of private companies, which are allowed up to fifty shareholders, cannot be offered for sale to the public nor transferred without the company's consent. In a public company there is no restriction on the number of shareholders, shares may be sold to the public, and shares are freely transferable. Public companies are required to publish more comprehensive accounts than private. In addition to these various forms of privately owned firm there exist also in the United Kingdom the public corporation, legally owned by the state, and two types of co-operative: consumer and producer.

The different institutional forms of the privately owned firm originated at different stages in the development of capitalism in order to cater for the changing technical and economic requirements of capitalist production. The majority of firms are unincorporated, being sole proprietorships or partnerships, and tend to be very small. Such firms are mainly to be found in agriculture, retail trade, other services and the professions, where capital requirements are small. Indeed, the modern concepts of the company and of limited liability arose in the nineteenth century in response to the growing scale of production and the consequent need for larger blocks of capital under centralised control.

A high correlation exists between plant size and the depth of investment on the one hand and the extent of incorporation on the other.[74]

At the end of 1976 there were in Great Britain 621,683 companies, of which 15,585 were public.[75] As shown in the next sub-section, a large proportion of economic activity in present-day capitalist economies is concentrated in a relatively small number of absolutely large firms. These firms are virtually all public companies, and this fact is significant for the analysis of business behaviour since the institutional form of the public company embodies characteristics that call into question the appropriateness of the traditional concept of the firm. In the first place, the corporate form of organisation carries with it the possibilities of a separation of ownership from control and of a potential conflict of interest between shareholders and managers. In the second place, the corporate form focuses attention on the firm as an organisation, thus reinforcing the potential relevance of organisation theory and the concept of behaviourism. These two questions are examined in sections 3.4 and 3.5.

THE SIZE DISTRIBUTION OF FIRMS AND OVERALL CONCENTRATION

As noted in section 3.2, the traditional theory is a partial equilibrium theory of the firm in different market structures. Under the influence of this theory most of the empirical work on concentration has been on market or industry concentration, on the grounds that the extent of such concentration is an important determinant of business behaviour. More recently, however, the phenomenon of growing overall or aggregate concentration and its significance for the way in which the economy works have received increasing attention.[76]

The most comprehensive data for the United Kingdom are to be found in the

Table 3.1   *Analysis of enterprises[a] by total employment size: manufacturing industry in the United Kingdom, 1972.*

Size of enterprise (no. employed)	Enterprises		Employment (% of total)
	(no.)	(% of total)	
10,000 and over	85	0·12	35·02
2,000–9,999	375	0·52	21·75
500–1,999	1,047	1·45	13·77
200– 499	1,823	2·52	7·96
100– 199	2,852	3·94	5·55
1– 99	66,119	91·45	15·96
All enterprises	72,301	100·00	100·01

Source: Department of Industry, *Report on the Census of Production 1972: Summary Tables,* Business Monitor PA1002 (London, HMSO, 1977), table 8, p. 118.

Note:
(a) An enterprise is one or more firms under common ownership or control.

Census of Production and relate primarily to manufacturing industry. The figures for 1972 are summarised in Table 3.1 and indicate the general characteristics of the size distribution of firms today. Most firms in manufacturing are relatively small, with those employing fewer than 100 workers accounting in 1972 for 91 per cent of all firms but only 16 per cent of total employment. At the other extreme 460 firms each employing 2,000 or more and constituting only 0·6 per cent of all firms accounted for 57 per cent of total employment. Although the details vary, the general picture remains much the same when size is measured in terms of assets or net output instead of employment.

Not only are the dominant firms large, but the trend has been towards ever larger firms. Between 1935 and 1958 the proportion of total employment in manufacturing accounted for by firms with over 10,000 employees rose from 14 to 25 per cent;[77] by 1972 it had risen further to 35 per cent.[78] The number of such firms increased between 1958 and 1972 from seventy-four to eighty-five. At the other end of the size distribution the Bolton Committee, inquiring into small firms, has documented the dramatic decline in the number of manufacturing firms with fewer than 200 employees. Table 3.2 shows that the reduction between 1935 and 1963 of 76,000 in the total number of firms was more or less entirely due to the fall in the number of small firms. However, although the clear trend towards larger firms in manufacturing has been repeated in other sectors, the small firm remains of continuing importance in the economy.

The Bolton Committee, reporting in 1971, has estimated that there were at least 1¼ million small firms in the United Kingdom, which employed some 6 million people or 25 per cent of the employed population and were responsible for nearly 20 per cent of the gross national product (GNP).[79] Moreover, in the most recent period the downward trend in the number of small firms may have halted or even been reversed. Census of Production data for 1972 put the total number of manufacturing enterprises at 72,000, of which 69,000 were small on the Bolton Committee criterion, accounting for over 21 per cent of total manufacturing employment, and 3,000 were 'larger'.[80] Unfortunately, changes

Table 3.2   *Relative importance of small[a] enterprises: manufacturing industry in the United Kingdom, 1935–68.*

| Year | Enterprises (thousands) | | | Employment in small enterprises (% of total employment) |
	Total	Small[a]	Larger	
1935	140	136	.4	38[b]
1958	70	66	4	24
1963	64	60	4	20

Source: J. E. Bolton (Chairman), *Report of the Committee of Inquiry on Small Firms,* Cmnd 4811 (London, HMSO, 1971), tables 5.I and 5.II, pp. 58 and 60.

Notes:
(a) For manufacturing industry 'small' enterprises were defined by the Bolton Committee as those employing fewer than 200 workers.
(b) Estimated figure subject to a substantial margin of error.

in the Census of Production, in particular a wider coverage of small firms, make direct comparison with the figures in Table 3.2 invalid.

In the past few years an increasing amount of information on overall concentration has become available, enabling both its extent and historical trend to be assessed. Table 3.3 reproduces three alternative estimates of the proportion of manufacturing net output accounted for by the 100 largest enterprises at various dates. The figures for the earlier years are less reliable than those for the more recent period, but the long term trend is clear. There has been a strong tendency for the share of the 100 largest enterprises to increase, particularly in the years since the Second World War. Thus, their share was about 16 per cent in 1909, about 22 per cent in 1949 and over 40 per cent in the early 1970s.[81]

Another but less reliable way of presenting the trend in overall concentration is to calculate the number of enterprises that would have accounted for half of total manufacturing output in different years. Prais has given the following estimates: pre-First World War, 2,000; 1935, 800; 1958, 420; 1963, 240; 1968, 160; and 1970, 140.[82]

Perhaps the method of estimating overall concentration used most extensively in recent years is that based on quoted companies. Different populations of companies have been used, and of course the level and trend of concentration recorded in the same period have varied as the make-up of the population has varied. The results of the more important studies are summarised in Table 3.4. They confirm the existence of a clear tendency for the share of the 100 largest enterprises to rise. The only exception is the estimate by Hannah and Kay for the period 1930–48, paralleled by the fall in the share of the 100 largest enterprises in manufacturing net output between 1935 and 1948/9 in Table 3.3.

Table 3.3 *Percentage share of the 100 largest enterprises in manufacturing net output, 1909–72.*

	1909	1924	1935	1948/9[a]	1953	1958	1963	1968	1970	1971	1972
Hannah	15	21	23	21	26	33	38	42	45	—	—
Prais	16[b]	22[b]	24	22	27	32	37[c]	41	40/1[d]	—	—
DOI	—	—	—	—	—	—	36·0	38·6	37·7	38·6	41·0

Source: L. Hannah, *The Rise of the Corporate Economy* (London, Methuen, 1976), table A.2, p. 216; S. J. Prais, *The Evolution of Giant Firms in Britain,* National Institute of Economic and Social Research, Economic and Social Studies[30] (Cambridge, Cambridge UP, 1976), table 1.1, p. 4; Department of Industry, 'The importance of the "Top 100" manufacturing companies', *Economic Trends,* no. 274 (August 1976), table 4, p. 90; and Department of Industry, *Report on the Census of Production 1972: Summary Tables,* Business Monitor PA1002 (London, HMSO, 1977), tables 8 and 10, pp. 119 and 217.

Notes:
(a) 1948 for Hannah, 1949 for Prais.
(b) Approximate figures.
(c) Includes steel companies; their exclusion would reduce the figure to approximately 36·5.
(d) Provisional estimate; the higher figure includes and the lower excludes steel. The estimate is artificially low, by about 1 per cent, compared with previous years due to the increased coverage of small firms by the Census of Production in 1970.

Table 3.4 *Percentage share of the 100 largest enterprises in various populations of mainly quoted companies by market value or net assets, 1919–76.*

Study	Population	Year	% share	Variable
Aaronovitch and Sawyer	Quoted manufacturing companies with 1957 assets ≥ £5 m.; various adjustments	1957 1968	58·25 73·20	Assets
Moyle	All companies quoted on the London Stock Exchange	1963 1969	51·1 60·0	Market value
Hannah and Kay	(1) London quoted companies with additions	1919 1930	56·4 77·4	Market value
	(2) As in (1) but about four times as many companies (due to greater data availability)	1930 1948	65·7 56·9	Market value
	(3) Quoted manufacturing companies with 1957 assets > £1 m. or 1969 assets > £2 m., with additions	1957 1969	60·1 74·9	Net assets
	(4) Quoted manufacturing companies with 1969 assets >£2·5 m. or 1973 assets > £2 m.; various adjustments	1969 1976	78·9 80·9	Market value

Source: S. Aaronovitch and M. C. Sawyer, *Big Business* (London, Macmillan, 1975), table 6.4, p. 119; J. Moyle, *The Pattern of Ordinary Share Ownership 1957–70*, University of Cambridge Department of Applied Economics, Occasional Paper 31 (Cambridge, Cambridge UP, 1971), table 3.1, p. 11; and L. Hannah and J. A. Kay, *Concentration in Modern Industry* (London, Macmillan, 1977): (1) table 5.1, p. 65; (2) table 5.3, p. 73; (3) table 6.1, p. 86; and (4) table 6.6, p. 96.

Apart from the period spanning the Second World War, during which overall concentration appears to have fallen somewhat,[83] the largest firms have become progressively more important until today they occupy a predominant position in the economy of the United Kingdom. The Department of Industry has gathered together data from several sources to provide a picture of the 'top 100' private-sector manufacturing companies in the early 1970s. These companies then accounted for about 40 per cent of manufacturing industry's net output, net assets, employment and inward direct investment from overseas (excluding oil companies' investment); 40–50 per cent of visible exports; 70 per cent of expenditure on industrial scientific research and development; and about 75 per cent of direct investment by UK companies (excluding oil) in manufacturing industry overseas.[84]

This picture may in fact underestimate the extent of overall concentration in that it takes no account of interlocking financial and personal ties. It has been suggested that such ties may take the form of minority shareholdings, subordination to a common financial institution (normally an investment or merchant bank) and interlocking directorships. Empirical evidence relating to this general area is rare, and the studies that exist relate to other countries. A classic study of the United States has concluded that in the 1930s four financial groups – namely, those associated with the Rockefeller, Du Pont, Mellon and Mather families – between them effectively controlled roughly one-seventh of the total assets of all manufacturing corporations.[85] In Japan before the Second World War four holding companies controlled one-quarter of all paid-up capital in industry and finance. In Sweden in the 1960s one family controlled eight of the ten largest industrial firms.[86] Similar information for the United Kingdom is not available, perhaps because such relationships may have been less important in Britain than elsewhere.

The significance of marked overall concentration arises from the domination of economic activity as a whole by a relatively small number of absolutely large firms, reinforced by the fact that such firms are typically diversified and operate in oligopolistic markets. Evidence has recently become available on the connection between overall and market concentration in the United Kingdom. Using a sample of thirty product groups from the 1963 Census of Production, Utton has found that in half of the cases one or more of the three largest firms within the product group was also one of the 100 largest manufacturing firms overall, while in about 23 per cent of the sample two or all three of the three largest firms within the product group were among the largest 100 overall.[87] The behaviour of a large diversified firm in any one market is unlikely to be independent of its overall position. Marketing strategy – both pricing policy and sales promotional activities – can be subsidised for a time until the firm becomes established.[88] Bargaining in an oligopolistic market will be influenced by the firm's interests outside that market. A large diversified firm will tend to have more resources to draw upon than a smaller specialist firm and hence is likely to have greater bargaining strength.[89] On the other hand, large diversified firms are likely to confront one another in several markets and will have to take account of their overall relations, not merely of their relative positions in a single market. It has been suggested that in such circumstances 'spheres of influence'[90] will develop, with firms respecting their rivals' positions in particular markets for fear of precipitating the onset of expensive general hostilities.

Firms, of course, operate in factor markets as well as in product markets, and in these markets especially it is likely to be the overall size of the firm rather than its size in any particular product market that matters. It has been suggested that larger firms will have a competitive advantage in the market for managerial labour, due to the greater possibilities for promotion and greater security,[91] but the major advantages enjoyed by larger firms in factor markets occur in the capital market. Larger firms, with their greater degree of diversification, tend to be less risky than smaller firms, experiencing less variability in their earnings and growth rates. As a result of this greater security larger firms are able to raise a higher proportion of their capital requirements in the form of loans, and this higher 'gearing' can be very beneficial when there is a differential tax advantage in favour of debentures and in times of rapid inflation. It is also well established that the cost of equity capital falls as the size of firm rises. In addition, the financial institutions appear to have a clear preference for the shares of larger firms.[92]

In an economy characterised by a high level of overall concentration the special position of the larger firms in product and factor markets constitutes a major competitive advantage of great economic significance. There are, thus, important economic implications arising from high overall concentration, as well as the more familiar social and political considerations such as the growth of alienation and the concentration of power.[93]

The dominant position of a relatively small number of absolutely large firms is of especial significance when considering the 'international' firm and relations between business and government. These two phenomena are now examined in turn.

THE 'INTERNATIONAL'[94] FIRM

Although international trade and capital flows have a long history the character of the overseas interests of firms has changed over the years. Since the Second World War international trade and portfolio investment have become relatively less important, with large firms increasingly involved in operating overseas subsidiaries engaged in production. While such international firms were nothing new in extractive industries like oil and non-ferrous metals, they were relatively new in manufacturing industry.

An international firm may be defined as 'an enterprise which owns or controls producing facilities, i.e. factories, mines, oil refineries, distribution outlets, offices, etc., in more than one country'.[95] For the most part international firms, thus defined, retain a clear nationality in the sense that they are controlled and predominantly owned by the nationals of a single country, although there may be minority shareholdings spread over several countries. There are, however, a few large enterprises with, in effect, internationally shared control, and their number may be increasing. Among the best-known firms of this type, with their dates of formation, are the Royal Dutch/Shell Group (1906), Unilever (1928), Agfa-Gevaert (1964), Fokker-VFW (1970) and Dunlop-Pirelli (1971).[96]

Before considering the implications for theory of the distinctive characteristics of the international firm the empirical evidence on the extent of the phenomenon is briefly set out. Much of the available data is on direct investment overseas, and it should be noted that this tends to result in an understatement of the overseas interests of international firms since these include resources financed both by direct investment and by locally raised funds. For instance, in the late 1960s only roughly one-third of the growth of US subsidiaries in Europe was financed by new capital export and retained profits.[97] Some of the more striking facts relating to the international firm have been summarised by the United Nations. In 1971 the value added by all such firms was roughly equal to one-fifth of non-socialist world GNP, while the value added by each of the largest ten international firms exceeded the GNP of over eighty countries. In the same year over 50 per cent of the stock of direct foreign investment belonged to US firms, nearly 15 per cent was owned by UK firms and virtually all the rest was shared between Canadian, Japanese and other European firms. Of the total stock of direct investment in 1966 some 40 per cent was in manufacturing, 29 per cent in petroleum and 7 per cent in mining and smelting, while in 1967 over two-thirds was in the developed capitalist countries and under one-third in the less developed countries. Four broad industries – namely, chemicals, machinery, electrical products and transport equipment – accounted for half of UK firms' 1965 and 60 per cent of US firms' 1970 stock of overseas investment in manufacturing. Finally, the overseas output of international firms grew more rapidly during the 1960s than non-socialist world GNP or exports, and in 1971 total overseas production exceeded total non-socialist world exports.[98]

A more detailed picture of the importance of overseas sales and in particular of overseas production can be obtained from Table 3.5. Although the estimates shown in the table are somewhat rough, they indicate that in all the countries included except France the 'average' manufacturing firm in the period 1957–65 relied to a considerable extent on overseas sales for its expansion (column 7). It is clear that in the United Kingdom, the Netherlands, the United States and Canada overseas production was relatively important (column 6) whereas in the other four countries reliance was almost entirely on domestic production. A further point of interest is the fact that overseas production was more important than exports for the growth of US and UK manufacturing sales (columns 5 and 6). This finding has been supported by more recent data, not confined to

Table 3.5 *The contribution of exports and overseas production to the growth of manufacturing industry sales, 1957–65.*

Country	Change ($ billion) in:				% of increase in total sales due to:		
	Exports (1)	Overseas production (2)	Total overseas sales[a] (3)	Total sales (4)	Exports (5)	Overseas production (6)	Total overseas sales[a] (7)
USA	4·2	24·0	28·3	183·9	2	13	15
UK	3·5	5·4	8·9	27·6	12	20	32
France	3·9	0·4	4·3	59·3	6	1	7
West Germany	8·4	1·4	9·8	62·9	14	2	16
Italy	4·0	0·9	4·9	16·6	24	5	30
Netherlands	2·0	1·2	3·1	7·2	27	17	43
Canada	1·5	0·6	2·1	4·6	33	13	46
Japan	5·2	0·6	5·8	29·6	17	2	20

Source: R. Rowthorn, *International Big Business 1957–67: A Study of Comparative Growth,* University of Cambridge Department of Applied Economics, Occasional Paper 24 (Cambridge, Cambridge UP, 1971), table 22, p. 62; and R. Rowthorn, 'Imperialism in the seventies: unity or rivalry?', *New Left Review,* no. 69 (September–October 1971), table 1, p. 37.

Note:
(a) The figures for total overseas sales overstate the extent to which national firms benefited from expansion overseas, since exports include those of foreign-owned subsidiaries and no account is taken of overseas production imported into the domestic economy.

manufacturing, which show that in 1971 total overseas production as a percentage of total non-socialist world exports was 396 per cent for the United States and 215 per cent for the United Kingdom, with Switzerland the only other country for which overseas production exceeded exports, although France and Sweden were almost in that position.[99]

Of course, overseas expansion is a two-way process, with each country not only exporting but also importing goods and capital. Gains made by firms in overseas markets may be offset by losses sustained in domestic markets. Indeed, at the overall or average level this is largely what appears to have happened. When account is taken of imports and production in the domestic economy by the subsidiaries of foreign firms the gains recorded in column 7 of Table 3.5 are more or less cancelled out, with the exception of Canada where they are swamped by the exceptionally heavy domination of domestic production by US subsidiaries.[100] This phenomenon of interpenetration is of great importance when considering the development of oligopolistic rivalry on a world scale, discussed below.

The data in Table 3.5 on overseas expansion and the relative importance of exports and overseas production are rough estimates for manufacturing industry as a whole and hence relate to the position of the 'average' firm. This average, however, conceals significant differences between the experience of different categories of firms. In particular most of the firms engaging in direct investment overseas are very large.

In 1971 more than 200 international firms, mainly American, had sales of $1,000 million or more, and 500–700 firms accounted for the bulk of overseas production. Nearly 200 firms had overseas subsidiaries in twenty or more countries. Some 250–300 firms accounted for over 70 per cent of US foreign direct investment, and 165 firms accounted for over 80 per cent of UK and 82 firms for over 70 per cent of West German direct investment overseas. Over one-third of US manufacturing output was produced by the top 187 US international firms, and 264 firms were responsible for about half of US manufacturing exports.[101]

Moreover, not only is the large international firm clearly an important phenomenon, but its importance is also increasing. A study of 187 US parent companies, between them probably accounting for over 80 per cent of US overseas direct manufacturing investment outside Canada, has traced their activities back to 1900. The number of their overseas subsidiaries was found to have increased as follows: end of the First World War, over 250; 1929, 500; 1945, just under 1,000; 1957, 2,000; and 1967, over 5,000.[102]

In the light of the domination of overseas direct investment by a relatively small number of large firms, it has been argued that the interpenetration of national economies by means of reciprocal direct investment can be viewed as a process whereby large firms, which tend to engage in overseas production, gain at the expense of smaller firms, which do not. This view has been supported by the finding that the 100 largest US and the 100 largest non-US industrial firms grew over the period 1957–67 at an average rate of about 1 per cent per annum more than their domestic economies and that the faster rate of growth was due more to rapid overseas expansion than to an increasing share of the domestic market.[103]

What are the distinctive features of international firms? Why has internationally organised production grown so rapidly in the postwar period? Answers to these questions are suggested by the fact that direct investment overseas is predominantly undertaken by firms operating in oligopolistic industries characterised by high-technology production processes and/or a high degree of product differentiation. In such conditions firms typically possess firm-specific knowledge, which constitutes a competitive advantage that may be realisable to its full extent only by engaging in overseas production rather than in the alternatives of licensing the knowledge to a foreign firm or exporting. At the same time the growth of direct foreign investment and overseas production has been a dynamic process in which innovation in science and technology, in distribution and marketing techniques, and in administrative structure and organisational methods has interacted with oligopolistic market structures to bring about the increasing internationalisation of production on a world scale.

Although theories of direct investment have been developed that rely exclusively on elements of 'foreignness',[104] for the most part explanations relating to the international firm can be traced back to the literature on industrial organisation, oligopolistic rivalry and the growth of the firm. Early attempts at explanation inevitably tended to concentrate on US firms, reflecting the fact that the initial postwar surge of direct foreign investment in the 1950s was the period of greatest US domination. Vernon's product-cycle model proposes a sequence in which the production of high-income or labour-saving new products takes place first in the United States, then in other developed countries and finally in less developed countries. Initially, in the innovation stage, when the production process or the product is still subject to substantial modification, there are advantages in producing close to input suppliers and consumers. As the product begins to become standardised the growing US market continues to be supplied by US production, but in other developed-country markets local production increasingly replaces US exports. Finally, when the product is completely standardised production is located according to relative production costs and may increasingly move to less developed countries, with the US and other developed-country markets themselves being supplied by imports.[105] In his later work Vernon has placed growing stress on the importance of oligopolistic market structures in his account of the product cycle, with oligopolistic interdependence providing the dynamic for a continuous stream of innovations and product-differentiating activities, at first in the domestic market but increasingly overseas as rivalry extends to the world market and the contenders match one another's every move. He has also allowed for the possibility of innovations that originate outside the United States, in response to specific characteristics of the European or Japanese economies, becoming the starting point for a product cycle.[106]

The second major strand in the literature is that which seeks to explain the rise of international firms in terms of the concepts of industrial economics, emphasising in particular the origin of their competitive advantage in firm-specific assets associated with features of the oligopolistic markets in which they typically operate. Such firm-specific assets are seen as necessary in order to enable the firm operating an overseas subsidiary to compete successfully against indigenous firms, which possess superior knowledge of the indigenous economy and do not have to incur the costs of operating across national boundaries. Building on the pioneering work of Hymer,[107] Caves has suggested two conditions that need to hold for a firm-specific asset to result in overseas investment. First, the asset must have something of the character of a public good within the firm; that is, it must be internally transferable at little cost in relation to its potential quasi-rent in servicing overseas markets. Second, the return or quasi-rent in overseas markets must depend to some extent on overseas production for its realisation. Knowledge is the archetypal firm-specific asset possessing these characteristics. Caves has argued that the knowledge associated with product differentiation is especially likely to give rise to direct investment overseas. The initial costs of differentiation, whether in the form of minor product development or of advertising and other forms of marketing, will be incurred and covered in catering for the home market. Overseas subsidiaries producing the already differentiated product can then compete successfully against indigenous producers that do not possess the asset created by the initial differentiating expenditure. If the firm-specific knowledge can be easily transferred to another firm, as in the case of a particular patent, and readily valued, licensing an indigenous firm to produce the product may be preferable to direct investment. However, if the knowledge consists of the ability to create a stream of process or product innovations and cannot be separated from managerial personnel, or if uncertainty precludes agreement on valuing the information, overseas production will be the only way in which the firm can obtain the full return on the use of its unique asset in overseas markets.[108]

Attempts have recently been made to draw together the various explanations offered for the development of the international firm. Buckley and Casson have suggested that the concept of the 'internalisation' of a market when the external market is characterised by imperfections can embrace most of the considerations discussed above. In particular they have argued that the market for knowledge is very imperfect and that direct investment overseas occurs when the benefits to the firm from internalising the transfer of knowledge exceed the costs.[109] Hirsch has developed a model exploring the conditions under which a profit-maximising firm will choose to service overseas markets, and the determinants of whether overseas servicing, if it occurs, will be through exports or overseas production. His model takes account of differences in production costs between countries, firm-specific assets such as know-how, the extent to which export-marketing costs exceed local-marketing costs, and the cost of exercising control across national boundaries. He has concluded that two conditions are necessary for overseas production to occur. First, the costs of domestic production plus export rather than local marketing must be higher than the costs of overseas production plus international co-ordination, so that exporting is unprofitable. Second, the benefit arising from firm-specific assets must be greater than the costs of international co-ordination, so that the overseas subsidiaries of the international firm have a competitive advantage over indigenous producers. Once firms are established overseas they acquire some of the local knowledge of indigenous firms, and the cost of exercising control across national boundaries falls. The possession of firm-specific assets emerges unequivocally as the key determinant of overseas investment, and this emphasises once again the importance of those high-technology and highly product-differentiated industries where such assets are likely to be present – industries with oligopolistic market structures, e.g. chemicals, pharmaceuticals, instruments, computers, cars, tobacco and cosmetics.[110]

Thus, the postwar rise of the international firm can be attributed in general terms to major advances in technology, marketing and above all organisation, occurring in a context of domestic and, increasingly, international oligopolistic rivalry. Initially, US firms made the running, but this in turn gave rise to a European response. Hymer and Rowthorn have referred to 'the dialectics of the multinational corporation, the thrusts and counterthrusts of US and non-US corporations as they compete for shares in the world market using direct foreign investment as one of their chief instruments'.[111] It is worth quoting at some length their interpretation of the years 1957–67, since it illustrates the importance of oligopolistic consciousness of interdependence. During this period, they have argued, there was a growing feeling in Europe that European firms were up against a severe 'American challenge'.[112] Yet, on average European firms were growing at a faster rate than American firms, and the latter also felt themselves threatened. The explanation offered for this paradox is the fact that, while the growth rate of US subsidiaries in Europe was somewhat greater than that of European firms, this latter growth rate was higher than that of the total operations of US firms, i.e. parents plus subsidiaries. Hymer and Rowthorn have continued:

To the short-sighted European firm, whose markets are mainly European, US investment seems to be an aggressive move to dominate Europe. To the long-sighted American firm, on the other hand, this investment appears to be a desperate attempt to defend its existing world share and keep up with the dynamic Europeans.

A more interesting interpretation of the ten years between 1957 and 1967 would recognise that a firm can be challenging and challenged at the same time, just as a military strategy can be both offensive and defensive. The rapid growth of the Common Market and Japan in the 1950s challenged the dominance of the US giants, who responded with an aggressive policy of foreign investment. Their great strength, their past experience with continental and multinational markets, plus the open-door policy of European governments made this counter strategy successful.

This invasion of Europe threatened the position of European firms which have now begun their countermeasures.[113]

Since 1967 the process of oligopolistic rivalry on an international scale has continued, with non-US firms expanding their overseas production at a faster rate than US firms. At the same time there has been growing unease at the increasingly dominant position occupied by the international firm within national economies and on a world scale. International firms have been increasingly operating on a global basis with highly centralised administrative structures planning the sourcing, production and marketing of products without regard to national boundaries.[114]

As a consequence, Hymer has suggested, there is a tendency for the heirarchical organisational structure of the international firm to be paralleled by an hierarchical relationship between countries. Production and the associated routine management become widely spread across countries; middle level co-ordination requiring access to white collar labour and good communications is geographically more concentrated in regional centres; and the central headquarters in which the key strategic decisions are made are located in the world's few major cities close to capital markets and the world's most powerful governments. This analysis, of course, introduces wider questions than are usually considered by the theory of the firm. Hymer has concluded his discussion of the political economy of the international firm on a sombre note:

> The multinational corporation, because of its great power to plan economic activity, represents an important step forward over previous methods of organising international exchange. It demonstrates the social nature of production on a global scale. As it eliminates the anarchy of international markets and brings about a more extensive and productive international division of labour, it releases great sources of latent energy.
>
> . . . But the multinational firm is still a private institution with a partial outlook and represents only an imperfect solution to the problem of international co-operation. It creates hierarchy rather than equality, and it spreads its benefits unequally.
>
> In proportion to its success, it creates tensions and difficulties. It will lead other institutions, particularly labour organisations and government, to take an international outlook and thus unwittingly create an environment less favourable to its own survival. It will demonstrate the possibilities of material progress at a faster rate than it can realise them, and will create a world-wide demand for change that it cannot satisfy.
>
> The next round may be marked by great crises due to the conflict between national planning by governments and international planning by corporations.[115]

The possibility of a conflict between global planning by international firms and national planning by governments has been widely recognised. Indeed, both the United Nations and the Commission of the European Economic Community (EEC) have produced reports on the problems that arise in relations between international firms and national governments.[116] However, while consideration of the relationship between international firms and nation states has proved unavoidable, serious discussion of the more general issue of the nature of the relations existing between business and government, i.e. between the firm and the state in a single country, has been largely neglected. This question is now briefly examined.

RELATIONS WITH THE STATE

The traditional theory of the firm embodies a concept of the firm as an entity passively adapting to its environment in terms of its objectives. Hence, it is consistent for the theory to abstract in relation to the state in a way that initially excludes all aspects of the role of the state other than those which set the overall framework on the basis of which this adaptation takes place. This overall framework is concerned with the structure of property rights over productive services, the forms of business organisation legally recognised and the law of contract. It can, of course, be changed by the state, e.g. when legislation is enacted relating to the conditions under which labour can be employed, to consumer protection or to company law. Although some such framework must be assumed in order to construct any theory of the firm,[117] the traditional theory of the firm is usually presented without its framework being made explicit, with the result that the institutional specificity of the theory is sometimes overlooked.

It is, then, on the basis of a specific state-established institutional framework that the traditional theory conceives of the firm as adapting to its environment. Once the theory has been elaborated other aspects of state activity may be introduced – both indirect intervention (e.g. monetary and fiscal policy or policy on foreign trade and payments) and direct intervention (e.g. policy to control monopoly and restrictive practices, to promote rationalisation or to regulate wages and prices). However, the approach of the traditional theory of the firm is to regard these aspects of state activity as modifying the environment to which the firm passively adapts. The relationship is seen as one way; the state acts for good or ill, and the firm makes the best of the new situation in terms of its objectives.

This general approach has been retained by Cairncross when considering the implications for the firm of the growth of the 'mixed economy', even though he has placed more emphasis on the importance of the state than is usual:

> . . . it is no good shutting our eyes to the increasing influence of the State . . . Firms are not independent of the state and solely engaged in trying to supply a market at minimum cost. They have to keep one eye on what the State is doing or may decide to do and their success as productive enterprises may depend almost as much on their success in conforming to government policy (or even in divining it) as in adopting more efficient methods of production.[118]

However, once the importance of the state has been recognised it is difficult to see why there should be a stop at acknowledging the need for firms to take account of (i.e. to 'conform to' or 'divine') state policy. If firms are able to do so, they will presumably seek to influence what the state does, not take it as given, just as they will seek to shape other aspects of their environment.[119] The oligopolistic relationship in which absolutely large firms stand to one another may be seen as supplemented by an oligopolistic relationship existing between these firms and the state. Such a situation has been noted by Streeten in the context of 'less-developed' countries: 'it must be remembered that the relation between companies and host governments is often one of bilateral oligopoly'.[120] But the point has also been made in a more general context. Discussing alternative views of the relationship between the firm and the state, Marris has commented:

. . . it makes little difference whether the State is seen as having been taken over by the corporations, or vice versa. In the writer's view, the essential point is that any system which grants units of delegated authority [i.e. autonomous firms] the right of organisational growth will inevitably experience concentration and hence the development of 'oligopolistic' interdependence between the organisation and the State itself.[121]

An illustration of the oligopolistic relationship in operation can be found in the way in which recommendations of the Monopolies Commission have been dealt with. Typically, the government has entered into negotiations with the firms in question, and the outcome has usually been agreement on a course of action that has fallen well short of that recommended by the Commission but has been more acceptable to the firms.[122]

Galbraith is the best-known contemporary economist to have placed the relationship between the firm and the state at the centre of his analysis, and it is not accidental that he has remained largely outside the mainstream of traditional orthodoxy. In his *American Capitalism* Galbraith has developed his concept of 'countervailing power': a dynamic process by which the concentration of power in one sector of the economy calls forth the development of an offsetting concentration of power in a related sector, thus neutralising the adverse effect of the initial concentration. The role of the state is envisaged as the promotion of countervailing power where this is needed but does not develop unaided.[123] Subsequently, in his *The New Industrial State,* Galbraith has argued that a subtle accommodation of the interests of the state to those of the firm has occurred, with the state having been harnessed to the pursuit of policies that furthered the objectives of those running the firm so that harmony prevails.[124] It is possible to reject much of Galbraith's overall analysis and many of his conclusions while nevertheless recognising his insistence on discussing real phenomena of contemporary social reality as a salutary antidote to the sterility of much traditional theory.[125]

Phillips has suggested an approach to the analysis of the relationship between market structure, conduct and performance that draws upon Galbraith's concept of countervailing power and the role of the state in promoting it but sees such state action as the response to a failure of private, not public, goals. Instead of taking structure as given and, together with conduct, determining performance, Phillips has proposed reversing the direction of causality. If performance is unsatisfactory from the standpoint of private objectives, the firms involved will seek to regulate conduct or alter structure in order to improve performance. If they are unable to effect such changes themselves they will seek the aid of the state. Thus, much regulation or reorganisation of private industry by the state may be seen as the state acting on behalf of private firms to improve private performance, rather than on behalf of the public to improve public performance.[126]

Such a change in theoretical framework is potentially of great importance. Instead of concentrating exclusively on the analysis of how firms adapt to government policy, emphasis is shifted towards the study of the way in which firms seek to influence that policy. So far, however, rather more interest has been shown in this approach by political scientists and sociologists than by economists. As an example of their work a study of the United States by Reagan may be quoted. He has distinguished four major ways in which firms influence government policy: through expert knowledge deployed in the negotiation of contracts and the proceedings of state regulatory agencies; through the exchange of personnel between industry and government; through campaigns to influence public opinion and legislators in relation to specific proposals affecting either an individual firm or firms in general; and through activities designed to influence the overall climate of opinion in a direction that is favourable to business interests.[127] Reagan has summed up his discussion of this last point as follows:

> . . . corporations are not only much concerned to protect their own immediate legislative interests, but are reaching out in an attempt to create a business-oriented political and social framework within which all public decision-making would be constrained. Instead of the society channelling business decisions within the bounds of public interest, the corporations seek to channel public-interest decisions within business-interest bounds.[128]

What implications does this brief discussion of the relationship between firm and state have for the theory of the firm and for public policy? In the first place, it suggests that any theory seeking to explain business behaviour, or at least the behaviour of the relatively small group of large oligopolistic firms, must be able to comprehend action designed to influence government policy. That such action is of importance may be signified by the remark of the chairman of the Beecham Group in 1968 that relations with the government absorbed between one-quarter and one-third of his time.[129]

In the second place, attention is drawn to the possibility that the state, far from acting on behalf of the public interest, may at times be used as an instrument of oligopolistic rivalry, either between rival firms or between nationally based firms and foreign governments. Consider, for instance, the record of intervention in Central and South America by agencies of the US government on behalf of US firms. Such intervention is by no means solely a matter of historical interest. Perhaps the best-known recent example is the attempt in 1970 by the International Telephone and Telegraph Corporation (the largest US non-financial corporation), the Central Intelligence Agency, the US ambassador and the State Department to prevent the late, then newly elected, left-wing President Allende of Chile from assuming office.[130] The general theoretical point was underlined in 1947 by Rothschild: 'The oligopolistic struggle for position and security includes political action of all sorts right up to imperialism. The inclusion of these "non-economic" elements is essential for a full explanation of oligopoly behaviour.'[131]

Finally, the growth of absolutely large firms in an oligopolistic relationship with the state raises questions about the direction of development of capitalism as a political–economic system. Marris has remarked on one possibility: 'This is the inevitable consequence of telling people to run things in their own interests, leaving the State or an invisible hand to look after Society. The State is taken over and the invisible hand withers away.'[132] Bain has drawn attention to the more general methodological dilemma with which the traditional theory and most other theories of the firm may be confronted:

> If now it were true that the very sort of industrial organization which economic theory analyses tended to undermine and eventually alter or destroy the political basis for the economic systems being analysed, economic theory would have overlooked much. Its predictions would have at best a very temporary validity, and a theory of political–economic evolution would be required to elicit the longer-term implications of contemporary industrial organization.[133]

It seems likely that the growth of overall concentration, the increasing internationalisation of production and the growing influence of the state in every aspect of economic activity are well on the way to transforming this conditional statement into an accurate description of the theoretical challenge facing economics.

3.4   OWNERSHIP, CONTROL AND OBJECTIVES

PROFIT MAXIMISATION

The assumption of profit maximisation as the objective of the firm is one of the cornerstones of the traditional theory. The justification for this assumption is twofold. On the one hand, the firm in the traditional theory is identified with the entrepreneur – the owner–manager who takes the risks, makes the decisions and receives the rewards. The entrepreneur in turn is assumed to be 'economic man', interested solely in maximising his profits. Since the entrepreneur is in complete control, his subjective motivation, i.e. the maximisation of his profits, becomes the objective or goal of the firm. On the other hand, the traditional theory of the firm was initially created to analyse imperfect or monopolistic competition and was subsequently applied primarily to perfect competition. In atomistically competitive markets profit maximisation is a survival condition. Since only firms that maximise profits survive, profit maximisation becomes an objective requirement irrespective of the subjective motivation of the entrepreneur.

There are, thus, two mutually reinforcing reasons for the traditional theory's assumption of profit maximisation as the firm's goal: the subjective motivation of the entrepreneur, and the objective requirement for survival in an atomistically (perfectly) competitive environment.[134] Of course, the possibility obviously arises that the entrepreneur's subjective motivation is to some extent moulded by the objective situation in which he is operating.

MONOPOLY POWER AND DISCRETION

As long as attention is confined to the traditional theory's analysis of the firm in perfect competition the assumption of profit maximisation as the firm's objective is unexceptionable. The firm is fully constrained by its environment and has no discretion. However, once monopoly power is admitted the situation changes radically. A firm that is able to obtain an element of monopoly profit can survive within the framework of the traditional theory without maximising its profits. It is no longer fully constrained, and there exists an area of discretion within which alternative policies that are conducive to the achievement of differing objectives can be pursued. The behaviour of the firm will now depend to some extent on the objective of those running it.

If the traditional theory's identification of the firm with the entrepreneur is retained, the question of the entrepreneur's subjective motivation now arises. Of course, his objective may be the maximisation of his profits as the traditional theory assumes. However, entrepreneurs may also have other goals – such as the pursuit of power, status, prestige, independence or a quiet life – which may be furthered by policies different from those which are conducive to profit maximisation. On the other hand, if the 'representative' firm is recognised as having the institutional form of the joint stock company, the question becomes divided into two parts: which person or group of persons actually controls the firm (i.e. determines the policies to be pursued), and what is the objective of that person or group?

The relationship between the ownership, control and objectives of the corporate firm will be considered shortly. First, however, it may be instructive to examine briefly a simple formal model that illustrates the proposition that different assumptions about objectives can lead to different behaviour when there exists an area of discretion.

Profit maximisation and sales maximisation compared
The model, developed by Baumol,[135] derives conflicting predictions about behaviour according to whether the firm's objective is assumed to be profit maximisation or the maximisation of the money value of the firm's sales, i.e. of its total revenue, subject to a minimum profit constraint. The sales-maximising level of output is the level at which the elasticity of demand is unity and marginal revenue is zero. This contrasts with the profit-maximising level of output, at which marginal revenue is equal to marginal cost. If marginal cost is greater than zero, then at the profit-maximising output marginal revenue will also be greater than zero. Hence, given that marginal revenue falls as output increases, the profit-maximising output will be smaller than the sales-maximising output. Once the profit constraint is introduced two types of equilibrium position for the firm are possible. First, if at the sales-maximising level of output profits are sufficient to satisfy the constraint, the constraint will not be effective and will not prevent the firm from settling at that output. Second, however, if at the sales-maximising level of output profits are below the required level, output will have to be reduced until profits rise sufficiently to satisfy the constraint. In this case, when the constraint is effective, the firm's equilibrium position will be at the level of output that just enables the profit constraint to be met. In the limiting case, when only maximum profits satisfy the constraint, there will be no difference between the profit-maximising and the profit-constrained sales-maximising levels of output. The model is set out diagrammatically in Figure 3.1.

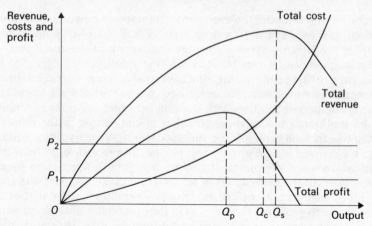

Fig. 3.1 Profit and sales maximisation compared.
OQ_p = profit-maximising output,
OQ_s = sales-maximising output, unconstrained (profit constraint of P_1),
OQ_c = sales-maximising output, constrained (profit constraint of P_2).

Baumol has argued that the unconstrained equilibrium position normally will not occur. This is due to the possibility of advertising expenditure, which, it is assumed, can always increase physical sales, although beyond a certain level only at a rapidly diminishing rate. Given this assumption, total revenue will increase with advertising expenditure, also at a diminishing rate. Thus, there is no upper limit to total revenue; the firm will continue to increase total revenue, by increasing advertising, until it runs up against the profit constraint. There is no possibility of an unconstrained sales-maximising equilibrium. It follows that, unless the minimum profit constraint is in fact the maximum level that is attainable, the sales-maximising firm will advertise more than the profit-maximising firm. A further contrast is evident when considering the firm's reaction to an alteration in fixed costs. The equilibrium level of output of the profit-maximising firm will be unaffected by an increase in fixed costs since neither marginal cost nor marginal revenue will change. However, if the firm is initially at a profit-constrained sales-maximising level of output, the increase in fixed costs will mean that the profit constraint is no longer being met. The firm will have to reduce output until the constraint is once again satisfied – or approached as nearly as possible if the maximum level of profit that is now attainable is below the level of the profit constraint.

This model demonstrates clearly that different assumptions about the objectives of the firm can lead to different predictions about behaviour. Given the theoretical structure into which the objective is to be inserted, the assumption of sales maximisation subject to a profit constraint results in the prediction of a larger output and advertising expenditure than does the assumption of profit maximisation, unless the level of the profit constraint coincides with the maximum profit attainable. It is, of course, precisely when the two coincide that the area of discretion reduces to zero and the behaviour of the firm (i.e. output and advertising expenditure) is the same irrespective of which of the objectives is assumed to be operative.

THE LABOUR-MANAGED ENTERPRISE

Another example of the way in which predictions about firm behaviour depend on the assumptions made about objectives is evident in the analysis of the labour-managed firm. In such firms the ultimate power of decision making is vested in the firm's workers, and their objective is most commonly assumed to be the maximisation of income per worker. It has been shown that a perfectly competitive economy consisting of labour-managed firms will result in a Pareto-optimal long-run equilibrium identical with that of the more familiar, perfectly competitive, neoclassical economy of profit-maximising firms.[136] However, the different objectives of the two types of firm give rise to differences in short-run adjustment behaviour.

Figure 3.2 illustrates the long-run equilibrium position of the two types of firm.[137] Curve *RR* is the average revenue product of labour for both firms, i.e. output per head multiplied by the price of the product. Consider now the labour-managed firm. Such a firm can be thought of as hiring its capital at a fixed rental, with the capital cost per worker obviously depending on the number of workers. This is represented by the rectangular hyperbola *CC*, with the area of any rectangle below the curve, i.e. capital cost per worker multiplied

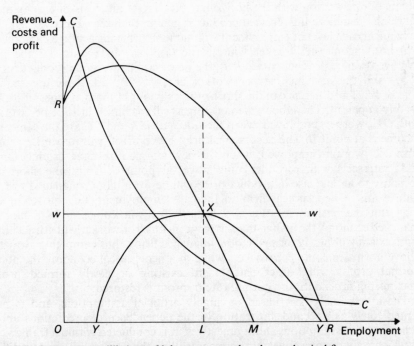

Fig. 3.2 Long-run equilibrium of labour-managed and neo-classical firms.
OL = long-run equilibrium employment of both labour-managed firms maximising income per worker and neo-classical firms maximising profit.

by the number of workers, equal to the fixed rental. If capital and labour are the only two inputs, income per worker will be the vertical distance between RR and CC, represented by curve YY, and will be maximised when the slopes of RR and CC are the same and OL workers are employed. In long run equilibrium the rental on capital and income per worker will be equalised throughout the labour-managed economy and will correspond to the normal rate of profit and equilibrium wage of the perfectly competitive neoclassical economy. Similarly, there will be a correspondence between the distribution of capital and labour between firms in the two types of economy.

Consider next the position of the profit-maximising firm that hires workers at the going wage. Since in long run equilibrium the going wage will be the same as the maximum income per worker of the labour-managed firm, it can be represented by line ww, which is tangential to YY at point X. The profit-maximising firm will adjust its employment until the marginal revenue product of labour equals the wage. Since the long-run equilibrium position of the two types of firm is the same, curve RM, representing the marginal revenue product of labour, passes through X, so that it intersects with ww when OL workers are employed. Thus, Figure 3.2 illustrates the long-run equilibrium positions of the two types of firm at which they both employ OL workers.

Suppose, now, that the price of the final product increases. This will cause the average and marginal revenue product curves to rise to the right except at the points of intersection with the horizontal axis, i.e. at all levels of employment at which the underlying physical product is greater than zero. Since the average revenue at each level of employment will increase, whereas average capital cost will not, income per worker will rise accordingly. In Figure 3.3 the new average revenue product curve, $R'R$, the new marginal revenue product curve, $R'M$, and the new income per worker curve, $Y'Y'$, are superimposed on Figure 3.2. The difference in the short-run behaviour of the two types of firm is readily apparent. The labour-managed firm will maximise income per worker with OL_m workers employed, when the slopes of $R'R$ and CC are the same and income is at point B. The neoclassical firm, by contrast, will maximise profits with OL_n workers employed, when the new marginal revenue product curve $R'M$ intersects with ww, the going wage, at point S. Thus, the short-run response to an increase in product price will be for a labour-managed firm to reduce and a neoclassical firm to increase employment. Of course, in the long run the position of the two firms will again coincide. In a labour-managed economy the higher-than-average income per worker will attract entry from existing or newly formed labour-managed firms, thus competing away the above normal income per worker, while in a neoclassical economy the above normal profits will attract entry from existing or newly formed profit-maximising firms until the normal rate of profit is restored.

The above analysis is based on highly artificial assumptions and is presented solely as a second illustration of the dependence of predictions about behaviour on assumptions about objectives. It is conducted within a framework in which only the objectives of those controlling the firm are allowed to differ. However, the reasons for the growth of interest in the labour-managed firm in recent years are far broader than can be captured by such 'dehumanised'

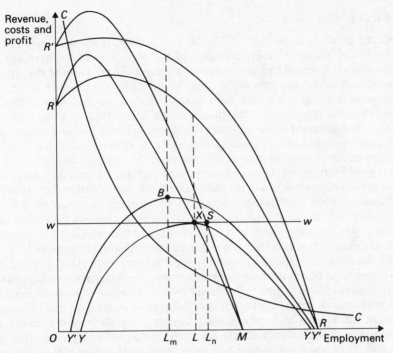

Fig. 3.3 Short run equilibrium of labour-managed and neo-classical firms compared.
OL = long-run equilibrium employment of both types of firm,
OL_m = short-run equilibrium employment of labour-managed firms,
OL_n = short-run equilibrium employment of neo-classical firms.

analysis.[138] In fact the main interest of the labour-managed, or worker-controlled, firm is the argument that only in a context of self-management can alienation be overcome and the 'economic liberation of man' be achieved.[139] Although there have been occasional examples elsewhere, the principal practical inspiration for this argument has been the Yugoslav experience.[140] The major economic claim made for the labour-managed firm is that a context of self-management provides the possibility for a transformation of values and motivation which can release hitherto untapped human energy and creativity, thus greatly enhancing the productivity of human labour.

Of course, the question of what is the appropriate form of relationship between decentralised units and centralised state institutions is not removed by worker self-management. Although the formal analysis of the labour-managed economy has been conducted largely within the framework of an unplanned market economy, the potential gains in labour productivity and human dignity arising from worker control have historically been associated largely with the argument for planned socialist economies. In either case it is inconceivable that the central government will not continue to play a major role; hence, the problem of how to develop effective democratic control over centralised institutions remains.[141]

MANAGERIAL THEORIES

Since the publication in 1932 of *The Modern Corporation and Private Property* by Berle and Means[142] the discussion of the objectives of the firm has been increasingly influenced by the concept of 'managerialism'. Despite the proliferation of managerial theories differing in detail[143] it is legitimate to speak of managerialism in general, since such theories share a common logical structure. This falls into three parts: the thesis of the separation of ownership from control; the assertion of a divergence of interest between 'owning' shareholders and 'non-owning' but 'controlling' managers; and the assumption that firms operate in an environment that affords them an area of discretion in their behaviour. Managerial theories differ in the assumptions that they make about managerial objectives and in the nature of the relationship that they postulate between shareholders, managers and the firm's external environment. What they have in common is the view that managers are not fully constrained by the external environment and the influence of shareholders but possess an area of discretion, which they use to pursue their distinct objectives.[144]

All three stages of the managerialist argument are important. If there exists no separation of ownership from control, the foundation disappears. If shareholders and managers have the same or compatible objectives, behaviour will presumably be little affected by the precise nature of the relationship between them. Finally, even if there is a clear separation of ownership from control and shareholders and managers do have conflicting subjective goals, this will be of small consequence if the environment within which the firm is operating allows little scope for discretionary behaviour. These three parts of the structure of managerialism are now examined in turn.

The separation of ownership from control

The thesis that there is a separation of ownership from control in the (large) public joint-stock company stems from the observation that in many companies share ownership is widely dispersed, with no individual or group accounting for a dominant proportion of voting strength. It follows, according to the thesis, that the board of directors, which typically owns only a few per cent of voting strength, effectively controls the company, relying on its own holdings and proxy votes to maintain its position. The directors' position is further strengthened by their greater possession of relevant knowledge about the company's affairs: directors are 'insiders', most shareholders are 'outsiders'. Thus, in companies where there is no individual or group holding a controlling proportion of voting strength, ownership (i.e. shareholders) is said to be separated or divorced from control (i.e. directors and/or top management).

The most comprehensive study of the distribution of share ownership and voting strength in English companies remains that undertaken by Florence.[145] Table 3.6 summarises his main findings. It relates to English 'commercial and industrial' public joint-stock companies listed in the Stock Exchange *Year Book* for 1951, whose issued share capital had a nominal value of £200,000 or more. The companies are classified into seven grades of vote concentration, with 'very large' firms (issued capital £3 million or more) distinguished from 'medium and smaller large' firms. The data are for 1951 and, in the case of the very large

Table 3.6   *Vote concentration of large[a] English commercial and industrial companies, 1936 and 1951.*

Type of company[a] and year	No. of companies	Largest holding (% of vote)		Largest 20 holdings (% of vote)				
		50% or more (1)	20–49% (2)	50% or more (3)	30–49% (4)	20–9% (5)	10–19% (6)	0–9% (7)
Very large:								
1936	92	9	13	15	13	17	15	10
1951	92	6	10	4	15	13	27	17
Medium and smaller large:								
1951	135	1	12	13	31	37	32	9

Source: P. Sargant Florence, *Ownership, Control and Success of Large Companies* (London, Sweet & Maxwell, 1961), table IIIC, pp. 68–9.

Note:
(a) All the companies included had issued share capital of a nominal value of £200,000 and were deemed 'large'. Those with an issued capital of £3 million or more were styled 'very large', the remainder being 'medium and smaller large'.

companies, for 1936. The table details the percentage of the total vote held by the largest single holding, where this exceeds 20 per cent, and by the largest twenty holdings in all other companies. It is clear from Table 3.6 that in 1951 there was only a handful of companies in which the largest single holding accounted for 50 per cent or more of the total voting strength. Furthermore, in 62 per cent of the 'very large' and 58 per cent of the 'medium and smaller large' companies the largest twenty holdings accounted for less than 30 per cent of the voting strength. Between 1936 and 1951 the extent of vote concentration in the 'very large' companies diminished. The overall picture that emerges from the table is one of considerable dispersion in the distribution of voting strength.

This overall picture has been supported by the incidental results of a study of share issues quoted on the London Stock Exchange in 1963. In the thirty-nine largest companies the twenty largest shareholdings typically held 5–25 per cent of market value. At the other end of the size distribution, in three-quarters of the 2,134 smallest companies the twenty largest shareholdings accounted for over 50 per cent of market value.[146] Of course, market value is not the same thing as voting strength. Nevertheless, the figures are consistent with Florence's finding that concentration of shareholding and company size were inversely related, and they perhaps suggest that the trend towards wider dispersion that Florence noted among 'very large' companies they have continued after 1951.

Data on directors' holdings provide further support for this view. Prais has examined the extent of voting shareholdings by the directors of the 100 largest quoted manufacturing companies, in terms of 1970 net assets, in 1968 and 1972. Between the two years the proportion of voting capital held by the board of directors fell in two-thirds of the companies, the mean board holding fell from 7·3 to 5·4 per cent and the median remained unchanged at 0·46 per cent. However, in 1972 there were still fourteen of the 100 largest companies in which the board held over 10 per cent of voting shares.[147]

Voting strength also appears to be widely dispersed in the United States, and again the trend has been away from concentration. A study by Larner[148] has compared the original findings of Berle and Means for 1929 with the position in 1963. Berle and Means distinguished various forms of corporate control and defined 'management control' as a situation in which no individual, family or group of associates held 20 per cent or more of the voting strength. On this basis, 44 per cent (eighty-eight) of the largest 200 non-financial corporations in 1929 were found to be management-controlled. Larner decided that the greater absolute size of the 200 largest non-financial corporations in 1963 and the wider dispersion of their stock meant that individual or group control could probably be exercised with much less than 20 per cent of voting strength. Accordingly, he redefined management control as a situation in which no individual or co-ordinated group held 10 per cent or more of the total voting strength, and on this more restricted basis 84·5 per cent (169) of the largest 200 non-financial corporations in 1963 were designated as management-controlled.

Larner's study provides a convenient introduction to the central and un-resolved problem in discussions of the relationship between ownership and control. As has been noted, he considered 10 per cent of voting strength sufficient to ensure control in 1963, as compared with Berle and Means's

Table 3.7 *Companies that are owner-controlled, according to two different criteria, 1936 and 1951.*

| Type of company^a and year | Criterion of owner-control: largest 20 holdings | | | |
| | 20% or more (columns 1–5 of Table 3.6) | | 30% or more (columns 1–4 of Table 3.6) | |
	(no.)	*(%)*	*(no.)*	*(%)*
Very large:				
1936	67	73	50	54
1951	48	52	35	38
Medium and smaller large:				
1951	94	70	57	42

Source and Note: As for Table 3.6.

20 per cent in 1929. What proportion, then, *is* required to exercise effective control? Gordon has constructed a situation in which, on certain assumptions, a company may be effectively controlled by the ownership of the equivalent of as little as 3 per cent of its stock.[149] However, the matter cannot be resolved *a priori;* it is an empirical question, and so far little work has been done in this area.[150] It is also an important question since different answers will produce markedly different pictures of the extent to which companies are owner controlled. Florence in his earlier work considered companies in which the twenty largest voteholdings accounted for 20–29 per cent of voting strength to be owner-controlled, but in his later work he had second thoughts.[151] The difference made to the incidence of owner control by whether 20 or 30 per cent is taken as the minimum that is necessary for control is set out in Table 3.7.

While the actual proportion of voting strength required to ensure control in any specific situation is a matter for empirical investigation, the general proposition that ownership is separated from control also raises difficult conceptual problems. What does it mean? That not all 'owners' are involved in control? That none are? What if some are and some are not? Beed has attempted to clarify the situation:

From the evidence presented, two possible and contradictory conclusions can be drawn: (i) following Berle, that in most companies 'a compact group of individuals' was not able to 'select the board of directors (or its majority)', *or* (ii) contradicting Berle, that a small individual or combined ownership, e.g. 1 to 5% was sufficient to exercise control provided it was not challenged by an unlikely combination of the vast numerical majority of minute owners; the wider the dispersion of ownership, the greater the possibility of control by absolutely large but relatively small shareholders. In the first case there has been a total separation of ownership from control; in the second, the 'large' owners constitute the control and the minute owners are powerless.[152]

Does Beed's second case count as a separation of ownership from control? In one sense it does, since an overwhelming majority of shareholders owning a large majority of the firm's shares are effectively disenfranchised. In another sense it does not, since a handful of 'large' shareholders are able to determine the company's policy. Florence has estimated that in 1951 in the 'representative' company the largest twenty shareholders constituted one-sixth of 1 per cent of all shareholders.[153] In this way, as Sweezy following Marx has observed, rather than ownership being separated from control it may be that the 'concentration of control over capital is not limited by the concentration of ownership'.[154]

In this discussion of the relationship between ownership and control two separate but inter-related questions, both unsettled, have emerged: first, there is the question of the proportion of the voting strength required to ensure control; and second, there is the possibility that a distinction should be drawn between the position of large and small shareholders. On the first question systematic evidence is sparse. Beed has reported an estimate by the Secretary of the Australian Shareholders' Association that in the absence of dispute the directors of Australian management-controlled companies typically collect around 15 per cent of the total votes when up for re-election.[155] Midgley, in a survey of fifty-five large companies drawn from *The Times 500* for 1969, has found that the proportion of voting capital held by shareholders attending the annual general meeting was typically below 1 per cent and that there were few instances in which returned proxies exceeded 20 per cent of the total.[156] The second question is closely connected with the issues discussed shortly under the subheading 'conflicting objectives?' However, a word on the role of institutional holdings may first be helpful.

Institutional holdings are in fact becoming rapidly more important.[157] The distribution of the market value of shareholdings by beneficial ownership is set out in Table 3.8 for companies quoted on the UK Stock Exchange in 1957, 1963, 1969 and 1975. Over the eighteen-year period the share of the personal sector fell from 67·7 to 39·8 per cent while that of the financial sector rose from 21·3 to 47·9 per cent. The continuing increase in importance of pension funds and insurance companies is evident. A similar overall trend has been noted for the United States by Baldwin, who has commented on its significance:

> The institutional investors, like other stockholders, should be primarily interested in profits; and unlike many small individual investors, however sophisticated, the institutions should find it a rational allocation of staff and executive time to devote much observation and study to the policies and prospects of firms in which they have invested or may invest.[158]

It has, of course, often been argued that institutional holdings, although frequently relatively large, are for investment rather than control and should, therefore, be discounted.[159] This is not a very plausible argument, and it has perhaps gained currency as a result of the normally passive role played by the

Table 3.8   *Market value of ordinary shares quoted on the UK Stock Exchange,*
by sector of beneficial ownership, 1957, 1963, 1969 and 1975.

Sector of beneficial holder	% of market value			
	1957	*1963*	*1969*	*1975*
Personal	67·7	56·1	49·5	39·8
Financial sector	21·3	30·4	35·9	47·9
of which:				
Pension funds	3·4	6·4	9·0	16·8
Insurance companies	8·8	10·0	12·2	15·9
Investment trusts and other				
financial companies	6·8	10·0	8·7	10·0
Unit trusts	0·5	1·3	2·9	4·1
Banks	0·9	1·3	1·7	0·7
Stock Exchange	0·9	1·4	1·4	0·4
Overseas	4·4	7·0	6·6	5·6
Public	3·9	1·5	2·6	3·6
Industrial and commercial	2·7	5·1	5·4	3·0
Total	100·0	100·1	100·0	99·9

Source: M. Erritt and I. Alexander, 'Ownership of company shares: a new survey', *Economic Trends*, vol. 287 (September 1977), table 2, p. 100; and J. Moyle, *The Pattern of Ordinary Share Ownership, 1957–1970*, University of Cambridge Department of Applied Economics, Occasional Paper 31 (Cambridge, Cambridge UP, 1971), table 4.2, p. 18.

institutions. However, passivity over long periods in which there may be no reason for intervention is quite consistent with decisive action at critical moments.[160] This is dramatically illustrated from time to time in the context of a contested takeover bid. The successful £400 million takeover bid by Grand Metropolitan Hotels for Watney Mann in July 1972 was the largest successful bid in the United Kingdom to that date. At the end of the four-month contest Watney's Chairman stated: 'What swung the battle in favour of Grand Metropolitan was the institutions, not the individual shareholders. The majority of them remained loyal to Watney.'[161]

Comprehensive evidence on the role played by the institutions is lacking. This may be because the institutions prefer to operate discreetly behind the scenes in friendly co-operation with management whenever possible. Such is the declared intention of the Institutional Shareholders' Committee formed in 1973, which then represented over one-third of ordinary shares. Midgley in his survey has found it rare for the institutions to attend company annual general meetings, but he has very interestingly reported that a spokesman for one of the largest insurance companies estimated that it had intervened in the affairs of the companies in which it held shares twenty-five times in the eighteen-month period to December 1971.[162] Thus, it seems likely that the institutions play a more important role than is usually evident and that any discussion of the relationship between ownership and control that ignores institutional holdings will be deficient.

Conflicting objectives?

Large corporate firms are in general run by managers. Even in the few remaining family firms the concept of the entrepreneur – the owner–manager – is probably inappropriate. The large company is a complex organisation, not an individual, and it may be expected to display qualitatively different behavioural characteristics from those of an individual.[163] In companies that are 'manager-controlled', of course, managerial motivation will be decisive in determining behaviour. However, even in 'owner-controlled' companies, day-to-day decisions will be in the hands of top management, and strategic decisions will be taken by the board of directors. Unless owner control is illegitimately equated with entrepreneurial 'owner–managership', the behaviour of owner-controlled companies is also likely to be influenced to some extent by the subjective motivation of their managers and directors. Thus, the second stage of the managerial argument, i.e. the assertion that there is a divergence of interest between shareholders and managers, is of perhaps greater potential significance than is often realised. If the assertion is well founded, it may have implications for understanding the behaviour of large companies in general, without prejudice to the question of the extent to which ownership and control can be said to be separated.[164]

The argument that shareholders and managers have conflicting objectives usually retains the traditional theory's assumption that the owners of capital, now *rentier* shareholders, seek to maximise their profits. However, in the context of a corporate firm this assumption requires some interpretation. If it is taken to mean the desire to maximise the return to capital invested, the question arises of the weight to be attached to current and future dividends and to capital gains. This in turn focuses attention on the time period over which the return is to be maximised and on the related issue of how to deal with uncertainty. One common way of handling these problems is to take profit maximisation to mean the maximisation of the present market value of the firm's shares.[165] Such an interpretation is a long way from the simple-minded profit-maximisation assumption of the traditional theory and requires a theory of the way in which share prices are determined.[166] So far theories of the stock market have assumed certainty, or a probabilistic certainty equivalent, over an infinite time horizon; thus, the ambiguities inherent in the traditional concept of maximisation, which relate precisely to time period and uncertainty, have remained unresolved.

However, although the problems of how to construe shareholder objectives remain, the principal preoccupation of managerialism has been with the question of managerial objectives. The literature may be summed up in the statement that managers are motivated by the pursuit of 'salary, security, status, power, prestige and professional excellence'.[167] These in turn, it has been argued, are more closely related to company characteristics such as size or growth rate than to profitability. Thus, perhaps the three best-known suggested alternatives to profit maximisation as the objective of the firm are Baumol's sales maximisation subject to a profit constraint, Marris's growth maximisation subject to a security constraint and O. Williamson's maximisation of a generalised managerial utility function subject to a profit constraint.[168]

Two points are worth noting at this stage. First, there is a good deal of agreement that growth is likely to be a central objective. Marris, of course, has made this explicit, but it is also implicit in the arguments of Baumol and Williamson. In the fuller statement of his static sales-maximising model, Baumol has indicated that a formalisation of the long run considerations influencing the level of the profit constraint will incorporate profit as a variable in a dynamic model,[169] and he has subsequently sketched the outline of a simple dynamic model with the rate of growth of sales as the objective.[170] Williamson too has recognised that the maximisation of his managerial utility function will involve growth.[171] Second, virtually all managerial theories allow an important role for profitability, whether as a means of achieving growth, of satisfying shareholders or both. Thus, growth and profitability emerge as key variables for the study of company behaviour. Managerial theories of the growth of the firm and the relationship between growth and profitability are examined in Chapter 4.

To what extent is the view that shareholders and managers have conflicting objectives well founded? Early attempts to obtain statistical evidence that is relevant to the hypothesis that managerial objectives are more closely related to sales or growth than to profits were based on US data. In a well-known study of forty-five out of the 100 largest US industrial corporations, McGuire, Chiu and Elbing have sought to relate the income (including income from stock) of chief executives to company sales and profits over the period 1953–9. They have concluded that there was a significant relationship between executive income and sales but not between executive income and profits, although the latter was not absolutely ruled out.[172] At first sight this study appears to provide support for the managerialist position. However, this appearance has been challenged by Dean and Smith, who have argued that, since profitability varies with industry, i.e. for reasons outside the immediate control of the firm's managers, and since managers are paid to administer, managerial compensation may be expected to be less closely related to profitability than to size.[173]

Comprehensive information about directors' remuneration and shareholdings first became available in the United Kingdom under the disclosure provisions of the Company Act 1969. Such information is available from 1969 and forms the basis of two recent studies. Cosh has examined the relationship between the remuneration of the highest-paid executive, the rate of return and net assets over the period 1969–71 for some 1,600 companies accounting for about two-thirds of the net assets of UK industrial and commercial companies. Separate analyses were undertaken for seventeen industry groups of quoted companies and five industry groups of unquoted companies and for fourteen industry groups of quoted companies divided into larger (net assets >£8·5 million) and smaller companies. Company size was found to be the major determinant of chief executive remuneration, 'explaining' 49 per cent of the variance, with the inclusion of profitability as an additional explanatory variable improving the degree of 'explanation' only to 54 per cent. In only seven of the seventeen industry groups of quoted companies was the profitability coefficient significant at the 5 per cent level. For the larger companies size emerged as even more dominant, 'explaining' 44 per cent of chief executive remuneration, with profitability adding only a further 4 per cent, significant at the 5 per cent level in only two of the fourteen industry groups and actually negative in five industry groups. For the smaller companies, however, size 'explained' 19 per cent of chief executive remuneration, with profitability improving the degree of 'explanation' to 34 per cent, significant at the 5 per cent level in eight and positive in all fourteen industry groups.[174]

Since profitability was clearly associated with chief executive remuneration in the case of smaller but not in the case of larger companies, Cosh has argued that the findings were *prima facie* fully consistent with neither the profit-maximising nor the managerial-objective-maximising hypothesis. However, while he has suggested for various reasons that neither could be confidently rejected, he is clearly inclined towards the managerial hypothesis, his final conclusion being that, 'if remuneration either influences or reflects the goals of the chief executives of the major companies in the economy, increased company size rather than increased profitability will be the major objective of these companies'.[175]

In a less sophisticated study based on much the same data, but not disaggregated to industry level, Meeks and Whittington also have concluded that 'size is confirmed as being of overwhelming importance in the explanation of the level of directors' pay'.[176] However, they have argued that for the purpose of understanding managerial behaviour the relevant comparison is between the effect on management pay of changes in size, that is growth, on the one hand and of changes in profitability on the other. Their estimates suggested that, when considering the effect on management pay of 'comparable achievements in terms of growth or profitability within the period, the premium on profitability is . . . at least as great as that for growth'.[177] Even taking account of the asymmetry between growth and profitability – in that growth contributes to size and, therefore, management pay even if it is not subsequently maintained, whereas profitability does not – they have concluded that 'the influence of profitability on the average level of directors' pay is non-trivial either in itself, or in relation to the corresponding influence of growth'.[178]

From a somewhat different angle Lewellen's study of fifty of the 500 largest US industrial firms as listed by *Fortune* in 1963 has cast further doubt on the hypothesis of a fundamental conflict of interest between managers and shareholders. He has accepted that there are few large companies in which management holds even a substantial minority of stock but has argued that small relative holdings may amount to large absolute holdings that are important for the personal wealth position of their owners. For instance, the average stock held by the top five highest-paid executives over the years 1960–3 was in the range of $2–3 million. He has also argued that management income is increasingly related to company stock. Over the period 1953–63 top executives' income, i.e. their addition to wealth, resulting from holdings of their companies' shares was twice as great as their income in the form of compensation for services rendered, i.e. their 'earned' income; for the top five executives it was three times as great. The performance of a company's shares became an even more important contributory factor to the financial position of its top executives when account was taken of the substantial proportion of compensation that was stock based.[179] Lewellen has concluded that: 'A separation of ownership and management *functions* clearly exists; it seems that a significant separation of their pecuniary interest does not.'[180]

Executives' income derives from the share performance of the companies for which they work to a lesser extent in the United Kingdom than in the United States; hence, Lewellen's rejection of the view that shareholders and managers have conflicting objectives may apply with less force in Britain. Nevertheless, at a general level his study has called into question the very concept of shareholders and managers as distinct groups. Their absolutely large holdings of shares in their own companies suggest that top managers as a group overlap significantly with the group of large property owners. This view is reinforced by the fact that their holdings in their own companies typically constitute only a small proportion of their total wealth.[181] The Oxford Savings Survey found that in 1952 a higher proportion of managers than of any other occupational category covered (namely, self-employed, clerical and sales, skilled manual, unskilled manual, retired) owned shares and that the average size of managerial holdings was larger than that of any other group.[182] A survey of upper income groups in 1956 found that the mean value of shares held by a sample of directors (£28,087) was over twice that of a sample drawn from Debrett (£13,620) and even more in excess of that for the other groups covered (namely, heirs, accountants, doctors, dentists).[183] For the United States a similar situation prevails.[184]

Of all forms of property ownership the distribution of company stocks and shares is most unequal, as is shown in Table 3.9 for 1954. Eighteen years later it remained true that the likelihood of wealth owners holding securities yielding dividends or taxed interest increased markedly with net wealth, as did the proportion of net wealth held in the form of such assets. In 1972 the top 9·6 per cent of wealth owners, with net assets of £15,000 or more, held 91·3 per cent of all securities yielding dividends or taxed interest.[185] In 1975 wealth owners with £200,000 or more held 26·9 per cent of their assets in the form of listed ordinary shares and 17·5 per cent in other company assets, compared with 5·9 and 3·7 per cent respectively for all wealth owners. Correspondingly, 29·3 per cent of listed ordinary shares and 30·3 per cent of other company assets were held by wealth owners with £200,000 or more.[186] While this says nothing directly about the relationship between managers and shareholders, in

Table 3.9 *Distribution of various forms of assets in Britain, 1954.*

Type of asset	% of total owned by:		
	Top 1%	*Top 5%*	*Top 10%*
Stocks and shares in companies	81	96	98
Government and municipal securities	42	71	83
Land, buildings and trade assets	28	58	74
Cash and bank deposits	23	48	64

Source: H. F. Lydall and D. G. Tipping, 'The distribution of personal wealth in Britain', *Bulletin of the Oxford University Institute of Statistics,* vol. 23 (February 1961), table V, p. 90.

conjunction with the data referred to in the previous paragraph it lends support to the argument that the managerial group is a significant element in the property-owning class. There is, of course, considerable differentiation within both the managerial and the property-owning groups. Hence, the picture emerges of top management as an integral part of the class of large property owners.[187] It is this picture that has led Miliband, while recognising the existence of some differences of interest between shareholders *qua* shareholders and managers *qua* managers, to write: 'But these are tactical differences within a strategic consensus . . . the differences of purpose and motivation which may exist between them are overshadowed by a basic community of interest.'[188]

Further support for this conclusion can be found in the work of Nichols. On the basis of an examination of the social experience and values of managers prior to their entry into company employment, and of the influences to which they are subjected once within the corporation, he has concluded that it is over-simplified to distinguish too sharply between 'propertied' and 'non-propertied' businessmen:

> A defining characteristic of both propertied and non-propertied directors is that their status, their prestige, their security, and not least their wealth are all directly dependent upon the continued existence of the large private enterprise corporation . . .
>
> The norms which govern his [the hired manager's] conduct derive in part from the shareholder interest and in normative, relational, and to some degree economic terms his position approximates to that of the propertied director. Managerialists have written of a 'divorce' or 'separation' of ownership and control. In this context we find it more fitting to write of a 'marriage of convenience.'[189]

The extent of discretion

The discussion of the managerialist argument so far has revealed ambiguities in the concept of the separation of ownership from control and cast doubt on the existence of a serious conflict of objectives between shareholders and managers. However, perhaps the most fundamental question is the extent to which the environment in which firms operate affords scope for discretionary behaviour. As noted at the beginning of this section, within the framework of the traditional theory of the firm it is the relaxation of the assumption of perfect competition that prompts a re-examination of the appropriateness of profit maximisation as the firm's assumed objective. This is because within that framework monopoly power enables survival at less than maximum profit.

Baumol's static model, as has been seen, results in different predictions about certain aspects of behaviour according to whether profit maximisation or sales maximisation subject to a profit constraint is assumed as the objective. J. Williamson has constructed a formal growth model in order to examine in a dynamic context the extent to which differences in assumed objectives result in differences in behaviour. He has concluded that: 'in all cases except where profitability is at best the minimum sum necessary to prevent takeover, the policies the firm pursues will depend on the form of its objectives. Profit-, growth- and sales-maximisers will act differently.'[190] Thus, whether a static or a dynamic setting is considered, the behaviour of the firm appears to depend on the objectives of those running it.

However, it will have been noticed that where profit is not selected as the objective some form of profit consideration is always retained, whether in the form of an externally imposed constraint or of an endogenous variable. The reason for this is the inescapable fact that a certain level of profit is necessary for the survival of the firm and its managers; a firm cannot survive as an independent entity in the face of sustained losses, and a management is unlikely to survive unless a minimum level of profitability is attained. Only after the level of profit that is necessary for survival has been achieved can other objectives be attended to. Both Baumol and Williamson have assumed that the environment within which the firm operates or grows is known with certainty, and both have also ignored the complications arising from oligopolistic interdependence.[191] Given this framework, it is possible to ascertain precisely the conditions under which the profit required for survival will be forthcoming and to explore the consequences for the behaviour of the firm of alternative objectives once these conditions have been met.

An interesting insight into the possible consequences for this approach of relaxing the assumption of certainty is provided by Lintner's analysis of the effect on the short-run behaviour of the firm of introducing uncertainty in the sense of risk into the traditional theory's framework. He has concluded that:

> . . . under risk-averse profit-maximisation, these effects of uncertainty concerning unit sales parallel the effects of non-profit goals, such as sales maximisation or management's concern with its own emoluments and empire-building, emphasized in the recent 'revisionist' literature by Baumol, Williamson, and others. The results in the present paper concur with the conclusions of such authors concerning the need for revisions and extensions of the traditional theory of the firm. On the other hand, our results suggest that, after the traditional profit-maximising theory has been revised and extended to incorporate risk aversion and uncertainty, the incremental contribution of the other non-profit revisionist goals may be less significant than previously expected.[192]

It should be stressed that while Lintner's analysis is suggestive it is restricted to the short-run and introduces only 'measurable uncertainty', i.e. risk rather than uncertainty proper.

A prerequisite for discussing the extent of discretion that is open to firms is an adequate theoretical framework for analysing the determinants of their behaviour. The adequacy or otherwise of any given framework is, of course, a matter of judgement. It has been implicit in the argument of this chapter that to be adequate a framework must not abstract from certain phenomena that appear to be essential characteristics of contemporary capitalist economies. Such phenomena may be divided into two categories: those relating to the firm, and those relating to the environment. In the former category are included the corporate institutional form and large absolute size of the dominant firms, as well as the diversified and international character of their operations. In the latter category come: the oligopolistic nature of interfirm relations; the inherent uncertainty arising from the continuously changing state of technology, input supply and market conditions; and the increasingly pervasive role of the state. The two categories are linked by the active attempts of oligopolistic rivals to shape the environment to their own purposes and to dominate their competitors. Only in the context of a theoretical framework, whether of this or some other sort, that captures the essence of the competitive process and its imperatives can the extent of the discretion that is open to the 'representative' firm be defined.[193]

It is unlikely that there would be much dissent from Baldwin's judgement that the present state of theory is inadequate, and there may even be increasing agreement with his view that 'the remedy lies in further exploration of the relevant characteristics of modern giant corporations and of their environments, rather than new motivational assumptions'.[194] Many of the elements out of which a more adequate theory may be constructed are explored in subsequent chapters. On the question of objectives, it seems likely that the need for any adequate theory to come to terms with change and uncertainty, not just risk, will ensure that profitability continues to be regarded as of central importance. Profitability is a *sine qua non* for survival in capitalist economies, and in the conditions postulated attention is likely to be constantly focused on the need to increase profit, if only to prevent a decline. This is not to argue for the retention of the traditional theory's concept of profit maximisation as the firm's assumed objective. On the contrary, it is to argue that only in the context of a much richer theory, oriented towards the analysis of the long-run developmental tendencies of the capitalist corporate system as a whole, can economists begin to formulate the appropriate questions to ask about the complex relationships between business motivation and behaviour.

CONCLUSION

The traditional theory's concept of the profit-maximising entrepreneur is inappropriate for the analysis of the corporate firm. It makes no sense to compare the modern corporate manager with the traditional entrepreneur, at least not when discussing ownership, control and objectives in the contemporary firm. Rather, the institutional complexity of the joint stock company – the overlapping relationship between shareholders, directors and top managers – is the appropriate area of investigation. This area has been divided into three aspects: the concept of the separation of ownership from control; the hypothesis of a conflict of objectives between shareholders and managers; and the extent to which firms enjoy an area of discretion in their behaviour. With respect to each aspect, examination reveals a situation that is considerably more complex than is often realised. The extent to which ownership and control are separated, indeed the meaning of the concept of separation in this context, is by no means clear. Room for doubt exists as to whether or not shareholders and managers form distinct social groups and, *a fortiori*, as to whether they can be said to have antagonistic interests. Finally, a convincing demonstration that different assumptions about objectives lead to different predictions about behaviour must await the creation of a more adequate theoretical framework for the analysis of the corporate system than at present exists.

What does emerge from the discussion of business objectives is that in conditions of change and uncertainty profitability is likely to be to the forefront of corporate concern, whether the firm is regarded as owner-controlled or manager-controlled. This is not least because of the relationship between profitability and growth, which is the subject matter of the next chapter. However, before turning in that direction the position of the behavioural school, which draws the most far-reaching conclusions from the recognition of the firm as a complex organisation, is considered.

3.5 BEHAVIOURISM

Once the firm is recognised as an organisation the possibility arises that its organisational characteristics may have implications for its behaviour. Thus, the organisational form of the public joint-stock company gives rise to discussion of the relationship between shareholders, managers, objectives and behaviour.[195] The behavioural school has taken this line of argument to its logical conclusion. Starting from the observation that large firms are complex organisations, appropriately conceived as administrative units with problems of internal co-ordination and decision making, it has sought to examine the firm explicitly as an organisational structure, using organisation theory to develop a behavioural theory of the firm.

Central to the approach of this school is the thesis that the continuing viability of an organisation is premised on the satisfaction of certain requirements generated by the relationships involved in its internal functioning and that the satisfaction of these requirements may, indeed almost certainly will, result in contradictory behaviour that is inconsistent with the perfectly co-ordinated pursuit of any 'higher level' objectives. Furthermore, once the assumption of perfect knowledge or a certainty equivalent is abandoned, the problems posed by the need to acquire and process information must be analysed to discover whether they have any significant consequences for the theory of the firm. The behavioural school has concluded that these problems are so immense that the assumption of an objective to be maximised is inappropriate and must be replaced by the assumption of a number of acceptable-level goals to be 'satisficed'. Thus, emphasis is placed on analysing how the individuals comprising an organisation are induced, given their cognitive situation and the information available to them, to behave in a way that is conducive to the survival of the organisation. The intention is to develop a theory of the firm based on 'realism' with respect to motivational and cognitive assumptions and on the processes of information gathering and internal decision making. Since work based on the behavioural approach is referred to from time to time in this book, it may be helpful at this stage to give a brief outline of the best-known application of this approach to the theory of the firm, namely, that developed by Cyert and March.

A BEHAVIOURAL THEORY OF THE FIRM[196]

The firm is conceived as a coalition of individuals and groups of individuals. It is taken as self-evident that individuals have goals and that organisations *per se* do not. Hence, there exists the possibility of goal conflict between the individuals constituting the coalition. The resolution of this potential conflict by assuming that a supreme authority is able to enforce conformity in the behaviour of subordinates to a higher level goal or by assuming a happy coincidence of consensus is rejected. Instead, it is argued that organisational goals are formed in the process of bargaining between the members of the coalition. This bargaining is over the distribution of 'side payments', i.e. inducements in the form of money or policy commitments. At a certain level of generality the distinction between the two forms of side payment disappears; commitments to pay money are reducible to policy commitments in the form of constraints. It is the pattern of policy commitments emerging from the bargaining process that specifies the goals of the organisation. However, because of the way in which agreement is reached the organisational objectives that emerge are imperfectly rationalised and expressed either in the form of 'aspiration levels' or in non-operational form. These organisational goals change in two ways as the bargaining process, which is continuous, proceeds: aspiration levels with respect to existing goals, i.e. the levels of achievement regarded as acceptable by the coalition members, will be modified in the light of the levels actually achieved; and new goals will be introduced as the attention focus of coalition members alters. The organisation is able to survive with unrationalised conflicting goals partly because some of the objectives are expressed in non-operational form, partly because at any one time some of the objectives will be assuming a non-active form, but mainly because objectives are considered sequentially and not simultaneously. Sequential rather than simultaneous consideration is one of the central characteristics of the theory and is discussed further below. Closely allied to the hypothesised ability of the organisation to survive in the face of conflicting goals is the concept of 'organisational slack', i.e. the notion that, due to ignorance and market imperfections, the payment made to coalition members will normally be in excess of that needed to keep them within the coalition. The existence of organisational slack enables the organisation to survive adverse changes in the external environment without disintegrating.

Decisions taken within the organisation are explicitly made dependent on the information available to and the expectations formed by the decision takers within the organisation. Emphasis is placed upon the fact that the expectations formed on the basis of any given information, and indeed the type of information gathered, will not be independent of the subjective situation and interests of the individuals or groups involved. The theory argues that change is typically only considered when a problem arises, although it is recognised that, if a solution comes to hand, a search for an appropriate problem may be induced. Once a problem has arisen, usually in relation to the non-achievement of one of the organisational goals or subgoals, 'search activity' is triggered off to discover possible solutions; that is, information is sought. It is here that the concept of sequential as opposed to simultaneous consideration becomes again relevant. The alternatives thrown up by search activity are considered in turn as they arise, and the first alternative that enables the aspiration level with respect to the goal in question to be achieved is accepted. Hence, the procedure of decision making has been described as 'satisficing' rather than maximising; it is designed to satisfy multiple, changing, acceptable-level goals, not to maximise a consistently specified objective function. This is not to say that the firm's behaviour is 'irrational'. Given the problems of information gathering and processing and the desire to reduce uncertainty, some sort of satisficing procedure may be the best possible in practice, and for this reason the approach outlined here has been designated 'qualified' or 'bounded' rationality.[197]

The result of this analysis is that the firm is seen as an adaptive organisation. Changes in the environment raise problems, and the organisation reacts to these problems according to certain established routines, known as 'standard operating procedures', which have been evolved in the course of a long-run adaptive process. The theory has been developed deliberately for the analysis of short-run behaviour, and consequently little attention has been paid to the exploration of the long-run adaptive process.

The significance of the behavioural approach is difficult to assess.[198] There is no doubt that it provides useful insights into some aspects of business behaviour. Cyert and March have claimed considerable short-run predictive success with their theory and have suggested that this is due to the realism of their assumptions about the internal workings of the firms in question.[199] However, several problems remain. In order to predict any specific firm's behaviour a rather detailed knowledge of the goals and standard operating procedures of that specific firm is required, and the latter, especially, are by their nature highly particularised, providing little scope for generalisation. Changes in goals and standard operating procedures occur in response to fairly immediate problems, within an essentially short-run framework. Of course, the changes are made in accordance with higher level rules, but these somehow just emerge from a long-run adaptive process that is not explored,[200] and they are presumably still very firm specific. Although not explored, it is clear that the long-run adaptive process is not to be regarded as tending towards long-run 'rationality', since in an uncertain and unstable environment, it has been argued, short run adaptation is the key.[201] There may, nevertheless, be interest in the relationship between the short-run and the long run, and it has yet to be demonstrated that the behavioural approach can be adapted in this direction.

Associated with the short-run orientation of the behavioural approach is its concept of the firm as essentially passive. The stress is overwhelmingly on the process of short-run response to environmental stimuli, with longer-run considerations of survival conditions and strategic planning explicitly excluded. Yet, as is argued earlier in this chapter, the characteristics of the large dominant firm suggest the need for a concept of the firm as an active entity, consciously seeking to influence its environment in ways that are favourable to the achievement of its objectives. By focusing on the way in which stimuli from an exogenous environment call forth responses from an isolated individual firm, attention is firmly directed away from the properties of the system as a whole, in particular from the characteristics that arise from the competitive interaction of active oligopolistic rivals. The environment exists somehow 'out there', and its properties are placed beyond the scope of the inquiry.

It is, of course, possible to recognise the force of the observation that large firms are complex organisations and yet to avoid recourse to behaviourism. If a firm's organisational characteristics have no implications for its behaviour, or more probably have implications that can be taken into account without adopting a behaviourist approach, a holistic concept of the firm can be retained. Thus, although organisational characteristics such as the relationship between shareholders and managers may need to be analysed in order to determine what the firm's objective is, once this has been done the firm can be viewed as a unit acting consistently in pursuit of a clearly specified objective. Similarly, internal administrative processes can be regarded as a separate area of study, in the same way that technical processes of production or marketing are regarded as separate areas of study, and can be abstracted from in the development of a theory of the firm.[202] Of course, the study of internal administration may lead to conclusions with relevance for a theory of the firm, such as that there exists an absolute size or a rate of growth above which the administrative efficiency of the firm declines, but once established these conclusions can be regarded as part of the initial set of assumptions required for the construction of any theory.

Perhaps the two principal insights of the behavioural school will turn out to be its emphasis on the importance of uncertainty and its insistence that the behaviour of the firm can only be understood as a continuing process. Although the way in which the behavioural approach itself comes to terms with these considerations appears unlikely to prove satisfactory, the recognition of uncertainty, not risk, and the rejection of microequilibrium theory are probably essential prerequisites for the development of an adequate understanding of business behaviour.

3.6   CONCLUSION

This chapter has considered the current state of economic theory in relation to the firm and some of the more important characteristics of actual firms in modern capitalist economies. The purpose of the theory of the firm is obscure. If the traditional theory is confined to the analysis of a perfectly known and perfectly competitive economy, it is merely the old general-equilibrium theory of value with no place for actual firms. On the other hand, if it is intended to aid in understanding the actual behaviour of actual firms, it is probably desirable to incorporate realism in process; the behavioural theory appears to be called for. The problem may perhaps be traced back to the normative legacy of the old theory of value; the purpose of the theory of the firm is construed as the analysis of the pattern of resource allocation, thus enabling the evaluation of alternative patterns according to the criteria of standard welfare economics. Orthodox economic theory is shot through with references to 'economic efficiency' or 'allocative efficiency' or the 'efficient allocation of resources'. This clearly explains the traditional theory's preoccupation with the prices and quantities of a given set of commodities. It is not by chance that the traditional theory of the firm and the 'theory of price' are the same thing.

However, analysis of the pattern of resource allocation requires general equilibrium analysis. It must be general because the focus of interest is the overall allocation of resources; it must be equilibrium because a determinate analytic solution is needed if anything is to be said. Unfortunately, it is only possible to have both with perfect competition. The theory of the firm, as distinct from the theory of value, retains the method of equilibrium analysis while abandoning generality. It, therefore, is of litttle help in analysing the overall pattern of resource allocation, and no alternative use has come to light. Furthermore, the traditional theory of the firm and most of the modifications, extensions and alternatives to it fall within the constrained maximisation paradigm, and this method of analysis is inappropriate in the presence of oligopolistic interdependence. Oligopolistic interdependence is, of course, one specific cause of uncertainty; and uncertainty, incalculable uncertainty, cannot be handled within the paradigm. The inter-related phenomena of oligopoly and uncertainty call into question the validity of the entire microequilibrium approach.

The characteristics of the decisive modern firms are such that oligopoly and uncertainty cannot legitimately be abstracted from. The size distribution of firms is highly skewed, with a relatively small number of absolutely large firms dominating most aspects of economic activity. This is true not only at the national level but increasingly also at the international level, as the mushrooming literature on the international firm testifies. The theoretical significance of this is that it underlines the need to make non-atomistic oligopolistic structures the focus of attention. In addition, it becomes decreasingly plausible to engage in economic analysis in abstraction from the interconnections between the economic and political systems; the nature of the relationship between firm and state – i.e. between the economic, social and political aspects of capitalist society – poses serious questions about the long-run developmental tendencies of the system as a whole.

Analysis of the *modus operandi* of the system as a whole is also a prerequisite for making any sense of the controversy over ownership and control. Preoccupation with the partial equilibrium analysis of an individual firm in isolation diverts attention away from the two key questions: the extent to which top management and large shareholders share a common economic interest and social situation as part of Wright Mills's 'very rich'; and the extent to which an oligopolistically competitive environment allows scope for residual differences in subjective motivation to affect behaviour.

The general conclusion to be drawn from this chapter is that, if a theory is to be applicable to the firm in modern capitalist economies, it must not abstract from the essential characteristics of those economies. The characteristics relate both to the firm and to its environment. Among the former are the corporate form and large absolute size of the dominant firms and the diversified and international nature of their activities. Included in the latter are: the oligopolistic nature of relations between the dominant firms; the existence of a significant 'competitive' sector made up of small firms; the inherent uncertainty that is due to continuously changing technology, input supply and market conditions in the context of an essentially unplanned economy; and the increasingly pervasive role of the state. Linking the two are the active attempts of oligopolistic competitors to control their environment and dominate their rivals. A general theory encompassing these characteristics remains to be constructed,[203] although many of the elements of such a theory already exist in the literature, and some are explored in subsequent chapters.

FURTHER READING

The literature covering the subject matter of this chapter is very large, and although the given references are quite extensive they are not intended as a comprehensive bibliography. The following suggestions are designed to provide readers with some help in getting their bearings.

On the historical development of the traditional theory of the firm there is no substitute for Shackle.[1] The classic 'revisionist' works are by Baumol,[24] Marris[24] and O. Williamson[24] and Cyert and March.[25] They are compared and contrasted by Wildsmith.[204] Prais provides a fascinating account of the development of the large firm and overall, or aggregate, concentration.[76] The development of concentration at all levels within the economy is traced by Hannah and Kay.[83] A stimulating discussion of the issues arising in the ownership–control controversy is to be found in Nichols.[160] The United Nation's recently updated survey provides a good introduction to the multinational corporation.[205]

NOTES AND REFERENCES

1 For more detailed discussions, on which the earlier part of this section draws heavily, see G. L. S. Shackle, *The Years of High Theory* (Cambridge, Cambridge UP, 1967), chs 2–6 and 18; and B. J. Loasby, 'Hypothesis and paradigm in the theory of the firm', *Economic Journal,* vol. 81 (December 1971), pp. 863–85.

2 For example, Shackle, op. cit. (n. 1), p. 4.

3 Shackle, op. cit. (n. 1), p. 69.

4 P. Sraffa, 'The laws of returns under competitive conditions', *Economic Journal,* vol. 36 (December 1926), pp. 535–50.

5 J. R. Hicks, *Value and Capital,* 1st edn (Oxford, Oxford UP, 1939).

6 J. R. Hicks, *Value and Capital,* 2nd edn (Oxford, Oxford UP, 1946), pp. 83–5.

7 Although general equilibrium analysis is extremely difficult without the assumption of perfect competition, a proof of the existence of a general equilibrium solution for monopolistic competition has been presented. See, for example, K. J. Arrow, 'The firm in general equilibrium theory', in R. Marris and A. Wood (eds), *The Corporate Economy* (London, Macmillan, 1971), ch. 3.

8 J. Robinson, *The Economics of Imperfect Competition* (London, Macmillan, 1933); E. H. Chamberlin *The Theory of Monopolistic Competition* (Cambridge, Mass., Harvard UP, 1933). The two appear to have been developed quite independently. They have generally (see Shackle, op. cit., n. 1, p. 62) but not always (see Loasby, op. cit., n. 1, pp. 875–8) been regarded as essentially the same theory in the large group, no selling expenditure form.

9 Shackle, op. cit (n. 1), p. 11.

10 Shackle, op. cit. (n. 1), p. 65 The sentence quoted by Shackle is from Robinson, op. cit. (n. 8), p. 15.

11 Loasby, op. cit. (n. 1), p. 879.

12 Shackle, op. cit. (n. 1), pp. 65–7.

13 Shackle, op. cit. (n. 1), p. 69.

14 G. C. Archibald (ed.), *The Theory of the Firm* (Harmondsworth, Penguin Books, 1971), introduction, p. 10.

15 Shackle, op. cit. (n. 1), p. 43.

16 P. M. Sweezy, 'Demand under conditions of oligopoly', *Journal of Political Economy*, vol. 47 (August 1939), pp. 568–73.

17 Shackle, op. cit. (n. 1), p. 61. The point is developed on pp. 76–7 of this book.

18 R. L. Hall and C. J. Hitch, 'Price theory and business behaviour', *Oxford Economic Papers*, no. 2 (May 1939), pp. 12–45.

19 Loasby, op. cit. (n. 1), p. 879.

20 For example, R. H. Barback, *The Pricing of Manufactures* (London, Macmillan, 1964). See Chapter 6 for detailed discussion of price case studies.

21 For a discussion of the implications for the theory of the firm of normative microeconomics and organisation theory, see H. A. Simon, 'New developments in the theory of the firm', *American Economic Review*, vol. 52 (May 1962), pp. 1–5.

22 See, for example, F. Machlup, 'Theories of the firm: marginalist, behavioral, managerial', *American Economic Review*, vol. 57 (March 1967), pp. 1–33.

23 A. A. Berle and G. C. Means, *The Modern Corporation and Private Property* (New York, Macmillan, 1932).

24 The classic works are W. J. Baumol, *Business Behavior, Value and Growth* (New York, Macmillan, 1959); R. Marris, *The Economic Theory of 'Managerial' Capitalism* (London, Macmillan, 1964); and O. E. Williamson, *The Economics of Discretionary Behavior: Managerial Objectives in a Theory of the Firm* (Englewood Cliffs, Prentice-Hall, 1964).

25 The term 'behavioural school' refers to a group of behavioural scientists whose leading figure is H. A. Simon. For the best-known application of their approach to the theory of the firm, see R. M. Cyert and J. G. March, *A Behavioral Theory of the Firm* (Englewood Cliffs, Prentice-Hall, 1963), a summary of which is presented in section 3.5. For a discussion of the foundation of much of their work, see H. A. Simon, *Administrative Behavior*, 3rd edn (New York, Macmillan, 1976); and H. A. Simon, *Models of Man* (New York, Wiley, 1957).

26 For a detailed discussion of these alternative concepts of the firm, see J. W. McGuire *Theories of Business Behavior* (Englewood Cliffs, Prentice-Hall, 1964), ch. 2.

27 Hicks, op. cit. (n. 6), p. 116.

28 See J. Johnston, *Statistical Cost Analysis* (New York, McGraw-Hill, 1960) for a review of the evidence on statistical cost curves.

29 E. T. Penrose, *The Theory of the Growth of the Firm* (Oxford, Blackwell, 1959).

30 For a critical discussion of 'orthodox' treatments of oligopoly, see P. W. S. Andrews, *On Competition in Economic Theory* (London, Macmillan, 1964), pp. 43–54.

31 See Chapter 2 for a review of the evidence on market structure.

32 Cf. R. Marris, 'Why economics needs a theory of the firm', *Economic Journal*, vol. 82 (March 1972), supplement, p. 324.

33 See H. A. Simon, 'Theories of decision making in economics and behavioral science', *American Economic Review*, vol. 49 (June 1959), pp. 253–83.

34 Andrews, op. cit. (n. 30), p. 71.

35 Shackle, op. cit. (n. 1), pp. 135–6.

36 For a non-mathematical exposition of a 'non-marginal' optimisation technique, see R. Dorfman, 'Mathematical or "linear" programming: a non-mathematical exposition', *American Economic Review*, vol. 43 (December 1953), pp. 797–825.

37 K. J. Cohen and R. M. Cyert, *Theory of the Firm: Resource Allocation in a Market Economy* (Englewood Cliffs, Prentice-Hall, 1965), p. 29.

38 The use of the term 'marginalist' in this chapter differs from that of Machlup,

op. cit. (n. 22), who has contrasted 'marginalist', by which he has meant what is here termed 'traditional', and 'managerial' theories. However, he has ended his discussion by proposing a marriage between the two.

39 The best-known examples are to be found in, respectively, Baumol, op. cit. (n. 24); Marris, op. cit. (n. 24); and Williamson, op. cit. (n. 24).

40 F. Machlup, 'Marginal analysis and empirical research', *American Economic Review,* vol. 36 (September 1946), pp. 519–54.

41 Simon, op. cit. (n. 25, 1957), pp. 196–206.

42 Cohen and Cyert, op. cit. (n. 37), p. 312.

43 The concept of present value is considered in Chapter 7.

44 For a review of work in this area, see M. Nerlove, 'Lags in economic behavior', *Econometrica,* vol. 40 (March 1972), pp. 221–51.

45 R. Marris, 'An introduction to theories of corporate growth', in Marris and Wood, op. cit. (n. 7), ch. 1, p. 13.

46 F. H. Knight, *Risk, Uncertainty and Profit* (Boston, Mass., Houghton Mifflin, 1921), p. 20.

47 For a survey of decision theory in certainty, risk and uncertainty, see McGuire, op. cit. (n. 26), ch. 6.

48 J. Lintner, 'The impact of uncertainty on the "traditional" theory of the firm: price-setting and tax shifting', in J. W. Markham and G. F. Papanek (eds), *Industrial Organisation and Economic Development* (Boston, Mass., Houghton Mifflin, 1970), p. 238.

49 For example, E. S. Mills, 'Uncertainty and price theory', *Quarterly Journal of Economics,* vol. 73 (February 1959), pp. 116–29; and R. R. Nelson, 'Uncertainty, prediction and competitive equilibrium', *Quarterly Journal of Economics,* vol. 75 (February 1961), pp. 41–62. For a more extended treatment, see E. S. Mills, *Price, Output, and Inventory Policy* (New York, Wiley, 1962).

50 See Chapter 7.

51 It is possible to 'solve' zero-sum two-person games but not other types of game by casting them in linear-programming form. However, this is merely a computational device, and no maximum – in the sense of the 'best' of a consistently ordered set of possible outcomes – is involved. Hence, although linear programming is a technique for finding a maximum, even the theory of zero-sum two-person games is probably best regarded as falling outside the constrained maximisation paradigm. In general, of course, economic situations involve more than two 'players', and the combined 'payoff' is likely to be affected by their behaviour. Thus, if the game-theoretic approach is to be used for economic analysis, it will have to be based on non-constant-sum many-person games.

52 For a survey of this work, see, for example, F. M. Scherer, *Industrial Market Structure and Economic Performance* (Chicago, Rand McNally, 1970), esp. ss 5.1–5.15.

53 The well-known sales-maximisation model, which is outlined in section 3.4, was first presented in W. J. Baumol, 'On the theory of oligopoly', *Economica,* vol. 25 (August 1958), pp. 187–98. The title, however, is misleading since oligopolistic interdependence is abstracted from and the firm's demand curve is assumed to be precisely known. This is made explicit in the fuller version of the model in Baumol, op. cit. (n. 24), p. 36.

54 McGuire, op. cit. (n. 26), p. 157. His Chapter 7 is a simple introduction to the theory of games. For an advanced analysis of oligopoly in terms of game theory, see M. Shubik, *Strategy and Market Structure* (New York, Wiley, 1959).

55 J. von Neumann and O. Morgenstern, *Theory of Games and Economic Behavior* (Princeton, Princeton UP, 1944).

56 O. Morgenstern, 'Foreword' to Shubik, op. cit. (n. 54), p. viii.

57 For an example of such hopes, see K. W. Rothschild, 'Price theory and oligopoly', *Economic Journal,* vol. 57 (September 1947), pp. 306–7, n. 4.

58 R. Marris, 'The modern corporation and economic theory', in Marris and Wood, op. cit. (n. 7), ch. 9; and Marris, op. cit. (n. 32), p. 331, citing Shubik, op. cit. (n. 54), chs 10 and 11.

59 Simon, op. cit. (n. 25), pp. 204–5.

60 P. W. S. Andrews, *Manufacturing Business* (London, Macmillan, 1949), ch. 5. The approach has similarities with the later development of 'limit pricing' theory; see Chapter 6.

61 Andrews, op. cit. (n. 30), p. 42.

62 Andrews, op. cit. (n. 60), p. 172.

63 Andrews, op. cit. (n. 30), p. 36.

64 Andrews, op. cit. (n. 30), p. 39.

65 Andrews, op. cit. (n. 30), p. 60.

66 A. Marshall, *Principles of Economics,* 8th edn (London, Macmillan, 1920), e.g. pp. 317–18 and 359–60.

67 Andrews, op. cit. (n. 30), pp. 17 and 57. For further exposition of Andrews's approach, see P. W. S. Andrews and Elizabeth Brunner, *Studies in Pricing* (London, Macmillan, 1975), chs 1–3.

68 Loasby, op. cit. (n. 1), p. 880.

69 Loasby, op. cit. (n. 1), p. 873.

70 'Its subject matter is, of course, allocation and income distribution, but it deals, usually in partial equilibrium, with complications that general equilibrium theory has not yet managed to incorporate' (Archibald, op. cit., n. 14, p. 11).

71 Although logically distinct, the 'positive' analysis of perfect competition has been closely associated historically with the demonstration of its 'efficiency' according to the 'normative' criteria of theoretical welfare economics.

72 Cf. Machlup, op. cit. (n. 22), p. 6.

73 Cf. Loasby, op. cit. (n. 1), pp. 881–5.

74 P. S. Florence, *The Logic of British and American Industry,* rev. edn (London, Routledge & Kegan Paul, 1961), p. 170.

75 Department of Trade, *Companies in 1976* (London, HMSO, 1977), table 2, p. 9.

76 See, for example, K. D. George, 'The changing structure of competitive industry', *Economic Journal,* vol. 82 (March 1972), supplement, pp. 353–68; M. A. Utton, 'Aggregate versus market concentration', *Economic Journal,* vol. 84 (March 1974), pp. 150–5; S. Aaronovitch and M. C. Sawyer, *Big Business* (London, Macmillan, 1975), ch. 6; and S. J. Prais, *The Evolution of Giant Firms in Britain,* National Institute of Economic and Social Research, Economic and Social Studies 30 (Cambridge, Cambridge UP, 1976), chs 1 and 7.

77 A. Armstrong and A. Silberston, 'Size of plant, size of enterprise and concentration in British manufacturing industry, 1935–58', *Journal of the Royal Statistical Society,* series A, vol. 128, pt 3 (1965), p. 401.

78 Department of Industry, *Report on the Census of Production 1972: Summary Tables,* Business Monitor PA1002 (London, HMSO, 1977), table 8, p. 118.

79 J. E. Bolton (chairman), *Report of the Committee of Inquiry on Small Firms,* Cmnd 4811 (London, HMSO, 1971), para. 13, p. xix. The definition of 'small' adopted by the Committee varied according to sector. Thus, in manufacturing industry it was firms with fewer than 200 employees, in construction those with fewer than twenty-five employees, in retailing those with a turnover of less than £50,000 per annum and in road transport those with fewer than six vehicles.

80 See Table 3.1.

81 In an attempt to discredit the conclusion that there has been a trend towards increased overall concentration, Jewkes has noted that between 1972 and 1976 Prais

twice revised downwards his estimate for 1970 and, further, that Prais's latest estimates are slightly below those of the Department of Industry (J. Jewkes, *Delusions of Dominance,* Hobart Paper 76, London, Institute of Economic Affairs, 1977, pp. 22 and 24). However, the trend in Table 3.3 is unmistakable, not least when the Department of Industry's figure of 41.0 per cent for 1972 is considered (for some reason Jewkes has given 38.7 per cent as the Department's figure).

82 Prais, op. cit. (n. 76), p. 7. The pre-Second World War estimates are very rough.

83 Prais has considered that due to the margin of error attached to the estimates it may be 'more prudent to speak of a freezing of the industrial structure during the war-period' (op. cit., n. 76, p. 6). Hannah and Kay were dubious about the accuracy of their estimates for 1930–48 and made adjustments in an attempt to compensate for a suspected under-representation of smaller firms. They have concluded that 'there is a genuine ambiguity about the direction of change. While larger firms were losing ground, the tendency towards the elimination of very small firms, already evident in the 1920s, was sustained throughout the 1930s and 1940s' (L. Hannah and J. A. Kay, *Concentration in Modern Industry,* London, Macmillan, 1977, pp. 76–8).

84 Department of Industry, 'The importance of the "top 100" manufacturing companies', *Economic Trends,* no. 274 (August 1976), pp. 85–91.

85 See J. Bain, *Industrial Organization,* 2nd edn (New York, Wiley, 1968), pp. 93–100, for this study and a general discussion of 'supercorporate control'.

86 See Scherer, op. cit. (n. 52), pp. 45–7, for the Japanese and Swedish studies and a general discussion of the area.

87 Utton, op. cit. (n. 76), pp. 150–5.

88 For a discussion of 'conglomerate bigness and pricing behaviour', see Scherer, op. cit. (n. 52), ch. 11, pp. 273–83. For a recent discussion of possible effects on resource allocation, see George, op. cit. (n. 76), pp. 355–60.

89 See, for example, Marris, op. cit. (n. 32), pp. 330–2.

90 C. D. Edwards, 'Conglomerate business as a source of power', in National Bureau of Economic Research, *Business Concentration and Price Policy,* Special Conference Series 5 (Princeton, Princeton UP, 1955), p. 335.

91 Aaronovitch and Sawyer, op. cit. (n. 76), p. 232.

92 For an excellent survey, see Prais, op. cit. (n. 76), ch. 5.

93 For a recent discussion of the social and political effects of concentration, see Hannah and Kay, op. cit. (n. 83), ch. 3.

94 Other terms used include 'multinational' and 'transnational'.

95 J. H. Dunning, 'The multinational enterprise: the background', in J. H. Dunning (ed.), *The Multinational Enterprise* (London, Allen & Unwin, 1971), ch. 1, p. 16.

96 See M. Whitehead, 'The multinationally-owned company: a case study', in Dunning, op. cit. (n. 95), ch. 12, p. 314.

97 Dunning, op. cit. (n. 95), p. 26.

98 United Nations Department of Economic and Social Affairs, *Multinational Corporations in World Development* (New York, UN, 1973), ch. 1 and appendix; reprinted in K. P. Sauvant and F. G. Lavipour (eds), *Controlling Multinational Enterprises* (London, Wilton House, 1976), pp. 7–28 and 243–85.

99 United Nations, op. cit. (n. 98), table 17, p. 267.

100 R. Rowthorn, *International Big Business, 1957–1967: A Study of Comparative Growth,* University of Cambridge Department of Applied Economics, Occasional Paper 24 (Cambridge, Cambridge UP, 1971), table 23, p. 64.

101 United Nations, op. cit. (n. 98), *passim.*

102 R. Vernon, 'Future of the multinational enterprise', in C. P. Kindleberger (ed.), *The International Corporation* (Cambridge, Mass., MIT Press, 1970), ch. 15, p. 381. The figures may slightly overstate the trend since some of the added subsidiaries were probably converted branches.

103 See Rowthorn, op. cit. (n. 100), pp. 72 and 79–80.
104 R. Z. Aliber, 'A theory of direct foreign investment', in Kindleberger, op. cit. (n. 102), ch. 1, p. 20. Aliber has developed a theory based on differences in the estimates of exchange risk associated with different currencies.
105 R. Vernon, 'International investment and international trade in the product cycle', *Quarterly Journal of Economics,* vol. 80 (May 1966), pp. 190–207.
106 R. Vernon, *Sovereignty at Bay* (New York, Basic Books, 1971), ch. 3, pp. 60–112. See also F. T. Knickerbocker, *Oligopolistic Reaction and Multinational Enterprise* (Boston, Harvard Business School Division of Research, 1973) for an interesting empirical investigation of the extent to which and reasons why US international firms in the postwar period countered their rivals' overseas investment with defensive foreign investment of their own.
107 The classic work always cited is S. Hymer, 'The international operations of national firms: a study of direct investment', unpublished PhD thesis (Cambridge, Mass., Massachusetts Institute of Technology, 1960).
108 R. Caves, 'International corporations: the industrial economics of foreign investment', *Economica,* new series, vol. 38 (February 1971), pp. 1–27, esp. s. 1.
109 P. Buckley and M. Casson, *The Future of the Multinational Enterprise* (London, Macmillan, 1976), ch. 2, esp. pp. 32–56.
110 S. Hirsch, 'An international trade and investment theory of the firm', *Oxford Economic Papers,* new series, vol. 28 (July 1976), pp. 258–70.
111 S. Hymer and R. Rowthorn, 'Multinational corporations and international oligopoly: the non-American challenge', in Kindleberger, op. cit. (n. 102), p. 57.
112 Cf. J. J. Servan-Schreiber, *The American Challenge* (London, Hamish Hamilton, 1968).
113 Hymer and Rowthorn, op. cit. (n. 111), pp. 72–3.
114 For an interesting discussion of one aspect of the global planning of international firms' activities, see G. K. Helleiner, 'Manufactured exports from less developed countries and multinational firms', *Economic Journal,* vol. 83 (March 1973), pp. 21–47.
115 S. Hymer, 'The multinational corporation and the law of uneven development', in J. Bhagwati (ed.), *Economics and World Order from the 1970s to the 1990s* (New York, Collier-Macmillan, 1972); reprinted in H. Radice (ed.), *International Firms and Modern Imperialism* (Harmondsworth, Penguin Books, 1975), pp. 37–62.
116 United Nations, *The Impact of Multinational Corporations on Development and on International Relations* (New York, UN, 1974); and Commission of the EEC, *Multinational Undertakings and Community Regulations,* Document COM (73) 1930 (Brussels, EEC, 1973). For a convenient survey, see J. Dunning, 'The future of the multinational enterprise', *Lloyds Bank Review,* vol. 113 (July 1974), pp. 15–32.
117 Murray has distinguished six primary economic functions for the state in capitalist economies, namely:
(1) 'the guaranteeing of property rights';
(2) 'economic liberalisation' – essentially the abolition of restrictions on mobility and the promotion of standardisation (e.g. of currency, law and weights and measures) in order to facilitate exchange;
(3) 'economic orchestration' – essentially macromanagement;
(4) 'input provision' – of labour, land, capital, technology, infrastructure and basic manufactured inputs (e.g. steel);
(5) 'interventon for social consensus'; and
(6) 'the management of the external relations of a capitalist system'
(R. Murray, 'The internationalisation of capital and the nation state', in Dunning, op. cit., n. 95, ch. 10, pp. 267–76).
118 A. K. Cairncross, 'The optimum firm reconsidered', *Economic Journal,* vol. 82 (March 1972), supplement, p. 316.

119 For an interpretation of the evolution of US trade policy in terms of the outcome of the relative strengths of international firms and organised labour, with the former usually winning out in cases of conflict, see G. K. Helleiner, 'Transitional enterprises and the new political economy of US trade policy', *Oxford Economic Papers,* new series, vol. 29 (March 1977), pp. 102–16.

120 P. Streeten, 'Costs and benefits of multinational enterprises in less developed countries', in Dunning, op. cit. (n. 95), ch. 9, p. 248.

121 Marris, op. cit. (n. 32), p. 329.

122 See Chapter 9.

123 J. K. Galbraith, *American Capitalism,* rev. edn (Harmondsworth, Penguin Books, 1963), esp. chs 9–12.

124 J. K. Galbraith, *The New Industrial State* (Harmondsworth, Penguin Books, 1969), esp. chs 26 and 27.

125 See, for example, the devastating attack on the traditional theory of consumer demand in J. K. Galbraith, *The Affluent Society* (Harmondsworth, Penguin Books, 1962), chs 10 and 11.

126 A. Phillips, 'Structure, conduct, and performance – and performance, conduct and structure?', in J. W. Markham and G. F. Papanek (eds), *Industrial Organization and Economic Development* (Boston, Mass., Houghton Mifflin, 1970).

127 M. D. Reagan, *The Managed Economy* (New York, Oxford UP, 1963), chs 5–7 and 9.

128 Reagan, op. cit. (n. 127), pp. 129–30.

129 Mr. H. Lazell, quoted in *The Times* (3 May 1968), p. 21.

130 See Bertrand Russell Peace Foundation, *ITT–CIA Subversion in Chile* (Nottingham, Spokesman Books, 1972).

131 K. W. Rothschild, 'Price theory and oligopoly', *Economic Journal,* vol. 57 (September 1947), p. 319.

132 Marris, op. cit. (n. 32), p. 335.

133 Bain, op. cit. (n. 85), p. 35.

134 It may be possible for an entrepreneur to survive without maximising profits if he is prepared to accept less than he could obtain by working and using his capital elsewhere. However, the margin between survival at below the 'normal' return on his labour and capital and bankruptcy is likely to be small enough for this situation to remain relatively unimportant, especially once uncertainty is introduced.

135 Baumol, op. cit. (n. 53, 1958), pp. 187–98.

136 J. Vanek, *The General Theory of Labor-Managed Market Economies* (Ithaca, Cornell UP, 1970), ch. 7. For an extension of the analysis, which develops a dynamic model and allows for the separation of ownership and control in both types of firm, see A. B. Atkinson, 'Worker management and the modern enterprise', *Quarterly Journal of Economics,* vol. 87 (August 1973), pp. 375–92.

137 Figures 3.2 and 3.3 are based on J. Meade, 'The theory of labour-managed firms and of profit sharing', *Economic Journal,* vol. 82 (March 1972), supplement, fig. 1, p. 407. Meade's article is an excellent exposition of the basic argument.

138 Cf. Vanek, op. cit. (n. 136), p. 382.

139 See J. Vanek (ed.), *Self-Management: Economic Liberation of Man* (Harmondsworth, Penguin Books, 1975), esp. P. Blumberg, 'Alienation and participation: conclusions', ch. 21.

140 See Vanek, op. cit. (n. 139), chs 4, 9, 17 and 26.

141 Cf. J. Shackleton, 'Is workers' self-management the answer?', *National Westminster Bank Quarterly Review* (February 1976), pp. 56–7.

142 A. A. Berle and G. C. Means, *The Modern Corporation and Private Property* (New York, Macmillan, 1932).

143 For the best-known managerial theories, see Baumol, op. cit. (n. 24); Marris, op. cit. (n. 24); and Williamson, op. cit. (n. 24).

144 Cf. W. L. Baldwin, 'The motives of managers, environmental restraints, and the theory of managerial enterprise', *Quarterly Journal of Economics,* vol. 78 (May 1964), p. 238.

145 P. Sargant Florence, *Ownership, Control and Success of Large Companies* (London, Sweet & Maxwell, 1961).

146 J. Revell and J. Moyle, *The Ownership of Quoted Ordinary Shares,* University of Cambridge Department of Applied Economics, A Programme for Growth, No. 7 (London, Chapman & Hall, 1966), p. 4.

147 Prais, op. cit. (n. 76), table 5.1, p. 89. A 'mini-survey' of thirty of the 100 largest quoted companies in 1975, undertaken by the Royal Commission on the Distribution of Income and Wealth, found 69 registered holdings of between 1 and 2 per cent of issued ordinary capital, 27 of between 2 and 5 per cent and 16 of 5 per cent and over. These large holdings were overwhelmingly registered in the names of insurance companies or nominee companies, and there were no large holdings registered in the names of directors. However, due to the large number of nominee holdings no firm conclusion about the position of directors could be reached (Royal Commission on the Distribution of Income and Wealth, *Income from Companies and Its Distribution,* Report No. 2, London, HMSO, July 1975, table 3, p. 11).

148 R. J. Larner, 'Ownership and control in the 200 largest non-financial corporations, 1929 to 1963', *American Economic Review,* vol. 56 (September 1966), pp. 777–87.

149 R. A. Gordon, *Business Leadership in the Large Corporation* (Berkeley and Los Angeles, California UP, 1961), p. 37.

150 Cf. 'their [Berle and Means's] method is unable to separate ownership from control because it does not establish empirically the proportion of votes needed for control' (C. S. Beed, 'The separation of ownership from control', *Journal of Economic Studies,* vol. 1, no. 2, Summer 1966, p. 30).

151 Florence, op. cit. (n. 145).

152 Beed, op. cit. (n. 150), p. 33. Cf. also: 'Since ownership is very widely dispersed . . . in management-controlled companies, either it could mean, with Berle and Means, that no one individual or small group could gain sufficient votes for control, or, contradicting Berle and Means, that only a few percent of votes was required for control' (p. 31).

153 Florence, op. cit. (n. 145), p. 66.

154 P. M. Sweezy, *The Theory of Capitalist Development* (London, Dobson, 1962), pp. 261–2.

155 Beed, op. cit. (n. 150), p. 31.

156 K. Midgley, 'How much control do shareholders exercise?', *Lloyds Bank Review,* vol. 114 (October 1974), pp. 28–31.

157 For a useful summary of this development, see Prais, op. cit. (n. 76), pp. 113–24.

158 Baldwin, op. cit. (n. 144), p. 251.

159 Cf. Florence, op. cit. (n. 145), p. 130.

160 Cf. T. Nichols, *Ownership, Control and Ideology,* Studies in Management, No. 8 (London, Allen & Unwin, 1969), p. 104.

161 Mr M. Webster, quoted in *The Times* (3 July 1972), p. 17.

162 Midgley, op. cit. (n. 156), pp. 28 and 36, n. 1.

163 Cf. Marris, op. cit. (n. 24), pp. 1–5, on 'The disappearance of the entrepreneur'.

164 Cf. Nichols, op. cit. (n. 160), p. 136, for the argument that the appropriate comparison is not between the traditional entrepreneur and present day manager but between the present-day 'propertied' manager and present-day 'non-propertied' manager.

165 Cf. J. Williamson, 'Profit, growth and sales maximisation', *Economica,* new series, vol. 33 (February 1966), p. 9.

166 See, for example, M. H. Miller and F. Modigliani, 'Dividend policy, growth and the valuation of shares', *Journal of Business*, vol. 34 (October 1961), pp. 411–33.

167 Nichols, op. cit. (n. 160), p. 96, summarising the arguments of Gordon, op. cit. (n. 149), pp. 305–16; Marris, op. cit. (n. 24), p. 147; and Williamson, op. cit. (n. 24), pp. 29–30.

168 W. Baumol, *Business Behavior, Value and Growth*, rev. edn (New York, Macmillan, 1967), p. 49; Marris, op. cit. (n. 24), p. 4; and Williamson, op. cit. (n. 24), p. 37.

169 Baumol, op. cit. (n. 24), p. 53.

170 W. J. Baumol, 'On the theory of expansion of the firm', *American Economic Review*, vol. 52 (December 1962), pp. 1078–87.

171 Williamson, op. cit. (n. 24), p. 36.

172 J. W. McGuire, J. S. Chiu and A. O. Elbing, 'Executive incomes, sales and profits', *American Economic Review*, vol. 52 (September 1962), pp. 753–61.

173 J. Dean and W. Smith, 'The relationship between profitability and size', in W. W. Alberts and J. Segall (eds), *The Corporate Merger* (Chicago, Chicago UP, 1966), ch. 1, pp. 7–8.

174 A. Cosh, 'The remuneration of chief executives in the United Kingdom', *Economic Journal*, vol. 85 (March 1975), pp. 75–94.

175 Cosh, op. cit. (n. 174), p. 90.

176 G. Meeks and G. Whittington, 'Directors' pay, growth and profitability', *Journal of Industrial Economics*, vol. 24 (September 1975), p. 10.

177 Meeks and Whittington, op. cit. (n. 176), p. 6.

178 Meeks and Whittington, op. cit. (n. 176), p. 11.

179 W. G. Lewellen, 'Management and ownership in the large firm', *Journal of Finance*, vol. 24 (May 1969), p. 313 and tables 9 and 10, pp. 317–18.

180 Lewellen, op. cit. (n. 179), p. 320.

181 Marris, op. cit. (n. 24), p. 18.

182 H. F. Lydall, *British Incomes and Savings* (Oxford, Blackwell, 1955), table 46, p. 95.

183 L. R. Klein, K. H. Straw and P. Vandome, 'Savings and finances of the upper income classes', *Bulletin of the Oxford University Institute of Statistics*, vol. 18 (November 1956), table VIII, p. 308.

184 Cf. G. Kolko, *Wealth and Power in America* (London, Thames & Hudson, 1962), p. 67.

185 Royal Commission on the Distribution of Income and Wealth, op. cit. (n. 147), table 17, p. 37.

186 Royal Commission on the Distribution of Income and Wealth, *Third Report on the Standing Reference*, Report No. 5 (London, HMSO, November 1977), tables 29 and 30, pp. 71–2.

187 Cf. P. A. Baran and P. M. Sweezy, *Monopoly Capital* (Harmondsworth, Penguin Books, 1968), pp. 46–8, for an elaboration of this point. They have relied on C. Wright Mills's concept of the 'very rich' and referred to his *The Power Elite* (New York, Oxford UP, 1956), esp. chs 6–8.

188 R. Miliband, *The State in Capitalist Society* (London, Weidenfeld & Nicolson, 1969), p. 35.

189 Nichols, op. cit. (n. 160), pp. 141–2. For a more recent general discussion in a similar vein, see J. Westergaard and H. Resler, *Class in a Capitalist Society* (London, Heinemann, 1975), pt 3, ch. 2.

190 Williamson, op. cit. (n. 165), p. 15.

191 For the latter, see Baumol, op. cit. (n. 168), ch. 5; and Williamson, op. cit. (n. 165), pp. 2 and 8.

192 J. Lintner, 'The impact of uncertainty on the "traditional" theory of the firm: price-setting and tax shifting', in Markham and Papanek, op. cit. (n. 126), p. 264. See also R. H. Day, D. J. Aigner and K. R. Smith, 'Safety margins and profit

maximisation in the theory of the firm', *Journal of Political Economy,* vol. 79 (November–December 1971), pp. 1293–301, who have argued that full cost pricing can be derived from profit maximisation under conditions of risk.

193 For a study of the extent of discretion allowed by the operation of stock market discipline in the form of takeover, see A. Singh, *Take-overs,* University of Cambridge Department of Applied Economics, Monograph 19 (Cambridge, Cambridge UP, 1971). This study is discussed in Chapter 4.

194 Baldwin, op. cit. (n. 144), p. 255.

195 See note 25.

196 This is a summary of Cyert and March, op. cit. (n. 25), chs 3–6.

197 Simon, op. cit. (n. 25, 1957), pp. 196–206.

198 For one of the few attempts at an assessment, see W. J. Baumol and M. Stewart, 'On the behavioural theory of the firm', in Marris and Wood, op. cit. (n.7), ch. 5.

199 Cf. Cyert and March, op. cit. (n. 25), ch. 7.

200 Cf. 'The behavioural analysis . . . has, up to this point, provided no theory of the determination of the rules of thumb themselves. It has not suggested how these rules will vary with changes in the values of exogenous economic variables' (Baumol and Stewart, op. cit., n. 198, p. 119).

201 Cyert and March, op. cit. (n. 25), p. 100.

202 Cf. 'they [Cyert and March] may turn out to be talking about what is essentially "technology" from the point of view of economics' (C. Kaysen, 'Another view of corporate capitalism', *Quarterly Journal of Economics,* vol. 79, February 1965, p. 50).

203 For two attempts in the Marxist tradition, see Baran and Sweezy, op. cit. (n. 187); and Aaronovitch and Sawyer, op. cit. (n. 76), ch. 2. For a 'post-Keynesian' attempt, see A. Eichner and J. Kregel, 'An essay in post-Keynesian theory: a new paradigm in economics', *Journal of Economic Literature,* vol. 13 (1975), pp. 1293–312; and A. Eichner, *The Megacorp and Oligopoly* (Cambridge, Cambridge UP, 1976).

204 J. R. Wildsmith, *Managerial Theories of the Firm* (London, Martin Robertson, 1973).

205 United Nations, *Transnational Corporations in World Development: A Re-examination* (New York, UN, 1978).

4 Corporate Growth

In Chapter 3, especially in sections 3.2 and 3.4, reference is made to the increasing importance assumed by growth in discussions of the modern corporate firm. The traditional theory of the firm emphasises the concept of 'optimum size' – the size at which economies of scale have been exhausted and diseconomies of scale have not yet set in, i.e. the minimum point on the U-shaped long-run average-cost curve, 'with growth part of a loosely defined adjustment mechanism which operates in a yet more loosely defined time dimension'.[1] By contrast, the theories of growth discussed in this chapter centre on the rate of growth, with size at any given moment being the incidental result of a continuing process of growth through time.

Although the theory of the growth of the firm has been most fully developed by Marris on the basis of a managerial approach, theories of this type are readily generalisable and, Radice has argued, 'are basically theories of the large modern firm, not theories of the managerial firm'.[2] This chapter is concerned with theories and empirical evidence relating explicitly to corporate growth. In section 4.2 the creation of the underlying conceptual framework is traced through the work of Downie, Penrose and Marris, and each of their contributions is assessed. In section 4.3 the basic structure of the family of models comprising the 'economic' theory of the growth of the firm[3] is set out, and some developments are considered. In section 4.4 some of the empirical work on the relationships between growth, profitability and size, which are the key variables isolated by the theory, is reviewed, and the phenomenon of takeovers is examined in order to throw light on the nature of stock market discipline. Although not the principal subject of this chapter, size must be included in any empirical consideration of the relationship between growth and profitability since the absolute size of the firm may have an independent influence on these, and other, aspects of behaviour and performance. Finally, in section 4.5 some conclusions are drawn both of a general character and about the special position of the large firm.

4.2 THE THEORY OF THE GROWTH OF THE FIRM: BASIC CONCEPTS

The concept of 'optimum size' provides an explanation, within the framework of the traditional theory of the firm, of why firms are of limited size. Once this concept is abandoned the question arises as to whether there is any limit to the size of the firm. The theories of the growth of the firm considered in this section and the next are based on the assumption that 'although there may be no effective constraints on the sizes of firms there are certainly constraints on their rates of growth'.[4] Hence, since a given size has to be attained by growth, the size of the firm at any moment in time can be explained by its past size, the nature of the constraints limiting the rate at which it can grow from that size, and the objectives of those running it.

The development of a theory of the growth of the firm requires the creation of a conceptual framework within which the nature of the constraints on growth can be analysed. Once this has been done the effect of alternative assumptions about objectives can be examined. It will be recalled that, apart from static profit-maximisation and static sales-maximisation, the alternative assumptions proposed have been within a growth context. The principal objectives in question are profit-, growth- and sales-maximisation. Profit-maximisation in a growth context is interpreted as the maximisation of the present value of the firm on the stock market; growth-maximisation presents no problem since in steady state models (see section 4.3) sales, profits and assets all grow at the same rate; sales-maximisation in a growth context has been treated analogously to profit-maximisation and interpreted as the maximisation of the present value of current and future sales.[5]

It can be argued that growth is a necessary condition for the long-run survival of the firm in an uncertain and constantly changing environment.[6] The spirit of this approach has been well expressed by Downie: 'The most fundamental characteristic of a capitalist economy is growth and change . . . [it] is characterised by a restless urge to do better, to change the conditions lest, through inactivity, they are changed against you.'[7] That there are firms that do not grow, or do not seek to grow, is not inconsistent with the general hypothesis of growth as a long-run survival condition for the firm. At any moment of time, of course, there will also be firms that are stagnant or in decline, but it is precisely such firms whose survival potential will be most in doubt. In general firms that survive do grow. Moreover, analysing the growth of firms is not a separate activity from analysing their decline and death. Growth and decline are complementary aspects of the competitive process in the economy as a whole; an understanding of one contributes to an understanding of the other. Hence, although the theories of the growth of the firm discussed in this chapter are focused on firms that grow, such theories may have, at least potentially, general relevance for the analysis of business behaviour in contemporary capitalist economies.

THE CONCEPT OF THE FIRM

The three writers most closely associated with laying the foundations of an explicit theory of the growth of the firm are Downie, Penrose and Marris.[8] Their approach is first distinguished from that of the traditional theory of the firm with respect to the concept of the firm adopted. The analysis of the traditional theory is conducted largely in terms of firms operating in a specific product market. Multiproduct firms are, of course, recognised; but since the framework is essentially static and the assumed objective is static profit-maximisation, the single market case is usually demonstrated, or just stated, to be generalisable should profit-maximisation require it. The size and any growth of the firm are merely the indirect results of static profit-maximisation.

Central to the analysis is the identification of the industry with all the single product firms supplying a particular market.

Downie started the change in emphasis by defining the industry as consisting of a 'group of firms whose techniques of production are sufficiently alike for it to make sense to conceive of one as being able to do the business of another'.[9] It will be noted that this definition is very similar to that used in the Census of Production, stressing gaps in the chain of substitution on the supply side as opposed to the traditional theory's definition in terms of gaps in the chain of substitution on the demand side. For Downie the firm is essentially a specialist organisation possessing specific technical and market experience. Each firm has a technological horizon that circumscribes the set of activities in which it is at least potentially interested. The larger the firm and the greater the division of managerial labour, the less technologically specialised will be its higher management and the wider will be its technological horizon.[10]

Penrose completed the change in emphasis by bypassing the industry and starting straight in with the firm. For her the firm is 'a collection of productive resources the disposal of which between different uses and over time is determined by administrative decision'.[11] She has underlined the significance of this concept of the firm:

In a sense, the final products being produced by a firm at any given time merely represent one of several ways in which the firm could be using its resources, an incident in the development of its basic potentialities. Over the years the products change, and there are numerous firms today which produce few or none of the products on which their early reputation and success were based. Their basic strength has been developed above or below the end-product level as it were – in technology of specialised kinds and in market positions. Within the limits set by the rate at which the administrative structure of the firm can be adapted and adjusted to larger and larger scales of operation, there is nothing inherent in the nature of the firm or of its economic function to prevent the indefinite expansion of its activities.[12]

Marris has largely adopted the Penrosian concept, and since his summary of her view is particularly clear and concise it is worth reproducing here:

... [Mrs Penrose] sees the firm as an administrative and social organisation, capable, in principle, of entering almost any field of material activity. The firm is not necessarily limited to particular markets, industries or countries; indeed, there is no theoretical reason why firms should not venture anywhere in the universe. In practice, of course, they find advantages in specialisation, but this represents a deliberate choice whose direction and degree may be varied at will. Every firm, at any one moment, inherits a degree and direction of specialisation from its own past, and this is represented in the knowledge and talents of the existing members and the sphere of technical and commercial activity with which they are familiar (as well as, of course, in the nature of the physical assets). But new members and new assets can always be recruited; the firm is a changeable bundle of human and professional resources, linked through the corporate constitution to a corresponding bundle of material and financial assets.[13]

The essence of this concept of the firm is that the firm is no longer confined to a single market. In the presence of constant returns to scale there is no 'optimum' size in the sense of a unique size at which long-run average costs are at a minimum; hence, no reason for the existence of an upper limit to the size of the firm is to be found on the cost side. If the firm is not restricted to a single market, i.e. is not limited by the size of its existing market, no reason for the existence of an upper limit to its size is to be found on the demand side either. Hence, there appears to be no upper limit to the size of the firm at all. Once the concept of the firm as an entity with no upper limit to its size and with the capacity to initiate its own growth is adopted, however, the question arises as to whether there is an upper limit to its rate of growth. The general answer provided by growth theorists is that there will be an upper limit to the rate of growth of the firm because growth is subject to various 'dynamic restraints'.[14] The interaction between these restraints – essentially between the means for growth and the costs of growth – sets an effective upper limit to the rate at which the firm *can* grow. Of course, the rate at which it *will* grow may also depend on the objectives of those running it. Three broad categories of restraint have been isolated: financial, demand and managerial. Differences in the way in which these restraints are interpreted and combined account for many of the differences between the theories of Downie, Penrose and Marris. It is convenient to introduce the discussion of the financial and demand restraints by way of an examination of Downie's theory of the competitive process.

DOWNIE: THE FINANCIAL AND DEMAND RESTRAINTS

Downie's contribution to the theory of the growth of the firm is incidental to his principal purpose: the analysis of the way in which alternative sets of 'rules of the game', i.e. market structures and conventions governing business behaviour, affect the dispersion of efficiency between firms and the rate of technical progress. Within an industry defined in terms of a similarity of technical process he has postulated a dispersion of efficiency, by which he means that there exist firms of differing efficiency levels below and above the industry average.[15] The extent of the dispersion of efficiency within any industry will depend both on the size of any differences in efficiency (roughly speaking, unit costs) between individual firms and on the relative sizes (roughly speaking, outputs) of the more or less efficient firms.

The source of differences in efficiency between individual firms is to be found in the advantageous access of some firms to technologically superior processes and/or products. Such advantageous access arises from past innovation, which is retained in the firm for a period by patent or, more probably, by industrial secrecy. An initial lead is strengthened by accumulating skill and experience in the activity in question. It will be noted that this framework is inconsistent with the traditional theory's assumption of a perfectly known production function, based on a given technology, which is freely accessible to all firms. Indeed, a large part of the explanation of efficiency differences, Downie has suggested, is to be found in the existence of widespread ignorance about what other firms are doing and the results that they obtain.

Next, Downie has introduced the concept of the 'transfer mechanism'. This is the process whereby the more efficient firms in the industry steadily encroach, more or less rapidly, on the market share of the less efficient firms. Since in his model all firms are assumed to have the objective of maximum growth, the more rapid rate of growth of the more efficient firms – a corollary of their encroachment on the market share of the less efficient firms – must be due to their advantageous access to the means for growth. In Downie's model the means for growth are on the one hand capacity and on the other customers. In order to expand capacity finance is required. Whether raised internally or externally, access to finance will depend on the rate of profit. Hence, the rate of growth of capacity will be related in a definite if complex way to the rate of profit. At the same time new customers can be attracted from rivals only by price reduction. (Downie has not mentioned expenditure on sales promotion, but it makes no significant difference to his analysis if this method of obtaining customers is chosen.) Beyond a certain point the further attraction of customers will be at the expense of the rate of profit, and thereafter a conflict exists between the growth of capacity and the growth of the markets to be supplied with the capacity. Since the rate of capacity expansion varies directly with the rate of profit and the rate of profit varies inversely with the rate of customer expansion, there will be a maximum sustainable rate of growth at which the simultaneously determined price and rate of profit are such as to enable customers and capacity to grow at the same rate. The more efficient the firm, the faster will be this maximum sustainable rate of growth and the more rapidly, if the firm is above the average level of efficiency, will it add to its share of the market. Thus, in the course of elaborating his transfer mechanism Downie has developed a theory of the growth of the firm in which the maximum rate of growth is set by the interaction of the financial restraint (i.e. funds to acquire capacity) and demand restraints (i.e. customers).

It should be noted that this argument does not ignore oligopolistic interdependence. It merely asserts that the more efficient firms will be in a position to grow faster than the less efficient and that as long as efficiency differences persist there is little that the latter can do about it. If the process is taken to occur in the context of a set of growing markets, the less efficient firms may for a time actually increase their absolute sales even though their share of the market is falling. The obvious outcome of the unchecked operation of the transfer mechanism is the ever-growing concentration of industry. However, at this point Downie's approach again recognises the existence of interdependence. As he has put it, any 'given historical situation will contain within itself the seeds of its own transformation'.[16] The operation of the transfer mechanism itself brings into play a counterforce called the 'innovation mechanism'. This is the process whereby the less efficient firms, increasingly compelled to recognise their relative inefficiency by their diminishing market share, will actively seek to reverse the efficiency difference. Downie has suggested that for this reason the next technological breakthrough in the industry is more likely to be made by the less efficient firms, which will have the incentive, than by the more efficient firms, which may tend to become complacent and whose pace of expansion may inhibit flexibility and experimentation. If this does happen, i.e. if one of the less efficient firms does make the next technological breakthrough, relative efficiencies will be reversed, and the transfer mechanism will start up again in the opposite direction.

Downie has made two major contributions to the theory of the growth of the firm, one of which has provided the foundation for subsequent work and one of which has been largely forgotten. The first is his identification of the two-way relationship between growth and profitability: the growth of capacity is directly related to the rate of profit; and the rate of profit, possibly after an initial direct relationship, is inversely related to the growth of demand. Notwithstanding the important developments made subsequently in exploring the nature of the financial and demand restraints and elaborating formal models, the relationship between growth and profitability has remained the cornerstone of all theories of the growth of the firm.

The second major contribution made by Downie is his insistence on rooting the analysis of the growth of the firm in the wider context of the competitive process. Oligopolistic interdependence, which is a continuing process of active rivalry, underlies both the transfer and the innovation mechanisms. Both mechanisms have, of course, been criticised. The transfer mechanism operates within an industry defined in terms of a similarity of technical process and does not encompass diversification outside the industry. Thus, profitability falls as growth increases because of the increasing difficulty of obtaining a larger share of the set of markets corresponding to the firm's industry. It was left to Penrose to remove the demand restraint in this form by invoking diversification as a general phenomenon, although this possibility was already implicit in Downie's work. In its place she has espoused the managerial restraint (see below) as the reason why profitability and growth become inversely related. The transfer mechanism has also been criticised, not for its recognition that innovation is an important form of competition, but for the particular role assigned to it by Downie. It has been widely held that innovation stems in the main from individuals and small new firms and/or from established and successful giants; there has been little support for the view that existing uncompetitive firms in difficulty are the major source of innovative breakthrough.[17]

However, despite these criticisms Downie's insistence that the analysis of the individual firm must be set in the context of the competitive process as a whole remains a major and distinctive contribution to the theory of the growth of the firm. It is distinctive because, while his first contribution – the relationship between growth and profitability – has been incorporated in the work of later theorists, the competitive process as a whole has in the main been lost sight of. Subsequent refinement and formalisation of the growth-profitability relationship have concentrated on the individual firm largely isolated from its rivals, and oligopolistic interdependence has been effectively assumed away. Thus, although much has been gained, perhaps even more has been lost, for the major strength of Downie's approach – his recognition of the paramountcy of the competitive process, the predominance of oligopolistic interdependence and the continuity of change – has disappeared in a plethora of steady-state permanent-growth models (see section 4.3).

In Penrose's work considerations that are external to the individual firm have deliberately been assumed away in order to concentrate exclusively on the internal characteristics of the firm. As indicated above, she has made diversification a central aspect of the behaviour of the firm and introduced the managerial restraint as the operative limit on the rate at which the firm can grow. These contributions are now examined.

PENROSE: THE MANAGERIAL RESTRAINT AND DIVERSIFICATION

Penrose has assumed 'a desire to increase total long-run profits' as the objective of those running the firm. Since 'total profits will increase with every increment of investment that yields a positive return, regardless of what happens to the marginal *rate* of return on investment', it follows that 'firms will want to expand as fast as they can take advantage of opportunities for expansion that they consider profitable'.[18]

Productive opportunity: resources and services
It will be recalled that the firm is conceived as a pool of productive resources organised within an administrative framework. The set of activities that the firm is both aware of and able to undertake at a profit is termed its 'productive opportunity'. It is around the analysis of the factors limiting this productive opportunity in any given period and causing it to change over time that Penrose's theory of the growth of the firm is constructed. In order to explore the concept of the productive opportunity a distinction between productive resources and productive services is introduced:

> Strictly speaking, it is never *resources* themselves that are 'inputs' in a productive process, but only the *services* that the resources can render. The services yielded by resources are a function of the way in which they are used – exactly the same resource when used for different purposes or in different ways and in combination with different types or amounts of other resources provides a different service or set of services. The important distinction between resources and services is not their relative durability; rather it lies in the fact that resources consist of a bundle of potential services and can, for the most part, be defined independently of their use, while services cannot be so defined, the very word 'service' implying a function, an activity. As we shall see, it is largely in this distinction that we find the source of the uniqueness of each individual firm.[19]

The uniqueness of each individual firm, then, consists in the fact that each firm's managerial team will have acquired experience and skill in combining and operating resources on the basis of the firm's particular historical development. Hence, even if the resources organised within the administrative framework of two distinct firms are identical, the services flowing from these resources will differ. Since both the possibilities for profitable activity perceived by a firm's managers and the productive services that they can utilise to exploit such possibilities will be to a considerable extent a function of their previous experience in the firm, the productive opportunity of each firm will also differ. To say that each individual firm is unique is to say that each individual firm has a unique productive opportunity.

The managerial restraint

While obviously aware of the existence of external environmental restraints on the rate at which the firm can grow, Penrose has placed the emphasis firmly on the internal restraint. She has disposed of the financial and demand restraints by assuming that the resources required for expansion are available at a price and that there exist opportunities for profitable investment, given the prevailing resource and product prices.[20] This has enabled her to concentrate solely on the managerial restraint. In what, given the conditions assumed, does this restraint consist?

Growth does not occur automatically; it has to be planned, and then the plans have to be carried out. In any given period the planning and execution of expansion must be undertaken by the existing managerial team. The top managers know each other and the organisation; indeed, as an administrative structure it is their creation. Only they can organise the growth of the firm. The collective experience of the managerial team will determine the character and extent of the productive services that are available for expansion, given the firm's productive resources. In particular the character and extent of the managerial services that are available, both entrepreneurial in the form of the contribution of viable new ideas and administrative in the form of the execution of such ideas, will shape the rate and direction of the firm's expansion. Of course, the managerial team itself can be expanded by the recruitment of new managerial resources, but no outsider can be absorbed instantaneously into the managerial team at full efficiency. Time is needed to gain experience in managing the particular firm that the newcomer has joined, i.e. for the outsider to become an insider. Such experience can only be acquired 'on the job' by learning from working with the existing managerial team. However, since the existing management does not have unlimited time and will not wish to allow too large a proportion of managerial activity to be undertaken by relatively inexperienced (in that firm) personnel, its capacity to absorb outsiders is limited. Hence, the rate of efficient managerial expansion is limited. In Penrose's words:

> . . . if a firm deliberately or inadvertently expands its organisation more rapidly than the individuals in the expanding organisation can obtain the experience with each other and with the firm that is necessary for the effective operation of the group, the efficiency of the firm will suffer, even if optimum adjustments are made in the administrative structure.[21]

Even on the assumption, then, that there exist no external restraints on the firm's rate of growth, the managerial restraint ensures that the firm's productive opportunity in any given period is finite, i.e. that there is, nevertheless, an upper limit to the rate of growth. However, the productive opportunity is continually renewed and enlarged, and the managerial limit continually recedes. There are two reasons for this. On the one hand, managerial services that are specific to the planning and execution of expansion are released as particular growth projects are realised and become part of the firm's routine operations. On the other hand, the managerial services available to the firm will alter over time due to the experience acquired both by the original members of the managerial team and by the newcomers absorbed into it. Consequently, the firm will have a new productive opportunity – a new set of activities of which it was not previously aware and/or that would not previously have been profitable for it to undertake. There is no contradiction between the existence of a managerial limit on the rate of growth in any particular period and the possibility of continuous growth over time.

The direction of expansion

Given that the firm will grow continuously, although at a rate that is subject to an upper limit, what will determine the direction in which it will expand? The answer to this question is to be found in an examination of the inducements and obstacles to expansion, which will be both external and internal. External inducements include changes in demand, technological innovation and other alterations in market conditions that enable the firm to improve its competitive position or ward off a threat from rivals; external obstacles include keen competition from rivals, patent or other restrictions on knowledge and on the use of technology, other inhibitions on entry into new areas and any scarcities of necessary factors. Internal obstacles are to be found in a scarcity of the specific managerial services required for the project envisaged; internal inducements are to be found in the existence at any given moment of an unused pool of productive services that can be employed by the firm only in the course of expansion. It is the balance of external and internal inducements and obstacles that determines the direction and method of the expansion of the firm. However, while recognising the importance of external pressures, which may be overriding in particular cases, Penrose has placed the emphasis on the internal pressures at work – pressures that derive from the resources inherited by the firm at any given moment from its past operations.

The firm hires and pays for productive resources. It utilises in the course of its operations productive services. The services obtained from the resources will vary according to the way in which and the skill with which the resources are combined. Resources are never fully utilised; there are always services that could be but are not being obtained. Thus, if expansion enables the firm's resources to be combined in a way that yields more profitable services, there will be an incentive to expand. As Penrose has put it: 'Unused productive services available from existing resources are a "waste", sometimes an unavoidable waste (that is to say, it may not pay to try to use them) but they are "free" services which, if they can be used profitably, may provide a competitive advantage for the firm possessing them.'[22]

A pool of unused productive services will always exist for a number of interconnected reasons. Since resources are 'indivisible' a complex operation involving the services of many different resources is likely to have an extremely large 'least common multiple'; that is, the smallest rate of activity at which the productive services of each resource employed are fully utilised is likely to be large. If the firm is currently operating below that rate of activity, there will be an incentive to grow. However, as the firm grows and its managerial team gains new experience and possibly hires additional resources (including managerial), the productive services that are potentially available from the firm's resources will change, and the target 'multiple' will recede. This will be especially so if in the course of expansion the firm's use of resources becomes more specialised, for the greater degree of specialisation – in particular, managerial specialisation – is likely to result in the creation of new managerial services of the entrepreneurial kind, i.e. viable new ideas. As the firm through its managers acquires specialist experience and a knowledge of an increasing number of areas, not only will the internal productive services that are available to it change, but in addition the external possibilities, i.e. demand conditions, will also change. This is because the demand conditions that are relevant to the firm's decisions are those 'seen' by it, and these will be determined largely by the experience and knowledge of its managers. Thus, the opportunities, i.e. the products considered by the firm, depend in part on its existing resources and on the productive services flowing from them. The relevant demand for the firm will be determined by its 'inherited resources', i.e. by the productive services (including management) that are available to it, and these will be continually changing.

This discussion of the source of unused productive services leads to the conclusion that the general direction of expansion will not be haphazard but will be closely related to the nature of the firm's existing resources, the type and range of productive service that these resources can render and the characteristics of the productive services currently unused. In Penrose's words:

> Unused productive services are, for the enterprising firm, at the same time a challenge to innovate, an incentive to expand, and a source of competitive advantage. They facilitate the introduction of new combinations of resources – innovation – within the firm. The new combinations may be combinations of services for the production of new products, new processes for the production of old products, new organisation of administrative functions.[23]

Diversification

It is implicit in the whole of Penrose's presentation of her theory that diversification is the normal way in which firms grow, not merely a reaction to the saturation of their existing markets. A firm is said to diversify 'whenever, without entirely abandoning its old lines of product, it embarks upon the production of new products, including intermediate products, which are sufficiently different from the other products it produces to imply some significant difference in the firm's production or distribution programmes'.[24] The incentive to diversify is to be found in 'the changing opportunity cost to the firm of its own resources',[25] which occurs whenever existing markets become relatively less profitable than other opportunities for new investment. This change in relative profitability is just as likely to be due to the rise of new opportunities as to the decline in profitability of old markets, and the rise of new opportunities is related both to external and to internal changes. However, where the competitive environment is oligopolistic a connection is established between the external and internal pressures; for if a firm's environment is such that in order to remain competitive and profitable it must keep abreast with technological innovation, it will engage in research-and-development activity, which will influence significantly the nature of the new productive services created within the firm.

Penrose's analysis of diversification starts from the concept of the areas of specialisation that it has been advantageous in the past for the firm to develop. These areas may be technological bases or market areas, productive or marketing activities, in which the firm has acquired experience and knowledge. Each base may provide more than one product, and each market may be the destination of more than one product. Thus, diversification may be of four basic types: additional products within the firm's existing techno-logical bases and market areas, products involving the same technological bases but new market areas, products involving new technological bases but the same market areas, and products involving new technological bases and new market areas. Since opportunities to add new products arise from changes in the productive services that are available to the firm as experience and know-ledge are accumulated, and from changes in the external environment as perceived by the firm, the type of diversification undertaken by the firm will be closely related to the nature of its technological bases and market areas. When the technological bases are such that there is scope for fruitful research-and-development activity, or the market areas are such that selling effort produces results, the type and direction of diversification are likely to differ significantly from those when these characteristics are not present.

In addition to the opportunities arising from the experience and knowledge accumulated in the process of past operations, particularly specialist technical or marketing activity, the exigencies of competition and the existence of specific problems, such as changes in the demand for specific products, provide further reasons why profit-seeking growing firms will diversify. However, for the theory of the growth of the firm the key significance of diversification is that it:

> . . . frees the firm from the restrictions on its expansion imposed by the demand for its existing products, although not from the restrictions imposed by its existing resources . . . Existing markets may be profitable and growing, but all that is required to induce diversification is that they do not grow fast enough to use fully the productive services available to the individual firm.[26]

Once the firm has achieved the maximum rate of profitable growth by means of internal expansion and has come up against the managerial restraint, it may be that the growth rate can be increased and that the restraint can be eased, by recourse to external expansion, i.e. expansion via acquisition or merger. More generally, the firm will choose the direction and method of expansion that enable it to grow most profitably; this expansion may be within existing markets or via diversification and in either case may take the form of installing new capacity or of acquiring existing capacity by means of merger. Thus, a new perspective arises for the analysis of merger activity. In addition to its relevance for market structure and the problems of monopoly and competition, such activity may be approached from the standpoint of the role of merger in the growth of the firm.

Downie's theory of the growth of the firm emerges incidentally from his theory of the competitive process as a whole and is set firmly within this broader context. The relationship between growth and profitability is explored by analysing the interaction between the two external restraints: financial and demand. Penrose's emphasis is quite the opposite. While recognising the existence of the two external restraints she has made the internal managerial restraint the centre of her analysis. Penrose's theory has been criticised for a lack of rigour in the specification of some of the relationships embodied in it, especially for its identification of the objective of maximum long-run profit with that of maximum long-run growth.[27] Perhaps for this reason and perhaps more generally because of her literary, non-formalised presentation, her distinctive contribution has been neglected in subsequent work.

Of course, Penrose's treatment of diversification as the normal method by which firms grow, her suggestions as to the role of innovation in the growth process and her discussion of merger within the context of the growth of the firm have formed the basis of much of the economic reasoning underlying later formal model building. However, Penrose's major emphasis is on managerial activity. She has related the behaviour of the firm to the environment as perceived by its management, i.e. to the firm's productive opportunity, and stressed that this productive opportunity will change not only with changes in the environment itself but also as the management's perception changes with accumulating experience. In this her approach has obvious similarities with that of the behavioural school, discussed in section 3.5. However, the similarities should not be overstated; for while the behavioural approach stresses short-run adaptation to routine subgoals by means of standard operating procedures, Penrose has emphasised above all the long-run strategic aspects of managerial activity: diversification, innovation and merger.

However, while Penrose's concern is with strategic activity, she has made no attempt to construct a formal equilibrium-growth model within the constrained maximisation paradigm. Instead, she has presented a rich verbal discussion of the way in which managements seek to modify the environment as perceived by them, and in the course of doing this she has illuminated many of the central characteristics of modern business behaviour. Her 'learning by doing' developmental approach emphasises the firm's existing position and the possibilities for development contained within it rather than any clearly identifiable ultimate destination or steady state.[28] There is no attempt to specify the internal and external constraints with the precision that would be necessary for her theory to qualify for inclusion within the constrained maximisation paradigm, for that would require a knowledge of the present and future that was more certain than is consistent with her view of the reality about which she is theorising.

Penrose's theory, then, is not a microequilibrium theory. Much of her work, including to some extent the managerial restraint, has been incorporated in subsequent developments, but her rejection of the microequilibrium approach has not been followed. Marris, while acknowledging her contribution, has described her theory as 'organisational' and distinguished it from 'strictly economic' theories such as his own.[29] Marris's earlier work consists in welding together the three basic restraints already discussed – financial, demand and managerial – into a rigorously specified theory. In the course of doing so he has completed the basic conceptual framework of the economic theory of the growth of the firm by developing his theory of takeover. This early contribution is now examined, and the basic structure of the family of formal models stemming from it is then set out in section 4.3.

MARRIS: THE STOCK MARKET AND THE GROWTH OF THE FIRM

Marris's major original contribution to the theory of the growth of the firm is his elaboration of the nature of the financial restraint. Downie has assumed that the firm's ability to raise finance is inversely related to its rate of profit, with the implication that eventually no further finance will be obtainable. Penrose has assumed away the financial restraint in order to concentrate on the role of management. In his theory Marris has sought to locate the financial restraint firmly in the reality of contemporary capitalist financial practice by developing a theory of takeover.

Marris was among the first to realise that a theory of the growth of the corporate firm requires a theory of stock market valuation, i.e. a theory of the determination of share prices. In general, theories of stock market valuation are constructed on the assumption that the market value of a firm is determined by the discounted stream of future earnings, i.e. dividends plus capital gains, of its current shares. This is because shareholders are assumed to value a firm's shares according to the return that they expect to receive on their investment in it, and this return consists of future dividends and capital gains. From this it follows that the current stock-market value of the firm will be maximised when the return expected by shareholders is at its maximum. Now, in Marris's theory, while shareholders are assumed to have the objective of maximising the return on their investment in the firm, which is equivalent to maximising its market value, the firm's managers are assumed to have the objective of maximising its rate of growth, subject to a security constraint.[30] What, then, is the relationship between market value and rate of growth? Marris has considered this question by examining the ways in which managers are able to raise funds for expansion.[31]

The firm's managers have three sources from which to finance their firm's growth: borrowing, new share issues and retained profit. Marris has argued that each of these sources is finite. There is a definite limit to the amount of borrowing that a firm can undertake. As the ratio of borrowed to equity finance (known as the firm's 'leverage' or 'gearing') rises, so does the risk to both borrower and lender. Since interest payments on debt are a legal claim on the firm, whereas dividend payments are optional, the greater the relative importance of such compulsory payments the greater will be the danger of bankruptcy in adverse circumstances. As a corollary, the larger the interest payment due, relative to total normal earnings, the greater will be the risk of non-payment in bad years run by the lenders. Hence, beyond a certain point the firm will not wish to incur additional debt, and lenders will not wish to lend.

The effect of a new issue of shares on the market value of a firm's existing shares will depend upon the expected profitability of the expansion to be undertaken with the funds raised. If the stock market expects the profitability of the new investment to be high enough to enable earnings on existing shares to be maintained or increased, the price of the existing shares will stay the same or rise. On the other hand, if the expected profitability is below that needed to sustain earnings on existing shares, the price of these shares will fall. This latter phenomenon is known as 'dilution'. Since shares of the same type, whether old or new, have the same price, continuous growth by dilution is impossible; eventually there will be no takers for the new issue.

The final source of finance that is available to the firm's managers is undistributed profits. On the assumption that the current market value of the firm depends on future dividends and capital gains, there will be a trade-off between dividends and retentions. If the shareholders are satisfied that the projects for which the retained profits are to be used are profitable enough to give rise to future dividends or capital gains with a present value that is equal to the dividends currently forgone, they will be content. If not, there will be only two courses of action open to them: to band together in order to dismiss the management – an eventuality that does occur, but only rarely – or to sell their shares. If sales occur on a large enough scale the market value of the firm's shares will fall. It is this process that Marris has regarded as the crucial discipline under which managers operate; for if the stock market valuation of the firm's shares falls too low, the situation will be ripe for a takeover raid, and most successful takeover raids, he has argued, result in the fairly rapid shedding of most of the taken-over firm's top management. Thus, the threat of a takeover bid is a restraint on the management of the firm, preventing it from raising finance externally or retaining it internally for use on what the stock market regards as insufficiently profitable growth projects. In Marris's words, 'the institutional framework, as specifically represented in an organised market for voting shares, restrains managerial independence in general and, more particularly, the freedom to grow'.[32]

Of course, a firm's absolute market value indicates nothing by itself about the stock market's assessment of the firm, since it obviously depends to a considerable extent on the firm's size. What is needed is a relative measure, and for this Marris has developed the 'valuation ratio', i.e. the ratio of stock market value to book value. Stock market value represents the market's assessment of the firm's performance and prospects under its existing management. Book value, on the other hand, represents in some sense the value of the resources tied up in the firm.[33] Marris's theory of takeover consists essentially in the proposition that a firm will be taken over if its actual valuation ratio falls below the subjective valuation ratio put upon it by a potential bidder. This, of course, will be the case if the potential bidder expects to obtain a better performance from the resources controlled by the firm than is being obtained by the existing management. The lower a firm's valuation ratio, the easier it will tend to be to improve its performance, and the more likely it is to be taken over. The minimum level of valuation ratio that a management is prepared to tolerate is determined by the maximum takeover threat that it is prepared to live with, and this in turn will depend on the importance that it attaches to security.[34]

It is clear that the financial restraint, in the form of the threat of a takeover bid, only becomes effective if the profitability of investment falls with the rate of growth of the firm. Why should profitability and growth be inversely related? Downie's answer is that in order to attract additional customers price must be decreased and that beyond a certain point this will cause profitability to fall. Marris, following Penrose, has argued that this demand restraint can in general be overcome by diversification. He has invoked the image of firms that continually offer new products progressing 'by successive "jumps" to appropriate positions among an ever-growing family of otherwise static demand curves'.[35] However, as the rate of diversification increases, profitability eventually falls. This is because: 'The planning of diversification is *par excellence* a typical function of high management. Characteristically, it has been found, these decisions are taken at higher levels within the management hierarchy than are, for example, pricing decisions.'[36] Thus, the managerial restraint, developed by Penrose and adopted by Marris, limits the extent to which diversification can overcome the demand restraint without profitability falling;[37] and as soon as profitability starts to fall the financial restraint, in the form of Marris's takeover threat, comes into play.

Of course, the launching of a takeover bid will cause the firm's existing management to consider ways of increasing profitability and will usually lead to the promise of increased dividends. The raiders will need to possess not only a supply of finance but also proved managerial ability. If shareholders are to accept the raiders' offer, they will need to be convinced that the raiders' managerial ability will result in greater profitability than the existing management is capable of achieving. Thus, the relative efficiency of the existing management will have an important influence on the rate of growth that can be undertaken without fear of the firm being taken over. Relatively efficient managements will be able to grow rapidly with safety; less efficient managements will be able to grow less rapidly with safety; inefficient managements are likely to be taken over. The parallel with Downie's view that the extent of the dispersion of efficiency is an important determinant of the speed with which his transfer mechanism will work and of the rate at which firms will grow should be clear.[38]

SUMMARY AND CONCLUSIONS

Once the concept of an optimum size for the firm is abandoned, size becomes merely a byproduct of growth. The problem then is to analyse the process by which firms grow and in particular to determine what limits their rate of growth. If an understanding of the growth process can be obtained, insights are likely to be gained into many of the central phenomena of modern capitalism, including decline. Growth, diversification, merger and innovation are all aspects of the competitive process. A theory explicitly designed to analyse growth is able to encompass the other phenomena more easily than the static traditional theory, which can handle them only with strain. Furthermore, only within a theory of the growth of the firm can the implications of alternative non-static assumptions about objectives be derived.

In this section the basic concepts of the theory of the growth of the firm are identified in the work of Downie, Penrose and Marris. Given constant returns to organisational size and a firm not confined to any given market or set of markets, there is no upper limit to the ultimate size of the firm. However, there is a limit to the firm's size at any moment because there is an upper limit to its rate of growth. The reason for this upper limit to the growth rate is to be found in the relationship between growth and profitability, which is the cornerstone of all theories of the growth of the firm. There are in fact two relationships: on the one hand, growth depends on profitability; on the other hand, growth above a certain rate adversely affects profitability. To grow requires finance, and to raise finance requires profitability; but there are costs involved in growth, which increase as the rate of growth increases, and these costs reduce profitability.

The costs of growth arise from the expense of obtaining a larger share of existing markets and of increasing the rate of diversification, i.e. because of the demand restraint. They increase as the rate of growth increases, partly because of increasing resistance from other firms and partly because the ability of the management to carry through expansion is limited, i.e. because of the managerial restraint. Hence, growth and profitability are inversely related. In a non-corporate firm falling profitability will cause the supply of finance to dry up. Within a corporate framework, however, the financial restraint takes the form of an increasingly acute threat of takeover as falling profitability, either actual or expected, produces a reduction in market value and the valuation ratio. This is the basic conceptual framework of what has come to be known as the economic theory of the growth of the firm. It incorporates original contributions by all three economists whose work has been referred to in this section, and it is the foundation on which the formal models of Marris and others rest.

However, both Downie and Penrose have also offered contributions to the understanding of the growth of the firm that have been largely neglected in later work. Penrose's concept of the changing productive opportunity perceived by the management places emphasis on the possibilities for growth and development present in the firm's inherited resources. These possibilities will be influenced by the firm's history and by the environment in which it operates. The stress is on the uniqueness of the possibilities that are open to each firm, but without prejudice to whether or to what extent the possibilities will be realised. Following Marshall, Penrose has drawn an analogy between firm and tree: 'one can never certify in advance whether the tree will or will not survive all possible vicissitudes and how they will affect its growth – the next winter may be severe, the spring rains may fail, or blight may set in'.[39] Thus, while Penrose's concern is apparently with the growth of the individual firm and the internal restraint, it is actually with the process of growth within an advanced capitalist economy.[40] Hence, her approach via the individual firm may not be incompatible with that of Downie, whose principal concern is with

the system as a whole. Downie's insistence on growth and change as fundamental characteristics of capitalist economies is noted at the beginning of
this section. For him, any theory that abstracts from those essential characteristics is likely to be of limited value. The competitive process as a whole
involves growth; but it also involves decline, both relative and absolute, and
sometimes death. There is no room in his scheme of things for steady-state
permanent-growth models. It is precisely successful growth that heightens
competitive pressure and threatens a transformation of the hitherto-existing
balance of strength and relative capacities for growth. The competitive
process proceeds by way of a dialectical thrust and counterthrust[41] as oligopolists seek to defend their positions in the face of change and to seize new
opportunities for dominating their rivals.

Neither Penrose nor Downie has constructed microequilibrium growth
models. In this sense their break with the traditional theory is more fundamental
than Marris's, for they have effectively abandoned the constrained maximisation paradigm whereas Marris has built a new theory within the old paradigm.
This difference is also relevant to the question of 'testing'. Downie's theory
stands or falls by whether or not he has succeeded in capturing the essential
characteristics of the competitive process as a whole. Penrose has appealed
largely to business histories and biographies of individual businessmen as
evidence for her theory. On the other hand, although attempts to test
Marris's theory have so far been confined to examining the relative growth–
profitability performance of owner-controlled and management-controlled
firms and to comparing the characteristics of taken-over and non-taken-over
firms, hope apparently persists of specifying a model in a way that will enable
econometric 'testing' on the basis of the limited data available.[42]

4.3   A SIMPLE MODEL AND SOME DEVELOPMENTS

The basic conceptual framework of the economic theory of the growth of the
firm and the reasoning underlying it are set out in the previous section. The
essential structure of the theory is to be found in the relationship between
growth, profitability and stock market valuation. Formal models incorporating
these relationships can be used to explore the effect of alternative objectives as
expressed in alternative utility functions. Thus, although the theory received its
initial impetus from the attempt to build a managerial theory, it has a general
application to growing corporate firms.[43]

The models in question are all 'steady-state' models. In a steady-state
model, once a policy has been decided, i.e. once values have been set to the
variables under the control of those running the firm, 'the main quantifiable
variables either grow at a common constant rate or, being variables defined as
ratios between other variables, themselves remain constant'.[44] Such models
are sometimes referred to as permanent growth models, since the values of the
policy variables are determined as if for all time on the basis of the objectives
of those running the firm and certain or certainty-equivalent knowledge about
the present and future environment, and permanent growth at a given rate
results. If objectives and/or the exogenous environment change, a new set of

'permanent' values of the policy variables is chosen, and a new rate of 'permanent' growth results.[45] The assumptions underlying steady-state permanent-growth models are discussed later in this section.

A SIMPLE MODEL

Radice has developed a diagrammatic exposition incorporating the essential structural relationships of a simple steady-state Marris-type model.[46] In Figure 4.1 the two-way relationship between growth and profitability is represented by the 'demand growth' and 'supply of capital' curves. The demand growth curve portrays the way in which the rate of profit is assumed to vary as the growth rate increases. At low growth rates an increase in the rate of growth causes the rate of profit to rise; above a certain growth rate, however (for reasons discussed in the previous section), further increases in the rate of growth cause the rate of profit to fall away. The supply-of-capital curve portrays the way in which the rate at which the firm is able to raise capital to finance capacity is assumed to vary as the rate of profit increases; the higher the rate of profit, the more rapidly will it be possible to increase capacity. Since there will be a maximum permissible retention-ratio – determined by the need to keep shareholders happy, i.e. to provide enough dividends to prevent the valuation ratio from falling below the minimum level that is tolerable – then, if internal finance only is considered, the relationship between the rate of profit and the rate of capacity expansion will be linear. If the maximum retention ratio rises, e.g. because managers for some reason are prepared to accept a lower valuation ratio and hence a more acute threat of being taken over, the supply-of-capital curve will pivot to the right. In general there will be a different supply-of-capital curve for each retention ratio. External finance complicates matters but does not alter the essential relationship.

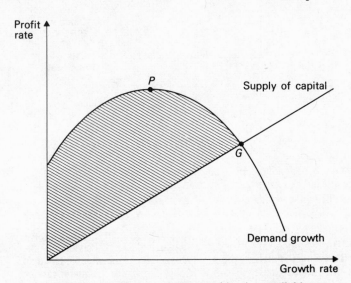

Fig. 4.1   Profit–growth rate combination available.

The shaded area in Figure 4.1 represents the profit–growth rate combinations that are open to the firm. Since it is a steady-state model, whichever profit and growth rates are selected will persist. The highest attainable profit rate is at point P, and the highest growth rate is at point G. If owners are solely interested in dividends, owner-controlled firms will choose P, since with a given retention ratio the point of maximum profit rate is also the point of maximum dividends. However, if owners are also interested in capital gains, assumed to arise from growth, they will choose the point to the right of P that corresponds to their rate of trade-off between profits and growth, i.e. between dividends and capital gains. If managers are assumed to have the objective of growth maximisation, subject to a security constraint, manager-controlled firms will choose G; the security constraint in the form of a minimum level of valuation ratio, which implies a maximum level of retention ratio, is, as seen above, embodied in the position of the supply-of-capital curve. Of course, managers will only be restricted to G if their concern for security takes the form assumed so far of a minimum valuation-ratio constraint. More generally they too may be assumed to have a trade-off relationship, in their case between growth and valuation ratio, i.e. security. These two types of trade-off – shareholder and managerial – are represented in Figure 4.2, derived by Radice from Marris.

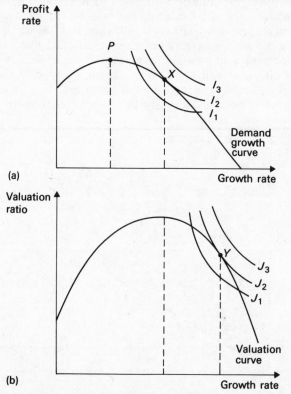

Fig. 4.2   (a) Shareholder indifference (b) Manager indifference.

In Figure 4.2a shareholder utility, which is a function of both profits (dividends) and growth (capital gains), is maximised at point X, which is the point of tangency between the demand growth curve and the highest attainable shareholder-indifference curve, I_2. Following the standard argument as to the determination of share prices sketched in the previous section, the point of maximum shareholder utility will be the point of maximum stock-market valuation. Since the book value of the firm is given, this point, X, will be the peak of the valuation ratio curve drawn in Figure 4.2b. Managerial utility, which is now a function of growth rate and valuation ratio level, will be maximised at point Y, which is the point of tangency between the valuation ratio curve and the highest attainable manager-indifference curve, J_2. Only if the threat of takeover is over-riding at any level of the valuation ratio other than the maximum will shareholder-selected and manager-selected growth and profit rates coincide.[47]

This simple model brings out all the essential features of the family of steady-state growth models. The relationships embodied in it may be set out formally as follows:

(1) *The finance–supply relationship*

$$g = rp \qquad (4.1)$$

underlies the supply-of-capital curve in Figure 4.1. If only internal finance is considered, the maximum rate of capacity growth g is equal to the rate of profit p multiplied by the retention ratio r. Since r is constant at $\bar{r}$, which is the maximum that is consistent with enabling the valuation ratio constraint to be met, the relationship between g and p is linear.

(2) *The growth-profitability function*

$$p = p(g) \qquad (4.2)$$

underlies the demand growth curve in Figures 4.1 and 4.2a. As the rate of demand growth increases the rate of profit first rises and then falls.

(3) *The stock-market discount function* determines the nature of the relationship between the growth–profitability function (see 2 above) and the growth–valuation function (see 4 below). In effect it governs the translation of the demand growth curve in Figure 4.2a into the valuation curve in Figure 4.2b by specifying the nature of shareholder indifference between alternative profit–growth combinations.[48]

For expository purposes Marris[49] has presented a *present value function*

$$Y = Y(g) \qquad (4.3)$$

where Y is the reciprocal of the dividend yield, which is the ratio of current dividend to market price; that is, Y is the amount by which current dividend must be multiplied in order to obtain share price. The dividend is expected with certainty to grow at g. Since the market is assumed to be interested in both current dividend and future growth in dividends, Y increases with g. If for some reason the growth element in dividends is ignored, Y will be independent of g.

(4) *The growth–valuation function* underlies the valuation curve in Figure 4.2b. It specifies the nature of the relationship between the valuation ratio and the rate of growth. Making use of the present value function (see 3 above) the growth–valuation function can be expressed as

$$v = D(g). \ Y(g) = v \ (g) \tag{4.4}$$

where $D = D(g)$ is a general dividend function in which current dividend D first rises and then falls as g increases.[50] Since D eventually falls and Y increases as g increases, v may have a maximum with respect to g, as in Figure 4.2b.

(5) *The utility function* underlies the indifference curves in Figure 4.2. In the case of managers the function is

$$U_1 = U_1(v, g) \tag{4.5}$$

with managerial utility depending on both the valuation ratio and the growth rate. The trade-off relationship between v and g will determine the nature of the managerial indifference curves in Figure 4.2b. If managerial utility is not contributed to by growth at all until a certain level of security is obtained, a minimum valuation ratio $v = \bar{v}$ can be designated as a constraint that must be met. Such a minimum valuation ratio, implying a maximum retention ratio, underlies the position of the supply-of-capital curve in Figure 4.1.

In the case of the shareholder indifference curves in Figure 4.2.a the utility function is

$$U_2 = U_2(p, g) \tag{4.6}$$

with shareholder utility depending on both the profit rate and the growth rate. The trade-off relationship specified by the stock-market discount function (see 3 above) reduces this to

$$U_3 = U_3(v) \tag{4.7}$$

since the combined effect of profit rate and growth rate on shareholder utility is captured by the valuation ratio. This simplified shareholder utility function is the one that is relevant to Figure 4.2b, and it will be noted that by comparison with the managerial utility function g has dropped out of the argument. This is because any contribution that growth may have to make to shareholder utility is through its effect on the valuation ratio v and has already been captured in the valuation curve.

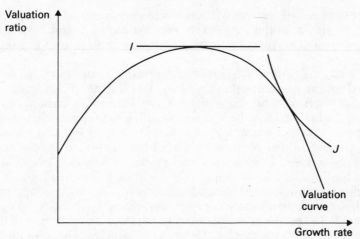

Fig. 4.3   Shareholder and manager indifference compared.

Shareholder 'indifference curves' that are appropriate to Figure 4.2b will therefore be horizontal, and the highest attainable shareholder indifference curve will be tangential to the valuation curve at its peak, indicating that shareholder utility is maximised at the highest possible valuation ratio – the most preferred available combination of profit rate and growth rate.

Thus, what Marris has termed 'the most general statement of the basic model'[51]

$$\text{maximise } U = U(v, g) \text{ subject to } v = v(g)$$

can be represented in Figure 4.3, where the valuation curve represents the constraint, J is an indifference curve representing managerial utility at a maximum and I is a shareholder 'indifference curve' in which only v contributes to utility, the g argument in the utility function being redundant.

SOME DEVELOPMENTS AND PROBLEMS

While Radice's diagrammatic exposition exhibits the essential features of the family of steady-state growth models, subsequent discussion has increasingly centred on two relationships that remain implicit in his treatment: the operating-profit function and the cost-of-growth function, which together determine the growth–profitability function. At first sight the analysis of the relationships determining the form of these functions and the connections between them appears straightforward. The operating profit rate, defined as the profit rate with no 'demand-growth-creating' expenditure, is given by a demand function, a production function and factor prices. The costs of growth are defined as the costs of shifting the firm's demand curve over time, which involves demand-growth-creating expenditure on advertising, research and development, personnel expansion, administrative reorganisation and the like.

These costs of growth increase with the rate of growth and eat into the operating profit rate. Hence, as the growth rate rises the recorded profit rate falls; the growth–profitability function is therefore a growth-recorded profitability function.[52]

The analytical distinction between 'operating' and 'growing' has been provided with an institutional analogue by O. Williamson.[53] He has set up two broad categories of firm: the unitary (U) and the multidivisional (M). The U-firm specialises functionally with separate divisions for manufacturing, sales, finance etc.; thus, for example, in a diversified U-firm the sales division will handle promotion and distribution for all lines produced by the firm. The M-firm, by contrast, is organised into product divisions, each of which is responsible for all the functional activities relating to its given product, with a head office responsible for 'strategic decisions involving planning, appraisal and control, including the allocation of resources among the (competing) operating divisions'.[54] The product divisions carry out the 'operating' activity of the firm, and the head office undertakes the 'growing' activity. The operating profit obtained by the product divisions is appropriated by the head office and used to extend the range of the firm's activities by demand-growth-creating expenditure culminating in the establishment of new product divisions, i.e. for growth, and to satisfy the capital market, i.e. for dividends.

Although Williamson has regarded the M-firm as a superior organisational form, in fact, of course, by no means all firms fall into this category. Even in those that do the separation of functions will not be complete: existing product divisions may grow with their existing markets without incurring any demand-growth-creating expenditure and/or may be allocated resources for such expenditure if prospects for increasing their market share seem good; the head office will not confine itself to 'growing' activity but will also evaluate and control the existing product divisions. Nevertheless, the distinction between product divisions and the head office does provide a convenient framework for discussing some of the analytical problems associated with the use of steady-state growth models.

As in the case of the static partial-equilibrium traditional theory of the firm, the principal problems stem from the existence of uncertainty and interdependence.[55] Both are effectively assumed away in steady-state growth models, and this is broadly true at both stages in the analysis: the determination of the operating profit rate, and the specification of the cost-of-growth function. The product, i.e. operating, divisions of the M-firm have been called 'quasi-firms', and Marris has suggested that most of the previous theory of the firm 'could well be described as "the theory of the quasi-firm" '.[56] The operating profit rate of each product division or quasi-firm is obtained from a demand function and an 'operating-cost' function, i.e. production function plus factor prices. Since each quasi-firm is assumed to have a determinate demand curve the problem of oligopoly is assumed away.

Marris has rightly regarded this as a serious problem for a theory intended to encompass absolutely large firms operating typically in oligopolistic markets. He has argued in terms of game-theoretic reasoning that a co-operative solution is likely, with the particular outcome that emerges from the set of possible co-operative solutions depending on the 'threat strength' of the firm as a whole. Hence, for example, in a 'game' between a quasi-firm and an independent single-product firm whose position in the given market is the same in all other respects, the quasi-firm is likely to come off better because of the greater resources that its head office is able to place at its disposal.[57] More generally, it is clear that the behaviour of a diversified firm in any one of its separate markets will not be independent of its overall position. Furthermore, it may not be merely the overall position in a static sense that is relevant. Although demand-growth-creating expenditure is envisaged above as reducing the recorded profit rate, Marris has suggested that this will only be the case when growth rises above a certain rate; at low growth rates an increase in the rate of growth may enable the operating profit rate to increase by more than enough to offset the costs of inducing the extra growth and so may be associated with an increase in the recorded profit rate.[58]

While the problem of oligopolistic interdependence is serious at the quasi-firm level it may be even more acute at the level of head office 'growing' activity, although so far it has not been analysed at this level. What is at issue here is the legitimacy of the steady state approach and the constrained maximisation paradigm. The use of a game-theoretic solution to the determination of the operating profit rate has already involved the abandonment of this paradigm at the quasi-firm level. However, the paradigm has been retained at the level of head office activity by means of the cost-of-growth function. It will be recalled that the most general statement of the basic model consists of a utility function that is to be maximised, subject to a constraint, namely:

$$\text{maximise } U = U(v, g) \text{ subject to } v = v\,(g)$$

The constraint is derived by means of a stock-market valuation function from a growth–profitability function, which in turn is obtained from an operating profit function and a cost-of-growth function. The determination of the operating profit rate is discussed above. What can be said about the cost-of-growth function?

The cost-of-growth function relates the rate of growth of demand for the firm's output to the rate of demand-growth-creating expenditure. It is assumed that a constant rate of such expenditure will produce a constant rate of demand growth and that a higher rate of expenditure will produce a higher rate of growth, although the increase in growth will be less than in proportion to the increase in expenditure. However, although there will be 'dynamic diminishing returns'[59] at any moment in time, through time each given rate of demand-growth-creating expenditure will produce a corresponding given rate of demand growth, which will continue 'permanently'. This is an essential characteristic of steady state models, and it requires the assumption that the exogenous environmental conditions determining the properties of the cost-of-growth function remain permanently constant. Marris has commented on the oddity of this assumption:

We are accustomed to the concept of *ceteris paribus* in the exogenous conditions of static theory, but the extension of 'constancy' over long periods of time, during which the firm is supposed actively to attempt to *change* its own static environment – shift its demand curve – presents obvious difficulties.[60]

The answer provided to this paradox is to distinguish between two sorts of environment. On the one hand, there is the static or immediate environment, which the firm is able to change continuously. On the other hand, there is the 'superenvironment', which determines the rate at which the firm can change its immediate environment but which is itself not subject to change by the firm. The superenvironment is conceived as 'a loose collection of general circumstances governing limits on the firm's environment-changing capacity'.[61] The concepts of the superenvironment, steady-state growth and a policy – i.e. the choice of a sustainable set of values for the variables controlled by the firm, including the rate of demand-growth-creating expenditure and hence growth rate – are inseparably linked:

> ... if the super-environment is constant, a constant policy will produce for the firm a steady state . . . The steady state will be sustained until either the super-environment changes or the policy changes, or both. Analysis takes the form of comparative dynamics, that is, the comparing of alternative steady-state values.[62]

The properties of the cost-of-growth function depend on the nature of the superenvironment; if the superenvironment is constant, so also will be the cost-of-growth function. Since the superenvironment 'by definition is beyond the influence of individual firms',[63] all that the firm can do is to adapt 'passively' to its environment in terms of its objectives, i.e. maximise its utility function subject to the growth-valuation constraint. The constrained maximisation paradigm can be retained because the superenvironment and hence the cost-of-growth function are exogenous to the individual firm and known with certainty or certainty equivalence.

Yet, for any individual firm the extent to which the superenvironment is responsive to its attempts to change its immediate environment will largely depend on what other firms are doing. As Wood has put it, 'the factor which determines the *form* of the micro cost-of-growth function is the existence and behaviour of other firms; it exhibits diminishing returns because other firms are also competing for sources of demand.'[64] Now, if competition from other firms produces diminishing returns to demand-growth-creating expenditure at any moment in time, it is difficult to see why this should not also be the case through time. Of course, the steady-state models under discussion 'are all models of the behaviour of the *single firm*; they are set in partial equilibrium and take the activities of other firms as given'.[65] However, this restriction may turn out to vitiate the entire steady-state approach; for the assumptions underlying the approach must at least be consistent with the existence of more than one firm, and the general responsiveness of the super-environment is unlikely to remain for long unchanged in the face of steady-state growth by several firms.

A comparison with the 'steady-state' static partial-equilibrium analysis of a single perfectly-competitive market may be instructive. In the short run the market environment, i.e. the cost curve and price facing the individual firm, is given and is beyond the influence of the firm. In the long run, changes in the number of firms may change the short-run market supply-curve and hence the price confronting the individual firm; while the market environment remains beyond the influence of the individual firm it is changed by the actions of firms in the aggregate. If there is an optimum size for the firm,[66] a long-run static partial-equilibrium solution will exist, determined by the underlying market demand and cost conditions. It is these underlying conditions that are exogenous with respect not only to the actions of the individual firm but also to those of firms in the aggregate. The partial equilibrium method of analysis is legitimate only if it is reasonable to assume that what happens in a single market as a whole – the aggregate effect of the actions of all firms in that market, e.g. the contraction or expansion of aggregate supply – has no significant effect on the market's underlying demand and cost conditions, e.g. by increasing aggregate demand or altering the cost function. In the case of steady-state growth models no distinction analogous to that between the short run and the long run is drawn. The immediate environment is subject to influence by the individual firm, while the superenvironment is unaffected by the actions of the individual firm or, presumably, of firms in the aggregate. Yet logically, the superenvironment is analogous to the single market; while conditions in the superenvironment may not be subject to influence by the actions of the individual firm, they will eventually be altered as a result of permanent growth by firms in the aggregate.

The upshot of this argument is the conclusion that steady-state growth by all firms is logically incompatible with the assumptions required to enable steady-state growth by any one firm. This is because the properties of the cost-of-growth function of the individual firm depend on the 'existence and behaviour of other firms', and in a system made up of firms following a steady-state permanent-growth path these properties will be endogenous, not exogenous. Thus, the structure of steady-state growth models is flawed by an internal logical contradiction. The point is greatly strengthened, of course, when the relatively small number of giant oligopolists dominating most sectors of industry is recalled, for it now becomes unlikely that each firm will determine the scale of its demand-growth-creating activity independently of what its rivals are doing. Rather, there is likely to be oligopolistic interdependence at the cost-of-growth level of analysis as well as at the operating profit level; and in the presence of oligopolistic interdependence, partial equilibrium analysis that 'take[s] the activities of all other firms as given' is illegitimate.

One possible way forward may be 'a general [as opposed to partial] analysis of a growing economy composed of growing firms and markets . . . [but] there is a considerable risk that it would be an exercise in arid formalism'.[67] Another perspective may be to concentrate on constructing limited models for particular purposes, eschewing any attempt to develop overall or 'complete' models of the economy as a whole.[68] On the other hand, it has been argued that 'the pattern . . . of firm behaviour cannot be studied independently of the total system and prior to the analysis of its *modus operandi*'.[69] This would be in the spirit of Downie's approach, but it may be thought to suffer from undue indeterminacy. Of course, the quest for determinacy and the related attractions of the constrained maximisation paradigm at the level of micro-equilibrium analysis are not unconnected with normative issues. This has been clearly recognised by Marris:

> . . . the desire for determinacy . . . is not merely a product of the professional style; it also arises from the knowledge that indeterminate theories cannot easily be subjected to qualitative analysis, a failing which may be of great political importance if we desire to prescribe for improvement. A determinate theory is therefore particularly needed by those who wish to evaluate and prescribe as against those whose aim is merely to describe.[70]

This is perhaps the heart of the problem. It brings the discussion back to the doubts about the relevance of a microequilibrium approach within the constrained maximisation paradigm that emerges in the conclusion to section 3.2; for in the context of a process through time, the effect of this approach is to focus attention on the determination of present action by the future environment rather than on the determination of the future environment by present action. A change of focus to the analysis of the *modus operandi* of modern capitalism as an integrated system, the economic analysis of which assumes relevance only when related to the other aspects of its overall structure, might have disadvantages from the standpoint of 'prescriptions for improvement'. However, it might also point the way forward to an integration of economic analysis and economic policy. Far from enabling policy to be prescribed in the 'public interest', it would rather enable a start to be made in explaining the policy actually pursued. Thus:

> The study of the interaction between monopolistic firms' strategies and structural change in the economy can also contribute to understanding the new orientation of economic policy which is *induced* by the development of the system. In fact we shall get beyond neo-voluntarism in the approach to the problems of economic policy.[71]

4.4 SOME EMPIRICAL FINDINGS

The theories of the growth of the firm discussed in the previous two sections have not yet yielded models cast in a form susceptible to direct confrontation with empirical data.[72] However, a good deal of empirical work has been done on the relationship between growth, profitability and size, with results that are broadly consistent between studies. These results form the basic facts for which any theory of the modern firm should be able to account. In addition comparisons have been made of the characteristics of 'taken-over' and 'non-taken-over' firms in the hope of throwing light on the role played by the stock market in constraining corporate behaviour. The general findings of these empirical studies are presented in this section. No attempt is made at a comprehensive survey.[73] Rather, one or two of the more important studies are reported in some detail in an attempt to convey an impression of the nature of the data and the problems of empirical analysis in this area. In particular, considerable reference is made to work undertaken at the University of Cambridge Department of Applied Economics, based on the standardised annual accounts of all public companies quoted on a UK stock exchange plus a small number of larger non-quoted and private companies. The original work covered the period 1948–60,[74] but it has in some cases been extended to cover later periods.[75] Data are first presented to indicate the complementarity of growth and decline or death. The relationship between growth, profitability and size is then examined. Finally, the characteristics of taken-over firms are considered. Throughout, the special position of very large firms, as suggested in the empirical studies, is noted. Although size is irrelevant in some of the relationships under discussion, in others it emerges as a key independent variable. This foreshadows to some extent the discussion of diversification, merger and innovation in Chapter 5, in which size plays a prominent role.

GROWTH AND DECLINE

The competitive process is marked by growth and decline. This is what is expected on theoretical grounds, and this is what is observed in fact. Table 4.1 relates to the population of companies used in the original University of Cambridge Department of Economics studies referred to above. Although the table gives data only for the aggregate of all manufacturing industries, it is important to note that many questions are best studied within an industry, since the 'same' levels of, say, size or profitability for firms in different industries may have widely differing economic implications if conditions differ widely between the industries. For this reason the empirical studies referred to have frequently drawn conclusions based on data disaggregated to the industry level.[76]

Of the 3,754 companies that were present at any time during the period

Table 4.1 *Companies in manufacturing, construction, distribution and miscel-laneous services quoted on UK stock exchanges: births, deaths and continuing companies, 1948–60.*

	No.	% of row 5
(1) Companies in 1948	2,825	75·3
(2) Continuing companies[a]	1,955	52·1
(3) Births[a]	929	24·7
(4) Deaths[a]	1,052	28·0
(5) Total in population	3,754	100·0
(6) Double counting[a]	182	
(7) Companies in 1960	2,702	72·0

Source: G. Whittington, *The Prediction of Profitability*, University of Cambridge Department of Applied Economics, Occasional Paper 22 (Cambridge, Cambridge UP, 1971), table 1.2, p. 7.

Note:
(a) For definitions of terms, see text. Births and deaths are from 1949 onwards.

2,825 existed at the beginning, and of these 1,955 continued throughout. The consideration of the relationship between growth, profitability and size during any period was most conveniently undertaken on the basis of 'continuing' companies – companies that were in existence throughout the period. It is important to note, however, that 'existence' has been defined with respect to inclusion in the population of companies in the study, not to existence as an economic unit. Thus, the 929 'births' refer to companies first qualifying for inclusion in the population from 1949 onwards; similarly, the 1,052 'deaths' refer to companies ceasing to qualify. The double-counting entry refers to the 182 firms that were born and also died within the period 1948–60.

It is clear that, of all the companies qualifying for inclusion at any time during the period, roughly one-half continued in the population throughout, while one-quarter entered and rather more than another quarter left at some time during the period. The incidence of births and deaths thus appears to have been roughly the same. However, from the standpoint of economic significance this appearance may be misleading. The overwhelming majority of 'deaths' really were deaths, in the sense that the companies concerned ceased to exist as independent economic units, mainly due to acquisition or merger; genuine deaths, especially those due to acquisition, are of considerable economic significance and are considered later in this section. On the other hand, the bulk of 'births' were accounted for by existing enterprises newly qualifying for inclusion in the population due to a change of status, e.g. from a private to a public company or from a non-quoted to a quoted company; at this level births are a statistical rather than an economic phenomenon.[77] Of course, companies included in the population were normally relatively large while newly created economic units were likely to be relatively small. However, since the number of small firms has been subject to secular decline,[78] at the lower end of the overall size distribution the rate at which new economic units were being created was insufficient to replace economic units that had ceased to exist.

Genuine deaths and newly created economic units are only one aspect of the working out of the competitive process. The differing fortunes of already existing firms that survive must also be taken into account. If 'births' into the population, while not genuine in the sense of representing the creation of new economic units, were the result of growth by previously existing firms, this would be of economic significance. Unfortunately, the data on which the studies under discussion have been based have not allowed this possibility to be investigated. Evidence on growth has been confined to 'continuing' companies, i.e. those that were present in the population throughout. Table 4.2 sets out the growth experience of continuing companies in the period 1948–60. A complication in the interpretation of the table is that no allowance has been made for inflation. However, the rising price level must have affected all firms, even if not necessarily to the same extent, and:

> Even allowing for the effects of inflation, there is a very appreciable increase in the size of firms by the end of the period. For instance, the average size of the firm in the food industry increased from nearly £2·5 million in 1948 to nearly £7 million in 1960, which is a high rate of growth notwithstanding the continuous inflation over the period.[79]

Table 4.2 *Percentage frequency distribution of continuing companies classified by growth of net assets,ᵃ 1948–60.*

Growth of net assets (%)	% of sample
< 0	6·1
< 2·5	15·0
< 5·0	18·9
< 7·5	19·2
< 10·0	15·7
< 12·5	10·6
< 15·0	7·0
< 20·0	5·2
> 20·0	2·4
Total	100·0
Mean growth (%)	6·9
Standard deviation of growth (%)	5·7

Source: G. Whittington, *The Prediction of Profitability,* University of Cambridge Department of Applied Economics, Occasional Paper 22 (Cambridge, Cambridge UP, 1971), table 2.4, p. 26.

Note:
(a) Growth equals the compound annual rate of growth of net assets measured in such a way as to mitigate the influence of the revaluation of fixed assets by some firms. Growth is measured in money terms rather than in real terms. Net assets equal total fixed assets plus current assets net of current liabilities, valued at historic cost net of depreciation.

It will be seen from the table that growth rates differed considerably between firms. Disaggregated data show that only a small part of this difference was due to differences between industries. Nevertheless, average growth rates and the relative dispersion of growth rates did differ between industries. 'Electrical engineering' had the highest growth rate (10·8 per cent) and a relative dispersion of growth that was equal to the average (5·7 per cent), while 'Entertainment and sport' had the lowest growth rate (1·3 per cent) and also the lowest relative dispersion (3·4 per cent).[80]

Of some interest, particularly when continuous inflation is borne in mind, is the persistence of non-growing firms; of the 1,955 continuing companies over the period 1948–60 covered in Table 4.2, 119 or 6·1 per cent had growth rates below zero.[81] However, when the two subperiods 1948–54 and 1954–60 are considered, both the number of continuing companies and the proportion of non-growing companies were greater.[82] Thus, not surprisingly, the chances of a non-growing company surviving decreased the longer the period considered.

Finally, on the subject of growth and decline it is worth noting that the probability of birth and death,[83] the relative mobility of firms (i.e. the extent to which they changed their ranking in the size distribution),[84] and the proportion of non-growing firms[85] all declined with size. This raises the possibility that size may have an independent influence on the growth and profitability performance of firms. Hence, before the relationship between these two variables is considered the relationship of each one to size is examined.

GROWTH, PROFITABILITY AND SIZE

Growth and size

A systematic relationship between the rate of growth and size of firms might take the form of an association between the average rate of growth and size class or between the extent of dispersion of growth rates and size class.[86] Samuels has examined a sample of 400 firms quoted on the London Stock Exchange over the period 1950–1 to 1959–60.[87] Only continuing companies were included, although Samuels has judged that the inclusion of non-continuing firms would not have made any significant difference to the results.[88] The firms were grouped into four size classes on the basis of net assets at the start of the period, measured by issued capital, but not into separate industry groups. Samuels has found that larger firms grew at a significantly faster rate than smaller firms and that the degree of variability of growth within a given size class did not differ between larger and smaller firms.

Singh and Whittington have classified growth by opening size according to twenty-one separate industry groups as well as for all firms together. Their aggregate results are reproduced in Table 4.3. The tendency for the rate of growth to increase and for the standard deviation to decrease with size was on the whole significant in both cases – a finding confirmed by the results for the separate industries and by regression analysis. However, the strength of the tendency differed, being much weaker for the positive relationship between average growth rates and size than for the negative relationship between dispersion of growth rates and size. The finding that there was a positive relationship between average growth and size has revised that reported by Singh and Whittington at an earlier stage of their work, based on the analysis of only three large industries, to the effect that there was no systematic relationship between mean growth rates and firm size.[89]

A more recent study by Meeks and Whittington has compared the growth

Table 4.2　*Growth of net assets*[a] *by opening size class: all firms, 1948–60.*

Opening size of net assets	No. of firms	Mean growth (%)	Standard deviation of growth (%)
<　£250,000	483	6·1	6·6
<　£500,000	464	6·5	5·2
< £1,000,000	389	7·0	5·3
< £2,000,000	271	7·2	5·4
< £4,000,000	167	7·9	5·4
> £4,000,000	181	8·4	4·9
All sizes	1,955	6·9	5·7

Source: A. Singh and G. Whittington, 'The size and growth of firms', *Review of Economic Studies,* vol. 42 (January 1975), table 1, p. 18.

Note:
(a)　See note to Table 4.2.

experience of 'giant' companies, i.e. those of the 100 largest that survived between 1948 and 1969, and the 'rest' of the survivors in the population of companies referred to in note 75. They have found that the 'giants' had a faster rate of growth than the 'rest' in 1964–9 but not in 1948–69 and that the 'giants' experienced less variability in their growth rate in both periods.[90]

A well-known study of the United States by Hymer and Pashigian has examined the relationship between firm size and growth rate for the 1,000 largest US manufacturing firms over the period 1946–55. Grouped by the size of net assets the firms were further classified according to industry, with ten industries having a sufficient number of firms for statistical analysis. Hymer and Pashigian have found that average growth rates did not differ for firms of different sizes but that there was a systematic tendency for variance to decrease with size.[91] Thus, the American study based on individual industries agrees with Singh and Whittington on the relation between the dispersion of growth rates and size but not on that between average growth rates and size, whereas Samuels's study agrees with them on the relation between average growth rates and size but not on that between the dispersion of growth rates and size. Possible explanations for the differences are that the US study is concerned only with the largest firms and that Samuels's study is based on firms in the aggregate, whereas Singh and Whittington have embraced a much wider size range and disaggregated to the industry level.

The general conclusions to be drawn from empirical studies on the relationship between growth and size are:

(1) there is probably a tendency for larger firms to have a somewhat higher average growth-rate than smaller firms, although the relationship is rather weak; and
(2) larger firms experience less variability of growth rates than do smaller firms.

Profitability and size
Before discussing the relationship between growth and profitability the possibility of a relationship between profitability and size is now considered. Samuels and Smyth have examined a sample of 186 continuing UK companies in manufacturing, distribution and mining for the ten years 1954–63. The firms were grouped into ten size classes on the basis of net assets. Samuels and Smyth have found that profit rates and the size of firm were inversely related, as were the variability of profit rates within a size class and the size of firm.[92]

The results of the Singh and Whittington study are based on more extensive data and a larger number of tests. They have used two measures of profitability: the pretax rate of return on net assets, and the post-tax rate of return on equity assets, the former of which is classified according to opening size in Table 4.4. On the basis of these and other results Singh and Whittington have found that in general the degree of dispersion of profitability decreased with size of firm, which agrees with the results of Samuels and Smyth. They have also detected a slight tendency for profitability to fall with size; but since the differences in average profitability between size classes were on the whole not statistically significant, they have concluded that there was no systematic relationship

Table 4.4 *Rate of return, pretax on net assets,[a] by opening size class: all firms, 1948–60.*

Opening size of net assets	No. of firms	Mean rate of return (%)	Standard deviation of rate of return (%)
< £250,000	483	17·0	9·8
< £500,000	464	17·1	7·5
< £1,000,000	389	17·4	8·1
< £2,000,000	271	16·7	9·0
< £4,000,000	167	16·1	6·6
> £4,000,000	181	15·8	5·4
All sizes	1,955	16·6	8·5

Source: G. Whittington, *The Prediction of Profitability,* University of Cambridge Department of Applied Economics, Occasional Paper 22 (Cambridge, Cambridge UP, 1971), table 3.5, p. 45.

Note:
(a) Rate of return equals trading profits and investment and other income, net of depreciation and charges for current liabilities, but before taxation, long-run interest payments and payments to minority interests in subsidiaries.

between average profitability and size. Thus, although their findings on this point are in the same direction as those of Samuels and Smyth, they cannot be regarded as positive support for them. Singh and Whittington, in any case, have suggested two reasons why their results are probably biased in favour of smaller firms appearing to have a higher rate of return than larger. First, loss-making companies, which were excluded from some of their tests (but not from Table 4.4), tend to be small. Second, the revaluation of assets, which has the effect of reducing the rate of return, tends to be concentrated in the larger companies.[93]

It may be that the apparent conflict between Samuels and Smyth (average profitability and the size of firm are inversely related) and Singh and Whittington (they are not) is due to lack of disaggregation to the industry level in the former study.[94] As in the case of growth there are strong arguments for conducting studies of profitability on an industry basis: the extent of scale economies and monopoly power is likely to differ between industries; demand conditions are unlikely to be the same in all industries; and errors due to differences in accounting conventions, especially those relating to asset valuation, are likely to be smaller within an industry than between industries.[95] Therefore, it is not surprising that, while 'across-the-board' studies have found contradictory negative, positive or parabolic relationships, 'when individual industry groups are analysed, any systematic relationship between mean class profitability and size disappears'.[96] However, it is worth noting that the study by Meeks and Whittington referred to above has found that the 'giants'' average rate of return and variability of profit rate were both lower than those of the 'rest'.[97]

The general conclusions to be drawn from empirical studies on the relationship between profitability and size, then, are:

(1) while there is no systematic relationship between average rates of return and the size of firm, there is perhaps a tendency for average profitability to decline with size; and
(2) larger firms in general experience less variability of profit rates than do smaller firms.

Before leaving these two relationships it is interesting to note that the largest firms on average have similar growth and profitability records irrespective of industry:

> There was found to be a remarkable similarity in the growth and profitability experience of large firms (as opposed to small or medium-sized firms) in different industries in every time period. The inter-industry differences in the post-tax profitability and rates of growth of large firms (with opening net assets greater than £2 million) were negligible in every period.[98]

This is not altogether surprising and will be taken up again later.

Growth and profitability
The evidence considered so far in this section suggests that there is a weak tendency for average growth rates to increase and for average profit rates to decrease as firm size increases and a more marked tendency for the variability of these rates to decline with size. These findings are of some theoretical significance since they are perhaps more consistent with the emphasis of the theories of the growth of the firm, discussed in sections 4.2 and 4.3, than with the emphasis on optimum size of the traditional theory. On the basis of the Downie–Penrose–Marris approach a dual relationship between growth and profitability would be expected to exist. On the one hand, profits are necessary for growth; hence, the more profitable the firm, the faster the maximum possible rate of growth will be. On the other hand, growth eats into profits; hence, the faster the rate of growth, the less profitable the firm will be. Thus, growth depends on profitability, and profitability depends on growth.

In empirical studies:

> . . . when we examine the contemporaneous long-run average growth–profitability records of a cross-section of corporations, we should expect to find a scatter engendered by the simultaneous operation of the two relationships discussed above, which, in simple linear form, may be formulated as

$$G = \alpha + \beta P + \epsilon$$

and

$$P = \gamma + \delta G + \mu.[99]$$

As noted earlier, the testing of comprehensive models embodying these two relationships, in which growth and profitability are simultaneously determined, has so far not proved possible. Singh and Whittington have explicitly disclaimed attempting to do so.[100] They have, however, examined the relationship between the two variables on the assumption that profitability explains growth. Before considering their results, Tables 4.5 and 4.6 respectively set out growth classified by the rate of return and the rate of return (on both net and equity assets) classified by growth for the aggregate of the 364 companies in four manufacturing industries covered in their earlier study.[101] These two tables provide *prima facie* evidence for the existence of a strong positive association between growth and profitability.

Several regression models were tried in a more sophisticated analysis of the relationship. A simple linear equation relating growth to profitability was found most appropriate, with post-tax return on equity assets providing a better 'explanation' of growth than pretax return on net assets. On average, profitability was found to 'explain' about 50 per cent of the variation in growth rates between firms, a 1 percentage point increase in post-tax equity return being associated with a 0·7 percentage point increase in growth rate. Both the degree of 'explanation' (R^2) and the regression coefficient varied considerably between industries and over time.[102]

There can be no doubt, on the basis of these results, that a strong positive relationship existed between growth and profitability. There was no obvious evidence to show a negative relationship appearing beyond a certain point. At first sight this may seem to conflict with the expectations of the growth

Table 4.5   *Growth by the pretax rate of return on net assets:[a] aggregate of four industries,[b] 1948–60.*

Pretax rate of return on net assets (%)	Growth of net assets (%)
< 0	−4·4
< 5·0	−0·2
< 10·0	3·5
< 15·0	6·1
< 20·0	7·7
< 25·0	9·7
< 30·0	11·0
< 35·0	13·5
< 40·0	16·1
> 40·0	17·0
All firms	8·0

Source: A. Singh and G. Whittington, *Growth, Profitability and Valuation,* University of Cambridge Department of Applied Economics, Occasional Paper 7 (Cambridge, Cambridge UP, 1968), appendix F, table F. 5, pp. 260–1.

Notes:
(a) See notes to Tables 4.2 and 4.4.
(b) 'Non-electrical engineering', 'Clothing and footwear', 'Food' and 'Tobacco'.

Table 4.6 *Rate of return, pretax on net assets and post-tax on equity assets, by growth:[a] aggregate of four industries,[b] 1948–60.*

Growth of net assets (%)	Pretax rate of return on net assets (%)	Post-tax rate of return on equity assets (%)
< −5·0	2·0	−5·1
< −2·5	7·6	3·0
< 0	8·9	−5·2
< 2·5	9·3	3·9
< 5·0	13·5	5·6
< 7·5	18·2	9·3
< 10·0	20·4	10·7
< 15·0	23·4	12·4
< 20·0	26·3	14·6
< 20·0	30·3	17·1
All firms	18·7	9·3

Source: A. Singh and G. Whittington, *Growth, Profitability and Valuation,* University of Cambridge Department of Applied Economics, Occasional Paper 7 (Cambridge, Cambridge UP, 1968), appendix F, table F. 3, pp. 256–7.

Notes:
(a) See notes to Tables 4.2 and 4.4.
(b) 'Non-electrical engineering', 'Clothing and footwear', 'Food' and 'Tobacco'.

theorists discussed above. However, there are convincing reasons for expecting that in the observed relationship between the two variables the positive effect of profitability on growth $[G=f(P)]$ will dominate the negative effect of growth on profitability $[P=\Phi(G)]$. This is because the first relationship, which is essentially the supply-of-capital function, will depend largely on conditions in the capital market and will be relatively independent of the individual firm; whereas the second relationship, which is essentially the demand-growth function, will depend on conditions that are more specific to the firm (notably the quality of management) and will hence tend to be much more variable between firms.[103] The point is illustrated in Figure 4.4. The supply-of-capital curve is assumed to be the same for all firms, and three demand-growth curves are shown, relating to firms facing different market conditions or with different levels of managerial quality and hence internal efficiency. Points P_1 to P_3 and G_1 to G_3 indicate the maximum attainable profit and growth rates respectively. Each firm will locate itself on its demand growth curve somewhere between P and G in accordance with the objectives of those running it (see section 4.3). Thus, the individual profit-growth combinations will fall within the shaded area, and the cross-sectional relationship observed between profitability and growth will tend to be positive.

Marris has argued quite explicitly that the dominant variation between firms is with respect to efficiency, with greater efficiency enabling both a higher growth rate and a higher rate of return. The effects of differences in efficiency will swamp any inverse relationship between growth and profitability:

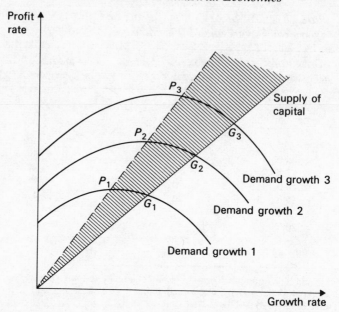

Fig. 4.4　Cross-sectional relationship between profitability and growth.

'In actual data we shall see mainly a distinction between "efficient" firms and less efficient firms; the former will tend to show higher growth rates, higher profit rates.'[104] Tentative support for this conclusion is to be found in Radice's comparison of the growth–profitability performance of owner-controlled and management-controlled companies, using as his sample all firms with 1963 net assets greater than £5 million in 'Electrical engineering', 'Textiles' and 'Food'. On the basis of managerialist reasoning about motivation and assuming similarity of environmental conditions, owner-controlled firms may be expected to achieve, on average, higher profit rates and lower growth rates than management-controlled firms. In fact Radice has found that owner-controlled firms tended to have higher profit rates *and* higher growth rates. One possible explanation for this is clearly better management quality and hence greater internal efficiency.[105]

The general conclusion to be drawn is that there is a strong positive relationship between growth and profitability, which is, nevertheless, subject to considerable variation between industries and over time. However, the simultaneous existence of a negative relationship between profitability and growth cannot be ruled out since there are good reasons for expecting the negative to be dominated by the positive relationship in actual cross-sectional data. A further conclusion relates to the position of large firms. It has already been noted that large firms enjoyed a similar growth and profitability experience irrespective of industry in a way that medium-sized and small firms did not. The same was found to be true of the relationship between growth and profitability in large firms:

... for these large firms, and at least for the industries which we have examined, the available data do not reject the hypothesis that growth–profitability observations in different industries and over different time periods come from the same basic population or the same statistical structure. This finding lends support to a tentative conclusion of the last chapter that as far as the analysis of growth and profitability is concerned, the conventional industrial classification is less relevant for the largest firms.[106]

THE CHARACTERISTICS OF TAKEN-OVER FIRMS

Although no direct 'test' of the theory of the growth of the firm set out in sections 4.2 and 4.3 has yet proved possible, studies of taken-over companies provide indirect evidence. It will be recalled that the stock market plays a central role in theories of the corporate firm. When the traditional theory is extended to embrace the corporate firm in a growth context, profit maximisation is interpreted as the maximisation of the present stock-market value of the firm. When managerial motivation of the sort advocated by Marris is postulated, the threat of takeover is the major restraint on growth-seeking managerial behaviour. Conflict between the two types of theory largely stems from different assumptions about the nature of the 'selection mechanism' in the capital market. As Singh has put it:

> Given oligopolistic conditions in many of the product markets in which the large modern corporation typically operates, an essential difference between the neoclassical theory and the new theories of the firm thus turns on the degree of efficacy of the capital-market discipline. In the limiting case, when this discipline is perfect, the neoclassical theory and Marris' theory, for instance, will yield the same predictions.[107]

Since most quoted companies that disappear 'die' as a result of being taken over, a study of the characteristics of taken-over firms may throw light on the degree of severity of stock market discipline.

In order to establish that acquisition *is* the most frequent reason why firms disappear, Table 4.7 sets out the causes of death of the 1,052 companies listed in Table 4.1 as having died. The picture that emerges for the period 1948–60 has also been confirmed for the two subperiods 1948–54 and 1954–60; in all periods acquisition was easily the most frequent cause of death. It is only in recent decades that acquisition has replaced liquidation as the principal cause of death. Singh has suggested that the relative stability of the level of economic activity since the Second World War and the greater ease of acquisition due to widely dispersed shareholding are probably responsible for this change, and he has predicted that the trend will continue.[108]

The most authoritative work on the characteristics of taken-over and non-taken-over firms in the United Kingdom has been undertaken by Singh, covering the periods 1955–60 and 1967–70.[109] A very detailed comparison of the two categories of firm in the earlier period established that non-taken-over firms had on average a higher valuation ratio and growth and profit rate, were larger and had a lower retention ratio. However, although the average

Table 4.7 *Cause of death of companies in manufacturing, construction, distribution and miscellaneous services quoted on UK stock exchanges, 1948–60.*

Cause of death	No.	%
(1) Acquisition	709	67·4
(2) Liquidation	92	8·7
(3) Other[a]	251	23·9
(4) Total deaths	1,052	100·0

Source: G. Whittington, *The Prediction of Profitability,* University of Cambridge Department of Applied Economics, Occasional Paper 22 (Cambridge, Cambridge UP, 1971), table 1.4, p. 9.

Note:
(a) In general other covers withdrawals from the population, for various reasons, of companies that nevertheless continued to exist.

values of these variables were 'significantly' different, the extent of overlap between the two groups of firms was so great that none of the variables could be deemed a 'good' discriminator.[110] The implications of this for the theory that the threat of takeover is expressed as a valuation ratio constraint have been commented on by Singh thus:

> In a strong form the constraint has been expressed as follows: unless a firm achieves a certain minimal valuation ratio it is almost bound to be acquired, but once it has achieved this value it is more or less safe from acquisition. However, in some versions of his model, Marris has expressed the valuation ratio constraint in a weaker form, *viz* the higher the valuation ratio of a firm, the lower the chance of its being acquired.
>
> The results of our investigation indicate that although the valuation ratio of the taken-over firms is significantly less than that of the non-taken-over firms, there is a very considerable degree of overlap between the two groups. In the period studied, there was a relatively large number of acquired firms with above average valuation ratios, and a similarly large proportion of non-taken-over firms whose valuation ratios were below the average for their respective industries. This evidence clearly refutes the valuation-ratio constraint in the strong form described above. It also suggests that the inverse relationship between the valuation ratio and the probability of take-over is likely to be very weak. Thus the achievement of a relatively high valuation ratio, far from guaranteeing a firm against takeover, may not even greatly reduce its chance of being acquired.[111]

It is of considerable interest that an even stronger conclusion has been drawn by Newbould, based on a study of quoted UK companies in 1967 and 1968 for which a final bid of £10 million or more was made.[112] There were seventy-four 'victim' firms, of which sixty-four were taken over and ten were not. The valuation ratios of the victim firms were compared with those of the bidding

Table 4.8 *Relative valuation ratios: victim firms (quoted companies valued at £10 million or more), bidding firms and industry averages, 1967–8.*

	No. of firms	% with valuation ratio:			Total (%)
		<1	<2	>2	
Taken-over firms	74	15	43	42	100
Bidding firms	92	11	47	42	100
Industry averages	74	9	69	22	100

Source: G. D. Newbould, *Management and Merger Activity* (Liverpool, Guthstead, 1970), tables 3.2 and 3.3, pp. 102 and 104.

firms (sometimes more than one per victim) and with industry averages, as set out in Table 4.8. The valuation ratio of the successful bidding firm exceeded that of its victim in thirty-three cases and was below it in thirty-one. The valuation ratio of actual victim firms exceeded the industry average in thirty-eight cases and was below it in twenty-six. The picture was not affected by inclusion of the firms involved in the ten failed bids; nor was it affected when genuine takeover raids (twenty-seven) were distinguished from other forms of merger. In Newbould's words: 'The conclusion is that the valuation ratio . . . is irrelevant to the incidence of mergers in 1967 and 1968.'[113]

The only contrary result reported is by Kuehn, based on a study of 1,554 takeovers of quoted UK companies during the period 1957–69. He has found a strong inverse relationship between the valuation ratio and the probability of acquisition.[114] However, Singh has drawn attention to the fact that Kuehn has measured the valuation ratios (and sizes) of taken-over and non-taken-over firms over different time periods: one year before takeover for the former, but the average of the thirteen-year period for the latter. When allowance is made for the biases thus introduced into Kuehn's study, the available evidence suggests that the degree of overlap between the valuation ratios of taken-over and non-taken-over firms was, if anything, greater in the late 1960s than in the earlier period.[115]

If the valuation ratio is of little help in discriminating between taken-over and non-taken-over firms, neither at first sight are the other potential discriminators. Singh has found that all the more important discriminators showed a markedly greater degree of overlap between the two groups of firms in 1967–70 than in 1955–60. However, two variables – size and profitability – were thought to merit further investigation at a disaggregated level in order to test for non-linear relationships between them and the probability of acquisition. Table 4.9 sets out the relationship between the relative size of a firm within its own industry and its probability of being acquired within one year. In the period 1967–70 the overall probability was 6·7 per cent compared with 3·4 per cent for 1955–60. In both periods firms in the smallest size quintile had a lower probability of being taken over within one year than those in the second quintile, and in the later period their probability of being acquired was lowest of all. This relative immunity of the smallest quoted companies

Table 4.9   *Average probability of a company being taken over within a year for each size quintile, and for the top 10 and 5 per cent: all industries, 1967–70 and 1955–60.*[a]

	Size category							All companies
	Q_1	Q_2	Q_3	Q_4	Top 20%	Top 10%	Top 5%	
1967–70 probability of acquisition (%)	3·0	10·1	9·7	6·5	4·5	2·6	1·4	6·7
1955–60 probability of acquisition (%)	3·6	4·2	3·5	3·1	2·5	1·6	0·8	3·4

Source: A. Singh, 'Take-overs, economic natural selection and the theory of the firm: evidence from the post-war United Kingdom experience', *Economic Journal,* vol. 85 (September 1975), table 4, p. 505.

Note:
(a)   Figures for 1955–60 are only roughly comparable with those for 1967–70.

was probably due to a greater incidence of family-controlled firms or of firms with an inactive market in their shares. From the second quintile upwards the probability of acquisition declined monotonically with size, moderately at first and then more sharply once the larger firms of the top 20 per cent were reached. Thus, an important curvilinear relationship between the two variables has emerged, reinforcing the general finding of earlier studies that among large companies size and the probability of acquisition are inversely related.[116]

Table 4.10 sets out the relationship between the relative profitability of a firm within its own industry and its probability of being acquired within one year. During 1967–70 the probability of acquisition was roughly the same until the level of profitability of the fourth decile was reached, when it fell significantly; thereafter, it remained much the same. Thus, a firm in the highest profitability decile had only a slightly lower chance of being taken over within one year than a firm with average profitability. In the earlier period the probability of acquisition fell significantly at the profitability level of the third decile; then it remained much the same until the tenth decile, when it again declined.

Since it has been established that there is no strong systematic relationship between size and average profitability, the evidence on the relationship of size and profitability to the probability of acquisition must be considered together. Singh's results for 1967–70 essentially confirm the conclusion of his earlier work about the best strategy for survival and the efficacy of stock market discipline:

For most small firms with a poor record of long-term profitability, there appears to be little effective choice if they wish to *appreciably* reduce the danger of take-over, except to attempt to improve their profits performance to a level above the average for the industry. The alternative course of increasing size is unlikely to be of much use to such firms, since they would

Table 4.10 *Average probability of a company being taken over within a year for each two-year average-profitability decile: all industries, 1967–70 and 1955–60.[a]*

	Profitability decile										All companies
	Lowest								Highest		
	1	2	3	4	5	6	7	8	9	10	
1967–70 probability of acquisition (%)	8·6	11·0	9·8	4·3	5·5	7·4	4·9	6·1	4·9	6·1	6·9
1955–60 probability of acquisition (%)	7·4	5·3	2·9	4·4	4·0	3·4	3·4	2·7	2·9	1·7	3·8

Source: A. Singh, 'Take-overs, economic natural selection and the theory of the firm: evidence from the post-war United Kingdom experience', *Economic Journal*, vol. 85 (September 1975), table 5, p. 506.

Note:
(a) Figures for 1955–60 are only roughly comparable with those for 1967–70.

have to become several times larger before they could attain any significant reduction in the chances of acquisition . . .

On the other hand, the results of this investigation suggest that the best strategy for survival of a large firm or a largish medium-sized firm . . . with a poor record of long-term profitability might be to increase its size. As in the case of small firms, these firms would require a very large proportional increase in their rate of profit to appreciably reduce the danger of take-over. But unlike the small firms, since the probability of acquisition for these firms is known to fall fairly sharply and continuously with an increase in firm size, they might find it relatively much easier to increase their chances of survival by becoming bigger . . .

To sum up, the take-over mechanism on the stock market, although it provides a measure of discipline for small firms with below average profitability, does not seem to meet the motivational requirements of the orthodox theory of the firm as far as the large firms are concerned. The evidence indicates that these firms are not compelled to maximise or to vigorously pursue profits in order to reduce the danger of take-over, since they can in principle achieve their objective by becoming bigger without increasing the rate of profit.[117]

This judgement is reinforced by the fact that, while takeover discipline on smaller unprofitable firms was probably as strong in 1967–70 as in 1955–60, overall and especially for large firms it was, if anything, weaker, since the differences between taken-over and non-taken-over firms were smaller.[118]

The implications of these conclusions may be pursued a little further. Updated versions of the traditional theory receive little support from the finding that the stock-market selection process allows considerable scope for firms, especially large firms, to survive without maximising profits. On the other hand, although the survival value of size, and hence growth, appears to lend support to the managerialist position on motivation, the valuation ratio does not appear to play the constraining role assigned to it in Marris-type models. Neither type of theory emerges with flying colours. However, the special position of large firms once again stands out clearly in the empirical evidence. The possible significance of this consistent finding is taken up in the conclusion to this chapter, which now follows.

4.5 CONCLUSION

This chapter has been primarily concerned with corporate growth. However, the influence of large size, while not expected on the basis of the theory, thrusts itself to the fore in the empirical work. It seems clear that there is no 'optimum' size in the traditional static sense. That being so, the theory of the growth of the firm has regarded size as incidental to growth rather than growth as incidental to size. The basic structure of the economic theory of the growth of the firm has been revealed as a dynamic constrained-maximisation problem in which the constraints are imposed by the exogenous characteristics of the 'superenvironment'. The firm is active with respect to its immediate environment but passive with respect to the superenvironment. It is the latter environment that determines the costs of growth, with dynamic diminishing returns playing the same constraining role as static decreasing returns play in the traditional theory's analysis of perfect competition.

A distinction must be drawn between the steady state framework of Marris's economic theory of the growth of the firm and the apparently similar theories of Downie and Penrose. Both of the latter have eschewed any attempt at constructing a microequilibrium model within the constrained maximisation paradigm. Downie's object of study has been not the firm but the competitive process, the essential characteristics of which are oligopolistic interdependence and continuous change. Penrose has been concerned to analyse the unique productive opportunity of each firm, stressing the importance of managerial perception and learning and the developmental character of the firm's behaviour. Neither has been prepared to be confined within the restricting paradigm of constrained maximisation, which seeks to determine today's action on the basis of tomorrow's environment rather than recognising that tomorrow's environment is partly determined by today's action. The logical flaw on which steady-state partial-equilibrium permanent-growth models rest is the assumption that there exists a superenvironment that depends on 'the existence and behaviour of other firms' but is independent with respect to oligopolistic interdependence and exogenous with respect to permanent growth. The conclusions of Chapter 3 on the dubious value of microequilibrium analysis receive further support from an examination of growth models. It will be noted from section 4.3 that once again the method of analysis chosen is not independent of normative purpose.

The empirical evidence confirms the existence of a strong relationship between growth and profitability. Moreover, the two most striking conclusions to emerge are the apparent irrelevance of the valuation ratio to the incidence of takeover and the special position of large firms. While there may be a weak tendency for average growth rates to increase and an even weaker tendency for average profitability to decrease with firm size, there seems to be no doubt that larger firms experience less variability in their growth and profitability performance than do smaller firms. Furthermore, the growth and profitability experience of large firms is much more independent of industry than is the case for small and medium-sized firms, and this is also true for the relationship between growth and profitability. It has frequently been suggested that the relative independence of large firms from the performance characteristics of specific industries is due to the diversified nature of their activities, and there is probably something in this. A greater degree of diversification may also be responsible for the smaller variability of profit rate over time experienced by large firms as compared with that experienced by small firms, although doubts have been raised on this score.[119]

However, other aspects of the differential experience of large and small firms must also be considered. Relative mobility, the proportion of non-growing firms and the probabilities of birth and death (notably death by acquisition) all decline with size. While diversification is certainly more important in larger firms, it is likely to be only one component of a general competitive advantage conferred by large size. Of course, this is not to suggest that there is a continuous relationship between size and competitive advantage; rather, it is to suggest that there exists a threshold above which firms on average enjoy advantages by comparison with those below. Whittington, in a special investigation of the relationship between size and profitability in firms with assets greater than £4 million, has found that the tendency for the variability of profit rate to fall with size was much less pronounced than was the case for smaller firms.[120] It may well be that a theory of the competitive process as a whole needs to distinguish between big business, i.e. the oligopolistic sector, and small business, i.e. the competitive sector, with the relationship between the sectors of some importance. Once again attention is directed away from the analysis of microequilibrium towards that of the system as a whole.

FURTHER READING

The original theoretical works considered in this chapter are those by Downie,[8] Penrose[8] and Marris.[8] More advanced material is to be found in Marris and Wood.[1] The most comprehensive empirical work on the growth of firms in the United Kingdom is that undertaken at the University of Cambridge Department of Applied Economics by Singh and Whittington.[74] Singh's 1975 article is an excellent discussion of the significance of postwar takeover experience for the theory of the firm.[75]

NOTES AND REFERENCES

1 J. Eatwell, 'Growth, profitability and size: the empirical evidence', in R. Marris and A. Wood (eds), *The Corporate Economy* (London, Macmillan, 1971), appendix A, p. 399.

2 H. Radice, 'Control type, profitability and growth in large firms: an empirical study', *Economic Journal,* vol. 81 (September 1971), p. 561.

3 Cf. R. Marris, 'An introduction to theories of corporate growth', in Marris and Wood, op. cit. (n. 1), ch. 1, pp. 4–5.

4 R. Marris, 'Why economics needs a theory of the firm', *Economic Journal,* vol. 82 (March 1972), supplement, p. 325. For there to be an 'optimum' size, decreasing returns to scale must set in above a certain size; however, the empirical evidence suggests that in general firms are operating under conditions of constant or increasing returns to scale; see, for example, A. Silberston, 'Economies of scale in theory and practice', *Economic Journal,* vol. 82 (March 1972), supplement, esp. p. 376.

5 Cf. J. Williamson, 'Profit, growth and sales maximisation', *Economica,* vol. 33 (February 1966), p. 9.

6 Cf. 'Marris asserts that over time the process of selection will drive out those who maximise profits and leave those who maximise growth' (A. Singh, *Take-overs,* University of Cambridge Department of Applied Economics, Monograph 19, Cambridge, Cambridge UP, 1971, p. 9).

7 J. Downie, *The Competitive Process* (London, Duckworth, 1958), p. 29.

8 Downie, op. cit. (n. 7); E. Penrose, *The Theory of the Growth of the Firm* (Oxford, Blackwell, 1959); and R. Marris, *The Economic Theory of 'Managerial' Capitalism* (London, Macmillan, 1964).

9 Downie, op. cit. (n. 7), p. 31.

10 Downie, op. cit. (n. 7), ch. 8.

11 Penrose, op. cit. (n. 8), p. 24.

12 Penrose, op. cit. (n. 8), pp. 149–50.

13 Marris, op. cit. (n. 8), p. 113. The concept of the firm under discussion here is quite consistent with the wide scope of activities normally allowed under a company's memorandum of association.

14 Cf. Marris, op. cit. (n. 3), p. 5, where 'restraint' is preferred to 'constraint'.

15 Cf. Downie, op. cit. (n. 7), ch. 3, for the definition of efficiency used, the details of which are of no significance for the present discussion.

16 Downie, op. cit. (n. 7), p. 59.

17 See the work on innovation discussed in section 5.4. As far as is known, Downie's hypothesis about the source of innovative breakthrough has not been explicitly tested.

18 Penrose, op. cit. (n. 8), p. 29.

19 Penrose, op. cit. (n. 8), p. 25.

20 Penrose, op. cit. (n. 8), pp. 43–4.

21 Penrose, op. cit. (n. 8), p. 47.

22 Penrose, op. cit. (n. 8), pp. 67–8.

23 Penrose, op. cit. (n. 8), pp. 85–6.

24 Penrose, op. cit. (n. 8), pp. 108–9.

25 Penrose, op. cit. (n. 8), p. 105.

26 Penrose, op. cit. (n. 8), p. 145.

27 For example, W. J. Baumol, 'On the theory of the expansion of the firm', *American Economic Review,* vol. 52 (December 1962), p. 1087, n. 15; and R. Marris, 'Review' of Penrose, op. cit. (n. 8), *Economic Journal,* vol. 71 (March 1961), pp. 147–8.

28 Cf. B. J. Loasby, 'Hypothesis and paradigm in the theory of the firm', *Economic Journal,* vol. 81 (December 1971), pp. 882–3.

29 Marris, op. cit. (n. 3), pp. 4–5.

30 Marris, op. cit. (n. 8), p. 47.

31 Marris, op. cit. (n. 8), pp. 18–40.

32 Marris, op. cit. (n. 8), p. 45.

33 The sense is likely to be rather loose. For instance, a necessary assumption for a reasonable degree of accuracy is that assets are valued at replacement, not historical, cost.

34 See Marris, op. cit. (n. 8), p. 48.
35 Marris, op. cit. (n. 8), p. 120.
36 Marris, op. cit. (n. 8), p. 120.
37 Marris's concept of diversification is clearly marginalist; that is, he has postulated diminishing marginal returns to diversification in any period. Cf. R. Marris, 'A model of the "managerial" enterprise', *Quarterly Journal of Economics,* vol. 77 (May 1963), pp. 196–7.
38 Cf. Marris, op. cit. (n. 8), p. 45.
39 Penrose, op. cit. (n. 8), p. 8.
40 Penrose, op. cit. (n. 8), p. 6.
41 Cf. the analysis by Hymer and Rowthorn of oligopolistic competition between multinational corporations, discussed in section 3.3.
42 Cf. A. Wood, 'Economic analysis of the corporate economy: a survey and critique', in Marris and Wood, op. cit. (n. 1), ch. 2, pp. 43–8, for a discussion of the problems of directly estimating these models. The attempts at indirect testing referred to are examined later in this chapter.
43 Cf. Marris, op. cit. (n. 3), pp. 3–4.
44 Marris, op. cit. (n. 3), p. 13.
45 Cf. Williamson, op. cit. (n. 5), p. 2.
46 Radice, op. cit. (n. 2), pp. 547–9.
47 The model presented here, Radice's, differs from Marris's original model in that the valuation curve peaks *after* the demand growth curve. For the original, see Marris, op. cit. (n. 8), p. 255; for argumentation to the effect that Radice's version is more plausible, see S. Aaronovitch and M. Sawyer, *Big Business* (London, Macmillan, 1975), pp. 49–52.
48 Cf. Marris, op. cit. (n. 3), pp. 17–19; and Wood, op. cit. (n. 42), p. 44.
49 Marris, op. cit. (n. 3), pp. 17–18.
50 This is because the dividend is positively related to the rate of profit, which is directly related to the growth rate at low rates of growth but inversely related to it at high rates of growth.
51 Marris, op. cit. (n. 3), p. 19.
52 Cf. Wood, op. cit. (n. 42), pp. 40–1.
53 O. Williamson, 'Managerial discretion, organization form, and the multidivision hypothesis', in Marris and Wood, op. cit. (n. 1), ch. 11.
54 Williamson, op. cit. (n. 53), p. 354.
55 These characteristics are, of course, related in that some uncertainty results from interdependence. The significance of uncertainty, as opposed to risk, is considered in section 3.2 and is not discussed again here.
56 R. Marris, 'Preface for social scientists', in Marris and Wood, op. cit. (n. 1), p. xxv. The term 'quasi-firm' was first proposed by R. Heflebower, 'Observations on decentralization in large enterprises', *Journal of Industrial Economics,* vol. 9 (November 1960), pp. 7–22. It was subsequently adopted by Williamson, op. cit. (n. 53), in the context of his analysis of the M-firm.
57 See R. Marris, 'The modern corporation and economic theory', in Marris and Wood, op. cit. (n. 1), ch. 9, s. 2.
58 See Marris, op. cit. (n. 3), p. 11, n. 2. The form of the relationship envisaged here is the one represented by the demand growth curve in Figure 4.1.
59 Marris, op. cit. (n. 3), p. 10.
60 Marris, op. cit. (n. 3), p. 12.
61 Marris, op. cit. (n. 3), p. 13.
62 Marris, op. cit. (n. 3), p. 13.
63 Marris, op. cit. (n. 57), p. 280.
64 Wood, op. cit. (n. 42), p. 58. It should be noted that 'Penrose effects', i.e. the

effects of the 'managerial restraint', are explicitly excluded as a contributory factor to diminishing returns at any given moment (p. 58, n. 1).

65 Wood, op. cit. (n. 42), p. 38.

66 Sraffa's demonstration that the assumptions that are necessary to ensure the existence of a partial equilibrium are incompàtible with the assumptions of perfect competition should be recalled; see section 3.2.

67 Wood, op. cit. (n. 42), p. 56.

68 This was apparently the view of the conference whose proceedings form the content of *The Corporate Economy* (Marris and Wood, op. cit., n. 1). See Wood, op. cit. (n. 42), p. 48.

69 S. Lombardini, 'Modern monopolies in economic development', in Marris and Wood, op. cit. (n. 1), ch. 8, p. 247.

70 Marris, op. cit. (n. 56), p. xx.

71 Lombardini, op. cit. (n. 69), p. 269.

72 Cf. Wood, op. cit. (n. 42), pp. 43–7.

73 See, for example, J. Eatwell, 'Growth, profitability and size: the empirical evidence', in Marris and Wood, op. cit. (n. 1), appendix A.

74 See A. Singh and G. Whittington, *Growth, Profitability and Valuation*, University of Cambridge Department of Applied Economics, Occasional Paper 7 (Cambridge, Cambridge UP, 1968); Singh, op. cit. (n. 6); G. Whittington, *The Prediction of Profitability*, University of Cambridge Department of Applied Economics, Occasional Paper 22 (Cambridge, Cambridge UP, 1971); and A. Singh and G. Whittington, 'The size and growth of firms', *Review of Economic Studies*, vol. 42 (January 1975), pp. 15–26.

 A detailed description of the data used and their limitations is provided in Singh and Whittington, op. cit. (n. 74, 1968), appendix A, pp. 203–25. The population of companies studied covered public companies quoted on UK stock exchanges that were not consolidated subsidiaries of other quoted companies, with a few exceptions, plus a few of the larger non-quoted and private companies. There were 3,754 companies in the full population, of which thirty-seven were non-quoted and fifty-three were privately owned (Whittington, op. cit., n. 74, table 1.2, p. 7). The standardised accounts used were those prepared by the National Institute of Economic and Social Research and the Board of Trade. Although they have recognised various limitations to the accounting data, particularly as regards asset valuation, Singh and Whittington have argued that these 'need not vitiate the significance of the data for particular purposes' (Singh and Whittington, op. cit., n. 74, 1969, p. 221).

75 See G. Whittington, 'Changes in the top 100 quoted manufacturing companies in the United Kingdom, 1948 to 1968', *Journal of Industrial Economics*, vol. 21 (November 1972), pp. 17–34; A. Singh, 'Take-overs, economic natural selection, and the theory of the firm: evidence from the post-war United Kingdom experience', *Economic Journal*, vol. 85 (September 1975), pp. 497–515; and G. Meeks and G. Whittington, 'Giant companies in the United Kingdom, 1948–69', *Economic Journal*, vol. 85 (December 1975), pp. 824–43. Since 1960 the population has been restricted by the exclusion of many small firms – those with assets less than £500,000 and gross income less than £50,000 in 1960 or 1964.

76 The four industry groups used by Singh and Whittington, op. cit. (n. 74, 1968), were 'Non-electrical engineering', 'Clothing and footwear', 'Food' and 'Tobacco'. Singh, op. cit. (n. 6), has used the first three of these plus 'Electrical engineering' and 'Drink'. Whittington, op. cit. (n. 74), for the most part has used all industry groups, but for some purposes he has used these last two plus 'Vehicles', 'Clothing and footwear' and 'Food'.

77 Cf. Singh and Whittington, op. cit. (n. 74, 1968), table A.4, p. 211; and Whittington, op. cit. (n. 74), table 1.4, p. 9. For deaths, see also Table 4.8 below.

78 See Table 3.2.
79 Singh and Whittington, op. cit. (n. 74, 1968), p. 22.
80 Whittington, op. cit. (n. 74), table 2.4, p. 26.
81 Whittington, op. cit. (n. 74), p. 26.
82 Singh and Whittington, op. cit. (n. 74, 1968), tables 4.7 and 4.8, p. 87.
83 Singh and Whittington, op. cit. (n. 74, 1968), table 4.10, p. 89; and Singh and Whittington, op. cit. (n. 74, 1975), p. 23.
84 Singh and Whittington, op. cit. (n. 74, 1968), p. 113.
85 Singh and Whittington, op. cit. (n. 74, 1968), tables 4.7–4.9, pp. 87–8.
86 Broadly speaking, the absence of either type of relationship is required if the 'law of proportionate effect' or 'Gibrat's law' is to hold. This law asserts that the probability of a firm growing at a given rate is independent of its initial size. As will be clear from the subsequent text, the law does not in fact appear to hold. See Singh and Whittington, op. cit. (n. 74, 1968), ch. 4; and Eatwell, op. cit. (n. 73), pp. 400–7.
87 J. Samuels, 'Size and growth of firms', *Review of Economic Studies,* vol. 32 (1965), pp. 105–12.
88 Hymer and Pashigian, whose study is not confined to continuing companies, have stated that if it were so confined their results would be essentially the same (S. Hymer and P. Pashigian, 'Firm size and rate of growth', *Journal of Political Economy,* vol. 70, December 1962, p. 557, n. 6). Singh and Whittington, whose study was confined to continuing companies, were not able to say whether the restriction had affected their results (op. cit., n. 74, 1968, p. 90).
89 See Singh and Whittington, op. cit. (n. 74, 1968), pp. 78–80.
90 Meeks and Whittington, op. cit. (n. 75), tables 2 and 4, pp. 830 and 833.
91 Hymer and Pashigian, op. cit. (n. 88), pp. 558–9.
92 J. Samuels and D. Smyth, 'Profits, variability of profits and firm size', *Economica,* vol. 35 (May 1968), pp. 127–39.
93 See Singh and Whittington, op. cit. (n. 74, 1968), ch. 6, ss 2–3; and Whittington, op. cit. (n. 74), ch. 3, s. 6.
94 M. Barron, 'The effect of the size of the firm on profitability', *Business Ratios,* no. 1 (Spring 1967), pp. 13–15, has urged that conclusions drawn from all-industry samples be treated with a degree of scepticism.
95 See Singh and Whittington, op. cit. (n. 74, 1968), pp. 114–15.
96 Eatwell, op. cit. (n. 73), pp. 393–5.
97 Meeks and Whittington, op. cit. (n. 75), tables 3 and 4, pp. 832–3.
98 Singh and Whittington, op. cit. (n. 74, 1968), p. 145.
99 Eatwell, op. cit. (n. 73), p. 410.
100 Singh and Whittington, op. cit. (n. 74, 1968), pp. 181 and 197.
101 See note 76.
102 Singh and Whittington, op. cit. (n. 74, 1968), ch. 7, s. 2.
103 Cf. Eatwell, op. cit. (n. 73), p. 410; and Radice, op. cit. (n. 2), p. 549. Both authors have cited A. Singh and G. Whittington, *Growth, Profitability and Valuation: A Note* (Cambridge, University of Cambridge Department of Applied Economics, mimeo, 1970).
104 R. Marris, 'Profitability and growth in the individual firm', *Business Ratios,* no. 1 (Spring 1967), pp. 10–11.
105 See Radice, op. cit. (n. 2), *passim.* Radice's results are in general confirmed by Holl, although in his study the differences between the mean values of the profit rates and growth rates of the two types of firm were not statistically significant. See P. Holl, 'Effect of control type on the performance of the firm in the UK', *Journal of Industrial Economics,* vol. 23 (June 1975), pp. 257–71.
106 Singh and Whittington, op. cit. (n. 74, 1968), p. 189. The cautious tone of this

conclusion should be noted. In particular, it should be remembered that the analysis of interindustry differences was on the basis of only three industries: 'Non-electrical engineering', 'Clothing and footwear' and 'Food'.

107 Singh, op. cit. (n. 6), pp. 12–13.
108 Singh, op. cit. (n. 6), pp. 33–4. The possibility that much acquisition is of loss-making companies and, therefore, is in effect hidden liquidation is ruled out, at least for quoted companies, on the basis of an examination of the profitability record of taken-over firms.
109 Singh, op. cit. (n. 6); and Singh, op. cit. (n. 75), pp. 497–515.
110 Singh, op. cit. (n. 6), p. 133.
111 Singh, op. cit. (n. 6), p. 81.
112 G. D. Newbould, *Management and Merger Activity* (Liverpool, Guthstead, 1970), pp. 97–107.
113 Newbould, op. cit. (n. 112), p. 105.
114 D. Kuehn, *Take-overs and the Theory of the Firm* (London, Macmillan, 1975), ch. 2.
115 Singh, op. cit. (n. 75), pp. 507–8.
116 See Singh, op. cit. (n. 75), pp. 505–6. For other studies confirming the existence of an inverse relationship between size and the probability of acquisition among large firms, see Aaronovitch and Sawyer, op. cit. (n. 47), table 8.6(a), p. 186; and Whittingon, op. cit. (n. 75), table IV, p. 21. For a contrary result, see Kuehn, op. cit. (n. 114), ch. 2. However, as in the case of the valuation ratio this result must be treated with caution, given the biases imparted by the different ways in which the size of taken-over and non-taken-over firms was measured.
117 Singh, op. cit. (n. 6), pp. 142 and 144. Several possible reservations to these conclusions were considered; and the two most important, concerning the fate of taken-over management and the distinction between voluntary and involuntary takeovers, were investigated further. None of the reservations appeared likely to affect the conclusions to any extent (pp. 144–52).
118 Singh, op. cit. (n. 75), p. 511.
119 Cf. Whittington, op. cit. (n. 74), ch. 3, ss 7–8, pp. 66–72; section 8 establishes the empirical conclusion, and section 7 presents doubts as to whether diversification is responsible.
120 Whittington, op. cit. (n. 74), ch. 3, s. 5, pp. 55–9.

5 Diversification, Merger and Innovation

5.1 INTRODUCTION

One conclusion of the discussion in Chapters 3 and 4 is the need for a theory of the competitive process as a whole – for a theoretical framework within which the active attempts of oligopolistic competitors to control their environment and dominate their rivals can be analysed. A comprehensive theory of this sort remains to be constructed, but a good deal of work has been done on some aspects of business behaviour that are likely to play a part in such a theory. In this chapter three central characteristics of business behaviour are considered. Section 5.2 examines the available data on the extent of diversification, the reasons advanced for diversification and the part played by it in the competitive process. Section 5.3 is concerned with the phenomenon of merger: its extent, alternative theories of merger and its effects, particularly its role in the competitive process. Section 5.4 considers innovation, reviewing the literature on the relationship between industrial structure and innovation and concentrating on the analysis of innovation as a major weapon of competition in modern capitalism.

The chapter suffers from the absence of a comprehensive theoretical framework, which would enable the discussion to be integrated by exhibiting diversification, merger and innovation as different aspects of a single competitive process. The discussion is conducted at different levels – that of the firm, the industry or the economy as a whole – depending on the level at which the subject matter has been approached in the literature. Similarly, the perspective of the analysis varies; sometimes the activity is viewed primarily from the standpoint of the behaviour of the individual firm and sometimes from the standpoint of industrial structure. However, it is the intention throughout to focus on the way in which the aspect of business behaviour under consideration fits into the competitive process. Not surprisingly the actions and interactions of the dominant group of large oligopolists emerge as an ever present feature of that process.

5.2 DIVERSIFICATION

In an early attempt to develop a theory of diversification Fisher has referred to 'the ubiquitous multi-product firm, the characteristic, not the atypical, unit of enterprise'.[1] Diversification is now recognised as a phenomenon of great importance in the contemporary capitalist economy. At the theoretical level the traditional theory's preoccupation with the single product firm has to a considerable extent been counterbalanced by the emphasis placed on diversification in the new theories of the growth of the firm. The possible implications of increasing diversification for the competitive process have also come to the forefront of discussion.[2] However, empirical evidence on the extent of diversification in the United Kingdom is not plentiful, although the position has improved in recent years.

MEASUREMENT PROBLEMS

Conceptually, the meaning of diversification appears to present no great difficulties. Amey has defined it as 'the spreading of its operations by a business over dissimilar economic activities'.[3] However, what are to count as significantly dissimilar activities are not given independently of the type of firm and the context in which the firm operates. On the basis of her concept of areas of specialisation Penrose has distinguished several different types of diversification: within an existing technological base or market area; into a new technological base or market area; and into a new technological base and market area.[4] It is clear that the extent of diversification will vary with the 'width' of the activity – the industry, market or product definition adopted. In practice the definition used in the relevant national Census of Production has normally been adopted since these censuses have provided most of the data for diversification studies.

A further problem arises over the way in which diversification is to be measured. The two most commonly used measures are the proportion of activity undertaken outside the firm's primary industry and the number of industries in which the firm is active. The first method indicates the relative importance of non-primary activities but gives no indication of the range of activities undertaken. The second method conveys the full extent of distinct activities but may be misleading if a high proportion of the activities comprises relatively small activities. In order to overcome these shortcomings various summary measures combining both aspects of diversification have been proposed. Since the major study of diversification in the United Kingdom is that by Utton, the measure

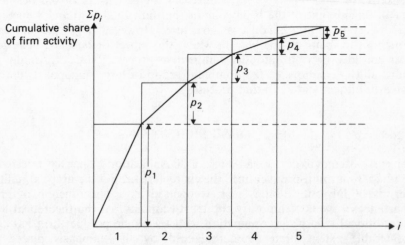

Fig. 5.1   Enterprise cumulative diversification curve.

that he has used is now outlined. It is based on the 'enterprise cumulative diversification curve' shown in Figure 5.1 and is defined as twice the area above [*sic*] the curve. The diversification index can be expressed as

$$W = 2 \sum_{i=1}^{n} ip_i - 1$$

where p_i is the proportion of the firm's activity in the ith industry and n is the number of industries in which the firm is active. It is a weighted average with the different activities weighted by their relative importance as indicated by their rank. It will equal 1 for a completely specialised industry and can be interpreted as a 'numbers equivalent', with, for example, $W = 4$ meaning that the firm is diversified to an extent equivalent to a firm that is equally active in four industries.[5]

THE EXTENT OF DIVERSIFICATION

Studies of the extent of diversification in the United Kingdom are based on the Census of Production for various years. Enterprises are classified to the industry that accounts for the largest proportion of their employment. 'Specialist' firms are active only in their primary industry, whereas 'diversified' firms, although classified to their primary industry, are also active in one or more secondary industries. Table 5.1 sets out the ratio of secondary to total output, averaged over manufacturing industry as a whole, as estimated in three different studies. Although in both the studies that have examined changes over time the extent of diversification was found to increase, the actual degree of diversification measured by Sawyer and Hassid for 1963 differed markedly, being 19·3 and 14 per cent respectively. This is due to differences in the industry definition used. In the 1958 and 1963 censuses enterprises were classified to fifty-one manufacturing industries of a breadth somewhere between Standard Industrial Classification (SIC) Order (two-digit) and Minimum List Heading (three-digit) industries. The 1968 census classified enterprises to seventeen manufacturing Orders (two-digit industries) and provided summary 1963 data on a comparable basis. It is this broader definition of primary industry that is responsible for the lower degree of diversification in 1963 shown in the later study.[6]

Using unpublished data provided by the Business Statistics Office, Utton has estimated the extent of diversification among the 200 largest UK manufacturing enterprises in 1974. Each firm was classified to one of fourteen SIC Orders (two-digit industries), and each firm's local units[7] were classified to one of 121 SIC Minimum List Headings (three-digit industries). Classification was on the basis of the Order or Minimum List Heading that accounted for the largest proportion of employment. The average share of total employment accounted for by the 200 firms' primary three-digit industries was 57 per cent, the average for their three largest industries was 80 per cent, and for subsequent industries average employment shares were below 10 per cent. Since each three-digit industry is fairly narrowly defined, Utton has judged that firms were on the whole rather more specialised than might have been expected, and this conclusion was strengthened by the extent of diversification

Table 5.1   *Percentage ratio of secondary to total output: average for UK manufacturing industry, 1958–68.*[a]

Study	1958	1963	1968
Amey	14·2		
Sawyer	14·6	19·3	
Hassid		14·0	16·9

Source: L. R. Amey, 'Diversified manufacturing business', *Journal of the Royal Statistical Society,* Series A, vol. 127, Pt 2 (1964);

M. C. Sawyer, 'Concentration in British manufacturing industry', *Oxford Economic Papers,* new series, vol. 23 (November 1971), p. 367, n. 1; and

J. Hassid, 'Recent evidence on conglomerate diversification in UK manufacturing industry', *Manchester School,* vol. 43 (December 1975), table 1, p. 375.

Note:
(a) Enterprises employing 100 or fewer were excluded from the data on which the studies have been based.

indicated by the W-index. The weighted average of W for manufacturing industry as a whole was 4·39; that is, the average manufacturing firm was diversified to an extent equivalent to a firm whose employment was shared equally between about four three-digit industries. Four of the fourteen Orders had $W > 5$, namely: 'Coal and petroleum products' combined with 'Chemicals and allied products', 9·12; 'Textiles', 6·69; 'Metal manufacture', 5·87; and 'Electrical engineering', 5·13. In the first three of these there is reason to suppose that some of the secondary industries represented vertical integration rather than diversification. The three least diversified orders were: 'Vehicles', 1·65; 'Instrument engineering', 1·69; and 'Shipbuilding and marine engineering', 2·98.

It is important to remember the difference made by the measure of diversification used. Hassid, like Utton, has found 'Metal manufacture' and 'Coal and petroleum products' at the head of his list of the most diversified industries, as measured by the ratio of secondary to total output in 1968. However, he has also found 'Electrical engineering' and 'Instrument engineering' to have the same extent of diversification, whereas Utton, using his W-index and data disaggregated to the three-digit rather than the two-digit level, has found the former among the most and the latter among the least diversified.[8]

While recognising both the necessary arbitrariness inherent in the studies discussed in this section and the formidable problems that arise in seeking to assess the economic significance of their results, it is clear that diversification is an important and growing phenomenon. This conclusion is strengthened by the fact that diversification appears to be particularly characteristic of large firms.

DIVERSIFICATION AND THE LARGE FIRM

In the two pioneering studies of diversification, by Gort for the United States

Table 5.2 *Diversification and size among the 200 largest manufacturing firms in the United Kingdom, 1974.*

Firms of rank	Mean	Diversification, W Maximum	Minimum
1– 50	3·85	14·29	1·00
51–100	3·33	16·67	1·00
101–150	2·94	12·50	1·00
151–200	2·63	8·33	1·00
1–200	3·23	16·67	1·00

Source: M. A. Utton, 'Large firm diversification in British manufacturing industry', *Economic Journal,* vol. 87 (March 1977), table 3, p. 106.

and Amey for the United Kingdom, it was established that diversification is strongly associated with firm size,[9] and this has been confirmed in more recent work. For instance, Hassid has found that in UK manufacturing industry in 1968 the average ratio of secondary to total output increased systematically with size, from 3 per cent for firms with 100–499 employees to 22 per cent for firms employing 5,000 or more. Larger firms, with 1,000 or more employees, accounted for over 90 per cent of the output of diversified manufacturing firms and were virtually the only firms active in more than three secondary industries.[10]

Utton has examined the relationship between diversification and firm size within the 200 largest manufacturing firms in 1974. His results are reproduced in Table 5.2 and show the mean value of the *W*-index of diversification increasing consistently with rank group. However, within each group there was considerable variation in the degree of diversification, as is evident from the maximum and minimum values. It will be noted that the most diversified firm, to an extent equivalent to operating equally in 16·67 three-digit industries, fell within the second rank group and that in each group there was at least one firm that operated in only one three-digit industry.

Thus, there is general agreement that diversification increases with firm size. However, it may be that among the largest firms the relationship between diversification and size, although still present, is not very strong. This is an interesting possibility since it once again suggests that the very largest firms may be in a class of their own, with characteristics significantly different from those of smaller firms.

REASONS FOR DIVERSIFICATION

Growing recognition of diversification as a widespread phenomenon has been accompanied by attempts to develop theoretical explanations for it and, less frequently, attempts to examine the hypotheses advanced in the light of the empirical evidence available. The essence of the theoretical problem has been seen as the specification of circumstances in which the objectives of the firm can be better achieved by increasing the range of activities in which it is engaged. The principal objectives proposed have been survival, profitability, growth and some combination of these. Not surprisingly, therefore, the major reasons suggested for diversification have been the pursuit of stability, profitability and growth. What circumstances may make it more attractive, in terms of these criteria, for a firm to extend the range of its activities rather than to concentrate on its existing operations?

Stability

A firm may seek to mitigate the effects of cyclical instability by spreading its activities over industries that reach their peak at different phases of the cycle or, alternatively, by concentrating on industries characterised by minimal cyclical variation. There is, however, no *a priori* reason why increased diversification should increase stability. The stabilising effect of a diversification on a firm's overall position can only be judged in the light of the cyclical characteristics of its existing activities.

Since diversification is most frequent in large firms it may be that longer term considerations than cyclical instability are more important. Concentration on a single product or a narrow range of closely related products makes a firm more dependent on the fortunes of a single market area and thus more vulnerable to unexpected adverse changes. Diversification, in principle, enables such risks to be pooled, although there is always the danger of diffuseness setting in. Of course, changes in demand are frequently predictable within broad limits, with many products having a more-or-less certainly known life cycle. A firm's stability may be increased if it is able to operate products at differing stages of their life cycle and may be further increased if it follows the same policy with respect to industries.

Profitability

The most obvious circumstances in which a firm may be able to achieve a higher level of profitability by diversifying than by concentrating on its existing activities occur when its current operations are in relatively stagnant or declining industries. However, it may be that a firm possesses unused specialist resources or services that give it a competitive edge relative to other potential entrants or existing firms in the industry that it proposes to enter. If so, it may be more profitable for the firm to enter the new industry than to concentrate on its existing activities, even if the new industry is not currently giving rise to above normal profits. Traditionally, the competitive advantage has been viewed as stemming from a similarity of production processes, raw materials or market areas. Increasingly, however, stress has been placed on the similarity of the technical and managerial skills and experience required by the existing and new activities.

Growth

It is already clear from Chapter 4 that diversification provides an avenue for growth in the face of restrictions on a firm's ability to grow in its existing activities. These restrictions may be either a limited rate of growth of industry demand or a competitive situation making difficult the expansion of the firm's market share, or both.

Despite the considerable difficulties that arise in seeking to estimate empirically the relative importance of different influences on the extent to which firms diversify – difficulties due mainly to the inadequacies of the available data and the association of so many of the relevant variables with firm size – a number of hypotheses have been drawn from the theoretical considerations above and subjected to some sort of test. The results of the tests are in general far from conclusive, with findings frequently conflicting. Studies of UK manufacturing industry based on the Census of Production have been undertaken by Amey (1958 data), Gorecki (1958 and 1963 data), Hassid (1963 and 1968 data) and Utton (1974 data).

Hassid has found that for industries from which firms diversified there was no relationship between profit stability or profitability and the extent of diversification. For industries into which firms diversified there was a positive relationship between profit stability and diversification, a negative relationship between profitability and diversification and a positive relationship between changes in profitability and changes in diversification.[11] Although Amey has found no tendency for more diversified firms to grow faster, Hassid has found a clear relationship between growth and diversification, while Gorecki has found that the main determinant of entry into an industry, particularly for diversifying firms, was the industry's growth rate.[12] The evidence from US studies tends to support the finding that growth and diversification are positively related but, contrary to Hassid, suggests that there may also be a tentative positive relationship between diversification and profitability.[13]

Gorecki has proposed an approach to the analysis of diversification that is analogous to the approach that seeks to explain direct investment overseas in terms of the best way to exploit a unique firm-specific asset (see Chapter 3). Following the argument that product differentiation and innovation are the most likely sources of firm-specific assets, he has hypothesised that diversification is likely to be positively associated with advertising intensity and research-and-development intensity. In fact there was a negative relationship between advertising and diversification, also reported by Hassid, and a strong positive relationship between research and development and diversification.[14] This latter relationship is the only one to have emerged consistently in all studies, for both countries, and is now considered further.

DIVERSIFICATION, TECHNOLOGY AND SKILLED MANPOWER

Measures of the extent to which an industry is science based have repeatedly been found to have the strongest (positive) association with diversification of any suggested 'explanatory' variable. In the United Kingdom Amey for 1958 and Hassid for 1963 and 1968 have found that between one-fifth and nearly two-thirds of the variation in the extent of diversification, as measured by the ratio of secondary to total output, was 'explained' by variation in the technical personnel ratio. Hassid's results implied that a 10 per cent increase in the employment of scientific manpower was associated with an increase of 3–4 per cent in diversification.[15]

What are the reasons for the strong relationship found to exist between diversification and science-based industries? It is likely that those sectors of the economy characterised by rapidly changing technology will also be growing rapidly. Such sectors are also likely to have a flexible internal structure in the sense that the relative positions, i.e. competitive strengths, of the constituent firms will be subject to continuous change as first one and then another establishes temporary technical superiority in one or other of its spheres of activity. This is not, of course, to say that permanent displacement will normally occur. The dominant elite of large firms can be envisaged as engaging in a continuing competitive struggle ranging over a more-or-less wide, more-or-less closely related set of activities. Large firms will tend at any moment in time to be engaging in activities in which they enjoy temporary competitive superiority, activities in which they are subjected to increasing challenge or that are declining in importance, and activities that are at an early stage of development, among which it is hoped are to be found the firm's future staple activities as they develop or maintain their competitive advantage. Thus, the leading group of firms can be expected to be constantly both crossing existing industry boundaries and establishing entirely new branches of industry. It is this sort of reasoning that has led to growing stress on the importance of existing, as opposed to newly established, firms as the major source of entry threat for oligopolistic industries.[16] Occasionally, of course, an outsider may enter the magic circle on the basis of an outstanding innovation. More frequently, however, such brilliant independent innovators will be allowed to take the high initial risks and, once having demonstrated the potentialities of their discovery, will be bought up by one of the established giants.[17]

The close association between diversification and the science-based sectors of the economy thus stems from the interconnection between oligopolistic competition, research and development, and the creation of new productive services, to use Penrose's terminology:

> The expected actions of competitors are a part of the external environment of an individual firm, and the techniques adopted by the firm to maintain its position in the face of competition have themselves a significant influence on the kind of new productive services that are created within the firm. The relationship between competition and the internal supply of productive services is of particular significance wherever the individual firm must keep abreast of new technical developments to compete successfully, and where the continued profitability of the firm is likely to be associated with the possibilities of innovation. The result of such conditions of competition has been the almost universal adoption by larger firms of the industrial research laboratory, which immeasurably speeds up the creation of productive services and knowledge within the individual firm.[18]

In short, there are more opportunities for diversification in science-based industries, and firms with research-and-development experience are better able to recognise and exploit them as weapons in the competitive battle. As Utton has put it:

> . . . since the outcome of research cannot be predicted with any certainty, a wide range of activities by a company may well increase the chance that a

new technological development can be employed within the framework of the existing product range. This may thus be a true economy of diversification since it is a function of the *range* of goods produced, · rather than an economy of size in terms of output, and *an increasing importance attached to research and development is therefore likely to bring with it an increase in diversification.*[19]

Increasing attention has been given in the recent literature to the connected question of the extent to which diversification is into more closely related industries, i.e. narrow spectrum, or into less closely connected industries, i.e. broad spectrum. For the purpose of statistical analysis narrow spectrum is defined as diversification into industries within an enterprise's primary industry Order and broad spectrum as diversification into industries in other Orders. For the 200 largest UK manufacturing enterprises in 1974 Utton has calculated that on average 55 per cent of diversified employment was broad spectrum and 45 per cent narrow spectrum, with broad spectrum employment exceeding 60 per cent of diversified employment in over half the Orders. However, if the intention of the analysis is to distinguish between diversification where close technological or marketing links are and are not present, this finding may be misleading. In particular there are likely to be close technical links between the several engineering and vehicles Orders. Accordingly, Utton has combined 'Mechanical engineering', 'Electrical engineering', 'Vehicles' and 'Metal goods not elsewhere specified' into one 'Engineering and vehicles' Order. On this basis average broad-spectrum diversification fell from 55 to 42 per cent. Taking into account other modifying considerations, especially the influence of integration, Utton has concluded that broad spectrum diversification probably accounted on average for about one-third of total diversified employment.[20]

This finding that the diversification of the 200 largest UK manufacturing enterprises in 1974 was still largely within closely related industries is consistent with Gorecki's finding for all UK manufacturing firms with over 100 employees in 1963 and with Berry's finding for 460 large US industrial corporations in 1961.[21] Thus, although conglomerate diversification into areas that are relatively remote from the firm's existing activities certainly occurs, and may be increasing, most diversification is probably in areas closely linked to the firm's existing technical and marketing expertise and knowledge. This suggests that managerial ability remains to a considerable extent industry specific, with the corollary that references to generalised non-specialised managerial ability should be treated with caution.

CONCLUSION

Despite the problems involved in measuring its extent there can be no doubt that diversification is widespread and increasing. The extent of diversification increases with size of firm and is also closely associated with the degree to which firms and industries are science based. Although no adequate theory of diversification yet exists, it is likely that understanding will be advanced by focusing on diversification as an integral part of the process of oligopolistic competition between giants. Large firms are able to deploy the resources, especially of capital and skilled manpower, that generate new productive services and enable diversification to be undertaken internally or to be achieved by merger externally. They are also obliged to keep their own and their rivals' activities, both existing and potential, under continuous review for fear of being left behind.

It is often suggested that diversification is an important motive for merger, although, of course, not all diversification occurs through merger and not all merger is for diversification. The next section considers what is known about merger activity in general: its extent, causes and consequences.

5.3   MERGER

Writing in the mid-1950s Markham has observed that 'the paths of economic theory and merger literature have rarely crossed'.[22] Since then the merger wave that gathered strength during the 1950s and 1960s has resulted in a rapidly growing body of work, both theoretical and empirical, that has increased understanding of the forces influencing merger activity, at least in the United Kingdom. In this section the historical record of merger activity in the United Kingdom is set out first. The various explanations advanced for merger are then considered. The section ends with a discussion of the effects of merger.

THE HISTORICAL RECORD OF MERGER ACTIVITY

Merger activity has been measured in several ways: by the number of mergers occurring per year; by the number weighted by some index of the scale of the individual mergers – usually the (stock market) value of the combined concern or the price paid by the acquiring firm; or by a measure of this latter type expressed in relation to some other economically meaningful magnitude – frequently expenditure on acquiring other companies as a percentage of total capital expenditure. By merger is usually intended the amalgamation of two or more firms, whether by consolidation into a new legal entity or by the acquisition of one firm by another. When data are presented in terms of acquisitions the largest firm involved in a consolidation is normally considered to be the acquirer.[23] Since the Second World War a growing volume of data has been available from official sources. For earlier periods, however, series have in the main had to be constructed from a variety of sources – principally the financial and trade press of the day.

A merger series for UK manufacturing industry in the twentieth century, produced by Hannah, is shown in Figure 5.2. The number of firms disappearing as a result of merger is seen to have varied considerably over time. On the basis of the number-disappearing series in Figure 5.2, and alternative series of the value of firms disappearing and the proportion of total investment expenditure accounted for by acquisition, the 1920s and 1960s have emerged as the peak decades for merger activity.[24] More recent data set out in Table 5.3 show that merger activity in the industrial and commercial sectors, after having reached its 1960s peak in 1968, remained at a very high level until its all time high in

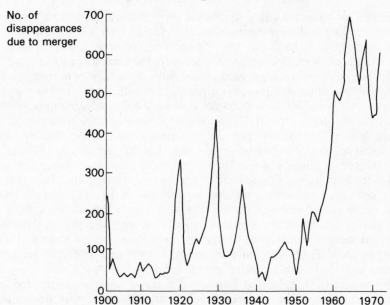

Fig. 5.2   Merger activity in UK manufacturing industry, 1900–73.
Source: L. Hannah, *The Rise of the Corporate Economy* (London, Methuen, 1976), fig. 7.2, p. 107.

1972. It then fell sharply, although there were signs of a recovery by 1977, and it seems likely that the 1970s overall will at least equal the 1960s in merger intensity. A striking indication of the importance of merger activity is the fact that over the period 1964–71 the average continuing quoted company grew more by merger than by net investment in fixed assets.[25]

Some interest attaches to the relative frequency of different types of merger. During the period 1966–73 mergers in distribution, property and finance

Table 5.3   *Acquisitions and mergers of industrial and commercial companies in the United Kingdom, 1969–77.*

Year	No. of companies acquired	Value of companies acquired (£ m.)
1969	846	1,069
1970	793	1,123
1971	884	911
1972	1,210	2,532
1973	1,205	1,304
1974	504	508
1975	315	291
1976	353	427
1977	482	812

Source: Trade and Industry vol. 30 (10 February 1978), table 1, p. 325.

accounted for an increasingly significant proportion of all mergers, with their value exceeding that of mergers in manufacturing after 1970.[26] However, the main focus of discussion has been on the relative importance of horizontal, vertical and conglomerate merger. Evidence for the United Kingdom establishes firmly that mergers in the postwar period have been mainly horizontal. Singh has found that, of the 488 quoted companies in manufacturing industry acquired between 1948 and 1960, nearly 60 per cent involved amalgamations within the same industry group. Of the 643 quoted companies acquired in the period 1954–65, Utton has classified 69·8 per cent by number and 81·1 per cent by value as horizontal acquisitions. Newbould has identified 407 mergers in 1967 and 1968 that involved victim firms valued at £1 million or more and mainly operated in the United Kingdom; of these over 80 per cent were horizontal. Of a sample of 593 takeovers, representing all the acquisitions of the 117 companies with three or more acquisitions during 1957–69, nearly 74 per cent have been classified by Kuehn as horizontal. Finally, Gribbin has reported that, of 798 proposed mergers considered by the Mergers Panel of the Board of Trade/ Department of Trade and Industry between 1965 and 1973, 78 per cent by number and 71 per cent by value were horizontal.[27]

The consistent finding that horizontal mergers have predominated in the United Kingdom in the postwar period, and show no sign of becoming less important, conflicts with the evidence for the United States, which suggests that conglomerate mergers have been of increasing importance there.[28] One possible reason for this apparent discrepancy is the impact of US antitrust legislation, which until recently was interpreted as favouring conglomerate as opposed to horizontal or vertical mergers. By contrast, in Europe and Japan governments have adopted a largely permissive attitude towards merger and have frequently encouraged it.[29]

It is likely that the impact of a changing economic environment interacting with different industrial and market structures has also played a part. The postwar merger wave, documented above for the United Kingdom, has not been confined to Britain. Similar developments have occurred in the United States, the rest of Western Europe and Japan. Indeed, Singh has referred to a worldwide merger movement and has attributed it in part to the intensification of international competition associated with the trade liberalisation and increased capital movements dating from the late 1950s. He has pointed to evidence that in Western Europe and Japan merger has been seen as the way to attain larger size in order to face competition from larger US firms. It is possible that US firms in turn have resorted to merger in order to safeguard their competitive position, although this has not so far been positively established as an explanation for the increase in US merger activity.[30] There is an obvious connection between such a process of oligopolistic interaction with respect to merger activity and the analogous process with respect to the postwar growth of the international firm discussed by Hymer and Rowthorn and considered in section 3.3 above.

REASONS FOR MERGER

The fact that merger activity has occurred in waves and that the relative frequency of different types of merger has altered over time has led some economists to eschew the search for a general theory of merger. Markham, in his survey quoted at the start of this section, has warned against attempts at unicausal explanation:

Mergers, however, are not monolithic in character. Some have been socially undesirable, others have been an integral part of competitive adjustment and may have been highly desirable; still others have had no recognisable effect on either industrial structure, market behaviour, or anything outside the particular firms involved.[31]

He has suggested that each period of high merger activity should be considered separately since it is likely that there will be specific factors in each case from which it would be misleading to abstract. It is in this spirit that Stigler has categorised the turn-of-the-century merger wave in the United States as merger for monopoly and the late 1920s wave as merger for oligopoly.[32] The more important explanations advanced for merger are now considered.

Synergy: monopoly power and scale economies
Profit-maximising firms, within the framework of the traditional theory of the firm, will further their objectives by merger if monopoly power enabling monopoly profit is created or if economies of scale, broadly construed, yielding lower costs are realised. These consequences of merger are together sometimes referred to as 'synergistic' effects, i.e. effects resulting from the meshing together of firms in such a way that their profits when merged exceed what the sum of their individual profits would have been had the firms remained un-merged.[33] The creation of market power is most likely to be a consequence of horizontal merger, although it may also be associated with vertical merger if, for example, the acquisition of a common supplier or distributor gives a firm a competitive advantage over its rivals. Scale economies may result with almost equal likelihood from horizontal or vertical merger.

Empirical studies are often contradictory and inconclusive. Nelson has concluded that his findings on the turn-of-the-century merger wave in the United States 'tend to demonstrate the existence of a fairly strong desire to avoid rigorous competition'.[34] He has based this conclusion on the proportion of merger activity accounted for by merged firms that achieved a dominant market position – a minimum of one-half in terms of the number of firms disappearing and seven-tenths in terms of capitalisation value. Markham, on the other hand, speaking of the same period, has concluded:

Hence, out of every five mergers ostensibly monopolistic in character, only one resulted in considerable monopoly control. Either one of two conclusions seems inescapable: (1) if the purpose of all mergers was monopoly power, four out of every five were unsuccessful in obtaining their initial objective, or (2) many mergers were formed for other purposes.[35]

His general conclusion for all mergers up to the mid-1950s was that relatively few had market monopoly as their goal.

Direct evidence on the importance or otherwise of scale economies as a motive for merger is sparse. Stigler has argued that the conspicuous ability of different-sized firms to survive in the same industry suggests *prima facie* that economies of scale are relatively unimportant over a wide range of American industry.[36] This, however, is not direct evidence. Cook and Cohen, on the basis of a very detailed series of industry case studies, have concluded: 'The case studies have indicated that mergers are unlikely to be successful unless there are considerable economies of scale, and that they are unlikely to take place unless those economies of scale are difficult to realise in the absence of mergers.'[37]

A study by Gort has sought to test the hypotheses that merger activity is a function of attempts to reduce competition or to reap economies of scale. He has argued that, if the motive is monopoly power, merger activity should be associated with industries in which there are a few dominant firms, high entry barriers and slow growth; whereas merger for scale economies should be associated with industries in which the average firm size increases, there are many entrants and growth rates are slow. On the basis of simple correlation coefficients and regression analysis, merger activity was found to be most closely related to a measure of technical change (i.e. the technical personnel ratio), high concentration ratios and rapid rates of growth. No important connection was found between merger activity and change in the concentration ratio, the rate of change of average firm size or the rate of change in the number of firms. On the basis of these results Gort has concluded that the evidence is inconsistent with either the monopoly power or the economies-of-scale hypothesis.[38] More generally, studies of the effects of merger, considered below, have provided no support for the existence of important economies of scale resulting from merger.

Expectation and market valuation

In place of the monopoly power and scale economies hypotheses, Gort has advanced his own hypothesis that 'forces which generate discrepancies in valuation are decisive in determining variations in merger rates both among industries and over time'.[39] By discrepancies in valuation are meant situations in which the potential buyer and seller, although neither foresees a rise in stock market valuation resulting from the merger, both expect to gain from the transaction: 'Discrepancies in valuation for income-producing assets arise from differences in expectations about future income streams and the risks associated with expected income. When such discrepancies are characterised by a higher value being placed on the assets of a firm by non-owners than by owners, acquisition becomes possible.'[40] Gort has argued that economic disturbances generate the sort of valuation discrepancies required to bring about mergers. On the one hand, they affect individuals' expectations differently; on the other hand, they increase the degree of uncertainty about the future. In the course of the readjustment that follows a major economic disturbance the relative valuation of some owners and non-owners may alter in such a way as to cause them to seek to change places. The types of economic disturbance that Gort has contended will produce merger-conducing discrepancies in valuation are above all technical change, historically high levels of security prices and industry growth. Hence, he has regarded his finding, referred to above, that merger activity is most closely associated with the technical personnel ratio, the concentration ratio and industry growth as consistent with his hypothesis.[41]

The business cycle and the stock market

Although not discussed by Gort, the controversy in the literature over the relationship between merger activity and the business cycle seems to be relevant to his theory in so far as security prices and industry growth rates are influenced by the cycle. Markham has found little support for the view that 'merger cycles are timed closely with business cycles'.[42] On the other hand Nelson, for the period 1895–1956, has found that of twelve clear cycles in merger activity eleven showed a definite timing relationship to business cycles and that the few business cycles to which merger activity did not respond were the weakest.[43] Maule's explicit comparison of these two studies has come down fairly heavily in support of Markham's position that there was no obvious relation between merger cycles and business cycles.[44]

However, what is well established and generally agreed is that there is a very close relationship between merger activity and stock market conditions.[45] An early attempt to explain this relationship was the hypothesis that merger when security prices were buoyant 'permitted a capitalisation of prospective monopoly profits and a distribution of a portion of these capitalised profits to the professional promoter'.[46] Although most favoured as an explanation of the turn-of-the-century merger wave in the United States, the role of promoters' profits in the UK merger boom of the 1920s has also been remarked.[47] Markham has identified such profits as in general the most important single motive at merger peaks; but this hypothesis has been dismissed by Gort on the grounds that, since most acquisitions are financed by share exchange and any cash used has in the main been accumulated internally by the acquiring firm, the scope for gains by the promoters of mergers is too small to provide an adequate basis for a general theory of merger.[48] His alternative, as indicated above, is that high levels of security prices are a contributory factor in creating a situation in which valuation discrepancies are large enough to call forth merger transactions.

It may be, of course, that stock market phenomena are essentially superficial influences – proximate causes affecting the timing of merger activity rather than the basic or underlying causes of mergers. This possibility has been well expressed by Nelson:

> The findings do not conclusively demonstrate, however, that underlying industrial factors were not an ultimate factor in merger behaviour. It is possible that merger movements represent a burst of industrial reorganisation toward which underlying economic and technological developments have been accumulating a long time. A favourable capital market may, under these circumstances, trigger the massive reorganisation. Thus, while the findings of the study may have demonstrated clearly the importance of the capital market as a proximate factor in merger movements, they have not so clearly demonstrated its importance as an ultimate cause.[49]

Merger for growth

The discussion of the reasons for merger has so far been based on the assumption of profit maximisation as the objective. In the case of the hypotheses of merger for monopoly and merger for scale economies the discussion has been conducted within the framework of the traditional theory of the firm, in which the firm is, among other things, conceived holistically. The hypothesis of merger for promoter's gain and Gort's hypothesis of valuation discrepancies among shareholders both retain the profit maximisation assumption, although in rather more complex forms. However, explanations of merger activity have also been advanced on the alternative assumption of growth maximisation as the firm's objective. The importance attached by Penrose to merger as a means of raising the level of the managerial constraint on the rate of growth of the firm is discussed in section 4.2. Although highly suggestive, Penrose's work has not sought to develop a theory to account for variations in the extent and type of merger. Subsequently, however, Mueller has presented just such a theory.[50]

Mueller's theory is premised on the assumption of a separation of ownership from control, shareholders seeking profit and managers seeking growth. He has argued that: 'The essence of the difference between growth and stockholder-welfare-maximising behaviour is the lower cost of capital or discount rate employed by the growth-maximising managers.'[51] The cost of capital or discount rate employed is lower for the managers than for the shareholders because the former consider only internal investment opportunities, being interested in the growth of the firm they control, whereas the latter consider both internal and external investment opportunities, being interested in the return on their investment. While conceding that the assumption of profit maximisation, i.e. in the context of his model assuming the same cost of capital for managers as for shareholders, makes sense if there exist 'synergistic' effects – accretions of monopoly power or economies of scale usually associated with horizontal or vertical mergers – Mueller has contended that such effects are unlikely in the case of many conglomerate mergers. Where these effects are absent 'the only justification for a merger can be to take advantage of managerial economies. For these economies to exist, managerial ability must be a non-specialised proclivity, and the leaders of the acquiring company must be men of much greater talent than those of the corporations they absorb.'[52]

It is rather fashionable just now to regard managerial ability precisely as 'a non-specialised proclivity', although more careful formulations refer to specialist financial or managerial skills of fairly widespread applicability.[53] However, for those who reject this view Mueller has offered as an alternative the growth-maximising assumption. Given this assumption, merger will occur in situations that are devoid of 'synergistic' effects or superior managerial skills due to the lower rate of discount of the managers of the acquiring firm relative to that of the sellers of the acquired firm, who may be either managers wishing to get out or shareholders. In support of his hypothesis Mueller has referred to the growing relative importance of conglomerate mergers in the United States, which, given his views on managerial ability, appear best accounted for by a growth-maximisation assumption about managerial objectives.

An attempt to discriminate between the alternative hypotheses of merger for growth and merger for profit has been made by Reid.[54] He has used as a sample the 478 of the 500 largest US industrial firms in 1961 as listed in *Fortune* for which the necessary data were available. The period covered was 1951–61, during which time the firms involved made over 3,300 acquisitions – more than half of the 6,176 mergers reported by the Federal Trade Commission in that period. The firms were divided into four groups according to the number of mergers undertaken: no mergers, 1–5, 6–10 and 11 or more. The average growth and profitability performance of each group was then calculated. Firms that relied solely on internal growth grew on average faster than firms with a low merger intensity (1–5) but more slowly than those with a high merger intensity (6 or more). On the other hand, non-merging firms had a strikingly better record than merging firms from the standpoint of the original shareholders. When merging firms only were considered, the most active achieved the highest rate of growth, the largest increase in market price and the smallest increase in the profits attributable to original shareholders. Further analysis suggested that firms engaging in pure conglomerate-type mergers grew most rapidly, while firms engaging in pure internal growth grew most profitably, although growth by conglomerate-type merger was more profitable than growth by other types of merger.[55]

Some caution is needed in evaluating Reid's study.[56] In particular it is necessary to consider the possibility that differences in the incidence of merger were due to differences in the environmental conditions confronting firms rather than to differences in motivation. When firms were classified on an industry basis the significance of the results was somewhat reduced. If further standardisation of the situation of firms, e.g. with respect to the quality of management and competitive strength, had been possible, the apparent direct relationship between merger and growth and inverse relationship between merger and profitability might have disappeared. Reid has made no attempt to classify firms as manager-controlled or shareholder-controlled; he has merely argued that the results are consistent with the hypothesis that merger tends to be for growth, not for profitability. However, they are also consistent with the hypothesis that merger is the result of the internal and external pressures and opportunities confronting the firm.

The environment, uncertainty and rivalry
Reference has already been made to Singh's suggestion that the worldwide merger movement that became evident in the 1960s was a response to intensifying international competition. Other authors have explored in some detail the relationship between changes in the economic environment, associated increases in uncertainty and rivalry, and merger. A characteristic of such approaches is an insistence that merger can only be understood as part of a process of oligopolistic interaction, rather than as an aspect of behaviour that can be derived from a microequilibrium theory of the firm within the constrained maximisation paradigm as discussed in sections 3.2, 3.6, 4.2 and 4.6. Newbould, for instance, has rejected explanations of merger that rely on 'rational' economic or financial assessments, e.g. carefully calculated estimates of probable synergistic returns or discrepancies in market valuation. Instead, he has regarded merger as typically a rapid, frequently defensive move to offset increases in uncertainty by obtaining greater control over the firm's

environment. Sophisticated financial and economic assessment is held to be largely beside the point:

> For example, there is defensive strategy. If the management of a firm sees its market position being threatened, say by a merger between two competitors, it will be obvious if life is going to be more competitive and difficult; and how much financial analysis would it take to deter the management from taking expensive defensive action? What premium should be paid to acquire perhaps the only firm remaining in the market that can offer the necessary defensive potential?[57]

Newbould's own theory may be summarised as follows. Changes in the environment in which a firm has been operating, which may include merger by competitors, cause the firm's managers to experience increased uncertainty. This increased uncertainty produces a desire to merge in order to reduce uncertainty. Merger occurs if the desire to merge is accompanied by managerial ability and willingness to carry through an actual merger. This ability and willingness depends in part on the number of other mergers currently being undertaken and the extent of managerial uncertainty. Two processes are at work. On the one hand, as the degree of uncertainty increases the desire to merge increases; this tends to increase the number of actual mergers, and this in turn increases the degree of uncertainty. On the other hand, the more that uncertainty increases the more hesitancy there is in undertaking any actual merger, while the more actual mergers there are the lower is the ability to carry through further mergers. An increase in uncertainty sets in motion both a self-sustaining process of merger and pressures tending to curb that process. Of course, to the extent that uncertainty-increasing changes are a permanent feature of the environment, the two tendencies will coexist continuously.[58]

George and Silberston have argued that mergers occur when the relationship between firms and their environment is disturbed by changes in the latter. They have suggested that the amount of competition that is acceptable is limited:

> Firms will attempt by means of restrictive agreements, or by monopolisation, or both, to restrict competition to the extent necessary to yield an 'acceptable' or 'normal' or fair return on capital. Patterns of market structure and business conduct which do not result in orderly competition and acceptable returns will be unstable and result in fundamental change. Similarly, any marked or sudden changes in the environment will lead to changes in industrial structure or business behaviour.[59]

One obvious way to respond to adverse changes in the environment is merger. This is a clear example of how an inadequate performance from the standpoint of the firm will result in a change in structure. George and Silberston, like Newbould, have recognised the repercussive effects of merger:

> If one firm substantially increases its size as a result of merger then this will tend to trigger off defensive mergers by competing firms. This competitive element may mean that the market structure is changed far more than is

required to reduce the risks of competition facing firms to the minimum acceptable level. But in a world characterised by uncertainty too much monopoly power is always better, from the firm's point of view, than too little.[60]

Finally, Aaronovitch and Sawyer have advocated an approach to merger that, although in many respects similar to that of Newbould and of George and Silberston, differs in one crucial respect: the concept of 'the costs of rivalry'. These are costs generated by the process of oligopolistic rivalry which fall on the firms involved and would be reduced if rivalry were reduced. It is argued that many costs arising at the firm as opposed to the plant level are primarily costs of rivalry and that the ability to sustain such costs constitutes the principal advantage of firm size. The costs in question are those of undesired excess capacity, research and development (mainly the latter), and promotion and marketing. Destabilising pressures and the associated increase in uncertainty will cause the costs of rivalry to increase, and firms will respond by seeking to increase their control over the market in order to curb the cost increase. In conditions of overall stagnation or decline the quest for increased control is likely to take the form of price agreements and cartels, whereas in conditions of overall growth the response is more likely to be merger.

This is because in periods of sustained overall growth the relative positions and competitive strengths of firms, and national economies, tend to be subject to marked and continuous change. Indeed, the major destabilising force to which Aaronovitch and Sawyer have drawn attention is the intensification of international competition, through both international trade and international capital movements associated with the overseas production of international firms. Thus, while all three studies considered in this subsection emphasise environmental changes leading to increased uncertainty, Aaronovitch and Sawyer have placed particular stress on the connection between these and oligopolistic rivalry in their explanation of merger.[61]

Environmental explanations for merger activity have not been, nor is it easy to see how they could be, cast in the form of formal models that are susceptible to formal statistical estimation. However, some empirical analysis has been undertaken. Newbould has attempted to get at the relationship between merger and uncertainty. The proportion of managers surveyed in the *Financial Times* 'Monthly survey of business opinion' who were 'neutral', rather than more-or-less optimistic, about the current general business situation as compared with that four months earlier was taken as a proxy for the level of uncertainty, on the grounds that 'neutral' was interpreted to mean 'don't know' rather than 'no change'. This proxy for uncertainty was found to be highly and significantly correlated with monthly series for both potential and actual mergers during 1967 and 1968. Newbould, and Aaronovitch and Sawyer have examined the relationship between indices of international competitiveness and merger activity. For the period 1954–68 Newbould has used the balance on current account and the level of imports as indicators of the extent of the difficulties facing firms, on the grounds that they may have reflected the intensity of competition. The expectation that there would be more mergers the worse the balance on current account and the higher the level of imports was confirmed.

Aaronovitch and Sawyer have conducted a series of tests using a 'trade pressure' index (exports minus imports divided by exports plus imports) and various other indices as explanatory variables, covering the manufacturing sector over the period 1955–68. At the aggregate and two-digit industry levels the trade pressure variable was in general confirmed as an influence on merger activity, although the statistical significance of the results was limited.[62] Thus, there is some limited empirical support for the view that merger activity in the United Kingdom during the 1950s and especially the 1960s was related to the degree of uncertainty and competitive pressure.

An assessment

It is not easy to assess the present state of economic theory relating to merger activity. No generally agreed theory has been developed. In the main what is offered is a series of partial, sometimes incompatible, theories designed to provide explanations for particular types of merger in fairly specific circumstances or concerned with merger activity at different levels of analysis. Such theories have sought to explain merger in terms of the motives of those running or controlling the firm, i.e. within a utility-maximising framework. Thus, given the assumption of profit-maximisation, the quest for monopoly power or for economies of scale will result in horizontal or vertical mergers, whereas conglomerate mergers will stem from the possession by some firms of a competitive advantage in specialist managerial skills. If there are no such 'synergistic' effects present – if the effects of merger are not 'multiplicative' but simply 'additive' – recourse must be made to the alternative of a growth-maximisation assumption in order to account for merger. Recognition of the role of the stock market in merger activity, of course, focuses attention on the influence of financial considerations. Thus, the profit- and growth-maximisation hypotheses have been recast in terms of their effect on share prices and hence the probability of takeover, as seen in Chapter 4. The influence of professional promoters has also been considered. Differences in expectations between shareholders have been advanced as an explanation of merger motivated by the objective of profit-maximisation even when synergistic effects are absent.

More recently, however, increasing recognition has been given to the importance of historical explanation. In particular the growing postwar unification of the world economy and associated intensification of competition have been advanced as the principal reasons for the merger wave in the United Kingdom during the 1960s and 1970s. As Hannah has put it:

> With the further revival of overseas competitors, British firms no longer faced the sellers' markets of the immediately postwar years but had to meet increasing competition both at home and abroad. Competition was also intensified by a further influx of foreign (principally American) capital into the British market, which stimulated rapid growth of (often technically and managerially superior) competitors for British firms. There was a widespread desire to reduce such competitive pressures within the British market, and the merger waves of these years were undoubtedly in part a response to these feelings. Such compensating mergers need not imply that there was a net decrease in competition, but certainly the initial impact of the restrictive

practices legislation and tariff reductions on the level of competition was in some degree neutralized by the increased level of concentration which followed them.[63]

The link between these developments and merger has been traced through the effect of increasing competition in increasing uncertainty and the costs of oligopolistic rivalry. Although these more recent analyses have been developed primarily as explanations of horizontal merger, their approach may perhaps be applied more generally. The view that horizontal merger leads to greater control over the environment whereas the other types of merger do not is surely a hangover from the traditional theory's emphasis on the single product firm in static equilibrium. In an economy dominated by diversified oligopolists competing in a continuously changing environment, gains to competitive strength and survival potential are unlikely to result only from this one type of merger. The effect on a firm's overall strength of diversification and hence of one type of merger is considered in section 5.2. The part played by merger in the process of competition by innovation is referred to in section 5.4.

THE EFFECTS OF MERGER

Interest in the effects of merger has for the most part been motivated by welfare considerations, although more recently their role in shaping the longer term evolution of the socioeconomic system, e.g. in contributing to the development of a 'corporate economy', has been highlighted. Of course, assessing the effect of merger is not easy. Cook and Cohen have pinpointed the general difficulty in the introduction to their detailed case studies: 'mergers are a reaction to a changing situation . . . judgement depends upon comparing the effects of what actually happened with the effects of what might have happened'.[64] Most effort to date has been given to the evaluation of individual mergers in terms of some criterion of success. There has also been a good deal of work on the consequences of merger activity for concentration. Finally, there have been attempts to assess the relationship between merger and the large firm.

The 'success' of individual mergers

The evaluation of individual mergers requires some criterion of success. Most studies have taken some indicator of profitability or shareholder benefit as their criterion, but some have also considered growth, as a presumed better reflection of the motives of those involved. Summaries of the empirical work on the relationship between merger and profitability or shareholder benefit, virtually all based on US data, have been undertaken by Utton and Meeks.[65] Both have concluded that in general merger does not improve profitability performance, with Utton's more comprehensive summary reporting six studies in which performance did not change after merger, five in which it worsened and only two in which it improved.

There are four main studies relating to the United Kingdom, of which only that by Singh is included in Utton's summary. Singh has examined the pretax return on net assets of seventy-seven firms that acquired other firms in the same industry during 1954–60, expressing profitability relative to the industry average. He has compared the profitability of the acquiring firms in the year of acquisition and the two subsequent years with the weighted average profitability of the two firms in the year before acquisition. In at least half of the cases there was a decline in relative profitability after merger. Newbould has compared twenty-four non-financial firms in the top 200 that had taken over another firm valued at over £5 million during 1967–8 with twenty-four firms of a similar size that had not. In terms of return on assets and earnings per share, but not in terms of relative movement in share price, the non-merging firms did better than those merging. Utton has considered the postmerger profitability performance of a non-random sample of thirty-nine merger-intensive firms over the period 1961–70. He has compared (1) the pretax net profitability of each firm in his sample in 1966 and 1967 with the profitability of each firm's primary industry in the same years, and (2) the average profitability of his merger-intensive sample over 1961–70 with that of a random sample of thirty-nine non-merging firms. In both 1966 and 1967, 58 per cent of the merger-intensive firms had profitability lower than their industry's median level, although in neither year was the result statistically significant. However, the merger-intensive sample had a lower average profitability than the non-merging sample, which was statistically significant. Finally, Meeks has compared the premerger and postmerger profitability of 233 mergers between 1964 and 1972. In order to allow for influences other than merger, profitability was standardised as a proportion of the industry average. Results were adjusted to take account of the accounting bias caused by the practice of entering the premium in excess of book value paid by the acquiring firm as 'goodwill', thus inflating the asset base on which the rate of profit was calculated and so reducing recorded profitability. In all seven post-merger years considered the average profitability, adjusted as well as unadjusted, of the sample was lower than the premerger level, and in many cases the decline was statistically significant.[66]

Thus, there is no evidence to support the view that mergers are in general successful from the standpoint of increasing profitability. If anything, merger has been associated with deteriorating profitability performance. On the other hand, there is accumulating evidence that merging firms grow faster than non-merging firms. This was clearly the case in Newbould's and Utton's studies for the United Kingdom and also in Reid's study for the United States.[67] Of course, these conclusions are dependent on the assumption that the comparisons made are legitimate. It may be the case, for instance, that firms that merge do so for reasons that are specific to them and that do not apply to other firms in the industry and that their profitability performance would have been even worse than it turned out to be had they not merged.

The success or otherwise of a merger in private terms is not at all the same thing as its worthwhileness in social terms. In particular there are well-known problems associated with the use of profitability as an indicator of social performance, which are discussed in Chapter 8. Nevertheless, postmerger profitability has been widely used as an indication of whether or not the merger has been socially beneficial in the sense of increasing productivity. Since any social benefits are usually held to stem from economies of scale in the broadest sense it is worth considering the evidence on the circumstances in which such economies are likely to be realised. Cook and Cohen, presumably referring to horizontal mergers, have been fairly definite: 'The studies have shown the importance of the early years of combines; they appear to require true monopoly power until such time as real economies of scale are realised; where these do not exist a big multi-firm combine is only successful in very special circumstances.'[68] A study by Kitching of the experience of twenty-two companies over the period 1960–5 has produced some interesting results. In response to a questionnaire managers claimed that 'synergy' was easiest to obtain with respect to finance and most difficult with respect to production facilities. In 84 per cent of the failures there was a 'size mismatch'; that is, the acquired firm's sales were less than 2 per cent of those of the acquiring firm. The most critical element in determining the success or failure of a merger was undoubtedly thought by the managers to be the quality of management.[69] This judgement has been supported by Pratten's detailed case study of a conglomerate merger between Slater Walker Securities and Greengate and Irwell, at the end of which Pratten has concluded: 'The ability of SWS to increase profits was attributable to its financial and management expertise.'[70] Further confirmation of the key role of management is to be found in Newbould's study. The results of a survey of thirty-eight firms 'suggested that substantial synergy could be *created,* but the emphasis is on the creation of it by management action. There was nothing to suggest that synergy was an automatic concomitant of merger.'[71] Indeed, Hart, Utton and Walshe in a series of case studies have found evidence of managerial diseconomies following merger in five out of ten product groups studied in which concentration increased between 1958 and 1963 primarily as a result of merger.[72] Thus, even though merger may create the possibility of achieving economies of scale, empirical evidence suggests that there is no guarantee that they will actually be realised, particularly in the short and medium term.

The effect of merger on concentration
Until fairly recently it was widely held that since the turn of the century mergers had had little effect on concentration.[73] However, empirical studies of the association between increasing concentration and merger activity in the period since the mid 1950s have largely discredited this view. In the United States a large proportion of mergers have been conglomerate, and this is reflected in the fact that overall concentration has increased much more than concentration at the industry level. In Britain concentration increased rapidly at all levels during the 1960s, and evidence appearing during the 1970s has established beyond doubt the predominant role of merger in bringing this about.

The method used to assess statistically the effect of merger on concentration over a given period is normally as follows. A hypothetical distribution of firms is calculated by treating all firms that merged during the period as if they had already merged at the start of the period. The effect of merger is then taken as the difference between the index of concentration for the actual opening distribution of firms and the index for the counterfactual hypothetical distribution. On this basis Utton, using the variance of the logarithms of firm size as his index of concentration, has found that between 1954 and 1965 merger accounted for over 40 per cent of the increase in concentration in UK manufacturing industry.[74] Hart, Utton and Walshe, on the basis of forty-two product-group case studies covering the period 1958–63, have concluded that mergers and internal growth were equally important in increasing concentration within product groups. However, to arrive at the change in the average level of concentration a third, equally important, influence – namely, that of product groups in which concentration decreased – had to be taken into account.[75]

The major UK study is that of Hannah and Kay, using the same basic method as Utton but with concentration ratios and a numbers-equivalent index of their own as indices of concentration. Their results provide very strong evidence of the connection between mergers and concentration. Between 1919 and 1930 concentration in UK manufacturing industry increased very substantially, with merger responsible for over 50 per cent of the increase. During 1930–48 the influence of merger was still in the direction of increasing concentration but to a much lesser extent, and its effect was in many cases more than offset by the deconcentrating effect of internal growth, so that the actual concentration indices tended to fall. However, the trend in actual concentration was somewhat ambiguous with both larger and very small firms losing ground to medium-sized firms. Between 1957 and 1969 as the postwar merger wave gathered strength, concentration again increased substantially, almost entirely due to merger. In fact overall and in many industries the effect of internal growth was deconcentrating, but this was more than offset by the effect of merger. Finally, in the period 1969–73 there was a moderate increase in concentration, entirely due to merger, with the large firms marking time and middle-sized firms gaining at the expense of smaller firms. In summary, during the years when merger had a predominant effect concentration increased sharply, whereas in those when merger was relatively unimportant concentration tended to remain much the same or even fall somewhat.[76]

At a more intuitive level George has examined the increase in concentration as measured by Census of Production five-firm sales concentration ratios between 1963 and 1968 – a period of unprecedentedly high merger activity. Once again the coexistence of merger and increasing concentration was found to be unmistakable.[77]

Merger and the large firm

Since merger emerges as a major contributory factor to increasing concentration, it is hardly surprising that merger has also played a major role in the emergence of large firms. Firm size can be measured overall or in relation to a particular industry or market. To a considerable extent large firms owe their dominant position, i.e. their overall size in relation to that of smaller firms, to key mergers at some stage in their history. Hannah has referred to 'the importance of mergers in the growth of the larger firms' on the basis of an analysis of increasing overall concentration in UK manufacturing between 1919 and 1930.[78] Whittington, in an analysis of quoted UK manufacturing companies over the period 1948–68, has concluded that the net assets of the top 100 grew rapidly by comparison with those of the rest of the company sector, by 620 as against 450 per cent, and that this was almost certainly due to the effect of mergers.[79] This judgement has been supported by Meeks and Whittington's comparison of the performance of 'giant' companies and the 'rest' in the United Kingdom from 1948 to 1969. The 'giants' were those of the top 100 companies in 1948 and 1964 which survived to 1969, numbering 58 and 75 firms respectively. The 'rest' were the remaining quoted companies in each period. Over the entire twenty years the differences between the 'giants' and the 'rest' were not great, but sizable differences opened up in the latter part of the period when the postwar merger wave was well under way. Between 1964 and 1969 the 'giants' grew at 10·2 per cent per annum compared with 8 per cent per annum for the 'rest'. Over half of the growth in the 'giants'' net assets was accounted for by acquisitions, which was significantly more than in the case of the 'rest', while the typical 'giant' acquired another quoted company once every $2\frac{1}{2}$ years compared with once every 33 years for a typical member of the 'rest'.[80]

While the evidence linking merger to the emergence of the largest firms overall is fairly clearcut, the relationship between merger and relative size in a particular industry is slightly more problematic. Evely and Little, on the basis of a sample of thirty-six high-concentration trades in 1951 have concluded: 'There are few firms indeed among the leaders in the trades surveyed which were not created by amalgamations or have not resorted to acquisition and merger at some stage during their development.'[81] Walshe, on the other hand, has found that in only eleven out of thirty-two high-concentration products had the dominant firms emerged primarily as the result of merger. However, taking into account possible errors of classification and considering his results together with those of Evely and Little, Walshe's final conclusion was that 'internal and external expansion have been about equally responsible for the promotion of monopoly, near-monopoly and tight oligopoly'.[82] US studies have tended to agree with Evely and Little. Stigler, measuring size of firm relative to the size of industry, has commented: 'There are no large American companies that have not grown somewhat by merger, and probably very few that have grown much by the alternative method of internal expansion.'[83] Weston has concluded that, although the absolute size of large firms at any moment was largely due to internal growth, their relative size had mainly been achieved by past merger.[84]

Not only have mergers been on balance an important means of establishing a dominant position; but, in addition, once established large firms tend to occupy a special place in the merger process. Large firms take over small firms, not the other way round. The generally inverse relationship between the probability of being acquired and size is noted in section 4.4. At the same time acquiring firms are generally very much larger than acquired firms.[85] Furthermore, most large firms appear to engage in merger activity, and dominant firms tend to use merger to maintain their dominant position.[86] Thus, merger activity emerges as an important instrument in the rise of firms to a dominant position and as an important activity of firms once a dominant position has been achieved. The possible implications of this for the role of merger in the competitive process are touched on in the conclusion to this section.

CONCLUSION

Adapting Newbould's terminology, the traditional theories of merger may be classified as 'economic' or 'financial'. 'Economic' theories are concerned with merger for monopoly or for scale economies, 'financial' theories with the influence of stock market valuation and other financial variables. Of course, the two are not necessarily contradictory since economic factors will be reflected in financial variables, especially when the firm is a quoted company. Theories have also been developed in which merger is a means to growth, with growth seen as serving managerial interests as opposed to those of shareholders. The traditional approach to merger has been from the standpoint of its effect on market structure and hence the allocation of resources. This approach, not surprisingly, has been largely associated with the adoption of a normative framework intended to enable 'good' mergers to be distinguished from 'bad'; merger is judged 'bad' to the extent that it conveys monopoly power and 'good' to the extent that it enables economies of scale to be realised. In either case, on the assumption of profit-maximisation as the objective, profitability sh   d increase as a result of merger. In fact, however, the evidence suggests that p   merger profitability has at best been unaffected and at worst has decli   d. The principal explanation offered for this have been that firms sacrifice profitability to growth (a merger) and/or that merger results in managerial dise

However, in   years a number have discussed why the worldwide merger wave of the 1960s being seen as a threat to competition in the world economy. Theories have been advanced, merger as an attempt by firms to reduce uncertainty and increase control over an environment de tabilised by external competition, ing develop-ments. Such theories have the major advantage of draw er activity to be analysed as one aspect of the process of eraction and rivalry between the giant firms that dominate the advanced capitalist world. Furthermore, emphasis on the need for rical analysis directs attention to the role of industry structure in development of the socioeconomic system. The available evidence suggests that merger has played an important part in the growth of concentration and the rise of the giant corporation.

5.4 INNOVATION

The phenomenon of innovation is of great significance for the analysis of business behaviour in capitalist economies. As Schumpeter has put it: 'Innovation is the outstanding fact in the economic history of capitalist society,' or again: 'What dominates the picture of capitalistic life . . . is innovation, the intrusion into the system of new production functions.'[87] On the one hand, innovation is such a widespread aspect of reality that theories that abstract from it run a grave risk of irrelevance; on the other hand, theories that do not abstract from it must seek to embrace a process of continuous change and the associated uncertainty as an integral part of the reality that they are concerned to explain. The implications of this for the traditional theory of the firm are far reaching. The concept of the firm as an entity passively adapting to an exogenously determined environment – the very concept of a given and perfectly known production function – becomes largely irrelevant for the analysis of business behaviour. Instead, the firm must be conceived as to a greater or lesser extent involved in the enterprise of seeking to change its environment – specifically here the production function on the basis of which it operates – in a direction calculated to further its objectives. In the words of Burns and Stalker, 'the undefined and passive notion of "meeting the conditions set by the world around it" becomes the more familiar "ways in which the firm achieves its purpose" '.[88]

This is not to say, of course, that firms can manage the process of innovation with assurance, to achieve any outcome desired. On the contrary, one of the major characteristics of innovative activity is the uncertainty associated with it. Some indication of the uncertainty involved has been given in a study of twenty large American firms by Booz, Allen and Hamilton. They have reported that fewer than 2 per cent of the proposals initially considered for new products were forwarded for development; while of every ten products emerging from research and development five failed in product and market tests, and of the five that passed only two were eventually a commercial success.[89] Another indication is the finding by Carter and Williams of a large discrepancy between the predicted and actual yields of investments in innovations made by firms. The difference between the actual and expected return was 50 per cent of the expected return in 75 per cent of the cases studied, with a correlation coefficient between actual and expected return of only 0·13. They have found that in general underestimation and overestimation were equally likely.[90] Freeman, reviewing the (mainly American) empirical work, has concluded that 'wide margins of error (with an optimistic bias) are characteristic of the experimental development process' but that even so 'the market uncertainty is frequently far greater than the technical uncertainty'. As an example of market uncertainty he has cited IBM's 'optimistic' estimate made in 1955 of a total 1965 US computer stock of 4,000, compared with the actual outcome of over 20,000.[91]

Schumpeter's concept of innovation is much wider than that at present in vogue. In emphasising as a defining characteristic of innovation the setting up of a new production function, Schumpeter has intended to cover the doing of any new thing, or old thing in a new way, whether 'by exploiting an invention or, more generally an untried technological possibility, . . . by opening up a new source of supply of materials or a new outlet for products, by reorganising an industry and so on'.[92] He has been very concerned to distinguish innovation from invention:

It is entirely immaterial whether an innovation implies scientific novelty or not. Although most innovations can be traced to some conquest in the realm of either theoretical or practical knowledge that has occurred in the immediate or remote past, there are many which cannot. Innovation is possible without anything we should identify as invention.[93]

In this Schumpeter has differed from presently favoured usage in two ways.

First, his definition covers anything that has not been done before, including, for example, a specific merger, whereas in current usage the term 'innovation' is usually restricted to the set of events connected with the appearance of new processes or products that are assumed to have at least some 'technological' content. Second, Schumpeter's rigid distinction between invention and innovation is widely regarded as unhelpful in that it directs attention away from the interdependence that is normally present between the various stages of the innovation process.[94]

For the purpose of the following discussion innovation may be defined as 'the technical, industrial and commercial steps which lead to the marketing of new manufactured products and to the commercial use of new technical processes and equipment'.[95] Innovation is increasingly regarded as a process, one of the early stages of which is invention: the generation of new scientific principles, new techniques or new ideas. If the innovation process is to continue beyond the stage of invention, action must be taken to apply the invention in a way that results in its successful utilisation. This will normally involve development, followed in turn by investment in productive capacity and by commercial launching. Very little evidence is available on the relative cost of the different stages, but in two of the most innovation-based industries, i.e. chemicals and electronics, Freeman has estimated that 'R and D costs typically account for about fifty per cent of the total costs of launching a new product'.[96]

Two further preliminary remarks are worth making before examining the available data on the extent of innovation. In addition to the damaging implications of the phenomenon of innovation for the relevance of the traditional theory of the firm to the positive analysis of business behaviour, the relevance of the normative analysis of standard welfare economics is, if anything, brought even more strongly into question. At the very foundation of the standard welfare analysis is the assumption that the 'state of the arts', i.e. production functions, and individual preferences are exogenous with respect to the workings of the economic system. Not only does innovation violate the first part of this assumption, but its effect in changing preferences also violates the second part. Standard welfare analysis is essentially static and requires certainty or its equivalent. Innovation is uncertain and by definition involves change. The two do not mix.

Finally, it should be borne in mind that this section is concerned essentially with innovation at the micro level. The macroeconomic aspects of innovation or technological change are not considered; nor, except in so far as they are relevant for the analysis of the competitive struggle, are the factors influencing diffusion, i.e. the process whereby an innovation spreads once it has been first introduced.[97]

THE EXTENT OF INNOVATION: PROBLEMS OF MEASUREMENT

In order to estimate the extent of innovation it is necessary to have both conceptual clarity over what precisely it is sought to measure and data that approximate reasonably closely to the theoretical variables adopted. In principle a distinction should be drawn between the inputs into the innovation process and the outputs from that process. The inputs comprise the resources devoted to the various stages of the process; the outputs consist of those projects which complete the whole process and emerge as successful innovations.[98]

It would thus be desirable to have an index of total inputs into the innovation process. In fact, however, the only directly relevant data that are available relate to the early stages of the process. For most countries it is possible to obtain statistics of expenditure on research and development (R and D), and for some countries it is also possible to obtain information on personnel employed in R and D. The major problem with these statistics is that all official series relate only to formally organised activity and hence exclude the contribution both of non-organisation individuals and of those members of organisations not classified to R and D. Despite this defect R and D statistics are in general the major source of information about innovative activity to the production stage.

On the output side a number of measures have been used relating to different stages in the innovation process. The most common measure of inventive output adopted has been statistics of patents issued. These statistics have a number of well-known drawbacks: they refer primarily to inventions, and inventions frequently do not lead on to innovation; they are inevitably partial in their coverage since the propensity to patent varies considerably between firms and many inventions may not be patentable anyway, as is the case in the United States for inventions derived from government-sponsored R and D; and the varying economic importance of different inventions is not reflected in the patent data.[99] Once again, despite these defects patent statistics have been widely used as an index of inventive output. An increasingly popular alternative is the procedure of directly listing the major, and sometimes also minor, inventions and/or innovations in a particular industry or within a given time-span. In principle this is the most satisfactory measure of all. It has the advantages of hindsight and the flexibility of a case-by-case examination in seeking to estimate the economic significance of each innovation. The major problem with this approach is the need to agree criteria for determining what are to count as major, or minor, innovations and for attributing weights to them. However, there may well be advantages in making the element of judgement explicit. Other measures adopted have been the frequency of publication in scientific or trade journals and the indirect method, at the level of the economy or by sector or industry, of estimating the savings of factor inputs per unit of output. Both these approaches are subject to very great shortcomings and have been less frequently used than those discussed above.[100]

Before leaving the problem of measurement it is instructive to note the findings of a study by Mueller which has sought to relate the patents issued in 1962–4 to various measures of R and D activity in 1958–60 for six US industry groups with different technical characteristics. Mueller has observed that 'the most interesting finding of this paper must be the high correlations between R and D and patents, i.e. that there appears to be a significant relationship between what goes into the inventive process and what comes out of it'.[101] This conclusion is generally supported by the empirical evidence on this issue.[102]

THE EXTENT OF INNOVATION : EMPIRICAL ESTIMATES

In the United Kingdom in 1972–3 total R and D expenditure, at over £1,300 million, was 2·3 per cent of gross national product at factor cost – a somewhat smaller proportion than the consistent 2·6 per cent of the 1960s.[103] International comparisons in absolute terms are particularly hazardous with respect to R and D expenditures. At the official exchange rate UK expenditure is very roughly one-tenth of that in the United States; but if a 'research exchange rate' is used to allow for the relatively higher cost of research in the United States, the fraction rises considerably. As a proportion of gross national product R and D expenditure in the United Kingdom is significantly lower than that in the United States but somewhat higher than that in the other major capitalist countries, although the gap is narrowing.

Table 5.4 analyses UK R and D expenditure in 1972–3 according to the sector performing the work and the sector financing it. The importance of the state emerges clearly, with the government sector carrying out roughly 25 per cent of total R and D and financing almost 50 per cent. If the public corporations are included a further 5 percentage points are added in each case. By contrast, private industry performed 55 per cent of R and D but financed less than 40 per cent. The position in the United States was broadly similar.

Table 5.4 *Scientific R and D expenditure by sector in which work performed and by which finance provided, United Kingdom, 1972–3.*

	Work performed		Finance provided	
Sector	*(£ m.)*	*(%)*	*(£ m.)*	*(%)*
Government:				
Defence	133·0	10·2	327·3	22·2
Civil	203·7	15·6	394·6	26·7
Adjustment*a*	—	—	−81·9	—
Total	336·7	25·8	640·0	48·9
Universities and further education	115·6	8·8	13·2	1·0
Public corporations	69·2	5·3	76·1	5·8
Research associations	18·8	1·4	—	—
Private industry	739·2	56·4	491·8	37·5
Overseas	—	—	72·6	5·5
Other	30·6	2·3	16·4	1·3
Total	1,310·1	100·0	1,310·1	100·0

Source: Central Statistical Office, *Annual Abstract of Statistics 1977* (London, HMSO, 1978), table 11.11, p. 303.

Note:
(a) Discrepancy between government funds provided as returned by the government and as returned by the sectors performing the work. The percentage for total government finance provided is based on the adjusted total (i.e. that returned by the sectors) and has been apportioned *pro rata* between defence and civil.

R and D expenditure is very unevenly spread between industries. In the United Kingdom in 1975, of a total of £1,350 million industrial R and D expenditure, over 60 per cent was accounted for by three industries: aerospace, 21·6 per cent; electronics, including computers and telecommunications, 20·7 per cent; and chemicals and allied products, 18·6 per cent.[104] On the basis of estimates of R and D expenditure as a percentage of net sales and value added, and R and D personnel income as a percentage of total earned income, the three most research-intensive industries were aerospace, electronics and petroleum products, followed by industrial engines, pharmaceutical and toilet preparations, and plastics.[105] Freeman, in his excellent survey of industrial innovation, has provided a fascinating historical-descriptive account of the major science-based industries, with chapters on chemical and oil process plant and nuclear energy, synthetic materials and electronics. He has argued that it is these industries *par excellence* that exemplify the trend towards the professionalisation of R and D and the replacement of craft-based processes of production by science-based ones.[106]

There is, of course, a connection between the important role of the state in financing R and D and the industries with the largest R and D expenditures. The two industries that spend most on R and D are aerospace and electronics, both intimately involved in defence and prestige civil aerospace production. In the late 1960s in the United Kingdom over 70 per cent of aerospace and 40 per cent of electronics R and D were financed by the state, while almost 60 per cent of state R and D went on military, space and nuclear R and D and a further significant amount on civil aviation.[107] However, although it is obviously still of major importance, the share of 'big science' in total government R and D expenditure has been declining, partly due to the relaxation of tension as détente has replaced the cold war and partly due to changes in public opinion and social values.[108]

The growth of state involvement in R and D has had an important effect on the relationship between government and business. Commenting on the situation in the United States, where the percentage of private industry R and D financed by the government is even higher than that in the United Kingdom, Mansfield has written:

> The tremendous increase in Federal contracting has resulted in a blurring of the distinction between the private and public sectors. Some major contractors, particularly in the defence and space fields, do practically all of their business with the government. In many cases, their products – aircraft, missiles, and the like – have no civilian markets, much of their capital is provided by the government, and the government has agents involved in the managerial and operating structure of their organisations. Because of the great uncertainties involved in military R & D and the impossibility of competitive bidding for R & D contracts, the mechanism of the free market has been replaced largely by administrative procedure and negotiation.[109]

The implications for our understanding of business behaviour of such intertwining of the private and public sectors, and the associated suspension of the

Table 5.5　*Percentage of total industrial R and D performed in firms ranked by size of R and D programme.*

Country	4 largest firms	8 largest firms	20 largest firms	40 largest firms	100 largest firms	200 largest firms	300 largest firms
USA	22·0	35·0	57·0	70·0	82·0	89·0	92·0
UK	25·6	34·0	47·2	57·9	69·5	75·0	77·0
France	20·9	30·5	47·7	63·4	81·0	91·2	95·6
Japan[a]				47·7	52·1	63·1	71·4
Italy	46·4	56·3	70·4	81·6	92·5		

Source: Organisation for Economic Co-operation and Development, *The Overall Level and Structure of R & D Efforts in OECD Member Countries* (Paris, OECD, 1967), table 4, p. 46.

Note:
(a)　Figures for the largest 54, 85, 180 and 289 firms respectively.

automatic working of the market over a large area of economic activity, are considered in the conclusion to this section.

The uncertainty and cost of much R and D partly explain why innovative activity provides a classic case of extremely close relations between business and the state. More fundamentally, however, the inherent uncertainty and the scale of resources required mean that the business involved in innovation is in general big business. Unfortunately, the available data on R and D by firm size are rather scanty. Table 5.5 sets out for five countries the percentage of R and D expenditure undertaken by firms ranked according to the size of R and D programme. In each country, apart from Japan, the forty largest programmes accounted for well over 50 per cent of total R and D, with the four largest programmes accounting for over 20 per cent and the eight largest for over 30 per cent. Firms ranked by size of R and D programme do not assume exactly the same order as when ranked in terms of the standard measures of firm size, i.e. assets, employment, sales, and the degree of concentration of R and D expenditure is in fact significantly less marked on the latter basis. Nevertheless, it is generally true that R and D are largely performed by large firms, while small firms do not normally undertake R and D.[110]

INDUSTRIAL STRUCTURE, TECHNOLOGICAL OPPORTUNITY AND INNOVATION

The nature of the connection between industrial structure and innovation has been the subject of a great deal of discussion. Much theorising and, more recently, empirical work have been devoted to examining the influence of the absolute size of firms and the degree of market power in determining the extent of innovation. However, the empirical studies soon identified interindustry differences in 'technological opportunity' as perhaps the major determinant of variations in the extent of innovative activity.

Absolute size has been considered from the standpoint of the resources required for innovation. On the one hand, stress is laid on the role of individual insight in invention, on the entrepreneurial ability and boldness required to recognise a potentially successful innovation and back a hunch, and on the need for flexibility and quick decisions that stems from the uncertainty of the innovation process. On the other hand, emphasis is placed on the possibility of managing innovation, on the advantages of the large scale deployment of resources for R and D, and on the fact that large absolute size enables the adoption of a longer term perspective and the pooling of risks.

Market power is traditionally considered in terms of a contrast between atomistic, frequently perfect, competition and monopoly. On the one hand, it is claimed that in an atomistically competitive situation, with its powerful tendency towards a uniform 'normal' rate of profit, there will be strong pressures making for cost-reducing innovation which will diminish as market power increases. On the other hand, it is argued that since innovation is risky it will be undertaken not in atomistically competitive situations, where any advantage derived will be only momentary, but rather when there is the prospect of monopoly profit, at least for a period. The need to ensure an adequate return on the resources devoted to inventive activity is, of course, the principal argument adduced in favour of a patent system.[111]

Although conceptually distinct, the influences of absolute size and market power have often been fused into a 'neo-Schumpeterian' hypothesis to the effect that, the larger the firm and the greater the degree of market power, the greater will be the intensity of innovative activity.[112] Of the many empirical investigations of this 'neo-Schumpterian' hypothesis two, by Hamberg and Scherer, are now briefly summarised. Hamberg has considered the 340 of *Fortune*'s list of the 500 largest industrials in 1960 for which R and D data were available, classified into seventeen manufacturing industry groups. Using employment as the size variable he has examined the way in which absolute R and D activities and a measure of R and D intensity varied with firm size and industry concentration. His findings included: that 'among the large companies R and D employment tends to increase with size of firm' but 'there is considerable variation among industry groups in the strength of this association'; that in fifteen of the seventeen industries 'no solid evidence' existed 'for the hypothesis that research intensity (as measured by the ratio R and D employment/total employment) increases with size among the larger firms'; and that, 'though positive association between R and D intensity and industrial concentration apparently exists it must be described as weak'.[113] While Hamberg has used a measure of *input* into the innovation process – namely, R and D employment – Scherer has used a measure of *output* – namely, patents issued in 1959 to 448 of *Fortune*'s list of the 500 largest industrials in 1955. The size variable – 1955 sales – is lagged four years to allow for the average delay between the date on which a patent application is lodged and the date on which the patent is granted. Scherer has concluded that either 'corporate patenting has not been shown to increase either more or less than proportionately with sales' or 'after a stage of slightly increasing returns extending to 1955 sales of approximately $500 million, corporate patenting tends to increase less than proportionately with sales, except in the case of a few giant firms which led their two-digit sectors in sales' and that 'if structural market power has a beneficial effect on the output of patented inventions, it is a very modest effect indeed'.[114]

The general conclusions of empirical work on the relationship between research intensity and firm size may be summarised as follows. Among firms that undertake R and D innovational effort initially tends to increase more than in proportion to size; but above a certain size, among the largest firms, this tendency does not continue, and innovational effort may even increase less than in proportion to size. However, the size at which the change occurs varies between industries, and in some industries, notably chemicals, innovational effort continues to increase more than in proportion to size throughout the size range. These conclusions relating to innovational effort also appear to hold for the relationship between innovational output and firm size.[115] The position with respect to the relationship between innovational activity and market power, at least as measured by concentration ratios, is more problematic. The empirical studies taken together are rather inconclusive, although based on their survey Kamien and Schwartz have suggested that in the case of market structure, as of firm size, 'the sought after relationships are quite likely nonlinear. Intermediate values of the market structure elements may be most conducive to research effort and its success, with extreme values providing less incentive'.[116]

One possible explanation for the non-linearity of the relationship between innovational activity and firm size and market structure may be the existence of a 'threshold'. While some level of absolute size and some degree of market power may be required for successful innovation, beyond such threshold levels further increases may not be associated with proportional increases in innovative activity, and the effect may even be negative. Freeman has advanced the concept of a 'threshold' level of R and D expenditure in those science-based industries in which innovation is the major form of competition. In such industries in order to survive a firm must be able to innovate, if not in advance of the other firms in the industry, then at least not too far behind the industry leaders. Freeman, who developed the concept in the course of his study of the electronics capital-goods industry, has argued that:

> In this situation every firm must have a minimum level of R and D work in progress, sufficient to keep abreast of the technical changes in components, to introduce a flow of improvements and to launch completely new models when forced to do so by the competition. This minimum level of 'defensive' research and development may be termed the 'threshold'. It is an *absolute* level of resources, not a *ratio* of sales.[117]

To obtain an annual R and D expenditure threshold level the estimated total development cost is divided by the estimated maximum 'lead time', i.e. the time from the start to the completion of a project. Total development cost will be determined by the state of knowledge in the relevant scientific and technical fields, given prevailing factor prices, while maximum lead time will be determined by the intensity of competition in the industry. Thus, the threshold level R and D expenditure depends on both the scientific–technical characteristics of the industry and the characteristics of its competitive struggle.

Freeman has calculated notional threshold annual R and D levels for various electronic capital goods in the early 1960s. They ranged from between £33,000 and £66,000 per annum for a marine radar set, through between £333,000 and £666,000 per annum for a small scientific computer and between £400,000 and £775,000 per annum for a television colour camera, to between £2 million and £8 million per annum for a communication satellite. Since firms will normally be involved in a range of products the overall threshold-level R and D expenditure will, of course, be many times higher. Firms that are unable to maintain such high levels of R and D expenditure will experience lengthening lead times and declining market shares and will eventually be forced out of the industry. The figures quoted are for a 'defensive' R and D capacity. An 'offensive' strategy, i.e. one seeking to drive other firms out of the industry by increasing the frequency and reducing the lead time of innovation, will tend to be even more expensive. Freeman has suggested that although this analysis was developed in relation to the electronic capital-goods industry it applies also to other science-based industries, particularly electrical machinery and chemicals.[118]

The level of the threshold for R and D expenditure is in part determined by the scientific and technological basis of the industry, and the fact that threshold levels vary is in part due to differences between industries in their scientific and technological bases. Such differences have an independent influence on the rate of innovation. 'Science-based' industries (e.g. aerospace, electronics and telecommunications, chemicals and pharmaceuticals, and motor vehicles) are likely to have a higher rate of innovation irrespective of market structure or firm size than are industries based on a more conservative technology (e.g. textiles, food and drink, timber and furniture, clothing and footwear). Scherer in his study has found that the most important cause of 'observed inter-industry differences in patenting, holding firm sales constant' was 'a set of influences best described under the heading "technological opportunity" ', which he has judged to be ultimately dependent on 'the broad advance of scientific and technical knowledge'. Of the overall variance in corporate patenting more than 30 per cent was attributed to interindustry differences in technological opportunity as against 42 per cent to interfirm differences in sales and 12 per cent to interindustry differences in the propensity to patent.[119]

Although agreement with Scherer's conclusion that interindustry differences in technological opportunity are the major determinant of interindustry differences in the rate of innovation is widespread, it is not unanimous. An apparent exception is Schmookler, who has argued that demand-induced profit expectations determine the performance characteristics of the commodities to be developed, with the state of scientific and technical knowledge merely determining how these performance characteristics are to be achieved. Thus, if inventions are classified to the industries in which the commodities incorporating them are to be used, rather than to the industries in which the commodities are to be produced, the rate of invention will be largely determined by the growth of demand. Invention is seen as essentially a response to demand with technological opportunity providing little of the stimulus.[120] However, it may be that Schmookler is only an apparent exception since he has accepted that technological opportunity will determine the allocation of innovative resources between industries once a profitable final demand has been established.

Rosenberg, in a critique of Schmookler, while not denying the importance of demand has challenged any attribution of primacy to the demand side. He has argued that:

> . . . the allocation of inventive resources has in the past been determined jointly by demand forces which have broadly shaped the shifting payoffs to successful invention, together with supply side forces which have determined both the probability of success within any particular time frame as well as the prospective cost of producing a successful invention.[121]

The supply side cannot be neglected because 'society's technical competence at any point in time constitutes a basic determinant of the kinds of inventions which can be successfully undertaken', and hence 'inventions are *not* equally possible in all industries'.[122]

Are there any general conclusions that can be drawn from the empirical investigations of the relationship between industrial structure, technological opportunity and innovation? One possible explanation of the likely non-linear relationship between the intensity of innovative activity on the one hand and firm size and industry concentration on the other, first increasing then decreasing, is that the rate of innovation may be affected by the degree of rivalry. Kamien and Schwartz have presented a model in which a profit-maximising firm's decision on when to innovate depends on the expected time of innovation by rival firms. The sooner this time, the greater the degree of rivalry. Their model predicts that for profitable projects the development period will initially shorten as the intensity of rivalry increases, but beyond a certain intensity it will lengthen. Although based on the unsatisfactory assumption that the costs of development and aggregate benefits of the innovation are known, the model does give results that are consistent with the empirical evidence, since a shorter development period implies a higher rate of innovation.[123] Grabowski and Baxter have examined the role of rivalry by testing for the existence of interdependencies in firms' R and D expenditures. On the basis of 1947–66 data for eight of the sixteen largest US chemical firms they have found 'some direct evidence that firms increase R and D expenditure in response to rivals' outlays and that the top two firms in the industry are particularly responsive to each other'.[124] In a subsidiary cross-sectional analysis of twenty-nine three-digit industries using 1954–5 data they have found a significant negative rank correlation between industry concentration and the coefficient of variation of industry R and D intensity. There was also a similar relationship between industry research intensity and the coefficient of variation of industry research intensity, holding the level of concentration constant. Grabowski and Baxter's overall conclusion was that 'in research intensive industries, each firm's R and D expenditures are sensitive to what competitors allocate to this activity'.[125]

Recognition of the relationship between innovation and rivalry is, of course, only a start. The inadequacies of the present state of oligopoly theory – the absence of a relevant theory of business behaviour in economies dominated by big business – render the answers to many questions still problematic. For instance, is the direction of causation from an oligopolistic industry of a few large firms to a rapid rate of innovation, or is it from a technological opportunity enabling rapid innovation to an oligopolistic industry of a few large firms? The discussion of technological opportunity above suggests that the latter possibility merits further investigation.

INNOVATION AND COMPETITION

In order to analyse the way in which the interaction of opportunities for innovation and industrial structure influences the nature of the competitive struggle a change of focus is needed. The relevant question is not whether large oligopolists are responsible for relatively more innovative activity or inventive output than smaller, more atomistically competitive firms; rather it is whether the existence of opportunities for innovation gives rise to competitive advantages for any particular category of firm. The significance of this change of focus may be illustrated by a consideration of the controversy about the sources of invention.

The sources of invention

The argument has been over the relative merits of large-scale organised and directed activity, e.g. in the research laboratories of large oligopolists, as contrasted with the inspiration and persistence of the creative individual, e.g. in small entrepreneur-based firms or as private inventors. Both Schumpeter in his later work and Galbraith have expounded the merits of organised research:

Technological progress is increasingly becoming the business of teams of trained specialists who turn out what is required and make it work in predictable ways.[126]

Technical development has long since become the preserve of the scientist and the engineer. Most of the cheap and simple inventions have, to put it bluntly and unpersuasively, been made.[127]

The best-known advocates of the small person are Jewkes and his associates. They have examined sixty-one inventions, selected as the major inventions of the period 1900–56, and concluded that the majority were made not by the research departments of firms but by private inventors acting for themselves.[128] This study has been criticised by Freeman on the grounds that it ignores a trend towards corporate inventions in the latter part of the period, the selection of major inventions was biased, it ignores (explicitly) development and it adopts an unduly individualistic or 'heroic' theory of invention.[129] However, despite these criticisms, which were initially made in the context of a defence of the possibility of a planned science policy, there seems to be strong evidence that a disproportionate number of major as opposed to minor or derivative inventions have tended to originate outside the dominant oligopolies.

A study by Adams and Dirlam of the major invention in steelmaking this century has found that 'the invention was neither sponsored nor supported by large, dominant firms'. On the contrary: 'The oxygen process was developed in continental Europe and perfected by the employees of a nationalised enterprise, in a war-ravaged country, with a total steel ingot capacity of about 1 million tons – by a *firm* that was less than one-third the size of a single *plant* of the United States Steel Corporation.'[130] Mueller has found that, of twenty-five major product and process innovations by Du Pont – one of the world's largest chemical companies – in the period 1920–50, ten were based on the inventions of Du Pont scientists and engineers: five out of eighteen new products, and five out of seven product or process improvements. The more detailed analysis contained in the study suggests that much of Du Pont's success has been due to the vigorous development of inventions drawn from outside the firm rather than to its own inventions.[131] In a study of the major inventions in the petroleum-refining industry Enos has found that: 'In almost all cases the inventions were made by men close to the oil industry but not attached to the major firms.'[132] Finally, a summary of Freeman's study of the electronic capital-goods industry, after noting the dominant position of American firms in this field, comments: 'The history of the principal innovations suggests that the American lead has been due less to original invention than to more rapid development of greatly improved models and more efficient technical service and marketing.'[133]

The common feature of these and other case studies is that in general major inventions have not originated in the large oligopolistic firms. However, large corporations have without doubt carried out the vast bulk of the subsequent development work up to the point of the successful commercial launching of the associated innovation, and in the course of this work they have made numerous minor and derivative inventions that cumulatively have been of great importance. The quantitative domination of corporations is reflected in the change that has occurred in the statistics of patents issued. In the United States the proportion of patents issued to individuals fell from about 80 per cent of the total in 1900 to about 40 per cent in 1957; in the United Kingdom patent applications from companies accounted for about 15 per cent of the total in 1913 and about 70 per cent in the late 1960s.[134] As noted above, qualitative differences do not show up in patent statistics. If they are to be detected at all, it is likely to be in the sort of case studies just considered.

An interesting attempt at directly estimating the relative importance of innovation according to firm size was undertaken by Freeman for the Bolton Committee of Inquiry on Small Firms. A survey of important innovations between 1945 and 1970 in some fifty three-digit industries covering about half of the total net output of British industry unearthed 1,100 innovations carried through by over 700 firms. Small firms, with fewer than 200 workers, accounted for 10 per cent of all innovations, compared with roughly one-quarter of total employment and one-fifth of net output. Large firms, with 1,000 or more workers, accounted for 80 per cent and very large firms, employing over 10,000 workers, for one-half of all innovations. There were, of course, wide variations between industries in the contribution of small firms, with two-thirds of all their innovations being in the machinery, instruments and electronics industries. On the other hand, in industries like aircraft, pharmaceuticals, dyes, synthetic resins and plastics, and vehicles the contribution of small firms was virtually non-existent. Thus, Freeman has concluded that, while

Jewkes is right, so too is Galbraith. Small firms still have a role in industrial invention and innovation – indeed, their innovative efficiency on average seems to be greater than that of larger firms since their 10 per cent of total innovations was achieved with only 3–4 per cent of total R and D expenditure – but there is no doubt that the innovative process today is dominated by the large corporation.[135] It is perhaps worth noting that, although in the end the historical record is not really in dispute, there remains an important difference between Jewkes and Freeman, with the former emphasising the continuing central role of non-corporate invention and the latter stressing the historical tendency towards the professionalisation of R and D and with it of invention as well as innovation.[136]

The subordination of innovation to commercial objectives
A reason for this state of affairs, in which corporate laboratories are responsible for a minority of major and a majority of minor or derivative inventions, is not hard to find. The nature of the innovation process is such that, the further back the stage, i.e. the more basic or fundamental the invention, the greater the uncertainty involved; whereas the closer the stage to the final point innovation, although the resources involved may be greater, the more predictable is the outcome. Thus, in a capitalist economy in which firms have at least to avoid continuing losses if they are to survive, corporate R and D will be concentrated on projects closely related to the firm's more immediate commercial requirements and will tend to eschew the less predictable, more basic research.

There is a variety of evidence for this proposition. Carter and Williams have found that: 'To be successful R & D must be related to the financial position and commercial objectives of the firm,' and that: 'The firm which is speedy and successful in scientific and technical progress is one in which research, production and sales are co-ordinated.'[137] A survey by the Federation of British Industry has reported that in 1959 over 50 per cent of industrial R and D in Britain was devoted to 'major and minor improvements' and to technical services.[138] Based on questionnaire replies from eighty-one of *The Times* top 300 companies in 1972, Schott has found that 60 per cent of R and D expenditure on projects successfully completed in the UK private sector in 1972 was on projects finished in two years or less, while only 11 per cent was on projects taking four years or more. She has concluded that 'with such short-term programmes the likelihood of some radical new innovation occurring must be fairly small'.[139] Gibbons and Johnston have found that, of 1,000 new product announcements in UK technical journals on a given date in 1971, only 18 per cent were new products involving technical change and developed in the United Kingdom and half of these were in fact modifications of the firms' existing products.[140]

In addition to a general propensity to avoid uncertainty as far as possible, two related reasons for the emphasis on relatively minor short-term projects have been advanced. Hamberg has drawn attention to the influence of vested positions:

. . . no firm is likely to be willing to conduct research that will result in the obsolescence of products that are highly profitable and the markets for which may have been painfully built up in the fairly recent past. Instead, such firms are likely to confine their research activities largely to extensions and refinements of the profitable products, that is, to improvements within the existing framework, in the interests of consolidation of past gains.[141]

Many writers have stressed the connection between innovation and product differentiation. Hamberg has remarked:

... it is apparent that the growth of industrial spending on R & D has to a considerable extent been motivated by the search for another means of achieving product differentiation. Once some firms turn to R & D for this purpose, the pressure is on their competitors to follow suit. The result is a stream of product improvements or 'new' products ... In either case, much of the research involved is inevitably defensive in nature, aimed at protecting market positions, and the emphasis is therefore on rush projects that secure immediate benefits.[142]

Comanor has cast the hypothesis in a form that is susceptible to empirical investigation:

Product differentiation, it is well known, has the effect of insulating submarkets and creating entry barriers. While research expenditures may serve many functions, an important one is to foster and promote a rapid rate of new product introductions, which then serves to facilitate the achievement of differentiation. In this manner, firms aim to repulse the competitive thrusts of their rivals. When joined with the restrictive privileges conferred by the patent system, this prospect is likely to provide an even stronger incentive to allocate funds for research. And therefore, research outlays should be higher in industries where products are differentiable.[143]

In order to test this proposition Comanor has drawn on Bain's finding [144] that the consumer non-durables and material inputs sectors of industry are less differentiated and the consumer durables and investment goods sectors more differentiated. He has assumed that new product and product improvement projects will be more likely than new process projects when differentiation is the object. A McGraw-Hill survey has found that in 1958 new processes were the aim of 18 per cent of firms in consumer non-durables and of 24 per cent in materials inputs but of only 13 per cent in consumer durables and 5 per cent in investment goods.[145] Comanor has also found that research levels tended to be far greater in the first two sectors than in the last two and concluded that 'our results support the view that differentiability is a major element in the decision to undertake extensive research'.[146]

The importance of linking R and D to commercial possibilities has emerged very clearly from the Sappho project carried out at the Science Policy Research Unit in the University of Sussex. The initial project examined twenty-nine 'pairs' of successful and unsuccessful innovations in the chemical and scientific instrument industries, with the pairing based on similarity of intended market and success defined in commercial terms. Subsequently, a further fourteen pairs from the same industries were added. The strongest discriminator between success and failure was the extent to which 'user needs' had been understood, which reflected the overall quality of R and D work, marketing and management (in the sense of the personnel performing the role of entrepreneur–innovator). Freeman has interpreted the results of the project as support for the view that innovation is a 'coupling process' in which:

> The critical role of the 'entrepreneur' (whatever individual or combination of individuals fulfil this role) is to 'match' the technology with the market, i.e. to understand the user requirements better than competitive attempts, and to ensure that adequate resources are available for development and launch.[147]

Innovation as a competitive weapon: the advantages of size
In general innovation is undertaken by large firms, although small firms continue to play a role in some industries. This suggests that large firms tend to have a competitive advantage in those industries where there is scope for continuing innovation. This advantage stems from the resources that large firms are able to deploy, whether for the purpose of developing major innovations in the form of new generations of equipment or entirely new products, or for the purpose of launching a continuous stream of minor product-differentiating 'innovations'.

Even in the case of major advances there are pressures resulting in the concentration of corporate research on relatively short-run development work, summed up by Andrew Carnegie in the phrase: 'Pioneering don't pay.' Freeman has come across this phenomenon in his study of the electronic capital-goods industry:

> The performance of the first laboratory prototypes and early commercial deliveries almost always leaves a great deal to be desired, so that the scope for improvement is very great. For this reason some entrepreneurs have followed a deliberate policy of being *second* with a new development rather than first. Success in such a policy often requires a greater capacity for moving fast with new developments once the time is considered ripe.

It is here that the advantages of the largest firms begin to tell:

> . . . it is not necessary to invent everything in order to secure a strong technical or commercial lead. It is quite possible to recover from a temporary lag . . . What is necessary is to have a strong development and engineering capacity, so that inventions made elsewhere may be rapidly assimilated, imitated, utilised and improved upon.[148]

This analysis is likely to have fairly general application for firms operating in fields where there are substantial technological opportunities. Mansfield has written that: 'Empirical studies substantiate the hypothesis that large firms are quicker, on the average, than small ones to begin using new techniques.'[149] He has also noted that: 'Independent inventors often turn their inventions over to larger companies for development, because they lack the financial resources and necessary facilities.'[150] This phenomenon has been widely observed. In his study of the plastics industry Freeman has found that 'those small firms which have patented new inventions have often subsequently been absorbed.'[151] Baran and Sweezy have quoted a former vice-president of General Electric: 'I know of no original product invention, not even electric shavers or heating pads, made by any of the giant laboratories or corporations . . . The record of the giants is one of moving in, buying out and absorbing the smaller creators.'[152]

There are very great competitive advantages to be gained from leaving the uncertain pioneering work to others. However, this is only consistent with survival if the firm is aware of new developments proving successful and is able to move quickly into the field at the appropriate time. The larger firms are able to maintain 'industrial laboratories . . . acting as information monitors and funnels for work done elsewhere and . . . providing the basis for further development work and adaptation to their companies' specific needs.'[153] They are also likely to be in a stronger position to acquire the individual entrepreneurs or small firms that have survived the uncertain process of pioneering and emerged with an invention or innovation of proved commercial potential. Finally, the larger firms are likely to be in a stronger bargaining position over patent exchanges or licensing arrangements should these prove to be the best way forward.

One of the varied ways in which size confers a competitive advantage in the case of minor product-differentiating 'innovation' has been illustrated by an interesting study of the US automobile industry in the 1950s. Menge has examined the use of 'new' products, i.e. style changes or new models, as a competitive weapon of the largest firms. He has found that, even if small firms were large enough to obtain all the usual production economies of scale, style changes put them at a disadvantage. This was because the fixed capital equipment (i.e. dies) for body stamping is very expensive and has a given life in terms of the number of bodies stamped. The largest firms have to replace their dies, say, every two years. They are then able to change style at no extra cost. Small firms can only compete by changing style if they scrap their dies before they are worn out. Hence, style changes will cost them extra.[154] More generally, product-differentiating 'innovation' is part of the overall process of product differentiation, including branding and advertising, and the competitive advantages of size arise from the familiar characteristics of the process as a whole. Of course, product differentiation also provides the possibility for small firms to survive on a specialist basis.

It is now possible to return to the question of the direction of causation between innovation and industry structure, including firm size. Although there is likely to be a relationship of interdependence between the rate of innovation and the structural characteristics of an industry,[155] the existence of significant opportunities for technological innovation appears to have an important independent effect on industry structure. Carter and Williams have put it rather cautiously: 'We suggest that the technical opportunities open to industry react, though no doubt slowly and imperfectly, on its organisation.'[156] Stoneman has commented on the effect of continuous technological change on the structure of the computer industry:

The two salient features of the industry that we have isolated are increasing returns to scale through fixed R and D expenditures and the technological nature of the competition promoting these R and D expenditures. A market share equal to 10% of the world market has been estimated as the minimum scale for long-run profitability. The fact that the industry has experienced heavy merger activity is, one can hypothesise, the result of these factors. It is perhaps significant that having captured a large market share very early IBM never had to engage in merger activity.[157]

Phillips has provided an admirable summary of the overall argument:

It is suggested, then, that a progressing science which is related to the products and processes of particular industries operates on markets in ways such that some firms tend to become larger, more profitable and more technologically progressive while others experience increasing difficulties in remaining viable. The latter tend either to remain small, in 'corners' of the market protected by various forms of product differentiation, or to disappear through mergers and failures. These results are not because 'the modern industry of a few large firms' is 'an almost perfect instrument for inducing technical change' [Galbraith]. The results are instead because continuity in technical change made possible by a changing scientific environment is an almost perfect instrument for inducing a modern industry of a few large firms which, in turn, contribute to technology.[158]

CONCLUSION

The study of innovation at the microeconomic level cannot abstract from uncertainty. In industries characterised by continuous technological change firms are constantly faced with both technical and market uncertainty. Work in this area seldom makes use of neoclassical theory. The assumption of perfect knowledge or a certainty equivalent and the concepts of maximisation and equilibrium are inherently unsuited to the analysis of continuous, frequently radical and, over all but the shortest period, largely unpredictable change. Similarly, the role of innovation in the competitive process can only be understood in a context of active oligopolistic rivalry, with which the neoclassical paradigm is unable to cope. Nelson and Winter have put it as follows:

The role of competition seems better characterised in the Schumpeterian terms of competitive advantages gained through innovation, or early adoption of a new product or process, than in the equilibrium language of neoclassical theory . . . The competitive environment within which firms operate is one of struggle and motion. It is a dynamic selection environment, not an equilibrium one.[159]

In an attempt to develop a formal model incorporating the Schumpeterian approach, they have proposed an evolutionary theory of the behaviour of firms and sectors of the economy based on a 'behavioural' approach to individual firms and an economic selection mechanism: 'Through the joint action of search and selection, the firms evolve over time, with the condition of the industry on each day bearing the seeds of its condition on the day following.'[160] The similarities between this approach and that suggested in the conclusions to Chapters 3 and 4 are evident, but whether this particular attempt will in the end prove fruitful remains to be seen. What does seem certain, however, is that an understanding of corporate innovation requires a theory in which innovation is incorporated as an integral part of the competitive process in advanced capitalist economies.

The emphasis of industrial R and D activity on short run projects geared to the firm's immediate competitive situation has far-reaching normative implications. In public policy discussion innovation is invariably regarded as desirable, and firms with a 'good' record of technical 'progressiveness' tend to be treated favourably by agencies set up to safeguard the 'public interest'. However, to the extent that innovation is of a trivial character, designed primarily to differentiate the product, it may well be considered as socially undesirable. A study of the US automobile industry has distinguished between innovations that would have enabled 1949 models to be produced more cheaply and those whose major purpose was to enable new models to be marketed. The cost of model changes in the late 1950s has been estimated at more than 25 per cent of purchase price.[161] Hamberg has stressed that 'the broad interpretation given "new products" by most firms' includes items like a new shade of lipstick, a higher octane petrol, a new car model.[162] Freeman has been rather more cautious and drawn a distinction between capital goods and consumer goods industries, since product-differentiating innovation is largely concentrated in the latter where R and D expenditures are relatively small. However, even he has suggested that because of the uncertainty and long term character of radical R and D 'it must be expected that there will be a tendency in a private capitalist economy to underinvestment in long-term research and innovation'. He has also pointed out that since 98 per cent of the world's R and D is undertaken in the developed countries, very little of it is directed towards satisfying the basic human needs of the majority of the world's population.[163]

This raises sharply the role of government in R and D. Breakdowns of publicly funded R and D by objective have revealed a remarkably low *de facto* priority for welfare and environmental R and D. Freeman has reported a fascinating study undertaken in the German Federal Republic, in which:

> . . . the priorities both of the public and of the civil servants responsible for science policy were found to be the almost exact reverse of those implied by the actual pattern of expenditures. That is to say that military, nuclear and space objectives were rated very low and a much higher priority accorded to 'welfare' objectives – research on the environment, medical research and education.[164]

It seems that neither the market mechanism nor the political process ensures that the allocation of R and D resources corresponds to what people regard as socially desirable. At the end of his invaluable book Freeman has rasied the question of how the process of innovation can be made more socially accountable.

He has suggested that the development of effective methods of 'technology assessment', incorporating aesthetic, work satisfaction and environmental criteria, is an urgent need if 'alienated technology' is to become 'human technology'.[165] Instead of taking it for granted that innovation – any innovation it often seems – is *per se* desirable, the attempt needs to be made to assess the contribution of different sorts of innovative effort, both actual and potential, to human welfare.

5.5 FURTHER READING

Utton's article[5] is the best source for information on diversification in the United Kingdom. For a discussion of merger and its significance for the working of the economic system, see Aaronovitch and Sawyer[23] and Hannah.[24] Freeman's work on innovation[91] is outstanding.

NOTES AND REFERENCES

1 M. R. Fisher, 'Towards a theory of diversification', *Oxford Economic Papers,* new series, vol. 13 (October 1961), p. 293.
2 For example, K. George, 'The changing structure of competitive industry', *Economic Journal*, vol. 82 (March 1972), supplement, pp. 355–60.
3 L. R. Amey, 'Diversified manufacturing business', *Journal of the Royal Statistical Society*, series A, vol. 127, pt 2 (1964), p. 252.
4 E. Penrose, *The Theory of the Growth of the Firm* (Oxford, Blackwell, 1959), pp. 109–11.
5 See M. A. Utton, 'Large firm diversification in British manufacturing industry', *Economic Journal*, vol. 87 (March 1977), pp. 102–3. The expression for W is derived as follows. The area under the diversification curve, V, is

$$V = \tfrac{1}{2}p_1 + [(n-1)p_1 + \tfrac{1}{2}p_2] + [(n-2)p_2 + \tfrac{1}{2}p_3] \ldots$$

$$= \tfrac{1}{2} + n - \sum_{i=1}^{n} ip_i$$

since

$$\sum_{i=1}^{n} p_i = 1$$

Since the height of the figure is 1 and the width is n the area above the curve, Y, is

$$Y = n - V = \sum_{i=1}^{n} ip_i - \tfrac{1}{2}$$

and twice the area above the curve, W, is

$$W = 2 \sum_{i=1}^{n} ip_i - 1$$

6 An incidental result reported by Utton is that in 1974 the average ratio of secondary to total employment among the 200 largest manufacturing enterprises was 24 per cent (see Utton, op. cit., n. 5, table A1, p. 112). Although based on employment and the 200 largest firms rather than on output and all firms with over 100 employees, and therefore not directly comparable with Table 5.1, Utton's figure suggests a further increase in diversification since 1968.

7 Local units are in general establishments, although in some instances an establishment might constitute two or more local units. Since local units are classified to a three-digit industry on the basis of their most important activity, no account is taken of diversification *within* a local unit.

8 J. Hassid, 'Recent evidence on conglomerate diversification in UK manufacturing industry', *Manchester School*, vol. 43 (December 1975), table 1, p. 375; and Utton, op. cit. (n. 5), table 2, p. 104.

9 M. Gort, *Diversification and Integration in American Industry, 1929–54*, National Bureau of Economic Research, General Series 77 (Princeton, Princeton UP, 1962); and Amey, op. cit. (n. 3), p. 262.

10 Hassid, op. cit. (n. 8), pp. 386–7.

11 Hassid, op. cit. (n. 8), pp. 387–8 and 392–3.

12 Amey, op. cit. (n. 3), pp. 274–6; Hassid, op. cit. (n. 8), p. 390; J. Hassid, 'Diversification and the firm's rate of growth', *Manchester School*, vol. 45 (March 1977), esp. pp. 21–6; and P. Gorecki, 'The determinants of entry by new and diversifying enterprises in the UK manufacturing sector, 1958–1963: some tentative results', *Applied Economics*, vol. 7 (1975), esp. pp. 143–6.

13 Gort, op. cit. (n. 9); C. H. Berry, *Corporate Growth and Diversification* (Princeton, Princeton UP, 1975), p. 70; S. Rhoades, 'The effect of diversification on industry profit performance in 241 manufacturing industries, 1963', *Review of Economics and Statistics*, vol. 55 (May 1973), pp. 151–3; and J. Carter, 'In search of synergy: a structure–performance test', *Review of Economics and Statistics*, vol. 59 (August 1977), pp. 284–8.

14 P. Gorecki, 'An inter-industry analysis of diversification in the UK manufacturing sector', *Journal of Industrial Economics*, vol. 24 (December 1975), pp. 132–3 and 140–2; and Hassid, op. cit. (n. 8), pp. 388 and 392–3.

15 Amey, op. cit. (n. 3), p. 268; and Hassid, op. cit. (n. 8), p. 389.

16 Cf. H. Hines, 'Effectiveness of "entry" by already established firms', *Quarterly Journal of Economics*, vol. 71 (February 1957), pp. 132–50. An interesting more recent study has found that the entry of diversifying firms into new industries was not affected at the level of statistical significance by the conventional barriers to entry (Gorecki, op. cit., n. 12, p. 144).

17 See section 5.4.

18 Penrose, op. cit. (n. 4), p. 106.

19 M. A. Utton, 'Diversification, mergers and profit stability', *Business Ratios*, issue 1 (1969), p. 24.

20 Utton, op. cit. (n. 5), pp. 108–10.

21 Gorecki, op. cit. (n. 14), pp. 134–6; and C. H. Berry, 'Corporate growth and diversification', *Journal of Law and Economics*, vol. 14 (1971), p. 379.

22 J. W. Markham, 'Survey of the evidence and findings on mergers', in National Bureau of Economic Research (NBER), *Business Concentration and Price Policy*, Special Conference Series 5 (Princeton, Princeton UP, 1955), p. 143.

23 For a discussion of the measurement of merger activity, see S. Aaronovitch and M. Sawyer, *Big Business* (London, Macmillan, 1975), pp. 130–40.

24 L. Hannah, *The Rise of the Corporate Economy* (London, Methuen, 1976), pp. 106–11 and appendix 1, pp. 203–14.

25 G. Meeks, *Disappointing Marriage: A Study of the Gains from Merger*, University

of Cambridge Department of Applied Economics, Occasional Paper 51 (Cambridge, Cambridge UP, 1977), table 2.B, p. 5.

26 Aaronovitch and Sawyer, op. cit. (n. 23), table 7.13, p. 145.

27 A. Singh, *Take-overs*, University of Cambridge Department of Applied Economics, Monograph 19 (Cambridge, Cambridge UP, 1971), p. 34; Utton, op. cit. (n. 19), table 2, p. 25; G. Newbould, *Management and Merger Activity* (Liverpool, Guthstead, 1970), p. 33; D. Kuehn, *Takeovers and the Theory of the Firm* (London, Macmillan, 1975), p. 24; and J. Gribbin, 'The operation of the Mergers Panel since 1965', *Trade and Industry*, vol. 14 (17 January 1974), table 5, p. 71.

28 See, for example, S. Reid, *Mergers, Managers and the Economy* (New York, McGraw-Hill, 1968), table 5.1, p. 76; and L. W. Stern, 'Mergers under scrutiny', *Harvard Business Review*, vol. 47 (July–August 1969), p. 19.

29 For the UK record, see Chapter 9.

30 A. Singh, 'Takeovers, economic natural selection, and the theory of the firm: evidence from the post-war United Kingdom experience', *Economic Journal*, vol. 85 (September 1975), p. 499.

31 Markham, op. cit. (n. 22). Incidentally, this quotation is a good illustration of the way in which the consideration of merger has been greatly influenced by implicit normative assumptions.

32 G. Stigler, 'Monopoly and oligopoly by merger', *American Economic Review (Papers and Proceedings)*, vol. 40 (May 1950), pp. 23–34.

33 The concept of synergy $(2+2=5)$ is often restricted to situations in which merger enables a saving of resources and hence lower costs (cf. Newbould, op. cit., n. 27, p. 163). From the standpoint of the individual profit-maximising firm, however, synergy should surely be interpreted as a situation in which merger enables combined profits to be higher than would otherwise be the case. If so, increased monopoly power would also be counted a synergistic effect.

34 R. Nelson, *Merger Movements in American Industry, 1895–1956*, National Bureau of Economic Research, General Series 66 (Princeton, Princeton UP, 1959), p. 102.

35 Markham, op. cit. (n. 22), p. 161.

36 Stigler, op. cit. (n. 32), p. 26.

37 L. Cook and R. Cohen, *Effects of Mergers* (London, Allen & Unwin, 1958), p. 442.

38 M. Gort, 'An economic disturbance theory of mergers', *Quarterly Journal of Economics*, vol. 83 (November 1969), pp. 624–42.

39 Gort, op. cit. (n. 38), p. 624.

40 Gort, op. cit. (n. 38), p. 626.

41 It has been suggested that Gort's results are also consistent with a traditional entrepreneurial view of merger. See B. Hindley, 'Recent theory and evidence on corporate merger', in K. Cowling (ed.), *Market Structure and Corporate Behaviour* (London, Gray-Mills, 1972), pp. 14–15.

42 Markham, op. cit. (n. 22), p. 151.

43 Nelson, op. cit. (n. 34), ch. 5, esp. pp. 108–12.

44 C. J. Maule, 'A note on mergers and the business cycle', *Journal of Industrial Economics*, vol. 16 (April 1968), pp. 99–105.

45 Cf. Nelson, op. cit. (n. 34), pp. 116–24; and R. L. Nelson, 'Business cycle factors in the choice between internal and external growth', in W. Alberts and J. Segall (eds), *The Corporate Merger* (Chicago, Chicago UP, 1966).

46 Stigler, op. cit. (n. 32), p. 30.

47 Hannah, op. cit. (n. 24), pp. 67–8.

48 Markham, op. cit. (n. 22), p. 181; Gort, op. cit. (n. 38), p. 638.

49 Nelson, op. cit. (n. 34), p. 125.

50 D. C. Mueller, 'A theory of conglomerate mergers', *Quarterly Journal of Economics*, vol. 83 (November 1969), pp. 643–59.

51 Mueller, op. cit. (n. 50), p. 656.
52 Mueller, op. cit. (n. 50), pp. 652–3.
53 Cf. Gort, op. cit. (n. 9), p. 58; and Amey, op. cit. (n. 3), p. 280.
54 Reid, op. cit. (n. 28), pt 2.
55 Reid, op. cit. (n. 28), table 8.2, p. 159 and ch. 9.
56 Cf. F. M. Scherer, *Industrial Market Structure and Economic Performance* (Chicago, Rand McNally, 1970), pp. 121–2; and Aaronovitch and Sawyer, op. cit. (n. 23), pp. 170–2.
57 Newbould, op. cit. (n. 27), p. 95.
58 Newbould, op. cit. (n. 27), pp. 143–52.
59 K. George and A. Silberston, 'The causes and effects of mergers', *Scottish Journal of Political Economy*, vol. 22 (June 1975), p. 184.
60 George and Silberston, op. cit. (n. 59), p. 186.
61 Aaronovitch and Sawyer, op. cit. (n. 23), chs 10–12. A summary of their argument is set out on pp. 239–40.
62 Newbould, op. cit. (n. 27), pp. 153–9; and Aaronovitch and Sawyer, op. cit. (n. 23), pp. 287–90 and appendix 12.1, pp. 293–304.
63 Hannah, op. cit. (n. 24), pp. 169–70.
64 Cook and Cohen, op. cit. (n. 37), p. 11.
65 M. A. Utton, 'On measuring the effects of industrial mergers', *Scottish Journal of Political Economy*, vol. 21 (February 1974), table I, p. 18; and Meeks, op. cit. (n. 25), table C.A, p. 88.
66 Singh, op. cit. (n. 27), pp. 161–5; Newbould, op. cit. (n. 27), table 5.14, p. 91; Utton, op. cit. (n. 65), pp. 20–5; and Meeks, op. cit. (n. 25), pp. 18–33.
67 Reid, op. cit. (n. 28), table 8.2, p. 159.
68 Cook and Cohen, op. cit. (n. 37), p. 436.
69 J. Kitching, 'Why do mergers miscarry?', *Harvard Business Review*, vol. 45 (November–December 1967), pp. 84–101.
70 C. F. Pratten, 'A case study of a conglomerate merger', *Moorgate and Wall Street* (Spring 1970), pp. 27–54.
71 Newbould, op. cit. (n. 27), pp. 192–3.
72 P. Hart, M. A. Utton and G. Walshe, *Mergers and Concentration in British Industry*, National Institute of Economic and Social Research, Occasional Paper 26 (Cambridge, Cambridge UP, 1973), p. 102. For a recent survey of the evidence, see Meeks, op. cit. (n. 25), pp. 30–2.
73 For a summary of the literature, see L. Hannah and J. Kay, *Concentration in Modern Industry* (London, Macmillan, 1977), appendix 2, pp. 126–8.
74 Utton, op. cit. (n. 65), pp. 47–53.
75 Hart, Utton and Walshe, op. cit. (n. 72), pp. 37 and 158.
76 Hannah and Kay, op. cit. (n. 73), pp. 65–71, 73–9, 85–6, 88–93 and 95. See also Hannah, op. cit. (n. 24), appendix 2, pp. 222–5.
77 K. George, 'A note on changes in industrial concentration in the United Kingdom', *Economic Journal*, vol. 85 (March 1975), pp. 124–8.
78 Hannah, op. cit. (n. 24), p. 113.
79 G. Whittington, 'Changes in the top 100 quoted manufacturing companies in the United Kingdom, 1948–1968', *Journal of Industrial Economics*, vol. 21 (November 1972), pp. 31–2.
80 G. Meeks and G. Whittington, 'Giant companies in the United Kingdom, 1948–69', *Economic Journal*, vol. 85 (December 1975), pp. 829–30. These authors have commented on the contrast between the results of their study and those of Utton's analysis of the growth of the 320 largest UK companies in 1954 over the period 1954–65. Utton has found, if anything, 'an inverse relationship between size and importance of growth by merger' (M. A. Utton, 'Mergers and the growth of large

firms', *Bulletin of the Oxford University Institute of Economics and Statistics,* vol. 34, May 1972, p. 193). Meeks and Whittington have suggested that the discrepancy may be due to differences in the company population and period covered.

81 R. Evely and I. Little, *Concentration in British Industry,* National Institute of Economic and Social Research, Economic and Social Studies 16 (Cambridge, Cambridge UP, 1960), p. 129.

82 G. Walshe, *Recent Trends in Monopoly in Great Britain,* National Institute of Economic and Social Research, Occasional Paper 27 (Cambridge, Cambridge UP, 1974), p. 99; see also p. 88 and ch. 5, pp. 91–9.

83 Stigler, op. cit. (n. 32), p. 23.

84 J. F. Weston, *The Role of Mergers in the Growth of Large Firms* (Berkeley, California UP, 1953), chs 2 and 3.

85 Singh, op. cit. (n. 27), p. 154; and Meeks, op. cit. (n. 25), table 3.A I, p. 20.

86 Walshe, op. cit. (n. 82), p. 88.

87 J. A. Schumpeter, *Business Cycles,* Vol. 1 (New York, McGraw-Hill, 1939), pp. 86 and 91.

88 T. Burns and G. Stalker, *The Management of Innovation* (London, Tavistock, 1961), p. 52.

89 Booz, Allen and Hamilton, *Management of New Products* (New York, Booz Allen and Hamilton, 1968); cited in E. Mansfield, *The Economics of Technological Change* (New York, Norton, 1968), pp. 65 and 105.

90 C. Carter and B. Williams, *Investment in Innovation* (London, Oxford UP, 1958), ch. 7.

91 C. Freeman, *The Economics of Industrial Innovation* (Harmondsworth, Penguin Books, 1974), pp. 231–3.

92 J. A. Schumpeter, *Capitalism, Socialism and Democracy,* 4th edn (London, Allen & Unwin, 1954), p. 132.

93 Schumpeter, op. cit. (n. 87), p. 84.

94 For a comparison of Schumpeter's view with that of A. P. Usher, who has advanced a theory explicitly based on the recognition of interdependent stages, see V. W. Ruttan, 'Usher and Schumpeter on invention, innovation and technological change', *Quarterly Journal of Economics,* vol. 73 (November 1959), pp. 596–606. For an extremely entertaining case study of innovation as a process, see R. Houlton, 'The process of innovation: magnetic recording and the broadcasting industry in the USA', *Bulletin of the Oxford University Institute of Economics and Statistics,* vol. 29 (February 1967), pp. 41–59.

95 Central Advisory Council for Science and Technology, *Technological Innovation in Britain* (London, HMSO, 1968), p. 1.

96 Freeman, op. cit. (n. 91), p. 265. The present author, in earlier editions of this book, made the error criticised by Freeman of wrongly citing much lower estimates of the relative importance of R and D costs, based on a misreading of a US Department of Commerce report.

97 For discussion of these matters, see C. Kennedy and A. P. Thirlwall, 'Technical progress: a survey', *Economic Journal,* vol. 82 (March 1972), pp. 11–72.

98 The terminology can become confusing. The *innovation process* – a series of inter-related stages – is to be distinguished from a *point innovation* – the final stage of the process at which a particular project is launched. Of course, the initial point innovation may be the start of a series of imitations – part of the process of *diffusion.* Presumably only successful innovations, however defined, should count as part of the output of the innovation process.

99 Bosworth has constructed an index of the commercial importance of patents by assuming that a patent's commercial importance will be reflected in the number of times that it is renewed (D. Bosworth, 'Changes in the quality of inventive output

and patent based indices of technological change', *Bulletin of Economic and Social Research,* vol. 25, November 1973, p. 98).

100 For a more detailed discussion of the problems of measurement, see S. Kuznets, 'Inventive activity: problems of definition and measurement', and B. Sanders, 'Some difficulties in measuring inventive activity', together with the 'Comment' of J. Schmookler, all in National Bureau of Economic Research (NBER), *The Rate and Direction of Inventive Activity,* Special Conference Series 13 (Princeton, Princeton UP, 1962). See also Freeman, op. cit. (n. 91), appendix, pp. 311–87.

101 D. Mueller, 'Patents, research and development, and the measurement of inventive activity' *Journal of Industrial Economics,* vol. 15 (November 1966), p. 36. Mueller has concluded that, if anything, R and D expenditures are to be preferred to patent statistics due to their greater stability.

102 See, for example, Carter and Williams, op. cit. (n. 90), p. 16; E. Mansfield, *Industrial Research and Technological Innovation* (New York, Norton, 1968); and M. Kamien and N. Schwartz, 'Market structure and innovation: a survey', *Journal of Economic Literature,* vol. 13 (March 1975), p. 5.

103 Central Statistical Office (CSO), *Annual Abstract of Statistics, 1977* (London, HMSO, 1978), p. 302.

104 CSO, op. cit. (n. 103), table 11.12, p. 306.

105 Department of Industry, 'Resources devoted to research and development by manufacturing industry', *Economic Trends,* vol. 247 (May 1974), table I, p. xliii.

106 Freeman, op. cit. (n. 91), esp. chs 2–4.

107 Freeman, op. cit. (n. 91), tables 2 and 41, pp. 34 and 290–1.

108 Freeman, op. cit. (n. 91), pp. 292–6.

109 Mansfield, op. cit. (n. 89), p. 188.

110 Freeman, op. cit. (n. 91), pp. 199–202 and 205.

111 See, for example, C. Taylor and A. Silberston, *The Economic Impact of the Patent System,* University of Cambridge Department of Applied Economics, Monograph 23 (Cambridge, Cambridge UP, 1973), p. 25.

112 See J. W. Markham, 'Market structure, business conduct and innovation', *American Economic Review (Papers and Proceedings),* vol. 55 (May 1965), pp. 323–4.

113 D. Hamberg, 'Size of firm, oligopoly and research: the evidence', *Canadian Journal of Economics and Political Science,* vol. 30 (February 1964), pp. 70 and 74–5.

114 F. Scherer, 'Firm size, market structure, opportunity, and the output of patented inventions', *American Economic Review,* vol. 55 (December 1965), pp. 1110 and 1120.

115 See Markham, op. cit. (n. 112), p. 329; and Kamien and Schwartz, op. cit. (n. 102), pp. 16–19.

116 See Kamien and Schwartz, op. cit. (n. 102), pp. 19–24, quotation p. 24.

117 Freeman, op. cit. (n. 91), p. 153.

118 This discussion of R and D threshold levels is taken from Freeman, op. cit. (n. 91), pp. 152–7. For the original study, see C. Freeman, 'Research and development in electronic capital goods', *National Institute Economic Review,* no. 34 (November 1965), pp. 40–91.

119 Scherer, op. cit. (n. 114), pp. 1100 and 1102–3. For discussion of the concept of 'opportunity to innovate', see B. Williams, *Technology, Investment and Growth* (London, Chapman & Hall, 1967), chs 2 and 7.

120 See J. Schmookler, *Invention and Economic Growth* (Cambridge, Mass., Harvard UP, 1966). For a summary and discussion of Schmookler's work, see Kamien and Schwartz, op. cit. (n. 102), pp. 7–8; and N. Rosenberg, 'Science, invention and economic growth', *Economic Journal,* vol. 84 (March 1974), pp. 90–108.

121 Rosenberg, op. cit. (n. 120), p. 103.

122 Rosenberg, op. cit. (n. 120), pp. 105–6.

123 M. Kamien and N. Schwartz, 'On the degree of rivalry for maximum innovative activity', *Quarterly Journal of Economics,* vol. 90 (May 1976), pp. 245–60. See also F. Scherer, 'Research and development resource allocation under rivalry', *Quarterly Journal of Economics,* vol. 81 (August 1967), pp. 359–94.

124 H. Grabowski and N. Baxter, 'Rivalry in industrial research and development', *Journal of Industrial Economics,* vol. 21 (July 1973), p. 228.

125 Grabowski and Baxter, op. cit. (n. 124), p. 233.

126 Schumpeter, op. cit. (n. 92), p. 132.

127 J. K. Galbraith, *American Capitalism* (Harmondsworth, Penguin Books, 1956), p. 100.

128 J. Jewkes, D. Sawers and R. Stillerman, *The Sources of Invention,* 2nd edn (London, Macmillan, 1969), esp. pts 2 and 3.

129 C. Freeman, 'Science and policy at the national level', in Organisation for Economic Co-operation and Development (OECD), *Problems of Science Policy* (Paris, OECD, 1968), pp. 61–5; and Freeman, op. cit. (n. 91), pp. 69–71 and 208.

130 W. Adams and J. B. Dirlam, 'Big steel, invention and innovation', *Quarterly Journal of Economics,* vol. 80 (May 1966), p. 174. For a criticism of this article by A. K. McAdams and a reply by Adams and Dirlam, see *Quarterly Journal of Economics,* vol. 81 (August 1967), pp. 457–82.

131 W. F. Mueller, 'The origins of the basic inventions underlying Du Pont's major product and process innovations, 1920 to 1950', in NBER, op. cit. (n. 100), pp. 323–46.

132 J. L. Enos, 'Invention and innovation in the petroleum refining industry', in NBER, op. cit. (n. 100), p. 304.

133 Freeman, op. cit. (n. 118), p. 3.

134 See Mansfield, op. cit. (n. 89), p. 91, for the US data; and A. Silberston, 'The patent system', *Lloyds Bank Review,* no. 84 (April 1967), p. 31, for the UK figures.

135 Freeman, op. cit. (n. 91), pp. 210–18. For the original study, see C. Freeman, *The Role of Small Firms in Innovation in the United Kingdom since 1945,* Committee of Inquiry on Small Firms (the Bolton Committee), Research Report No. 6 (London, HMSO, 1971).

136 Freeman, op. cit. (n. 91), pp. 71 and 219–20.

137 C. Carter and B. Williams, *Industry and Technical Progress* (London, Oxford UP, 1957), pp. 47 and 160.

138 Federation of British Industry, *Industrial Research Survey* (London, CBI, 1960); cited in P. S. Johnson, 'Firm size and technological change', *Moorgate and Wall Street* (Spring 1970), p. 11.

139 K. Schott, 'Investment in private industrial research and development in Britain', *Journal of Industrial Economics,* vol. 25 (December 1976), p. 86.

140 M. Gibbons and R. Johnston, *The Interaction of Science and Technology* (Manchester, University of Manchester Department of Liberal Studies in Science, mimeo, 1972); cited in Freeman, op. cit. (n. 91), p. 244.

141 D. Hamberg, 'Invention in the Industrial Research Laboratory', *Journal of Political Economy,* vol. 71 (April 1963), p. 105.

142 Hamberg, op. cit. (n. 141), pp. 100–1.

143 W. S. Comanor, 'Market structure, product differentiation, and industrial research', *Quarterly Journal of Economics,* vol. 81 (November 1967), p. 646.

144 J. Bain, *Barriers to New Competition* (Cambridge, Mass., Harvard UP, 1956), pp. 121–5 and appendix D.

145 McGraw-Hill Department of Economics, *Business Plans for New Plant and Equipment, 1958–1961* (New York, McGraw-Hill, 1958); cited in Comanor, op. cit. (n. 143), p. 647.

146 Comanor, op. cit. (n. 143), p. 648.

147 Freeman, op. cit. (n. 91), pp. 171–94, has outlined the project and summarised its findings; quotation p. 191. For the original study, see Science Policy Research Unit, *Report on Project SAPPHO,* 2 vols (University of Sussex, mimeo, 1971); and

Science Policy Research Unit, *Success and Failure in Industrial Innovation* (London, Centre for the Study of Industrial Innovation, 1972).

148 Freeman, op. cit. (n. 118), p. 63.

149 Mansfield, op. cit. (n. 89), pp. 123–4.

150 Mansfield, op. cit. (n. 89), p. 91.

151 C. Freeman, 'The plastics industry: a comparative study of research and innovation', *National Institute Economic Review,* no. 26 (November 1963), p. 32.

152 T. K. Quinn, *Giant Business: Threat to Democracy* (New York, Exposition Press, 1963), p. 117; cited in P. Baran and P. Sweezy, *Monopoly Capital* (Harmondsworth, Penguin Books, 1968), p. 60.

153 Hamberg, op. cit. (n. 141), p. 114.

154 J. A. Menge, 'Style change costs as a market weapon', *Quarterly Journal of Economics,* vol. 76 (November 1962), pp. 632–47.

155 Buxton has presented a three-equation model in which research intensity is a function of industry structure, the rate of technical change is a function of research intensity and industry structure, and the rate of change of industry structure is a function of the rate of technical change (A. Buxton, 'The process of technical change in UK manufacturing', *Applied Economics,* vol. 7, 1975, p. 62).

156 Carter and Williams, op. cit. (n. 137), p. 127.

157 P. Stoneman, *Technological Diffusion and the Computer Revolution,* University of Cambridge Department of Applied Economics, Monograph 25 (Cambridge, Cambridge UP, 1976), p. 98.

158 A. Phillips, 'Patents, potential competition, and technical progress', *American Economic Review (Papers and Proceedings),* vol. 56 (May 1966), p. 304. The quote from Galbraith is from J. K. Galbraith, *American Capitalism* (London, Hamish Hamilton, 1952), p. 91.

159 R. Nelson and S. Winter, 'Neoclassical *vs* evolutionary theories of economic growth: critique and prospectus', *Economic Journal,* vol. 84 (December 1974), pp. 888 and 890.

160 Nelson and Winter, op. cit. (n. 159), pp. 893–4.

161 F. M. Fisher, Z. Griliches and C. Kaysen, 'The cost of automobile changes since 1949', *Journal of Political Economy,* vol. 70 (October 1962), p. 450.

162 Hamberg, op. cit. (n. 141), p. 100. Hamberg's article is extremely interesting and suggestive. It is a devastating attack on the triviality of much industrial R and D. However, the argument contains an apparent inconsistency. Section 2 details the economic factors accounting for the tendency to triviality – essentially the pursuit of profit. Section 3 then examines certain non-economic factors claimed to be relevant, all of which are derived from an 'odd-ball eccentric' image of the 'creative individual'. Unfortunately, Hamberg has not considered whether his economic factors may not in themselves by a sufficient explanation. While creative individuals may well be able to work better on their own than in a profit-oriented corporate laboratory, they may operate even more effectively in an organised environment designed to serve objectives other than profitability.

163 Freeman, op. cit. (n. 91), pp. 252, 279 and 298.

164 Freeman, op. cit. (n. 91), pp. 290–1 and 295–6.

165 Freeman, op. cit. (n. 91), pp. 308–9.

6 Pricing and Advertising

6.1 INTRODUCTION

In this and the following chapter two major areas of decision making by firms are examined: the pricing and marketing of products, and the investment appraisal and financing of production. Product pricing has always been a major topic of interest in economic analysis, but a consensus view on pricing behaviour and its determinants has not yet emerged:

> The determination of prices has played a central part in economic theory for a hundred years or more. It forms the core of microeconomics and is often the first topic in economics that students are taught . . . Yet it has been, and remains, a subject of considerable controversy.[1]

By contrast, economists have paid relatively little attention to the non-price aspects of product marketing, with the partial exception of promotional advertising, despite growing evidence that the price decision plays a subsidiary role in selling in many oligopolistic markets.[2]

In reviewing current thinking on pricing and advertising particular attention will therefore be paid to the following issues:

(1) To what extent does the neoclassical theory of the firm provide a satisfactory theoretical framework for the analysis of price determination?
(2) What methods of empirical investigation are most appropriate to the study of pricing behaviour?
(3) To what extent is it meaningful to analyse the pricing behaviour of firms without reference to the other (non-price) competitive strategies in which firms engage?
(4) What are the factors influencing the type and intensity of non-price competition (notably advertising), and what are the welfare implications of such behaviour?

The structure of the chapter is as follows. Section 6.2 contains an overview of the current state of price theory, focusing mainly upon the continued reliance on many of the features of the neoclassical tradition (notably marginal analysis) and on the unsatisfactory nature of alternative theories that attempt to take account of more realistic oligopolistic market structures. This is followed in section 6.3 by an analysis of the empirical evidence on pricing behaviour, with particular attention to the reliability of that evidence and the extent to which it substantiates or casts doubt on the usefulness of marginal analysis. Next the relationship between price and non-price competitive behaviour is examined in both theoretical and empirical terms in section 6.4. Then, in section 6.5 one form of non-price competition – advertising – is examined in greater detail by analysing its extent, its relationship to market structure and performance, and its welfare implications. The chapter concludes with a summary of the main findings and with recommendations on further reading (section 6.6).

The subject matter of the chapter is restricted to business pricing and advertising in the private sector. Price theory and behaviour in the public sector are examined in Chapter 10. Analyses of government policies to influence or control pricing behaviour in the private and public sectors are contained in Chapters 9 and 10 respectively.

6.2   AN OVERVIEW OF PRICE THEORY

Price theory has been most fully developed for the theoretical limiting cases of perfectly competitive and single-firm monopoly markets.[3] In a perfectly competitive market there exists a very low degree of seller and buyer concentration and no entry barriers or product differentiation. Also, firms possess perfect knowledge and unbounded rationality when making business decisions. Since the individual firm is too small to influence market price by its own actions it is a *price taker* rather than a *price maker*, adjusting its sales volume to the profit-maximising level where marginal cost, marginal revenue and market price are equal (Figure 6.1a). Market price is determined by the interaction of market demand and market supply: changes in market demand, or in the marginal costs of production of all firms in the market, cause a change in market price in the same direction.

The single-firm monopoly market is characterised by a high degree of seller concentration and high entry barriers. In this situation the firm is a price maker and, assuming perfect knowledge, unbounded rationality and a desire to maximise profits, will choose the price-sales combination where marginal cost and marginal revenue are equal. However, in this situation market price will exceed both marginal and average cost, and monopoly profit will be earned in long run equilibrium (Figure 6.1b). Changes in market demand or in the monopolist's marginal-cost function will cause a change in market price. Normally price will change in the same direction as the change in demand or costs that has brought it about. However, an increase in demand may be accompanied by a fall in price if the monopolist is able to obtain substantial further economies of large scale production.

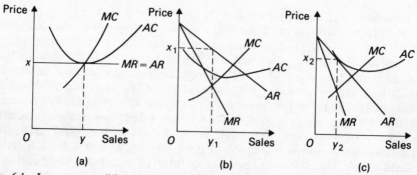

Fig. 6.1   Long run equilibrium of the firm under conditions of (a) perfect competition, (b) monopoly and (c) monopolistic competition.

The marginalist calculus has also been applied to the 'large group' situation of imperfect competition in which many firms sell differentiated products within the same general market.[4] Given the same behavioural assumptions as above, relating to perfect knowledge, unbounded rationality and profit maximisation, each firm will charge a price for its product brand that equates the marginal revenue and marginal costs (including selling costs) of its provision. Assuming freedom of entry into the general market, individual firms will only earn normal profits in the long run (Figure 6.1c), unlike the single firm monopolist, but changes in demand and cost conditions will be expected to have the same directional influence on brand price as in the monopoly situation.

Attempts to extend the use of marginal analysis, in the form outlined above, to the more realistic 'small group' situation of oligopoly have been less widely accepted, for the following reasons:

(1) In the 'small group' situation the actions of individual firms within a market are not, as tacitly assumed so far, independent of each other. Each firm is sufficiently large to affect the market conditions facing other firms, through its own price and output policies. Therefore, an oligopolistic firm, in determining its own prices, is expected to take account of the reaction that this may precipitate among its market rivals.

(2) The existence of high degrees of seller concentration combined with high entry barriers gives oligopolistic firms, or their senior management, a degree of discretion in the objectives that they pursue. Therefore, it is not safe to assume that, in general, prices are determined *as if* firms are seeking to maximise their profits.

(3) Firms in realistic market situations possess neither perfect knowledge nor unbound rationality and therefore are incapable of applying, in any precise sense, the marginalist calculus described above. The pricing rules that they use may result in patterns of price behaviour that are different from those which would result from the application of marginalist rules.

Various attempts have been made to develop alternative theories of oligopolistic behaviour that take one or more of the above elements into account; but, as described below, no generally accepted alternative has yet been evolved.

RIVALRY AND COLLUSION IN OLIGOPOLISTIC MARKETS

Cournot has analysed the situation of two competing firms producing a homogeneous product at zero marginal cost where each firm consistently assumed that the *output* level of its rival would remain unchanged, irrespective of its own action, and on this basis determined the price–output level that would maximise its own profit. In this situation it can be shown that an equilibrium position is reached where the market price charged by each firm is equal to two-thirds of the price that would be charged by a single firm monopolist.[5] Edgeworth has taken the same situation; but instead he has analysed the implications of each firm consistently assuming that the *price* charged by its rival would remain unchanged, irrespective of its own action, and on this basis determining its own profit-maximising price–output level. In this case he has shown that a single-market equilibrium price would not emerge and that price could fluctuate between quite wide limits.[5] Another approach to rivalrous market behaviour has been developed through game theory based upon work by von Neumann and Morgenstern.[6] In this case attitudes to the uncertainty that is inherent in rivalrous behaviour are included as explicit determinants of the pricing strategies that individual firms adopt and therefore of the market price solution eventually reached. For example, individual firms might select the pricing strategy that, were their rivals to choose the reactive strategy that was most harmful to them, would have the least harmful effect on their profits. This cautious response to uncertainty, sometimes referred to as 'maximin behaviour', can be contrasted with the excessively optimistic view of a rival's likely response contained in the Cournot and Edgeworth models.

The weaknesses shared by most of these types of models are that they assume that rivalrous reactions in oligopolistic markets are simple, are of a uniform nature and do not change through experience or in different market circumstances. In the Cournot model, for example, each firm acts as if its rival will never change his sales level although, according to the analysis, the firm must repeatedly observe such reactive changes in output taking place. However, once it is conceded that the reactive behaviour of firms may change over time the price–output equilibrium in that market becomes indeterminate unless the nature of this change can itself be specified.

From the standpoint of the individual firms in an oligopolistic market each of the three types of solution to price determination described above is not the most preferred solution, in the sense that the firms could make greater aggregate profit by co-ordinating their price–output decisions rather than by engaging in ill-informed competitive rivalry. Assuming that there are high entry barriers to the market, such firms could, if they were sufficiently well-informed and rational, maximise their aggregate profit by collusion, through treating their production units as if they belonged to the same single-firm monopoly and basing their price–output decisions on the common decision rule that

$$MR = MC_A = MC_B = MC_N \qquad (6.1)$$

where MR is the market marginal revenue and MC_A, MC_B, etc. relate to the marginal costs of production of the different production units serving the market.

Such price collusion, however, is more difficult to achieve where:

(1) there are more than a very small number of firms selling in the market;
(2) the firms have different costs of production;
(3) the firms engage in product differentiation;
(4) overt methods of sustaining price collusion are precluded by law, and covert methods are less effective.[5, 7]

If one firm is considerably larger than other firms in a market, it may act as a price leader; that is, the larger firm is the price maker and the

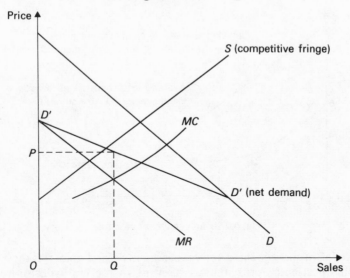

Fig. 6.2   Price determination under conditions of price leadership.

smaller firms, forming a competitive fringe, are price takers. If it is assumed that the price leader is a profit maximiser and has perfect knowledge and unbounded rationality, price will be determined as in Figure 6.2. The price leader will, as shown, deduct the expected supply of the competitive fringe from market demand at each price level to obtain a *net* market demand function. Then, it will determine the market price that corresponds to the point of equality between its marginal costs of production and marginal revenue, as derived from its net demand function.

However, this analysis ignores the possible influence on pricing behaviour of potential new entrants, the threat of which may cause oligopolistic firms to engage in limit (i.e. entry-deterring) pricing.[8] Whether or not such firms are influenced in their pricing policy by the threat of new entry depends in part on their willingness to sacrifice some reduction in profit during the more immediate short run, through charging lower prices to discourage entry, in order to secure higher profits and sales in the longer run, in the absence of new entrants. Assuming that the threat of entry is a pricing consideration, the extent to which existing firms can charge prices above the average cost level (including normal profit) of new entrants without that threat being realised depends upon the extent of indivisibilities in production and the expected output response by existing firms confronted by new entry.

Bain[9] and Sylos-Labini[10] have assumed that existing firms will respond to new entry by maintaining their pre-entry output level, so that the total production placed on the market increases by the full amount of the new entrant's initial production. *Ceteris paribus*, this increase in production will tend to be greater the more substantial are the cost economies that can be achieved through large scale production by new entrants. Given that total production is expected to increase while demand remains unchanged, the post-entry price is

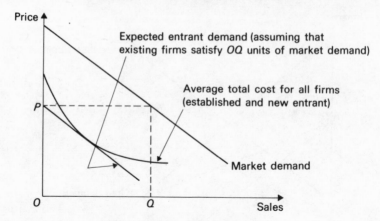

Fig. 6.3   Entry-deterring pricing.

expected to fall in consequence; and according to Sylos-Labini it is the expected level of this post-entry price that is relevant to the entry decision of new firms. It therefore follows that established firms within a market may be able to charge prices in excess of average costs (including normal profit) of production without attracting new firms into the market, even if their cost conditions are the same. However, above a certain price limit this ceases to apply (Figure 6.3). If established firms produce *OQ* or less and charge a price of *OP* or greater, the new entrant can make a profit because his expected demand will be greater than that shown in Figure 6.3. If the pre-entry output is greater than *OQ* and the price less than *OP*, it cannot make a profit.

For this pricing system to apply it is necessary that both established firms and potential new entrants believe that these responses to new entry will occur and possess the relevant information to determine the appropriate level of the entry-deterring price. However, such responses may not apply, or new firms may enter the market at different price levels because of incomplete information. If entry does take place, established firms may not maintain their pre-entry level of output since it may not be in their financial interests to do so. Alternatively, they may collude with the new entrant to maximise their joint profits or engage in competitive rivalry through price cutting. Hence, limit-pricing theory also provides an incomplete explanation of price behaviour in rivalrous situations.

BUSINESS OBJECTIVES

The nature of business objectives in oligopolistic markets is reviewed in section 3.4. In such markets the opportunity exists to pursue objectives other than profit maximisation, and the motivation to do so arises in larger companies with the separation of management control from ownership. In the literature this has been interpreted to imply that oligopolists are more likely to pursue an objective of constrained sales or asset maximisation than of profit maximisation.[11] The effect of these different business objectives on pricing behaviour is illustrated in Figure 6.4, where *P* is the profit-maximising

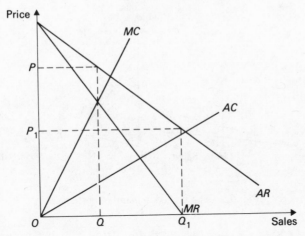

Fig. 6.4   Pricing according to profit-maximising and sales-maximising objectives.

price, P_1 is the unconstrained sales-maximising price, and the profit-constrained sales-maximising price lies between P and P_1.

However, a change in business objectives will also affect the optimal values of non-price variables such as advertising and other forms of sales promotion (see section 6.4), and so it will alter the oligopolist's demand and cost schedules and through these his market price.[12] Similarly, the model ignores the possible impact on price behaviour of existing or potential oligopolistic rivalry. It also still assumes the possession of perfect knowledge and unbounded rationality by the price maker.

UNCERTAINTY AND BOUNDED RATIONALITY

The uncertainty created by rivalrous behaviour in oligopolistic markets is considerable, and the cost to firms arising from the incorrect anticipation of competitors' reactions may be very high. However, this is only part of the more pervasive uncertainty relating to future demand and cost conditions that faces each price maker. Additionally, he has limited time, mental and other resources available in which to collect and analyse information of relevance to his pricing decisions. These elements have been largely neglected in the analyses reviewed so far, with the partial exception of game theory analysis. Unfortunately, the attempts made to give uncertainty and bounded rationality more explicit consideration have suffered either from oversimplification, by reducing the problem to one of probability analysis[13] or of the application of the marginalist calculus to information gathering,[14] or from an insufficiently developed analytical framework, as in the case of the kinked demand and full-cost-pricing hypotheses discussed below.

The kinked demand hypothesis, developed by Sweezy[15] and Hall and Hitch,[16] is an attempt to explain price inflexibility, particularly in the short run, where there is considerable uncertainty about competitors' reactions. It does not explain why prices are at their existing level, nor does it make clear what

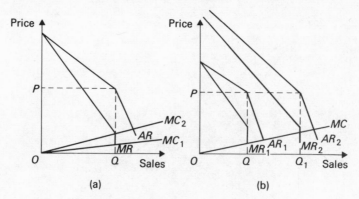

Fig. 6.5   The kinked demand hypothesis.

changes in demand or cost circumstances may cause a change in price levels in the longer term. It is based upon the notion that businessmen are extremely pessimistic about the likely reactions of their competitors, were they to change their prices. On the one hand, they believe that if they raise their price their competitors will not do likewise; therefore, the oligopolist believes that the demand for his products is highly price elastic immediately *above* the existing price. Conversely, they believe that if they lower their price their competitors will reduce their price correspondingly; hence, their demand immediately *below* the existing price will be highly price inelastic. Consequently, there is a 'kink' at the existing price in their demand function, which in turn causes a discontinuity in the corresponding marginal-revenue function (Figure 6.5). This may result in price inflexibility in two situations:

(1)   Increases or decreases in the marginal cost function may occur, within a range, without bringing about any change in the price or output of a firm (Figure 6.5a).
(2)   Increases or decreases in demand may occur that, provided the kink remains at the same price level, change the level of output but not the level of price (Figure 6.5b).

A different kind of response to conditions of uncertainty and bounded rationality is envisaged in the full-cost (or 'cost-plus') pricing principle.[16] This principle, of which there are many variations, has largely developed from observations of pricing practices; it is therefore examined more fully in the next section, although it has also been incorporated into the behavioural theory of the firm.[17] In essence it states that price is determined by first estimating unit costs, direct or total, of production and then adding a percentage markup for profits, plus overheads if not previously included in unit costs. This pricing procedure is used, so it has been argued, because:

(1)   it avoids the complexity and uncertainty involved in demand and marginal revenue estimation;
(2)   it 'facilitates oligopolistic co-ordination by making rivals' decisions more

predictable and by providing common guide-lines as to appropriate price levels';[18] and

(3) it discourages new entrants during periods of expansion by restricting price increases to the same amount as increases in full costs.

The predictions relating to price changes that can be deduced from the full cost principle depend upon its precise formulation. For example, it is necessary to determine whether the unit cost is to be calculated on the basis of actual, normal or expected output, whether temporary changes in variable costs are to be taken into account and whether the mark-up percentage is fixed or adjustable according to market conditions. If the crudest form of the full cost principle is used – the extent to which this is justified is discussed in the next section – and it is therefore assumed that the full cost is based upon actual output, prevailing cost levels and a fixed markup, the following results will apply:

(1) An increase in the demand for a product will not cause an increase in its price, provided that factor price levels do not also rise. If unit costs fall, because of a decline in unit overhead costs as output rises, price should fall.
(2) A decrease in the demand for a product will not cause a decrease in its price. If unit costs rise, because of an increase in unit overhead costs as output falls, price should rise.
(3) If unit costs increase or decrease, price should change by the same percentage irrespective of the price elasticity of demand for the product.

The predictions relating to price behaviour that can be derived from the oligopolistic theories reviewed above are not always consistent with each other; nor in many cases are they apparently consistent with the pricing behaviour predicted by marginal analysis in more competitive markets. This has focused attention on the following topics of empirical research, which are examined in the next section:

(1) Are prices less flexible in oligopolistic markets than in competitive markets; and, if so, what are the consequences of this inflexibility?
(2) Are price changes in oligopolistic markets responsive to cost changes but unresponsive to changes in demand?
(3) Is marginal analysis inappropriate to the prediction of price behaviour in oligopolistic markets?

6.3 PRICING IN PRACTICE

In reviewing studies of pricing practice it is convenient to distinguish between those based upon:

(1) questionnaires and interviews with the management of individual businesses (referred to as business surveys); and
(2) statistical analyses of the changes in actual prices recorded by groups of businesses (referred to as statistical analyses).

The methods of investigation used in these two types of study are different, and they tend to have different uses and shortcomings.

During the 1930s a group of Oxford economists gathered information, through personal interviews, on the pricing behaviour of thirty-eight businesses mainly engaged in the manufacturing sector and concluded that:

> It casts doubt on the general applicability of the conventional analyses of price and output policy in terms of marginal cost and marginal revenue, and suggests a mode of entrepreneurial behaviour which current economic doctrine tends to ignore. This is the basing of price upon what we shall call the 'full cost' principle.[19]

In the early 1960s Barback investigated the pricing practices of a small number of UK manufacturing firms, using a combination of questionnaire and personal interview techniques. He started his investigations on the presumption that it would be possible to reconcile full-cost pricing and marginal analysis but on their conclusion rejected this view:

> The continuous and many-sided state of flux in a firm's environment involves it in such ignorance and uncertainty that in a theory of pricing it is necessary to abandon the demand curve, and with it the possibility of supposing that marginalist adjustments can be made or marginal equalities achieved, unless by accident – and then surely temporarily. Equally, there is evidence that the basic postulate of profit maximisation is, for pricing theory, unsatisfactory.[20]

In the early 1970s Hague published a study of the pricing practices of thirteen manufacturers having links with the Manchester Business School. Eight of the thirteen firms are described as satisficers rather than maximisers, and a proportion of the remainder are described as 'half-hearted' maximisers. The study highlights the potential complexity of the pricing decision for a multi-product firm if it is to take all relevant considerations into account, and it observes that most of the investigated firms had formally or informally devised means of simplifying the pricing procedure used and that the nature of this simplified procedure was itself an important determinant of the prices actually charged.[21] Therefore, Hague has replaced marginalism by behaviourism as the dominant explanation of pricing practice.

The most recent UK studies of the pricing practices of individual businesses are contained in the reports of the National Board for Prices and Incomes[22] and of the Price Commission.[23] However, these studies are primarily concerned with the admissability of price increases rather than with detailed investigation of the determinants of prices. Nevertheless, one interesting feature of the Price Code that has been enforced is the qualified approval tacitly given to the use of the crude version of the full cost principle in justifying price increases:

This meant that if turnover *increased*, the benefit went to consumers. Unit allowable costs would be lower to the extent that fixed costs were spread over higher sales, and only the net increase resulting from increases in other costs could be added to prices. If turnover *decreased*, unit allowable costs would rise by the spreading of fixed costs over smaller sales, and would add to cost increases due to direct labour and materials. Both these increases could then be added to prices – if the market would allow.[24]

Although there have been a considerable number of UK pricing studies, as indicated above or elsewhere,[1, 25, 26] the sample of firms in most cases was small and non-random, and therefore it would be difficult to generalise from their findings even if the studies were methodologically acceptable. In the United States there have also been a considerable number of pricing studies, and certain of these are more acceptable from this point of view.

Kaplan, Dirlam and Lanzillotti have examined the pricing behaviour of twenty large American companies during the mid 1950s.[27] They have observed significant differences between the pricing policies and pricing procedures of large corporations, which they have attributed to differences in corporate objectives, the products produced and the competitive nature of the markets in which the corporations were involved. The most frequently encountered pricing policy was to achieve a target (i.e. satisfactory) rate of return on investment, while a number of companies had the subsidiary objective of stabilising the price charged and/or the price–cost margin. A third type of price policy aimed to maintain or improve the company's market share, even at the expense of the short term rate of return on investment. Fourth, for some of their products large firms were price takers, following the actions of the price leader in that market. Finally, for many large companies, although to varying degrees, pricing policies were inextricably linked to other dimensions of marketing policies and couldn't be meaningfully interpreted except in this context. In these cases:

> . . . the officials who discussed policy with the interviewers found it difficult to analyse pricing as a separate activity distinct from others entering into their company policy . . . Pricing policy and 'non-price' (quality and style) competition appear to be closely linked in the majority of the companies surveyed.[28]

These pricing policies were frequently reflected in more specific pricing formulae, among which standard cost formulae were prominent. However, Kaplan *et. al.* have emphasised that the profit performance achieved by a number of companies demonstrated that these cost-based pricing formulae were modified when competitive pressures were strong:

> General Motors has developed an elaborate technique for handling costs, which sometimes has been presented as its basic pricing guide. Yet, the selection of the price, as an examination of the company's earnings statements appears to demonstrate, must deviate by a wide margin from the level that would result from the use . . . of standard cost pricing . . .

International Harvester, by its own account, has been unable to price as it would like, in an industry in which its sales of specific pieces of farm equipment are often smaller than those of a close competitor.[29]

A parallel study by Lanzillotti of the pricing practices of 256 small manufacturing firms in Washington, DC, has revealed a number of points of similarity and contrast with the large company study.[30] Typically, the great majority of firms had a pricing policy of achieving a predetermined profit rate on sales or predetermined markup on unit costs. At the same time the majority of firms indicated that they matched their prices to those of their principal competitors; in other words, in the final analysis they were forced to modify their pricing policies to take account of competitive pressures in the market.

FULL COST PRICING AND THE DEFENCE OF MARGINALISM

The findings of many of these business surveys have come under attack on the grounds that:

(1) small and non-random business surveys using questionnaires and interviews are an unreliable method of obtaining data on price determination;
(2) the results of such surveys have been misinterpreted or misrepresented; and
(3) the marginalist explanation of price determination has been incorrectly presented and therefore unduly criticised.

These arguments have been most clearly articulated by Machlup, and therefore attention will be mainly focused on his defence of marginalism.[31, 32]

It has already been observed that most of the business surveys of pricing behaviour undertaken, particularly in the United Kingdom, have been based upon small non-random samples. A more fundamental criticism, however, is that studies of this kind, unless accompanied by skilful in-depth interviewing, may result in the supply of 'socially acceptable' but otherwise unreliable information:

> Questions of business policy are particularly difficult objects of inquiry because the businessman usually is anxious to show by his answers that he is intelligent, well-informed, and fair. The standards of fairness and business ethics to which he wishes to conform are often those which he believes are accepted by his lawyers, accountants, customers, competitors, fellow citizens, economists and whatnot. Only through detailed discussion of different situations and decisions, actual as well as hypothetical, will an investigator succeed in bringing out true patterns of conduct of the individual businessman.[33]

Similarly, Machlup has argued that the lack of knowledge among businessmen of marginalist terminology and of calculations of marginalist magnitudes, which has been widely observed in many business surveys, is not inconsistent with their behaving *as if* they understood and used these concepts in settling their prices. He has asserted that:

> . . . the technical terms used in the explanation of an action need not have any part in the thinking of the acting individual. A mental process in every-day life may often be most conveniently described for scientific purposes in a language which is quite foreign to the process itself.[34]

He has illustrated this viewpoint by analogy with the routine decision of a motorist considering whether to overtake a lorry. A 'theory of overtaking' would include a large number of variables, such as the respective speeds of car and lorry, the distance between the two vehicles, the width of the road, and the volume and speed of the traffic moving in the opposite direction. The motorist in 'sizing up' the situation prior to overtaking would take these variables into account without necessarily formally identifying and measuring them and without necessarily even being able to do so in a precise scientific manner. A similar situation, Machlup has argued, applies when businessmen reach pricing decisions; they 'size up' the situation, taking cost, consumer and competitive circumstances into account without using economists' terminology or placing numerical estimates on all the elements in the situation.

This argument implies that the various practices of administered pricing that have been observed in business surveys merely 'cloak' the application of marginalist criteria. In order to explore this argument further it is necessary to examine more closely the nature of the full-cost-pricing convention and the manner in which it is used in price determination.

The Hall and Hitch study has observed that:

> The formula used by the different firms in computing 'full cost' differs in detail . . . but the procedure can be not unfairly generalised as follows: prime (or 'direct') cost per unit is taken as the base, a percentage addition is made to cover overheads (or 'oncost', or 'indirect' cost) and a further conventional addition (frequently 10%) is made for profit. Selling costs commonly, and interest on capital rarely, are included in overheads; when not so included they are allowed for in the addition for profits.[35]

In a number of cases the markup on direct costs was based on achieving a target rate of return assuming a 'normal' or 'expected' level of output, whereas in other cases the markup was based upon the actual level of output achieved. The implications of a rigid adherence to this pricing criterion in changing cost and demand conditions can be illustrated in terms of Figure 6.6. Provided that the firm correctly anticipates its initial sales level, determined by the demand function DD, it will charge OP and sell OQ units of its product. If demand increases to D_1D_1, it will still charge the same price if its full cost estimate is based on the originally expected output level, but it will lower its price to OP_1 if its costing is based on the realised sales level. Similarly, if demand decreases to D_2D_2, it will either charge the same price as previously or charge a higher price of OP_2 in order to maintain its price–cost margin.

Therefore, the price movements predicted by the full cost principle to result

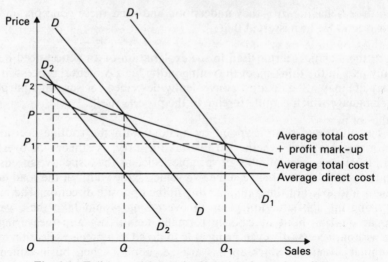

Fig. 6.6   Full cost pricing under changing demand conditions.

from demand changes are inconsistent with those normally indicated by marginal analysis. However, this inconsistency only holds true if the full cost principle is rigidly applied. In fact there is now considerable evidence that some businesses at least vary the size of the markup in the prices that they actually charge according to market and competitive conditions. In the Hall and Hitch study[16] only twelve of the thirty-eight businessmen interviewed adhered 'rigidly' to the full cost principle, and both the Kaplan *et al.*[27] and Lanzillotti[30] studies in the United States have indicated that price–cost margins of both large and small manufacturing companies were adjusted in the light of market conditions.

It is therefore *logically possible* that the application of a flexible form of the full cost principle, in which the markup is variable, will result in a fall in price when demand contracts and a rise in price when demand increases. However, on the basis of the business survey evidence that is available it would be dangerous to deduce that this will *necessarily* and *generally* be the case. A proportion of businesses do appear to adhere fairly rigidly to the full cost principle, and the degree of flexibility exercised by other businesses in adjusting their markup percentages will be restrained by fears of compensatory price cutting by rivals in times of declining demand and of intervention by public controlling authorities in times of general expansion.

The most that can be deduced from the evidence above is that different patterns of price behaviour are observable and that these vary according to the type of market, product and business objectives involved. This view suggests not that the marginalist explanation of pricing behaviour should be rejected but that its role and area of application should be redefined. Machlup, for example, has concluded that:

The simple marginal formula based on profit maximisation is suitable where (1) *large groups* of firms are involved and nothing has to be predicted about particular firms, (2) the effects of a *specified change* in conditions upon prices, inputs and outputs are to be explained or predicted rather than the values of these magnitudes before or after the change . . . and (3) only *qualitative answers*, that is, answers about directions of change, are sought rather than precise numerical results.[36]

This view will be examined further below in the light of various statistical studies of pricing behaviour undertaken.

STATISTICAL ANALYSES OF ADMINISTERED PRICING

Statistical studies of administered pricing have largely originated from Means's investigations of the behaviour of prices in a wide range of American industries immediately before and during the major depression of the early 1930s.[37] On the basis of an analysis of the price changes recorded for the 447 commodities forming the BLS Wholesale Price Index between 1926 and 1933, he has drawn the following conclusions:

(1) There was a tendency for the prices of most products to change either very frequently or very infrequently (the former being referred to as 'market' prices and the latter as 'administered' prices).
(2) There was a direct relationship between the frequency of change and the amplitude of change: 'The items which changed frequently in price showed a large drop during the depression while those having a low frequency of change tended to drop little in price.'[38]
(3) There was an inverse relationship between price and production declines: 'for industries in which prices dropped most during the depression, production tended to drop least, while for those in which prices were maintained, the change in production was usually greatest.'[38]
(4) Price rigidity was due to the combined influence of a number of factors, which included the degree of seller concentration in the market.

The implications, therefore, were that firms in more concentrated markets applied an administered pricing system that resulted in a downward inflexibility in prices during depressed economic conditions, and that this both resulted in a misallocation of resources within the American economy and, Means believed, retarded recovery from the depression.

Given such wider policy implications, this study attracted a great deal of comment. Central to many of the criticisms made of it are: the somewhat arbitrary selection of products to which the administered price hypothesis is supposed to apply; the limitations of the BLS Wholesale Price Index as an indicator of prices *actually paid*, as distinct from prices *publicly quoted*; and the failure to disentangle, in a sufficiently systematic way, the influence of seller concentration from that of other variables on price determination. The tentative conclusion reached by Scherer therefore appears to do reasonable justice to the available evidence:

It seems fairly clear that concentrated industries did exhibit somewhat less deflationary pricing behaviour during the early 1930s, although direct relationships between market power and price were obscured by variations in other variables with a more potent impact on price. The main effect of market power was to minimise downward deviations in that relatively small fraction of price representing profit margins.[39]

Since 1945 attention has mainly been focused on the relationships between seller concentration, administrative pricing and inflation. Further analysis of the BLS Wholesale Price Index during the 1950s and 1960s led Blair and others to conclude that differences between the behaviour of administered and market prices had continued.[40] Although there were exceptions to the broad pattern, Blair has suggested that in those markets where price changes were less frequent:

(1) price reductions in periods of recession had been least – indeed, in certain instances price increases had been observed;
(2) price increases during periods of upturn in the economy had been more modest; and
(3) longer term increases in price levels had been the greatest.

This study, however, has not established whether other variables were also contributing to these observed differences in pricing behaviour; nor has it directly related price behaviour to seller concentration levels.

De Podwin and Selden have analysed the relationship between seller concentration and price movements for 322 manufactured product groups and concluded that: 'There seems to be no indication that administered prices, as measured by degree of industrial concentration, increased appreciably more in the 1953–1959 period than prices determined under supposedly more competitive conditions.'[41]

Weiss has questioned the findings of this study on the grounds that it has neglected the influence of other important variables, notably changes in factor prices and in productivity. Weiss has drawn the different conclusion that firms in concentrated industries showed more than average willingness to concede wage increases, which they then more than recouped in administered price increases: 'The main occasion (excuse) for increases in margins in concentrated industries in the 1950s was wage-rate increases and the price increases which accompanied these wage increases more than covered the increase in unit labour costs.'[42]

In 1970 Stigler and Kindahl published a new set of transactions price series (NB series), compiled from purchasers' records, which they regarded as superior to the BLS data used in previous studies. They have drawn the conclusion that the administered price hypothesis is not upheld by these new data.[43] This has been challenged by Blair,[40] Means[44] and Weiss,[45] who have claimed that the NB and BLS price series are basically consistent with each other and that the previously hypothesised relationship between pricing behaviour and administered markets still holds, particularly during periods of recession.

In the United Kingdom support for an administrative price hypothesis is associated with the work of Nordhaus and Godley, who in their 1972 study have attempted to test the hypothesis that, for UK manufacturing industry over the period 1953–69, 'the mark-up of price over normal historical current average cost is independent of the conditions of demand in the factor and product markets and is independent of the deviations of actual cost from normal cost'.[46] The testing procedure adopted was to adjust unit cost estimates for any reversible cyclical influences and to use this as a predicted price variable. The actual price index was then regressed on the predicted price variable and a demand variable. The observed significance of the predicted price variable was taken as interim support for the normal cost-pricing principle and the observed non-significance of the demand variable as an indication that short run changes in the level of aggregate demand did not influence price levels.

This finding has since been questioned, notably by Laidler and Parkin[47] and Smith,[48] whose criticisms are that:

(1) the hypothesis was mis-specified in such a way that the significance of the demand variable was unlikely to be established;
(2) the coefficient of the expected price variable in the reported regression results was considerably less than unity, which indicates that the price–cost margin did not remain constant over the period investigated; and
(3) the regression model only succeeded in explaining a relatively small pro-portion of observed price changes, which suggests that there may be other important influences at work.

Smith has developed an alternative model in which the proportionate change in the general level of prices is determined by excess demand and expectations of price changes, and when the model was tested both variables were found to be significant and of expected sign.[48]

More recently Coutts, Godley and Nordhaus have completed a fuller study, which, while essentially using the same methodology as previously, has dis-aggregated the analysis to seven industrial groups and widened the range of statistical tests used. Their conclusions have remained substantially unchanged:

Taken together these results give strong support to the normal price hypo-thesis. The effect of short-run changes in demand through the period of a typical business-cycle as a separate influence on price, if it exists at all, is small – almost certainly no greater than 0·5 per cent from trough to peak.[49]

However, it seems likely that these findings will be subject to criticisms similar to those levelled at the earlier study by Nordhaus and Godley,[46] and it therefore seems premature to eliminate the demand variable from explana-tions of short-run industrial price behaviour.

CONCLUSIONS ON PRICING PRACTICE
The conflicting findings on price behaviour presented above partly reflect the limitations of both business surveys and aggregate statistical analyses as methods of establishing the nature and determinants of pricing practice. Business surveys have frequently been based on small and non-random samples

of firms and cannot easily distinguish between the pricing procedures used by firms and the determinants of the prices finally charged. Statistical analyses have been mainly restricted to aggregate price data of debatable quality and have experienced difficulty in taking account of all the main variables that may cause price changes. For these reasons the following conclusions on the three issues identified at the end of section 6.2 are necessarily tentative.

First, the balance of evidence supports the view that prices are altered less frequently in oligopolistic markets than in competitive markets. However, the differences may not be as great as originally supposed, since in oligopolistic markets the prices actually charged will alter more frequently than published or quoted prices. There are also other factors additional to seller concentration, such as the nature of the product and the characteristics of buyers, that influence the frequency with which prices change.

Second, the balance of evidence also suggests that short-run price changes of industrial products in oligopolistic markets are primarily brought about by changes in unit costs and that, compared with the situation in competitive markets, prices in the short run are less responsive to changes in demand. However, the evidence does not yet justify the view that demand influences on short run behaviour in these markets are generally insignificant. The influence of the full-cost-pricing principle has been most evident in resistance to price reductions during periods of recession, but once other factors are taken into account its impact appears to have been considerably less than that estimated in the early studies by Means. The impact of full-cost pricing during periods of economic expansion is not yet sufficiently understood to permit a reliable conclusion to be drawn.

Third, these findings lend further support to the view that the role of marginal analysis in explaining price changes should be carefully circumscribed. As previously indicated by Machlup, marginal analysis is most useful in explaining the direction of longer-term price movements in competitive markets. It is of more questionable value in predicting short-run price movements in oligopolistic markets. However, a satisfactory alternative to the use of marginal calculus in these markets has not yet been established.

6.4   NON-PRICE COMPETITION

Up to this point the pricing decision has been mainly treated as a self-contained element in the decision-making process. However, in practice pricing decisions frequently form an integral part of a more general marketing strategy,[28, 50, 51] which includes a 'mix' of the following components:

(1) the design and quality of the product;
(2) product advertising;
(3) sales and distribution activities, including such support facilities as market research;
(4) the quality of service, including the reliability of delivery, credit terms and after sales service; and
(5) product pricing.

In Udell's survey of 200 US producers of industrial and consumer goods, listed in *Martindell's Manual of Excellent Management*, each senior manager was asked to select the five areas that he regarded as most vital to his company's marketing success.[52] His findings, summarised in Table 6.1, suggest that the most vital areas of marketing are not pricing but relate to product development and servicing or to sales effort; and that the relative emphasis on product and sales effort varies according to the nature of the product and the characteristics of the buyers.

The first of these points has been supported by the case study evidence collected by Kaplan *et al.* on pricing in big American businesses:

> American Can, having relegated price to the background, and having enjoyed a position as price leader, was able to concentrate on the provision of service and the devising of innovations . . . Du Pont points out that, while heavy chemicals may sell mainly on a price basis, it is the missionary work with dealers and first-hand demonstrations to farmers that permit the company to compete effectively, in the sale of agricultural chemicals, insecticides, and fungicides . . . General Foods feel the need for developing high-margin novelties that will serve to pick up sales and make more than a proportionate contribution to profits . . . The rôle of style competition in the automobile industry dominates competitive relationships at the manufacturers' level.[53]

Table 6.1 *Percentage of firms choosing, as vital, specific marketing areas.*

	Producers of:		
Policy area	Industrial goods	Non-durable consumer goods	Durable consumer goods
Product			
Product research and development	79	83	75
Product service	79	14	36
Sales effort			
Advertising and sales promotion	37	89	73
Management of sales personnel	49	64	91
Sales research and sales planning	63	82	73
Pricing	47	50	46
Other areas			
Organisational structure	50	39	27
Distribution channels and their control	34	54	46
Finance and credit	18	11	9
Marketing cost budgeting and control	12	29	9
Transport and storage	9	4	9

Source: J. Udell, 'The role of price in competitive strategy', *Journal of Marketing*, vol. 28 (1964).

Table 6.2 *Advertising and marketing expenses as a percentage of sales in selected US industries, 1963.*

Industry	Total marketing costs	Advertising and sales promotion
Producer goods		
Rubber and plastic	13·1	1·5
Fabricated metal	16·6	3·0
Machinery, except electrical	15·6	2·2
Electrical machinery and supplies	15·6	2·4
Instruments, photographic and optical goods	15·6	2·1
Consumer goods		
Breakfast cereals	27·0	17·0
Biscuits	24·3	4·2

Source: J. Backman, *Advertising and Competition* (New York, New York UP, 1967), p. 19.

The second of these points has been supported by American data collected by Backman,[54] which show how both the marketing mix and its overall relative importance vary between industries (Table 6.2).

DETERMINANTS OF THE MARKETING MIX

A change in the intensity of one element in the marketing mix of a firm, such as a product style or sales promotion change, will normally cause a change in *both* its demand (marginal and average revenue) and cost (marginal and/or average cost) functions. This in turn may lead to an adjustment in the price and output level of the firm and in the levels of other marketing elements. In other words, there are interdependencies between the quantities of the different marketing elements.

If a firm wishes to maximise its profits and possesses perfect knowledge and unbounded rationality, it should *simultaneously* equate the marginal costs and marginal revenue associated with each of its price and non-price decision variables. The simultaneity condition is important because, for example, equating the marginal costs and marginal revenue of product style changes without at the same time equating the marginal costs and marginal revenue for the determination of price, advertising, etc. would result in a style expenditure level that was inconsistent with the objective of maximum profits. This is illustrated in Figure 6.7, where for purposes of simplification there is only one non-price variable: advertising. The initial equilibrium position of the firm in Figure 6.7a, at which price and sales levels are OP_0 and OQ_0 respectively, is derived from the original revenue and cost functions (AR_0, MR_0, AC_0 and MC_0). The new revenue and cost functions in Figure 6.7a (AR_1, MR_1, AC_1 and MC_1) are based on the profit-maximising quantity of the non-price variable of OQ_1 units (see Figure 6.7b), and the total revenue function of the

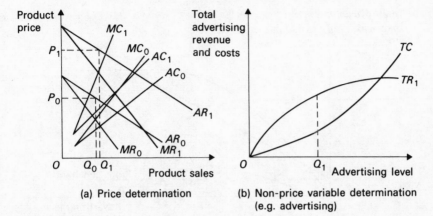

Fig. 6.7 Simultaneous determination of price and other elements in the marketing mix by a profit-maximising firm.

non-price variable in Figure 6.7b assumes the new profit-maximising product price of OP_1 (see Figure 6.7a).

If firms behave in the way assumed above, then, using a form of analysis originally developed by Dorfman and Steiner,[55] the determinants of the marketing mix and of each of its elements can be specified. Assuming, for example, that advertising is the only non-price variable, it can be deduced that

$$\frac{A}{PQ} = \frac{P-MC}{P} \cdot E_a \qquad (6.2)$$

which indicates that the profit-maximising ratio of advertising (A) to sales (PQ) depends upon the excess of price (P) over the marginal cost of the firm's product (MC) as a proportion of price and upon the advertising elasticity of demand for the firm's product (E_a). Thus, the advertising–sales ratio will be higher, other things being equal, if:

(1) the firm's price-cost margin is increased;
(2) its advertising elasticity of demand rises;
(3) its price elasticity of demand falls; or
(4) the reactions of competing firms to an increase in its advertising level are reduced.[56]

However the usefulness of this type of model in relation to price behaviour in oligopolistic markets has already been questioned above because of the indeterminate nature of rivalrous behaviour, the pursuit of objectives that differ from profit maximisation and the prevalence of uncertainty and bounded rationality in decision making (section 6.2). These same considerations also require examination in relation to non-price behaviour.

The behaviour of market rivals in oligopolistic conditions will affect both a firm's price–cost margin and its advertising elasticity of demand and through

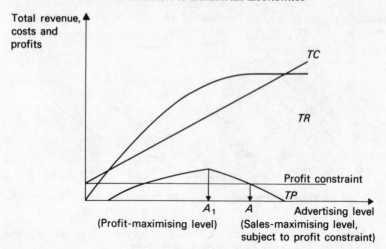

Fig. 6.8 Comparison of advertising levels under conditions of profit maximisation and sales maximisation subject to profit constraint.

these its advertising–sales ratio. Other elements in the marketing mix will be similarly affected. However, as indicated in section 6.2, this rivalrous behaviour may take a variety of forms that affect the level and mix of a firm's marketing activities quite differently. As in the case of price behaviour, little progress can be made in identifying the most likely outcome until the reactive behaviour itself is better understood.

If firms do not pursue profit-maximising objectives, both price and non-price variables are expected to diverge from their profit-maximising levels. This divergence is illustrated in Figure 6.8 where it is shown that a firm that aims to maximise sales while being subject to a profit constraint will normally undertake more advertising and other forms of sales-expanding marketing activities than a firm in identical market circumstances that aims to maximise profits.

More generally, Needham has shown that a change in the *level* of the constraint will affect the optimal level of the marketing activities by the firm (as above) whereas a change in the *form* of the constraint may also change the optimal mix of marketing activities.[57]

In the case of price behaviour the most commonly observed response to uncertainty and bounded rationality is the use of simple pricing conventions such as the full cost principle. A parallel response appears to occur in the case of advertising. After reviewing the available evidence Schmalensee has concluded that:

> This research creates the net impression that businessmen follow rules of thumb in deciding how much to advertise. An advertising–sales ratio is selected *ex ante* and management tries to maintain it *ex post*. Advertising is cut in recessions even though firms have idle capacity.[58]

Whether or not these findings are inconsistent with the use of marginalist analysis is, as in the area of pricing, a matter of dispute. Schmalensee has shown that under specified conditions, e.g. long run stability in the price and advertising elasticities of demand for a firm's product, stability in the advertising–sales ratio will be consistent with profit maximisation.[59] However, the logical possibility of consistency should not be confused with its realisation. The information and rationality requirements implicit in the Dorfman and Steiner model[55] are particularly exacting and suggest that marginal analysis may be of questionable value in examining short-run marketing behaviour in oligopolistic markets. However, it may be helpful in explaining longer term changes in marketing behaviour and major differences in the levels of marketing activity between different industries and markets.

6.5 ADVERTISING

Of the different forms of non-price competition, advertising has been most fully investigated and is therefore examined in further detail in this section. A review of the nature and extent of advertising is followed by an analysis of its relationship to market structure and market performance and, finally, of the wider policy issues raised by its use.

NATURE AND EXTENT

vertising has been defined as 'mass paid communication, the ultimate purpose which is to impart information, develop attitudes and induce action beneficial he advertiser (generally the sale of a product or service)'.[60] This distinguishes vertising from other promotional activities such as salesmen's personal lls and sales demonstrations that do not involve mass communication.

practice, however, advertising data are not collected on a basis that is nsistent with this definition since they are largely restricted to advertising rough the mass media of press, television, radio, cinema and transport. These atistics normally include 'classified' advertisements in the press that are not ntended to sell products but exclude such items as catalogues and shop window and interior advertising.

Total advertising expenditure, as defined above, was approximately £1,200 million in 1976, which is slightly in excess of 1·6 per cent of total consumer

Table 6.3 *Total advertising expenditure in the United Kingdom, 1956–76.*

Year	Total advertising expenditure (£ m.)	Advertising expenditure as a proportion of total consumer expenditure (%)
1956	197	1·44
1966	447	1·84
1976	1188	1·62

Sources: Advertising Association, *Advertising Expenditure 1960–76* (London AA, 1977), p. 5.

Table 6.4 *Allocation of total advertising expenditure by media and type of expenditure, 1976.*

Expenditure by media	(%)	Expenditure by type	(%)
Press	68·1	Display advertising	68·5
of which:		of which:	
National newspapers	16·6	Press	36·6
Regional newspapers	27·6	Television	25·8
Other	23·9	Other	6·1
Television	25·8	Financial notices	1·3
Poster, transport, cinema, radio	6·1	Classified advertising	21·5
		Trade and technical journals	8·7
Total	100·0	Total	100·0

Source: Advertising Association, *Advertising Expenditure 1960–76* (London AA, 1977), p. 7.

expenditure and 1 per cent of gross national product (Table 6.3). These proportions have remained relatively stable during the last twenty years, never exceeding 2 per cent of total consumer expenditure or 1·5 per cent of gross national product. However, these statistics include expenditure on classified advertisements, financial notices and certain advertisements in trade and technical journals, which if excluded leave approximately two-thirds (£800 million in 1976) of total advertising expenditure in the form of display advertising (Table 6.4).

Of display advertising it is the proportion undertaken by manufacturers that is directed to final consumers (MCA) that attracts the greatest public interest. According to Advertising Association estimates, this accounted for approximately 40 per cent of total advertising expenditure in 1976, which was 0·7 per cent of total consumer expenditure. The smallness of this percentage has sometimes been used to suggest that this type of advertising has an insignificant influence on resource allocation. However, as shown below, this average percentage conceals considerable variations between product groups. Additionally, the percentages increase considerably in size if expressed as a proportion of manufacturers' costs, i.e. before wholesaling and retailing distributive expenditures have been included.

Advertising expenditure data relating to product groups have to be treated with additional caution because of the difficulty in matching advertising data to manufacturers' sales data on a consistent basis. However, on the basis of evidence derived from the 1963 Census of Production it seems that the three manufacturing product groups with the highest advertising–sales ratios in 1963 were toilet preparations (16·4 per cent), soap and detergents (13·8 per cent) and pharmaceuticals (8 per cent).[61] A larger number of product groups, mainly within the food and drink industries (e.g. soft drinks, chocolate and sugar confectionary, fruit and vegetable products), together with domestic electrical appliances had advertising–sales ratios within the range of 3–6 per cent.[61] Backman has observed a similar pattern of advertising intensity in the United States: 'the biggest relative users of advertising are concentrated in

Table 6.5   *Manufacturers' advertising and other marketing expenses as a percentage of manufacturers' total costs (including profit margins) for proprietary non-ethical medicines, 1977.*

Products	Advertising expenditure	Other marketing expenditure	Total (excluding packaging)
Analgesic products	20·0	7·2	27·2
Cough and cold products	22·6	4·7	27·3
Digestive and laxative products	11·9	9·2	21·1
Vitamins and tonics	16·6	7·7	24·3
Eye treatment products	9·9	4·3	14·2

Source: Price Commission, *Prices, Costs and Margins in the Production and Distribution of Proprietary Non-ethical Medicines* (London, HMSO, 1978).

five industries – drugs, cosmetics, soaps, soft drinks, and gum and candies'.[62]

Within each product group further variations in advertising–sales ratios exist between products, between firms and according to the stage in the life cycle of the products involved. The Price Commission in its 1977 study of proprietary non-ethical medicines has observed advertising–sales ratios ranging from 10 to 23 per cent and marketing–sales ratios ranging from 14 to in excess of 27 per cent (Table 6.5).[63] At the time when the cosmetics industry in the United States was spending on average 15 per cent of its sales on advertising, Avon spent less than 3 per cent because of its greater reliance on house-to-house selling in its marketing mix.[64] Similarly, the advertising–sales ratio is normally much higher during the early stages of product introduction and sales growth in the life cycle than during the later stages of product maturity and sales decline.[65]

Therefore, it seems that for certain types of products, particularly during the formative early stages in their life cycle, the advertising–sales ratio is very high, and the possibility that this has a significant influence on resource allocation and community welfare cannot be summarily dismissed.

ADVERTISING, MARKET STRUCTURE AND PROFITABILITY

The aspect of the economics of advertising that has received most detailed attention is the relationship between advertising intensity, market structure and market performance, measured by profit rates or margins.[66] In addition to being an important topic in its own right the many studies made of it well illustrate the practical difficulties involved in obtaining agreed answers to contentious and complex economic issues. This situation has prompted one reviewer of the subject, Butters, to comment somewhat contentiously that:

The economics of advertising is marked by the same emotional commitment to conflicting schools of thought that is usually associated with monetary theory and the economics of speculation. To all appearances, the choice of both the axioms used and the data to be interpreted has been made in order to justify pre-existing conclusions rather than to make an unbiased test between alternative theories.[67]

As an illustration of this point the reader should be aware that 'the level of advertising' may be defined differently between different studies. It may be expressed as an absolute amount or as an advertising–sales ratio; it may relate to a firm or industry; or it may be treated as a current or capital item of expenditure.

Before reviewing the evidence it may be helpful to summarise the three main interpretations of the relationship between advertising intensity, market structure and profit margins that have been advanced:

(1) High levels of advertising intensity help to bring about and sustain high entry barriers and high degrees of seller concentration, which in turn result in higher-than-average profit margins.
(2) High levels of advertising intensity are a consequence, not a cause, of structural imperfections in the market. Such high advertising levels result from a situation in which the structural imperfections in markets enable above-average profit margins to be earned.
(3) Differences in advertising intensity are not correlated with market imperfections or profit levels but are to be explained by other factors, such as the nature of the product or buyer characteristics.

The policy implications of these three interpretations are different. In the first situation a case may be made for controlling the level of advertising expenditure because of its monopolising influence. In the second case policy should be directed at the more fundamental source of the problem by reducing the level of market imperfection. In the third case there is no apparent need to regulate advertising intensity directly or indirectly through changes in market structure.

Both in Britain[61, 66, 68-70] and the United States[66, 71-6] a considerable number of empirical studies have been undertaken of the relationship between advertising intensity and market structure. Certain of the early studies have explored the relationship between advertising intensity and seller concentration without making clear the direction of the line of causality that they were hypothesising, but in general most empirical investigations have been concerned to establish whether seller concentration is a determinant of advertising intensity rather than whether advertising intensity affects seller concentration. Although some of the studies have established a significant positive linear relationship between concentration and advertising intensity, in many others this relationship has not been confirmed. It has been suggested, however, that the true relationship may be non-linear, because at high levels of seller concentration greater recognition of the shortcomings of rivalrous advertising behaviour between competitors may reduce the financial incentive to advertise. Some empirical studies support this view, having found evidence of an inverted U-shaped relationship,[61, 68, 70, 75] but this conclusion has also been challenged.[69, 71] A further development in recent years has been the suggestion of a two-way relationship between advertising intensity and seller concentration, such that high advertising intensity is both the consequence of high seller concentration and the means by which it is reinforced and extended.[66, 68, 70, 75] Strickland and Weiss[75] have presented some empirical evidence that supports this view, but the two-way relationship has not yet been widely tested.

More frequently it has been argued that advertising intensity influences market structure by raising entry barriers rather than by directly increasing seller concentration.[77, 78] This may come about in two ways. First, if there are economies of scale in advertising activities that favour existing large sellers within the market relative to smaller potential entrants outside it; or second, if advertising has a cumulative long-term impact on buyer loyalty that cannot be readily eroded through advertising campaigns by new entrants.

The evidence available suggests the existence of a threshold level below which the unit costs of advertising rise. However, there is no clear general evidence that economies of scale in advertising progressively increase with firm size or that the largest sellers in a market engage in the greatest level of advertising.[70, 72, 78, 79] A number of writers have suggested that advertising activity possesses an investment quality, and Lambin has found that current advertising influences future as well as current sales; hence, 'this capital of goodwill may represent a barrier of entry for the potential entrants who have to overcome this consumer inertia created by advertising'.[80] Therefore, the possibility that advertising intensity may reinforce pre-existing imperfections in market structure cannot be ruled out, but at present the evidence is insufficient to deduce that advertising activity necessarily has a substantial effect on either entry barriers or seller concentration.

The relationship between advertising intensity and profitability has also been explored on a number of occasions, particularly in the American literature, and the studies have generally supported the view that there is a significant positive correlation between them.[70, 73, 75, 81, 82] However, the inference that increased advertising intensity increases profit margins has been challenged on two grounds. First, it has been argued that advertising expenditure should be treated as an investment rather than as a current cost of production. If annualised advertising costs and profit ratios are recalculated on this basis, the above relationship may cease to hold. Second, it has been suggested that advertising intensity will be greater where the price–cost margin is greater (see equation 6.2 in section 6.4); therefore, the direction of the line of causality assumed above may be incorrect.

The first of these arguments has been supported by Telser[83] and Bloch;[84] but it has been counterargued by Siegfried and Weiss[85] and Comanor and Wilson[86] that, when such adjustments to advertising and profits data have been made, the original finding still holds. The force of the second argument has been widely acknowledged, and studies by Comanor and Wilson,[87] Vernon and Nourse,[73] and Strickland and Weiss[75] have attempted to distinguish the main elements in the two-way relationship between advertising intensity and profit margins. Each of the studies indicates both that advertising intensity influences profit margins and that profit margins are a determinant of advertising intensity. However, in certain instances the former relationship is relatively weak, and further evidence is needed before this relationship can be confirmed.

Insufficient findings exist to make a confident choice between the three interpretations of the relationship between market structure, advertising activity and market performance presented at the beginning of this subsection (p. 260), but the following tentative conclusions seem justified:

(1) Differences in advertising intensity between industries are due to a considerable degree to differences in the characteristics of the products and buyers concerned (see hypothesis 3).
(2) Differences in advertising intensity are also related to differences in profit margins, which in turn are linked to certain pre-existing features of market structure, notably entry barriers and seller concentration.
(3) To this extent advertising behaviour is a profit-maximising response to exogenously determined characteristics of the market (see hypothesis 2).
(4) Some limited and conflicting evidence exists to suggest that firms above a threshold size are able to use advertising to modify the structure of markets to their commercial advantage, by raising entry barriers and, more speculatively, by increasing seller concentration (see hypothesis 1).

PRODUCT ADVERTISING AND THE PUBLIC INTEREST

The desirability or otherwise of product advertising, from the standpoint of the public interest, is one of the most longstanding and hotly disputed of economic issues. Ideally, an objective assessment should be based upon estimates of the magnitude and distribution of the social benefits and social costs of different kinds of advertising activity.[88] However, as observed above, both the nature and the magnitude of advertising impacts are still disputed. Therefore, it is only possible to indicate the main benefits and costs of advertising as claimed in the literature[89-91] and to submit these claims to critical examination, without striking the final balance of advantage between them.

It has been claimed that the following kinds of benefit may result from advertising activities:

(1) It performs an informative role by supplying consumers with data on product availability, characteristics, quality and price. The use of mass communication for this purpose is socially advantageous where it consumes less resources than if each consumer undertook his own information search for such data.
(2) The use of advertising to project the image of branded goods may encourage producers to maintain adequate product-quality standards; otherwise, the 'image differentiation' in which they engage may dissuade consumers from purchasing their brands.
(3) By expanding the level of sales of a product through advertising, economies of large scale production may result, which may enable its producer to price the product at a lower level than would otherwise be charged without advertising.
(4) By rapidly creating markets for new products and thereby enabling

them to become profitable more quickly than would otherwise be the case, advertising may strengthen the incentive to innovate.

(5) It subsidises the mass media, enabling them to charge prices for newspapers, etc. that are substantially below their average financial costs. This may constitute a social benefit to the extent that increased newspaper, etc. sales result in a better informed and educated community.

(6) Advertising involves a form of art that may have cultural or entertainment value in its own right.

However, it has also been suggested that product advertising may have the following socially-adverse qualities:

(1) A significant part of advertising activity may be *persuasive* rather than *informative* and to this extent yield no social benefit.

(2) It may change the pattern of consumer tastes to the advertiser's, but not necessarily to the community's, advantage by instilling or entrenching hedonistic values and stimulating consumers to make unfavourable comparisons between their own well-being and that of people whom they are encouraged to emulate.

(3) It may reinforce and extend existing market imperfections (e.g. by raising entry barriers), which may result in a welfare loss through the restriction of sales, a decline in productive efficiency and a transfer of consumer surplus to producers.

Certain of these effects are illustrated in Figure 6.9. In the pre-advertising situation the firm could maximise its short run profits by charging price OP, but it only charges OP_1 because of the ease of new entry into the market. The expenditure of P_1P_3 unit advertising costs does not change the demand function in this instance, but by raising brand loyalty it increases entry barriers and enables the firm to charge OP_2 without fear of new competition. Three types of impact are shown: the resource costs of the persuasive advertising, the welfare loss through the restriction of sales, and the transfer of consumer surplus to producers. Additionally, if productive efficiency falls, resulting in a further increase in marginal costs of production, this will be an additional social cost of advertising, although there will probably be an equivalent reduction in the transfer of consumer surplus.[92]

Both the alleged benefits and socially adverse qualities of product advertising have been challenged. Those who have questioned the social value of advertising have argued that only a small part of advertising activity is informative, that product branding is not a sufficient guarantee of quality and reliability and that, while the reduction of prices in conditions of heavy advertising is a theoretical possibility, the more general expectation is that such prices will increase. Similarly, although advertising intensity may stimulate innovative activity, such innovations may take the form of minor style changes that themselves may be costly and of dubious public advantage.[93] The social benefits derivable from subsidising the mass media have also been questioned on the grounds both that advertising may encourage the media to reduce the informative (as distinct from the entertainment) quality of their services in

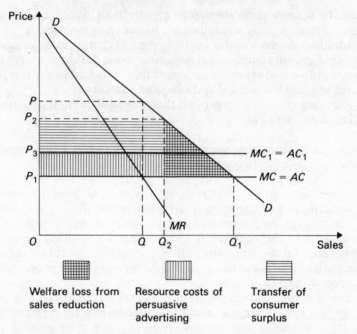

Fig. 6.9   Impact of advertising activities that raise entry barriers to a market.

order to tap the mass market that advertisers seek and that it may influence editorial policy on news topics on which major advertisers have strongly held views.

Those who have upheld the social benefits of product advertising have questioned the value of the distinction between informative and persuasive advertising on the grounds that all advertising activity involves both elements, which in the last resort are inseparable. It has also been claimed that the extent to which product advertising conditions buyer attitudes has been exaggerated and that sales are more profoundly influenced by other elements in the marketing mix, notably product quality.[94] Finally, it has been argued, advertising activity is not a proven source of market imperfection, and therefore it is incorrect to assign the social costs of market imperfections to it.

6.6   CONCLUSION

This chapter is concerned with one of the main topics in microeconomic analysis: pricing behaviour – its determination and relationship to other forms of competitive behaviour. At the theoretical level the limitations of simple marginal analysis in the explanation of pricing behaviour in oligopolistic markets have been reviewed. These arise from the need to take into account the existence of interdependent rivalrous behaviour, the pervasiveness of uncertainty and bounded rationality in the business environment and the pursuit by firms of objectives that diverge from profit maximisation. A variety of alternative theoretical approaches that attempt to take some or all of these different conditions into account have been developed, but as yet none of these commands wide acceptance as a replacement for the marginalist pricing model (section 6.2).

Empirical research into pricing behaviour has taken two different forms: business surveys, and statistical analyses of price changes. In both cases the majority of the studies has cast doubt on the marginalist interpretation of short-run pricing behaviour, particularly in the manufacturing sector. However, the evidence also indicates that demand variables have a subsidiary influence in bringing about price changes, which therefore do not always correspond exactly to changes in 'normal' or 'full cost' levels (section 6.3).

Empirical studies have also indicated that prices are only one component in the marketing mix used by firms and, in the view of many businessmen, are frequently not the most important element. By retaining the assumptions of certainty, unbounded rationality and profit maximisation it is possible to establish the equilibrium position of the firm by the simultaneous equation of marginal costs and marginal revenue for each price and non-price decision variable. What has not yet been sufficiently explored is how price and marketing behaviour would be modified if the more realistic features of oligopolistic environments, described above, applied (section 6.4).

Advertising activity is the best-documented and most controversial form of non-price competition, although it is not necessarily the most important component. The average cost incidence of product advertising by manufacturers in the UK economy is quite low, but for particular product groups it reaches 20 per cent or more of sales revenue. Increased levels of advertising may reinforce pre-existing imperfections in market structure and so enable larger profits to be earned, but this has not yet been widely established in empirical studies, although a number of them have drawn this conclusion. The magnitude and distribution of the social benefits and costs arising from advertising activity have not been reliably determined, and therefore it is not possible to establish in a definitive way whether particular types of advertising behaviour are in the public interest or not (section 6.5).

FURTHER READING

Reviews of the theory of price determination in different types of market are to be found in a number of microeconomic textbooks, including Baumol[3] and C. E. Ferguson.[3] An up-to-date general survey of empirical studies of the pricing decision is not available, but readers may first consult Silberston[1] and Blair[40] before turning to the more specialised literature on the subject. Needham[50, 57] should be consulted on the determinants of the price and non-price components of the marketing mix. J. M. Ferguson[66] and Cowling *et al.*[70] have provided a useful background survey of the literature on the relationship between advertising intensity, market structure and market performance, but they should be supplemented by more recent specialised articles on the subject.

NOTES AND REFERENCES

1 A. Silberston, 'Surveys of applied economics: price behaviour of firms', *Economic Journal,* vol. 80 (September 1970), pp. 511–82.
2 See references in section 6.4.
3 Price determination in perfectly competitive and monopoly markets has been analysed in most basic microeconomic textbooks, such as C. E. Ferguson, *Micro-economic Theory* (Homewood, Ill., Irwin, 1972); and W. J. Baumol, *Economic Theory and Operations Analysis* (Englewood Cliffs, Prentice-Hall, 1977).
4 E. H. Chamberlin, *The Theory of Monopolistic Competition* (Cambridge, Mass., Harvard UP, 1933); and J. Robinson, *The Economics of Imperfect Competition* (London, Macmillan, 1933).
5 Ferguson, op. cit. (n. 3), ch. 11.
6 F. M. Scherer, *Industrial Market Structure and Economic Performance* (Chicago, Rand McNally, 1970), pp. 140–5.
7 Scherer, op. cit. (n. 6), pp. 158–64. Also see section 9.3.
8 D. Needham, *The Economics of Industrial Structure, Conduct and Performance* (London, Holt, Rinehart & Winston, 1978), pp. 159–72.
9 J. S. Bain, *Barriers to New Competition* (Cambridge, Mass., Harvard UP, 1956).
10 P. Sylos-Labini, *Oligopoly and Technical Progress* (Cambridge, Mass., Harvard UP, 1962).
11 Baumol, op. cit. (n. 3), ch. 15.
12 Needham, op. cit. (n. 8), ch. 1.
13 J. W. McGuire, *Theories of Business Behavior* (Englewood Cliffs, Prentice-Hall, 1964), ch. 6.
14 D. de Meza and M. Osborne, *Problems in Price Theory* (Deddington, Phillip Allan, 1978). .
15 P. M. Sweezy, 'Demand under conditions of oligopoly', *Journal of Political Economy,* vol. 47 (1939), pp. 568–73.
16 R. L. Hall and C. J. Hitch, 'Price theory and business behaviour', *Oxford Economic Papers,* vol. 2 (1939), pp. 12–45.
17 R. M. Cyert and J. G. March, *A Behavioral Theory of the Firm* (Englewood Cliffs, Prentice-Hall, reprinted 1970).
18 Scherer, op. cit. (n. 6), p. 178.
19 Hall and Hitch, op. cit. (n. 16), p. 12.
20 R. H. Barback, *The Pricing of Manufactures* (London, Macmillan, 1964), p. 169.
21 D. C. Hague, *Pricing in Business* (London, Allen & Unwin, 1971).
22 J. Pickering, 'The Prices and Incomes Board and private sector prices: a survey', *Economic Journal,* vol. 81 (1971), pp. 225–41.
23 J. Mitchell, *Price Determination and Prices Policy* (London, Allen & Unwin, 1978).
24 Mitchell, op. cit. (n. 23), pp. 175–6.
25 P. W. S. Andrews and E. Brunner, *Studies in Pricing* (London, Macmillan, 1975).
26 A. Gabor, *Pricing: Principles and Practices* (London, Heinemann, 1977).
27 A. D. H. Kaplan, J. B. Dirlam and R. F. Lanzillotti, *Pricing in Big Business* (Washington, DC, Brookings Institution, 1958).
28 Kaplan, Dirlam and Lanzillotti, op. cit. (n. 27), pp. 3 and 260.
29 Kaplan, Dirlam and Lanzillotti, op. cit. (n. 27), pp. 277–8.
30 R. F. Lanzillotti, *Pricing, Production and Marketing Policies of Small Manufacturers* (Washington, DC, Washington State UP, 1964).
31 F. Machlup, 'Marginal analysis and empirical research', *American Economic Review,* vol. 36 (1946), pp. 518–53.
32 F. Machlup, 'Theories of the firm: marginalist, behavioral, managerial', *American Economic Review,* vol. 57 (1967), pp. 1–33.

33 Machlup, op. cit. (n. 31), p. 538.
34 Machlup, op. cit. (n. 31), p. 537.
35 Hall and Hitch, op. cit. (n. 16), p. 19.
36 Machlup, op. cit. (n. 32), p. 31.
37 The evidence and argument advanced by Means have been summarised by J. M. Blair, *Economic Concentration: Structure, Behavior and Public Policy* (New York, Harcourt, Brace, Jovanovich, 1972), pp. 419*ff*.
38 G. C. Means, *Industrial Prices and their Relative Inflexibility* (74th Congress, 1st Sers. S.Doc.1, 1935).
39 Scherer, op. cit. (n. 6), p. 296.
40 Blair, op. cit. (n. 37), pp. 438*ff*.
41 H. J. De Podwin and R. P. Selden, 'Business pricing policies and inflation', *Journal of Political Economy*, vol. 71 (April 1963), pp. 116–27.
42 L. W. Weiss, 'Business pricing policies and inflation reconsidered', *Journal of Political Economy*, vol. 74 (April 1966), pp. 177–87.
43 G. J. Stigler and J. K. Kindahl, *The Behavior of Industrial Prices* (New York, National Bureau of Economic Research, 1970).
44 G. C. Means, 'The administered price thesis re-confirmed', *American Economic Review*, vol. 62 (1972), pp. 292–306.
45 L. W. Weiss, 'Stigler, Kindahl and Means on administered prices', *American Economic Review*, vol. 67 (1977), pp. 610–19.
46 W. D. Nordhaus and W. Godley, 'Pricing in the trade cycle', *Economic Journal*, vol. 82 (1972), pp. 853–82. This version of the full cost principle has sometimes been referred to as the *normal cost* principle. Its distinguishing feature is that temporary (or cyclical) cost increases do not precipitate price changes.
47 D. E. W. Laidler and M. Parkin, 'Inflation: a survey', *Economic Journal*, vol. 85 (1975), pp. 741–809.
48 G. W. Smith, 'Price determination', in M. Parkin and M. T. Sumner (eds), *Inflation in the United Kingdom* (Manchester, Manchester UP, 1978).
49 K. Coutts, W. Godley and W. Nordhaus, *Industrial Pricing in the United Kingdom* (Cambridge, Cambridge UP, 1978), p. 72.
50 Needham, op. cit. (n. 8), ch. 4.
51 Scherer, op. cit. (n. 6), ch. 14.
52 J. Udell, 'The role of price in competitive strategy', *Journal of Marketing*, vol. 28 (1964), pp. 44–8.
53 Kaplan, Dirlam and Lanzillotti, op. cit. (n. 27), pp. 261–2.
54 J. Backman, *Advertising and Competition* (New York, New York UP, 1967), ch. 2.
55 R. Dorfman and P. O. Steiner, 'Optimal advertising and optimal quality', *American Economic Review*, vol. 44 (1954), pp. 826–36.
56 Needham, op. cit. (n. 8), pp. 83–91.
57 Needham, op. cit. (n. 8), pp. 24–30.
58 R. Schmalensee, *The Economics of Advertising* (Amsterdam, North-Holland, 1972), p. 18.
59 Schmalensee, op. cit. (n. 58), p. 43.
60 R. H. Colley, quoted in P. Doyle, 'Economic aspects of advertising: a survey', *Economic Journal*, vol. 77 (1968), pp. 570–602.
61 C. J. Sutton, 'Advertising, concentration and competition', *Economic Journal*, vol. 84 (1974), pp. 56–69.
62 Backman, op. cit. (n. 54), p. 15.
63 Price Commission, *Prices, Costs and Margins in the Production and Distribution of Proprietary Non-ethical Medicines*, House of Commons 469, Session 1977–8 (London, HMSO, 1978).
64 Backman, op. cit. (n. 54), p. 18.

65 J. J. Lambin, *Advertising, Competition and Market Conduct in Oligopoly over Time* (Amsterdam, North-Holland, 1976), p. 124.

66 J. M. Ferguson, *Advertising and Competition: Theory, Measurement, Fact* (Cambridge, Mass., Ballinger, 1974).

67 G. R. Butters, 'A survey of advertising and market structure', *American Economic Association Papers and Proceedings*, vol. 66 (1976), pp. 392–7.

68 J. Cable, 'Market structure, advertising policy and inter-market differences in advertising intensity', in K. Cowling (ed.), *Market Structure and Corporate Behaviour* (London, Gray-Mills, 1972), pp. 105–24.

69 W. D. Reekie, 'Advertising and market structure: another approach', *Economic Journal*, vol. 85 (1975), pp. 156–9; and R. D. Rees, 'Advertising, concentration and competition: a comment and further results', *Economic Journal*, vol. 85 (1975), pp. 165–72.

70 K. Cowling *et al.*, *Advertising and Economic Behaviour* (London, Macmillan, 1975).

71 W. S. Comanor and T. A. Wilson, *Advertising and Market Power* (Cambridge, Mass., Harvard UP, 1974).

72 Lambin, op. cit. (n. 65).

73 J. M. Vernon and R. E. M. Nourse, 'Profit rates and market structure of advertising intensive firms', *Journal of Industrial Economics*, vol. 22 (1973), pp. 1–12.

74 B. C. Brush, 'The influence of market structure on industry advertising intensity', *Journal of Industrial Economics*, vol. 25 (1976), pp. 55–65.

75 A. D. Strickland and L. W. Weiss, 'Advertising, concentration, and price–cost margins', *Journal of Political Economy*, vol. 84 (1976), pp. 1109–21.

76 T. S. Friedland, 'Advertising and concentration', *Journal of Industrial Economics*, vol. 26 (1977), pp. 151–9.

77 Comanor and Wilson, op. cit. (n. 71), ch. 5.

78 Ferguson, op. cit. (n. 66), ch. 4.

79 Comanor and Wilson, op. cit. (n. 71), ch. 9.

80 Lambin, op. cit. (n. 65), p. 95.

81 Ferguson, op. cit. (n. 66), ch. 6.

82 Comanor and Wilson, op. cit. (n. 71), ch. 6.

83 L. G. Telser, 'Advertising and the advantages of size', *American Economic Review*, vol. 59 (1969), pp. 121–3.

84 H. Bloch, 'Advertising and profitability: a re-appraisal', *Journal of Political Economy*, vol. 82 (1974), pp. 267–86.

85 J. J. Siegfried and L. W. Weiss, 'Advertising, profits, and corporate taxes revisited', *Review of Economics and Statistics*, vol. 56 (1974), pp. 195–200.

86 Comanor and Wilson, op. cit. (n. 71), ch. 8.

87 Comanor and Wilson, op. cit. (n. 71), ch. 7.

88 These criteria and their application are examined in Chapters 8–11.

89 Scherer, op. cit. (n. 6), pp. 325–32.

90 P. Doyle, 'Economic aspects of advertising: a survey', *Economic Journal*, vol. 77 (1968), pp. 570–99.

91 Comanor and Wilson, op. cit. (n. 71), ch. 11.

92 D. Morris, 'Some economic aspects of large-scale advertising', *Journal of Industrial Economics*, vol. 24 (1975), pp. 119–30.

93 F. M. Fisher, Z. Griliches and C. Kaysen, 'The costs of automobile model changes since 1949', *Journal of Political Economy*, vol. 70 (1962), pp. 433–51.

94 Lambin, op. cit. (n. 65), pp. 100*ff.*

7 The Investment Decision

7.1 INTRODUCTION

Investment may be defined as any act involving 'the sacrifice of an immediate and certain satisfaction in exchange for a future expectation'.[1] The distinguishing feature of an investment is the expenditure of valuable resources in the anticipation of future gain or a stream of benefits to be realised over time. The business firm undertakes investment because it is believed by management that it will contribute to the achievement of the firm's objective. Traditionally this objective has been recognised as the maximisation of profit. The assessment of investment appraisal criteria carried out in section 7.4 is conducted in these terms. In so doing no value judgement about the desirability of profit maximisation is being made, and it is clear that investment criteria can be related to other objectives (e.g. business growth, as discussed in Chapter 4).

Investment may also be considered as a macroeconomic phenomenon, and there is some evidence of an association between the volume of investment and the national rate of economic growth.[2] This evidence is in fact far from conclusive, but the acceptance of such a relationship guarantees government interest in the level of investment. The involvement of central government in investment decision making is considered in the concluding section of this chapter.

It is possible to make a distinction between various kinds of investment decision, e.g. investment in new capital, investment in replacement capital and investment in working capital. These distinctions are important in practice. It has, for instance, been traditional in the United Kingdom for banks to look more favourably upon involvement in investment in working capital because of the relatively greater probability of rapid recovery thereby entailed. There is also some evidence that different investment criteria are applied to different types of investment. Investments also differ in scale, and there is evidence that the investment criteria employed vary with the scale of the commitment. Conceptually, the methods of investment appraisal described below can be applied to any form of expenditure that conforms to the definition of investment given in the opening paragraph. However, in practice the decision to vary the criteria according to circumstances may also be logical. Thus, for a very small investment with a relatively insensitive rate of return the expenditure of large resources on a discounting calculation may not be justified.

Two of the most important issues in the examination of the investment process are investment appraisal and the funding of investment programmes. Appraisal techniques materially affect the decisions taken on the allocation of investment funds, which are a valuable scarce resource (see sections 7.2–7.4). The issue of the availability of investment capital is equally important; lack of funds, perhaps partially because of institutional inadequacies, may inhibit growth, while the particular pattern of funding adopted by firms may itself affect resource allocation (see section 7.6).

Accordingly, the structure of the remainder of this chapter is as follows.

A number of methods of investment appraisal developed by economists and others are reviewed in section 7.2, and the evidence that is available on the relative importance of these methods in practice is examined in section 7.3. In section 7.4 an assessment is made of the relative strengths and weaknesses of the different appraisal techniques described, and this is followed in section 7.5 by a more detailed examination of the difficulties encountered, under conditions of uncertainty, in investment appraisal. The sources of business finance used by UK industry, with some international comparisons, are analysed in section 7.6. The special problems faced by small firms in raising capital and the behaviour of very large firms in the capital market are then examined in section 7.7. The concluding section (7.8) examines the level of aggregate investment in the United Kingdom, the debate over its determinants and the implications for government policy to be drawn. The chapter is primarily concerned with investment and finance in the private sector of industry; investment in the nationalised sector is analysed in Chapter 10.

7.2   METHODS OF INVESTMENT APPRAISAL

The distinguishing feature of an investment is that the costs that it incurs and the revenues that it generates arise over a period of time. Capital, i.e. accumulated wealth, is an input whose use necessarily involves the passage of time, and the major problem of investment appraisal follows from this fact. Most investment decisions are taken in the light of a set of figures that express some form of relationship between the cost of the project – initial outlay plus working capital – and the incremental profit expected to accrue to the firm as a result of undertaking the project. The central problem is, therefore, one of evaluating uncertain future cash flows and relating these to outlays in the immediate and near future. The forms in which this relationship can be expressed are considered below. The assessment of the relative merits of these investment criteria is based upon the assumption that the objective of the decision maker is to maximise profits. Furthermore, the substantial problems introduced by imperfect foresight, risk and uncertainty are ignored until section 7.5.

As Shackle has observed, the task of evaluating alternative opportunities is 'in high degree a resort to conjecture. Conjecture itself, however, can be systematised.'[3] In this section four criteria of investment appraisal that attempt to systematise this process are examined. This is not an exhaustive list, but it is believed that these criteria both are most frequently encountered in practice and adequately illustrate the relative merits and disadvantages of the two main categories of investment criteria in use. Investment criteria may be placed into one of two categories, which are referred to under a variety of titles, i.e. 'rules of thumb' or 'quickies' on the one hand and 'scientific' or 'sophisticated' methods on the other. Into the latter groups are placed all criteria that utilise the procedure known as discounting. This is essentially a means of allowing for the deferment of the receipts or costs that are inherent in an investment project. In the next two subsections certain 'rule of thumb' criteria are outlined.[4] This is followed by a description of discounting and its use in more 'sophisticated' appraisal methods. The assessment of the relative merits of the different methods is carried out in section 7.4.

THE PAYBACK METHOD[5]

The payback period is the period of time, usually expressed in years, required to generate sufficient additional profits to recover the initial capital outlay of the investment. It is customary to calculate profits net of tax but inclusive of depreciation. The shorter the payback period, the more favourably the project is regarded.[6]

THE BOOK RATE OF RETURN

This may be defined as the ratio of (1) the average annual profit that is attributable to the investment (after tax and net of depreciation) to (2) the initial capital outlay. The rate of return is thus obtained as a percentage figure, which can be compared to the initial cost of capital. For example, if a project earns £180 over ten years on an outlay of £100, the rate of return may be expressed as 18 per cent per annum. Alternatively, the average profit (£18) may be related to some concept of average capital employed (say £500), in which case the rate of return will be calculated as 36 per cent.

TIME PREFERENCE AND DISCOUNTING

The main deficiency of the two methods of investment appraisal considered above is that they fail to take adequate account of the timing of receipts and outlays. It is not correct to assume that money received in the future is equivalent in value to an equal sum received in the present. If two projects have the same total return but this return is distributed differently over time, the two projects cannot be regarded as equally profitable. Money has a time value; that is, money now is worth more than an equal sum in the future because it can be employed profitably in the interval. The central problem is to determine the *present value* equivalent of any given sum of money due at some future date. The solution to this problem is to convert amounts due in the future to their base year equivalents. This process is known as *discounting*.[7]

Consider the investment of a capital sum of £100. This may be invested for one year at a rate of interest, (r), and the total sum will then be $£(100+r)$ after one year. In generalised terms, if a sum of money, P, becomes $P(1+r)$ in one year's time, it can be concluded that the time exchange is $1:(1+r)$ one period hence. The rate of exchange, r, is almost always positive and is referred to as the *rate of interest*. In the example, if $r=5$ per cent, the present value of £100 invested last year is £105. By the same reasoning the present value of £100 due next year is the sum that, invested at 5 per cent, will be worth £100 in one year's time; £95·24 invested for one year will produce the required £100. In other words, if the present value of a future sum of Z is denoted by Y, then Y invested now at compound interest will grow to Z in one year; Y now is worth the same as a certain promise of Z in one year.

This proposition may be expressed in a more general form. There is clearly a close relationship between the processes of *discounting* (i.e. finding the present value of a sum that is due in the future) and *compounding* (i.e. finding the terminal value of a sum invested now). Let P be invested at r per cent compound. The yield after one period is

$$rP + P = P(1+r) \tag{7.1}$$

Similarly, after two periods the yield is

$$P(1+r) \times (1+r) = P(1+r)^2 \tag{7.2}$$

and after n periods the yield is

$$P(1+r)^n \tag{7.3}$$

If a sum of money due now is denoted by P and one in the future by S, then after one period

$$S = P(1+r) \tag{7.4}$$

and after n periods

$$S = P(1+r)^n \tag{7.5}$$

or

$$P = S/(1+r)^n \tag{7.6}$$

The fraction $1/(1+r)^n$ is known as the *discount factor* and must be applied to sums that are due in the future to reduce them to their present value. For example, if in the above $r = 5$ per cent the present value of £100 due in one year's time is given by

$$£100 \times \frac{1}{1 \cdot 05} = £95.24$$

Similarly, the present value of £100 due in two years' time is

$$£100 \times \left(\frac{1}{1+r} + \frac{1}{1+r} \right) = £100 \times \frac{1}{(1+r)^2} = £100 \times \frac{1}{(1 \cdot 05)^2} \approx £91$$

In order to calculate the present value, P, of sum S due in the future over n periods the following formula is employed:

$$P = \sum_{i=1}^{i=n} \frac{S_i}{(1+r)^i} \tag{7.7}$$

where Σ is the conventional sign for summation of the sums S_i from the first, $S_1(i=1)$, to the nth.

A table can be constructed showing the discount factors that are appropriate to any interest rate and time period. These factors can then be applied to any time series of cash flows to give their present values.[8]

The discounting process, therefore, aims to take account of the timing of cash flows. The major defect of not discounting is to discriminate against projects that give profits immediately relative to projects that do not. Two methods of investment appraisal that incorporate the discounting process are the *net present value (NPV)* and the *internal rate of return (IRR)* criteria, and a considerable debate has been conducted over their relative merits.

NET PRESENT VALUE

The NPV is defined as the present value equivalent of all cash inflows less all cash outlays associated with a project. If the NPV is greater than zero, the project is worthwhile from a profit-maximising standpoint. If a choice has to be made between projects, the one with the greatest NPV should be selected.

In the following example a three-year project is described. The initial and only outlay is £1,000, annual receipts are £400 and $r = 5$ per cent. Accordingly,

$$P = \frac{S_1}{1+r} + \frac{S_2}{1+r^2} + \frac{S_3}{1+r^3} \tag{7.8}$$

$$= \sum_{i=1}^{i=3} \frac{S_i}{(1+r)^i} \tag{7.9}$$

Let

$$\text{NVP} = \sum_{i=1}^{i=3} \frac{S_i}{(1+r)^i} - C \tag{7.10}$$

Thus the NPV is $+£90$, as shown by the calculations in Table 7.1. This project is acceptable according to the above criterion because the NPV is positive. However, in accepting a positive NPV as an indicator that a project is viable certain simplifying assumptions should apply. At no time in the life of the project should the cash flows assume a form that jeopardises the long term existence of the company. If a choice between projects has to be made, e.g. because projects are competitive or investment funds are limited, the projects should be ranked for selection purposes in order of their NPVs; that is, the greater the NPV, the higher the ranking of a competing project. If the competing projects differ in capital outlay, the relationship between the absolute difference in outlay and the expected improvement in NPV must be examined. If the comparison is between projects of different life spans, then, as long as it is feasible to renew the shorter-lived project, the correct procedure is to make a comparison between the NPV of the longer-lived project and the NPV of a series of short term investments supplying the same need over the same period.

Table 7.1   *Calculation of NPV with* r=5 *per cent.*

Year, i	Outlay, C (£)	Inflow, S_i (£)	Discount factor, $1/(1+r)^i$	Discounted value of inflow $S_i/(1+r)^i$ (£)
0	1,000	—	—	—
1	—	400	$\dfrac{1}{1\cdot05}$	381
2	—	400	$\dfrac{1}{1\cdot10}$	364
3	—	400	$\dfrac{1}{1\cdot16}$	345
$\Sigma=$	1,000			1,090

$$\text{NPV} = £1{,}090 - £1{,}000 = +£90$$

THE MARGINAL EFFICIENCY OF CAPITAL OR INTERNAL RATE OF RETURN

This method is also known as the '*solution*' *rate of interest*. It is defined as the rate of interest, r, that equates the discounted present value, P, of expected future receipts to the present value of the stream of cash outlays; that is, it solves the equation for the discount rate that makes NPV=0. Thus, the IRR is the solution for r in

$$£1{,}000 = \sum_{i=1}^{i=3} \frac{400}{(1+r)^i} = \text{IRR} \tag{7.11}$$

In this example all the expenditure occurs at the beginning of the project, and it is clear that the IRR must exceed 5 per cent because the NPV is positive at this discount rate. If $r=10$ per cent is substituted into the equation, the NPV is $-£4$. The solution rate is found to be 9·7 per cent, and the project would just break even if financed on the basis of an overdraft-type of loan at this interest rate (see Table 7.2). In ranking projects the one with the highest IRR over the cost of capital is selected according to the profit-maximising criterion.

Table 7.2   *Calculation of the IRR.*

Year	Outlay (£)	Plus interest at 9·7% (£)	Debt (£)	Less cash flow (£)	Balance (£)
1	1,000	97	1,097	400	697·0
2	697	67.6	764·6	400	364·6
3	364·6	35·4	400	400	0

Table 7.3 *Investment criteria and the selection of projects.*

		A	B	C	D
(a)	*Cash inflows associated with the four competing projects (£)*				
	Year 1	10	40	40	60
	Year 2	10	30	20	40
	Year 3	20	30	30	0
	Year 4	30	20	20	0
	Year 5	80	20	20	0
	Total	150	140	130	100
(b)	*Ranking of projects by investment criteria*				
	Payback	4	3	2	1
	Book rate of return	1	2	3	4
	NPV (5%)	1	2	3	4
	IRR	2	1	3	4

The choice of investment criteria may have a decisive effect upon the selection of projects. Consider Table 7.3a in which A, B, C, and D represent four competing projects, each involving an initial outlay of £100. These projects are ranked in Table 7.3b in order of preference according to the four investment criteria examined above. It can be seen that the payback method ranks project D as the best alternative even though it makes no incremental profit at all, whereas the other methods of appraisal place project D in the last position.

The total volume of investment in an economy and the impact of government policy on this may also be influenced by the techniques of appraisal that firms use. For example, since the 1960s there have been different systems of investment grants and tax allowances in operation that have favoured investment in manufacturing industry in the 'assisted areas' of the United Kingdom (see the calculations made by the present author in Table 7.4). These have affected both the net present value of individual projects and their payback period, but to differing and varying extents. For example, the financial incentives introduced in 1966, although they had a somewhat lower NPV value than the 1963 incentives, probably had a greater impact on the payback period and may, therefore, have had a greater influence on investment levels in the assisted areas. This is examined more fully in sections 11.6 and 11.7.

Table 7.4 *Government incentives to manufacturing industry, 1963–72.*

Incentive system (year)	Assisted areas (%)	Non-assisted areas (%)
1963	59·4	27·7
1966	44·8	26·4
1970	40.0	24·0
1972	60·0	40·0

7.3   THE INVESTMENT DECISION IN PRACTICE

The aim of this section is to ascertain, as far as the evidence allows, the relative frequency with which the various investment appraisal criteria outlined above are utilised. A fairly marked change appears in the picture conveyed by evidence from the early and mid 1960s and that of the early 1970s. In part this difference may be due to the difference in the size of enterprise providing evidence in the two sets of studies.

Williams and Scott, in a study of fourteen firms in the mid 1960s, have found that in only nine cases were serious calculations made of the expected return from capital investments.[9] Two firms used discounted cash-flow (DCF) criteria, but the vast majority relied upon pretax calculations of the average rates of return in 'typical' years. Nield's larger inquiry into capital replacement policies, covering 133 firms and conducted at approximately the same time, has attempted to determine whether or not firms in the engineering industry made detailed calculations, as opposed to relying on qualitative judgements.[10] Where detailed calculations were made Nield has attempted to identify the criteria employed. Over half of the sample did undertake quantitative analysis in all cases. However, 68 per cent of firms completing the questionnaire adopted the payback method of appraisal. Frequently, pretax calculations were employed. Only two firms employed discounting techniques, and this may be particularly significant given that the Nield survey was biased towards large firms.

A study of the response to investment incentives undertaken by Corner and Williams and reported in 1965 has confirmed the prevalence of the payback method; 73 per cent of the sample, which was biased towards the small firm, used this criterion.[11] These conclusions have been further confirmed by an investigation into investment in the machine tool industry in 1965, which has reported that over 20 per cent of the firms studied made no investment appraisal calculations at all while the remainder used the payback method.[12]

The conclusion drawn from these studies of the investment appraisal techniques that were characteristic of British industry in the mid 1960s is that unsophisticated techniques were then the rule. Discounting appeared to be practiced by a very small minority of firms.

To the extent that rationality in decision making is defined in terms of profit maximisation under conditions of certainty, the conclusions reached by these studies are extremely disturbing. The British Institute of Management has concluded with its impression that the techniques generally used by British industry for evaluating capital projects not only were crude but also could be positively misleading.[13] The evidence that pretax estimates were utilised is similarly disturbing to policy makers who place reliance on tax incentives to influence investment decisions. However, more recent work in both the United Kingdom and the United States indicates that some revision of these conclusions may now be called for.

The major new UK evidence has been produced by Carsberg and Hope.[14] This 1973 study is based on a random sample of 325 large companies selected from *The Times*'s 1,000 largest companies, to which 103 replies were received. Eight appraisal techniques were specified, and respondents were

Table 7.5   *Investment appraisal techniques in use in the United Kingdom, 1973.*

Method used	1	2	3	4	5	6	7	8 (not mentioned)	Points scored
Payback	19	7	10	9	5	4	7	42	533
Book rate of return (first-year profit only)	12	6	8	1	3	2	6	65	641
Book rate of return (average)	11	4	6	13	4	—	7	58	622
NPV	10	10	7	11	4	4	7	50	588
IRR	28	15	10	11	3	5	9	22	416
Qualitative judgement	34	6	15	20	6	5	2	15	365

The header spans: *No. of firms selecting score:*

Source: B. Carsberg and A. Hope, *Business Investment Decisions under Uncertainty* (London, Institute of Chartered Accountants, 1976), table 8.1.

asked to select a figure from 1 to 7 to indicate the importance in use of each criterion, a score of 1 indicating that the particular method was used on all occasions; a score of 8 was allocated to the method not mentioned. The results of this survey are summarised in Table 7.5 and lead to the following conclusions. First, quantitative calculations, as opposed to qualitative judgement, were extremely significant; seventy-six firms regarded them as fundamentally important in investment decisions, whereas only twenty-six regarded such calculations as providing only secondary confirmation of a decision already reached in principle. Second, the discounting methods of appraisal were shown to be much more widely used than earlier work had suggested. Carsberg and Hope have concluded that the 'results of our survey indicate

Table 7.6   *Single and multiple methods of investment appraisal in British industry, 1973.*

Method used	No. of firms
Single methods:	
Payback	11
Book rate of return (first-year profit)	2
NPV	2
IRR	6
Qualitative	9
Total (single)	30
Multiple methods	73
Total (single and multiple)	103

Source: B. Carsberg and A. Hope, *Business Investment Decisions under Uncertainty* (London, Institute of Chartered Accountants, 1976) table 8.2.

that considerably more use is now made by British firms of the two main discounted cash flow methods . . . Indeed 85% of respondents use one or both methods. It seems likely that there has been a significant movement to adopt discounted cash flow methods in the past few years.'[15] This trend may be taken as evidence of the greater interest in profit maximisation that some commentators have suggested. However, it must be recorded that the support for discounting techniques afforded by this study is somewhat tempered by the further revelation that, in those companies in which only one method was used, the payback method was the most popular (see Table 7.6). Also, the findings only relate to the companies that co-operated in the study, and those which did not may have used less sophisticated appraisal techniques.

The two broad conclusions drawn above have been supported by a number of recent American studies. Klammer has surveyed 369 large firms with large-scale investment programmes, obtaining 184 responses relating to three points in time: 1959, 1964 and 1970.[16] The results, summarised in Table 7.7, indicate that discounting techniques were most commonly used in 1970 and that their relative importance increased significantly over the time period covered by the study.

Table 7.7   *Methods of investment appraisal in American industry, 1959–70.*

	% using method in each year[a]		
Method used	*1970*	*1964*	*1959*
Discounting	57	38	19
Book rate of return	26	30	34
Payback	12	24	34

Source: T. Klammer, 'Empirical evidence of the adoption of sophisticated capital budgeting techniques', *Harvard Business Review* vol. 50 (1972), pp. 387–94.

Note:
(a)   Figures do not add up to 100.

The best generalisation that can be made from the available evidence is that in larger corporations there has been a significant movement towards the adoption of the more sophisticated techniques involving discounting. It would be interesting to know whether or not the same is true of smaller companies, but this cannot be discovered from the available evidence. There is some evidence to suggest that smaller companies do make relatively less use of discounting techniques; for example, Rockley's study of sixty-nine UK companies, summarised in Table 7.8, goes some way towards supporting this conclusion.[17] It has also frequently been contended that the technique adopted varies with the size and type of investment decision involved. There is insufficient evidence to confirm or refute this hypothesis, but it would be logical for a profit-maximising enterprise to take into account the relative costs and benefits associated with the use of these alternative techniques. This point is considered again in section 7.4.

Table 7.8   *Investment appraisal and company size.*

| | % of companies using: | | |
	Payback	Book rate of return	DCF
Size of company (employment)			
→1,000	63	57	42
1,000–1,500	57	32	50
←5,000+	68	64	77
Sales (£ m.)			
→10	62	42	35
10–50	64	41	64
50+	65	53	88

Source: L. E. Rockley, *Investment for Profitability* (London, Business Books, 1973) p. 136.

7.4   AN ASSESSMENT OF INVESTMENT APPRAISAL TECHNIQUES

In this section an assessment is made of the relative merits of the techniques outlined in section 7.2. It will be assumed in making this assessment that the objective of the firm is to maximise profits. Whenever it appears that the techniques may be appropriate to other objectives, this fact is noted.

THE PAYBACK METHOD

It has been claimed that this method has the virtue of simplicity. The calculation is admittedly simple, but it is less apparent that this is a virtue since there are very serious deficiencies associated with its use.

First, it takes no account of the time pattern of receipts. The detailed discussion of this point is reserved until later in the section. Second, it takes no account of any earnings that may accrue to a project after the expiration of the payback period. It favours, therefore, short term projects and ignores the possibility of long term growth in profits. In fact it is not a profitability criterion at all but rather the embodiment of a liquidity concept; that is, it is concerned with the rapid recovery of outlays. It is for this reason often referred to as a 'fish bait' criterion, because it concentrates on recovering the bait rather than on the size of the fish to be caught. However, where liquidity rather than profitability is an important business consideration the method has corresponding merit. It can also be argued that it has some value in allowing for uncertainty as to the size of future returns. However, it does not deal with this problem in a satisfactory manner, because the type of uncertainty situation to which it can most appropriately be applied is that in which substantial returns are followed by a complete cessation of positive cash flows, e.g. a project whose life is interrupted by nuclear war or immediate obsolescence. This is not the most common type of uncertainty encountered in business.

The payback method's deficiencies outweigh the advantages that it may have in simplicity of calculation. It may have some merit as an initial screening device, ruling out projects with payback periods of such great length that they will normally not be contemplated. It also has some value when maintaining liquidity, as opposed to maximising profit, is a stated objective of a firm's activities.[18]

THE BOOK RATE OF RETURN

It will be recalled that one of the problems encountered in using this technique is that there are a number of different ways in which the book rate of return may be calculated. The main deficiency of this technique, however, is that in common with the payback method it fails to take account of the time value of money. Accordingly, attention is now focused on the relative merits of discounting and non-discounting methods of appraisal.

DISCOUNTING *v*. NON-DISCOUNTING METHODS

It has already been shown that the choice of investment appraisal technique influences both the selection of investments from among alternative projects and the volume of investment in an economy. Also, the use of discounting techniques is increasing, at least in large companies, which are becoming more important in the economy. It is appropriate, therefore, at this point to summarise the main advantages and limitations of discounting methods over non-discounting techniques.

Although the most important advantage of discounting methods is that they make allowance for the time value of money they do have certain other subsidiary advantages. They avoid the need to make specific allowance for depreciation in investment appraisal. Furthermore, the prominence given to the timing of total cash flows introduces the possibility that expenditures upon working capital can be included in the calculation, while such items as tax payments and investment allowances can also be given their due consideration.

There are, on the other hand, a number of objections to the use of discounting procedures. It has frequently been argued that they attribute to the business-man powers of computation that he does not possess. Therefore, it has been argued, it may be more satisfactory to resort to the less precise, but more easily conducted, computations of, say, the payback method. It has also been contended that the very appearance of precision implied in the discounting process is both illusory and dangerous. This argument contains an important element of truth in that the data on expected returns utilised in the calculation are merely forecasts and may as such turn out to be false. It is clearly true that any method of investment appraisal is only as good as the data upon which it is based.

However, omniscience has never been a prerequisite for the adoption of scientific method. Recognition of the fact that data may retrospectively be seen to have been incorrect is not an argument for abandoning a rational approach, nor is it an argument for compounding the uncertainty associated with all attempts to forecast the future by adopting methods of appraisal that are obviously unsatisfactory.

The process of forecasting future cash flows that is necessary to the adoption of discounting methods highlights salient factors, and in many cases it will be possible to narrow imponderables to a definite range.

The lesson to be drawn from the above is not that 'sophisticated' methods ought to be discarded but rather that the decision to invest is essentially a matter for the exercise of managerial skill and expertise. This exercise may be aided by certain calculations, which will of necessity be only as good as the forecasts upon which they are based. The use of rational calculations does not oblige blind allegiance to a single figure. The final decision will remain a matter of intelligent compromise between hard facts and the wise interpretation of forecasts. The role of qualitative analysis should not be underestimated. Carsberg and Hope, for example, have noted that:

> ... replies to the questionnaire suggest that qualitative judgment is indeed important in practice. There are many good reasons why this should be so ... Projects will often have important effects which are 'remote' and hence not readily estimated in cash terms: for example, the favourable publicity associated with the development of an advanced technology or the advantage, in attracting customers, of offering for sale a product which will complement a range ... Effects such as these can best be considered ... by subjective judgment after carrying out as many explicit measurements as reasonably possible.[19]

No useful purpose will be served by employing 'quickies' that concentrate on the wrong questions and achieve simplicity only by ignoring the complex problems of investment appraisal. They frequently bear no close relationship to the objectives of the firm. Similarly, no harm can stem from the intelligent and considered use of logical calculations unless they divert attention from a crucial factor in the decision-making process. They should be rejected only if it is believed that the extra effort and expense involved outweigh the improvement in performance resulting from their application. Therefore, it may be entirely appropriate to use different techniques for investments of varying scales.

It is relevant at this point to refer back to the work of Rockley, which revealed that in the companies studied there was no association between the use of discounting techniques and the success (i.e. profitability) of investments

Table 7.9 *Methods of investment appraisal and their relation to corporate profitability.*

Return on capital (%)	% of companies using		
	Payback	Book rate of return	DCF
→6	57	57	62
6–10	70	45	55
10+	58	33	58

Source: L. E. Rockley, *Investment for Profitability* (London, Business Books, 1973), p. 136.

undertaken (see Table 7.9). This rather disturbing finding has been supported by evidence gathered by the Centre for Inter-Firm Comparison (CIFC).[20] This research was based on an analysis of the performance of 240 firms in seven industries. The differences in the profit records of the companies that had formal procedures for appraising investment proposals and those which did not was marginal only. The use of DCF techniques was not clearly related to good performance, whereas analysis based either on subjective judgement or on book rate of return was.

NET PRESENT VALUE *v*. INTERNAL RATE OF RETURN[21]

If it could be established that discounting methods were superior to non-discounting methods, it would still remain to consider the relative merit of the two discounting techniques examined. In the evaluation of investment opportunities two types of decision present themselves: the formal accept-or-reject question, and the problem of ranking alternative projects.

In the first case the two discounting criteria produce identical answers. All projects that have a yield in excess of the cost of capital must have a positive NPV when discounted at the marginal cost of capital. In other words, all projects accepted on an NPV basis have, by definition, a positive NPV and hence require a rate of discount higher than that given by the marginal cost of capital to reduce their NPV to zero. Thus, in Figure 7.1 both criteria indicate acceptance when the market rate of interest is 5 per cent because the NPV (represented by curve VV_1) is positive and the IRR (S) is greater than 5 per cent.

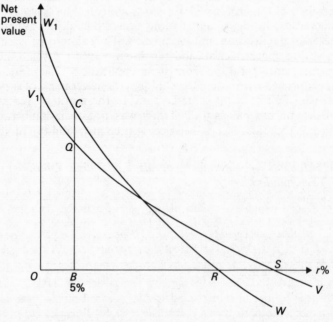

Fig. 7.1   Comparison of net present value and internal rate of return criteria.

When the decision is one of ranking, however, they may not give the same results. It has frequently been argued that the IRR method does not rank projects in their true order of profitability. The reason for this is that the NPV is an absolute figure whereas the IRR is related primarily to the amount of capital involved and the extent of the investment period; that is, a project may have a high rate of return in relation to initial investment but yield a low absolute amount of profit. It may be argued that most decisions will be of the accept-or-reject variety in which the additional information generated by the NPV method will be irrelevant. However, there are two situations in which the ranking of projects becomes important: when capital rationing prevails, and when mutually exclusive choices are encountered. The term 'capital rationing' is used to describe a situation in which a firm cannot raise capital beyond a fixed limit, in which case the true opportunity cost of capital is clearly in excess of the market rate. Under these conditions it is impossible to calculate a well-defined cost of capital with which to evaluate projects on an IRR basis, and, in the words of Merrett and Sykes, 'NPV is the only practical method of analysis'.[22]

Mutually exclusive projects arise when there is more than one method of achieving a given end and when it is not considered desirable to select more than one of the alternatives. The problem that is inherent in the use of the IRR solution in making a choice in these circumstances is illustrated in Figure 7.1. Curves VV_1 and WW_1 relate to two such mutually exclusive projects: respectively V and W. When $r=5$ per cent project W has the larger discounted present value ($BC>BQ$) whereas project V has the higher IRR ($OS>OR$). However, in order to maximise profits project W must be selected, given the value of r.

The final objection to the IRR is that under certain special conditions it may either give rise to multiple solutions or lose its meaning as the return earned on capital outstanding (as seen in Table 7.2). These possibilities do not arise when cash flows are normal, i.e. when an initially negative outlay is followed by positive cash flows.

Merrett and Sykes have argued that, under normal circumstances and notwithstanding certain recognisable special cases, the IRR method is superior to NPV. The reasons for this alleged superiority are as follows. First, the IRR solution may be superior to the NPV in risk situations because an essential characteristic of risk is that it is a function of time and of the amount of capital outstanding at any point in time. Thus, a rate of return expressed per unit of capital outstanding per period of time is essentially measuring the return in the same dimensions as are involved in producing the risk situation. This is exactly the figure provided under normal circumstances by the discounted yield method. It will be recalled that, if IRR is 8 per cent, a firm will break even on an 8 per cent overdraft-type loan. This is made clear above, and it follows that, as each £1 of outstanding debt earns 8 per cent, by definition the return per unit of capital is 8 per cent per period of time outstanding. Therefore, it is claimed that the yield method facilitates the task of determining whether or not the rate of return is adequate, given the risk, in a manner that the NPV, as an absolute quantity, is unable to do. Second, supporters of the yield method have argued that businessmen may more easily appreciate the concept of a rate of return upon capital employed. Third, the use of the yield method obviates the necessity to enter a dispute over the firm's cost of capital. The NPV calculation requires that a full range of present values be estimated for each possible cost. The yield, on the other hand, can quickly be compared to the estimated cost of capital.[23]

Therefore, it can be seen that the yield method has both advantages and disadvantages associated with its use. The majority of economists, however, have considered that the NPV method is superior. For example, the National Economic Development Council (NEDO) pamphlet on investment appraisal concludes that 'the project that should generally be chosen is the one which has the highest NPV'.[24] The reason for this preference is that it is generally assumed that the objective of investment is profit maximisation. Therefore, the projects that produce the highest NPV – which, as has been seen, are not necessarily those with the highest IRR – should be chosen. It is possible to concede this and yet to make a case for the yield method on the grounds that the instances when it can be demonstrated that the yield method breaks down are unlikely to be encountered frequently in practice. This is an empirical question. The contention that the yield method is easier for businessmen to understand is likewise *a priori* impossible to answer. A position that might attract wide support would be that the NPV method should be selected on the grounds that it can operate equally efficiently under all circumstances in which the IRR method is satisfactory also and under conditions that render the yield solution meaningless.

7.5　RISK, UNCERTAINTY AND DECISION MAKING

The analysis above largely ignores the effects of risk and uncertainty upon investment decision making. Every investment is to a greater or lesser degree a gamble because the future cannot be predicted with complete accuracy. However, the treatment of risk and uncertainty is a complex and imperfectly exposed area of economic analysis, and this section only indicates the main avenues along which this explanation is proceeding.[25]

In economics a distinction has long been drawn between 'risk' and 'uncertainty'.[26] 'Risk' is used to describe situations in which a plurality of outcomes is possible and in which objective probabilities of occurrence can be assigned to each potential outcome. 'Uncertainty' is used to describe a state of nature in which such objective probabilities cannot be determined. Most business decisions are characterised as involving uncertainty because they are unique decisions. However, many contemporary writers appear to be taking the line that this distinction should be ignored. Thus, Bierman and Smidt have argued that, if 'the concept of "probability" were applicable only to events that could be repeated a large number of times under controlled circumstances, the concept would be of relatively little use in analysing business investment decisions'.[27] Therefore, they have argued for the use of subjective probabilities in the place of objective probabilities. In the discussion of the use of probabilities in investment appraisal that follows the use of subjective instead of objective probabilities does not fundamentally alter the form of the techniques of analysis used.

The existence of uncertainty has a number of different implications for economic analysis. In a narrow sense it poses problems in formulating techniques of investment appraisal, but in another context it is relevant to the development of more broadly based theories of corporate policy making. For example, investment in business diversification may be a logical response to the uncertainty that is inherent in specialisation in production.[28] However, in this chapter attention is restricted to the impact of uncertainty upon appraisal techniques.

The simplest approach to the presence of uncertainty is to increase the discount rate used in appraisals. Such an addition, z, reduces the value of the discount factor, D, so that

$$D = \frac{1}{1+r+z} < \frac{1}{1+r}$$

Therefore, the greater the uncertainty, the more the expected return is reduced because expected cash flows are multiplied by a smaller fraction. However, in addition to the difficulty of determining the appropriate value for z this approach implies that uncertainty is a simple increasing function of time, which is frequently not the case.

Second, probabilities, relating to different possible outcomes, may be used as weights to be applied to a range of estimated cash flows for each year of a given project's life. From this may be obtained the expected monetary value of the cash flow, which can then be discounted to its present value equivalent in the usual manner. Alternatively, present value equivalents for each possible outcome may be calculated and then weighted according to the probability of their likely occurrence. For example, given the present value equivalents and probabilities for projects A and B contained in Table 7.10,

expected present value of A $= (£100 \times 0·35) + (£200 \times 0·15) + (£50 \times 0·50)$
$= £90$
expected present value of B $= (£150 \times 0·35) + (£100 \times 0·15) + (£70 \times 0·50)$
$= £102·50$

Thus, given these values a profit-maximising firm would prefer to invest in project B.

Table 7.10 *Present values and their probabilities associated with two competing projects of the same capital cost.*

	Possible outcomes (probabilities in brackets)		
Project	1 (0·35)	2 (0·15)	3 (0·50)
A	£100	£200	£50
B	£150	£100	£70

However, given that probabilities cannot be determined on an objective basis, the attitude of the decision maker to uncertainty in the formulation of his subjective probability values may be critical to the choice of project. In this regard the literature recognises a number of different investment strategies based upon different attitudes to the presence of uncertainty. For example:

(1) *Maximax criterion:* the project is selected on the assumption that the outcome that is most favourable to the investment will be realised; project A will be selected in the (subjective) belief that outcome $_2$ will occur.
(2) *Maximin criterion:* the project is selected on the pessimistic assumption that the outcome that is least favourable to the investment will occur; project B will be selected in the belief that outcome $_3$ will occur.
(3) *Laplace criterion:* the project is selected on the assumption that each possible outcome is of equal probability; project A will therefore be preferred.

A number of other theoretical approaches to the treatment of uncertainty are to be found in the growing literature on the subject.[29] However, relatively little is known about the treatment of uncertainty in investment appraisal in practice. The results of the survey conducted by Klammer (see Table 7.11) suggest that probability analysis in one form or another has increased in usage as a management science technique but show that by 1970 it was still only being used by one-third of large American companies. In terms of the specific risk-analysis techniques used, the more traditional methods of

Table 7.11 *The use of management science and risk analysis techniques by large American companies, 1959–70.*

	% of firms using technique in each year		
	1959	1964	1970
Risk analysis technique			
Short payback	9	9	10
Raising expected return	12	16	21
Probability distributions	7	7	13
Other	2	4	10
Management science technique			
Game theory	0	2	3
Linear programming	5	8	17
Non-linear programming	1	3	4
Computer simulation	4	7	28
Probability theory	5	8	32
Utility theory	0	1	4
Critical path analysis	4	13	28

Source: T. Klammer, 'Empirical evidence of the adoption of sophisticated capital budgeting techniques', *Harvard Business Review*, vol. 50 (1972), pp. 387–94.

shortening the payback period and raising the required rate of return were considerably more widely used than probability distribution analysis, which was only applied in this context in a small minority of large firms. To this it must be added that the relatively frequent use of the payback method as an appraisal technique, as described in section 7.3, may indicate that many decision makers dealt with uncertainty by trying to reduce its importance. In general it seems safe to conclude that the treatment of uncertainty in investment appraisal is commonly fairly unsophisticated in practice.

7.6 SOURCES OF FINANCE

In order to implement an investment decision the necessary capital must be acquired. In this section the alternative sources of capital are examined, and their relative importance is assessed.

The sources of finance can be divided into two main categories:

(1) Internal funds:
    (a) retained profits;
    (b) depreciation provisions; and
    (c) tax provisions.
(2) External funds:
    (a) long term or loan capital; and
    (b) short or medium term – bank credit, hire purchase or trade credit.

The methods chosen to finance a project vary according to the size of the outlay, the type of firm involved and the character of the project. Frequently, a variety of sources are employed simultaneously.

Internal funds comprise amounts retained in the company from income earned in past periods. This sum can be defined as any amount of income transferred to reserves above that which is necessary to maintain intact the net worth of the assets. Strictly speaking, therefore, depreciation provisions are not a source of investable funds. However, in a purely practical sense the majority of firms feel justified in treating such provisions as funds becoming available at a certain date and in using them as such. It is standard practice to define internal sources of funds as above.

The availability of retained profits depends, at any given time, on two factors: the absolute value of past profits, and the policy adopted by the company towards the distribution of such profits in the form of dividends. It will be shown that internally generated funds are the most important single source of the resources required for capital investment. Consequently, the determination of a distribution policy is a decision of considerable importance for the firm's future growth prospects. On the one hand, there is strong pressure to retain sufficient funds to guarantee future expansion. On the other hand, it will be appreciated that the distribution record is taken into account by investors in assessing the relative attractiveness of the company as an investment. Too cautious a dividend policy in the past may adversely affect a company's access to external funds in the future.

Table 7.12   *Sources of funds of industrial and commercial companies.*

Year	Total (£ m.)	Undistributed income (£ m.)	Undistributed income (%)	Banks (£ m.)	Banks (%)	UK capital issues Ordinary (%)	UK capital issues Debenture and preference (%)	Investment grants (£ m.)	Investment grants (%)
1971	7,361	4,382	59·5	732	9·9	2·2	2·9	526	7·1
1972	10,368	5,255	50·7	2,988	28·8	3·1	2·8	321	3·1
1973	15,074	7,442	49·4	4,504	29·9	0·7	0·4	227	1·5
1974	15,039	7,829	52·1	4,411	29·3	0·3	0·4	137	0·9
1975	12,303	8,064	65·5	418	3·4	7·9	0·6	96	0·8
1976	17,879	11,447	64·0	2,494	13·9	4·3	0·1	58	0·3

Source: Financial Statistics, vol. 187 (November 1977), table 9.2.

A study of the period 1949–53 has demonstrated that retained profits were then the single most important source of funds to quoted companies in the United Kingdom, accounting for 64 per cent of funds raised.[30] More recent data confirm the continued importance of internally generated funds (see Table 7.12). According to the Diamond Report, 'over the period we studied (1950–1972) internal funds accounted for an average 76% of total funds raised, about 40% being retained profit . . . Equity capital raised for cash accounted for 6·5%.'[31] Further confirmation is provided in Table 7.13, which is based on data prepared for the Bullock Committee and is of different coverage from Table 7.12.[32]

Table 7.13   *Sources of funds of larger quoted companies, 1950–75.*

Source of funds	% of total sources in each period 1950–4	1955–9	1960–4	1965–9	1970–4
Retained profit	56	44	36	32	39
Depreciation	25	32	37	40	36
Total internal	81	76	73	72	75
Banks	3	5	8	11	15
Ordinary shares	6	10	10	5	2
Preference shares and long term borrowing	10	9	9	12	8
Total external	19	24	27	28	25
Total sources	100	100	100	100	100

Source: Report of the Commission of Inquiry on Industrial Democracy (the Bullock Report) (London, HMSO, 1977).

Table 7.14   *The rate of self-financing in selected economies, 1959–65.*

Country	Average %
USA	117
UK	130
West Germany	79
Belgium	75
Netherlands	67
France	75
Italy	61
Japan	59
Spain	35

Source: Organisation for Economic Co-operation and Development, *Capital Market Study* vol. 1 (Geneva, OECD, 1967) p. 312.

International studies have shown that the degree of self-financing by businesses varies greatly from country to country. The *rate of self-financing* for 1959–65, reported in Table 7.14, is defined as the ratio of gross internally-generated funds to gross fixed-asset formation. It can be seen that the rate was highest in the United Kingdom and United States and lowest in Spain, Japan and Italy.

More recent evidence has been gathered by Morgan and Harrington in their study of capital markets in the European Economic Community (EEC).[33] It can be seen from Table 7.15 that the main conclusions of the earlier study by the Organisation for Economic Co-operation and Development (OECD) have generally been confirmed, as has the importance of internally generated funds. The importance of depreciation provisions in West Germany and the special role of the banks in Italy are features worthy of note that are not revealed in the table.

Table 7.15   *Sources of funds of non-financial corporations in the EEC, 1973.*

	% of total sources in each country			
Source	Denmark	France	West Germany	Italy
Retained earnings	} 37·7	37·5	} 55·5	} 42·1
Capital transfers		4·7		
Increases in debt:				
To banks	8·4	8·2	} 39·9	−1·8
To others	38·9	47·5		42·1
Increases in equity capital	15·0	2·2	4·5	17·7
Total sources	100·0	100·1	99·9	100·0

Source: E. V. Morgan and R. Harrington, *Capital Markets in the EEC* (London, Wilton House, 1977) p. 314.

EXTERNAL FUNDS

The major source of long-term external finance for public companies is the new issue market. Three types of shares are usual: ordinary (equity), preference and debenture (loan).

It will already be clear that in the United Kingdom the issue of shares of all types has been a relatively minor source of funds to companies. It can also be seen from Table 7.16 that the value of capital issues has fluctuated greatly from year to year. Many commentators have, however, been unwilling to conclude that the new issue market is as unimportant as these figures suggest. This point of view has been well represented by Morgan and Harrington, who have argued that the market is relatively more important to rapidly expanding companies and that, as a provider of finance for net fixed investment, the market is much more important.[33] Thus, in the United Kingdom in 1972 the value of new issues was 50 per cent of net fixed investment.

The relative importance of all types of longer-term external finance is shown in Table 7.16, from which it can be seen that the proportion of total new issues accounted for by the various categories of shareholding has varied considerably from year to year in the United Kingdom. The relative importance of loan capital declined significantly between 1970 and 1976, while equity achieved a peak in 1974. While a large number of factors have been suggested as contributing to these changes in behaviour (e.g. tax changes, the relative cost of different types of finance, government regulations, the reluctance of companies to reduce control by diluting equity) attempts to explain observed changes in these terms have not been very successful. Morgan and Harrington's study has confirmed the relatively low gearing ratio in British industry; but there is little evidence to suggest that this is an important factor producing variations in company performance, nor does the ratio appear to appreciably alter the cost of capital. The main conclusion that has emerged from studies of the UK capital market is that internal finance is the single most important source of funds to companies. In the next subsection the relative merits of internal and external financing are examined.

Table 7.16 *Total UK capital issues, 1970–6.*

Year	Total, net of redemptions (£ m.)	Type of issue (%)		
		Debenture	Preference	Ordinary
1970	363·6	73·7	3·4	22·9
1971	773·0	65·7	1·5	32·8
1972	1,100·2	34·7	3·0	62·3
1973	168·7	4·1	12·9	83·0
1974	78·2	−74·0	20·0	154·0
1975	1,551·0	14·6	2·6	82·8
1976	1,114·3	2·5	2·8	94·7

Source: Financial Statistics vol. 187 (November 1977), table 12.1.

SELF-FINANCING *V*. MARKET FINANCING

It has been demonstrated that, as a general rule, UK companies have preferred to rely on internal funds for investment purposes as opposed to raising capital externally. In some cases, of course, this has represented necessity rather than choice. Whatever the reason behind the decision to rely on internal funds, it has been argued that the practice results in an inefficient allocation of resources.[34] The basis of this contention is that entrepreneurs are more aware of the cost of external funds than of internal funds and that only externally generated capital is subject to 'the test of the market'. Finally, it has been argued that, because past success bears no close relationship to future prospects, the practice of locking up capital in existing companies produces rigidities in the capital market. In practice a high proportion of projects are financed from many sources, both internal and external, and the argument that management will use internal funds injudiciously should not be taken to extremes.

The most potent argument against restricting the availability of internal funds is that there are good *a priori* reasons to suspect that greater distribution of profits would result in a fall in the total supply of capital reinvested. This would be the case if, for example, individuals and corporations had different propensities to save. The case for greater reliance on external funds depends to a large extent on the assumption that investors possess the ability to reinvest in some optimum fashion. The fact that a growing proportion of investment is undertaken by institutions, as opposed to individuals, may strengthen the case for a greater distribution of profits.[42]

Any movement towards a greater degree of external financing must be associated with changes in company distribution policy. In the United Kingdom the corporate tax system has on different occasions been geared to encouraging the retention of earnings. For example, in the period 1947–58 distributed profits were taxed at a higher rate than retained earnings; the introduction of corporation tax in 1965 also had this effect. In 1973 the introduction of the imputation system of taxation removed this form of discrimination. There is a fairly substantial body of evidence to suggest that these types of tax change do have an appreciable effect on distribution policy.[35]

7.7 COMPANY SIZE AND INVESTMENT

In this section two aspects of the relationship between company size and the finance of investment are examined: the special problems faced by small firms in raising capital, and the behaviour of very large firms in the capital market.

CAPITAL AVAILABILITY FOR SMALL FIRMS

Private limited companies, the vast majority of which are small, do not have access to the new issue market while it may be impractical for many small- and medium-sized public companies to raise money in this way. Despite the growth in importance of large corporations, small companies are still a considerable source of employment (see Chapter 3) and have been, according to some studies, an important source of new innovation. There may, therefore, be pressing reasons for trying to alleviate the problems faced by small companies in raising finance for expansion. Interest in the financial problems of small firms has grown since the publication of the Bolton Report in 1971, and it has become 'fashionable' to express a belief in the desirability of promoting the small firm sector.[36]

The United Kingdom has a fairly long historical record of developing specialist institutions to assist companies of a particular size in raising capital. The best known have been the Industrial and Commercial Finance Corporation (ICFC) and the Finance Corporation for Industry (FCI). These were formed in 1945 as a somewhat belated response to the Report of the Macmillan Committee of 1931. This report publicised a gap, called the Macmillan Gap, in the capital market for the supply of long term capital in amounts that were too small to be treated as capital issues, which in those days meant amounts up to £2 million. The ICFC was established by the English and Scottish banks and the Bank of England together agreeing to provide up to £15 million in share capital plus additional borrowing facilities up to a further £30 million. The objective of the ICFC was to provide long term and permanent capital in amounts ranging from £5,000 to £2 million, particularly in cases where existing facilities were not readily available. The ICFC went public in 1960, thereby achieving independence from the banks, and in 1964–5 its upper lending limit was raised to £3 million. The FCI operated on a larger scale, with original capital reserves of £25 million and borrowing powers of up to £100 million. Finance was normally provided by means of long- or short-period fixed-interest loans. In January 1974 both corporations were merged into a new body with the title Finance for Industry.[37]

The Radcliffe Committee, while recognising that 'there is . . . no recognised and readily accessible channel, corresponding to the new issue market for large firms, through which the small industrialist can raise long term funds', concluded in 1959 that no proliferation of institutions was called for.[38] Approximately ten years later the Bolton Committee was established to seek out a 'Macmillan-type' gap in the capital market for very small firms. It has concluded that small firms did face some special problems in raising finance;[36] for example, they were normally more harshly affected by periods of credit restriction and normally faced higher interest charges than larger firms.[39] The Bolton Committee, however, did not believe that any proliferation of new institutions was called for, although it has acknowledged special areas of difficulty in the raising of mortgage funds and venture capital for new projects.

The publication of the Bolton Report marked the beginning of a revival of interest in the small firm sector rather than the conclusion of a period of investigation. The Wilson Committee, for example, which published its first Progress Report in December 1977, has indicated that the small firm's capital market would be a major area of study in its future deliberations.[46] The earlier Morgan and Harrington survey has shown that the small firm sector in other EEC countries received more government assistance than was the case in the United Kingdom.[33]

THE SUPPLY OF FINANCE AND THE LARGE COMPANY

Large and very large companies appear to exhibit relatively greater reliance on the capital market, i.e. on external funds, than do medium and smaller-sized companies. Whittington and Meeks, in a study of giant companies in the United Kingdom, have found that for the 'giants' new issues during the period 1964–9 represented 6·6 per cent of total net assets as opposed to 4·4 per cent for the 'rest' of the sample. Conversely, retentions represented 3·4 per cent of the net assets of the 'rest' but only 2·9 per cent in the case of the 'giants'.[40] Prais, in a study of the evolution of giant firms in manufacturing industry during 1950–73, has concluded that:

> (In 1970) as many as half of the hundred largest companies issued new capital for cash . . . Comparing this result with a study relating to 1949–53, one may infer that the proportion of giant companies going to the new issue market each year has perhaps almost doubled in the intervening period.[41]

The Bolton Committee has established that company size affects the cost of acquiring capital.[36] Larger companies usually obtain capital more cheaply; and although this difference must to a certain degree represent a risk premium, it has frequently been argued that one of the main advantages of large size in the corporate sector is in raising finance. Such advantages have sometimes been described as pecuniary economies of scale, but they may be better regarded as economies of buying power.

The more ready access of large companies to sources of finance may have wider implications for the structure of industry and the competitive process. Access to greater financial reserves and resources may bestow a competitive advantage on large firms and enable them to squeeze smaller companies, particularly in times of credit rationing.[34] Similarly, larger companies may find it easier than other firms to finance the research and development of new products, thus enabling them in the long term to enhance their dominant position in the economy. Therefore, conditions in the capital market may have been a contributory factor in the growing importance of the large firm, as documented and analysed in Chapters 3–5.

7.8 AGGREGATE INVESTMENT IN THE UNITED KINGDOM

This chapter focuses upon two main areas of investment behaviour: the techniques of appraisal used by individual firms, and the sources of investable funds that are available to them. Given the alleged association between the volume of industrial investment and overall economic growth, central government has inevitably taken a great interest in both the aggregate level and direction of investment within the economy and sought to influence this by a variety of measures. For example, it has a long-standing interest in the adequacy of the capital markets and, more particularly, in the difficulties experienced by smaller firms in securing external finance. It also has a long history of seeking

Table 7.17   *Governmental financial assistance to industry, 1977.*

Type of assistance	£ m.
Selective financial assistance	
(Industry Act, section 8)	160[b]
Accelerated projects scheme	84[b]
Regional development grants	408[a]
Regional selective assistance	164[b]
Industry schemes:[c]	
Clothing	15
Ferrous foundries	40
Machine tools	20
Paper and board	23
Textile machinery	20
Printing machinery	15
Poultry and meat	5
Wool textiles	23
Electronic components	20

Source: Trade and Industry vol. 28 (23 September 1977) p. 539.

Notes:
(a)   Payments in 1976–7.
(b)   Payments to 31 January 1977.
(c)   Finance allocated.

to stimulate investment, particularly in the industrial sector, through investment loans, grants and tax concessions. The level and industrial distribution of the main forms of government financial assistance to industry in the mid 1970s are summarised in Table 7.17.[43] This financial assistance is evaluated within the context of industrial policy and regional policy in sections 9.4 and 11.6–11.8 respectively; therefore, in this section attention is restricted to the issues of whether an insufficiency of investable funds has reduced the level of aggregate investment and, therefore, may justify some government assistance to industry for investment purposes.[42]

There have been a large number of studies that have attempted to explain changes in the level of investment in the United Kingdom in terms of such factors as changes in the rate of interest, the degree of capacity utilisation, the rate of profitability, the growth of demand and business expectations, and the level of confidence. The results of a recent study by Panic and Vernon are summarised in Table 7.18. These suggest that the degree of capacity utilisation was a major determinant of the amount of investment undertaken at both the aggregate and the industry level. The next most important factor was found to be the state of business expectations, measured on the basis of surveys of business intentions. A profit variable was included in the model as an indicator of the availability of internal finance and was a statistically significant factor in all but one industry, but not at the aggregate investment level.[44]

Table 7.18 *The determinants of investment in manufacturing industry, 1960–72.*

Industry	Constant	Capacity utilisation	Growth	Trend	Confidence CBI[a]	Confidence FT[b]	Profits	R^2
Chemicals	−175·57	1·6705		0·9883		0·2174	2·9388	0·84
Engineering	−212·60	1·1940		0·6985	0·0549			0·84
Metals	−161·12	1·9357		0·1566		0·3206	1·9960	0·84
Motors	0·88	5·9400				0·1877	1·0486	0·47
Textiles	−110·45	0·3600	0·7071	0·3585	0·1063		3·5818	0·78
Paper	−33·95	0·2196		0·2597			0·8870	0·66
All manufacturing	−585·65	8·3686		3·4232		1·2465		0·87

Source: M. Panic and K. Vernon, 'Major factors behind investment decisions in British manufacturing industry', *Oxford Bulletin of Economics and Statistics BOUIS* vol. 37 (1975), p. 196.

Notes:
(a) Survey by the Confederation of British Industry.
(b) Survey by the *Financial Times*.
(c) Values for which the 't' value exceeds unity have been included.

Table 7.19   *Company rate of return on capital, for all industrial and commercial companies, 1960–76 (%).*

Year	At historic cost[a]	Before stock appreciation[b]	After stock appreciation[c]
1960	18·8	13·5	13·2
1961	16·4	11·9	11·4
1962	14·9	10·8	10·4
1963	16·0	11·8	11·3
1964	16·7	12·5	11·7
1965	16·0	11·9	11·2
1966	14·3	10·6	9·8
1967	13·5	10·3	10·0
1968	14·7	11·0	9·9
1969	14·8	11·0	9·7
1970	14·1	10·1	8·3
1971	14·6	10·0	8·5
1972	15·5	10·2	8·5
1973	17·6	10·8	7·4
1974	17·3	9·6	4·3
1975	14·6	6·8	3·2
1976	16·3	7·0	3·3

Source: Trade and Industry, vol. 28 (16 September 1977) p. 519.

Notes:
(a)   Presents the rate of return calculated on capital employment valued at historic cost.
(b)   Presents the rate of return calculated to include the effects of stock appreciation.
(c)   Removes the contribution made by such appreciation to profitability.

After 1969 the return to investment in the manufacturing sector fell to historically low levels (see Table 7.19). King has concluded that 'there is strong evidence of a fall in the share of profits (in total income) net of both capital consumption and stock appreciation from 1969 onwards'.[45] Similarly, since 1970, with the exception of 1974, there has been a slump in aggregate investment levels (see Table 7.20).

As documented in section 2.5, there has occurred a relative decline in the manufacturing sector of the UK economy; and as described in section 9.4, it is an integral part of Britain's industrial policy that more investment resources should be channelled in this direction. Yet, in recent years the ability of the manufacturing sector to attract funds from the capital market appears to have fallen. However, it seems likely that the severe fall in profitability, illustrated above, has played an important part in this,[44] although this does not mean that other factors have been insignificant influences.

It seems clear that a major change in investment behaviour from the earlier 1970s situation depends primarily on changing the relationship between existing productive capacity and the expected future level of demand. If so, the major cause of the so-called 'investment famine' may have been a low level of demand for funds caused by low profitability and poor expectations rather

Table 7.20 *Gross fixed investment in manufacturing industry.*[a]

Year	Total (£ m.)	Plant and machinery (£ m.)	(% change)	Buildings (£ m.)	(% change)
1966	1,773·7	1,312·0	+6	363·4	−5
1967	1,737·7	1,318·6	+1	319·6	−12
1968	1,851·2	1,406·1	+7	335·9	+5
1969	1,977·5	1,471·5	+5	390·1	+16
1970	2,129·8	1,623·9	+10	391·2	−
1971	1,990·7	1,520·2	−6	357·1	−9
1972	1,739·2	1,310·4	−14	305·5	−14
1973	1,752·9	1,333·0	+2	289·3	−5
1974	2,025·4	1,529·2	+15	359·0	+24
1975	1,744·8	1,336·2	−13	302·7	−16
1976	1,654·2	1,297·7	−3	240·2	−21

Source: Economic Trends, vol. 288 (October 1977) p. 18.

Notes:
(a) At 1970 prices.

than a lack of supply caused by inadequacies in the capital market. Therefore, the focus of attention on the strengthening of existing financial institutions, or on the creation of new ones to improve the operations of the capital market, or on the improvement of financial investment incentives by government to industry, may be misdirected.

FURTHER READING

A very extensive literature exists on the theory, and to a lesser extent the practice, of investment appraisal. A detailed examination of the main appraisal techniques can be found in Bierman and Smidt[4] and Merrett and Sykes,[4] while Carsberg and Hope's book also includes useful survey material on current practice.[14] The basic issues involved in decision making under conditions of uncertainty have been examined in Shackle[3] and McGuire 1964.[25] A considerable literature also exists on business finance and capital markets, with the publications of the Wilson Committee providing much useful data and analysis,[46] the Bolton Committee analysing the finance problems of small businesses[36] and Morgan and Harrington supplying useful comparative data for other EEC countries.[33] The determinants of investment levels may be studied further in Panic and Vernon[44] and the references cited therein.

NOTES AND REFERENCES

1 A. Masse, *Optimal Investment Decisions* (Englewood Cliffs, Prentice-Hall, 1962), p. 1.
2 See, for example, theories of growth as described in such macroeconomics texts as G. Ackley, *Macroeconomic Theory*, Collier-Macmillan International edn (New York,

Macmillan, 1969), ch. 18; and A. P. Thirlwall, *Growth and Development* (London, Macmillan, 1972), ch. 2.

3 G. L. S. Shackle, *Expectation, Enterprise and Profit*, Studies in Economics, No. 1 (London, Allen & Unwin, 1970), p. 77. Chapters 4 and 5 of this book constitute a useful analysis of the problems of investment appraisal and the treatment of uncertainty.

4 For an extended discussion, see, for example, A. J. Merrett and A. Sykes, *The Finance and Analysis of Investment Projects* (London, Longmans Green, 1967); H. Bierman and S. Smidt, *The Capital Budgeting Decision* (London, Collier-Macmillan, 1975); and P. J. Curwen, *Managerial Economics* (London, Macmillan, 1974), ch. 5.

5 For more detailed discussion of this method, see M. J. Gordon, 'The pay-off period and the rate of profit', *Journal of Business*, vol. 28 (October 1955); and J. Hellings, 'The case for pay-back re-examined', *Journal of Business*, vol. 45 (Spring 1972).

6 To this extent it may, therefore, be an example of a formula that is appropriate to an objective other than profit maximisation under conditions of certainty.

7 See, for example, Shackle, op. cit. (n. 3), pp. 78–92; Merrett and Sykes, op. cit. (n. 4), ch. 1; and Bierman and Smidt, op. cit. (n. 4).

8 Tables of present value equivalents of 1 at different rates of interest can be found in Shackle, op. cit. (n. 3); Merrett and Sykes, op. cit. (n. 4); Bierman and Smidt, op. cit. (n. 4); National Economic Development Office (NEDO), *Investment Appraisal in the Clothing Industry* (London, HMSO, 1973); and NEDO, *Investment Appraisal*, 3rd edn (London, HMSO, 1970).

9 B. R. Williams and W. P. Scott, *Investment Proposals and Decisions* (London, Allen & Unwin, 1965).

10 R. R. Nield, 'Replacement policy', *National Institute of Economic Research*, vol. 30 (November 1961), pp. 30–43.

11 A. J. Corner and A. Williams, 'The sensitivity of businesses to initial and investment allowances', *Economica*, vol. 32 (January 1965), pp. 32–47.

12 British Institute of Management (BIM), *Capital Investment Projects: Methods of Appraisal*, Information Notes, No. 42 (BIM, 1965).

13 BIM, op. cit. (n. 12), p. 2.

14 B. Carsberg and A. Hope, *Business Investment Decisions under Uncertainty* (London, Institute of Chartered Accountants, 1976).

15 Carsberg and Hope, op. cit. (n. 14), p. 47.

16 T. Klammer, 'Empirical evidence of the adoption of sophisticated capital budgeting techniques', *Harvard Business Review*, vol. 50 (1972), pp. 387–94.

17 L. E. Rockley, *Investment for Profitability* (London, Business Books, 1973).

18 For a re-examination of the payback method's merits, see J. Hellings, 'The case for pay-back re-examined', *Journal of Business Finance*, vol. 28 (Spring 1972), pp. 99–102.

19 Carsberg and Hope, op. cit. (n. 14), p. 45; see also R. G. Walker, 'The judgment factor in investment decisions', *Harvard Business Review*, vol. 39 (1961), p. 99.

20 Centre for Inter-Firm Comparison (CIFC), *Management Policies and Practices and Business Performance* (London, CIFC, 1978).

21 For an extended discussion of this issue, see Merrett and Sykes, op. cit. (n. 4), ch. 5; Bierman and Smidt, op. cit. (n. 4), ch. 3; and J. F. Weston and E. F. Brigham, *Managerial Finance*, 3rd edn (New York, Holt, Rinehart & Winston, 1970), chs 6 and 7.

22 Merrett and Sykes, op. cit. (n. 4), p. 152.

23 The determination of the appropriate cost of capital is extremely controversial. A full discussion can be found in Shackle, op. cit. (n. 3); Merrett and Sykes, op. cit. (n. 4); and Bierman and Smidt, op. cit. (n. 4).

24 NEDO, op. cit. (n. 8, 1970), p. 6.

25 For more extended discussion, see, for example, Shackle, op. cit. (n. 3), ch. 5; J. W. M.

McGuire, *Theories of Business Behavior* (Englewood Cliffs, Prentice-Hall, 1964), ch. 6; J. W. M. McGuire (ed.), *Interdisciplinary Studies in Business Behavior* (London Ohio, E. Arnold, 1962), ch. 6; S. Reutlinger, *Techniques for Project Appraisal under Uncertainty*, International Bank for Reconstruction and Development, Paper No. 10 (London, J. Hopkins Press, 1970); and Bierman and Smidt, op. cit. (n. 4), ch. 9.

26 F. Knight, *Risk, Uncertainty and Profit* (Boston, Mass., Houghton Mifflin, 1921).

27 Bierman and Smidt, op. cit. (n. 4), p. 110.

28 See A. Alchian, 'Uncertainty, evolution and economic theory', *Journal of Political Economy*, vol. 58 (1950), pp. 211–22; and Chapter 3.

29 See in particular Shackle, op. cit. (n. 3).

30 B. Tew and R. F. Henderson, *Studies in Company Finance* (Cambridge, National Institute of Economic and Social Research, 1959).

31 *Report of the Commission of Inquiry into the Distribution of Income and Wealth* (the Diamond Report), No. 2 (London, HMSO, 1971), para. 326.

32 *Report of the Commission of Inquiry on Industrial Democracy* (the Bullock Report) (London, HMSO, 1977), p. 9, table 3.

33 E. V. Morgan and R. Harrington, *Capital Markets in the EEC* (London, Wilton House, 1977).

34 See in particular A. Rubner, *The Ensnared Shareholder* (London, Macmillan, 1965).

35 See, for example, A. Rubner, 'The failure of the British differential profits tax: a comment', *Economic Journal*, vol. 77 (December 1967), pp. 947–52; and A. Rubner, 'Corporate taxation and dividend policy', *Review of Economic Studies*, vol. 37 (January 1970), pp. 57–72.

36 *The Financial Facilities for Small Firms: Report of the Committee of Inquiry on Small Firms* (the Bolton Report) (London, HMSO, 1971).

37 For an assessment of the early work of the ICFC, see G. W. Murphy and D. Prusman, 'ICFC: a progress report', *Manchester School*, vol. 36 (September 1968), pp. 223–51.

38 *Commission on the Working of the Monetary System* (the Radcliffe Report) (London, HMSO, 1959).

39 This might be a proper reflection of risk.

40 G. Whittington and G. Meeks, 'Giant companies in the United Kingdom, 1948–69', *Economic Journal*, vol. 85 (December 1975), pp. 524, 843.

41 S. J. Prais, *The Evolution of Giant Firms in Britain* (Cambridge, Cambridge UP, 1976), p. 112.

42 What constitutes a 'sufficient' or 'desirable' volume of investment is, of course, a difficult question.

43 For a full list, see 'Government support for industry', *Trade and Industry*, vol. 28 (23 September 1977), pp. 538–542.

44 M. Panic and K. Vernon, 'Major factors behind investment decisions in British manufacturing industry', *Oxford Bulletin of Economics and Statistics* (1975), pp. 191–209.

45 M. A. King, 'The UK profits crisis: myth or reality?', *Economic Journal*, vol. 85 (March 1975), pp. 33–47.

46 Committee to Review the Functioning of Financial Institutions (the Wilson Committee), *Progress Report on the Financing of Industry and Trade* (London, HMSO, 1977); and Wilson Committee, *Evidence on the Financing of Industry and Trade* (London, HMSO, continuing), various volumes.

8 Performance Measurement

8.1 INTRODUCTION

The remaining chapters in this book are concerned with the analysis of government policy towards industry: in the private sector (Chapter 9), in the public sector (Chapter 10) and in its influence on industrial location (Chapter 11). One of the major aims of government intervention in industrial activities is to improve their performance. 'Performance', however, is an elusive and often ambiguous concept that is open to a variety of different interpretations and measurements. Therefore, the purpose of this chapter is to explore its meaning and the means by which it is estimated in practice.

Essentially, performance means the degree of success in achieving stated objectives, and this is what should be measured by performance indicators. A common, yet basic, difficulty in the use of performance indicators is the failure to make explicit, and to justify, the objectives and value judgements implied by the acceptance of particular indicators. Once these objectives and value judgements are uncovered the subjective and, therefore, potentially contentious nature of performance indicators becomes very apparent.

This review is mainly concerned with performance measurement at the level of the individual firm and industry, but the contentious qualities of performance indicators can be equally well illustrated at the macroeconomic level. The most frequently used performance indicators at this level relate to the *per capita* growth in national output, the rate of inflation, the general level of unemployment and the state of the balance of payments. The study of any elementary textbook in macroeconomics will show that 'good' performance in respect of one of these indicators may well, at least in the short run, be achieved at the expense of less satisfactory performance as measured by certain of the other indicators.[1] Therefore, for a time one performance indicator has to take precedence over the others, and the selection of this indicator implies that the objective upon which it is based is for the time being the most important. For example, in the shorter term the reduction of inflation may take precedence over the reduction in the general level of unemployment or over the acceleration of the *per capita* growth rate in national output.

Each type of indicator may be defined in different ways, and the selection of one definition in preference to another often also contains an implicit value judgement. Two examples may illustrate this point. First, recent studies relating to the quality of the environment have indicated that there is not a simple relationship between the increase in *per capita* real national output and the increase in well-being (even material well-being).[2, 3] This arises in part because some of the increase in national output may be absorbed in compensating for the adverse environmental impacts caused by increased national production. Attempts are being made to estimate changes in the value of national output taking these environmental impacts into account.[4] In the meantime the continued use of the traditional growth-rate indicator contains the implicit value judgement that these associated changes in environmental and other externalities are unimportant. Second, the inflation rate is normally measured by an index of the general level of prices, which may conceal divergent trends in the price movements affecting different sections of society. Over certain periods of time the cost of living of the poorer sections of society may increase substantially more or less than that of society generally.[5] The selection of a performance indicator that only measures price changes for society as a whole may imply an absence of concern for their effects on income redistribution.

Similar kinds of value judgements are implicit in the choice of performance indicators at firm and industry level, as is illustrated in subsequent sections of this chapter. It is the presence of such judgements that lies at the base of many of the disagreements, at the *conceptual* level, in performance measurement. In addition, however, there are important *empirical* difficulties in performance measurement, also illustrated later, which arise from the frequent inability to meet the demanding data requirements of the more refined measures of performance. Use of less satisfactory but more readily available data may result in a subtle redefining of the performance indicator itself. The empirical difficulties may be overcome, but at the expense of creating greater disagreements at the conceptual level.

There is, then, a basic dual problem involved in the evaluation of government policy towards industry, which is largely independent of the type of policy or industrial activity involved. First, as the previous chapters indicate, there are real limitations on the present ability to predict the impact of exogenous actions (of which changes in government policy are one category) on the *behaviour* of firms within markets. Second, even if this could be satisfactorily predicted, considerable difficulties would remain in evaluating that change in behaviour, to establish whether it would constitute a higher level of *performance* than achieved currently.

Appreciation of this dual problem should encourage an element of cautiousness in the evaluation of government industrial policies. This is in marked contrast to the strong assertions, encountered from time to time, that restrictive practices legislation, nationalisation, regional policy etc. necessarily have a favourable or unfavourable impact on economic performance.

The remainder of this chapter examines the main types of performance measure that are currently in use or under discussion, indicating their respective uses and limitations. These are:

(1) profit measures;
(2) productivity measures;
(3) indirect measures relating to market structure and pricing and investment rules; and
(4) measures of productive and 'X-efficiency'.

8.2 PROFIT MEASURES

Traditionally, it has been assumed in economic theory that the business objective of the privately owned firm is long-run profit maximisation (see Chapter 3).

Therefore, if profits are the barometer of success, it seems reasonable *from the private business's standpoint* to measure performance in the same units. In fact there are many studies, relating, for example, to the success of mergers or the shortcomings of conglomerates, that have used the profit rate achieved as a performance indicator.[6]

However, more recent research (also referred to in Chapter 3) has questioned whether profits are the sole element in business objectives or merely a constraint on the pursuit of other objectives, such as the maximisation of company sales or assets. In such circumstances the use of the profit measure as a performance indicator may be inappropriate since it cannot indicate the degree of success by the company's management in achieving their objectives. A sales or assets growth indicator may be more appropriate in these cases. Even greater problems may occur in identifying a suitable performance indicator for a firm pursuing multiple short-run performance targets, as hypothesised in the behavioural theory of the firm.

While under certain conditions high profit rates are an indication of satisfactory performance from the standpoint of a private business, they may be an indication of unacceptable performance from a *social* standpoint. For example, they may have been achieved through exercising monopoly power to obtain factor inputs at unduly low prices or through selling products at prices greatly exceeding those which would have been charged in competitive conditions. Equally, a reduction in profit rates cannot be interpreted unambiguously, from the social standpoint, as an improvement in performance; nor can an increase in profit rates be interpreted as a deterioration in performance. A fall in profit margins may result from reduced efficiency in the organisation and operation of production processes, leading to a rise in cost levels; it may also reduce the capital resources that are available for the re-equipment and modernisation of plant and so prejudice future improvements in technical efficiency.

For these reasons profit is an ambiguous performance indicator from both the private and the social standpoints. Additionally, difficulties can arise in its actual measurement and in profit comparisons between firms. These difficulties occur largely because the accounting conventions used in its calculation vary between firms and over time and because of divergences between the accountant's and economist's concept of profit.[7] The possible sources of deficiency in profit comparisons include the following:

(1) Differences may exist between firms in the treatment of managerial services in the calculation of their profits. This may be an important consideration when comparing the profits of large and small firms, because in the latter case a full deduction for managerial payments may not have been made before the calculation of profit.
(2) Differences may exist between firms in the importance of loan capital. If interest payments are deducted before the calculation of profit, comparisons between firms will be affected by differences in their gearing.
(3) Depreciation may be estimated on a different basis between firms and may not in any of the cases correspond closely to the opportunity cost of the capital assets used.

(4) Similarly, stock appreciation may be valued differently between firms and, particularly in periods of rapid change in price levels, may not closely reflect the change in the true value of stocks held.

(5) The shorter the time period of the analysis, the greater is the likelihood that temporary extraneous factors will intrude upon the profit comparison.

Measures of *total* profit, however defined, are of little value as performance indicators unless they can be related to the scale of business from which they are generated. Ratios that relate total profit to either total sales or total capital employed are most commonly calculated. Total sales may be measured either gross or net of particular input costs. Capital may be measured either as the nominal value of share capital issued or as the net or gross book value of capital assets. Capital assets may be defined either narrowly as fixed assets or more broadly to include stocks and other net circulating capital.

The selection of the most appropriate ratio should depend upon the objective or standpoint from which performance is being measured. The ordinary shareholder is directly interested in the relationship between profits (after fixed interest payments) and the nominal share capital issued. The manager concerned about the 'effective' utilisation of capital will be more interested in the relationship between profits (before interest payments) and the total real capital employed. The manager concerned with the 'effective' utilisation of all the resources that he uses may prefer to express profits as a ratio of either total receipts or total costs. In assessing the possible abuse of market power, regulatory agencies have used a variety of different profit measures[8] (see Chapter 9). Therefore, a single generally-appropriate profit ratio does not exist.

Ratios also have little value as performance indicators unless they can be set against agreed standards. The standard is usually established either on an *inter-temporal* basis, i.e. a profit ratio achieved at an earlier point in time, or on a *cross-sectional* basis, i.e. an average profit ratio achieved by a group of other firms at a similar point in time. The performance estimates obtained are, therefore, influenced by the choice of the time period over which comparisons are made and/or the selection of the sample of firms for comparison as well as by the comparability of the basic data used.[8]

For the above different reasons profit measures require careful and cautious use as performance indicators, particularly when used from the standpoint of community assessment. Before a profit measure is adopted as a performance indicator it should be evaluated by:

(1) identifying and making explicit the objective by which performance is to be judged;

(2) determining the degree of consistency between the profit measure as defined and the objective being pursued; and

(3) assessing the consistency between the profit measure as defined and its empirical measurement.

8.3   PRODUCTIVITY MEASURES AND GROWTH ACCOUNTING

Productivity can be briefly defined as the ratio of a measure of output to a measure of one or more of the inputs used to produce the output.[9] Productivity measures are usually expressed in index form to facilitate comparisons over time or place, and they may be classified in the following ways:

(1) According to the level of the activity to which the measure relates. The level of activity may be the national economy, an industry, a firm, a factory or a particular production process.

(2) According to the range of inputs included in the calculation of the productivity ratio. The main distinction usually made is between *partial* productivity measures, which relate output to a single factor input (frequently labour), and *total* factor productivity measures, which include capital as well as labour inputs.

(3) According to whether the productivity index is based upon an intertemporal or cross-sectional comparison, e.g. whether it compares the productivity ratio for the British steel industry at the present with its ratio for a decade previously or with the ratio for the US steel industry at the present.

(4) According to whether the inputs and outputs are measured in physical or monetary units.

THE LEVEL OF THE ACTIVITY

A productivity measure for a national economy may estimate productivity changes for a country over time or productivity differences between countries at the same point in time. The most common unit of measurement at this level of activity is *per capita* gross domestic product (GDP) or gross national product (GNP) at constant prices. At a more analytical level attempts have been made to explain increases in the GDP or GNP in terms of changes in the quantity and quality of factor inputs and 'residual' factors – the latter including such factors as education, health, research and development inputs etc., which might otherwise be treated as qualitative changes in factor inputs. The results obtained from such growth-accounting studies have varied considerably according to the way in which the quality of factor inputs and other less tangible variables have been estimated.[10, 11] Time-series and international cross-sectional productivity studies for industrial sectors have also been undertaken. Many of these have used partial productivity measures – commonly, labour productivity measures – but a number of total factor productivity measures for industrial sectors have also been carried out.[12]

Productivity measurement at the level of the firm or for smaller units of activity has been undertaken from the standpoint both of business management and of public policy. Early studies mainly prepared labour productivity measures, but total factor productivity measures are now much more common. In the United Kingdom the Centre for Inter-Firm Comparison (CIFC), established by the British Institute of Management in 1959, has undertaken productivity studies for business management in over sixty industries using a linked system of physical and financial ratios.[13] This section of the chapter is mainly concerned with productivity measurement from the public policy standpoint, at the levels of the industrial sector and individual firm. However, since the basic principles of measurement are the same at all levels, although the empirical problems of measurement vary in intensity from one situation to another, the discussions and conclusions reached are also broadly applicable at other levels.

PARTIAL AND TOTAL FACTOR PRODUCTIVITY INDICES

The partial factor productivity index, P, may be defined as

$$P = \frac{Y}{I} \times 100 \qquad (8.1)$$

where Y is an index of real output and I is an index of one of the factor inputs, e.g. labour, L, or capital, K. Thus, in the case of the labour productivity index

$$P_L = \frac{Y}{I_L} \times 100 \qquad (8.2)$$

and in the case of the capital productivity index

$$P_K = \frac{Y}{I_K} \times 100 \qquad (8.3)$$

Similarly, the total factor productivity index, P_T, may be defined as

$$P_T = \frac{Y}{\alpha L + \beta K} \times 100 \qquad (8.4)$$

where α and β are weights summing to unity. Alternative formulations of this index are possible based upon alternative specifications of the production function.

Therefore, it follows that a change in the productivity index, $\dot{P}_L$, $\dot{P}_K$ or $\dot{P}_T$, is the result of a change in output, $\dot{Y}$, relative to the change in one of the inputs, $\dot{I}_L$ or $\dot{I}_K$, or to the combined weighted change in all inputs $(\alpha \dot{L} + \beta \dot{K})$.

The use of these productivity indices as performance indicators implies the acceptance of certain important assumptions. First, it implies that there is an over-riding objective to minimise the resources, as identified as inputs in the production function, used to produce a given level of output – or, more generally, to minimise the input–output ratio given that the level of output may vary. A second implicit assumption is that only the resources that are identified in the production function are relevant to an assessment of performance. A third assumption is that conditions of constant returns to scale in production apply.

In the remainder of this section the principles and difficulties involved in productivity measurement are examined further, with particular reference to the selection and measurement of factor inputs, the weighting of labour and capital inputs and the measurement of output. The section concludes with a brief review of the methods used to compare productivity changes in British and West German manufacturing industries over the period 1954–72.

THE SELECTION AND MEASUREMENT OF FACTOR INPUTS

The simplest and most widely used form of productivity measurement relates a measure of output to a simple measure of labour inputs, e.g. the total number of employees. If this performance indicator is used, it implies that the objective is to maximise output per person, but without consideration for the total resource cost by which this may be achieved. For example, the productivity measure may improve over time because each employee is working longer hours, or because skilled labour has replaced unskilled labour or because capital has been substituted for labour.

Differences in the composition of labour inputs, either over time or between different situations, can be taken into account by adjusting the labour input index for changes in the length of the working week, in the duration of annual holidays and in the amount of part-time employment. It is more difficult to adjust the index for changes in the skill composition of the labour employed because of the problem of determining appropriate weights for the different skill categories in the labour force. Wage differentials may be used, but in imperfect factor markets there is no assurance that these accurately reflect the differences in productivity between the skill categories.

The inclusion of capital and other resources in the construction of a total productivity measure is in principle the appropriate means to take account of non-labour factor inputs. However, the problems involved in doing this are considerable, particularly in relation to the measurement of capital inputs:[10]

> Conceptually, the ideal approach to inputs of capital is similar to that of labour. In order to construct an index of capital inputs, we would like to have for each physical kind of capital (each kind of machine, building, etc.) the quantity of its services provided (in hours or years) and its rental price (per hour or year) . . . This is far removed from what is really available to producers of productivity comparisons.[14]

What *are* available are estimates of the capital stock of firms or industries at specified points in time, expressed in terms of their historic cost of acquisition. These are usually converted into measures of gross capital stock, sometimes net of depreciation, on a replacement cost basis. This measure is then used as a proxy for capital inputs on the assumption that the flow of capital services is proportional to this stock. However, this only holds to the extent that the weighted average life of the assets comprising the capital stock and the quality of the capital stock remain unchanged. Both aspects of this assumption are unrealistic, although in particular situations the errors that this causes may be small.[12]

Inputs of land are rarely taken into account in productivity measures, except in the agricultural sector where problems in making allowance for quality differences in inputs may also arise. Where such inputs are not included capital inputs may serve as a proxy for all non-labour inputs.

Productivity indicators, therefore, cannot take account of the quantities and qualities of all factor inputs, although this of itself is not a source of deficiency. At one time, possibly as an over-reaction to the very simplistic partial productivity measures originally used, there was a tendency to pursue this type of comprehensiveness in productivity measurement, but the end product was not necessarily particularly meaningful:

If we were able to standardise all the outputs and take account of all the inputs, including not only labour and capital but technological and managerial, climate and natural resource elements, there should be no remaining differences in productivity.[43]

When we turn to the efficiency concept we find that if the concept is to mean anything, input and output must be defined so that they are not equal. If all input is conserved as output, and all output originates as input, the efficiency ratio is always equal to unity and there can be no way of comparing the efficiency of alternatives.[15]

The productivity index therefore measures the impact of 'residual', i.e. excluded, variables combined with the impact resulting from the mis-specification or mis-estimation of the input variables, and of the production function itself, included in the calculation of the index. Therefore, because of the problems of interpretation resulting from mis-specification and mis-estimation it may be preferable to have a less comprehensive but more reliable productivity measure. For example:

. . . efforts at the international comparison of total factor productivity are bound to involve great uncertainties in view of measurement problems with respect to capital and hence to introduce margins of error that are greater than those that are to be expected in comparisons of labour productivity. In these circumstances the optimal research strategy for international comparisons may be to continue to produce comparisons of labour productivity and to treat capital services as one of the external variables in terms of which it is sought to explain the results.[44]

This is indicative of a possible change in emphasis in the way in which productivity measures are to be used. Instead of using them as a direct indicator of a firm or industry's performance, they may be better employed as an analytic tool in accounting for the contribution made by each contributory variable to the firm or industry's increase or decrease of output. Hence, productivity measures may be increasingly used for *growth accounting* rather than as direct *performance indicators*.

WEIGHTING PROBLEMS

If productivity measurement only involved comparisons between the outputs of a single homogeneous product and the inputs of a single homogeneous factor of production, a weighting system would not be required. Such a system is

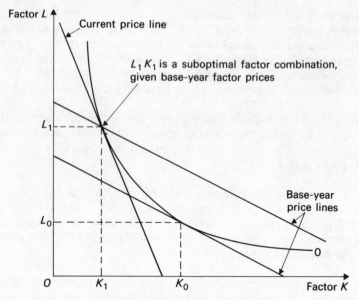

Fig. 8.1 Weighting of factor inputs.

needed to aggregate the output of dissimilar products and the inputs of the different types and qualities of the factors of production. The usual method of aggregation involves weighting units of input or output by their respective prices in a base period.[16] Therefore, where there are two factors of production, i.e. labour and capital, changes in aggregate input may be calculated by weighting the changes in labour and capital inputs by the shares of labour and capital respectively in net output in the base period.

The justification for this weighting system is that, according to marginal productivity theory, in perfect markets factor prices reflect the marginal products of the factor inputs used. It has been criticised both by those who have questioned the usefulness of marginal productivity theory[10] and because of the prevalence of imperfect market conditions. However, in the absence of a more suitable alternative this weighting system continues to be used.

Even if these weights are accepted they may not be appropriate if relative factor prices vary over time or between different situations, as illustrated below. Here, as illustrated in Figure 8.1,

$$I_0 = x_0 L_0 + y_0 K_0 \tag{8.5}$$

I_0 is the total input of a firm in the base period, L_0 and K_0 are the inputs of the two factors used in the base period and x_0 and y_0 are the factor prices in the base period.

Suppose that relative factor prices change, as illustrated in Figure 8.1, but that output level and the firm's production function remain unchanged. In order to minimise its costs of production the firm changes its inputs to L_1 and K_1 respectively in response to the change in relative factor prices, so that

$$I_1 = x_1 L_1 + y_1 K_1 \qquad (8.6)$$

The weighting system assumes that

$$I_1 = x_0 L_1 + y_0 K_1 \qquad (8.7)$$

However, as illustrated in Figure 8.1,

$$x_0 L_1 + y_0 K_1 > x_0 L_0 + y_0 K_0$$

Therefore, the productivity index records a *deterioration* in performance between periods 0 and 1.

Conversely, if the weights are derived from relative prices in the current period, the weighting system assumes that

$$I_0 = x_1 L_0 + y_1 K_0 \qquad (8.8)$$

Therefore, since

$$x_1 L_1 + y_1 K_1 < x_1 L_0 + y_1 L_0$$

the productivity index records an *improvement* in performance between periods 0 and 1.

Therefore, as Kendrick has indicated, 'at best, one can compare the changes in aggregate output and input in two periods using the prices of each as weights in order to bracket the range of uncertainty'.[16] If a single estimate is required, a mean of the weights may be used, which will reduce but not eliminate the error caused.

THE MEASUREMENT OF OUTPUT

So far, in examining the difficulties in productivity measurement, the analysis has mainly related to the treatment of inputs. The problems encountered in the measurement of outputs are generally smaller, but two important kinds of difficulty can arise.

First, the enterprise or industry whose performance is being assessed may produce an output that cannot be satisfactorily measured in either physical or monetary units. A number of service industries in the public sector – e.g. health, education, police and public administration – fall within this category. The services that they provide are heterogeneous and, therefore, cannot be meaningfully aggregated in physical units. Equally, they do not have market prices that might be the basis of a monetary weighting system. In such circumstances, as described in Chapter 2, statisticians may measure the output of a service industry – or such parts of its output to which this problem applies – as the value of the inputs used to produce the output.[17] If output is defined as input, the productivity measure remains constant over time and cannot be used as a performance indicator in any meaningful sense.

A second difficulty is in the use of price deflators in the measurement of changes of output over time. The price of a product may rise through time because the general price level is increasing or because the quality of the product is improving and is, therefore, valued more highly. The separation of the effects of these two influences is extremely difficult in practice; therefore, quality changes may be ignored by deflating the values of output by the full extent of any price changes that have occurred. Where quality improvements do occur and are ignored in this way, increases in output – and, therefore, of productivity – over time are understated; the converse applies if product quality declines. This second type of difficulty may arise more frequently in the services sector, where reliance on the monetary, as distinct from the physical, measurement of output is greatest.[3, 17]

PRODUCTIVITY MEASUREMENT AND GROWTH ACCOUNTING: A CASE STUDY

The principles and difficulties of productivity measurement can be more fully appreciated by examining particular productivity studies, such as those relating to the UK transport sector,[18] the comparative performance of UK and Swedish companies,[19] and the comparative growth of productivity in British and West German manufacturing industry.[12] The main features of the last of these three studies are briefly reviewed below.

The main purposes of the study were two-fold: to construct and compare indices of total factor productivity (TFP) growth for manufacturing industries in the United Kingdom and West Germany over the period 1954–72; and to estimate and compare the contribution of the different factors to the rate of output growth in these industries.

The TFP index was defined and estimated as in equation 8.4 and was then used in a growth-accounting framework to distinguish the respective contributions of changes in labour inputs, capital inputs and 'other factors' to output growth rates.

Output estimates for each manufacturing industry in both countries were derived from official statistics relating to net manufacturing output at constant prices. Statistics for the two countries were not completely consistent because of differences in the classification of industries and in the definition of net output. Also, in both countries the estimates of output changes may have understated output quality improvements; so there has been a general tendency to underestimate productivity improvements.

Inputs were defined to consist of labour and capital inputs, with capital acting as a proxy for all non-labour factors of production. The *labour input* was measured fairly crudely, because of data limitations, as the number of persons employed in an industry in each year. During the period 1954–72 the average number of employee hours per annum fell in both countries; therefore, the estimates have understated the increase in labour productivity that occurred, although probably to approximately the same extent in both countries. The *capital input* index measured, by industry, the gross fixed-capital stock at constant-price replacement cost. Such an index is subject to a number of limitations, as previously discussed, arising from the use of inappropriate price indices, estimates of asset lives and adjustments for capital quality. Labour and capital inputs were *weighted* to combine them into a single input index, according to the shares of labour and capital in net output in 1963. The weights differed between the two countries but not to an extent that materially affected productivity growth comparisons between the two countries.

It is obvious that many potential sources of deficiency existed in the preparation of these TFP indices, but it is a matter of judgement whether they were sufficiently important to render the estimates obtained valueless. Elliott, the author of the study, has drawn a cautiously optimistic conclusion:

> In spite of all the above weaknesses, the difficulty of calculating total factor productivity growth should not be overestimated. Although measurement of the growth of overall efficiency is full of conceptual hazards, and in spite of the usual data problems, the author is confident that the method used . . . is sufficiently well grounded in theory, and sufficiently robust in the presence of less than perfect data, for the results to be both meaningful and useful.[45]

If this judgement is accepted, the results of the study may be interpreted within a growth-accounting framework (Table 8.1). This table indicates, first, the relative importance of increases in TFP compared to increases in labour and capital inputs as contributors to output growth in both UK and West German industries. Second, it shows that the rate of growth in TFP was consistently much higher in West German than in UK industries. Finally, within both countries there were substantial differences in the rate of growth in TFP between industries.

The analysis of the causes of differences in TFP growth between industries and countries is beyond the terms of this review, but two matters that are relevant to this are evident from Table 8.1 and the previous discussion. First, TFP measures the whole of the residual impact on output growth after the effect of changes in labour and capital inputs, as estimated, have been taken into account. Therefore, it measures the aggregate impact of a large number of dissimilar factors, e.g. technical advances, other unaccounted-for changes in the quality of labour and capital inputs, and the economies of large scale production. The identification and assessment of the impact of these separate factors can often only be accomplished on an incomplete and partially subjective basis. Second, in Table 8.1 there is some evidence, although with exceptions (e.g. textiles), of a positive correlation between the TFP growth rate and the output growth rate in individual manufacturing industries. The direction of causality between these two variables, however, is not fully clear. Increases in total factor productivity improve an industry's competitiveness, which stimulates an increase in its sales and output. However – and many consider that this may be the stronger force[12] – a fast rate of growth, with the high investment that it entails, makes it easier to attract higher quality labour and managerial talent, to absorb the most recent technological advances and, possibly, to reap greater economies of scale – in short, to achieve a high TFP growth rate.

Table 8.1 Sources of output growth in selected UK and West German manufacturing industries, 1954–72 (% per annum).

Industry	United Kingdom				West Germany			
	Growth in output	Growth due to:			Growth in output	Growth due to:		
		Labour increase	Capital increase	Residual (TFP)		Labour increase	Capital increase	Residual (TFP)
Chemicals and allied industries	5·9	0·2	3·1	2·6	10·6	1·6	3·2	5·9
Engineering and electrical goods	3·9	0·7	1·6	1·5	6·8	2·6	2·3	1·9
Metal manufacturing	0·9	−0·4	1·4	−0·1	4·3	0·6	2·2	1·5
Textiles	1·1	−1·7	0·5	2·3	4·1	−1·1	1·7	3·6

Source: I. Elliott, 'Total factor productivity', in M. Panic (ed.), The UK and West German Manufacturing Industry, 1954–72 (London, National Economic Development Office, 1976), p. 68.

Note: In a few cases, due to rounding errors, the sum of components is not equal to the aggregate to which they refer.

8.4 PERFECT COMPETITION AND WORKABLE COMPETITION

Because of the practical difficulties involved in constructing direct indicators of performance, such as profit or productivity indicators, attempts have been made to use market models to provide indirect criteria for judging performance. The rationale upon which this is based is that it may be easier to construct indicators relating to the preconditions for satisfactory performance – e.g. to market structure, pricing and investment criteria – rather than relating to the measurement of performance itself. This approach has been most fully developed on the basis of the perfect competition model. Although it is not a realistic market form this has been used, often unjustifiably, to develop performance indicators for application in other kinds of market situation.

THE PERFECT COMPETITION MODEL

The principal assumptions of the perfection competition model that bear on the present analysis are that:

(1) there is freedom of entry and exit in the market;
(2) the individual firm sells its goods and obtains its factors of production within markets in which there is no differentiation in product or price; and
(3) the size of the individual firm's share in product and factor markets is too small for it to influence the level of prices.

These assumptions are implicit in the familiar equilibrium situation of the individual firm in perfectly competitive product and factor markets. The individual firm's demand function for a product is perfectly elastic and identical to its marginal revenue function (Figure 8.2). Profit maximisation is, therefore, achieved at an output level where marginal cost equals both marginal revenue and market price. In the long run equilibrium, assuming homogeneity of the factors of production, the firm's level of output will also correspond to the point of minimum average total cost where only normal profits are earned.

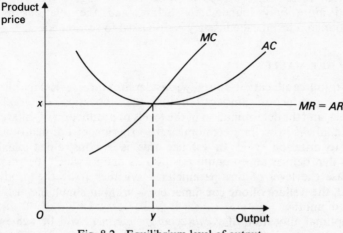

Fig. 8.2 Equilibrium level of output.

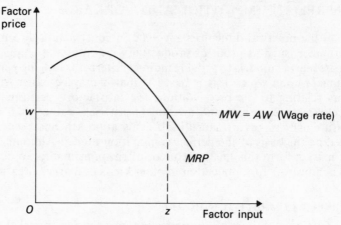

Fig. 8.3　Equilibrium level of factor employment.

Similarly, in a perfectly competitive factor market the profit-maximising firm will employ additional units of each factor up to the point where the marginal revenue product is just equal to the price of acquiring them (Figure 8.3).

The establishment of a perfectly competitive market, therefore, has three consequences that are of significance from a performance standpoint:

(1) It ensures in the long term that firms do not earn supernormal profits.
(2) It ensures that the Pareto conditions are satisfied for the optimal allocation of factor inputs in the production of goods and for the optimal allocation of such goods among consumers.
(3) It forces firms to be technically efficient, i.e. to produce each level of output with the minimum possible combination of factor inputs, in order to produce their outputs at least cost and earn normal profits.

The first of these consequences is illustrated in Figure 8.2, the second is examined more fully immediately below, and the relationship between competition and technical efficiency is discussed in section 8.4.

PARETO OPTIMALITY

Optimal resource allocation is usually considered at three levels: the allocation of factors of production among outputs, the allocation of goods among consumers, and the determination of the levels of production of different goods. In most analyses in welfare economics the criterion of optimality adopted is the Pareto criterion.[20, 21] In essence this is a constrained maximisation criterion that defines an optimum position as one in which it is not possible to increase the level of one parameter – whether it be the production of one good, the welfare of one consumer etc. – without simultaneously reducing the level of another.

The optimal allocation of *goods among consumers* will be achieved if the marginal rates of substitution among commodities are equal for all consumers.

In a perfectly competitive market the price of each good is identical for all consumers; thus, the price ratios confronting each consumer will be equal. To maximise total satisfaction consumers will purchase goods until the marginal utility derived from the last unit of expenditure on each good is identical. Therefore, if prices are equal, the ratios of marginal utilities must be equal for all consumers, assuming a constant marginal utility of money. That is,

$$\frac{MU_{x1}}{MU_{x2}} = \frac{MU_{y1}}{MU_{y2}} \tag{8.9}$$

where x and y are goods, 1 and 2 are consumers and MU is the marginal utility of each consumer. If equation 8.9 is satisfied, the marginal rates of substitution will be equal, and it will not be possible to make one consumer better off without making another worse off.

Similarly, the allocation of *factor inputs* will be optimal in conditions of perfect competition. The optimality conditions in a two-output, two-factor situation can be summarised as

$$\frac{MP_{ix}}{MP_{jx}} = \frac{MP_{iy}}{MP_{jy}} \tag{8.10}$$

where i and j are factor inputs and MP is the marginal revenue product of each factor input. Profit maximisation ensures that a firm hires each factor until its factor price equals its marginal revenue product. Also, perfect markets ensure that the price of a factor is identical for all firms. Hence, $MP_{ix} = MP_{iy}$ and $MP_{jx} = MP_{jy}$, and this ensures that equation 8.10 is satisfied.

Finally, the optimal combination of *goods produced* requires that

$$\frac{MU_x}{MC_x} = \frac{MU_y}{MC_y} \tag{8.11}$$

where MC is the marginal cost of production of each good. It has already been demonstrated that perfect competition ensures that the marginal utility–price ratio is identical for all products and that price is in all cases equal to marginal cost, as a condition of profit maximisation. Therefore, the relationship between marginal utility and marginal cost specified in equation 8.11 must also hold.

The performance that is achievable by firms within a perfectly competitive market system, therefore, has a number of apparently attractive features. In turn, despite the obvious dangers in transposing findings from this market model to more realistic market situations, this has had an important influence on thinking about performance measurement and the means of achieving better performance.

First, in the perfectly competitive market model the firm achieves maximum performance by pursuing its own commercial objective of profit maximisation. At one level of thinking this has been too simply transposed into the real world situation as the 'invisible hand' philosophy, whereby 'the private interests and passions of men' are led in the direction 'which is most agreeable to the interests of society'.[22] In some instances this has been interpreted to mean that business profits provide a satisfactory performance indicator for society as well as for individual firms. The limitations of the use of profit as a performance indicator are examined in section 8.2.

Second, the perfect competition model implies that satisfactory performance depends crucially upon market structure (as defined in Chapter 2). Transposed into the real world situation this has often been interpreted to suggest that deficiencies in performance can be attributed to deficiencies in market structure. Therefore, it has been suggested, the performance indicators that are likely to be most operational, although they are indirect, relate to the key variables of market structure. By the same argument government policy to raise industrial performance should be directed to the correction of identifiable deficiencies in market structures. The transposition of this type of thinking to realistic market situations has been most apparent in the use of the concept of 'workable competition' (discussed later in this section) and in the analysis of monopoly and restrictive trade-practices policies (see Chapter 9).

Third, the perfect competition model indicates that the optimal allocation of resources is achieved through firms applying certain pricing and investment criteria. These are to charge prices for products that are equal to the marginal costs of producing them (as in Figure 8.2) and to evaluate investment proposals according to the net present-value criterion (as defined in Chapter 7). Similar pricing and investment rules, modified to take account of deviations from perfectly competitive market conditions, have been used as performance indicators in the nationalised industries sector and are examined in Chapter 10

THE LIMITATIONS OF THE PERFECT COMPETITION MODEL

In view of its widespread influence in the establishment of performance indicators, it is important to appreciate the limitations of the perfect competition model when it is used for this purpose. Attention here is focused on three possible sources of weakness: income distribution assumptions, externalities and 'second best' problems.

Income distribution assumptions
The acceptance of Pareto optimality as a social welfare criterion is based upon the implicit assumption that the existing distribution of income within society is also optimal.[21] If this assumption is not satisfied, social welfare may be increased through the redistribution of income, which would change the pattern of demand, the structure of prices and, consequently, the way in which resources are allocated and used within the economy. Economists can provide little guidance on the 'best' distribution of income and, therefore, tend to ignore the issue by assuming that separate provision will be made through the government's fiscal system to achieve a socially acceptable income distribution, leaving market forces free to operate *as if* optimal income distribution had been achieved. However, in practice there may be both social costs and institutional difficulties in relying exclusively on the fiscal system for this purpose; therefore, the argument for using markets and pricing as an instrument of income redistribution re-emerges. The contentious issue of whether or not to subsidise

public transport – in other words, departing from the pricing rule, illustrated in Figure 8.2, on income distribution grounds – is an illustration of this point.

Externalities
The perfect competition model also assumes away the existence of externalities, which in real world situations may provide an important justification for departing from the simple pricing and investment rules that it enshrines. Externalities cause divergences between private opportunity costs, borne by the producers or consumers of a good, and social opportunity costs, borne by society as a whole. These divergences arise where the non-producers and/or non-consumers of a good are indirectly affected by production or consumption activities, as in the cases of road congestion and environmental pollution.

Each additional vehicle user on a congested road imposes additional time delays on all other road users, which in total exceed the additional delay that he personally experiences, i.e. his private opportunity cost. Similarly, a chemical-processing factory may discharge effluent into a river, causing a deterioration downstream in fishing facilities yet without cost to itself. The perfectly competitive market model assumes that the parties involved in the externality will bargain between themselves, on the basis of their respective legal rights, and that the financial settlement reached will 'internalise' the externality.[23] However, in less-than-perfect markets lack of knowledge and high transaction costs often make this impractical. If businesses apply the pricing and investment rules derived from the perfect competition model where these externalities still exist, a misallocation of resources will result. To correct this it has been suggested that prices should reflect social, not private, opportunity costs and that investment appraisal should be based upon comparisons of social benefits and social costs rather than financial receipts and expenditures to investors (see Chapter 10).

Problems of 'second best'
The attainment of optimal resource allocation, as previously defined, requires that all the conditions of perfect competition be achieved in all sectors of the economy. However, this is an realisable requirement, and unfortunately economic theory cannot identify the more realisable 'second best' alternatives to these market conditions.[24] For example, a policy move to satisfy one of the more realisable features of perfect competition will not necessarily improve welfare unless the other conditions are also satisfied. The difficulties that may be associated with partial moves towards perfectly competitive market conditions are illustrated by the following two examples:

(1) A monopolist pursuing profit maximisation produces a lower level of output than would be produced in perfectly competitive market conditions. The imposition of a pollution tax upon his activities, to internalise environmental externalities as in a perfectly competitive market, will cause a further reduction in his level of output.

(2) Measures may be taken to divide up large enterprises in order to remove

potential sources of monopoly power in markets. However, this may result in welfare losses through loss of the economies of large scale production (whose existence has to be ignored in the perfect competition model)[25] and through reduced co-ordination in investment planning[26] (due to the lack of perfect knowledge assumed to exist in the perfect competition model).

Hence, the full conditions of the perfect competition model are not realisable in the real world situation. Yet, it seems that there is no means of readily identifying either the types of markets that provide the best practicable alternatives to the perfect model, or the types of improvements to existing market arrangements that will unambiguously result in improvements to business performance.

WORKABLE COMPETITION

The recognition that perfect competition is not realisable in the real world has led to an examination, among those which *are* realisable, of the forms of competition that are likely to result in the highest level of performance. The task has been defined by Clark in the following terms: 'It seems that a contribution might be made . . . by attempting to formulate concepts of the most desirable forms of competition, selected from those that are practically possible, within the limits set by conditions we cannot escape.'[27] The 'most desirable forms of competition' Clark has termed 'workable competition', and this was to become the yardstick by which performance in actual markets was to be judged, rather than the theoretical limiting case of perfect competition.

Clark's thesis is not clearly stated, but in essence it consists of two main elements. The first is an early recognition of the second-best problem in pointing to the danger of regarding a move towards the structure of a perfectly competitive market system as necessarily an improvement:

If there are, for example, five conditions, all of which are essential to perfect competition, and the first is lacking in a given case, then it no longer follows that we are necessarily better off for the presence of any one of the other four. In the absence of the first, it is *a priori* quite possible that the second and third may become positive detriments; and a workably satisfactory result may depend on achieving some degree of 'imperfection' in these other two factors.[27]

Second, Clark has presented his own generic definition of workable competition and sought to indicate, *inter alia*, that this form of competition can be achieved in oligopolistic markets. Its essential ingredient is rivalry, either actual or potential, among profit-maximising suppliers, who vie among themselves for the customer's patronage:

Competition is rivalry in selling goods, in which each selling unit normally seeks maximum net revenue, under conditions such that the price or prices each seller can charge are effectively limited by the free option of the buyer to buy from a rival seller or sellers of what we think of as 'the same' product, necessitating an effort by each seller to equal or exceed the attractiveness of the others' offerings to a sufficient number of sellers to accomplish the end in view.[27]

Subsequently, a number of writers have put forward alternative definitions of workable competition, and a sample of these is included below:

An industry is workably competitive when (1) there are a considerable number of firms selling closely related products in each market area, (2) these firms are not in collusion, and (3) the long-run average cost curve for the new firm is not materially higher than that for the established firm.[28]

An industry may be judged to be workably competitive when, after the structural characteristics of its market and the dynamic forces that shaped them have been thoroughly examined, there is no clearly indicated change that can be effected through public policy measures that would result in greater social gains than social losses.[29]

. . . (a) the existence of alternative sources of supply (b) independence of action by vendors in seeking buyer custom (c) absence of substantial control of supply by any one seller and (d) easy access to markets.[30]

. . . the result of whatever gives rise to reasonably satisfactory or workable competition . . . patterns of market structure and conduct which may be expected to give rise to or be associated with workable performance.[31]

The usage of the term 'workable competition' is, therefore, quite widespread, and particularly in the United States it is a term that has been commonly used in discussing antitrust legislation and in court action.[32] The term has been used far less in Britain; but as the next chapter shows, the most commonly quoted parameters of workable competition have been frequently employed as indirect performance indicators in the regulation of monopoly and restrictive practices in Britain.

How valuable is the concept of workable competition? In general the 'second best' cautionary remark by Clark has not received sufficient emphasis. If it had, those who have defined workable competition would have felt the necessity to specify more precisely, and to work out the full welfare implications of, the particular competitive system that they have advocated in order to establish its superiority over any prevailing system. In fact this has never been done; and if it were attempted, certain difficulties would inevitably arise. Given the state of theories of business behaviour in non-atomistic markets, a unique relationship between non-perfect competitive systems and market behaviour and performance would be difficult to establish. In these circumstances it is not surprising to find that writers have retreated to definitions of workable competition that are either essentially tautological, e.g. those of Markham[29] and Bain,[31] or so vague that they are of little practical use.

The failure to specify, in definitions of workable competition, the level of knowledge possessed by purchasers and suppliers raises a range of awkward welfare issues relating to such matters as advertising, product differentiation and the co-ordination of output and investment decisions. At the more practical level terms such as 'considerable number', 'closely related', 'substantial control' and 'easy access' are of little value unless they can be more closely specified.

The competitive system may be viewed as a control mechanism constraining the freedom of opportunity of the individual economic actors in the system.[33] The perfectly competitive market system constrains these actors in a manner that enables the outcome to be uniquely identified, whereas workable competition does not yield a unique outcome. So long as competitive systems are relied upon as control systems, the need to identify the system characteristics uniquely identified with desired performance will remain. Until this is achieved the task of such organisations as the Monopolies and Mergers Commission and the Restrictive Trade Practices Court, whose task is to modify the existing competitive system on behalf of the public interest, is an unenviable one:

> . . . if technological and institutional conditions are not compatible with pure competition and, at the same time, are not deemed to be such as to justify a public utility regulation of the firms in question, there arises a problem of defining an acceptable kind of competition in terms of market structure such that it can normally be expected to be accompanied by the kind of performance considered acceptable in the use of resources.[34]

8.5   PRODUCTIVE EFFICIENCY AND X–EFFICIENCY

In the more recent literature relating to performance measurement there is frequent reference to productive efficiency and X-efficiency. In this section the meaning and measurement of these two types of efficiency are explored, and the influence of competitive market conditions upon their attainment is also examined. Some of the matters raised are closely linked to issues discussed in the two preceding sections.

PRODUCTIVE EFFICIENCY

Productive efficiency is defined in terms of its two main components: technical efficiency and factor price efficiency.[35] The former is a measure of the degree of economy in the use of resource inputs to produce a specified output, with a given state of technology. The latter measures the skill in achieving the best combination of the different inputs, having regard to their relative prices.

In Figure 8.4, AB represents the 'best practice' production function in the sense that it indicates the *minimum* combinations of the two factor inputs of given quality required by the firm, in the present state of technology, to produce the specified level of output. In the case of a firm at point P, OC_1

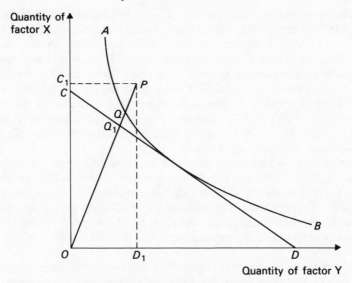

Fig. 8.4 Productive efficiency of the firm.

and OD_1 are the *actual* quantities of factors X and Y that it uses to produce that level of output. Thus, the technical efficiency of a firm at P, relative to 'best practice', can be measured by the ratio OQ/OP. Similarly, given the relative price of the two inputs, measured by the slope of the price line CD, the factor price efficiency can be measured by the ratio OQ_1/OQ. The productive efficiency of the firm is then measured by the product of these two ratios:

$$\frac{OQ}{OP} \times \frac{OQ_1}{OQ} = \frac{OQ_1}{OP} \tag{8.12}$$

The nearer the ratio moves towards unity, the higher is the productive efficiency of the firm.

This concept of productive efficiency is derived from the neoclassical theory of the firm, and its adoption implies a desired objective of producing any given output at least cost to the producer. It also subsumes a unified well-informed management structure that is responsible for departures from least cost solutions, which in principle could be eliminated if the management were fully efficient. Such efficiency would be 'forced' upon management in perfectly competitive markets as a condition of survival, but to varying degrees it is discretionary in other market forms.

The conceptual and practical difficulties in calculating the above ratios are evident from the earlier review of productivity measurement in section 8.3. These difficulties largely centre on two inter-related issues: the identification and measurement of factor inputs to take account of differences in quality, as well as in quantity, of such inputs; and the identification of the 'standard' production function and factor price line by which the performances of actual firms are to be assessed.

Standard production functions based upon engineering calculations can be very unreliable because they tend to neglect the less obvious factors, e.g. input quality and interdependencies between different stages in the production process. Standards based upon interfirm comparisons within an industry will not be valid if differences in product range and factor qualities between firms are ignored. Similarly, practical difficulties arise in identifying the most appropriate factor prices to use in the construction of the factor price line. Firms located in different areas may be faced by different prices; and some prices, i.e. those which are subject to long term contracts, may reflect market conditions over different time periods.

By way of illustrating these points, one study of municipal bus undertakings in Great Britain has indicated that important elements of the differences between them in costs per vehicle-mile were attributable to factors that were largely beyond the control of the individual undertakings rather than exclusively due to differences in managerial, technical or factor price efficiency.[36] These exogenously determined differences included the following:

(1) Differences in factor prices. Undertakings located in areas of high labour demand had to pay much higher wages than other undertakings.
(2) Differences in the terrain and traffic conditions. These caused cost differences due to variation in vehicle speeds, fuel consumption, maintenance etc.
(3) Differences in the pattern of demand. Variation in the structure of employment caused differences in the severity of the travel peak and hence in average operating costs.

Shapiro and Müller, in a study of farming practice in Tanzania, have argued that:

> . . . invocation of the term 'technical efficiency' may imply an admission of the analyst's incomplete understanding of the production process. Improved specification of the model may relate interfirm productivity variability to input variability, rather than to the somewhat enigmatic technical efficiency. This improved specification may be extremely helpful to policy makers in developing nations, where the list of proposed programs often includes many that aim at improving management . . . If policy makers know *why* some farmers are better managers (i.e. why there are technical efficiency differentials), they might have firmer grounds for choosing among such an array of programs.[37]

They have hypothesised that, although all firms in a given situation have *potential* access to the same technical knowledge, each firm only has *effective* access to a subset of this knowledge. The subset is mutually dependent upon the information at the disposal of its owner and his 'openness' to new ideas, as measured by his past record of farm modernisation. Their findings strongly suggest that these qualities of the business owner are important determinants of the differences in performance between firms. However, the link established between information possessed and technical efficiency was not always as expected because the possession of information did not always result in action. Part of the explanation appears to be that there were hidden costs, not necessarily of a financial nature, associated with the use of some of the new technical information, which owners preferred not to incur. Examples of this kind included:

(1) improvements that involved retiming the planting of cash crops where such retiming would then clash with the planting of food crops and involve breaking with the traditional notion that a man should grow his own food;
(2) improvements that required members of the family to depart from the traditional methods of undertaking their work; and
(3) improvements that involved using hired labour instead of the traditional co-operative work groups but that might result in social ostracism.

These examples are of more general significance in drawing attention to the incomplete nature, from both the individual and the social standpoint, of the objective of cost minimisation for a given output, which is implicit in the concept of productive efficiency. Also, they draw attention to the potential importance of internal organisational relationships and behavioural elements within the firm as influences on its technical performance. This is explored further below through the notion of X-efficiency.

X-EFFICIENCY

The term 'X-efficiency' was initially developed by Leibenstein to distinguish it from *allocative efficiency*; but, as discussed later, he has also considered it to be distinguishable from *productive* and *technical efficiency*.[38,39]

Allocative efficiency relates to the welfare gains that are obtainable if the monopoly elements causing a restriction in output are removed but production costs remain unchanged. Suppose (in Figure 8.5) that price is lowered from its monopoly level (OP) to its competitive level (OP_1) and that the cost functions

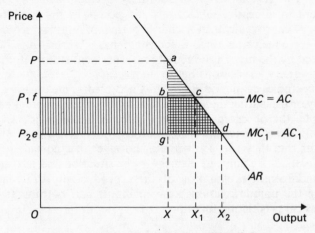

Fig. 8.5 Allocative efficiency and X-efficiency.

(MC and AC) remain unchanged; then there is an expansion in equilibrium output (from OX to OX_1) and a welfare gain (equivalent to area bac).

The size of the welfare gain depends on the extent to which price was originally above the competitive level and on the price elasticity of demand for the product. It is clear from the diagram, however, that unless both these values are very large the welfare gain will be small relative to the value of total output and sales. Leibenstein's review of empirical studies in this area has largely supported this expectation:

> The empirical evidence, while far from exhaustive, certainly suggests that the welfare gains that can be achieved by increasing *only* allocative efficiency are usually exceedingly small, at least in the capitalist economies. In all but one of the cases considered all of the gains are likely to be made up in one month's growth. They hardly seem worth worrying about.[38]

This conclusion has caused Leibenstein to explore the alternative, and possibly more significant, types of improved efficiency. These other types may be categorised as those due to technical change and those accruing independently of it. He has termed the latter type of improvement an improvement in X-efficiency, which shows itself in a downward shift in the firm's cost function (from MC to MC_1 in Figure 8.5). In a competitive market situation this causes a fall in price (to OP_2), an expansion in output (to OX_2) and a welfare gain (equivalent to area $efcd$) relative to the previous competitive-market equilibrium. If monopoly conditions remained in the market so that the original price (OP) and output level (OX) were unchanged, there would be a smaller welfare gain (equivalent to area $efgb$), which should accrue to the producer.

The size of the welfare gain from an improvement in X-efficiency varies according to the magnitude of the shift in the firm's cost function that it causes. However, it is clear from Figure 8.5 that an improvement in X-efficiency ($P_1 P_2$) that is equal to the price reduction achieved through allocative efficiency (PP_1) results in a substantially greater welfare gain than an improvement in allocative efficiency. This points to the potentially greater importance of improvements in X-efficiency than of improvements in allocative efficiency – a conclusion that, Leibenstein has claimed, has been broadly substantiated by the many productivity measurement studies undertaken.[46]

For the variety of reasons given in section 8.3, the findings of these productivity studies cannot be uncritically accepted as measuring differences in X-efficiency or measuring the scope for its improvement in practical situations. For example, the observed differences in total factor productivity between firms in an industry may reflect unrecorded differences in the quality of the factor inputs that they use. Leibenstein, however, has considered that factor quality differences are only one element in the situation and has suggested that a more fundamental explanation of these productivity differences involves questioning the unique relation between inputs and outputs as assumed in the neoclassical production function:

> The conventional theoretical assumption, although it is rarely stated, is that

inputs have a fixed specification and yield a fixed performance. This ignores other likely possibilities. Inputs may have a fixed specification that yields a variable performance, or they may be of a variable specification and yield a variable performance.[46]

The basic reason for the variable relation between inputs and output, in a given state of technical knowledge, is that contracts for labour and management are inevitably incomplete; 'a good deal is left to custom, authority and whatever motivational techniques are available to management, as well as to individual discretion and judgment',[46] to determine what the *actual* inputs of labour and management services are to be and what *precise level* of performance is to be obtained from them. In effect Leibenstein's distinction between the *resources* hired by a firm and the *services* actually used in its production is similar to that used by Penrose in her theory of the growth of the firm[40] (see section 4.2). The distinction is also related to the notion of organisational slack, used in the behavioural theory of the firm, which acknowledges that labour and managerial inputs will achieve different levels of output depending upon, *inter alia*, the network of organisational commitments within the firm and the external pressures, both market and otherwise, on its overall performance[41] (see section 3.5.). It is Leibenstein's reluctance to place the analysis of business efficiency within the theoretical framework provided by the neoclassical production function that has caused him to distinguish X-efficiency from productive efficiency, although not all other writers have maintained this distinction.[39]

What, then, are the determinants of the level of X-efficiency? A complete analysis has not yet been attempted, but Leibenstein has attached particular significance to the role of competitive market pressure:

. . . for a variety of reasons people and organisations normally work neither as hard nor as effectively as they could. In situations where competitive pressure is light, many people will trade the disutility of greater effort, of search, and the control of other people's activities for the utility of feeling less pressure and of better interpersonal relations. But in situations where competitive pressures are high, and hence the costs of such trades are also high, they will exchange less of the disutility of effort for the utility of freedom from pressure, etc.[47]

However, he has not provided any empirical evidence to support this presumed relationship between competitive pressure and X-efficiency. There are considerable difficulties in undertaking such an empirical test, since, for example, it requires examples of strictly comparable firms operating under differing market conditions. One such study, recently undertaken by Primeaux, involves comparison between the cost levels of municipally-owned electricity utility duopolists and of municipally-owned electricity utility monopolists in North American cities.[42] The results obtained suggest that, after other differences had been taken into account, the average power costs of the duopolists were on average 10 per cent lower than those of the monopolists.

This, however, is only one example and is limited to the comparison of monopoly and duopoly market conditions. Other studies exploring a broader spectrum of competitive conditions are needed. The interaction between competitive pressure and other sources of X-efficiency – e.g. interpersonal relations within firms, which promote work motivation – also requires to be examined.

Finally, it should be appreciated that improvements in X-efficiency are not invariably desirable. As Primeaux has demonstrated in the case of the electricity power industry, increases in X-efficiency achieved through increased market pressure may be bought at the expense of some loss in the economies of large scale production.[42] X-efficiency may also be bought at the expense of harder effort, a more routine work pattern, less satisfactory working and social relationships.[37] Changes in competitive pressure may alter the balance of the trade-off facing the members of an organisation and so cause a rise in X-efficiency. The new situation, however, is not necessarily socially preferred to the one superseded.

8.6   CONCLUSION

The cautionary tone of this chapter is intended to counterbalance the exaggerated claims and inexact use of performance indicators in the past. The need for performance indicators grows as the role of government intervention in the economic system widens, but such indicators as currently exist require careful construction and interpretation if they are not to be misapplied. None provide certain, unambiguous performance measures; at best they help to narrow down the critical area within which the inevitable judgement on performance has to be made and to systematise the information that is relevant to this judgement.

In using or evaluating particular performance indicators the following considerations are likely to be relevant:

(1) Any indicator of performance should be consistent with the objectives being pursued and should first of all be judged by this consistency. The objectives that are implicit in a number of performance indicators may not have the automatic and universal approval assumed in their use. In a number of cases the implied objectives are very restrictive.

(2) Profit has frequently been used as a performance indicator; but it is likely to be inappropriate where the objective, from either a private or a social standpoint, cannot be exclusively specified in profit terms. Even where this is possible there remains a number of conceptual and practical difficulties in profit ratio measurement.

(3) The significance of any partial or total-factor productivity measure, as a performance indicator, depends upon:
   (a) the inputs and outputs *excluded* from the calculation; and
   (b) the manner in which the items *included* in the calculation are estimated and weighted.

Increases in productivity ratios, or in productive efficiency or X-efficiency, do not necessarily imply an improvement in performance or an increase in social welfare. However, they may provide a growth-accounting framework that is useful for policy purposes, e.g. by providing a fuller and more systematic account of the different factors contributing to output growth in particular types of firm or industry.

(4) The use of the perfect competition model as a basis for deriving performance indicators, e.g. pricing and investment criteria, is limited by the need to make restrictive assumptions relating to income distribution, and to the structural and behavioural characteristics of markets. Once these assumptions have been relaxed the indicators derived from the perfect competition model are not strictly valid, and the modifications to them that are needed under 'second best' conditions are not easily identified.

(5) The notion of workable competition, although relating to more realistic market situations, is as presently formulated an unsatisfactory basis for establishing performance yardsticks, because of its imprecision, because it does not have a unique market outcome and because it encounters all the problems of a 'second best' solution.

FURTHER READING

A number of general reviews of the 'state of the art' of productivity measurement have been published, including the survey of international comparisons of productivity by Kravis.[14] A fuller understanding of total factor productivity measurement may be obtained by examining particular measurement studies, such as those by Elliott[12] and Deakin and Seward.[18] The further analysis of X-efficiency might commence with Leibenstein's original study,[38] supplemented by Primeaux's empirical study on its possible connection with competitive market pressure.[42] Further study of Pareto optimality conditions and the difficulties involved in interpreting these for use in real market conditions might be based on Leftwich,[20] supplemented by Millward,[21] although similar material is covered in a number of other texts on welfare economics.

NOTES AND REFERENCES

1 R. G. Lipsey, *An Introduction to Positive Economics,* 4th edn (London, Weidenfeld & Nicolson, 1975), ch. 51.
2 F. Hirsch, *Social Limits to Growth* (London, Routledge & Kegan Paul, 1976), ch. 4.
3 T. Juster, 'A framework for the measurement of economic and social performance', in M. Moss (ed.), *The Measurement of Economic and Social Performance* (New York, National Bureau of Economic Research, 1973).
4 W. D. Nordhaus and J. Tobin, 'Is growth obsolete?', in NBER *Economic Growth* (New York, National Bureau of Economic Research, 1972).
5 T. Lynes, *National Assistance and National Prosperity,* Occasional Papers on Social Administration (London, Bell, 1962).
6 J. F. Weston and S. K. Mansinghka, 'Tests of the efficient performance of conglomerate firms', *Journal of Finance,* vol. 26 (September 1971), pp. 919–46.

7 F. Bailey, *Current Practice in Company Accounts* (London, Haymarket Publishing, 1973), chs 2 and 3.

8 See, for example, C. K. Rowley, 'The Monopolies Commission and the rate of return on capital', *Economic Journal*, vol. 79 (March 1969), pp. 42–65; A. Sutherland, 'The Monopolies Commission: a critique of Dr Rowley', *Economic Journal*, vol. 81 (June 1971), pp. 264–72; C. K. Rowley, 'The Monopolies Commission: a reply', *Economic Journal*, vol. 81 (September 1971), pp. 602–8.

9 T. E. Easterfield, *Productivity Measurement in Great Britain* (London, Department of Scientific and Industrial Research, 1959).

10 M. I. Nadiri, 'International studies of factor inputs and total factor productivity: a brief survey', *Review of Income and Wealth*, vol. 18 (June 1972), pp. 129–54.

11 S. Fabricant, 'Perspective on productivity research', *Review of Income and Wealth*, vol. 20 (September 1974), pp. 235–49.

12 I. Elliott, 'Total factor productivity', in M. Panic (ed.), *The UK and West German Manufacturing Industry, 1954–72* (London, National Economic Development Office, 1976).

13 J. Teague and S. Eilan, 'Productivity measurement: a brief survey', *Applied Economics*, vol. 5 (June 1973), pp. 133–45.

14 I. B. Kravis, 'A survey of international comparisons of productivity', *Economic Journal*, vol. 86 (March 1976), p. 10.

15 K. E. Boulding, 'Some difficulties in the concept of economic input', in National Bureau of Economic Research (NBER), *Output, Input and Productivity Measurement* (Princeton, Princeton UP, 1961), p. 333.

16 J. W. Kendrick, *Productivity Trends in the United States* (Princeton, Princeton UP, 1961), p. 10.

17 G. Briscoe, 'Recent productivity trends in the UK services sector', *Oxford Bulletin of Economics and Statistics*, vol. 38 (1976).

18 B. M. Deakin and T. Seward, *Productivity in Transport* (Cambridge, Cambridge UP, 1969).

19 C. Pratten, *A Comparison of the Performance of Swedish and UK Companies* (Cambridge, Cambridge UP, 1976).

20 R. H. Leftwich, *The Price System and Resource Allocation* (Hinsdale, Ill., Dryden Press, 1973), ch. 16.

21 R. Millward, *Public Expenditure Economics* (Maidenhead, McGraw-Hill, 1971), chs 1–3.

22 A. Smith, *An Inquiry into the Nature and Causes of the Wealth of Nations* (London, Bell, 1921).

23 R. H. Coase, 'The problem of social costs', *Journal of Law and Economics*, vol. 3 (1960), pp. 1–44.

24 R. G. Lipsey and K. Lancaster, 'The general theory of the second best', *Review of Economic Studies*, vol. 24 (October 1956), pp. 11–32.

25 P. Sraffa, 'The law of returns under competitive conditions', *Economic Journal*, vol. 36 (December 1926), pp. 535–50.

26 G. B. Richardson, *Information and Investment* (London, Oxford UP, 1960).

27 J. M. Clark, 'Towards a concept of workable competition', *American Economic Review*, vol. 30 (1940), pp. 242–3.

28 G. J. Stigler, 'Extent and bases of monopoly', *American Economic Review*, vol. 32 (1942), supplement, pp. 2–3.

29 J. W. Markham, 'An alternative approach to the concept of workable competition', *American Economic Review*, vol. 40 (1950), p. 361. In this reference Markham has also quoted a lengthier definition of workable competition by C. Edwards.

30 R. Cassady, 'The role of economic models in micro-economic market studies', in A. R. Oxenfeldt (ed.), *Models of Markets* (London, Columbia UP, 1963), p. 44.

31 J. S. Bain, *Industrial Organisation* (New York, Wiley, 1959 edn), p. 15.
32 See, for example, *The Report of the Attorney General's National Committee to Study Anti-Trust Laws* (Washington, DC, US Government Printing Office, 1965), ch. 7, which defines workable competition in terms of the number and relative size of firms, the ease of entry and the extent of independence of action by rivals.
33 R. M. Cyert and K. D. George, 'Competition, growth and efficiency', *Economic Journal*, vol. 79 (March 1969), pp. 23–41.
34 E. S. Mason, 'The current state of the monopoly problem in the United States', *Harvard Law Review*, vol. 62 (1949), p. 1267.
35 M. J. Farrell, 'The measurement of productive efficiency', *Journal of the Royal Statistical Society*, series A, vol. 120 (1957), pp. 253–81.
36 N. Lee and I. Steedman, 'Economies of scale in municipal bus transport: some British results', *Journal of Transport Economics and Policy*, vol. 4 (January 1970), pp. 15–28.
37 K. H. Shapiro and J. Müller, 'Sources of technical efficiency: the roles of modernisation and information', *Economic Development and Cultural Change*, vol. 25 (January 1977), p. 293.
38 H. Leibenstein, 'Allocative efficiency *vs* "X-efficiency" ', *American Economic Review*, vol. 56 (June 1966), p. 394. An updated version of this article is to be found in H. Leibenstein, *Beyond Economic Man* (Cambridge, Mass., Harvard UP, 1976), ch. 3.
39 H. Leibenstein, 'X-efficiency, technical efficiency and incomplete information use', *Economic Development and Cultural Change*, vol. 25 (January 1977), pp. 311–16.
40 E. T. Penrose, *The Theory of the Growth of the Firm* (Oxford, Blackwell, 1959), pp. 25*ff*.
41 R. M. Cyert and J. G. March, *A Behavioral Theory of the Firm* (Englewood Cliffs, Prentice-Hall, 1963), chs 3–5.
42 W. J. Primeaux, 'An assessment of X-efficiency gained through competition', *Review of Economics and Statistics*, vol. 59 (February 1977), pp. 105–8.
43 Kravis, op. cit. (n. 14), p. 2.
44 Kravis, op. cit. (n. 14), pp. 12–13.
45 Elliott, op. cit. (n. 12), pp. 61–2.
46 Leibenstein, op. cit. (n. 38), p. 407.
47 Leibenstein, op. cit. (n. 38), p. 413.

9 State Intervention in the Private Sector

9.1 INTRODUCTION

This chapter is concerned with the activities of the government departments and state agencies that intervene generally in the private sector of the economy at the microlevel in order to influence industrial performance.[1] Two broad types of intervention can be distinguished: competition policy and industrial policy, although the distinction cannot be maintained too rigidly. Competition policy seeks to influence industrial performance indirectly, by maintaining or creating a framework within which the pursuit by independent firms of their private interests in accordance with market forces results in a desirable economic performance. The framework consists of both the market structures in which firms operate and the set of state-determined rules regulating their behaviour. Industrial policy, by contrast, involves state intervention at the level of specific industries or firms, designed to bring about directly a desired outcome that would not otherwise occur. It is not intended to create a framework within which the market can be left to operate; rather it is intended to supplement or supplant market forces, i.e. to assist or replace them. The traditional rationale for competition policy has been the argument that competition acts as a control mechanism limiting the power of individual firms, whereas monopoly gives an individual firm the power to behave in ways that may be harmful to the public interest. This argument rests on two propositions:

(1) There is some performance on the part of firms that is in the public interest.
(2) Competition between firms will result in that performance.

Thus, the case for competition is that it results in an economic performance deemed desirable.

The case is at its most rigorous in the demonstration that perfect competition throughout the economy will result in a Pareto optimum. Of course, rather stringent assumptions are required for this demonstration, and the fact that these assumptions do not hold and never have held renders this particular argument for competition largely irrelevant.[2] However, something of the argument from theoretical welfare economics lingers on in the form of specific criteria of desirable performance, e.g. that price should equal marginal cost. Several considerations render the adoption of such criteria a dubious course unless supported by further reasoning. Such considerations relate both to 'second best' matters[3] and to the value judgements involved, including those about the distribution of wealth and income and about what is to count as an increase in welfare. In addition to these objections to the use of such criteria as indicators of static 'allocative efficiency', it is also possible that their adoption would militate against the achievement of other, perhaps more important, objectives concerned with change and development. Hence, the argument from theoretical welfare economics and perfect competition provides support neither for a general presumption in favour of competition nor for the adoption of specific criteria, such as that price should equal marginal cost, purporting to be indicators of 'allocative efficiency'. Some other standard of desirable performance and appropriate industrial structure and conduct is needed.

One alternative approach proposed is that of 'workable competition'.[4] This is an attempt to avoid recourse to pure *ad hoc* pragmatism by seeking to develop a general framework in which aspects of market structure and conduct are related in a fairly systematic way to the performance regarded as desirable. Thus, workable competition is the combination of market structure and conduct that results in 'workable performance'. Workable performance is defined in terms of a set of ideals or norms relating to the important dimensions of performance,[5] which may include technical progressiveness, price policy, profitability, investment in relation to demand, foreign trade record or any other variable designated by the government as desirable. Among the aspects of market structure and conduct widely held to be relevant to the determination of whether or not workable performance will result, i.e. whether or not there is workable competition, are the number and relative size of firms, the ease of entry and the extent of independence of action by rivals.[6]

It may be doubted whether the approach of workable competition is of any assistance in the quest for criteria of what is in the public or national interest. In the first place the approach requires a definition of desirable performance as its starting point; and yet, what is to count as desirable performance is by no means self-evident. Consider the dimension of technical progressiveness. Is all 'innovation' to be regarded as desirable? Or is there a need for criteria to distinguish between developments that are socially desirable and those which are trivial, wasteful or even harmful? If preferences are assumed to be exogenous to the working of the economic system, as in theoretical welfare economics, and meeting such preferences is assumed to be desirable in itself, there is no problem. If, however, it is recognised that preferences are socially influenced in ways that make them endogenous to the socioeconomic system, it is not so plausible to argue that satisfying preferences should be regarded as an end in itself. An independent criterion is required if the proposition 'what is is thereby desirable' is to be avoided.

However, even if this problem is brushed aside and it is accepted that the state somehow or other decides on what is to be regarded as desirable performance, the approach of workable competition still has little to contribute; for the state of economic theory is such that the relationship between industrial structure, business conduct and performance cannot be unambiguously specified. Hence, the question of what sort of structure and conduct will result in a given performance, deemed desirable, is frequently a matter of considerable controversy among economists.[7]

It is perhaps partly for this reason that competition policy in the United Kingdom has been explicitly based on *ad hoc* pragmatism, i.e. the examination of each case on its merits. While such a policy, it has been claimed, has the advantage of avoiding any 'doctrinaire' inflexibility, it none the less has its problems. In particular the absence of a coherent theoretical framework within which to judge specific cases carries with it the danger of arbitrariness and inconsistency. One frequently gets the feeling that a given decision could easily have gone the other way had the composition of the relevant body been different or had economists with different views been heard,[8] which is not really surprising since neither the 'normative' nor the 'positive' clarity that is necessary for specific decisions to be consistently related to a common set of principles exists. More seriously, it may be that the *ad hoc* philosophy of UK competition policy has been a contributory factor to its continuing relative ineffectiveness, despite three major revisions since 1948.[9]

Economists concerned with industrial performance have traditionally been preoccupied with competition policy, but they have largely failed to come to terms with the rapid development of industrial policy in recent years. Such economic analysis of industrial policy as has been undertaken has tended to be within the neoclassical theoretical framework and has concentrated on pointing out the dangers of incoherence and political expedience, as seen from the perspective of orthodox neoclassical rationality, in direct state intervention at the microlevel.[10] However, despite this hostile stance, industrial policy has increasingly come to dominate government microeconomic intervention in the private sector, and it is not difficult to see why this has happened.

In the United Kingdom, at any rate, the basic reason for the development of industrial policy has been the rapidly worsening performance of the economy, particularly the manufacturing sector, by comparison with that of most other advanced capitalist countries. The poor performance of British industry has been well conveyed by the then chief economist of the National Economic Development Office (NEDO) in his introduction to a comparative study of UK and West German manufacturing industry:

> . . . starting from a level of efficiency which was not all that different, the two countries went through a period of almost 20 years in which German industry achieved a significant improvement in its relative position. Its productive capacity expanded much more than that of the UK. Moreover, it experienced a greater improvement in efficiency with which manufacturing resources are used – indicating a much greater absorption of new technologies. The improvements in efficiency have been reflected also, as one might expect, in the relatively slower increases in prices of manufactured goods in West Germany. Given all these differences, it is hardly surprising that there has been such a disparity in performance of the two manufacturing sectors in world trade. In 1955 the countries' shares of world trade in manufactures were as follows: UK 22·9 per cent and West Germany 19·2 per cent. By 1973 the German share had increased to 22·4 per cent, while the UK's was down to 7·5 per cent.[11]

Evidence of relative productivity performance is becoming more plentiful, although it requires careful interpretation, as demonstrated in Chapter 8. Comparisons have been made on the basis of both aggregate national-accounts data and studies of individual companies or plants. Jones has estimated that between 1955 and 1973 the value added per worker in manufacturing grew by roughly 3 per cent per annum in the United Kingdom compared with an average of 5 per cent per annum in the Five of the European Economic Community (EEC). By 1973 labour productivity in manufacturing in the EEC Five ranged between 54 and 93 per cent higher than in the United Kingdom.[12] In a more detailed two-country comparison Elliott and Hughes have concluded that: 'By 1972, labour productivity in West German manufacturing was probably between one-quarter and one-third higher than in the UK.'[13] In two studies based on 1972 data Pratten has compared labour productivity in the British and overseas factories of international companies and in British and Swedish companies. The weighted average of labour productivity in US factories was over 50 per cent higher than that in British factories (fifty observations), in West German factories over one-third higher (thirty-five observations) and in French factories over one-quarter higher (twenty-four observations). It should be noted that the estimates of productivity differentials between their factories in different countries were provided by the companies concerned and accepted at face value. In the second study a comparison of fifty companies in each country found that on average the output per employee was 50 per cent higher in the Swedish than in the British companies.[14] Finally, the Central Policy Review Staff have estimated that in the United Kingdom in 1973 overall labour productivity in the car industry, including components, was some 30 per cent below that in France, Italy and West Germany, while in car assembly plants: 'It takes almost twice as many man-hours to assemble similar cars using the same or comparable plant and equipment in Britain as it does on the continent.'[15]

There has also accumulated in recent years compelling evidence that Britain's balance-of-payments problems have been substantially contributed to by the poor international performance of the manufacturing sector. Panic has calculated that the United Kingdom's income elasticity of demand for manufactured imports over the period 1957–72 was about 50 per cent higher than that of West Germany and France.[16] Moore and Rhodes have shown that, while all the major capitalist countries except West Germany experienced an increase in manufacturing import penetration between 1969 and 1974, this was most marked in the case of the United Kingdom, with the share of manufactured imports in the domestic market increasing by almost two-thirds compared with the next highest increase of one-third in Italy.[17] Between 1964 and 1973 an index constructed by Campbell-Boross and Morgan, on the assumption that a change in the ratio of exports to imports indicates a change in competitiveness, declined at an average annual rate of 4·3 per cent for the UK manufacturing industry as a whole.[18] There was also the dramatic fall in the United Kingdom's share of world exports in manufacturing, quoted above. Overall, the poor performance of British manufacturing industry in the international economy is beyond dispute; and, if anything, the rate of deterioration has accelerated in the mid and later 1970s.

There is clearly no direct connection between relatively low productivity and poor trade performance. Price competitiveness is related to relative productivity levels through the intervening variables of domestic price levels and exchange rates. In fact, due primarily to the depreciation of sterling, UK manufactured goods were more cost and price competitive in 1977 than in 1972, having attained their most competitive position towards the end of 1976.[19] However, despite increased price competitiveness the international trading performance of UK manufacturing continued to decline in the mid 1970s, presumably due to competitive factors other than price. Fetherston, Moore and Rhodes, in a study of manufacturing exports and cost competitiveness during the period 1956–76, have found that effective devaluations and revaluations had modified but not reversed long run trends in export shares.[20] Moore and Rhodes, commenting on the poor performance of the UK manufacturing industry, referred to: 'A growing lack of competitiveness embracing not only (and perhaps not even mainly) relative prices, but also quality differences, design characteristics, delivery dates and after-sales service.'[21] Evidence on individual industries collected over the years by the NEDO supports the view that non-price factors have been a major cause of the United Kingdom's poor trade performance; and while there is limited evidence of a link between non-price competitiveness and productivity,[22] the associated connection between faster-growing economies and non-price competitiveness has been strongly argued.[23]

The development of industrial policy in the United Kingdom has occurred in a context of growing awareness of the international weakness of the British economy. The stated objective of industrial policy, repeated over and over again, has been to increase productivity and improve the balance of payments. A typical statement made in July 1978 was as follows:

> The Industrial Strategy is dedicated to increasing British industry's share of home and overseas markets by improving productivity and competitiveness through higher investment and better use of our productive resources. By supporting investment projects under Section 8 of the Industry Act 1972, the Government has made a major contribution towards improving the level and direction of investment in British manufacturing industry. But the evidence from the Sector Working Parties shows also that major improvements must be made in the way industrial assets are used.[24]

The rest of this chapter is organised as follows. Section 9.2 sets out the legal framework and public interest guidance with which the various government departments and agencies at work in 1978 operated. Competition policy, covering the work of the Restrictive Practices Court, the Monopolies and Mergers Commission and the Price Commission, is discussed in section 9.3. In section 9.4 the development of industrial policy is traced, from its beginnings in the National Plan and the Industrial Reorganisation Corporation of the 1960s to its 1978 form in the Industry Acts 1972 and 1975, the National Enterprise Board and the Industrial Strategy. Finally, some conclusions are drawn in section 9.5.

9.2   THE LEGAL AND INSTITUTIONAL FRAMEWORK

In this section the legislation and institutions relating to competition policy and industrial policy in the United Kingdom in 1978 are outlined. In any assessment of policy designed to improve industrial performance from the standpoint of the public or national interest, the interpretation of what counts as contributing to that interest is clearly crucial. To enable readers to form their own judgement, guidance given as to the public interest or statements of the purpose of legislation and institutions are set out as fully as possible.

COMPETITION POLICY[25]

The legislation governing competition policy in the United Kingdom in 1978 was primarily the Fair Trading Act 1973, the Restrictive Trade Practices Act 1976, the Resale Prices Act 1976 and the Price Commission Act 1977.[26] Matters relating to restrictive practices, resale price maintenance, monopoly and merger were generally overseen by the Director-General of Fair Trading through the Office of Fair Trading. Under the Fair Trading Act 1973 and the Consumer Credit Act 1974 the director also had various duties with respect to consumer protection, but these are not considered in this chapter.

Restrictive Trade Practices
The Restrictive Trade Practices Act 1976 – a consolidation of earlier legislation – requires certain categories of agreement between the suppliers of goods or services to be registered with the Director-General of Fair Trading. The categories comprise agreements with respect to the prices to be charged, the terms of supply, the quantity or type to be supplied and restrictions on the persons or areas to be supplied. Agreements providing for the exchange of information on such matters are also registrable. In the case of goods only, agreements relating to recommended prices are also registrable. Certain categories of agreement are exempt from registration, including agreements relating to exclusive dealing, patents, know-how, and legal, medical, architectural and engineering services. There is also provision for the Secretary of State* to exempt any agreement deemed to be important to the national economy, although the conditions that have to be met are closely specified. This provision was used only once between 1968, when it was enacted, and 1978. The director is charged with deciding the order in which registered agreements are brought before the Restrictive Practices Court and with preparing the case against any agreement that the parties concerned wish to continue. However, if the director is satisfied that a registered agreement is not significant enough to warrant Court proceedings, he may apply to the Secretary of State for a direction to that effect.

Restrictions or information provisions contained in registrable agreements are presumed to be against the public interest unless they can be shown to be otherwise. This can only be done by establishing before the Court that the restriction or information provision confers certain benefits, or does not restrict competition, and that there is no offsetting detriment. The eight 'gateways' or 'escape routes' for agreements relating to goods, embodied in the Restrictive Trade Practices Act 1976, are as follows:

*'Secretary of State' has been used throughout to stand for the relevant minister.

(*a*) that the restriction or information provision is reasonably necessary, having regard to the character of the goods to which it applies, to protect the public against injury (whether to persons or to premises) in connection with the consumption, installation or use of those goods;

(*b*) that the removal of the restriction or information provision would deny to the public as purchasers, consumers or users of any goods other specific and substantial benefits or advantages enjoyed or likely to be enjoyed by them as such, whether by virtue of the restriction or information provision itself or of any arrangements or operations resulting therefrom;

(*c*) that the restriction or information provision is reasonably necessary to counteract measures taken by any one person not party to the agreement with a view to preventing or restricting competition in or in relation to the trade or business in which the persons party thereto are engaged;

(*d*) that the restriction or information provision is reasonably necessary to enable the persons party to the agreement to negotiate fair terms for the supply of goods to, or the acquisition of goods from, any one person not party thereto who controls a preponderant part of the trade or business of acquiring or supplying such goods, or for the supply of goods to any person not party to the agreement and not carrying on such a trade or business who, either alone or in combination with any other such person, controls a preponderant part of the market for such goods;

(*e*) that, having regard to the conditions actually obtaining or reasonably foreseen at the time of the application, the removal of the restriction or information provision would be likely to have a serious and persistent adverse effect on the general level of unemployment in an area, or in areas taken together, in which a substantial proportion of the trade or industry to which the agreement relates is situated;

(*f*) that, having regard to the conditions actually obtaining or reasonably foreseen at the time of the application, the removal of the restriction or information provision would be likely to cause a reduction in the volume or earnings of the export business which is substantial either in relation to the whole export business of the United Kingdom or in relation to the whole business (including export business) of the said trade or industry;

(*g*) that the restriction or information provision is reasonably required for purposes connected with the maintenance of any other restriction accepted or information provision made by the parties, whether under the same agreement or under any other agreement between them, being a restriction or information provision which is found by the Court not to be contrary to the public interest upon grounds other than those specified in this paragraph, or has been so found in previous proceedings before the Court; or

(*h*) that the restriction or information provision does not directly or indirectly restrict or discourage competition to any material degree in any relevant trade or industry and is not likely to do so.[27]

If the Court is satisfied that one or more of these circumstances holds, it must then also satisfy itself that the 'tailpiece' is fulfilled, i.e.:

. . . that the restriction or information provision is not unreasonable having regard to the balance between those circumstances and any detriment to the public or to persons not parties to the agreement (being purchasers, consumers or users of goods produced or sold by such parties, or persons engaged or seeking to become engaged in the trade or business of selling such goods or of producing or selling similar goods) resulting or likely to result from the operation of the restriction or the information provision.[28]

The 'gateways' and 'tailpiece' applying to services are identical in all material respects.[29]

In the first legislation on competition policy in the United Kingdom – the Monopolies and Restrictive Practices (Inquiry and Control) Act 1948 – an agnostic attitude was adopted towards monopoly and restrictive practices, in line with the *ad hoc* approach discussed in section 9.1. The presumption that restrictive practices are against the public interest unless they can be shown to be otherwise was first introduced in the Restrictive Trade Practices Act 1956. However, although this was apparently a major change of policy in that a presumption in favour of competition seemed to be established, the criteria of the public interest in terms of which claims for exemption are to be judged remained general and vague, albeit less so than the guidance of the 1948 Act. What is to count as an injury (*a*) or a substantial benefit (*b*) to the public? With reference to what standard is the fairness of terms to be evaluated (*d*)? If clarity is achieved on these thorny conceptual problems, what sort of market conduct will result in the desired performance? This latter question arises equally with respect to the criteria that present *prima facie* fewer problems of interpretation, namely, the counteraction of the restrictions of others (*c*), the avoidance of local unemployment (*e*) and the promotion of exports (*f*). Even when it has somehow been decided that a particular restriction has passed one of the 'gateways', there remains the formidable problem of determining the considerations that should be taken into account when balancing the benefit established against any accompanying detriment. The 1976 Act gives no guidance on these questions of interpretation, apart from the general presumption in favour of competition. The issues of 'positive' economic analysis involved are so complex and often controversial that, not surprisingly, most economists have doubted whether a judicial procedure is the most appropriate method for dealing with them (see section 9.3). More importantly, perhaps, the absence of clear guidance on the 'normative' side as to what specifically is to count as being in the public interest presumably throws the members of the Court back on to their own 'assumptions, principles or prejudices' in making their decisions.[30]

Resale Price Maintenance
The Resale Prices Act 1976 – another consolidation of earlier legislation – prohibits collective resale price maintenance. It also creates a general presumption that individual price maintenance is against the public interest and prohibits the practice unless exemption is obtained from the Restrictive Practices Court. Applications for exemption may be made by the Director-General of Fair Trading, an individual supplier or a trade association

representing suppliers. Before granting exemption the Court must be satisfied that:

. . . in default of a system of maintained minimum resale prices applicable to those goods:

(a) the quality of the goods available for sale, or the varieties of the goods so available, would be substantially reduced to the detriment of the public as consumers or users of those goods; or

(b) the number of establishments in which the goods are sold by retail would be substantially reduced to the detriment of the public as such consumers or users; or

(c) the prices at which the goods are sold by retail would in general and in the long run be increased to the detriment of the public as such consumers or users; or

(d) the goods would be sold by retail under conditions likely to cause danger to health in consequence of their misuse by the public as such consumers or users; or

(e) any necessary services actually provided in connection with or after the sale of the goods by retail would cease to be so provided or would be substantially reduced to the detriment of the public as such consumers or users;

and in any such case that the resulting detriment to the public as consumers or users of the goods in question would outweigh any detriment to them as consumers or users (whether by the restriction of competition or otherwise) resulting from the maintenance of minimum resale prices in respect of the goods.[31]

It should be noted that all the 'gateways' except (d) require a judgement not merely as to the likelihood of a certain factual outcome – e.g. whether the quality and variety of goods (a), the number of outlets (b) or the services provided (e) would be reduced or whether prices would increase (c) – but also as to whether that outcome would be 'to the detriment of the public'. As with restrictive practices, once such preliminary questions have been decided there remains the 'tailpiece' requirement of balancing any specific benefit from the maintenance of minimum resale price in a particular case against any accompanying general detriment. The Act provides no further guidance on the criteria in terms of which detriment to the public is to be judged.

Monopoly
Under the Fair Trading Act 1973 monopoly is defined as a situation in which at least one-quarter of a given category of goods or services is supplied by or to a single firm, or two or more firms acting in such a way as to restrict competition, whether by agreement or not. The relevant market may be defined as a specific geographical area, thus bringing local monopolies within the scope of the legislation. If a monopoly situation is thought to exist, the Director-General of Fair Trading or the Secretary of State may refer the matter to the Monopolies and Mergers Commission for investigation. A reference may be limited to the facts of the situation or may also require a judgement with respect to the

public interest. The facts relate to whether or not a monopoly exists and, if so, also to any actions designed to maintain or exploit the monopoly and any actions that are attributable to the existence of the monopoly. References by the director are subject to veto by the Secretary of State. References relating to nationalised industries can only be made by the Secretary of State acting jointly with the minister responsible for the industry. Since 1973 monopoly references have been subject to a time limit for reporting, normally eighteen months, although extensions are permitted.

On receipt of a monopoly reference the Monopolies and Mergers Commission has first to decide whether a monopoly situation exists and, if so, in references not limited to the facts of the situation, whether any of the facts established are against the public interest. The guidance given in the Act on how to interpret the public interest is as follows:

In determining . . . whether any particular matter operates, or may be expected to operate, against the public interest, the Commission shall take into account all matters which appear to them in the particular circumstances to be relevant and, among other things, shall have regard to the desirability –
(*a*) of maintaining and promoting effective competition between persons supplying goods and services in the United Kingdom;
(*b*) of promoting the interests of consumers, purchasers and other users of goods and services in the United Kingdom in respect of the prices charged for them and in respect of their quality and the variety of goods and services supplied;
(*c*) of promoting, through competition, the reduction of costs and the development and use of new techniques and new products, and of facilitating the entry of new competitors into existing markets;
(*d*) of maintaining and promoting the balanced distribution of industry and employment in the United Kingdom; and
(*e*) of maintaining and promoting competitive activity in markets outside the United Kingdom on the part of producers of goods, and of suppliers of goods and services, in the United Kingdom.[32]

When the Commission finds facts relating to a monopoly situation that are against the public interest, it may include in its report recommendations on the action that it considers should be taken. On receipt of a report from the Commission specifying the adverse effects of facts found to be against the public interest, the Secretary of State may issue Orders designed to prevent or remedy them. Such Orders may require the publication of price lists, regulate prices, break up existing firms, impose conditions on or prohibit mergers, and prohibit specified uncompetitive practices. Before issuing such Orders the Secretary of State may ask the director first to seek voluntary undertakings from the firms in question.

In addition to references relating to specific monopoly situations, the Secretary of State may make general references to the Commission concerning practices that appear to be typical of monopoly situations or otherwise uncompetitive. Such references have in the past included those on collective discrimination, refusal to supply and parallel pricing.

The Monopolies and Mergers Commission has undergone two changes of name in its history. Originally set up as the Monopolies and Restrictive Practices Commission by the Monopolies and Restrictive Practices (Inquiry and Control) Act 1948, it was renamed the Monopolies Commission by the Restrictive Trade Practices Act 1956. Although it was reconstituted under the Monopolies and Mergers Act 1965, which expanded its terms of reference to include mergers, it retained the same name. However, when again reconstituted under the Fair Trading Act 1973, it was renamed the Monopolies and Mergers Commission.

Merger

The Fair Trading Act 1973 also enables the Secretary of State to refer a merger to the Monopolies and Mergers Commission if it would create or strengthen a monopoly situation, defined as control over at least one-quarter of a given category of supply, or if it would involve the acquisition of assets whose value exceeded £5 million. Merger references may be made only by the Secretary of State, but the Director-General of Fair Trading has a duty to recommend that a reference be made where he thinks such action desirable. References may require the Commission to confine its consideration of the public interest question to certain specified elements in the overall merger situation. The Secretary of State is enpowered to refer a merger to the Commission either before it has gone through, in which case he may prohibit the completion of the merger until the Commission has reported, or within six months of the merger being completed.

On receipt of a merger reference the Monopolies and Mergers Commission must report, normally within six months, on whether the merger satisfies either of the qualifying criteria (i.e. relating to monopoly or assets) and, if so, on whether it 'operates or may be expected to operate against the public interest'.[33] The guidance given in the Act on how to interpret the public interest in the case of merger is the same as that quoted above with respect to monopoly.

When the Commission reports adversely the procedure is the same for merger as that already outlined for monopoly. The Secretary of State may ask the director to seek undertakings from the parties concerned or may issue Orders. Undertakings and Orders may cover the prevention or breakup of the merger or may relate to the future conduct of the merged company.

The Fair Trading Act 1973 also covers newspaper mergers, but these are subject to separate procedure because of the particular public-interest questions involved and are not discussed in this chapter.

Prices

Competition policy in relation to restrictive practices, monopoly and merger in the United Kingdom in the postwar years has developed by building on what went before, thus displaying a fair measure of continuity. The Monopolies and Mergers Commission in one form or another and the Restrictive Practices Court have become established as stable features of competition policy under both Labour and Conservative governments. Policy in relation to the control of prices has been quite different.

The National Board for Prices and Incomes (NBPI) operated between 1965 and 1970 and was charged with assessing price or wage increases referred to it by the government against specified criteria as set out in various White Papers.[34] After a short gap during the 1970 Conservative government's period of disengagement, the Counter-Inflation Act 1973 introduced a new non-discretionary system of price control in the form of a Price Code administered by a Price Commission. The largest firms were required to prenotify proposed price increases, with medium-sized firms postnotifying and smaller firms maintaining records. Large and medium-sized firms were also required to submit financial statements at regular intervals. Increases were assessed in terms of the extent to which they were necessary to cover specified allowable cost increases, subject to deductions for assumed productivity increases and a maximum permitted profit margin. The detailed provisions set out in a series of Price Codes became increasingly complex, incorporating various profit safeguards and investment reliefs as attempts were made to deal with the changing economic and political situation.[35]

In 1977 the Price Commission was reconstituted under the Price Commission Act 1977, its power to refuse applications for price increases was removed, and it was given new powers. By mid 1978, after a transitional period, the Commission was operating a fundamentally different system from that which prevailed between 1973 and 1977. In some respects the new Price Commission resembled the old NBPI, shorn of its incomes side. It also shared the fate of the NBPI, being abolished in 1979 shortly after the newly elected Conservative Government assumed office.

The Price Commission Act 1977 conferred on the Price Commission powers to undertake investigations of individual firms on its own initiative, subject to veto by the Secretary of State, and examinations of specified sectors or industries referred to it by the Secretary of State. Investigations on the Commission's own initiative could be into price increases of which it had been prenotified under the provisions of the Counter-Inflation Act 1973, which remained in force, or into prices that were not subject to price increase prenotification, or into distributors' margins. The Commission had twenty-eight days in which to decide whether to investigate a prenotified increase; and if it decided to go ahead, it had to report within four months of the date of notification. Reports on investigations not arising from prenotification had to be submitted within three months of the decision to investigate. During an investigation prices were frozen, subject to certain safeguards for profits. In its report on an investigation the Commission had to recommend whether prices or profit margins should be restricted and, if so, for what period, up to a maximum of twelve months including the period of investigation. In reaching its recommendation the Commission was required to have regard to:

(*a*) the need to recover costs incurred in efficiently supplying goods and services and in maintaining the value of the relevant business;
(*b*) the desirability of encouraging reductions in costs by improvements in the use of resources and of securing reductions in prices of goods and charges for services in consequence of such improvements;
(*c*) the need to earn, from selling goods and providing services in the United Kingdom, profits which provide a return on capital employed in

producing profits which is sufficient, taking one year with another –

(i) to defray the cost of the capital (including compensation for the risk involved in producing the profits), and

(ii) to provide money for, and to encourage the production of, innovations and technical improvements in and the expansion in the United Kingdom of the enterprises which consist of or include the relevant businesses;

(*d*) the need to take account of changes in prices in determining the value of assets;

(*e*) the desirability of maintaining the quality of goods and services and satisfying the demands of users of goods and services;

(*f*) the need to safeguard the interests of users of goods and services by promoting competition between suppliers or, where competition must be restricted or cannot be promoted (either because certain suppliers control a substantial share of the relevant market or for any other reason), by restricting prices and charges;

(*g*) the desirability of establishing and maintaining a balance between the supply of goods and services and the demand for them; and

(*h*) the need to avoid detriment, from restraints on prices and charges, to the United Kingdom's balance of payments and the need to increase the share of United Kingdom enterprises in markets in the United Kingdom and elsewhere.[36]

When the Commission had reported on an investigation the Secretary of State after hearing representations from the firms involved, had to decide whether or not to accept any recommendations made by the Commission concerning restrictions on prices or profit margins.

Price Commission examinations of any matter relating to prices in sectors or industries referred to it by the Secretary of State are subject to the same guidelines, quoted above, as were its own-initiative investigations. Prices were not frozen while an examination was under way, but after representations the Secretary of State could issue Orders imposing restrictions in accordance with any recommendations made by the Commission. Such restrictions could, with the approval of Parliament, extend beyond twelve months. The Secretary of State could seek and accept undertakings instead of issuing Orders.

There were various provisions in the Price Commission Act 1977 to promote co-ordination with the Director-General of Fair Trading in the operation of competition policy. The Secretary of State could not refer matters to the Price Commission for examination, nor accept undertakings nor issue Orders relating to examinations, without first consulting the director. The Commission could be instructed by the Secretary of State to take over certain responsibilities for supervising undertakings placed on the director by the Fair Trading Act 1973. Finally, the director was required to make available to the Commission any relevant information, and the Commission was required to supply the director with any information that it came across in relation to unregistered agreements that appeared to be registrable.

It can be seen from this outline of the framework and public interest criteria f competition policy in the United Kingdom that in each area of control – estrictive practices, resale prices, monopoly, merger and other prices – a resumption in favour of competition exists, with regulation very much a econd best. The concept of competition as a control mechanism is ideally remised on the existence of atomistic market structures and non-collusive on-discriminatory behaviour, since only in such conditions can a given erformance be confidently expected from a given structure. However, the roblem with this is that the development of capitalist economies tends to esult in increasing market and also aggregate or overall concentration. his has had two consequences. At the theoretical level the ideological ttraction of the concept of the invisible hand as control mechanism, for hose who oppose the development of conscious social control over resource llocation, has resulted in endless attempts to arrive at a definition of ompetition that is compatible with the realities of advanced capitalist conomies in which most industries are dominated by a handful of firms and . small number of giant firms dominate the economy as a whole. At the ractical level the failure of competition policy to produce an acceptable erformance has resulted in the development of industrial policy with very ittle theoretical underpinning.

NDUSTRIAL POLICY

_ike policy towards prices, industrial policy in the United Kingdom has been ubject to sharp discontinuities. The first cycle started with the establishment f the National Economic Development Council (NEDC) and industry conomic Development Councils (EDCs) in the early 1960s, spanned the rise nd fall of the National Plan in the mid 1960s and reached its most developed orm with the activities of the Industrial Reorganisation Corporation (IRC) n the late 1960s. The fundamental preoccupation of industrial policy with roductivity and the balance of payments is clearly evident in the work of the RC, which has described the way in which it sought to discharge its tatutory functions of 'promoting industrial efficiency and profitability and ssisting the economy of the United Kingdom or any part of the United Kingdom'[37] as follows:

> IRC's client is the national interest where this is identifiable. To this end
> IRC is continuously reviewing and refining its priorities for action against
> two overall criteria: the scope for improving productivity and the scope for
> improving the balance of payments.[38]

The IRC was disbanded in 1971 as part of the 1970 Conservative government's hort-lived policy of disengagement. However, the problems confronting British capitalism were so acute that disengagement, despite its ideological ttractions, did not last long. The second cycle of industrial policy in the United Kingdom started with the Conservative government's Industry Act 1972 nd was continued with the 1974 Labour government's Industry Act 1975, which set up the National Enterprise Board (NEB), and its Industrial Strategy, aunched in 1975.

344　　　　　　　　*An Introduction to Industrial Economics*

The Industry Acts 1972 and 1975
Under the Industry Act 1972 the Secretary of State is empowered to provid
selective financial assistance to promote employment in the assisted are
(section 7) or, more generally, to promote the national interest (section 8
Although there are similarities in the provisions of the two sections the discussio
in this chapter is primarily concerned with national selective financial assi
tance under section 8. Regional assistance is discussed in Chapter 11. Section
assistance may be provided where:

(a)　the financial assistance is likely to benefit the economy of the Unite
　　　Kingdom, or of any part or area of the United Kingdom, and
(b)　it is in the national interest that the financial assistance should be provide
　　　on the scale, and in the form and manner, proposed.[39]

Assistance may take any form, but the Secretary of State may not acquire shar
in a company without its consent. The amount that is available in the fir
instance for section 8 assistance is set at £600 million, but with the agreeme
of the House of Commons this may be raised by up to £250 million on fo
occasions to reach a maximum of £1,600 million.[40] There is a limit of £
million for assistance to any one project unless a larger sum is agreed t
the Commons.

　　The 1972 Act established an Industrial Development Advisory Board, whi
must include persons with experience in 'industry, banking, accounting ar
finance'.[41] The Board has the power to insist that its recommendation be p
before Parliament if the Secretary of State decides to disregard its advic
At the beginning of 1976 the Department of Industry published its *Criter
for Assistance to Industry*, which the Industrial Development Advisory Boar
accepted as guidance for determining its advice. The basic principle enshrin
in the criteria is that the cost of assistance to enable an enterprise or proje
to become viable, i.e. profitable, has to be weighed against any relevant soci
considerations, including employment, the balance of payments, rationalisatio
research, and sectors of industry that are of special significance to th
economy.[42]

　　The Industry Act 1975 established the NEB, created powers for th
Secretary of State to prevent or reverse the overseas ownership
manufacturing enterprises, provided for the disclosure of information relati
to manufacturing enterprises to ministers and trade unions, and repeal
certain restrictions on the Secretary of State's powers under the 1972 Act.
Section 3 of the 1975 Act enabled the Secretary of State to direct the NE
to exercise any of his powers under sections 7 and 8 of the 1972 Ac
The 1975 Act also gave statutory recognition to planning agreements. The
are voluntary agreements between an enterprise and the governme
concerning the strategic plans of the enterprise over a specified perio
Financial assistance included in a planning agreement is safeguarded again
future alterations in the provisions governing such assistance. Consultati
with the relevant unions is intended to be part of the process of drawing up
planning agreement, if necessary making use of the 1975 Act's provision f
disclosure of information.[44]

The National Enterprise Board

The purposes of the NEB are set out in the Industry Act 1975 as follows:

a) the development or assistance of the economy of the United Kingdom or any part of the United Kingdom;

b) the promotion in any part of the United Kingdom of industrial efficiency and international competitiveness; and

c) the provision, maintenance or safeguarding of productive employment in any part of the United Kingdom.[45]

The main activities of the NEB are to provide finance for industrial investment, particularly for the expansion or modernisation of manufacturing, to promote industrial restructuring and to act as a state holding company for shares transferred to it by the government or acquired on its own initiative. The NEB may also be directed by the Secretary of State to exercise any of his powers under sections 7 and 8 of the Industry Act 1972. Assistance is normally provided in the form of share capital, but loans and guarantees may also be made. The sum available to the NEB in the first instance is £700 million, but this may be increased to £1,000 million with the agreement of the House of Commons. The NEB is reimbursed by the secretary of state for any expenditure arising as a result of directions to exercise his section 7 or 8 powers.

The Secretary of State is empowered to give the NEB directions concerning the performance of its duties, and in December 1976 a general direction containing NEB guidelines was issued.[46] These guidelines, together with the relevant provision of the 1975 Act, set the framework within which the NEB must act. The NEB is required to inform or obtain the consent of the Secretary of State before acquiring shares, or making loans, involving more than £10 million, 30 per cent of voting strength, or significant new policy decisions. Approval is also required before disposing of shares. The Director-General of Fair Trading must be consulted before the NEB becomes involved in a merger qualifying for reference to the Monopolies and Merger Commission. NEB companies are not to be given an unfair competitive advantage, and the NEB must charge a commercial rate of interest on loans and generally obtain an adequate rate of return on capital employed, although taking a longer term view than private enterprises, as laid down in the Secretary of State's financial directions.[47] The NEB is required to submit to the Secretary of State an annual Corporate Plan setting out its strategy for the following year, and this strategy must take account of the government's overall industrial strategy.

Industrial Strategy

The 1974 Labour government's Industrial Strategy was launched at a meeting of the NEDC in November 1975. The NEDC – tripartite body bringing together the government, the Confederation of British Industry (CBI) and the Trades Union Congress (TUC) – agreed to the publication of a White Paper, *An Approach to Industrial Strategy,* as the basis for future work. The prime objective of the Industrial Strategy was to help transform the United

Kingdom into a 'high output–high wage economy . . . by improving our industrial performance and raising the growth of our productive potential'.[48] A national strategy for industry was seen as involving:

(i) the better co-ordination of policies affecting the efficiency of industry. This will require us to identify the industrial implications of the whole range of Government policies. The feed-back of information from planning agreements with companies will be of particular value in this respect.

(ii) the more effective use of the instruments of industrial policy and the deployment of financial assistance to industry. Both planning agreements and the NEB will be important here.

(iii) ensuring that industry, both public and private, is able to earn sufficient profits on its investment to spur managements to expand and innovate and to provide them with the internal finance on which to base investment. Adequate sources of external funds are also vital: some will be provided through the National Enterprise Board and some through Finance for Industry, but it will also be essential that the market should be able to meet the needs of industry.

(iv) a more effective manpower policy, including measures to provide a better supply of skilled manpower for growth industries and to cope with the human problems of people transferring from contracting to expanding industries. Training and retraining will be crucial here, both in coping with the problems of the present recession and in enabling people to meet the needs of a re-oriented British industry. The Manpower Services Commission (MSC) and its agencies will have an important part in this.

(v) the improvement in planning, both in industry and by Government, which will flow from systematic and continuing tripartite discussion of the likely prospects of individual industries, allied to greater disclosure of information at company level, particularly, but not exclusively, in planning agreements.[49]

The approach to a strategy was to be transformed into an actual strategy in three stages. First, the NEDC would identify the industries or sectors that it considered to be the most important for the achievement of the strategy's objective. Next the individual industry EDCs or, where these did not exist, newly formed Sector Working Parties (SWPs), would undertake detailed analyses of the particular problems and possibilities of their industry or sector and recommend appropriate action to overcome the problems and realise the possibilities. Finally, the results of the detailed EDC or SWP discussions would be pulled together as a basis for general discussion and a means of influencing government policies. The approach to industrial strategy was, in effect, to promote discussion at industry level in order to stimulate action at that level and also to feed information upwards to help the government to assess its policies and determine its priorities. Thus:

When these proposals have been put into practice, the Government will be in a position to examine the problems of a wide range of industries and companies against a coherent framework. In playing its part in helping to deal with the problems the Government will use the whole range of its powers. It will be able to frame its general economic policies so as to take account more systematically of the needs of industry. The NEB will be able to provide finance for companies in key sectors. Selective financial assistance will be used to encourage and assist viable projects and the sectoral discussions should enable appropriate schemes, like those already adopted for the ferrous foundaries, machine tools, clothing, and textile industries to be developed. Public purchasing policies will be used constructively in order to develop the export potential of appropriate industries. The MSC and its agencies will have a major role to play in both meeting the needs of growth sectors for suitable trained manpower and in easing the problems arising from industries shedding labour. All those instruments must come into play immediately wherever they are appropriate. The Government is confident that they will make a still more valuable contribution to the necessary improvement of our industrial performance as the new strategy develops. But the main responsibilities will be with both sides of industry in the sectors and firms involved.[50]

It is difficult from this account of the relevant legislation and institutions to identify any clear operational criteria relating to industrial policy in the UK in 1978. In the provision of selective financial assistance virtually everything seemed to depend on the discretion of the Secretary of State or the NEB, and in general no reasons were given for the decisions made. In principle the Industrial Strategy might have been expected to provide guidance, but in fact it had not done and did not seem likely to do so, as is evident from the discussion in section 9.4.

9.3 COMPETITION POLICY

This section discusses the different areas of competition policy and considers some of the issues that have arisen in relation to them. The order of discussion is the same as that in the previous section, namely, restrictive practices, resale price maintenance, monopoly, merger and other prices.

RESTRICTIVE PRACTICES[51]

By the end of 1977 the Restrictive Practices Court had considered thirty-five contested agreements containing restrictions relating to goods and had found eleven of these not contrary to the public interest.[52] There remained on the Register of Restrictive Trading Agreements 428 agreements relating to goods that contained operative restrictions. Of these, in addition to the 11 found not contrary to the public interest, 187 had been subject to directions that enabled them to continue without being referred to the Court, 67 had been the subject of notices of reference to the Court and about 100 looked as if they would probably not need to be referred. Thus, there remained something like 60 agreements relating to goods for which the probable course of action had yet to be decided. Agreements relating to services became registrable for the first time in October 1976, and by the end of 1977 there were 206 such agreements on the register with the process of registration continuing. At that date twelve services agreements had been subject to direction enabling them to continue without reference to the Court, and no services agreement had yet been brought before the Court.[53]

In the contested goods hearings before the Court, gateway (b) – that the restriction conferred a specific and substantial benefit on the public – was pleaded in eight of the eleven successful cases: black bolts and nuts, cement, magnets, metal windows, net books, scrap iron, tiles and fish. Of the remaining three successful cases: sulphuric acid was originally allowed under (d) – necessary to obtain fair terms – and subsequently confirmed under (b); water tube boilers was allowed under (f) – of benefit to exports; and Scottish daily newspapers was allowed under (h) – not likely to discourage competition. In addition to the eleven successful agreements, which passed both a gateway and the tailpiece, one agreement, namely, yarn spinners, was allowed through (e) – necessary to prevent serious and persistent local unemployment – but failed to pass the balancing act of the tailpiece.[54] Supplementary restrictions have been allowed under (g) – necessary to maintain an agreement found not contrary to the public interest – in seven of the eleven successful cases. Overwhelmingly, firms wishing to maintain a restrictive agreement have chosen to argue gateway (b) before the Court, followed a long way behind by (f) and (d). In interpreting Table 9.1, which summarises the position, it should be remembered that more than one gateway has often been argued with respect to the same agreement.

It is impossible to discuss all the successful cases in any detail, let alone the unsuccessful ones. However, before considering some of the general issues that

Table 9.1 *Gateways argued before the Restrictive Practices Court, to end 1977.*

Gateway	Times argued	Times successful
(a) Protection of the public against injury	3	0
(b) Conferring specific and substantial benefit	32	9
(c) Counteracting other restrictive measures	1	0
(d) Necessary to obtain fair terms	6[a]	1
(e) Prevention of local unemployment	3	1
(f) Prevention of reduction in exports	8	1
(h) Not likely to discourage competition	1	1

Source: Registrar of Restrictive Trading Agreements, *Report of the Registrar, 7 August 1956 to 31 December 1959,* Cmnd 1273 (London, HMSO, 1961); *1 January 1960 to 30 June 1961,* Cmnd 1603 (1962); *1 July 1961 to 30 June 1963,* Cmnd 2246 (1964); *1 July 1963 to 30 June 1966,* Cmnd 3188 (1967); *1 July 1966 to 30 June 1969,* Cmnd 4303 (1970); and *1 July 1969 to 30 June 1972,* Cmnd 5195 (1973). Also Director-General of Fair Trading, *Annual Report for the Period November 1973 to December 1974,* HC 370 (London, HMSO, 1975).

Note:
(a) Argued twice with respect to the same agreement.

arise from a detailed scrutiny of the Court's deliberations, the judgement in one of the later major cases, i.e. fish, is now outlined in order to give some flavour of the Court's reasoning.

The Distant Water Vessels Development Association Judgement

This case concerned a reserve price scheme operated by the Distant Water Vessels Development Association which fixed minimum prices for the sale by auction at certain ports of specified categories of fish caught in distant waters. The Association sought to justify the agreement under gateway (*b*), arguing that if it were ended higher long-run prices would result, thus depriving the public as purchasers and consumers of a specific and substantial benefit. Special features of the white fish industry were adduced in support of the claim. While supply and demand were broadly in balance, there being no excess catching capacity, landings of fish fluctuated greatly not merely on a seasonal basis but also from day to day. This irregularity of supply assumed a particular importance due to the highly perishable nature of the commodity, which had to be sold immediately on landing. The demand for fish at the auction was relatively price inelastic, so that on days of heavy landings sharp falls in prices would produce little increase in sales. Although there existed at the ports processing capacity for filleting and freezing, this was limited, and it would be uneconomic to extend capacity to cope with days of heavy landings since it would be idle for much of the time.

In these circumstances, it was argued, the purpose of the scheme was to maintain revenue from fish sales at a higher level than it would otherwise have been, since without the reserve price days of heavy landings would result in uneconomically low prices. Of course, the fall in price would constitute a gain, not a loss, of benefit to the public, but the Association argued that the fall in the general level of prices would result in losses or reduced profitability and a loss of confidence such that trawler owners would run down their fleets. The resultant reduction in supply would cause an increase in price, which, persisting in the long run, would more than outweigh the benefit of lower prices in the short run.

In its judgement the Restrictive Practices Court considered that the abolition of reserve prices would lead immediately to a substantial fall in auction prices and that the demand for fish in the long run, as in the short, was relatively price inelastic. The reserve prices were determined annually by the Association's Development Committee subject to three limitations: that the general reserve prices for codfish and haddock must not exceed 85 per cent of the average auction prices in the previous three years; that the average of the reserve prices plus the average government subsidy must not exceed 85 per cent of the average cost of catching and selling the fish in the previous three years; and that the White Fish Authority must be consulted. The Court found that these safeguards, although somewhat arbitrary, achieved their purpose of providing an assurance of good faith and moderation in the fixing of reserve prices and that in any case there was evidence that it was the actual and potential competition facing the distant water vessels that effectively imposed limits on the reserve prices.

Given that revenue would fall in the absence of reserve prices, would this or any concomitant loss of confidence cause a reduction in catching capacity? The Registrar of Restrictive Trading Agreements argued that the five major groups, which between them accounted for over 80 per cent of the distant water catch and had substantial outside interests in merchanting, would do nothing that was likely to cause a shortage of the fish on which their merchanting interests depended and that they had the financial strength to maintain and modernise their fleets. The Court, however, accepted that there would be a substantial reduction in catching capacity resulting from the abolition of the reserve prices. It also considered that the shortage of supply envisaged would not be made up by imports except at prices substantially higher than those currently prevailing and, hence, that the prospective reduction in the catching capacity of the British trawler fleet would usher in a continuing era of substantially higher prices:

> Finally, the Court, having weighed the ultimate continuing higher average price level against the immediate substantially lower price level, decided that the benefit to the public from the avoidance of the former was properly to be described as substantial. The Court therefore held that the restrictions involved in the reserve price scheme were in the public interest.[55]

Some Central Questions

In examining the decisions of the Restrictive Practices Court economists have tended to single out a number of inter-related issues for discussion. The major preoccupation has been the consideration of the way in which the Court has interpreted the concept of 'competition' and the attitude that it has adopted towards the relationship between competition and co-operation. Central to this interest has been an analysis of the Court's view of the problems arising from the existence of uncertainty and the quest for information and/or security.[56] In the case of cement the Court found that the existence of a fixed price agreement resulted in a lower price level than would otherwise have been the case, since the greater security enabled capital for new investment to be raised at a return that was below that which would have been necessary had free competition prevailed. In the cases of magnets and metal windows the Court found that minimum price agreements were on balance necessary in order to ensure the continuation of beneficial exchanges of cost information and technical co-operation. With respect to the former agreement the benefit took the form of substantial technical progress, resulting in improved magnets; with respect to the latter it took the form of substantial cost reductions, leading to lower prices as a result of the enhanced competitive position of the parties to the agreement *vis-à-vis* a powerful independent manufacturer.

The question raised in the literature in relation to all three cases is whether the price agreement was necessary to achieve the benefit established. Both the cement and metal windows industries were dominated by a single oligopolist – Associated Portland Cement Manufacturers (APCM) making 62 per cent of UK deliveries of cement, and Crittalls having 43 per cent of the market for metal windows – and it has been argued that in the event of the abandonment of the price agreement the most likely outcome would have been a situation of price leadership. Similarly, it has been argued that it is not obvious why the ending of the price agreement in the magnet industry would have resulted in an end to technical co-operation; co-operation might, indeed, have become more beneficial in such circumstances.

The controversy over these three cases has centred on the 'positive' question of the analysis of business behaviour and the effect of different arrangements on certain dimensions of performance accepted as being in the public interest, namely, lower prices and technical progress. Other cases have involved, in addition to such 'positive' questions, 'normative' questions as to what is to count as being in the public interest. In the case of tiles, for instance, the Court accepted that a system of fixed prices enabled size standardisation, which resulted in substantial cost economies, which were largely passed on in the form of lower prices. On considering any offsetting detriments:

> The Court accepted that standardization of production must involve some restriction on freedom of choice and that this was to some extent detrimental. However, the Court found that in this case the detriment related only to freedom of choice as to size, not as to quality, colour or finish, and that this was much less important than the advantages the public gained as a result of the economies stemming from standardization.[57]

The 'normative' element was paramount in the cases of nuts and bolts and net books. The Court sustained a fixed price agreement between forty-four manu-facturers, accounting for the supply of about 90 per cent of black bolts and nuts, despite the fact that price levels were found to be marginally higher as a result, on the grounds that the agreement saved customers the inconvenience and expense of 'shopping around'. In the case of the net book agreement the Court found that, if the agreement ceased to operate, fewer books would be published and that:

> . . . inevitably, we think, the effects would be most severe in the higher reaches of literature. The new author with something important to say, the scholar with new knowledge to communicate, the poet or the artist seeking to bring more beauty into the world, the philosopher desiring to increase under-standing and illumine the minds of those who will read what he writes; these, we think, are the writers who would find it harder to get their work accepted for publication. In the more hazardous conditions that the termination of the agreement would create, many of them might not find publishers at all. We cannot doubt that this would deny to the reading public specific and substantial benefits.[58]

Many economists, as might be expected, have argued that the Court was mistaken in holding that books are different from any other commodity and was wrong to impose its own value judgement. Even when recognising the legitimacy of making decisions on the basis of value judgements, there is a tendency to persist with the mistaken view that such decisions may conflict with the 'principles of economic efficiency', as if these 'principles' were not themselves derived from value judgements.[59] It makes for greater clarity to recognise that what is involved is not a clash between economic efficiency and a value judgement but a clash between two different sets of value judgements.

After reviewing the work of the Court as a whole Sutherland has drawn some general conclusions about the characteristics of successful cases. He has noted that, in the cases concerning manufacturing industries, the agreements that were successful were usually in industries with a considerable degree of oligopoly and a long history of joint action. He has further noted that there was a tendency for successful cases to be presented positively, in the sense that the agreements were claimed to result directly in the public being better off, rather than negatively, in the sense of claiming that the abandonment of the agreement would have adverse effects on the producers, which would result indirectly in the public being worse off.[60] Hunter has argued that three categories of criteria making for success were discernible: lower prices, superior technology and convenience or value judgements about the public interest. He has suggested that lower prices were usually present, even when they were not regarded as the dominant benefit, and that superior technology was often seen as resulting in lower prices. Hunter has also isolated a number of 'ameliorative' factors: 'reasonable' prices in relation to costs, 'reasonable' profitability, 'reasonable' conduct by way of the exchange of information or the adoption of an 'objective' procedure for setting prices, and intensive competition – factors that, although in themselves not enough to save a restriction, were none the less influential at the tailpiece stage.[61] Leyland has set out a 'set of tests for adequate business performance' – namely, profits, cost–price relationships, cost structure, capacity–output relationships, buyer–seller relationships, entry conditions, general progressiveness – and has concluded that, while all the dimensions were examined in one or other case, they were not each examined in every case.[62]

The Court's Economic Model

One theme running through the literature has been the attempt to construct an economic model in terms of which the individual decisions of the Restrictive Practices Court can be exhibited as part of a coherent and consistent whole. The most ambitious exercise in this direction has been undertaken by Brock, who has summarised her conclusion as follows:

> . . . the competitive process is one in which the efficient firms undercut their rivals and force the inefficient firms out of the industry by selling goods at lower prices and capturing the market. If it is profitable, the firms will often undertake cooperative projects, for example in research, even when competing in this way. The firm's demand curve is usually considerably price elastic, and, in analysing the market, price is by far the most important variable to consider. The competition just sketched does not depend, as in Robinsonian or Chamberlinian theory, on having a large number of firms in the industry; it is likely to apply even with a few large firms. There is little discussion of the role of new entry in this economic model.
>
> With this arrangement, prices will be brought into equilibrium by the free workings of supply and demand at such a level as to cover costs (although there may be disequilibrium periods where this will not happen) and allow

a small percentage for profit. Long-run investment in innovatory equipment and research will continue at an optimum rate. This organization of industry will best promote the public interest in both the short- and long-run.[63]

While Brock has regarded this as an adequate account of the Court's attitude in the first seventeen cases, she has considered that later judgements rendered things less clearcut. In particular she has detected the development of a much greater willingness to recognise the frequent need to restrict price competition to enable co-operation – a development clearly welcomed by her.

Virtually all commentators have noted a discontinuity in the Court's judgements, some dating the changed emphasis from the thirteenth case, i.e. cement, in 1961 and some from the eighteenth case, i.e. magnets, a year later. Not all, however, have welcomed the change:

> ... one cannot forbear to contrast the emphasis on short-term, circumstantial solutions (notably in the *Net Books* decision but also in *Glazed and Floor Tiles* and the *Standard Metal Window Group* cases) with the attention given in early decisions to long-term economic considerations. In the *Yarn Spinners* case, confronted by an intrinsically difficult choice between equity and economic efficiency (between assisting local unemployment and permitting free competition to re-allocate resources) the Court took the view that the long-run competitive efficiency of the economy was the more important consideration and eventually, more beneficial for the ultimate consumer. To a lesser degree the early *Scottish Bread Agreements,* the *Chemists Federation* and *Associated Transformer Manufacturers* agreements demonstrated the same determination to rely on competition as the method of shaping trends in the industry concerned and the economy as a whole. Regrettably, later decisions appear to have drifted away from these objectives.[64]

The extraordinary persistence of the presumption in favour of competition has yet again been illustrated by Hunter's rather mournful summing up, which will serve to end this brief consideration of the attempts made to construct the Court's economic model:

> In sum, restriction is as good as competition providing there is evidence offered to show that it confers a specific and substantial benefit (or can meet the requirements of an exemption gateway). The presumptive superiority of competition after an ephemeral existence ... has gradually disappeared from the Court's doctrines to be replaced by a pragmatic weighing of circumstantial advantage and detriment.[65]

Justiciability

There has been a good deal of discussion in the literature as to whether it is appropriate for the process of examining restrictive practices from the standpoint of the public interest to be conducted by means of a judicial procedure. The general conclusion arrived at by economists and also by many lawyers has been that the issues involved are not 'justiciable', for two main reasons. First, the 'positive' issues of economic analysis have been said to be too complex;

the evaluation of alternative economic models and the conduct of hypothetical argumentation about the future course of events are unlikely to be competently undertaken by laymen in a legal setting. Second, it has been argued that the 'normative' issues relating to the interpretation of what is to count as the public interest are essentially political questions, to be decided in the usual political way. Of course, if it were possible for the law to be framed in a way that embodied clear principles that were susceptible to consistent and predictable application, a court would presumably be an appropriate body and would be able to develop a body of precedent and guarantee a large measure of certainty and stability in its judgements. However, it is precisely this possibility that has frequently been denied.

It is clear from the discussion in the first two sections of this chapter that policy in the United Kingdom has developed on extremely pragmatic lines. The general presumption in favour of competition that is apparently present in the Restrictive Trade Practices Act 1956 seems to have been seized upon by the Restrictive Practices Court as the basis for its interpretation of what is to count as the public interest in its early judgements relating to gateway (*b*) and in the balancing act of the tailpiece. However, in its later judgements, as suggested above, the Court appears to have returned to the highly pragmatic philosophy informing the mainstream of British policy in this area. It is the alleged absence of a strong, almost over-riding, presumptive principle in favour of competition that has underlain the attacks on justiciability. Once recourse is made to pragmatic *'ad hoccery'*, problems multiply:

> Not all criteria can be known in advance mainly because insufficient work has been done to evaluate the performance of free competition, or collaboration, in respect of these phenomena. The strength of the value judgements attaching to the various criteria would continue to turn largely on questions of fact in particular situations rather than on general rules.[66]

In summary, the argument against the justiciability of the issues dealt with by the Court is that a court is not an appropriate body to judge performance. The courts in the United States are able to operate effectively because of the *per se* rule; that is, they are called upon to judge structure and conduct, not performance. However, perhaps the argument should really be directed against any attempt to judge performance on the basis of the currently conventional view as to what the relevant 'positive' and 'normative' issues are. While the Court may leave much to be desired it is not obvious why any remotely likely alternative body would do any better, or any worse.

The Effects of the Legislation

A consideration of how effective the legislation has been must cover two stages: the effect on the number of agreements in operation, and the effect of any abandonment of agreements on the performance of the economy. As to the first stage, at the end of 1977 over 95 per cent of goods agreements on the Register of Restrictive Trading Agreements had either been terminated or were not likely to require consideration by the Restrictive Practices Court. Virtually all those that remained were almost certain to be abandoned, the last contested case having been in 1972. However, experience has shown that not all registrable agreements are in fact registered, and for this and other reasons enforcement activity is necessary. In the 1960s fines totalling £102,000 were imposed on eight members of the Galvanised Tank Manufacturers' Association for contempt of Court resulting from the breach of an undertaking given in an undefended case, and eight firms were each fined £10,000 for contempt stemming from the making of an agreement to the like effect of one condemned in the tyre manufacturers' case. More recently, in the late 1970s, investigations by the Monopolies and Mergers Commission and the Director-General of Fair Trading unearthed unregistered agreements relating to diazo copying materials, flour and bread, electric cable and ready-mixed concrete, which were largely in the form of unwritten understandings.[67] It is difficult to estimate how widespread illegal evasion is; but Swann *et al.,* on the basis of the detailed case studies outlined below, have referred to 'a fair amount of unregistered collusion' and suggested that 'a great many' of the information agreements ostensibly abandoned when such agreements were made registrable in 1968 'have simply gone underground'.[68]

As to the second stage, i.e. the effect of the ending of restrictive agreements on the performance of the economy, the position is also problematic. Soon after the legislation was introduced Heath conducted a questionnaire inquiry into the short term consequences of agreements abandoned up to mid 1959.[69] No clearcut conclusions emerged, although Heath has judged that there had been some consumer gain resulting from lower prices. Few mergers were found to have been closely related to the ending of agreements, but it was pointed out that merger was likely to be a long term, not a short term, consequence. In fact Newbould has subsequently argued that pressure on restrictive agreements by increasing uncertainty did contribute to the increase in merger activity.[70] Heath's principal finding was that information agreements had commonly re-placed restrictive agreements – a phenomenon eventually recognised when such agreements were brought within the scope of the legislation in 1968.

The major study of the effects of the restrictive practices legislation is that carried out between 1969 and 1971 by Swann *et al.,* based on forty case studies: eighteen major and twenty-two minor.[71] The studies consisted of general interviews with the agencies that were responsible for operating com-petition policy, the collection of background information for each case study and intensive interviews with firms and customers in each industry, plus a supplementary questionnaire where necessary. Swann *et al.* have first assessed the shorter run effects. In four of the thirty-four industries in which agreements were terminated competition was already increasing. In another fourteen or possibly seventeen industries competition was judged to have increased as a result of the termination. The assessment of the longer run effects of the legislation proved more difficult. In many industries competition continued to operate, and certain additional industries became more competitive when in-formation agreements became registrable in 1968. Of course, increased competition might have been due to factors other than the ending of restrictive agreements; for example, innovation was judged to have been an important stimulus to increased competition in about one-third of the industries. On the other hand, clear countertendencies towards various forms of collusion were evident, and merger had been important in the post-termination history of many industries. One interesting side result of the case studies was the opportunity to compare predictions made at the time of Court hearings with what subsequently happened. In virtually all cases predictions that dire consequences would follow the termination of an agreement – most frequently that quality would be debased – had not in fact been fulfilled. The general conclusion of Swann *et al.* is that:

> The Act can . . . be judged to have improved resource allocation, however incompletely, and to have done very little real harm. At the same time it must be clear that although the Act has gone *some* way along the path of improving resource allocation in most of the industries we have studied, a very great deal indeed remains to be done.[72]

The study by Swann *et al.* is clearly committed to the overall beneficial consequences of competition. It has, however, been argued that the restrictive practices legislation may be an obstacle to joint action in the national interest under the auspices of SWPs, as discussed in section 9.4 on industrial policy.[73]

RESALE PRICE MAINTENANCE

Under the Resale Prices Act 1964 suppliers wishing to continue with individual resale-price maintenance were obliged to register the relevant class of good and could then continue the practice until the Restrictive Practices Court had decided whether the class should be exempted from the general prohibition. About 500 classes were identified and registered, and these were then divided or combined into 157 references to be brought before the Court, consisting of subclasses, classes or groups of classes of goods. Eventually, only three cases were proceeded with, and by the end of June 1972 all these had been dealt with by the Court. In neither of the first two cases heard by the Court – chocolate and sugar confectionery, and footwear – was exemption granted, although in the course of them all five gateways were pleaded. However, in the third case, i.e. medicaments, exemption was granted on the grounds that for 'ethicals' the abolition of resale price maintenance would result in a substantial reduction in goods available – gateway (*a*) – and in necessary services (*e*) and that for 'proprietaries' it would result in a substantial reduction in the number of retail establishments (*b*). The only other exemption order related to books, under the section of the 1976 Act that provided that the Court might treat as conclusive any findings made under the restrictive trade practices Acts unless evidence of changed circumstances was given. In the event the Registrar of Restrictive Trading Agreements decided not to offer any evidence; so the exemption order was automatic.

Although resale price maintenance is now virtually a thing of the past in Britain, the practice of publicising recommended prices has been widely substituted. A report by the Monopolies Commission in 1969, *Recommended Resale Prices,* has concluded that this practice had different effects in different industries and did not always operate against the public interest. Not surprisingly, the Commission has suggested that a case-by-case review was merited. In 1973 agreements relating to recommended prices were made registrable and became subject to proceedings before the Court.[74]

MONOPOLY[75]

The Monopolies and Mergers Commission may be asked to investigate dominant firm situations in the supply of goods, restrictions on the supply of services other than those contained in registrable agreements, general practices of an uncompetitive character, and mergers. Dominant firm situations are defined as situations in which a single firm accounts for at least one-quarter of the reference goods in question. They have covered virtual monopoly (e.g. Pilkington producing 91 per cent by value of the reference goods involved) and various types of oligopoly (e.g. Unilever, 44 per cent and Procter and Gamble, 46 per cent; Imperial Tobacco, 63·5 per cent, Gallaher, almost 30 per cent and some twenty-three minute fringe firms). Although dominant firms may engage in restrictive practices – indeed, oligopolistic collusion of one sort or another is widely observed – since 1956 restrictive agreements have been within the jurisdiction of the Restrictive Practices Court, not the Monopolies and Mergers Commission or its predecessor.

By the end of 1977 the Commission had published seventy-six reports, excluding those relating to mergers. The first phase of its work dealt mainly with references involving restrictive agreements. Of the twenty-one reports completed prior to the Commission's reconstruction in 1956, eighteen dealt with such agreements, although six of these were in oligopolistic industries: electric lamps, insulin, pneumatic tyres, rubber footwear, electrical and allied machinery, and electronic valves; and a further four were agreements dominated by a single firm: dental goods (Amalgamated Dental), insulated electric cables (British Insulated Callender's Cables), calico printing (Calico Printers Association) and metal windows and doors (Crittalls). There was also a general report on collective discrimination, which led to the first Restrictive Trade Practices Act in 1956. In this first phase only two inquiries were concerned with dominant-firm monopoly situations: matches (British Match), and industrial and medical gases (British Oxygen).

From the 1956 reconstruction to the end of 1977 the Commission published fifty-five reports, of which four were on general references, nineteen related to services of one sort or another and thirty were on dominant firm situations in the supply of goods.[76] The dominant firm reports, together with the firms involved, were: chemical fertilisers (Imperial Chemical Industries, Potash, Fisons, British Basic Slag); cigarettes and tobacco (Imperial Tobacco, Molins); electrical equipment for land vehicles (Lucas, Smith, Chloride, Champion); wallpaper (Wall Paper Manufacturers); colour film (Kodak); electrical wiring harnesses (Lucas); cinema films (Rank, Associated British Picture Corporation); household detergents (Unilever, Procter and Gamble); infant milk foods (Glaxo, Cow and Gate); flat glass (Pilkington); cellulosic fibres (Courtaulds); electric lamps (Thorn); clutch mechanisms for road vehicles (Automotive Products); cigarette filter rods (Cigarette Components); metal containers (Metal Box); starch, glucoses and modified starches (Brown and Polson); asbestos (Turner and Newall); chlordiazepoxide and diazepam

(Hoffman–La Roche); footwear machinery (British United Shoe Machinery); breakfast cereals (Kelloggs); wire and fibre ropes (British Rope); primary batteries (Ever Ready, Mallory); plasterboard (British Plaster Board); contraceptive sheaths (London Rubber); building bricks (London Brick); frozen foods (Unilever); electrostatic reprographic equipment (Rank-Xerox); diazo copying materials (Ozalid); cat and dog foods (Mars, Spillers); and flour and bread (Associated British Foods, Rank-Hovis-MacDougal, Spillers). Thus, by the end of 1977 there had been thirty-two·reports on references relating to goods supplied under monopoly conditions by dominant firms, involving forty-six firms in all.

The investigations carried out by the Commission have been detailed, have normally taken several years and have usually resulted in fairly sizable reports. As in the previous section, before considering some of the general issues that arise an account is now given of a major report on a dominant firm.

Metal Containers

The report[77] was published two years and four months after receipt of a reference from the Board of Trade into the supply of metal containers. The Monopolies Commission was asked to investigate and report on whether monopoly conditions as defined in the 1948 Act prevailed; and if so, first, what things were done as a result of or to preserve those conditions and, second, whether the conditions or the things done operated or might be expected to operate against the public interest. The first chapter of the report sets out the general dimensions of the industry.

It was found appropriate to classify the reference goods into metal containers of three types:

(1) open top type, mainly for thermally processed foods, supplied with one open end, which is closed by seaming on a top after filling;
(2) general line type, with some kind of ordinary lid or cap; and
(3) aerosol containers, with a plastic valve assembly to be sealed on after filling.

In all three markets the Metal Box Co. Ltd. was dominant, accounting in 1968 for approximately 77 per cent by value of total UK sales. Imports of reference goods were negligible. Metal Box had extremely close relationships with Continental Can – the second-largest US can manufacturer. Competition in the industry was found to come from two sources. In the first place, each of the three types of container was supplied by at least one firm in addition to Metal Box. The major competitor in each category was, respectively, Reads Ltd, Clover Can Co. Ltd and Crown Cork Co. Ltd, all three of which, as it happened, were owned or controlled by American companies. In the second place, competition, both actual and potential, came from those can users which themselves manufactured or possessed the ability to manufacture metal containers. In 1968 this 'self-manufacture' by users accounted for some 12·5 per cent of the potential UK market for reference goods.

Chapter 2 of the report provides a detailed description of the historical development and current position and practice of the dominant firm – Metal Box. Such surveys have become established features of the procedure of the

Commission. Chapter 3 provides briefer descriptions of the other producers, both manufacturers/users and specialist manufacturers. In Chapters 4 and 5 two aspects of Metal Box's market behaviour are set out: its complex pricing practice, and its practice with respect to the supply of closing machines. Costs, profits and productivity are considered in Chapter 6. The case for Metal Box is given in Chapter 7, and in the final chapter the Commission presents its conclusions and recommendations.

Monopoly conditions clearly existed in that Metal Box supplied over one-third of the reference goods. However, the Commission concluded that these conditions in themselves neither operated nor might be expected to operate against the public interest. In arriving at this conclusion the following considerations were held to be relevant:

(1) Metal Box had achieved a satisfactory balance between capacity and demand such that excess capacity had been avoided while adequate capacity to meet long term growth and short term fluctuation had been installed. Furthermore, a reasonable compromise had been struck between decentralised production to minimise transport costs and concentrated production to exploit scale economies.
(2) The firm was found to have a good record of innovation, to possess a progressive and efficient management and to have achieved on balance an above average improvement in productivity. Thus, it enjoyed costs that were as low as could reasonably be expected.
(3) Metal Box's rate of profit had been consistently at a substantially higher level than the average for manufacturing industry in general – e.g. in 1968, 18·4 per cent compared with 14·3 per cent, calculated on a depreciated historic cost basis. However, this was not considered surprising for an efficient manufacturer in a growth industry, and profits were not regarded as having been excessive.

Although Metal Box's dominant position was not found to be against the public interest in itself, certain 'things done' were held to be objectionable. The firm's pricing arrangements for its open top cans involved a basic price list plus a complex scheme of discounts and rebates. It was claimed that these were designed to encourage large standardised steady orders, thus facilitating long runs, planned production and full capacity working. In general the Commission accepted that the prices charged to different customers were in line with costs and that the differential price structure did not create obstacles to competition not based on advantages accruing from scale and efficiency. However, discounts or rebates based on exclusive or fixed proportion purchases and long-term buying agreements in excess of two years were regarded as objectionable in that they were not related to cost differences and had the effect of discouraging buyers from using alternative sources of supply. On similar grounds Metal Box's aerosol 'incentive' scheme, which provided for a 1 per cent discount if the level of the previous year's purchases was maintained, was held to be objectionable.

The remaining 'thing done' to which the Commission objected related to the supply of closing machines by Metal Box. Until 1969 such machines had been hired to users at uneconomic rentals, with free spare parts and servicing, under agreements that precluded their use for closing cans other than those purchased from Metal Box. After a decade in which this formal restriction had been increasingly relaxed in practice, a new form of agreement was introduced based on economic rentals, economic charges for spare parts and servicing and no restrictions as to use. However, as an 'interim' measure to ease the transition to the new arrangements a special rebate on can purchase, not to exceed in total the machine rental, was introduced for those hiring closing machines. This rebate was found to be objectionable in that it was unrelated to cost and calculated indirectly to reduce the customer's freedom of action.

Following on from its conclusions the Commission recommended that exclusive or fixed-proportion purchase discounts, buying agreements in excess of two years, the aerosol 'incentive' discount and the discount to closing machine hirers should all be discontinued.

The Commission's Conclusions and Recommendations

The report on metal containers is fairly typical of the approach adopted by the Monopolies and Mergers Commission and its predecessors in dominant firm inquiries. The structure of the industry or market is examined to decide whether monopoly conditions exist and the behaviour or conduct of the firm(s) involved is set out. The performance of the firm(s) is then studied and the public interest question decided.

When attempting to assess the work of the Commission, in this area it is necessary to bear in mind the issues raised in section 9.1. In the absence of any coherent theoretical framework the Commission has necessarily adopted a pragmatic *ad hoc* approach, with the attendant dangers of arbitrariness and inconsistency. This has been very clearly demonstrated in a study by Sutherland of the major reports published between August 1965 and November 1968.

The relevant part of Sutherland's survey examined the Commission's reports on colour film, flat glass and man-made cellulosic fibres. Of the three firms involved, Kodak and Courtaulds were found to occupy a dominant position that was in itself contrary, and/or to engage in practices that were contrary, to the public interest, while Pilkington was given a clean bill of health. Sutherland has reviewed the structural position, the behaviour and the performance of the three firms, as reported by the Commission, in an attempt to discover the reasons for the different conclusions reached as to the public interest. His general conclusion is that there was insufficient difference in the factual findings to justify the Commission's view that nothing in Pilkington's position and practice was contrary to the public interest, whereas aspects of Courtaulds' and Kodak's were. The explanation of the inconsistency, he has suggested, was partly that the analysis was less rigorous in the case of Pilkington and partly that the Commission appeared to adopt different attitudes to the relative importance of structure and behaviour. He has particularly criticised the significance attached to managerial attitudes in the case of the family firm, Pilkington:

> . . . the public interest is affected rather more by the performance, such as the non-linking of price to cost . . . and the high level of profits in a low

risk situation . . . than by the fact that management 'is conscious of its responsibility, as a monopolist, to the public interest.'[78]

The possibility of inconsistency, however, has not been the principal difficulty; in fact the Pilkington decision was the only major inconsistency detected by Sutherland. The real problem has been the absence of any settled framework in terms of which to assess the public interest. A review of the conclusions and recommendations of the Commission shows that in practice it has come very close to concentrating exclusively on behaviour, with certain practices regarded as virtually *per se* contrary to the public interest.

The Commission was called upon to reach a conclusion as to the public interest in sixty-six of the seventy-six references reported on by end-1977, the other ten references not requiring judgement about specific cases. Five cases relating to agreements or service cartels and four relating to dominant firms (Pilkington, Cigarette Components, Brown and Polson, Mars/Spillers) were found to have no features contrary to the public interest. In only five cases was the monopoly position of a dominant firm found in itself to be objectionable (British Match, British Oxygen, Rank, Courtaulds, London Rubber). All the remaining fifty-two cases were found to have objectionable features in the form only of 'things done', either agreements or (common) practices. There were twenty-one cases relating to dominant firms in which, although 'things done' that were contrary to the public interest were found, no objection was raised to the monopoly position in itself.[79] Furthermore, in several of the cases relating to restrictive agreements, although aspects of the agreement were held to be objectionable, the monopoly position of a simultaneously existing dominant firm was not regarded as contrary to the public interest – e.g. dental goods (Amalgamated Dental), pneumatic tyres and rubber footwear (Dunlop), electrical and allied machinery (Associated Electrical Industries) and metal windows and doors (Crittalls).

From their reports the general position of the Monopolies and Mergers Commission and its predecessors can be inferred as follows. First, deliberately anticompetitive behaviour, especially in the form of artificial restraints on competition such as exclusive dealing and other entry-stopping conduct, has consistently been condemned. Although discriminatory pricing of various sorts has often been condemned, it has not always been. However, restrictions on the sale of competitors' goods, various forms of discount, bonus and rebate schemes designed to disadvantage potential competitors, tie-in sales, full-line forcing, and other practices that seek to foreclose part of the market, have invariably been criticised by the Commission. The same is true for other forms of anticompetitive behaviour.[80] Examples of this attitude are to be found in the condemnation of restrictions on distributive outlets in the cases of cinema film and colour film, of non-quantity discounts in the case of Metal Box, of the level of advertising and promotional expenditure undertaken by Unilever and Procter and Gamble in the detergent market, and of agreements with foreign suppliers entered into by Courtaulds. By and large behaviour of this type has been considered to be objectionable *per se* without reference to any assessment of performance. Exceptions, e.g. the failure to condemn restrictions on retail outlets for infant milk foods or to investigate Pilkington's informal arrangements with foreign suppliers, have been regarded by most commentators as aberrations.

Second, very high profits have usually been condemned. Unilever and Procter and Gamble obtained a rate of profit (on an historic cost basis) that was respectively twice and three and a half times as high as the average for all manufacturing industry. Kodak's 44 per cent (on an historic cost basis) on reference goods was three times the manufacturing average. However, generous rates of profit have been earned without disapproval. Molins's 1951–8 average of 36·2 per cent (on an historic cost basis) was getting on for, and Triplex's 1960–5 average of 33·2 per cent was, twice the rate for manufacturing industry as a whole.

Third, structural change has never been recommended. Possible qualifications to this statement are the recommendations that Wall Paper Manufacturers, Courtaulds, and Turner and Newall should undertake no further acquisitions without permission, that Imperial Tobacco should dispose of its minority (42·5 per cent) holding in Gallaher, and that the import tariff on colour film and cellulosic fibre should be cut. The possibility of breaking up the dominant firm was considered but rejected in the cases of British Match, Courtaulds, and Rank and Associated British Picture Corporation. Such a course of action might also have been considered – the reports are unclear on this question – in the cases of British Oxygen, Wall Paper Manufacturers and Imperial Tobacco. However, there has never been an actual recommendation to break up an existing monopoly, not even in the five cases where the monopoly position itself was found to be contrary to the public interest. Rather than structural change the Commission's norm has been to recommend some change in behaviour. In Hunter's words: 'Its collective judgement is that monopoly or oligopoly is a normal incident of contemporary industrial structure and is acceptable where it can give sufficient evidence of efficient performance and/or some degree of workable competition.' In fact the Commission has come to 'accept the monopolistic/oligopolistic pattern and set out to modify it in relatively minor respects'.[81] Perhaps not surprisingly, competition policy with respect to dominant firms in the EEC has developed along similar lines. As George and Joll have put it: 'UK and EEC policy are [sic] similar in that both aim to control the behaviour of large firms, rather than to control market structure and prevent firms acquiring the position of dominance which makes such anti-competitive conduct possible.'[82]

The Impact of the Commission on the Dominant Firm
The Commission's recommendations have had no force unless adopted by the government. For the most part they have been accepted, and the government has obtained from the firms involved voluntary undertakings to implement them. Statutory orders have been issued only in the cases of Total, allowed to lapse after a 'voluntary' undertaking was given, and Hoffman-La Roche (Librium and Valium). The latter was the subject of a bitter dispute between the government and the company, which was fought out in Parliament and the courts and was eventually revoked when a 'voluntary' agreement was reached.

However, a number of potentially far-reaching recommendations have not been accepted by the government.[83] The Commission's recommendations of price control for British Match and price and profit control for British Oxygen were rejected, as was the recommendation that the manufacturers of electrical equipment for land vehicles should publish prices and terms for their replacement goods. The government decided not to require Imperial Tobacco to divest itself of its holding in Gallaher. The Commission's recommendation that detergent prices should be cut by at least 20 per cent and sales expenditure by at least 40 per cent, with the Board of Trade to introduce long run sanctions, was not accepted. Instead:

> The Companies have undertaken to make fully available an alternative range of top-quality soap powders and synthetic detergent powders at a price 20% below the prices of existing products in these categories. The consumer will thus be able to choose freely between these cheaper products, the prices of which will reflect less expenditure on advertising and promotion, and the higher priced and more intensely advertised products.[84]

The government's decision not to follow the Commission's recommendation to cut tariffs on cellulosic fibre and colour film has already been mentioned.

The only study to date of the consequences of the Commission's activities in relation to dominant firms is that by Rowley. In his view 'the available evidence indicates that the direct and immediate impact of the Monopolies Commission has been slight' although the long-run effect may turn out to be greater.[85]

A slightly different impression has been given in a government inter-departmental working-party review of competition policy published in 1978:

> Remedial action following these reports has led to reduced prices (detergents, colour film, Librium and Valium); to the abandonment of discriminatory pricing (cellulosic fibres, clutch mechanisms); to relaxation of exclusive dealing and other monopolistic ties (wallpaper, petrol, colour film, metal containers); to wider availability of products (instant milk foods); and to prices more nearly reflecting costs, and sales policies allowing greater consumer choice (films for exhibition, electric lamps, plasterboard, cross channel ferries).[86]

MERGER

The basic approach to mergers in UK competition policy is set out in the Office of Fair Trading's guide to the Fair Trading Act 1973:

> The assumption behind the merger provision of the Fair Trading Act, and behind the earlier legislation on mergers, is that significant mergers raise economic, social, and other issues affecting the lives of many people and so merit consideration on grounds of public interest. There is no presumption that mergers, or any particular class or classes of merger, are bad in themselves. Many mergers can be to the country's benefit and in others no significantly adverse effects on the public interest can be foreseen . . .
>
> Each case falling within the scope of the Act is looked at on its own

particular merits and not in accordance with any fixed rules or assumptions; the aim in each case being to assess and balance the advantages and the disadvantages to the public interest. Although the maintenance of adequate competition is one of the important considerations in selecting mergers for reference, judgements on the competition aspects are made in a practical and not a theoretical way, in the light of actual market conditions and expectations; and weight is given also to other significant economic and social aspects.[88]

The procedure adopted is for the Office to scrutinise any mergers that come to its notice, which in practice means virtually all relevant mergers, and submit a report to an interdepartmental Mergers Panel chaired by the Director-General of Fair Trading. Drawing on the advice of the Mergers Panel, the director then either recommends to the Secretary of State that the merger be referred to the Monopolies and Mergers Commission or, in contentious cases, gives his reasons for not so recommending. The Secretary of State is not obliged to accept the director's advice, although he normally does so.

Between 1965, when mergers were first made subject to control, and the end of 1977, the Mergers Panel considered 1,542 mergers, excluding newspaper mergers, which are dealt with under separate provisions and not discussed in this chapter. Of these only forty-two, i.e. under 3 per cent, were referred to the Commission, despite the fact that over 10 per cent of those considered were eligible for investigation under the market share criterion.[89] In addition to the guidance on how to interpret the public interest given in the 1973 Act, quoted in section 9.2, the Commission has considered other matters when assessing proposed mergers. These have included the effects on efficiency, the balance of payments, total UK employment, industrial relations within the company to be taken over, the desirability of maintaining the largest company in an industry under British ownership, and the risk that the interests of a UK industry might be subjected to other interests of the bidding company.[90]

At the end of 1977 reports were awaited on three references, thirteen mergers had been found to be not contrary to the public interest, twelve had been found to be contrary, and fourteen had been abandoned before the Commission reported. The mergers allowed were: British Motor Corporation/Pressed Steel, Dental Manufacturing or Dentists' Supply/Amalgamated Dental, Guest, Keen and Nettlefolds/Birfield, British Insulated Callender's Cables/Pyrotenax, Thorn/Radio Rentals, Unilever/Allied Breweries, British Match/Wilkinson Sword, Eagle Star/Sunley, Charter/Sadia, NFU/FMC, Dentsply/Amalgamated Dental, Weidmann/Whiteley, and Freuhauf/Crane Freuhauf. Adverse reports were made in the cases of Ross/Associated Fisheries, United Drapery/Montague Burton, Barclays/Lloyds/Martins, Rank/De La Rue, British Sidac/Transparent Paper, Beecham or Boots/Glaxo, Davy/British Rollmakers, European Shipholdings/Furness Withy and Manchester Liners, Amalgamated Industrials/Herbert Morris, Pilkington/UK Optical, Babcock and Wilcox/Herbert Morris, and British Petroleum/Century Oils.

Serious obstacles stand in the way of any attempt to assess the working of the arrangements for controlling mergers. Since reasons have not been published it is difficult to arrive at an independent view as to whether the government's decisions on which merger situations to refer to the Commission and which not to refer have been consistent. It is also difficult to reach a view as to whether the criteria used by the government to decide whether or not to refer have been consistent with those used by the Commission to determine the public interest. If they have not, some mergers might not have been referred although the Commission would have found them contrary to the public interest had it investigated them. There are, however, two relevant questions that can be considered, at least provisionally, on the basis of the Commission's published reports. These are whether the Commission has applied the same criteria to merger references as to dominant firm references and whether it has acted consistently in relation to different merger references.

The only major study of this field is that by Sutherland.[91] By contrast with its lengthy investigation of dominant firms the Commission is statutorily obliged to report on merger references within six months, with the possibility of an additional three months in exceptional circumstances, and has in fact usually taken from three to five months. It has, therefore, been able to make only limited inquiries into the past behaviour and performance of the firms involved. In particular, Sutherland has argued, it has been unable to make its own independent investigation of the sort undertaken in relation to dominant firm references and has had to rely on its assessment of the case presented by the companies concerned. There has been little systematic analysis of the profit record, of whether costs were as low as they could be, of whether prices were satisfactorily linked to costs, of whether behaviour had created entry barriers or of how the market might develop in the absence of merger. Sutherland has discerned two strands in the Commission's approach. If no 'fairly tangible and immediate detriment' has appeared probable – evidence for which would usually take the form of complaints from interested parties, e.g. trade customers – then longer term and more general detriments which might arise from reduced competition have been given minimal weight. In such cases *prima facie* acceptable arguments advanced by firms about possible performance benefits have not been seriously probed. On the other hand, if some immediate detriment to trade customers has seemed possible, an attempt has been made to work out safeguards in the form of assurances from the merging companies about their future behaviour; for example, assurances played an important part in the Commission's decision to allow the merger in the British Motor Corporation/Pressed Steel and British Insulated Callender's Cables/Pyrotenax cases.

Thus, Sutherland has concluded that the Commission has adopted a formal approach, prohibiting mergers only when it found them to have features that were actually contrary to the public interest rather than allowing only those where a positive benefit was established. With respect to dominant firms the Commission has generally been insistent on modifying any behaviour restricting residual competition. Such behaviour is possible because of the dominant position of the firm(s) involved, i.e. because of the prevailing market structure. Hence, in the absence of reasonably strong evidence that positive benefit would result from and could only be obtained by merger, the Commission might have been expected to seek to preserve competition directly, by prohibiting structural change, rather than indirectly, by allowing the merger and imposing temporary codes of behaviour. Since it has in fact tended to do the opposite, Sutherland has convicted the Commission of inconsistency in its attitude to dominant firm and merger references. As to consistency within the Commission's reporting on mergers, the evidence is largely qualitative, being mainly in the form of testimony from interested parties, and it is difficult to distinguish possible inconsistency from differences in the assessment made of the evidence submitted.

During the 1970s dissatisfaction with competition policy towards merger grew. This was due to an increasing awareness of the role of merger in increasing concentration and to the accumulating evidence of disappointing results from merger, both discussed in section 5.3, together with a growing recognition that UK merger policy has been largely ineffective.[92] Despite the case-by-case approach on which UK merger policy has been explicitly based, the underlying presumption in fact has clearly been that mergers are in general beneficial. This is evident from the small proportion of mergers actually referred to the Commission, i.e. under 3 per cent, and from successive ministerial statements over the years.[93] This favourable stance towards merger has also been reflected in the practice of allowing major mergers without reference to the Commission, on the strength of assurances about good behaviour obtained from the firms seeking to merge. Such cases have included Chrysler/Rootes, General Electric Company/Associated Electrical Industries, International Computers, Electrical and Musical Industries EMI/Associated British Picture Corporation, General Electric Company/English Electric, General Foods/ Rowntree, Ross/Associated Fisheries (trawling interests only), and Distillers/ United Glass.

As already noted, Sutherland has raised the possibility of reversing the existing favourable presumption and allowing mergers only if positive benefit can be established. Swann *et al.* have proposed that the presumption should be against merger where any significant reduction in competition will result, with the Commission judging applications for exemption from the general presumption.[94] A reversal of presumption could be achieved by requiring the Commission to report on whether a merger was *in* the public interest and giving the Secretary of State power to allow the merger only if it had been found to be so.

In its 1978 review of competition policy a government interdepartmental working party considered the case for a complete reversal of presumption and rejected it on the grounds that a very high proportion of proposed mergers would then be referred to the Commission and since a high proportion of these would probably be found to be in the public interest this would be a waste of the Commission's time. Furthermore, the near certain prospect of being referred would deter many mergers that were potentially in the public interest. Instead, the working party recommended a change from a favourable to a neutral presumption. The working party's proposals involved providing the Mergers Panel with guidelines for identifying mergers that would have a significant effect on competition or economic power. Mergers with no significant effect would in general be allowed, while those with a significant effect would be referred to the Commission unless clearly established expected benefits would offset any detriments. Finally, the working party suggested that the 1973 Act's section 84 guidance as to the interpretation of the public interest should be supplemented in the case of merger references to include:

(*a*) the desirability of minimising the detriments of reduced competition and increased concentration; and
(*b*) the desirability of restructuring to improve the international competitiveness of British industry.[95]

Clause (*b*) clearly reflects the felt need to frame merger policy in a way that takes account of the government's industrial policy. The working party estimated that its recommendations would initially increase the rate of reference from under 3 to up to 12 per cent, with much the same proportion of cases referred being found contrary as the then prevailing one-third. It was expected that there would subsequently be a deterrent effect, resulting in fewer but better thought-out mergers coming forward.[96]

PRICES

As indicated in section 9.2, the Price Commission was reconstituted in the summer of 1977 and abolished in the summer of 1979.[97] In its first report the new Commission set out its general approach. Having noted the existence of fully competitive sectors on the one hand and monopoly situations on the other, it continued:

> Between the two extremes lie many situations in which pricing may be distorted by market imperfection or by defects of information which do not allow a fully competitive market to operate. It is here that the main thrust of the Commission's intervention should fall.[98]

This approach was further emphasised in the Commission's second report when attention was drawn to the especial relevance for its work of section 2(2)(f) of the Price Commission Act 1977, concerning the promotion of competition or, where that was not possible, the restriction of prices.

At the end of its first nine months the new Commission had initiated twenty-one investigations, and reports had been published on thirteen. It will be recalled that prices were frozen during an investigation subject to certain safeguards for profits. In fact, because the safeguards were still framed in accordance with the old Price Code system, the Commission had been obliged to allow interim increases in all but three cases, and it was clearly unhappy about this. Recommendations for restrictions on prices or margins were made in three of the thirteen reports on investigations, while in several others assurances about future price increases were recorded and/or suggestions for improving efficiency were made.

It is interesting to compare the Price Commission's 1978 investigation report on Metal Box Ltd with the Monopolies Commission's 1970 report on Metal Containers, summarised above. The Price Commission was favourably impressed by Metal Box's high standards of performance and judged that the company's substantial market power had been used responsibly. It found no evidence of the practices that the Monopolies Commission had considered objectionable, although it did suggest that Metal Box should review its system of uniform delivered prices for aerosol cans. Subject to an assurance that there would be no increase in aerosol can prices before September 1978, unless substantial cost increases occurred, the Price Commission made no recommendations for restrictions on prices.[99]

In addition to investigations, during its first nine months the Price Commission received eight references of industries or sectors for examination under the 1977 Act, reports on three of which had been published. The application of the criteria specified in the Act to examinations was proving difficult, since the criteria appeared to be more appropriate to specific firms than to the overall industries or sectors that were the concern of examinations.[100]

The reconstituted Price Commission existed for such a short period that there is no basis for any real assessment of its work. It is of considerable interest, however, to note that before it was abolished the issues of efficiency and of the need to ensure an adequate rate of return appeared to be emerging as central concerns of the Commission. In both cases there were clear similarities between the developing approach of the Commission and the experience of the NBPI, which operated between 1965 and 1970.[101] On the first issue there were already signs that the Commission was beginning to follow in the footsteps of the NBPI by concerning itself with detailed questions of internal efficiency. The NBPI, in seeking to devise a substitute for effective competition where this could not be realised, had as its major target not monopoly profit but the internal inefficiency that is likely to exist in situations where competitive pressure is muted by market power and cost minimisation is not a necessary condition for survival. Towards the end of its life the logic of the NBPI's approach was moving it steadily in the direction of advocating regular 'efficiency audits' for firms where competition was lacking.[102]

In assessing the adequacy of profitability the Price Commission had by 1978 begun to consider 'the need to encourage investment, to cover the cost of capital and to reward . . . risk'.[103] Here too the experience of the NBPI was highly relevant. Analysis of the private-sector pricing activities of the NBPI clarifies the nature of two key assumptions that must underlie any public interest assessment of pricing and investment performance. First, to the extent that the supply price of capital is influenced by attitudes, conventions and institutional arrangements, an assumption must be made about what the rate of return should be.[104] Second, an assumption must be made about what the future pattern of industry should be, thus determining what investment is to count as necessary.[105] In effect prior decisions have to be made, either explicitly or implicitly, about the desired distribution of income and wealth and about social priorities. The work of the NBPI, partly because the general characteristics and rationale of its approach were set out fairly clearly in its general reports, partly due to its recognition of the importance of equity, can be shown clearly to have rested on such assumptions. But the activities of the Price Commission, as of the other bodies discussed in this section, also depend on specific implicit normative judgements about distribution and priorities.[106]

A final similarity between the Price Commission and the NBPI was that they were both widely regarded as candidates for fusion with the Monopolies or Monopolies and Mergers Commission. In 1969 the Labour government proposed the merger of the NBPI and the Monopolies Commission to form a Commission on Industry and Manpower.[107] In 1978 the Labour government's interdepartmental working-party review of competition policy recommended that the Price Commission and the Monopolies and Mergers Commission should be brought together in due course. Meanwhile, the two bodies were seen as complementary, with the Price Commission concerned primarily with short-term pricing issues and with inadequately competitive situations not caught by the 25 per cent market-share definition of monopoly and therefore not qualifying for reference to the Monopolies and Mergers Commission.[108]

9.4 INDUSTRIAL POLICY

Industrial policy as discussed in this section is concerned with intervention at the level of the specific industry or firm and the extent to which this is related to an overall plan or strategy for the development of the economy. This means that some forms of assistance to industry, e.g. general investment incentives such as accelerated depreciation allowances against tax and most regional assistance, are not considered here. However, the distinction cannot be pushed too far, and it is of interest to have some idea of the magnitude of total government expenditure on or assistance to industry. Unfortunately, the relevant data are not readily come by. Denton has estimated the net subsidies to private industry in 1970–1 at £851 million, with a further £72 million indirect tax relief bringing the figure to approximately 7 per cent of central government expenditure.[109] Begg *et al.* have estimated the total expenditure in 1970–1 on special regional assistance at £302 million, although not necessarily on the same basis.[110] Roy has calculated that grants, investment allowances, employment premia, research-and-development subsidies and the imputed value to the private sector of public sector losses came to £2,100–2,300 million in 1972–3 – some 26 per cent of private-sector fixed-capital investment, excluding housing.[111] Looking at subsidies in the UK economy as a whole, not just to industry, Prest has presented estimates of UK subsidies by adjusting the official figures to include relevant current and capital grants. His results are (official figures in parentheses) £2,445 million (£895 million) for 1970 and £3,079 million (£1,133 million) for 1972.[112] Despite the real problems of estimation it seems clear that public financial assistance to private industry has become very important. Of course, financial assistance, although the most visible, is not the only form of state intervention. For instance, as detailed below, much of the activity of the IRC consisted of informal discussions leading to merger or other industrial reorganisation, with no involvement of public money.

This section outlines the development of industrial policy from its origins in the NEDC and the National Plan, through the IRC and the Industry Act

1972, to the Industry Act 1975, the NEB and the Industrial Strategy. It ends with an assessment of the problems that have become evident in the attempt to develop effective direct state intervention at the microlevel.

PLANNING AND MICROINTERVENTION

The National Economic Development Council and the National Plan
In November 1960 the Federation of British Industries proposed to the government the preparation of what was in effect a five-year indicative plan. As a result of this initiative the Conservative government of the day established the NEDC, consisting of representatives of the government, employers and unions. At its first meeting in March 1962 the then Chancellor of the Exchequer, Selwyn Lloyd, defined the NEDC's tasks as:

> To examine the economic performance of the nation with particular concern for plans for the future in both the private and the public sectors of industry.
>   To consider what are the obstacles to quicker growth, what can be done to improve efficiency, and whether the best use is being made of our resources.
>   To seek agreement upon ways of improving economic performance, competitive power and efficiency, in other words to increase the rate of sound growth.[114]

In 1963 it was decided to set up, also on a tripartite basis, a series of individual EDCs for key sectors of industry, with the following terms of reference:

> Within the context of the work of the NEDC, and in accordance with such working arrangements as may be determined from time to time between the Council and the Committee, each Committee will:
> (a) examine the economic   performance, prospects and plans of the industry, and assess from time to time the industry's progress in relation to the national growth objectives, and provide information and forecasts to the Council on these matters;
> (b) consider ways of improving the industry's economic performance, competitive power and efficiency and formulate reports and recommendations on those matters as appropriate.[115]

Thus, both the NEDC and the individual EDCs had a dual function, 'on the one hand projecting a national economic growth path and assessing the implications, and on the other hand analysing the practical obstacles to faster growth within the industrial and social structure'.[116]

Between 1962 and 1964 the NEDC, working in close harmony with the Conservative government, published the outcome of various exercises in indicative planning based on the exploration of the implications of an assumed overall growth rate of 4 per cent for different sectors of the economy, making particular use of discussions with seventeen key industries. With the election of a Labour government in 1964 the responsibility for planning was effectively transferred from the NEDC to a newly created Department of Economic Affairs. The department, in consultation with the NEDC, set about preparing a fully-fledged National Plan, eventually published in 1965. An overall growth target of 3·8 per cent per annum to 1970 was chosen, and discussions were then held with industry, through the EDCs where they existed or in other ways, to consider the implications of the overall growth rate for individual industries. As a result of these discussions individual industry estimates were adjusted upwards in order to conform to the overall target, although doubt has been expressed about the extent to which these adjustments represented a genuine revision of expectations.[117]

This was a critical question since the rationale for indicative planning is precisely that it affects expectations and thereby modifies behaviour. Expectations may be affected in two ways. First, agreement on an overall growth-rate target for the economy as a whole provides a basis for estimating the future demand for the output of individual industries or sectors. Second, discussion among the firms that are active in each industry enables them to become more aware of their respective plans and then to adjust these in order to realise between them an industry output that equals the output implied by the overall economywide growth rate. In effect, indicative planning is an attempt to achieve *ex ante* co-ordination between decentralised decision-making units, by contrast with the *ex post* co-ordination achieved through the market mechanism in the form of price, cost and profit signals reflecting the prevailing relationship between supply and demand.

The problem with pure indicative planning is that, in the absence of instruments to ensure that the overall, sectoral and industry targets are met, everything depends on the individual decision-making units voluntarily acting as they are supposed to act according to the plan. However, if there is doubt about whether the projected targets will in fact be met, as is almost inevitable, the rational thing for a self-interested enterprise to do may well be to wait and see; and if all enterprises act in this way, this will ensure that the targets are not achieved. Furthermore, even if there is confidence in the overall and industry growth targets, the more successful firms are likely to seek to increase their shares at the expense of the less successful, thus rendering genuine agreement unlikely.[118]

In the event, the 1965 National Plan lasted for less than a year. The prevailing rate of growth of exports was 4 per cent whereas that implied by the Plan was 5·25 per cent, and the Plan gave no indication of how the necessary increase in growth rate was to be achieved. In the summer of 1966 the worst sterling crisis since the Second World War developed and was met with the most severe deflationary measures. There was no possibility that the 3·8 per cent growth target could be achieved, and the National Plan was publicly abandoned.

With the collapse of the National Plan the Labour government concentrated on specific measures of microintervention unrelated to any overall perspective. The NBPI, restraining wages and increasing efficiency, was intended to assist in holding down inflation and increasing competitiveness, the EDCs concentrated on the detailed problems of their individual industries; and to intervene at the level of the individual firm the government had established the IRC.

The Industrial Reorganisation Corporation

As noted in section 9.2, the IRC was established for the purpose of 'promoting industrial efficiency and profitability and assisting the economy of the United Kingdom', and its overall criteria became 'the scope for improving productivity, and the scope for improving the balance of payments'. In the four and a half years or so of its active life the IRC was 'substantially involved' in about ninety projects.[120]

Three broad categories of work were identified in the IRC's third report: reorganisation, stimulation and selective investment. Selective investment involved backing single firm ventures, often following a government request, which the IRC regarded as furthering its overall objectives. Examples are the loans to Reed and to Dixon for de-inking plant to enable the more effective salvaging of printed paper, thus economising on imports, to Marwen for the further expansion of its numerically controlled machine tools, and to British Leyland Motor Corporation for machine tool purchase to modernise and expand its production facilities. Stimulation was concerned principally with rousing management in firms whose poor performance could not be attributed to fragmentation. Since such activity was largely behind the scenes, reliance must be placed on the IRC's own account of its work in this sphere:

> Low productivity, late delivery, slow switch of markets, mediocre products and a lack of management control characterise many companies more than large enough to be viable units. Long years of soft markets in the past – 'home and colonial' – have taken their toll and there are undoubtedly some sleeping giants and industrial coffins on the British industrial scene. IRC is using its influence to stimulate British industrial companies to effective and profitable reform, where appropriate, without recourse to merger or takeover by others.[121]

However, the major part of the IRC's work was devoted to effecting reorganisation by merger. Great stress was laid by the IRC on its view that there is no virtue in size for its own sake – that size may have disadvantages where it results in managerial diseconomies – but equal, if not greater, emphasis was placed on the need to gauge size on an international scale:

> Size in itself is no solution – indeed it is not without its disadvantages; but size, provided it is industrially appropriate and under effective management, can provide the essential base for the large scale of effort that is increasingly required to prosper in world markets and to proceed successfully to new generations of equipment. From IRC's contacts with industry in the UK and abroad, it appears that in three areas in particular – marketing, product development and investment – the scale and effectiveness of our effort has lagged behind that of our competitors abroad. IRC is convinced that these factors must be measured internationally.[122]

The IRC's continuing preoccupation with international competitiveness is strikingly illustrated by its approach to aggregate performance: 'The best measure of the performance of manufacturing industry is the visible trade account.'[123] Also, the IRC had no doubt that in Britain, in the late 1960s and early 1970s at least, larger size was likely to be necessary to improve this performance: 'The plain fact is that in more and more sectors we shall have to get accustomed to the difficulties of building and running large concerns.'[124]

The IRC operated very largely through confidential discussions with firms, sometimes on its own initiative but increasingly also on theirs as the initial mistrust and suspicion were overcome. From these discussions and its own research it formed a view about potentially beneficial lines of development in a large number of industries. Its most common form of activity was with firms that were or became willing partners. Sometimes it gave its support to projects that were already under way and sometimes it brought firms together for discussions on merger when it felt that this was the way to further its strategy in a given industry. Although it had funds available, in a majority of cases these were not involved. Examples of mergers that proceeded with the IRC's goodwill, often as a result of its good offices, but without its financial help, are Dunford and Elliott/Hadfields, Racal Electronics/Controls and Communications, Reyrolle Parsons/Bruce Peebles, Ross/Associated Fisheries (trawling interests), Rowntree/Mackintosh, and Portals/Permutit. However, the ability to provide financial help where appropriate was essential to the IRC's activity. Even with respect to some of the mergers just mentioned the IRC agreed to discuss finance should it become necessary, while two-fifths[125] of its projects involved finance in the form of actual payment. Examples of amicable mergers lubricated by IRC funds are English Electric/Elliott-Automation, British Oxygen/Edwards High Vacuum, Weir/Osborn-Hadfields, Plessey/Ferranti (numerical control interests), and Klinger/Qualitex.

Although the IRC sought to proceed 'by advice and persuasion which it has found effective in a rational society',[126] this did not always prove possible. On a number of occasions it felt the need to intervene in a contested situation. The best-known example of this is the General Electric Company (GEC)/Associated Electrical Industries (AEI) merger in 1967, which was opposed by the AEI Board. The IRC threw its weight behind GEC and was widely thought to have influenced the outcome, not least by holding a meeting of institutional shareholders at which it set out its case for the merger. As a result of its action in this case one member of the IRC Board, i.e. the chairman of AEI, resigned. This experience did not prevent the IRC from in 1968 again giving GEC very effective backing, this time in its contest with Plessey as to which firm should take over English Electric. On another occasion in 1968 the IRC went beyond moral support when it intervened in a contested situation in the instrument-making industry. Rank had bid for Cambridge, but the IRC held that a merger between Cambridge and Kent would be more beneficial. Agreement could not be reached; so the IRC acquired Cambridge shares in the market and agreed to participate in underwriting Kent's offer, which was successful.

The IRC was also prepared to acquire firms itself to achieve special objectives. In order to speed rationalisation in the ballbearing and special steel industries the IRC in 1969 made a bid in its own right for Brown Bayley, which through subsidiaries had interests in both industries. It then supported a merger between Ransome and Marles, and Pollard – the two remaining British-owned ballbearing manufacturers – and subsequently a merger between the combined firm and its own ballbearing firm – the Brown Bayley subsidiary Hoffmann. Thus, through temporary outright ownership the IRC achieved its objective – in this case a 'viable' British-owned ballbearing industry. At the same time the IRC was keenly interested in the promotion of European mergers. It was involved in the Dunlop/Pirelli, Laporte/Solvay, and Humphreys/Gütehoffnungshutte developments[127] and was also attracted by the possibility of a European IRC.[128]

Despite its activities at an international level the IRC has on occasion been accused of having adopted a narrowly insular attitude when considering structural reorganisation. Its investment in Rootes, to ensure a significant and continuing British participation when voting control passed to Chrysler, was made at the formal request of the government; but its lengthy and successful efforts, described above, to establish a 'viable' British-owned presence in the ballbearing industry were undertaken on its own initiative. The reasons advanced for this course of action are of some interest:

> One of the IRC's overriding considerations in promoting industrial reorganisation is to assist British industry to improve its export potential. Amongst those European countries for which information was available IRC observed that apart from Sweden, the only country with a strong surplus in its trade in ballbearings was Germany. The independent German company, Kugelfischer FAG made a strong contribution to this surplus. IRC was also aware that SKF [one of three powerful foreign-owned UK manu-facturers], as with any strongly based international group, acting in the interest of its own efficiency and profitability might well find it advantageous to rationalise its production facilities, locate its R & D, buy its raw materials and machine tools and direct its marketing policy in ways which would not necessarily benefit the UK economy.[129]

There is no doubt that the IRC had developed an acute awareness of national vulnerability. In one form or another it kept returning to the position of Britain as a nation state:

> Britain has also to protect her vital interests as a state, within whatever grouping she finds herself, Commonwealth, EFTA or EEC. If this was neglected Britain could find herself becoming a branch office economy where industries vital for growth, technology or defence were either absent or entirely directed from other parts of the world.[130]

Although in particular instances Britain's vital interests were held to require a specifically British solution, in general these interests were equated with as systematic as possible a reconstruction and modernisation of British in-dustry, with or without foreign participation as appropriate. The IRC had varying degrees of success. Comprehensive restructuring was largely achieved in nuclear construction, vehicles, ballbearings and parts of the electrical industry;

it was only partially achieved in trawler fleets, instruments, mining machinery, pumps, compressors and numerical control. Less headway was made in other industries – wool, rubber, paper, footwear, special steels and parts of mechanical engineering – where the changes that occurred were relatively less important and more piecemeal.[131] At the height of its activities the IRC had rather more than £100 million of the £150 million that were available invested in one form or another.

In order to satisfy itself that the underlying purpose for which an investment had been made was being fulfilled, a follow-up procedure was instituted. During the financial year 1969–70 thirty-nine follow-up reports were received by the IRC Board, covering all but its most recent investments. At the end of the year there existed arrangements for a twice-yearly checkup on forty-five investments in some twenty-five industrial sectors. In addition there were eight firms for which responsibility rested with an IRC-nominated director: Brown Bayley Steels, George Kent, Plessey Numerical Controls, Ransome Hoffman Pollard, Nuclear Power Group, British Nuclear Design and Construction, British United Trawlers, and Rootes.[132] During its final year only twenty or so investments were considered in detail, due to the running down of the IRC's staff after the announcement that it was to be disbanded. However, an overall review of its activities concluded that, of the ninety projects in which it had been substantially involved, at least seventy-five were turning out as expected, with the remainder labouring somewhat but still operating in the desired direction.[133]

From the very beginning the most important criterion of the public interest used by the IRC was the quality of the managements concerned. In the GEC/AEI dispute it was its judgement of the quality of GEC's management that determined the attitude of the IRC Board. This factor was returned to again and again: 'The quality of management is the key to success'; 'the critical element in IRC work is the capacity of industrial management to do the job'; 'The main criterion is a strong unified management willing and able to expand in the face of international competition.'[134] It could hardly have been otherwise, given the IRC's 'unusual status – created by government but directed by businessmen, free to make its own decisions about individual projects without political bias and not subject to government veto'.[135] Inevitably, this absence of 'political bias' and 'government veto' meant that the interpretation of the public interest arrived at corresponded closely to the currently conventional biases and prejudices of the directing businessmen.[136] Not surprisingly, they tended to support relatively successful managers like themselves. Furthermore, notwithstanding its role as an instrument of state, intervention the IRC was thoroughly imbued with the prevailing ideological commitment to the market. It saw its task as supplementing, very definitely not supplanting, the market.[137]

The IRC was run by businessmen; it was not linked to any strategic view of how the government wanted to see the economy develop; and it sought to assist, not to replace, market forces. Why, then, did the Conservative government elected in 1970 decide to disband it – a decision regretted by the wide sections of industry that had come to value it? The IRC, along with the NBPI, fell victim to the Conservatives' short-lived policy of disengagement, which lasted between 1970 and 1972. It seems likely that the underlying reason for the disengagement policy was ideological. Once state intervention assumes the form of detailed and continuous surveillance, as was implicit in the logic if not the intended practice of the Labour government's position, it is unlikely to be long before more far-reaching questions are raised. As Graham has put it, 'once one intervenes within the market system all those conflicts which are hidden by the invisible hand become more obvious and the Government becomes the clear object for blame whenever expectations are not fulfilled'.[138] The very concept of the economy as an essentially harmonious system is called into question, and sectional or class interests begin to thrust themselves to the fore. Such dangers may be reduced if state intervention is less direct, i.e. concerned mainly with the framework within which private enterprise operates apparently unfettered, so that the casualties of the system appear as an inevitable corollary of 'beneficial resource allocation' rather than as the victims of decisions from which others benefit.

However, the problems of British capitalism had become so deep seated that disengagement, despite its ideological attractions, did not last long.[139] In the spheres of both industrial policy and incomes policy a dramatic *volte face* occurred. The Counter-Inflation Act 1972 imposed a ninety-day standstill on prices, pay, dividends and rent and was followed by the Counter-Inflation Act 1973, which established the Pay Board, subsequently abolished by the 1974 Labour government, and the Price Commission, subsequently abolished by the 1979 Conservative Government. The Conservative government's Industry Act 1972 established virtually unlimited discretionary powers for the state to provide financial assistance to the private sector – powers that the 1974 Labour government found largely adequate for its purposes.

SELECTIVE FINANCIAL ASSISTANCE AND INDUSTRIAL STRATEGY

The Industry Act 1972

The nationalisation of Rolls Royce in 1971 after its final collapse, and the rescue of the constituent yards of Upper Clyde Shipbuilders in 1972 after the successful work-in by its employees, caused the Conservative government to abandon its policy of disengagement and recognise that general powers for selective microintervention were necessary.[140] The result was the Industry Act 1972, which, although primarily concerned with regional development grants and grants for shipbuilding, also created powers for regional and general selective financial assistance under sections 7 and 8. Applications for assistance were considered by an Industrial Development Unit created within the Department of Trade and Industry. The Unit was staffed by businessmen and in many ways resembled the IRC. The Act further provided for the establishment of an Industrial Development Advisory Board, also consisting of businessmen, to advise the government on applications for selective financial assistance. Finally, the initial criteria laid down by the government required that 'in all cases a realistic assessment of commercial viability, together with an analysis of any important external (including social) costs and benefits, should be the basis on which a decision to give selective financial assistance is given'.[141]

Although started under the Conservative government these arrangements continued virtually unchanged under the Labour government elected in 1974.[142] Until 1976 selective financial assistance under section 8 of the 1972 Act was used primarily for rescue operations, i.e. to support firms in financial difficulties. Rescue operations were also carried out under section 7 of the Act, making use of a clause in the regional selective-assistance guidelines enabling the normal commercial criteria to be disregarded. Among the firms helped in this way were British Leyland, Chrysler UK, Ferranti, and Kearney and Trecker Marwin Machine Tools.

It is not quite true that the advent of the 1974 Labour government made no difference. For a brief interlude, i.e. from spring 1974 to summer 1975, the Department of Industry, under Benn, pursued an interventionist strategy much less determined by market forces than before or since. In particular financial assistance was provided to five firms even though the Industrial Development Advisory Board had advised against it – in three cases to workers' co-operatives seeking to safeguard employment after the original firms had collapsed. However, after the defeat of the Left in the June 1975 EEC referendum Benn was replaced as Secretary of State for Industry and transferred to the Department of Energy.[143]

Although rescue operations claimed most public attention they were never intended to be the main purpose for which selective financial assistance would be provided. The other principal way in which assistance has been made available to industry under section 8 of the 1972 Act has been through a series of special schemes. The schemes have been of two sorts – general and sectoral – and have run for limited periods. Their purpose has been to accelerate or promote investment in general and to stimulate investment, modernisation, efficiency and rationalisation in specific industries considered to be of particular national importance.

The first general scheme – the Accelerated Projects Scheme – ran from April 1975 to July 1976. It was designed as a countercyclical measure to bring forward commercially sound projects that would benefit the balance of payments. Of the 350 applications received, after scrutiny by the Industrial Development Unit and the Industrial Development Advisory Board, 118 were accepted and 115 rejected, the rest having been withdrawn. The main reason for rejection was failure to establish that the project would not be started directly without assistance. Commitments were made to provide grants totalling £84 million towards projects involving a total capital expenditure of £495 million.[144] A second general scheme – the Selective Investment Scheme – with an initial allocation of £100 million was announced in December 1976 with a closing date of June 1978. It covered projects with significant benefits to the UK economy that would not be undertaken in the form proposed without government assistance. By the end of January 1978, 278 applications had been received, of which 48 had been approved, involving assistance of £23·7 million towards projects costing £236 million, while a further 127 were under consideration.[145]

By the end of March 1977 eleven sectoral schemes had been instituted under section 8 of the 1972 Act, covering the following industries: wool textile, clothing, ferrous foundry, machine tool, paper and board, non-ferrous foundry, electronic components, printing machinery, textile machinery, poultrymeat processing, and red meat slaughter. The amount allocated to the eleven sectoral schemes at that date was £221 million, and offers of assistance totalling £56 million had been made to 589 projects, involving a total expenditure of £272 million.[146]

In the summer of 1977 the financial limit on expenditure under section 8 of the 1972 Act was increased from £600 million to £850 million. Payments and undertakings at that time totalled £518 million,[147] about evenly divided between rescues and schemes, with rescues becoming less and schemes becoming more important.[148]

The National Enterprise Board

The principal purpose of the Industry Act 1975 was to establish the NEB. As originally envisaged by the Labour Party in opposition, the NEB and the planning agreement system were intended as instruments of positive public intervention and planning in the private sector. In addition to acting as a state holding company for existing state shareholdings, it was proposed that the NEB would take over some twenty-five of the 100 largest companies in order to give it sufficient leverage to influence the direction of the economy as a whole. At the same time a comprehensive system of planning agreements between the government and all large firms – certainly the top 100 – was envisaged, with sanctions against those refusing to co-operate.[149]

However, these far-reaching proposals were severely watered down as the Labour Party moved from opposition to office. The initial White Paper was published in August 1974 and the Industry Bill appeared at the start of 1975, both while Benn was still Secretary of State for Industry. The Industry Act, which was significantly different from the Bill, was passed in November 1975 after Benn's departure from the Department of Industry. Draft guidelines for the NEB were published in March 1976 and the final guidelines in December 1976. In the end the NEB was required to operate commercial criteria, denied compulsory powers and permitted to acquire majority shareholdings in firms only with the firm's consent. The role of planning agreements was downgraded to such an extent that it took fifteen months to conclude the first one – in March 1977 with Chrysler UK, which was at that time a firm so dependent on state finance as to have no real option. The irrelevance of this planning agreement was soon demonstrated when in 1978 the parent company reached an agreement to sell its European operations, including Chrysler UK, to Peugeot-Citroën, without bothering to discuss the matter with the UK government.

The NEB started operations at the end of 1975.[150] It had transferred to it state shareholdings in seven companies and state loans to four companies, valued in all at about £500 million. These transferred capital assets did not count towards the financial limit imposed on the NEB by the 1975 Act. Between November 1975 and the end of 1976 the NEB spent some £70 million on new investments, and in 1977 it spent a further £200 million. At the end of 1977 it was responsible for investments of £769 million in thirty-three companies and had spent £270 million of its available finance. The major companies with which the NEB was involved were British Leyland, Rolls Royce, Ferranti,

Herbert and International Computers. In the first quarter of 1978 it entered into further commitments, especially to British Leyland, bringing its expenditure by 31 March 1978 to £550 million out of the £700 million that was initially available to it. In April 1978 the financial limit was raised to its maximum, in the absence of new legislation, of £1,000 million.

The terms on which the NEB invested were strictly commercial, except where it was acting under direction from the government, as in the case of British Leyland. The only qualification to this is that it was prepared to take a longer-than-average view of investment opportunities. In December 1977 the government issued a financial directive laying down the rate of return on capital employed in companies other than British Leyland and Rolls Royce to be achieved by 1981. On the assumption that the average rate of return in manufacturing industry in 1981 would be 20 per cent, the NEB was required to earn a return of 15–20 per cent by that year, the lower limit being designed to take account of its longer-term view. This compared with a return of 11·4 per cent on non-British Leyland and Rolls Royce investments in 1977. The financial duty with respect to British Leyland was set in April 1978 at 10 per cent by 1981, compared with a loss of £42 million in 1977. The financial duty relating to Rolls Royce had not by then been determined.

Apart from specific directions, the NEB became accountable to the government in three ways: through its annual report and accounts, through discussion leading to agreement on its annual Corporate Plan, and through its submissions to the Secretary of State concerning proposals for investment requiring his consent. Similarly, the NEB sought accountability from its subsidiary and associate companies through their annual reports and through discussions leading to an annual strategic plan for each company. While seeking to avoid involvement in the day-to-day running of companies, the NEB took a keen interest in the quality of management and was prepared to intervene if necessary. In October 1977 it took the initiative in changing the top management of British Leyland, with Edwardes, who was then a part time member of the NEB, becoming British Leyland's chairman and chief executive.

In its first two years the NEB's strategy was difficult to discern, partly, perhaps, because of its preoccupation with the problems of British Leyland. It expressed its main tasks as being to concentrate on a limited number of sectors that were capable of becoming internationally competitive and to stimulate exports. It was also concerned to help smaller companies, particularly in areas of high unemployment, and to this end it established regional boards in the north and northwest with delegated powers to approve investments not exceeding £500,000. Although the NEB's guidelines required it to take account of the government's Industrial Strategy, as elaborated by the NEDC – and the NEB itself stated that it regarded a sectoral approach as fundamental – little that was concrete had emerged by the end of its first two years. The only sectors specifically mentioned by then as having received special attention were computers and electronics. Thus, in mid 1978 there was little evidence of the NEB relating its activities to any overall strategic view, any more than the IRC had done. But then, nearly three years of work on the government's Industrial Strategy had not yet produced anything resembling a strategic view, and there was no sign of one emerging in the foreseeable future.

The Industrial Strategy

The Industrial Strategy, launched in November 1975, was envisaged as proceeding from the identification of key industrial sectors, through analysis by tripartite SWPs, to action by the government and firms. By early 1978 thirty-seven SWPs were operating: automation and instrumentation, clothing, constructional steelwork, construction equipment and mobile cranes, domestic electrical appliances, electronic components, electronic computers, electronic consumer goods, ferrous foundries, fluid power, food and drink industries, food- and drink-packaging machinery, heavy electrical machinery, industrial electrical equipment, industrial engines, industrial trucks, iron and steel, knitting, machine tools, man-made fibres, mechanical-handling equipment, mining machinery, non-ferrous foundaries, office machinery, paper and board, petrochemicals, pharmaceuticals, printing machinery, process plant, pumps and valves, radio communications and radar and navigational aids, rubber, space-heating and ventilating and air-conditioning machinery, specialised organics, telecommunications, textile machinery, and wool textiles. In all the thirty-seven SWPs covered roughly 40 per cent of manufacturing output, 46 per cent of manufacturing employment and 50 per cent of manufacturing exports.[151]

For the first two years or so the Industrial Strategy and the SWPs were concerned primarily with analysis. At its July 1976 meeting the NEDC discussed reports submitted by the SWPs the previous month on the results of rapid surveys of the short-term problems facing their industries. It also agreed that work should start on developing a medium-term strategy for each industry. In February 1977 the NEDC discussed interim reports on the medium-term strategies that dealt with the problems and possibilities in home and overseas markets and the steps needed to ensure adequate price and non-price competitiveness. Arising from this meeting five sectors were singled out for special attention: construction equipment, domestic electrical appliances, electronic components, industrial engines, and office machinery. The Secretary of State for Industry met all five SWPs and some of the major firms.[152]

The February 1978 meeting of the NEDC was seen as a major landmark for the Industrial Strategy. It had before it reports on the SWP medium-term strategies for their industries, which included in many cases quantified targets for increasing exports and reducing import penetration. There was also widespread recognition of the importance of improving product technology and product range, as well as of the need for firms to orient themselves to world and not just domestic markets. Objectives were also set in relation to output and employment. In a joint memorandum to this meeting the Chancellor of the Exchequer and the Secretary of State noted that most of the earlier recommendations from SWPs had been directed to the government. They then detailed the ways in which the government had sought to respond to the requests from industry. These included fiscal changes to improve incentives and increase differentials, financial assistance in the form of the section 8 schemes outlined above and a £20 million product and process development scheme under the Science and Technology Act 1965, measures to assist small firms, improved export credit-guarantee facilities, and expanded industrial-training provision. The ministers argued that after two years of analysis and diagnosis, during which the government had made a significant contribution, the time had come for action at firm and plant level, focused primarily on increasing productivity. This was accepted by the NEDC, and the government made an additional £250,000 available to help the SWPs to get the message through to the individual firms in their industries.[153]

The tripartite sectoral approach adopted in the Industrial Strategy was in many ways a return to the consensus policies of the 1960s. Indeed, so tuned in was it to the susceptibilities of private sector industry that some of the TUC members on the NEDC 'thought they detected an undue amount of political lobbying in some of the sector reports'.[154] It was certainly very different from the strongly interventionist policies of Labour in the early 1970s – policies that still lingered on in the Labour Party despite having been abandoned by the government. It is ironic that, while the Labour government relaxed the Price Code in the summer of 1976 in order to increase profits, *Labour's Programme for Britain, 1976* was still calling for compulsory planning agreements and NEB control of one leading company in each major industry.[155]

Two issues stand out clearly from this review of the Labour government's Industrial Strategy. First, work on the strategy, along with selective financial assistance under the Industry Act 1972 and the activities of the NEB, was not related to any overall economic strategy. For instance, SWPs were asked to formulate their own macroeconomic assumptions, and since these varied the individual reports could not be aggregated to give an overall picture.[156] Still less was there any identification of priority sectors that would be given assistance to develop in ways that were radically different from what was implied by market forces. In short, the question of criteria for intervention remained unresolved. Second, little progress had been made in solving the problem of how to get individual firms to act in the way required. The points raised by the SWPs had a familiar ring, many of them having been around since the early exercises in indicative planning in the 1960s. While all involved were agreed that the time had come for action at the firm level, the only new ideas as to how this might be achieved had been ruled out as being incompatible with a mixed economy.[157]

AN ASSESSMENT

Industrial policy of some sort seems now to be established in the United Kingdom as a continuing part of the state's involvement in the economy. However, no settled framework of theory or criteria have emerged to inform its operation. Neoclassical theory is based on the implicit assumption that the market solution is the norm and that 'interference' in the market requires justification in terms of 'market failure' due to the existence of externalities, including public goods, or imperfections. It is not designed for the analysis of selective microintervention, at the level of the firm, directed towards maintaining employment, increasing productivity or improving the balance of payments. Analysis within the neoclassical framework has been largely concerned to point out the dangers involved in selective state intervention discriminating between firms, rather than to provide positive guidance for such intervention.[158] However, although neoclassical theory has been of little help in developing guidelines for industrial policy, no alternative coherent body of theory has been adopted.

What, then, have been the criteria guiding industrial policy in the United Kingdom? Overwhelmingly, official statements have emphasised the importance of intervening primarily in cases where commercial viability is in prospect. There are, of course, well-established exceptions to this general proposition. In many countries, including Britain, a number of high technology industries receive permanent subsidies. These include aerospace, computers and nuclear power. The high capital intensity and high risk of such industries is accepted as placing them effectively beyond the capacity of private capital, and governments support them for prestige, defence, technological spin-off and balance-of-payments reasons. Similarly, in many countries declining industries like shipbuilding, coal and steel are supported for social reasons.[159]

At the level of the firm, the form of intervention that is comparable to support for declining industries is the 'rescue operation'. In its January 1976 guidelines on the operation of industrial policy, *Criteria for Assistance to Industry*, the Department of Industry has identified three types of legitimate rescue operation: a limited number of exceptional cases in which 'the case for intervention speaks for itself' because of the scale of the social considerations involved; rather more cases where a reasonable amount of assistance would enable a company to become viable; and exceptional cases where a modest amount of assistance to a company in receivership would make all the difference between it continuing in operation and closing down.[160] Considerable doubt was expressed about the seriousness with which the government intended to keep to these criteria when in December 1976, despite the advice of the Industrial Development Advisory Board that there was no prospect of viability, a £160 million rescue operation for Chrysler UK was announced, on the grounds of balance-of-payments and employment considerations.

Notwithstanding these exceptions, the normal approach advocated by the government has been to 'invest in success', i.e. to provide assistance principally to profitable firms and projects whose commercial viability was not in doubt. This seems straightforward enough, but inevitably questions arise: If a firm or project is commercially viable, why does it need state assistance? If it needs state assistance, how can it be commercially viable?[161] Imperfections in the capital market and in information are possible answers in principle, but justifications along these lines arise within the neoclassical framework and have not normally been used as explanations for specific cases of selective intervention. In fact no clear answers or systematic principles have been developed, nor could they have been; for as long as commercial success in existing market conditions is the objective, legitimate state intervention is restricted to attempts to bring about what prevailing market forces would have brought about had they not somehow been prevented from operating effectively. There is scope only for marginal adjustment to supplement or assist market forces.

An alternative approach would have been to seek to intervene in a way that supplanted or replaced market forces, achieving an outcome that was different in major respects from what would have occurred without intervention. However, to be able to act in this way a government needs to have criteria that are different from those of the market. It may be, for example, that jobs, import substitutes and exports are considered to have a social value over and above that attached to them by the market. One way of expressing such a divergence between social and private costs and benefits is through a system of 'shadow pricing', in which shadow prices reflecting social valuation differ from preintervention market prices reflecting private valuation. The problems with this approach are that decisions may be inconsistent and that policy may be directed to dealing with symptoms rather than to tackling underlying causes. At a more fundamental level a government may have longer term objectives involving major structural changes in the economy, that greatly alter the opportunity costs reflected in currently prevailing market prices. These strategic objectives for the development of the economy and its major sectors would then determine the priorities for resource allocation, possibly incorporated in a medium or long term plan. Thus, criteria other than those of the market would be derived, either explicitly or implicitly, from the government's strategic aims.[162] In fact, of course, industrial policy in the United Kingdom has never been operated in this way. As Young has put it in his review of the IRC:

> The Government did not attempt to link the IRC's work to a view of what would be a desirable industrial structure in manufacturing industry as a whole in ten or twenty years time. A conscious decision could have been taken to tell IRC to concentrate on particular growth sectors. Attempts could then have been made to concentrate national resources behind them, relating IRC's work to government policies for manpower planning, R & D expenditure, and even location of industry. Instead the IRC was given a wide-ranging brief across the whole manufacturing sector, with the result that its Board judged individual cases on their merits in a vacuum.[163]

Apart from the problem of how to arrive at the criteria guiding industrial policy, the other main problem to have arisen is that of implementation. Industrial policy in the United Kingdom has operated almost entirely on the basis of consent. There have been very few cases where the independence of private sector firms has been over-ruled. All governments in the United Kingdom since the advent of industrial policy have been committed to a 'mixed economy', and this has imposed severe constraints on their ability to implement their policies. Government action to coerce private sector firms 'would endanger its working relationship with the private sector because such action would alienate firms and industrial interest groups far removed from the particular sector involved'.[164] This has had two consequences. First, government industrial policy has been unable to affect firms unwilling to co-operate. In the mid 1960s industrial departments and the EDCs became increasingly frustrated at the way in which their exhortation and advice was completely ignored by many firms. One of the most important reasons for the establishment of the IRC was the attempt to create an instrument that could operate directly at the level of the firm, but it too was 'quite helpless' in industries where there was no desire to co-operate.[165]

Second, the need to respect the autonomy of private sector firms has created difficulties even when government financial assistance has been accepted, for it soon became clear that the provision of financial assistance by itself solved nothing. An effective monitoring system was essential, and the logic of the situation was inescapable. If monitoring revealed that a firm or project for which financial assistance had been provided was going wrong, remedial action, if necessary over-ruling and replacing the existing management, was called for.[166] However, this was incompatible with the continued existence of a 'mixed economy' in any meaningful sense, a necessary condition for which is the commercial independence of the private sector. Young has summarised the position as follows:

> Thus a situation has emerged in which government seeks to work through the private sector because it sees its aims and the firm's aims as being similar, *but in practice there are many instances where the two are poles apart.* This means that basing industrial policy and the relationship between government and industry on the principle of consent, and relying mainly on persuasion and cajolery will not always achieve the government's end, because the independence and autonomy of the firm enables it to resist government's attempts to influence its decision-making. The reluctance that governments show to overrule the wishes of the firm, as for example in a takeover or follow-up situation, means that basic economic problems continue to exist because the independence of the firm frustrates the implementation of policy and its impact on the basic problems. It is *the search for means of bringing government influence to bear on the firm that do not involve the firm losing its commercial independence,* that has been at the heart of British industrial policy between the late 1950s and the election in February 1974.[167]

At the heart of the argument around Labour's industrial policy in the mid 1970s, in particular around planning agreements, was the question of whether this search would continue or whether an effective industrial policy would be developed on the basis of over-ruling, if necessary, the private sector.

Two interconnected problems have emerged from this discussion of the criteria guiding UK industrial policy and the approach adopted towards its implementation. In the case of criteria the central issue is whether intervention is intended to supplement existing market forces or to supplant them. In the case of implementation the issue is whether the independence of the firm should be respected even if government policy is thereby frustrated. The two issues are, of course, closely linked, since the likelihood of consent being withheld will be much greater if the government is seeking to over-rule market forces and impose its own strategic direction of development than if it is merely promoting marginal adjustments.

9.5 CONCLUSION

This chapter has examined the microinterventionist activities of the state under the two broad headings of competition policy and industrial policy. Although in official statements the two are presented as different aspects of the same policy, there has in fact been little connection between them.

Competition policy, faced with the underlying tendency in capitalist economies for concentration to increase, has been relatively ineffective. Dominant firms have never been broken up, and mergers have rarely been prevented. The agencies of competition policy have been almost exclusively concerned with the behaviour of firms rather than with structural change. Certain uncompetitive practices undertaken by dominant firms have been generally condemned, while agreements between firms to engage in restrictive practices have largely disappeared, or at least have been driven underground. Superficially, the most successful aspect of competition policy has been that concerned with restrictive agreements. However, this may have been counterproductive in the longer run since there is some evidence that the ending of restrictive agreements has been a factor contributing to subsequent merger in some industries.

Of course, competition policy has been of some benefit to people as consumers by checking the worst excesses made possible by monopoly power. However, it has also had an ideological function, namely, to keep alive the concept of a decentralised self-regulating economic system as the norm, with state action only as an exception to be kept to a minimum; and whatever contribution competition policy may have made to consumer welfare along traditional lines, there is no evidence that it has contributed to improved performance in the two areas of principal concern to successive governments: productivity and the balance of payments.

Three modifications to competition policy in the United Kingdom were under discussion in 1978. First, there was the proposal to create a category of practices engaged in by firms with monopoly power which would be regarded as contrary to the public interest unless shown to be otherwise. Second, there was a proposal to bring oligopolistic market structures within the scope of the legislation. Finally, there were proposals designed to strengthen policy towards merger, widely considered to be very ineffective. However, there was also concern in some circles, including the NEDC, to ensure that competition policy did not interfere with industrial policy, and this concern was finding expression in opposition to the proposed strengthening of merger policy.

Although influenced by factors that are common to all advanced capitalist countries, the development of industrial policy in the United Kingdom has been closely related to the particular problems associated with Britain's weakening international position. However, there is little evidence that industrial policy in the United Kingdom so far has had much impact on that position. One reason for this may be ideological. Industrial policy develops because the market mechanism is failing to produce an acceptable performance. For industrial policy to be effective there must be criteria other than those of the market, and the government must be prepared to over-rule the autonomy of private sector firms; but if this were to happen on any scale, the 'mixed economy' would be undermined, and the rationale for capitalism would be removed. Refusal to recognise this has led to endless attempts to square the circle, i.e. to develop an industrial policy that takes as given the very circumstances that have contributed to the need for such a policy in the first place, namely, private ownership and the autonomy of private sector firms interacting with one another through the market mechanism.

This is not to say that industrial policy has done nothing. Very large amounts of public money have been paid to private sector firms, but this has been on the private sector's terms. Given that the governments of both parties have been committed to the 'mixed economy' and to proceeding by consent, it could not have been otherwise. This provision of public money to private firms on the latter's terms has been aptly described by Young as 'state-supported capitalism'.[168]

Planning in advanced capitalist economies has also had an impact. In the United Kingdom there has been no effective overall or comprehensive planning since the Second World War, but there have been attempts at sectoral or partial planning. Such sectoral planning, undertaken by collective bodies representing the industries concerned, typically EDCs, has provided an apparent rationale for channelling resources to private firms. However, capitalist planning has also fulfilled a normative or ideological role. Watson has identified two distinct modes of planning – technocratic and corporatist – which coexist in varying proportions according to circumstances. *Technocratic planning* is concerned primarily with the technical problems of consistency in the sense of attempting to ensure an adequate balance between supplies and demands in a set of interlocking industries and markets. *Corporatist planning* is concerned primarily with the political problems of achieving consensus between potentially conflicting interest groups. Except in the case of incomes policies, Watson has argued, the technocratic mode has been dominant, and this has been associated with partial rather than comprehensive planning, i.e. the 'planning' of bits of the economy rather than of the economy as a whole. Although partial planning has by definition no overall technical-planning function, it has an overall social function, namely, legitimation; that is, it accustoms people to think of economic problems as technical rather than political and social and thereby contributes to acquiescence in the political and social *status quo*.[169]

Watson's analysis is very helpful for understanding the problems facing industrial policy, and planning, in the United Kingdom. The fundamental reason why such policies have not worked is that they have been authoritarian and elitist in conception and attempted execution.[170] In the United Kingdom, corporatist planning in relation to incomes policy has been directed towards achieving agreement between the government on the one hand and the CBI and TUC on the other, but the limited extent to which these latter bodies can commit those whom they represent has been largely responsible for the limited duration of any agreements reached. Technocratic planning, concerned with detailed sectoral problems, has also experienced difficulty in making contact with those whose action is decisive. This means not only management but, at least as important, also workers, particularly since in the process of technocratic planning the participation of the trade unions is frequently a formality observed for the purposes of legitimation.[171]

Predictably, as the 1970s drew to a close, there were two broad responses to the failure of industrial policy to have made any evident in-roads into the under-lying problems of British capitalism.[172] Neither, as of then, had been tried. The left-wing prescription was based on the premise that to be effective a policy for industry must be democratic. This meant the elaboration of democratically determined priorities for resource allocation, the development of mechanisms for ensuring the social accountability of enterprises and the involvement of workers in running their places of work. The 1972–4 Labour Party policy of NEB control of twenty or so of the largest companies, planning agreements and industrial democracy was an attempt to achieve this. At that time the strength of the forces committed to the *status quo* was great enough to prevent the implementation of this policy and the 1974 Labour Government adopted instead the ineffective policy discussed in Section 9.4.

The right-wing reaction to the failure of industrial policy was to advocate a more thorough-going disengagement than had been attempted by the Conservative Government between 1970 and 1972. British experience between 1960 and 1974 suggested that there were major structural obstacles to the implementation of such a policy. Young's conclusion certainly supports this interpretation:

'Thus, two different Governments with totally opposed views add to the utility of intervention came round to the view that in order to solve the basic economic problems they had no option but to develop increasingly detailed policies.'[173]

The election in 1979 of a right-wing Conservative Government ideologically committed to achieving a major reduction in the role of the State, however, threw industrial policy in the UK back into the melting pot. It heralded the start of the most determined attempt so far at thorough going disengagements. Whether the new approach could actually be implemented in practice or whether the obstacles would prove too great, remains a question for the experience of the early 1980s to answer.

FURTHER READING

For a fuller discussion of the difficulties associated with various performance criteria, especially profitability, see Chapter 8. A stimulating examination of the relationship between Britain's industrial sector and balance of payments is to be found in Singh.[23] The 1978 report of the government interdepartmental working party on monopolies and mergers policy is well worth reading.[25] For a discussion of policy towards restrictive practices, see Swann *et al.*[7] Papers presented at a 1974 conference on industrial subsidies have been edited by Whiting.[10] Indispensable for an understanding of industrial policy is the study by Young with Lowe of the IRC and the 1970–2 experiment in disengagement.[119] Equally valuable is the history of the NEDC and the various exercises in planning between 1960 and 1976 by Shanks.[113] Finally, for one version of the left alternative see Holland,[149] and for one version of the right alternative see Budd.[174]

NOTES AND REFERENCES

1 For discussion of other ways in which the government has sought to influence the private industrial sector, see S. Young, *Intervention in the Mixed Economy* (London, Croom Helm, 1974), ch. 2.

2 For a comprehensive discussion, see J. de V. Graaff, *Theoretical Welfare Economics* (Cambridge, Cambridge UP, 1957). See also Chapter 8.

3 Cf. R. Lipsey and K. Lancaster, 'The general theory of second best', *Review of Economic Studies,* vol. 24 (October 1956), pp. 11–32.

4 See, for example, J. M. Clark, 'Toward a concept of workable competition', *American Economic Review,* vol. 30 (June 1940), pp. 241–56. See also Chapter 8.

5 Cf. R. M. Cyert and K. D. George, 'Competition, growth and efficiency', *Economic Journal,* vol. 79 (March 1969), p. 25.

6 See *The Report of the Attorney General's National Committee to Study Anti-Trust Laws* (Washington, DC, US Government Printing Office, 1965), excerpt from ch. 7 reproduced in A. Hunter (ed.), *Monopoly and Competition* (Harmondsworth, Penguin Books, 1969), ch. 5.

7 For a discussion of the theory of competition policy that, while still critical, is more sympathetic to workable competition, see D. Swann, D. P. O'Brien, W. Maunder and W. Howe, *Competition in British Industry* (London, Allen & Unwin, 1974), ch. 3, esp. pp. 103–9.

8 It has been suggested that the attitude of the Restrictive Practices Court has changed since its composition altered; cf. R. Stevens and B. Yamey, *The Restrictive Practices Court* (London, Weidenfeld & Nicolson, 1965), p. 115, and ch. 6, s. 3, pp. 125–35. Cf. also: 'References to the Monopolies Commission have been like dipping into a bran-tub, the tone of the final report being decided by which of the available part-time members happened to be free at the time the reference was made', 'Fair's fair up to the time that I say it isn't' (*The Economist,* 9 December 1972, p. 85).

9 Hannah and Kay have suggested that the appropriate contrast between UK and US policies towards merger is not that one is *ad hoc* and the other *per se*, but that UK policy has been ineffective and US policy effective (L. Hannah and J. Kay, *Concentration in Modern Industry,* London, Macmillan, 1977, pp. 116–17).

10 See, for example, A. R. Prest, The economic rationale of subsidies to industry', in A. Whiting (ed.), *The Economics of Industrial Subsidies* (London, HMSO, 1976), pp. 65–74; and J. Wiseman, 'An economic analysis of the Expenditure Committee reports on public money in the private sector', in Whiting, op. cit. (n. 10), pp. 77–85.

11 M. Panic, 'Introduction' to M. Panic (ed.), *The UK and West German Manufacturing Industry, 1954–72* (London, National Economic Development Office, 1976), p. xi.

12 D. T. Jones, 'Output, employment and labour productivity in Europe since 1955', *National Institute Economic Review,* vol. 77 (August 1976), pp. 73–6. The EEC Five are Belgium, France, West Germany, Italy and the Netherlands.

13 I. Elliott and A. Hughes, 'Capital and labour: their growth, distribution and productivity', in Panic, op. cit. (n. 11), ch. 2, p. 30.

14 C. Pratten, *Labour Productivity Differentials within International Companies,* University of Cambridge Department of Applied Economics, Occasional Paper 50 (Cambridge UP, 1976), pp. 5–10; and C. Pratten, *A Comparison of the Performance of Swedish and UK Companies,* University of Cambridge Department of Applied Economics, Occasional Paper 47 (Cambridge, Cambridge UP, 1976), p. 125. For a summary of the two studies, see C. Pratten, 'The efficiency of British industry', *Lloyds Bank Review,* no. 123 (January 1977), pp. 19–28.

15 Central Policy Review Staff, *The Future of the British Car Industry* (London, HMSO, 1975), p. 79.

16 M. Panic, 'Why the UK's propensity to import is high', *Lloyds Bank Review,* no: 115 (January 1975), pp. 4–6.

17 B. Moore and J. Rhodes, 'The relative decline of the UK manufacturing sector', in Cambridge Economic Policy Group, *Economic Policy Review,* No. 2 (Cambridge, University of Cambridge Department of Applied Economics, March 1976), ch. 4, p. 37.

18 L. Campbell-Boross and A. Morgan, 'Net trade: a note on measuring changes in the competitiveness of British industry in foreign trade', *National Institute Economic Review*, vol. 68 (May 1974), p. 81. The index of competitiveness, C, is defined as

$$C = \frac{X_n/M_n}{X_o/M_o} \times 100$$

where X and M are respectively exports and imports, the subscript 0 refers to the base year, and the subscript n refers to the year for which C is calculated.

19 Information Division of the Treasury, 'The international competitiveness of UK manufactured goods', *Economic Progress Report*, no. 95 (February 1978), p. 2; reprinted in *Trade and Industry*, vol. 30 (17 February 1978), pp. 340–1.

20 M. Fetherston, B. Moore and J. Rhodes, 'Manufacturing export shares and cost competitiveness of advanced industrial countries', in Cambridge Economic Policy Group, *Economic Policy Review*, No. 3 (Cambridge, University of Cambridge Department of Applied Economics, March 1977), ch. 6, pp. 62–6.

21 Moore and Rhodes, op. cit. (n. 17), p. 36. See also National Economic Development Office (NEDO), *International Price Competitiveness, Non-price Factors and Export Performance* (London, NEDO, 1977).

22 See Information Division of the Treasury, 'Productivity and real earnings', *Economic Progress Report*, no. 93 (December 1977), p. 2.

23 See especially Panic, op. cit. (n. 16), pp. 9–11; and A. Singh, 'UK industry and the world economy: a case of deindustrialisation?', *Cambridge Journal of Economics*, vol. 1 (1977), pp. 131–2.

24 *Winning the Battle against Inflation*, Cmnd 7293 (London, HMSO, July 1978), pp. 5–6. The Industrial Strategy was one form assumed by industrial policy under the 1974 Labour government. The Industry Act 1972 and sector working parties are discussed in section 9.4.

25 For a quasi-official summary of the legislation covering competition policy, see *A Review of Monopolies and Mergers Policy*, Cmnd 7198 (London, HMSO, May 1978), annex F, pp. 123–30.

26 Supplementary legislation in 1978 included the Restrictive Practices Court Act 1976 and the Restrictive Trade Practices Act 1977.

27 Restrictive Trade Practices Act 1976, s. 10(1).

28 Restrictive Trade Practices Act 1976, s. 10(1).

29 Restrictive Trade Practices Act 1976, s. 19(1).

30 Cf. Allen commenting on his twelve-year membership of the Monopolies Commission: 'In fact, the guidance given by the Act consisted of a string of platitudes which the Commission found valueless, and it was left for the members themselves to reach their own conclusions by reference to the assumptions, principles or prejudices which their training and experience caused them to apply to economic affairs' (G. C. Allen, *Monopoly and Restrictive Practices*, London, Allen & Unwin, 1968, p. 66).

31 Resale Prices Act 1976, s. 14(2).

32 Fair Trading Act 1973, s. 84(2).

33 Fair Trading Act 1973, s. 74(2). Virtually the same phrase is used in the case of monopoly reports; cf. s. 54(3).

34 The principles varied over time, but in general the criteria for price behaviour remained essentially those contained in the first White Paper *(Prices and Incomes Policy*, Cmnd 2639, London, HMSO, April 1965, paras 9–10, p. 7). Although they fall outside the scope of this chapter, the activities of the NBPI relating to incomes were undoubtedly its main preoccupation. It is clear that prices were included within the scope of the policy largely as a *quid pro quo* for obtaining the co-operation

of the Trades Union Congress over wages in the initial stages; cf. A. Graham, 'Industrial policy', in W. Beckerman (ed.), *The Labour Government's Economic Record, 1964–70* (London, Duckworth, 1972), p. 194.

35 The Price Codes and the Price Commission were only one side of the Counter-Inflation Act 1973. The other side concerned incomes. It was administered by the Pay Board and was again in fact the main focus of the policy. The Pay Board was abolished by the 1975 Labour government, but the Price Commission was retained as part of the deal designed to achieve voluntary wage restraint. The Price Code became increasingly complex as the government wrestled with the problem of helping profitability while appearing to retain a firm control over prices.

36 Price Commission Act 1977, s. 2(2).

37 Industrial Reorganisation Act 1966, s. 2(1).

38 Industrial Reorganisation Corporation (IRC), *Report and Accounts for the Year ended 31 March 1969*, (London, IRC, 1968) p. 8.

39 Industry Act 1972, s. 8(1), as amended by the Industry Act 1975. Unless otherwise stated, references to the 1972 Act are to the Act as amended; see schedule 4 of the 1975 Act for the amended text.

40 The original figures were £150 million, £100 million and £550 million respectively, but these were increased to those in the text by the Industry (Amendment) Act 1976.

41 Industry Act 1972, s. 9(3).

42 Department of Industry, *Criteria for Assistance to Industry* (London, Department of Industry, January 1976), esp. paras 9, 12, 14, 18 and 32; reproduced in *Industry Act 1972: Annual Report by the Secretaries of State for Industry, Scotland and Wales for the Year ended 31 March 1976*, HC 619 (London, HMSO, 1976), appendix A, pp. 35–40.

43 The restrictions prohibited the provision of assistance under the 1972 Act except when no other source of finance was available, gave priority to forms of assistance other than shareholding, set a limit of 50 per cent on any state shareholding that could not be avoided, required the earliest possible disposal of any state shareholding, and placed an end-1977 termination date on any new section 8 assistance. They reflected the reluctance with which the 1970 Conservative government accepted the inevitable as well as a sop to backwoods opinion, while their repeal under the 1975 Act in turn reflected both a more interventionist posture on the part of the 1974 Labour government and a sop to the Labour left.

44 See *The Regeneration of British Industry*, Cmnd 5710 (London, HMSO, August 1974), for detailed proposals concerning planning agreements as they were originally envisaged.

45 Industry Act 1975, s. 2(1).

46 Secretary of State for Industry, *Industry Act 1975: the National Enterprise Board (Guidelines) Direction 1976* (London, Department of Industry, 1976); reproduced in National Enterprise Board (NEB), *Annual Report and Accounts, 1977* (London, NEB, 1978), appendix B, pp. 56–60.

47 See Secretary of State for Industry: *Financial duty relating to NEB investments in companies other than British Leyland Ltd and Rolls Royce Ltd* (London, Department of Industry, 1977); and *Financial duty in respect of British Leyland Ltd* (London, Department of Industry, 1978); both reproduced in NEB, op. cit. (n. 46), appendixes E and F, pp. 63–4, respectively. These were the only financial directions made by April 1978.

48 *An Approach to Industrial Strategy*, Cmnd 6315 (London, HMSO, November 1975), para. 1, p. 4.

49 Cmnd 6315, op. cit. (n. 48), para. 7, p. 6.

50 Cmnd 6315, op. cit. (n. 48), para. 31, p. 12.

51 A brief survey of some of the major issues arising in the Restrictive Practices Court's

work is given here. For more detailed discussion, see C. Brock, *The Control of Restrictive Practices from 1956* (London, McGraw-Hill, 1966); A. Hunter, *Competition and the Law* (London, Allen & Unwin, 1966), chs 5–9; Stevens and Yamey, op. cit. (n. 8); Swann *et al.*, op. cit. (n. 7); and symposia in the *Economic Journal*, vol. 70 (September 1960), pp. 455–84 and in *Oxford Economic Papers*, vol. 17 (November 1965), pp. 347–467. Fairly lengthy extracts from the Court's judgements in six cases are given in Hunter, op. cit. (n. 6).

52 The Restrictive Practices Court had delivered more than thirty-five judgements in contested cases, but some of these were concerned with further developments or variations in cases already considered and others with preliminary issues to be settled prior to substantive hearings.

53 Director-General of Fair Trading, *Annual Report for the Period January 1977 to December 1977*, HC 228 (London, HMSO, 8 March 1978), pp. 35–9.

54 A minor restriction in the Blanket Manufacturers' Agreements passed (*b*) but also failed the tailpiece.

55 Registrar of Restrictive Trading Agreements, *Report of the Registrar, 1 July 1966 to 30 June 1969*, Cmnd 4303 (London, HMSO, 1970), p. 20. The whole of this account follows closely the registrar's notes on the case (pp. 17–20).

56 For a discussion of the theoretical issues involved, see especially the work of G. B. Richardson: *Information and Investment* (London, Oxford UP, 1960); 'The theory of restrictive trade practices', *Oxford Economic Papers*, vol. 17 (November 1965), pp. 432–49; and 'Price notification schemes', *Oxford Economic Papers*, vol. 19 (November 1967), pp. 355–69.

57 Registrar of Restrictive Trading Agreements, *Report of the Registrar, 1 July 1963 to 30 June 1966*, Cmnd 3188 (London, HMSO, 1967), p. 18.

58 *Law Reports: Restrictive Practices*, vol. 1 (January 1959); reproduced in Hunter, op. cit. (n. 6), pp. 317–18.

59 Cf. 'Thus the *Net Books* case represents a genuine and serious collision between the principles of economic efficiency and consideration of equity' (Hunter, op. cit., n. 51, p. 130).

60 A. Sutherland, 'Economics in the Restrictive Practices Court', *Oxford Economic Papers*, vol. 17 (November 1965), pp. 385–431.

61 Hunter, op. cit. (n. 51), ch. 6.

62 N. Leyland, 'Competition in the Court', *Oxford Economic Papers*, vol. 17 (November 1965), pp. 461–7.

63 Brock, op. cit. (n. 51), pp. 131–2.

64 Hunter, op. cit. (n. 51), p. 149.

65 Hunter, op. cit. (n. 51), p. 154.

66 Hunter, op. cit. (n. 51), p. 155.

67 See Registrar of Restrictive Trading Agreements, op. cit. (n. 57), pp. 36–42; Cmnd 7198, op. cit. (n. 25), annex B, p. 72; and Director-General of Fair Trading, op. cit. (n. 53), p. 36.

68 Swann *et al.*, op. cit. (n. 7), pp. 199–200.

69 J. B. Heath, 'Restrictive practices and after', *Manchester School*, vol. 29 (May 1961), pp. 173–202. Heath has pointed out that his results should be treated with caution since the response rate was only about one-third and since replies to questionnaires in any case tend to be unreliable.

70 G. Newbould, *Managers and Merger Activity* (Liverpool, Guthstead, 1970), p. 145.

71 Swann *et al.*, op. cit. (n. 7), esp. ch. 4, pp. 145–214.

72 Swann *et al.*, op. cit. (n. 7), p. 195.

73 See Cmnd 7198, op. cit. (n. 25), pp. 32–3.

74 See Monopolies Commission, *Recommended Resale Prices*, HC100 (London, HMSO, 1969). For a fuller discussion, see J. Pickering, 'The abolition of resale price

maintenance in Great Britain', *Oxford Economic Papers,* vol. 26 (March 1974), pp. 120–46.

75 For detailed although rather dated discussion of the work of the Monopolies Commission, see Hunter, op. cit. (n. 51), ch. 10; A. Sutherland, *The Monopolies Commission in Action,* University of Cambridge Department of Applied Economics, Occasional Paper 21 (Cambridge, Cambridge UP, 1970); and C. K. Rowley, *The British Monopolies Commission* (London, Allen & Unwin, 1966). Extracts from Monopolies Commission reports on three dominant-firm references are given in Hunter, op. cit. (n. 6).

76 There was also a follow-up report on imported timber and a report on aluminium semimanufactures, which were found to be within the scope of the Restrictive Practices Court and not the Monopolies and Mergers Commission.

77 Monopolies Commission, *Metal Containers: A Report on the Supply of Metal Containers,* HC 6 (London, HMSO, 10 July 1970). Although the Monopolies Commission report on metal containers is not among its most recent, it is retained from earlier editions of this book since metal containers were the subject of one of the first reports of the new Price Commission (Price Commission, *Metal Box Ltd: Open Top Food and Beverage and Aerosol Cans,* HC 135, London, HMSO, January 1978).

78 Sutherland, op. cit. (n. 75), p. 46.

79 In six of these cases the reference was limited to certain 'things done', so that the dominant position itself was not considered from the standpoint of the public interest. In two further cases – diazo copying materials, flour and bread – the Monopolies and Mergers Commission formally found nothing contrary to the public interest under the Fair Trading Act 1973, but it did unearth unregistered agreements within the jurisdiction of the Restrictive Practices Court.

80 For a recent survey, see Cmnd 7198, op. cit. (n. 25), annex 3, pp. 73–5.

81 Hunter, op. cit. (n. 51), pp. 254–5.

82 K. George and C. Joll, 'EEC competition policy', *Three Banks Review,* no. 117 (March 1978), p. 61.

83 Graham has argued that 'it was rare for the recommendations of the Monopolies Commission to be carried out by the Government in anything like their original form' (op. cit., n. 34, p. 193).

84 This amazing statement, made by the president of the Board of Trade on 26 April 1967, is reproduced in Board of Trade, *Monopolies and Mergers Acts 1948 and 1965: Annual Report for the Year ended 31 December 1967,* HC 131 (London, HMSO, 1968), appendix 6.

85 Rowley, op. cit. (n. 75), p. 349.

86 Cmnd 7198, op. cit. (n. 25), para. 2.4, p. 6.

87 For further discussion, see Sutherland, op. cit. (n. 75), esp. pt 2; Office of Fair Trading, *Mergers* (London, HMSO, 1978); and Cmnd 7198, op. cit. (n. 25), esp. annex D, pp. 97–112.

88 Office of Fair Trading, op. cit. (n. 87), p. 13. For a well-known theoretical framework in terms of which to consider the balance of costs and benefits arising from merger, see O. Williamson, 'Economies as an antitrust defence: the welfare tradeoffs', *American Economic Review,* vol. 58 (March 1968), pp. 18–36.

89 See Cmnd 7198, op. cit. (n. 25), annex D, tables 3 and 4, pp. 108–9; and Office of Fair Trading, op. cit. (n. 87), annex 2, pp. 43–4. An additional twenty mergers were considered under a special confidentiality procedure. Rival bids for the same company were counted as one reference. The market share criterion was at least one-third until November 1973 and at least one-quarter thereafter.

90 Cmnd 7198, op. cit. (n. 25), annex F, pp. 128–9.

91 Sutherland, op. cit. (n. 75), pt 2.

92 See, for example, Hannah and Kay, op. cit. (n. 9), pp. 116–17.

93 See Cmnd 7198, op. cit. (n. 25), annex H, pp. 151–61.

94 Swann *et al.,* op. cit. (n. 7), p. 209.

95 Cmnd 7198, op. cit. (n. 25), p. 37.

96 For the working party's discussion, see Cmnd 7198, op. cit. (n. 25), paras 5.13–5.24, pp. 34–8.

97 At the time of writing the only systematic information available on the new Price Commission was that given in its quarterly reports; see Price Commission, *Report for the Period 1 August to 31 October 1977,* HC 117 (London, HMSO, 1977), and subsequent reports. For a discussion of the old Price Commission, which gave way to the new Commission in August 1977, see Price Commission, *Report for the Period 1 March to 31 May 1977,* HC 459 (London, HMSO, 1977), ch. 2, pp. 8–14; A. Cockfield, 'The Price Commission and the price control', *Three Banks Review,* no. 117 (March 1978), pp. 3–25; and R. Evely, 'The effects of the Price Code', *National Institute Economic Review,* vol. 77 (August 1976), pp. 50–9.

98 Price Commission, op. cit. (n. 97, *1 August to 31 October*), p. 1.

99 Price Commission, op. cit. (n. 77); and Monopolies Commission, op. cit. (n. 77).

100 Price Commission, *Report for the Period 1 February to 30 April 1978,* HC 516 (London, HMSO, June 1978), pp. 1–2. Examinations referred under the 1977 Act were wider in scope than the special references to the old Price Commission under the Counter-Inflation Act 1973, of which there were thirty-three.

101 For a fuller discussion of the NBPI's activities, see A. Fels, *The British Prices and Incomes Board,* University of Cambridge Department of Applied Economics, Occasional Paper 29 (Cambridge, Cambridge UP, 1972); J. Mitchell, *The National Board for Prices and Incomes* (London, Secker & Warburg, 1972); J. Pickering, 'The Prices and Incomes Board and private sector prices: a survey', *Economic Journal,* vol. 81 (June 1971), pp. 225–41; and A. Jones, 'Prices and incomes policy', *Economic Journal,* vol. 78 (December 1968), pp. 799–806.

102 For a discussion of the NBPI's activities in relation to managerial efficiency, see Fels, op. cit. (n. 101), ch. 11.

103 Price Commission, *Report for the Period 1 November 1977 to 31 January 1978,* HC 287 (London, HMSO, 1978), p. 12.

104 Cf. 'Within certain limits . . . it seems reasonable in the light of recent thinking to suppose that the overall rate of profit, in the longer term as in the short, contains, like the pay structure, an element which can be regarded as depending on contemporary attitudes and implicitly agreed conventions' (United Nations, Secretariat of the Economic Commission for Europe, *Incomes in Post War Europe,* Geneva, UN, 1967, p. 4).

105 Cf. Fels, op. cit. (n. 101), p. 214.

106 For a fuller discussion, see P. Devine *et al., An Introduction to Industrial Economics,* 1st or 2nd edn (London, Allen & Unwin, 1974 or 1976), pp. 477–82.

107 *Productivity, Prices and Incomes Policy after 1969,* Cmnd 4237 (London, HMSO, 1969), para. 24.

108 Cmnd 7198, op. cit. (n. 25), paras 5.36–5.38, p. 42.

109 G. Denton, 'Financial assistance to British industry', in W. M. Corden and G. Fels (eds), *Public Assistance to Industry* (London, Macmillan, 1976), ch. 5, p. 123.

110 H. Begg, C. Lythe, R. Sorley and D. Macdonald, 'Annual expenditure on special regional assistance to industry in Great Britain, 1960/1–1972/3: a note', *Economic Journal,* vol. 85 (December 1975), table 1, p. 885.

111 D. Roy, *State Holding Companies* (London, Fabian Society, 1974); cited in S. Holland, *The Socialist Challenge* (London, Quartet, 1975), pp. 66–7 and 73.

112 A. Prest, *How Much Subsidy?,* Research Monograph 32 (London, Institute of Economic Affairs, 1974), table 2, p. 29.

113 This subsection is taken largely from M. Shanks, *Planning and Politics: The*

British Experience, 1960–76 (London, Allen & Unwin, 1977), chs 1 and 2, pp. 17–46.

114 Quoted in Shanks, op. cit. (n. 113), p. 23. Shanks has noted that to the best of his knowledge these initial terms of reference were not subsequently changed.

115 Quoted in Shanks, op. cit. (n. 113), p. 25.

116 Shanks, op. cit. (n. 113), p. 25.

117 Shanks, op. cit. (n. 113), p. 43.

118 For a discussion of indicative planning in the context of the National Plan, see M. Surrey, 'The National Plan in retrospect', *Bulletin of the Oxford University Institute of Economics and Statistics,* vol. 34 (August 1972), pp. 249–68, esp. s. 2. For a theoretical discussion, see J. Meade, *The Theory of Indicative Planning* (Manchester, Manchester UP, 1970).

119 The major primary sources of information on the Industrial Research Corporation (IRC) are its *Report and Accounts for December 1966 to March 1968*, HC 252 (London, HMSO, 1968); *for the Year ended 31 March 1969*, HC 286 (London, HMSO, 1969); *for the Year ended 31 March 1970*, HC 310 (London, HMSO, 1970); and *for April 1970 to April 1971*, HC 443 (London, HMSO, 1971). See also S. Young with A. Lowe, *Intervention in the Mixed Economy* (London, Croom Helm, 1974); S. Young, 'Reshaping industry: the IRC in retrospect', *New Society*, vol. 16 (19 November 1970), pp. 906–8; and W. G. McClelland, 'The Industrial Reorganisation Corporation, 1966–71: and experimental prod', *Three Banks Review,* no. 94 (June 1972), pp. 23–42.

120 IRC, op. cit. (n. 119, *April 1970 to April 1971), p. 10.

121 IRC, op. cit. (n. 119, *Year ended 31 March 1970*), p. 6. The IRC discovered the crisis at Rolls Royce well before it came to a head and became public.

122 IRC, op. cit. (n. 119, *Year ended 31 March 1969*), p. 7. Cf. also McClelland, a member of the IRC Board: 'But it cannot be denied that in the main "reorganisation" was a euphemism for creating larger units, and the case for IRC stands or falls on the proposition that in many sectors British companies were not large enough, and that without intervention they would not become large enough, soon enough' (McClelland, op. cit. n. 119, p. 24).

123 IRC, op. cit. (n. 119, *Year ended 31 March 1970*), p. 5.

124 IRC, op. cit. (n. 119, *Year ended 31 March 1970*), p. 6.

125 Young, op. cit. (n. 119), p. 906.

126 IRC, op. cit. (n. 119, *Year ended 31 March 1970*), p. 6.

127 Young, op. cit. (n. 119), p. 907.

128 C. H. Villiers, managing director of the IRC, set out his ideas on the principles that might inform such a body in a speech delivered in Berlin in September 1969 (IRC, op. cit., n. 119, *Year ended 31 March 1970,* 3 April, pp. 37–8).

129 IRC, 'Statement on the UK ball and roller bearing industry'; reproduced in IRC, op. cit. (n. 119, *Year ended 31 March 1970*), 2 April, p. 34. Cf. also IRC, op. cit. (n. 119, *Year ended 31 March 1969*), p. 15.

130 IRC, op. cit. (n. 119, *Year ended 31 March 1970*), p. 14. Cf. also 'non-economic and longer-term considerations about the likelihood and desirability of a state of international helotry or vassalage have to be weighed' (McClelland, op. cit., n. 119, p. 26).

131 See Young, op. cit. (n. 119), p. 908.

132 See IRC, op. cit. (n. 119, *Year ended 31 March 1970*), pp. 12–13.

133 IRC, op. cit. (n. 119, *April 1970 to April 1971*), p. 10.

134 IRC, op. cit. (n. 119): *December 1966 to March 1968,* p. 7; *Year ended 31 March 1969*, p. 8; and *Year ended 31 March 1970,* p. 7.

135 IRC, op. cit. (n. 119, *December 1966 to March 1968*), p. 6.

136 Cf. 'The IRC's vague terms of reference meant that the personnel who operated it were crucial in determining its shape' (Graham, op. cit., n. 34, p. 211).

137 Cf. 'In dealing with the problem of the structure of industry the working of market forces remains the main instrument for change' (IRC, op. cit., n. 119, *Year ended 31 March 1969*, p. 17). See also S. Young, 'A comparison of the industrial experiences', in J. Hayward and M. Watson, *Planning, Politics and Public Policy* (Cambridge, Cambridge UP, 1975), ch. 7, p. 146; and Young with Lowe, op. cit. (n. 119), p. 168.
138 Graham, op. cit. (n. 34), p. 217.
139 For a discussion of the rise and fall of the Conservative government's disengagement policy, see Young with Lowe, op. cit. (n. 119), chs 11–13.
140 See Young with Lowe, op. cit. (n. 119), ch. 13.
141 As summarised in *Industry Act 1972: Annual Report by the Secretary of State for Industry for the Year ended 31 March 1975*, HC 620 (London, HMSO, 1975), p. 6.
142 For changes made by the Industry Act 1975, which removed certain restrictions on state intervention, see note 43. For revised criteria, see note 42.
143 See M. Stewart, *The Jekyll and Hyde Years: Politics and Economic Policy since 1964* (London, Dent, 1977), p. 218.
144 See J. Chapman, 'The Department of Industry's Accelerated Projects Scheme and Selective Investment Scheme', *National Westminster Quarterly Bank Review* (May 1978), pp. 27–34.
145 See Chapman, op. cit. (n. 144), pp. 34–7.
146 *Industry Act 1972: Annual Report by the Secretaries of State for Industry, Scotland and Wales for the Year ended 31 March 1977*, HC 545 (London, HMSO, 1977), pp. 9–12 and appendix U, p. 103.
147 See note 146, p. 5.
148 Department of Industry, 'Government support for industry', *Trade and Industry*, vol. 28 (23 September 1977), p. 539.
149 See Labour Party, Opposition Green Paper, *The National Enterprise Board* (London, Labour Party, n.d.); and Labour Party, *Labour's Programme, 1973* (London, Labour Party, 1973), pp. 17–19 and 33–4. For the most detailed account of the thinking behind these proposals that is available, see S. Holland, *The Socialist Challenge* (London, Quartet, 1975), esp. chs 7 and 8.
150 Information on the NEB in operation is scant. The most convenient source, on which what follows is based, is its annual reports. See National Enterprise Board (NEB), *Annual Report and Accounts, 1976* (London, NEB, 1977); and NEB, op. cit. (n. 46).
151 Information Division of the Treasury, 'The industrial strategy' *Economic Progress Report*, no. 96 (March 1978), pp. 4–5.
152 See A. Mueller, 'Industrial efficiency and government policy', *Trade and Industry*, vol. 29 (21 October 1977), p. 122.
153 See 'Industrial strategy: from analysis to action', *Trade and Industry*, vol. 30 (10 February 1978), pp. 268–71, which reproduces extracts from a memorandum by the chairman of the Industrial Strategy Staff Group on the SWP findings and from the joint memorandum of the Chancellor of the Exchequer and the Secretary of State for Industry; and also Information Division of the Treasury, op. cit. (n. 151), pp. 4–6.
154 Shanks, op. cit. (n. 113), p. 83.
155 Labour Party, *Labour's Programme for Britain, 1976* (London, Labour Party, n.d.), p. 4, supplement to *Labour Weekly*.
156 Shanks, op. cit. (n. 113), p. 82.
157 Cf. Shanks, op. cit. (n. 113), p. 78; and Stewart, op. cit. (n. 143), p. 219.
158 Cf. Prest, op. cit. (n. 10), pp. 72–4.
159 Cf. Young with Lowe, op. cit. (n. 119), pp. 176–7.
160 See note 42, p. 39.
161 Cf. J. Mitchell, 'Government intervention and industrial policy', in R. Griffiths (ed.),

Government, Business and Labour in European Capitalism (London, Europotentials Press, 1977), ch. 3, pp. 71–2.

162 Cf. I. M. D. Little and J. A. Mirrlees, *Project Appraisal and Planning for Developing Countries* (London, Heinemann, 1974).

163 Young with Lowe, op. cit. (n. 119), p. 87.

164 Young with Lowe, op. cit. (n. 119), p. 189.

165 Young with Lowe, op. cit. (n. 119), pp. 32, 34 and 82.

166 Young with Lowe, op. cit. (n. 119), pp. 201–5.

167 Young with Lowe, op. cit. (n. 119), p. 208.

168 Young with Lowe, op. cit. (n. 119), p. 168.

169 See M. Watson, 'The character and contradictions of Western-style planning', in Griffiths, op. cit. (n. 161), ch. 2, pp. 40–60; and M. Watson, 'A comparative evaluation of planning practice in the liberal democratic state', in Hayward and Watson, op. cit. (n. 137), pp. 445–83. See also L. Nizard, 'Planning as the regulatory reproduction of the status quo', in Hayward and Watson, op. cit. (n. 137), pp. 433–44.

170 Cf. Shanks, op. cit. (n. 113), p. 96; and Watson, op. cit. (n. 169, in Griffiths), pp. 51–9.

171 Watson, op. cit. (n. 169, in Griffiths), p. 45; and Watson, op. cit. (n. 169, in Hayward and Watson), pp. 468–9.

172 For a brief outline, see D. Morris, 'Industrial policy', in D. Morris (ed.), *The Economic System in the UK* (Oxford, Oxford UP, 1977), ch. 19, pp. 470–2; and Shanks, op. cit. (n. 113), pp. 94–7.

173 Young with Lowe, op. cit. (n. 119), pp. 174–5.

174 A. Budd, *The Politics of Economic Planning* (London, Fontana, 1978), chs 7 and 8, pp. 119–54.

10 Government Relations with the Public Industrial Sector

10.1 INTRODUCTION

The aim of this chapter is to examine the impact of government policy on the creation and control of the industry-based nationalised industries, with particular reference to their performance on the criteria discussed in Chapter 8. After a brief review of the extent of the nationalised industrial sector in the United Kingdom attention is focused mainly on the objectives of the industries, their financial performance and their pricing and investment policies. No attempt is made to present a comprehensive analysis of the nationalised industrial sector; instead, important points are illustrated in more detail by referring to the situation in a particular industry.

THE SCOPE OF THE NATIONALISED SECTOR

The nationalised industries fall mainly into four industrial sectors: fuel and power, transport and communications, steel, and shipbuilding and aircraft. The nationalised component of the fuel and power sector comprises the boards responsible for generating and distributing electricity, the British Gas Corporation, the National Coal Board and the British National Oil Corporation. The only major component of this sector that is not publicly owned is oil supply and refining.[1] The nationalised component of the transport sector comprises the British Railways Board, the British Airways Board, the British Airports Authority, the National Bus Company, the National Freight Corporation, the British Waterways Board and several ancillary undertakings. In addition, within public ownership but at local authority level there are substantial passenger-transport services, including those of London Transport and of the seven passenger transport authorities, and certain dock and airport interests. The great majority of *public* passenger-transport services are in public ownership, while the main concentration of private enterprise interests in *public* transport services is in road haulage and coastal shipping. There is also a very large supply of competing *private* transport services, derived principally from private cars and own-account lorries and vans, which are predominantly in private ownership. The British Steel Corporation has at present a virtual monopoly of the basic processes of steelmaking, but the private enterprise component is significant at the finishing stages, although still in a distinct minority. Shipbuilding and aircraft manufacture are sectors into which nationalisation has spread most recently. British Aerospace took over all major aircraft manufacturers, and British Shipbuilders most major shipbuilders, in 1977. In both these cases competition is fairly limited in domestic markets, but like British Steel both industries face considerable international competition.

The nationalised industries do not comprise the whole of the government's industrial 'portfolio'. Besides the industries comprising the nationalised-industry sector proper, defined as those financed under programme five of the public expenditure programme, there are the holdings of the National Enterprise Board (NEB), whose activities are discussed in Chapter 9 (pages 330 to 396). While it is difficult on most criteria to place a division between the NEB branch of the nationalised sector and that discussed in this chapter, the main difference seems to be that the NEB has holdings in companies rather than in whole sections of industries. In the rest of this chapter the analysis applies to the industry-based nationalised industries and excludes the NEB's holdings as well as the Bank of England and the Post Office.

A brief consideration of the extent of the nationalised industries within their own industrial sectors quickly leads to the conclusion that they play an important role in the economy as a whole. This is confirmed by the facts that they employ about 7 per cent of the labour force, contribute about 10 per cent of total output and account for 14 per cent of total fixed investment.[2, 3]

Apart from the recent additions mentioned above the great majority of the nationalised industries were brought into public ownership in the 1945–50 period by the then Labour government. Initially, this was treated as an ideological and party political issue, with the result that in transport and steel the degree of public ownership has changed according to the political persuasion of the ruling government. More recently, the ideological debate has softened sufficiently to permit a more considered appreciation of the objectives that the nationalised industries are supposed to achieve, although as yet the two main parties are far from reaching a consensus on these matters.

THE RATIONALE OF NATIONALISATION

There were four reasons for originating the nationalisation programme. First, it was believed that the prevailing market structure, characterised in transport, for example, by small units among which there was regulated competition, wasted resources. It was held that important resource savings could be achieved by creating larger units that were more capable of reaping the full economies of scale and by eliminating the 'unnecessary' duplication of facilities.[4] Second, it was believed that in order to plan the development of the postwar economy in an effective manner the government should be able to exercise effective control over the basic industries of the economy. Third, it was hoped that the establishment of the nationalised industries would make possible an improvement in the working and other conditions of the employees of those industries. Finally, it was seen as a move in the direction of the much broader socialist objective of creating a more egalitarian and co-operative society in Britain.

This thinking was reflected in some of the provisions of particular nationalising Acts in the late 1940s, but to varying degrees and often in an inexact way, as will become apparent in the next section. In practice little attention has been given to the fourth objective beyond providing for a system of worker consultation and strengthening the existing negotiating machinery. Conscious attempts have been made, particularly during the early years, to improve working conditions, but over the longer period the general terms and conditions of employment have been mainly determined by the operation of orthodox market forces. The establishment of the nationalised industries has effectively increased the degree of government control over industry – an asset probably welcomed by any harassed government, irrespective of its political persuasion – and has been widely exercised, but this begs the real question of what particular objectives have been pursued when these planning powers have been exercised. The short answer is: whatever particular short-run objective was being pursued by the government of the day, which could be restraining the increase in the cost of living, reducing the level of wage demands, regulating the level of investment in the country or conserving the financial resources of the Treasury. It is now widely accepted that this control has not always been exercised in the best long-term interests of the industries concerned or indeed of the economy. The first objective named above – that of reaping maximum economies of scale – has from time to time been found to conflict with other social and political objectives, e.g. when it was decided to build a number of smaller steel strip mills in Wales and Scotland, while at no time has the nationalised sector turned its back on the competitive market. In the energy, steel, shipbuilding, aircraft and transport sectors both domestic and international competition remain fierce.

The point that needs to be emphasised, therefore, is that the nationalised industries have never been called on to pursue 'narrow' clearly-defined economic or financial objectives; consequently, it is rather meaningless to judge their performance on the assumption that they have. At the same time their formal responsibilities, defined in legislation, have not constituted their effective objectives, which have been determined as a consequence of the close and continuous relationship with the appropriate minister and government department. In this situation a consensus of opinion has tended to develop on the sorts of criteria that ought to govern the decision making of the nationalised industries and on assessing their performance in terms of the degree to which they have approximated to these criteria in practice. This is a useful exercise, which is followed for a considerable part of this chapter, but the significance of the exercise should be fully appreciated at the outset. The point can best be made by a simple example. During the greater part of its history British Rail has made annual financial losses on its operation, which at certain periods have been very considerable in size. It is common to suggest that this indicates poor or unsatisfactory performance by British Rail. However, before accepting this statement it is first necessary to identify the more fundamental implicit objectives contained in the requirement that British Rail should pay its way in the circumstances that have prevailed; and second, it is necessary to take into account the reluctance of both political parties when in office to accept the service reductions and price increases judged necessary to achieve financial viability. This implies that in the government's preference function other objectives have taken precedence over the formal financial objectives placed on British Rail. Such an haphazard mixture of formal objectives and informal expectations was one of the main criticisms of the government control of nationalised industries made by the National Economic Development Office (NEDO) in its 1976 report. Many of the report's recommendations, discussed in detail later, were designed to broaden the criteria for judging the performance of the nationalised industries and to make the criteria more specific.[5]

LEGISLATION RELATING TO THE NATIONALISED SECTOR

To set the discussion of the ensuing sections in its institutional, legal and organisational contexts the rest of this section is devoted to a brief examination of the relevant legislation governing each of the four main sectors and to a discussion of the somewhat special nature of public corporations in the United Kingdom and the relationship that they enjoy with the ministers who are responsible for their control and, ultimately, with Parliament. Both are necessary, as they represent constraints that can affect the economic performance of the industries concerned.

Transport and Communications

The nationalising Act for the transport sector was the Transport Act 1947, which established the British Transport Commission. This comprised several executives such as the Railway Executive and the Road Haulage Executive, which were responsible for the various aspects of the Commission's activities. However, all these sectors of the transport industry were not immediately nationalised in their entirety. The details vary;[6] but in general the hotels and docks acquired were those formerly belonging to the railway companies, and apart from London Transport, which has been in public control since 1933, the only major bus undertakings acquired outright were again those owned by the railways.[7] In the case of road passenger transport the Act provided for the extension of public ownership in certain areas if the Commission saw fit. The only parts of the road haulage industry taken into public control were operators plying for public hire, and this did not occur until 1950.

The period of Conservative government from 1951 to 1964 was marked by two major reorganisations of the nationalised transport sector in 1953 and 1962. The main emphasis in the 1953 Transport Act was partial denationalisation (in road haulage) and decentralisation (particularly in the railways). It is significant that even at this early stage complete denationalisation was not suggested, which was as well in the light of experience with road haulage, in which about 30 per cent of the nationalised fleet could not be sold back to the private sector. In the 1962 Transport Act further decentralisation was the major emphasis, and the Commission was replaced by five separate boards.[8]

One of the first acts of the Labour Party administration after the 1966 election was to remove the restrictions on acquisition by the Transport Holding Company – the board that was responsible for road haulage and buses. This resulted in the company purchasing several transport undertakings, including the 1,600 vehicle Tayforth Group in the haulage sector and the bus companies owned by the British Electric Traction Company. The latter acquisition almost completed the nationalisation of major bus operators outside the local authority sector. These extensions to nationalisation were, however, achieved without the compulsion of legislation.

The main legislative measure of this period to affect the nationalised transport industries was the Transport Act 1968. This had been preceded by a series of White Papers on various aspects of transport policy,[9] which represented the most comprehensive review of transport policy as a whole undertaken by government to that date; and it is significant that the problems of the particular nationalised industries, e.g. railway deficits, were seen as part of the wider problems of transport policy as a whole.[10] Following this several organisational changes in the nationalised transport sector were made, including the splitting of road haulage and bus interests into separate companies. After this the only reorganisation was the merger of British European Airways (BEA) and the British Overseas Airways Corporation (BOAC) into British Airways in 1973.

Between 1968 and 1978 there was very little legislation affecting the nationalised transport industry. A major review of transport policy took place in 1976 and 1977; and the 1978 Transport Act put into effect some of the changes the review recommended.[11] The main impact on the nationalised transport industries was indirect – via the policy changes – rather than direct and it is fair to conclude from this process that measures affecting these industries are now placed more firmly in the context of transport policy rather than in the broader context of policy towards nationalisation itself.

Fuel and Power

Compared with the transport sector the fuel sector's legislative and organisational background is far less complicated. In the coal industry the original nationalising legislation – the Coal Industry (Nationalisation) Act 1946 – has been only slightly modified by the 1965 and 1967 Coal Industry Acts, which dealt with financial rather than organisational aspects. The 1946 Act set up the National Coal Board, which on 1 January 1947 acquired the assets of almost every coalmining company in the country together with a miscellaneous collection of other assets.

Both the gas and electricity industries have, however, undergone organisational changes since their original nationalisation, the latter as a result of a committee of inquiry and the former because of a radical technological change.

The gas industry was the last to be nationalised in the 1945 Labour administration's programme. The Gas Act 1948 set up twelve area gas boards, which were autonomous in almost every respect (production, pricing, marketing, investment) except industrial relations, and a Gas Council, which only had general powers to co-ordinate and supervise and responsibility for industrial relations. These boards took over the businesses of the more than 700 private companies and the smaller number of public authorities that had hitherto supplied gas. With the discovery of natural gas in the 1960s, followed by its import from abroad and still later by its pumping from the North Sea, the need for a national distribution grid became apparent, and the Gas Council emerged as both the supplier of this grid and the bulk purchaser of natural gas. The Gas Act 1965 strengthened the position of the Gas Council, giving it powers to manufacture and acquire gas and, more important, to supply area boards. The logical development of this was the Gas Act 1972, which combined the functions of the Gas Council and the area boards into the British Gas Corporation, which came into existence in 1973. As a result a single organisation is responsible for the whole UK gas industry.

The electricity industry was brought fully into public ownership in April 1948 by the Electricity Act 1947, but it had been subject to some degree of public ownership for a long time. First, 66 per cent of the 562 undertakings nationalised in 1948 were previously public authorities (mostly municipal); and second, since the Electricity (Supply) Act 1926 a Central Electricity Board had been responsible for the national distribution network (i.e. the national grid) and for controlling, but not owning, the power stations supplying it. The 1947 Electricity Act set up the British Electricity Authority, later to become the Central Electricity Authority, which was responsible for generation and for high voltage transmission to the twelve area boards established by this Act, which in turn were responsible for distribution.[12]

In 1956 the report of the committee of inquiry that had been looking into the industry prefaced the reorganisation contained in the Electricity Act 1957.[13] This established a tripartite organisation, with the area boards having the same responsibilities as before but with the Central Electricity Authority's sphere of influence divided between two bodies: the Electricity Council, responsible for labour relations and research for and advice to the industry as a whole; and the Central Electricity Generating Board, responsible for generation and transmission. All boards, including the area boards, were made financially autonomous.

In 1978 an attempt by the government to pass legislation to reorganise and further centralise the structure of the electricity industry failed to secure a parliamentary majority. In the future, therefore, the reorganisation of the electricity industry is a distinct possibility, although the technical grounds for it do not seem as strong as they were for the gas industry.

The British National Oil Corporation was probably more the result of technological development than of political ideology. The discovery of recoverable oil reserves in the North Sea in the late 1960s meant that the government had to devise a way of controlling exploration and the rates of extraction as well as of collecting the royalties due it as owner of the mineral rights. The Petroleum and Submarine Pipelines Act 1975 established the Corporation to do these tasks as well as to manage the government's direct investments in the oil industry.

Steel

The steel industry has probably had the most chequered history in respect of its progress towards nationalisation. It was first nationalised in 1951 under the Iron and Steel Act 1949. One hundred companies were taken over by the Iron and Steel Corporation, which was responsible for running the industry. Its activities were, however, short lived, as with the return of the Conservative Party to power in October 1951 denationalisation was promised in the King's Speech. Thus, in 1953 a further Iron and Steel Act was passed, authorising the denationalisation of the industry – a process completed in five years with the exception of one company – and setting up the Iron and Steel Board, which possessed only broad supervisory powers although it had a degree of financial control. In 1967 a third Iron and Steel Act renationalised the industry, although on this occasion only thirteen undertakings were acquired. They accounted for about 90 per cent of the industry's production of ores and heavy metals, but nevertheless this left a substantial private sector. Under the 1967 Act the British Steel Corporation was set up with responsibility for the industry.

Shipbuilding and Aircraft

The nationalisation of the aircraft and shipbuilding industries was part of the Labour Party's policy when it returned to power in 1974. It has been effected by the Aircraft and Shipbuilding Industries Act 1977. This formed two corporations – British Aerospace and British Shipbuilders – which took over the main companies in the respective industries in 1977. At present both are in the process of internal reorganisation.

Despite its length the above gives only a brief outline of the legislation and organisation of the nationalised industries in the four main sectors. It should not be assumed, however, that the legislation cited was only confined to the question of the transfer of assets from private to public ownership. Many other matters of importance were dealt with, to which passing mention has been made in a few cases. In particular the nationalising Acts dealt in detail with the financial aspects of the transfer and the financial structure of the industries concerned.[14] Two matters that they did not cover in any depth are: the relationship of the industries concerned with the ministers responsible for them, and their precise objectives. The discussion of the former in the following subsection concludes this introduction.

THE RELATIONSHIP BETWEEN THE NATIONALISED INDUSTRIES AND THE GOVERNMENT

The nationalised industries occupy a unique position in the hierarchy of state institutions. They are not government departments, yet, they depend entirely on the government for finance and ultimately for the authority to conduct their activities. This is not to say, however, that they can be thought of as autonomous and responsible to nobody. Control is exercised by the appropriate ministers as a result of powers given to them by the founding statutes and in other less formal ways.[15] The formal powers of ministers enable them to control finance, to give general directions to a board and to appoint board members. In practice such formal powers, especially the second one, have rarely been used explicitly, ministers choosing to use less formal ways of control. On occasion, however, e.g. with the Transport Commission in 1952, disputes have arisen, and the minister concerned has used his formal powers. In recent years with the issue of more detailed policy guidelines – particularly the 1961 and 1967 White Papers, discussed in section 10.2 below – the ministers concerned have become more intimately concerned with the performance of the industries, even more so because the position that these occupy in the economy has meant that their performance has sometimes been important to the achievement of the government's objectives for the economy as a whole. A further aspect of this is the fact that some industries – namely coal, railways and latterly steel – have been making financial losses and that the subsidies paid to them have inevitably been associated with further ministerial control.[16]

Ultimate control, however, rests with Parliament, which alone has the power to pass legislation to contract or expand an industry's activities. Obviously, if such powers were used other than on the initiative of the government of the day, it would indicate a breakdown of the political system. However,

Parliament has exercised the power at least to comment on the activities of the nationalised industries by virtue of the existence of the Select Committee on Nationalised Industries, whose objective is

> . . . to examine the Reports and Accounts of the Nationalised Industries established by Statute whose controlling Boards are appointed by Ministers of the Crown and whose annual receipts are not wholly or mainly derived from moneys provided by Parliament or advanced from the Exchequer.[17]

The workings and reports of this select committee are published as House of Commons Papers. The general pattern has been to select each major industry in turn for the subject of what has usually been a very detailed investigation culminating in a report and recommendations. At times the comments of the select committee have succeeded in airing some criticisms of the policies pursued by nationalised industries that might not otherwise have been given such publicity. In 1967–8 it investigated the whole subject of ministerial control, but in general it has been for the minister concerned to decide whether to adopt the select committee's recommendation.

In recent years the select committee has broadened the scope of its investigations. This is illustrated by its investigation in 1976 and 1977 into the role of British Rail in public transport.[18] This considered the activities of British Rail in the wider context of its contribution to transport policy objectives rather than in the narrow context of its financial performance. The report was an essentially forward-looking document, which considered the questions of the likely pattern of future demand for rail services and the future size of the rail network. It considered aspects of British Rail's relationships with other transport undertakings, including those in the local authority sector, and made recommendations that would, if implemented, also affect these operators. Much of the report was devoted to pricing, financial policy and investment, and many of its recommendations were accepted by the government. However, the report is more important in this context as an illustration of the broadening basis of Parliament's attitude to the nationalised industries, displaying an increasing emphasis on the efficiency with which the industries use their resources.

It is also worth noting that during the life of the National Board for Prices and Incomes (NBPI) many of its reports concerned the nationalised industries, especially in the period after September 1967 when all the industries' price increase proposals were referred to the NBPI.

The investigations, conclusions and recommendations of both these institutions form a useful body of knowledge on many aspects of the nationalised industries' activities and have undoubtedly had some influence on policy. Despite the existence of these bodies direct and effective control does rest with the ministers concerned, although, as emphasised above, the degree to which they have chosen to use it has varied with the circumstances.

Since 1970, however, there has been increasing criticism of the relationship between government departments and nationalised industries. A particular cause of this, although not the sole one, was the policies followed by the government in the early 1970s, which subordinated nationalised-industry pricing policies and financial performance to the needs of anti-inflation policy. Between 1974 and 1976 the directives were sharply reversed as there was a pressing need to reduce the public-sector borrowing requirement, again in the interests of macroeconomic policy objectives. In addition, in a report on capital investment procedures in 1973 the select committee criticised the government's handling of its relationship with the nationalised industries.

As a result the NEDO was requested to undertake a detailed study of the role of the nationalised industries in the economy, their relationships with the government and the ways in which they could be controlled in future. The findings of its report, published in 1976, can be summarised by the following quotation: 'Our enquiry has left us in no doubt that the existing framework of relationships, developed under governments of both main political parties, is unsatisfactory and in need of radical change.'[19] The main reasons for this conclusion were, according to the report,

> . . . a lack of trust and mutual understanding between those who run the nationalised industries and those in government (politicians and civil servants) who are concerned with their affairs;
> . . . confusion about the respective roles of the boards of nationalised industries, Ministers and Parliament, with the result that accountability is seriously blurred;
> . . . no systematic framework for reaching agreement on long term objectives and strategy, and no assurance of continuity when decisions are reached;
> . . . no effective system for measuring performance of nationalised industries and assessing managerial competence.[19]

A detailed critique of the NEDO report cannot be given here, and readers should study the report itself. The main recommendation of the study in the area under discussion was that each industry should be run by a policy council and the corporation board. The policy council would be responsible for corporate objectives, strategy, establishing performance criteria and monitoring performance. Within this framework the corporation board would be responsible for running the industry. Thus, the policy council would form a buffer layer between government and board. It was intended that in this way the day-to-day running of the industry could be insulated from the day-to-day running of the government. The policy council would comprise board members, civil servants from sponsoring departments and the Treasury, trade union representatives and independent members. The board would be appointed by the council and not by the government, as at present.

While the NEDO report has been valuable in highlighting the problems of the government–nationalised industry relationship its proposed solution does not seem to contribute much to solving them. Although the policy council would form a layer between boards and government there is nothing inherent in the NEDO proposals to prevent a government, if it so wished, from acting in the way criticised in the report. What is needed is a fundamental policy decision on the part of a government about the extent to which it will interfere with the policies of the nationalised industries on the one hand and about objectives and criteria for their performance on the other. At the same time many of the detailed criticisms of the NEDO report are valid and need action on the part of both government and industries.

The catalyst for this action may well be the White Paper published in March 1978,[20] which rejects the concept of policy councils, claiming they have not found favour with the nationalised industries themselves. At the same time the White Paper proposes several changes in the relationship between government and industries, some of which implement the NEDO proposals. First, ministers are to be given power to issue specific directives to boards as well as the general directives that they can issue at present. This should clarify the responsibility for certain policy decisions and show where and how ministerial intervention has affected an industry's performance. The costs of complying with such directives will be published and, where appropriate, compensation paid. Second, to strengthen the links between industries and sponsor departments civil servants from the latter and possibly from the Treasury may be appointed to industry boards. Whether this will have the desired effect of improving departmental knowledge of an industry's problems will depend among other things on how often departmental members are changed. Both trade union and consumer members may also be appointed to some boards.

To strengthen the effectiveness of the industries' forward-planning processes, especially concerning investment, the government intends to approve part of investment programmes for up to three years ahead. While this is a welcome measure it will not help industries where the lead time on major investments is longer than three years. However, industries will be given more freedom to allocate resources between investment and other uses, as emphasis will, in times of investment reductions in the public sector, be switched from the control of investment levels to the control of requirements for external finance.

Finally, far more factors that are relevant to assessing the performance of the industry – e.g. government instructions, financial targets, performance indicators agreed with the government and cash limits – will be published in each industry's annual report.

At this stage it is too early to assess how the new bases for the industry–government relationship will work in practice. Their merits are, first, that they recognise the political reality that governments will wish to control nationalised industries and from time to time force them to follow policies that they would not themselves choose. Second, they make such directives more specific and the subject of financial compensation. In this way they should enable the performance of the industry to be assessed much more clearly. If, for instance, an industry were directed to hold down its prices and paid specific compensation, then provided the latter was correctly calculated the overall financial performance of the industry could still be assessed, as in principle could the efficiency of its pricing policy in the absence of the directive. Overall, therefore, the framework may have been created in which the relationship between the nationalised industries and the government can be improved, but only time will tell whether this is true or not. Running through the White Paper, however, is a willingness on the part of the government to overcome the criticisms of the NEDO report. The five years following the White Paper should, therefore, be an interesting period in this respect.

10.2 OBJECTIVES OF THE NATIONALISED INDUSTRIES

OBJECTIVES IN THE LEGISLATION

In theory the objectives of the nationalised industries were set by government and Parliament in the legislation that established them. In practice it will not be surprising to learn that objectives with the degree of generality found in the original legislation would not be those actually governing the behaviour of the industries in their early years. In general two principal sets of objectives were specified in the nationalisation Acts, the first of which was with respect to the level of service:

It shall be the duty of every Area Board . . .
(a) to develop and maintain an efficient, coordinated and economical system of gas supply for their area and to satisfy, so far as it is economical to do so, all reasonable demands for gas within their area.[21]

In exercising and performing their functions the Electricity Boards shall . . .
(b) secure . . . the development, extension to rural areas and cheapening of supplies of electricity.
(c) avoid undue preference in the provision of such supplies . . .[22]

It shall be the general duty of the Commission so to exercise their powers under this Act as to provide, or secure or promote the provision of, an efficient, adequate, economical and properly integrated system of public inland transport and port facilities in Great Britain for passengers and goods with due regard for safety of operation.[23]

The above quotations are typical of the Acts of the late 1940s. Two common features seems to run through them. First, they specified the 'technical' areas of operation of the industry; and second, they made some stipulations about the service to be provided. It is the latter point in particular that was ambiguous. Although all the Acts listed several 'desirable features' of an ideal service – e.g. 'efficient', 'adequate', 'co-ordinated' – no definitions were given of the respects in which the undertakings were to achieve efficiency, adequacy or co-ordination. Furthermore, the statutory objectives contained inconsistencies; and it is quite possible to conceive of a situation where an electricity board had to meet all the demands for electricity in a rural area while trying to follow the conflicting aim of securing 'economical' supplies. Unless boards were given some economic criterion against which to make their judgements, the requirements to meet all reasonable demands and not to dicriminate in their provision were almost sure to lead to a misallocation of resources.

The second feature of the objectives concerns the financial provisions. Again, many similarities can be found among the various Acts, as the following indicate:

> It shall be the duty of each Area Board so to exercise and perform their functions under this Act as to secure that the revenues of the Board are not less than sufficient to meet their outgoings properly chargeable to revenue account taking one year with another.[24]

> All the business carried on by the Commission . . . shall form one undertaking, and the Commission shall so conduct that undertaking and, subject to the provisions of this Act, levy such fares, rates, tolls and other charges, as to secure that the revenue of the Commission is not less than sufficient for making provision for the meeting of charges properly chargeable to revenue, taking one year with another.[25]

Again, the two features that stand out are the similarity of the provisions for industries in widely differing markets and circumstances and the general vagueness and lack of precision in defining and specifying key words and phrases such as 'taking one year with another', which to be effective needed a statement of the number of years over which surpluses and deficits could be offset. Thus, the range of financial performance that could be construed as being compatible with these objectives was very wide indeed.

Of even greater potential importance for resource allocation than overall financial performance from year to year are pricing and investment policies. Although the Acts made some reference to the former, concern was largely with controlling the overall level of charges and in establishing safeguards, e.g. the Transport Tribunal, to ensure that increases were not excessive and that charges were 'reasonable', rather than with dealing with the more fundamental issues of pricing systems and the relationships of prices to costs. Little or no guidance, beyond exhortations to operate modern and efficient undertakings, was given on the question of investment criteria.

It may be argued that such vague objectives are a feature of any legislation and that it should lie with the appropriate ministers either directly or indirectly to give the nationalised industries more precise objectives. On the other hand, no general statements were in fact issued by any government until 1961 (see below), and in the interim period the boards of the nationalised industries were left to place their own interpretation on the legislation. This inevitably led to actual objectives differing in some respects from the nominal objectives set out in the legislation. Lack of guidance can be seen from the following quotation from a British Transport Commission Annual Report:

> During 1949, as in 1948, the Commission received no formal direction from the Minister of Transport in exercise of the powers under Section 4 of the Act which enable him to give directions of a general character as to the performance of the functions in relation to matters affecting the national interest.[26]

With hindsight it appears that most nationalised industries followed a policy that was akin to sales maximisation. Evidence of this comes from the fact that they operated unremunerative services that would have been closed down on profit maximisation criteria yet, at the same time, could not make out a specific case for their retention on social cost–benefit grounds. The following quotation illustrates this:

> We must conclude that the nationalised industries strive for simple objectives which have in them a strong uneconomic element. Up to 1957 the Coal Board was out to maximise output of coal at all costs . . . similarly, electricity policy was to maximise generating and distributing capacity . . . the plan was simple – capacity so ample that not even on the worst day of the most severe winter would it be necessary to cut loads. As a public utility service Electricity Boards dislike inability to supply and they are to be respected for their high standards in this respect.[27]

Effectively, the industries interpreted the needs of the nation as requiring them to meet all demands placed on them, but little was known about the most appropriate way of pricing such services. From time to time the government's interpretation of the national interest diverged from that of the industry, and policy changes were brought about as a result. Examples of this are given in section 10.1, and further instances from this period were the limits on railway tariff increases imposed by the Minister of Transport in 1952 and 1956.[28]

During the period to 1960 the only major legislation was the Transport Act 1953, which gave a slightly different emphasis to the objectives to be followed by the Commission. Section 25 of the Act gave a revised set of objectives, among which were:

(*a*) to provide railway services for Great Britain . . . due regard being had . . . to efficiency, economy and safety of operation and to the needs of the public, agriculture, commerce and industry.

Thus, the adequacy clause was dropped from the railways' objectives, which together with releasing them from the strictures of nineteenth-century anti-monopoly legislation resulted in their being able to pursue a much wider range of objectives that were more akin to profit maximisation. The conclusion of the Select Committee on Nationalised Industries in this respect is quite relevant:

> The operation of a railway is a public service . . . whoever undertakes this service has to make . . . the difficult decision about what size and shape of railways to provide. In deciding this the Commission could have based their decision on financial grounds and provided only such services as were profitable. They have however viewed their duty in a different light. They have been guided in a number of decisions by what seem to them to be social needs, as well as by what is economically wise; and it is in this way that they have considered proposals for new modernisation schemes, without asking the Minister for his views on the subject . . .

In earlier days it was possible within a railway system to make large profits on some parts of the service, and to use those to subsidise the losses on other parts . . .

For the Commission therefore to continue to provide some services that are bound to be run at a loss is to continue to drive the books into deficit. This makes it impossible for them to carry out their duty of balancing their revenue account, taking one year with another.[29]

Various nationalised industries had been the subject of a series of such reports from the select committee since its inception in 1956.[30]

THE 1961 AND 1967 WHITE PAPERS

The 1961 White Paper

Partly as a result of this potential conflict of objectives, the government published a White Paper in 1961 devoted specifically to the objectives of the nationalised industries.[31] Although the title of the paper was quite general, attention was concentrated on the financial objectives. The White Paper recognised that it might not be appropriate for the nationalised industries to act purely as profit maximisers and that they should also fulfil non-commercial obligations. However, it concluded that specific financial targets should be laid down so that the industries and the government would have some indication of how well the industries were meeting their objectives:

> Financial objectives or 'targets' were to be determined for each undertaking in the light of its needs and capabilities in relation to these criteria. In practice targets have normally been expressed as a rate of return on the undertaking's assets though other methods of expressing them were not ruled out.[32]

This represented a step forward in three respects. First, the specification of a definite time period replaced the haphazard system of 'taking one year with another'. Second, specific financial targets that could be understood by those running the industry were set. As such the government was implicitly making a policy decision on the allocation of resources to the nationalised sector as a whole and to it *vis-à-vis* the private sector; whether this decision was made explicitly is open to doubt. Finally, in target setting account could be, and was, taken of the non-commercial obligations of particular industries. For instance, factors such as the National Coal Board's obligations to keep open uneconomic collieries and BEA's losses on air services to the Scottish Highlands and islands were taken into account in setting their respective targets.[33]

The 1961 White Paper failed, however, to specify two important features of policy: pricing and investment. Although setting a broad rate of return effectively influenced the allocation of resources to an industry *vis-à-vis* the rest of the economy, within this broad base nothing was said about the allocation of resources within the industry. Considering the nature and importance of some of the nationalised industries, this may be construed as a fundamental error.

The 1967 White Paper

To some extent this criticism was overcome with the publication in 1967 of a second White Paper, which began with a statement of the government's objectives for industry as a whole and of the role that the nationalised industries were to play in this. Most significant of all it recognised that:

> In [the nationalised industries'] case the objectives outlined above cannot be achieved merely by maximising the financial returns of each industry: significant costs and benefits can occur which are outside the financial concern of the industry and it is the responsibility of the Government to ensure that these 'social' factors are reflected in the industries' planning.[97]

This, it appears, was a recognition that private and social costs and benefits do diverge and that profit maximisation would not necessarily lead to the maximisation of social welfare or, more to the point, to the achievement of the government's objectives for the economy as a whole. On the other hand, the need for a measure of financial discipline was still apparent.

Guidance on objectives also extended to investment and pricing. The policy recommended for investment decisions left the long term planning of investment in broad sectors of the economy to government departments and recommended that industries use discounted cash-flow techniques of appraisal to rank alternatives within this overall plan. To facilitate interindustry comparisons of projects a test rate of discount of 8 per cent common to all industries was specified. The rate itself was determined as that which was comparable with 'the average rate of return in real terms looked for on low-risk projects in the private sector in recent years'.

The use of the test rate did not preclude investment that did not yield a positive return on this criterion if the projects concerned were justified on 'social or wider economic' grounds. Social costs and benefits were also to be taken into account in circumstances where the government had grounds for believing that they diverged markedly from those of alternative projects (paragraph 14), with cost–benefit analysis being undertaken by government departments rather than the industries themselves.

Guidance on investment, therefore, was apparently very much in accordance with the general policy of obtaining the maximum possible social return from the investment in nationalised industries by using a mixture of commercial practices tempered by allowance for the divergences between social and private costs and benefits.

The pricing policy set out in the 1967 White Paper recognised the criticism of earlier policies that little attention had been given to the relationship between prices and the costs of providing individual goods and services. It started by restating the principle that prices should be fixed in such a way that 'revenues should normally cover . . . accounting costs in full – including the service of capital and provision for its replacement'.[34] This, however, was not all:

Prices, if they are to contribute towards a more efficient distribution of resources, must also attract resources to places where they can make the most effective contribution to meeting the demands of users. It is therefore important that . . . pricing policies should be devised with reference to the costs of the particular goods and services provided.[35]

Although the White Paper failed to present clearly-specified pricing principles it did recognise many of the difficulties that are inherent in such an exercise. In particular the following were discussed:

(1) the costs of administering a sophisticated policy;
(2) the problems of peak and off-peak prices and of spare capacity;
(3) the relationship of prices to both short-run and long-run marginal costs; and
(4) the problems arising when indivisibilities and joint costs occur, including the use of the two-part tariff.[36]

The recognition of the problems by the government was a welcome step, although the degree of autonomy accorded to the industries themselves meant that they too would have to be aware of the implications in their own particular case for the policy to be effective.

The rest of the White Paper dealt with costs and the setting of financial targets as a whole. The former was a straightforward exposition of the then current thinking on prices and incomes policies; and the latter was effectively a summary of the factors, most of them discussed in the White Paper, that influenced the setting of the targets.

To summarise, the 1967 White Paper encompassed two new areas – pricing and investment criteria – in which the government offered guidance to the nationalised industries. Within these spheres were introduced several concepts – e.g. the use of a test rate of discount, relating prices to the costs of individual services and taking into account social as well as private returns – which combined to give the nationalised industries a much clearer framework within which to work. On the other hand, few specific directions were given in the White Paper – it is possible that the concepts of short- and long-run marginal-cost pricing were not fully understood – and a whole range of performance by the individual industries could still be construed as being consistent with these objectives.

A further way in which objectives were clarified was with respect to some of the industries' services. Legislation passed in the same period specifically relieved the transport industry of the responsibility for services that, although justified on social grounds – that is, their social benefit exceeded their social cost – were not viable on commercial criteria and had hitherto been financed by cross-subsidisation from remunerative services provided by the same undertaking or by a general grant from the government to cover a deficit. One of the best examples of this was the Transport Act 1968, which contained several provisions of this nature. The philosophy of this policy can be found in two earlier White Papers dealing with transport policy.[37]

To summarise the position up to 1970, therefore, the objectives set for the nationalised industries by the government passed through three phases. The first and longest, lasting from original nationalisation in the period following 1946 to 1961, was one in which few clear economic or financial objectives were specified. Thus, it is difficult to comment on performance in this period as there were few standards to which it can be related. From 1961 financial performance can be assessed with respect to the targets set by the government for that period, although any such discussion must take place within the context of the implications of the targets themselves. The third phase, from 1967 to 1970, continued the system of financial targets and also put forward criteria against which pricing and investment performance can be assessed.

The progression of thought on objectives may also be split into two periods for the purpose of summary. In the first, up to 1962, the only objectives were the broad ones contained in the legislation, which clearly could be construed as a framework for achieving the even broader aims for nationalisation itself put forward in section 10.1. From 1962, still within the context of the objectives set out in the legislation, more detailed objectives were set by the government.

DEVELOPMENTS SINCE 1967: THE 1978 WHITE PAPER

In the 1970s there was little formal guidance from government to nationalised industries on objectives. During this period most industries evolved, with government encouragement, corporate plans for the future development of their businesses.

The 1978 White Paper[38] is, therefore, the first statement on official thinking on nationalised industry objectives and policy for eleven years. It represents a departure from the 1967 policies in several respects. First, it proposes that the government should take powers to give specific as well as general directives to the industries. This could, therefore, be used to specify objectives at more detailed levels than those contained in Acts of Parliament. As well, it could be used to give an industry a specific directive to deviate from its objectives if the government considered the circumstances warranted it. The White Paper, not unnaturally, does not indicate whether these powers would be used in the ways discussed above.

Second, the guidance on investment has changed from an emphasis on test discount rates to an emphasis on a required rate of return, in real terms, on an industry's whole capital stock. The reason put forward for this change is that the test discount rate had not been applied to the majority of capital expenditures. In particular a distinction seemed to have been made between essential replacement investment – which somehow, it is implied, did not require justification – and other investment, with the test discount rate applying to the latter only. The required rate of return, therefore, should mean that all investment is evaluated, although the White Paper clearly implies that cross-subsidisation among projects is permissible.

Guidance is much less specific about the circumstances where external costs and benefits should be taken into account in the investment appraisals. As the discussion of investment performance in section 10.6 below shows, this is a potentially serious omission. It is all the more serious in the context of remarks made in a report by Coopers and Lybrand Associates to NEDO and published as an appendix to their 1976 study.[39] This concluded that every major nationalised industry had significant externalities concerning its investment programmes and that social cost–benefit analysis was thus the most appropriate technique of appraisal. The industries will need much clearer guidance on their investment objectives than they have received.

Third, the detailed guidance on pricing policy given in 1967 has been diluted in the 1978 White Paper, and a return has been made to the 1961 system of setting financial targets and letting industries themselves determine pricing policies and principles in the light of market circumstances, product characteristics etc. Within this, however, industries will be encouraged to relate the structure of prices to the structure of costs and to use short-run marginal-cost pricing where appropriate. Arbitrary cross-subsidisation is specifically condemned.

It can be seen from the discussion so far that the extent to which the White Paper's proposals give the industries a framework of objectives depends on the way in which the financial target and the required rate of return are set. The latter has been set with the same objective as the discount rate in 1967, namely, to ensure that no capital is used in the nationalised sector when it could be used more efficiently in the private sector. In setting the financial target, however, the fourth difference in approach compared with the 1967 approach is apparent. This is that the financial targets will specifically take account of: 'any sectoral and social objectives set for that industry. These objectives will be published.'[40] If this is carried out in practice, it will at least mean that the non-commercial objectives that the government wishes an industry to pursue will be made clear. How they will affect the financial target remains to be seen.

To summarise, the 1978 White Paper combines features of both the 1961 and 1967 approaches. The main objectives set for the industries will be financial, and non-financial obligations will be taken into account in setting the financial targets and/or by specific subsidies, which can presumably be treated as revenue. Within this there is considerable scope for industries to pursue their own pricing and investment policies. Probably the main contribution of the 1978 White Paper is its recognition that non-commercial objectives and their influence on targets and directives to industries should be made explicit. If nothing else, this should encourage the government to give the effects of these obligations and objectives considerable thought and analysis and make the appraisal of performance, which is the subject of the rest of this chapter, much clearer in the future.

10.3   FINANCIAL PERFORMANCE OF THE NATIONALISED INDUSTRIES

The financial performance of the nationalised industries is relevant at two levels. First, the relative financial performance of the various industries within the sector may be helpful in indicating priorities for resource allocation among such industries; and second, the relative financial performance of the public and private sectors of industry may similarly be helpful in the context of the question of resource allocation between these sectors as a whole. It may be argued in fact that, as within the private sector financial performance is used as an indicator to guide resource allocation – resources tending to be put into uses where they can earn the largest positive financial return and taken out of uses whose financial return is low or even negative – such a criterion would be appropriate in the nationalised sector also. Finally, the role of a financial constraint as a discipline on the management of an industry must not be underemphasised.

Besides considering relative financial performance both within the nationalised sector and *vis-à-vis* the private sector, it should be noted that it is also possible to judge performance against the financial targets set out by the government. In the immediate postwar period and throughout most of the 1950s the only financial criterion was that of balancing costs and revenues, taking one year with another, as set out in the original nationalisation Acts. This was followed by periods during which more specific financial targets were set. This action was a recognition by the government, at least partly as a result of the work of the Select Committee on Nationalised Industries, that the vague financial constraints implied in the 'break-even' requirement were not conducive to the efficient management of the undertakings and that different levels of financial performance were appropriate for different industries. This led to the setting of individual target rates of return on assets for a period of up to five years for each industry. In 1967, while the system of targets was not abandoned, the relative importance and interdependence of pricing and investment policies were recognised explicitly. The 1967 White Paper said on the subject of financial objectives:

> . . . it follows from the fact that targets should reflect sound investment and pricing policies and not vice versa that if there are significant changes in the circumstances of an industry the Government would be ready to review its target.[41]

From the early 1970s financial targets were effectively abandoned as the nationalised industries were prevented from raising prices as part of the counterinflation policy. In 1974 this policy was reversed; and as already discussed, financial targets play a critical role in the 1978 White Paper's proposals, which effectively reverse the 1967 White Paper's views on the relationship between targets and pricing and investment policies.

However, there are several difficulties in attempting any systematic discussion of the financial performance of the nationalised industries in the period from nationalisation to the setting of targets in the early 1960s. The first is that the criterion of 'breaking even' was very vaguely worded, especially as the number of years to be taken into acccount was not specified. Second, the earlier part of the period at least was not one of normality in many sectors as a result of the aftermath of the Second World War and the reorganisations within many industries consequent upon nationalisation itself.[42] Finally, there is the question of differences in the accounting methods of the various industries – a problem still pervading comparisons in later periods. In general, however, it is true to say that most industries, with the notable exception of the British Transport Commission, had little difficulty in meeting the criterion provided that there was a reasonable degree of flexibility in the number of years considered.[43]

The 1961–7 period provides a better chance for comparing performance to targets as the latter were specified explicitly. The 1967 White Paper included data on financial performance that were drawn up on a comparative basis and from which the effects of differences in accounting practice had been removed. Information on a selection of industries is given in Table 10.1. It can be seen from the table that only British Rail and BEA failed markedly to achieve their targets while all other industries were fairly close to them and that in no case was any industry substantially above its target.

From 1967, particularly from 1970, the assessment of financial performance was more difficult for several reasons: first, because targets were not always made explicit and were often set for much shorter time periods; second, because changes in policy in, for example, the transport sector affected the relevance of the financial measures of performance; and third, because the nationalised industries were subjected to price restraint at a time of increasing general inflation. The latter was meant to help to reduce the rate of inflation as part of the government's macroeconomic strategy. Between 1970 and 1974 almost all nationalised industries were forced into deficits, which for the three hitherto

Table 10.1   *Selected nationalised industries: financial targets and performance, 1963–7 (%).*

| Industry | Target | Performance | | | |
		1963–4	1964–5	1965–6	1966–7
Post Office	8·0[a]	7·8	6·9	8·1	8·0
National Coal Board	—[b]	6·7	4·9	0·1	3·7
Electricity Council and boards	12·4[c]	12·4	12·0	12·5	10·7
Gas Council and boards	10·2[d]	9·7	10·5	9·8	9·0
British Rail	—[e]	−1·0	−0·1	−0·6	−0·4
BOAC	12·5[f]	−6·6	15·2	9·6	21·7
BEA	6·0[g]	8·3	5·8	5·4	4·8

Source: Nationalised Industries: A Review of Economic and Financial Objectives, Cmnd 3437 (London, HMSO, 1967), tables 3 and 4.

Notes:
(a) Net return on net assets.
(b) No rate of return set. Target was to break even and provide £10 million per annum to cover the difference between historic and replacement cost depreciation. Figures quoted are net returns on net assets.
(c) Gross return on net assets.
(d) Gross return on net assets.
(e) No rate of return set. Target was to eliminate deficit as soon as possible. Figures quoted are gross returns.
(f) Net return on net assets.
(g) Net return on net assets.

most profitable concerns – i.e. electricity, gas and the Post Office – totalled £1,182 million in this period.[44]

Since 1974 the government's first priority for the nationalised industries has been to eliminate their deficits, and by 1977 this had largely been achieved, although inevitably at the expense of real price increases. For the last years of the decade the 1978 White Paper quotes the current financial targets as follows:

British Airways	11 per cent average rate of return on mean net assets, 1975–6 to 1978–9.
British Transport Docks Board	At least 20 per cent return on mean net assets by 1980.
Telecommunications	6 per cent per annum real return on mean net assets revalued to replacement cost, 1976–7 to 1978–9.
Posts	2 per cent return on turnover in 1978–9 and 1979–80.
Giro	12·5 per cent annual average return on public dividend capital plus retained profits, 1975–6 to 1977–8.
British Rail	Break even after receipt of predetermined grants for passenger services.
National Bus Company	Break even after receipt of grants from local authorities for unremunerative services.

Financial targets for the other industries are to be set as soon as possible. The targets themselves again reflect the diversity of circumstances in which the industries, and in the case of the Post Office the different parts of a single industry, operate. At present it is difficult to follow the logic in the differences among industry targets; but as already stated, this should become clearer if the White Paper's proposals are implemented.

At this juncture it is difficult to monitor progress towards the targets as in many cases information on only a single year's performance is available, and single years can be atypical. However, the relatively uncomplex targets set for British Rail and the National Bus Company permit some assessment of performance between 1975 and 1977. These figures are given in Table 10.2. In both cases the industries managed to achieve more than their financial targets, although the National Bus Company was still recovering from the effects of counterinflation policies in 1975 while British Rail had just benefited from a further capital reconstruction following the Railways Act 1974.

Table 10.2 *British Rail and the National Bus Company: financial results after interest, grants etc., 1975–7 (£ m.).*

	1975	1976	1977
British Rail	+5·5	+5·3	+27·0
National Bus Company	−19·0	+5·8	+9·6

Source: Annual reports and accounts.

Thus, when not subjected to government controls on their pricing policies, in the periods when financial targets have been set the majority of nationalised industries have been able at least to approach them. The conclusions to be drawn from this, however, depend on whether the targets themselves are appropriate. As already argued in discussing objectives, financial targets will only be appropriate if they take into account the constraints on the industry. In particular two points need explicit consideration.

First, the arrangements for compensating the industry for any non-commercial obligations put on it need to be considered. If these comprise a specific subsidy, the way in which it has been calculated is important. For instance, if British Rail were to provide commercially unremunerative services, then either it could be paid the financial loss when this was known, or the government could determine how much the service was worth to it and pay a grant at this level.[45] The interpretation of British Rail's financial results would be different in each case. Under the first method any improvement in performance on the service would be reflected only in the grant and not in British Rail's overall financial results. Under the second method improvements in performance would be reflected in the financial results.

In the past governments either have not given specific subsidies or have usuallly subsidised nationalised industries (particularly in the transport sector) by the first method, although this has changed for British Rail since the Railways Act 1974 was passed. Even more serious is the criticism that when specific subsidies have been paid to nationalised industries – e.g. to the airlines for purchasing British aircraft and to the Central Electricity Generating Board for ordering power stations in advance of commercial requirements – the subsidies have been based on an arbitrary assessment of the costs involved or on the result of a bargaining process rather than on a rational assessment of benefits and costs.

Second, the capital structure of the industry is relevant to judging financial performance if net rates of return, i.e. returns after paying interest and depreciation, are to be the basis for the target. There is a clear division here between industries such as British Steel and British Airways, which are financed by public dividend capital that is akin to risk capital in the private sector, and the rest of nationalised industries, which have fixed interest payments to make on their capital. Dramatic differences in British Rail's financial performance have in the past been brought about by capital write-offs and restructurings. Many nationalised industries have argued strongly in favour of public dividend capital, but these arguments have been rejected by the government.[46] It is not impossible to make the necessary adjustments to the financial performances, or the financial targets, in any case. Nevertheless, this needs to be taken into account and has not always been done in the past.

It may be concluded that when financial targets have been set in the past these factors have not been fully taken into account, and whether they will in future remains to be seen. The discussion and interpretation of financial performance, therefore, need to be approached with considerable caution. In addition account must be taken of the shortcomings of profit as a measure of efficiency, discussed in Chapter 8. This has been recognised by Pryke in his study of the comparative performance of the public and private sectors.[47] He has admitted the difficulties of realistic comparison and discussed performance not in financial terms but in terms of the productivity of labour and capital. His conclusion is that the nationalised sector has with minor exceptions performed much better in this respect than private industry – especially the private manufacturing sector. The fact that this, in the case of some industries at least, may not have been fully reflected in financial performance, an example being the National Coal Board, seems to indicate the effect of other influences on financial performance, which can make it a poor indicator of relative efficiency, especially if Pryke's conclusions are correct.

Thus, the fact that the financial performance of the nationalised industries against their targets set by the government has generally been satisfactory, in periods when targets have been operative, does not necessarily reflect that the industries themselves have been efficient; nor does it reflect that the allocation of resources between the public and private sectors has been appropriate. If the government's stated intentions in setting targets are followed, this conclusion may not be so in future. For the present the whole area of financial performance has to be recognised as one of considerable ambiguity when assessing the economic efficiency of the industries and the effectiveness of the government control of them. For these reasons attention in the rest of the chapter is focused on the more central issues of pricing and investment performance.

10.4   CRITERIA FOR PRICING AND INVESTMENT POLICIES FOR THE NATIONALISED INDUSTRIES

The aims of this section are, first, to consider briefly the principles for pricing and investment in the nationalised industries that can be derived from economic theory and, second, to see to what extent the guidelines given to the industries conform to them. In the light of these discussions the performance of the nationalised industries in both pricing and investment is analysed in sections 10.5 and 10.6 with respect to both the principles and the constraints imposed by government policy.

The conditions under which an optimal allocation of resources may be achieved are discussed in Chapter 8, where it is also concluded that it is highly unlikely that the unrestricted operation of a free-enterprise economic system will achieve such allocation under any of the market conditions that are likely to prevail in present circumstances. The existence of a substantial publicly-owned sector of the economy presents a somewhat different picture in that it could in theory pursue objectives that were consistent with an optimal allocation of resources.

However, several issues are raised by such a policy, and it is necessary to discuss them briefly here for their relevance to pricing and investment policies. The most fundamental issue, as pointed out in Chapter 8, is that a criterion for optimality must be adopted. If, for the sake of argument and the want of alternatives, the Pareto criterion – that resources are allocated optimally if it is impossible to make one person better off without simultaneously making another person worse off – is taken, two further points arise.

One is that the adoption of this criterion implies that the distribution of income is acceptable. If not, it may be that making one person 'worse off' in money terms and making another 'better off' will be consistent with a better distribution of income than already exists. This matter has already been touched on in Chapter 8, but it is important here too; for almost every pricing and investment decision by a nationalised industry has distributional implications of this kind, and a policy that would be Pareto optimal could in every other sense be attacked on distributional grounds.

Second, implicit in the rationale of Paretian welfare economics is the assumption that the consumer is the best judge of his own welfare and that his reactions to the price system can thus be taken as truly indicative of his scale of preferences. This again may be challenged by some people.

Even assuming that the above problems can be overcome, there exists the more formidable one of the second best. Given that the government cannot control all the sectors of the economy, behaviour in the uncontrolled sector may deviate from that required for optimality, e.g. as a result of the existence of monopoly or oligopoly conditions in either or both of the factor and product markets. In these circumstances it has been shown that pursuit of behaviour rules that would be optimal in a first-best situation may not in fact necessarily improve the efficiency of resource allocation in the second-best situation.[48]

The extent to which this will affect the decision rules of a particular nationalised industry will depend on the degree to which it operates in markets with, or purchases factors from, private enterprise firms actually operating under second-best conditions. Thus, if the privately owned sector of the road haulage industry is not pursuing a first-best pricing policy and pricing according to marginal cost, it follows that marginal cost pricing may be inappropriate for the state-owned haulage industry too. Similarly, there is the case of transport undertakings competing with other modes that use an unpriced resource (e.g. road space), and in some cases use it themselves, where again the pursuit of first-best pricing policies may not be appropriate. When the extent of nationalised industries is considered it can easily be seen that these points are not merely theoretical but have considerable empirical significance. Almost all industries purchase factor inputs from private enterprise where, as the analysis of Chapter 2 points out, perfect competition is the exception rather than the rule. Many – e.g. coal, electricity, gas, road haulage, the airlines and railways – compete in the same markets as private industry, and all sell to private industry.

Is it correct to conclude from these arguments, therefore, that there is little scope for improving resource allocation by the pricing and investment policies of the nationalised industries? Several authors have suggested solutions to this problem, and the elements of one such synthesis of the issues involved is given here.[49]

As far as the assumption that consumers are themselves the best judges of their own well-being is concerned, although it can be argued that 'in areas of the public sector such as health and education . . . a paternalistic approach seems desirable',[50] in the areas where the majority of the nationalised industries operate it is the present author's value judgement that on the whole the consumer *is* the best judge of his own well-being and that his reactions to the price system are, therefore, indicative of his preferences.

The question of income distribution is more difficult. Millward has argued, in the present author's opinion correctly, that in routine matters of pricing and investment it is impossible to assess all the distributional consequences and that 'efficiency' rules for such decisions should thus be followed. There exist, however, several situations involving major areas of pricing and investment that have distributional implications that are of considerable significance, and in these cases such implications should be taken into account. Examples are:

(1) Specific once-and-for-all projects such as the third London Airport scheme, which often, in addition, involve 'externalities'.

(2) The *introduction* of pricing to goods and services previously subject to some kind of non-price rationing; examples in the UK would include the suggestions for pricing roads, water-supply and parking facilities.

(3) Major changes in pricing procedures, such as switching from average-cost pricing in electricity supply to time-of-day differentials, to reflect marginal costs.[51]

As far as the second-best problem is concerned, Millward has argued that:

. . . though the effects of the distortions are in principle widespread, some of the more 'immediate' and nearby effects are the most important. One tries, in other words, to optimise within broad sectors; to ensure, for example, that within the transport sector relative transformation rates are roughly related to relative substitution rates.[52]

An ultimate objective would therefore be to ensure that:

A public enterprise's product would be sold at a price whose relationship to marginal cost approximated to that in competing private enterprises, and adjustments in taxes on the latter would be used as far as possible to ensure, that for this group as a whole, the price/marginal cost ratio does not get too much out of line with the rest of the economy.[53]

Thus, it is clear that, when the actual position of the nationalised industries in the United Kingdom is considered in detail, while the problems of income distribution and consumer rationality do not disappear they do become much less important than they seem at first sight. The problem of the second best is still potentially serious, and it may be stated at this stage that Millward's criteria have not been met in full by any of the nationalised industries. However, they do give scope for the formulation of pricing rules. On the other hand, it is possible to put forward an even lower order set of pricing rules, which are a prerequisite for those suggested above: namely, that prices within a particular industry should as far as possible reflect the marginal costs of the products concerned. This is largely within the control of the industries themselves and was hinted at in the section on pricing in the 1967 White Paper. Such emphasis as there was on marginal cost pricing in that paper has been considerably diluted in the 1978 White Paper. Here, guidance on pricing takes much more account of the market circumstances of the industries concerned. While it does not explicitly mention the concept paragraph 67 can be interpreted as taking some account of second-best problems, albeit in a manner that is very informal and capable of divergent interpretations by the industries concerned. Within the financial target system there exists the potential for making much clearer the extent to which an industry should be constrained by conditions in the factor and product markets in which it operates.

The marginal-cost pricing principle has not been abandoned altogether. Paragraph 68 of the 1978 White Paper makes it clear that the structure of costs should be reflected in the structure of prices. Cross-subsidisation is condemned. Also central to pricing policy is the question of subsidies to cover externalities, discussed in section 10.1 when objectives are examined. The recognition that certain externalities exist and the payment of subsidies to cover them are features of the current guidelines and, as section 10.5 will show, will potentially overcome one major criticism of past performance.

So far as investment rules are concerned, optimal resource allocation necessitates that only projects showing a positive net discounted present value in terms of social rather than private benefits and costs should be undertaken. In situations where there is a financial constraint the rule should be to choose the projects that do in fact give the highest returns. This kind of analysis raises the same type of questions as those raised above for pricing policy, and that discussion applies. More emphasis, however, should perhaps be given to the point that the distributional effects of an investment policy, e.g. the choice of fuel for electricity generation, may be of greater significance than a routine pricing policy; thus, efficiency criteria may not be so relevant.

To some extent the pricing and investment principles set out in the 1967 White Paper were in accordance with this thinking. They did at least give the industries for the first time a broad framework in which to work and to fit their own decisions. Clearly, however, they failed fully to meet all the theoretical requirements of pricing and investment criteria, they were inevitably tempered by problems of application, and considerable scope had to be left to the individual industries.

The review leading to the 1978 White Paper made it clear that the criteria had not worked in practice. On pricing the problems of the 1971–5 price-restraint policies have already been discussed above. On investment the 1978 White Paper concludes that the early approach based on the test discount rate has not lived up to expectation because relatively little investment expenditure has been appraised using that method. Whether this is the fault of the government or of the industries is not discussed. This in itself is a rather weak reason for condemning the criterion; the fact that the method has not been used does not mean that it should not be used.

In place of the 1967 criteria the 1978 White Paper puts forward criteria on pricing and investment that seem to give even greater scope for interpretation by individual industries. Pricing policy is to be determined by market circumstances and the financial target, although concepts based on marginal cost pricing are not forgotten. The attention given to market circumstances may be a reflection of the second-best problem. Guidance on investment criteria moves away from project appraisal to attaining a required rate of return on capital. This, it seems, is an attempt to ensure that all investment is evaluated – including 'replacement' investment, which often appears to be sacrosanct in the eyes of many industries. The appraisal of individual projects is not to be ignored, and the use of discounted cash-flow techniques is still recommended.

To conclude, the two major sets of guidelines on pricing and investment policies and criteria that governments had given the nationalised industries reflect some of the principles discussed above. Both are attempts to help the industries to contribute to efficiency in resource allocation. The 1978 criteria also take account of other constraints more explicitly, e.g. in referring to 'sectoral and social objectives'.[54] However, because the 1967 guidelines were effectively suspended less than five years after their introduction as the first explicit guidance on pricing policy and because at the time of writing the 1978 guidelines remained to be implemented, the evaluation of pricing and investment policies is far from straightforward.

10.5   PRICING PERFORMANCE

INTRODUCTION

It may be concluded from section 10.4 that the spheres in which the pricing policies of the nationalised industries can improve the efficiency of resource allocation, without meeting other problems, are somewhat limited. They comprise:

(1) adjustments of prices to equal the marginal costs of producing each product that the industries supply, as far as this is practicable; and
(2) so far as is practicable, further adjustments so that the relationship of price with marginal cost for the industries' products corresponds to that of products with which they are competing.

Given that in the years up to 1961 the only financial objective was to break even, it is not surprising that many of the industries followed a pricing policy that was consistent with setting price equal to average cost. Furthermore, the pricing policies tended to be even further removed from those outlined above in that prices were often set in such a way that the total revenue from an industry's operations as a whole was sufficient to cover its total costs, without regard to the fact that the total revenue from the sale of an individual product might be considerably greater or less than the total cost of producing it.

This arose primarily for two reasons. First, many of the nationalised industries were under a statutory obligation not to discriminate among consumers; in the case of the railways at least this dated back to long before nationalisation.[55] Many of the industries had been or were natural monopolies.[56] For instance, the railways during the period up to 1914 had a virtual monopoly of all transport beyond purely intraurban traffic; but although the point can still to a great extent be argued today in the cases of electricity and gas, it no longer applies to the railways, whose monopoly was eroded in the 1920s by the advent of road transport.

Nevertheless, all the nationalisation Acts constrained the industries concerned not to show 'undue preference', or words to that effect, among consumers. Presumably this was an attempt to prevent them from expropriating consumer surplus and meant that they must charge the same rate to all consumers for the same service. This, however, taking the case of the railways as a detailed example, tended to be interpreted in such a way that a uniform rate per mile was charged for different passenger journeys and for different loads of the same commodity, with the result that rates were unrelated to the costs of providing the service as a whole or to the marginal costs of a particular consignment.

The net result of such pricing practices is a misallocation of resources within the industry as a whole and either the cross-subsidisation of one set of consumers by another, if it is breaking even, or the cross-subsidisation of the consumers of the product by taxpayers as a whole, if the industry is incurring a deficit. The misallocation occurs because the industry is producing some products whose marginal valuation is less than their marginal cost and thus devoting 'too many' resources to their production, and vice versa for the products whose consumers are cross-subsidising the unremunerative goods and services.

A second reason for this uniformity of pricing undoubtedly lay in the fact that the industries themselves did not until comparatively recently recognise that they were multiproduct enterprises. The reason lies in their failure to recognise the differences underlying the physical homogeneity of the products or services that they produced, e.g. a unit of electricity, a passenger-mile or freight-mile of transport services. The dimensions in which heterogeneity occurs are those of time and place. For instance, a railway journey from London to Manchester is not a substitute for one from London to Glasgow. Similarly, a unit of electricity supplied at 1500 hours is not a substitute for one provided at 0900 hours.

Not only demand but also cost conditions vary according to the place and time of production. For example, the costs of providing transport and electricity vary according to such factors as the physical characteristics of routes, supply lines and population densities. Similarly, the costs of producing peak period transport, electricity and gas services are greater than they are for off-peak services because output cannot be stored and must, therefore, be produced with extra equipment when demanded.

Several empirical studies demonstrating the prevalence of cross-subsidisation practices in the recent past have been published. Although its costing assumptions can be questioned,[57] the Beeching report on British Rail found that only long-distance intercity passenger traffic showed any surplus even over direct costs while other forms of rail passenger transport failed even to cover their direct costs.[58] The present author's studies of the structure of costs in the bus industry have found that the long-run marginal cost of providing peak traffics was not met by the marginal revenue from them, resulting in a deficit that was 43 per cent of cost.[59] The studies have also found evidence of cross-subsidisation among routes, more evidence of which has come from the fact that many operators of rural services now receive grant aid from local authorities in order to maintain unremunerative services.[60] The same point has been made in relation to the gas industry by the NBPI.[61]

Having reviewed the theoretical case and given some indication of the sources of evidence, it now remains to consider the degree to which the pricing policies of the industries have recently been modified to conform more closely to ideal pricing principles. The lack of space precludes a detailed discussion of all the nationalised industries; so attention here will be concentrated on three: electricity, gas and transport.

PRICING PRACTICE: ELECTRICITY

Of all the nationalised industries the electricity industry has probably been the most advanced in its pricing policies, largely because these were the first to be investigated by economists, particularly Boiteaux in France.[62] The sources of possible cross-subsidisation arise with respect to time and place. The pricing policies developed so far have attempted to relate prices to marginal costs in particular periods to reflect time differentials in costs rather than to make price equal the marginal cost of supplying electricity to particular areas.

The basis of the peak problem is that electricity cannot be cheaply stored; and as demand is unevenly distributed throughout the day and year, maximum capacity must equal peak capacity if all demands are to be met.[63] Furthermore, as the technical efficiency of generating stations varies the least efficient, and thus most costly, stations are used only at the peaks. Thus, not only is a substantial proportion of capital costs incurred for the purpose of supplying peak demands, but in addition marginal running costs are higher at the peaks.

In the United Kingdom there are two types of electricity tariff: the bulk supply tariff (BST) at which the Central Electricity Generating Board (CEGB) sells to the area boards, and the tariffs at which the latter sell to final consumers. The BST comprises two parts: running rates and capacity charges.[64] Running rates vary because short-run marginal cost varies with demand. Three scales apply: one for the winter peak period, one for daytime and one for night-time. Although this does not ensure that the running rate equals the marginal cost of electricity at any one time, it does at least vary with marginal cost. While it would be theoretically possible to make the running rate variable according to the actual cost at each point in time, it would be impossible to predict in advance what the rate would be at any time, and this would present area boards with difficulties, given that customers need to know in advance the cost of consuming electricity. On the other hand, a case could be made out for more variation in the running rates, e.g. between winter and summer as well as between day and night.

The second part of the BST, i.e. the capacity charges, was the subject of an investigation by the NBPI, which reported in 1968 that the capacity charges:

. . . do not precisely reflect fixed costs. They serve to recover the balance of what is estimated is required to meet the CEGB's financial obligations after allowing for the surplus of total income from the running rates over total running costs.[65]

The charges are apportioned among area boards in accordance with the demands that they make on capacity at times of peak demand and at times when system demand is at 90 per cent of peak demand. Again it must be questioned whether there should be a further division of the capacity charge into, say, winter and summer, day and night rates, as well as an absolute peak rate. On the other hand, the total system is a closer approximation to marginal cost pricing than, for instance, a uniform charge per unit would be. While a closer approximation to marginal cost pricing might be achieved, at this stage the basic approach adopted is to be welcomed.

Each area board is free to set its own tariff structure for the final consumer, and thus each varies. In general separate tariffs exist for industrial and domestic consumers. Industrial tariffs are more related to the marginal costs incurred by the area board in that they incorporate a capacity charge based on the user's maximum demand during any one period and a charge per unit. The main criticism of this is that the fixed charge is the same regardless of when the electricity is consumed; thus, a firm consuming in the off-peak pays the same fixed charge as a firm consuming at the same maximum rate in the peak. Domestic tariffs have only recently incorporated a 'time of day' element. In the main they comprise a two-part tariff with a fixed charge per quarter and a uniform rate per unit consumed, regardless of the time of consumption.[66] In recent years attempts have been made to introduce a time-of-day element into domestic consumption by offering cheaper electricity for storage heaters that only consume electricity in the off-peak and, from 1968–9, offering a tariff that meters day and night consumption separately with a lower rate for the latter. This has only been made possible by the advent of devices such as storage heaters, which store not electricity but heat – the ultimate product. The extent to which it would be possible to extend this system is severely limited; and it is difficult to support a more sophisticated tariff system, since with the large numbers of domestic consumers the cost would be very high and the potential benefits low.

The electricity industry's pricing policy was seriously affected by the price restraints of the early 1970s. Off-peak electricity was initially sold at a price that was very close to marginal generating costs, but when fuel costs increased and prices were restrained the industry was effectively forced to sell its product for less than marginal cost. When it was possible to rectify this the proposed percentage increases in off-peak electricity prices were considerably greater than those in peak prices, and at the government's request the off-peak increases were phased over a longer period. So that this situation will not arise again retail electricity tariffs now incorporate a fuel charge element adjusted automatically as average fuel costs change. This development does not, however, represent a radical departure from the pricing policy discussed above, and it appears that further moves towards marginal cost pricing are only constrained by the technological problems of obtaining frequent meter readings.

No attempt is presently made by the electricity industry to reflect differences in the marginal costs of supplying consumers at different locations in electricity tariffs. Thus, a rural consumer whose connection to the system may involve laying several miles of cable pays the same fixed charge per quarter, *ceteris paribus*, as an urban consumer within a few yards of a supply.

PRICING PRACTICE: GAS

In the case of the gas industry the demand at the time of writing was such that, even at times of peak demand, capacity was sufficient to meet it. By the early 1980s, however, if demand rises according to predictions, capacity constraints will be reached that will require the introduction of storage facilities and/or the expansion of the distributive network to cope with peak demands.

The optimal pricing policy in these circumstances seems to be for a relatively low charge now and an increased peak charge at such times when capacity shortages threaten and increased capacity becomes necessary: 'a BST which simply reflected the changing pattern of marginal costs would . . . be very low at first, but would be expected to jump upwards in two or three years'.[67] The conclusion of the NBPI on this question in 1968 was that the costs associated with the change in tariffs, which could be quite sharp, were greater than the costs of the inefficiency introduced by the policy that it advocated of charging according to long-run marginal cost immediately.

The other main conclusion of the NBPI was that there was no economic case for charging a uniform tariff to all area boards, as the cost of supplying a marginal unit depends on the distance of the demand point from the landing point for the natural gas, which varies from one area to another. Although it is recognised that charging a uniform tariff may achieve other aims of government policy, e.g. regional policy objectives, this should be the financial responsibility of the government, not the gas industry.

Thus, the main ways in which the BST in the gas industry deviates from marginal costs are that cost variations according to distance are not reflected in charges and that, at present, long-run marginal costs are being charged on the assumption that capacity constraints will be reached in the near future. Whether peak costing will be introduced when they are is an open question.

So far as the industry's retail tariffs are concerned, two ways in which they have tried to approximate more closely to marginal cost pricing are the introduction of tariffs for 'interruptible' supplies for industrial consumers[68] and of two-part tariffs for domestic consumers. They have still not achieved time-of-day nor time-of-year tariffs for the latter, but these involve considerable problems.[69] A further and fuller discussion of the structure of marginal costs in the gas industry is contained in appendix D of the NBPI's 1968 report on gas prices.[61]

PRICING PRACTICE: TRANSPORT

The transport industry has probably made least progress of all towards a pricing system based on marginal costs. In road haulage severe competition from the private sector has meant that pricing by the nationalised sector has been constrained by orthodox market forces, and it is likely that in stable market conditions prices will approximate long-run marginal costs, with relatively little scope for cross-subsidisation.

The bus industry has always been fairly conservative in its attitude towards pricing. Prices are generally uniform throughout large sections of an operator's network and only vary with the distance a passenger travels. Costs, however, vary considerably among individual services and between peak and off-peak periods. The peak problem, referred to briefly on page 424, is similar to that of the electricity industry: that is, demand levels vary over time, output cannot be stored, and capacity must therefore be enough to meet peak demands. Very few attempts have been made by the bus industry to reflect the higher marginal costs of peak travel in higher prices, with the aim of covering the long-run marginal costs of meeting peak demand from peak revenue and/or of encouraging passengers to shift from peak to off-peak. Some experiments in reduced off-peak travel have been made by the National Bus Co., but in almost all cases the criterion against which the results have been judged has been a comparison of total revenue before and after the experiment. No account has been taken of the fact that the original price was probably well above off-peak marginal cost and, thus, that the reduction could be justified on welfare grounds.

The railway industry has to some extent progressed further. The removal of responsibility for much of the small-unit freight traffic to the National Freight Corporation has had the effect of increasing the proportion of British Rail's business contained in wagon-loads and train-loads, which are easier costing units. Also, the nineteenth-century legal restrictions on cost-based tariffs were removed by the Transport Act 1953, and successive managements have subsequently made use of this greater freedom in charging policies.

From 1975 (at least), freight charges appeared to be initially estimated on the basis of the price charged by the railways' nearest competitor and were then checked against the appropriate measure of marginal cost to see if the traffic was in fact remunerative to the railway system. This system is, it is claimed, a realisation of the fact that long-run marginal costs, including the replacement of equipment, cannot be met and that a shorter time period for costing may be appropriate. At the same time it recognises British Rail's objective of earning a rate of return on its capital whenever it can.[70] Thus, in negotiating long term contracts British Rail would not accept traffic at a price that did not cover its marginal costs over the life of the contract.

The Railways Act 1974 was a significant development in this respect because it tackled the vexed question of the allocation of infrastructure costs, e.g. track and signalling. The decision made, with which some economists have quarrelled, was that the size and shape of the network are determined by the passenger service pattern that the government requires British Rail to maintain and for which it pays the railways board a specific sum each year to cover the public service obligation placed on it. In 1977 this grant amounted to £364 million against income from passengers of £593 million. Thus, where freight services share infrastructure with passenger services no track and signalling expenses, except to cover wear and tear, are charged. Only where freight services are the sole users of infrastructure is a charge made. Guidelines on freight-pricing policy are fairly clearcut, and British Rail is constrained not to lose money on its freight services.

The system of public service obligations imposed on the railways also has implications for passenger pricing. Given that the government obliges British Rail to operate a set network of services and compensates it for so doing, passenger pricing policy is now akin to constrained revenue maximisation.

Costs are, however, not completely excluded from the calculus because the payments from the government are fixed; thus, if British Rail is to enhance a particular service, marginal revenues must cover marginal costs.

The pervasiveness of indivisibilities in rail operation seriously reduces the usefulness of identifying the marginal cost of individual passengers and its use as a base for charging. In practice, therefore, British Rail's passenger-pricing policy is one of price discrimination rather than marginal cost pricing at the passenger level. Thus, it has a policy of offering low fares to particular groups characterised by high price elasticities of demand, e.g. pensioners and students. As well, reduced fares are offered for travel at times when empty seats are available, and in some cases this discrimination is so fine that it is confined to particular trains. In almost all cases British Rail appears to have been fairly successful in preventing a loss of income from its other markets into these low price sectors. For example, very few reduced-price tickets are available for first-class travel, thus effectively insulating the business travel sector. Restrictions on the times of availability also have the same effect.

Perhaps the greatest apparent weakness in British Rail's pricing policy concerns the pricing of commuter services into the large conurbations. These services have significant requirements for rolling stock and manpower, and in some cases track capacity, which are underutilised during the rest of the day. Peak pricing would necessitate high charges for these services, while in practice regular users can purchase season tickets that may not cost much more than the off-peak fare. It has been argued by the government that in London at least the cross-elasticity of demand is so low that parts of the market – principally longer distance commuters – would not divert to other modes if fares were increased.[71]

The consideration of this aspect of pricing policies in the transport industry does, however, raise the problem of the relationship between prices and marginal costs both within an industry and in other industries within broad sectors. The problem raised in passenger transport, as pointed out in Chapter 8, is that the marginal social cost of road travel on a congested road is greater than the marginal private cost and that this is not reflected in charges for road use.[72] Thus, it can be argued that the marginal social costs arising from a transfer of peak hour passengers from bus or rail, e.g. as a result of a price increase following the introduction of prices based on marginal private costs, would exceed the benefits to be derived by the public transport operators from the policy.

The 1976 consultation document attempted to discuss railway pricing policy in the context of pricing policies in the sector as a whole, although the government's attitude changed somewhat in the White Paper published in 1977.[73] However, it is now prepared to see some continuation of subsidies to commuter services, but policy in this area is far from satisfactory from a welfare point of view.[74] Further discussion of it, however, is within the realm of transport policy rather than that of nationalised industry pricing. It serves very well indeed to illustrate the fact that for many nationalised industries, not only transport, there are several factors that are external to the industries that must be taken into account in determining pricing policy. The 1978 review of nationalised industry policy has, as already discussed, provided a framework within which this may be achieved. Future performance in this sphere may, therefore, leave greater scope for analysing pricing policies within this broader context.

CONCLUSION

To sum up, it has been argued that the pricing policies pursued by nationalised industries should – subject to the possible constraints on income distribution, required financial performance[75] etc. – attempt to allocate resources within each industry in the most efficient way possible by relating prices to the long-run marginal cost of producing each product as closely as technical and cost considerations indicate to be feasible.

Performance with respect to the higher order criteria of attempting to equate the relationship of price to marginal cost in broad sectors such as fuel and power and transport has not been good, and little progress has been made. This is significant, for it is in this area that government influence and intervention are the only way of achieving optimal performance. It can be concluded that up to the time of writing governments have not used their relationships with the nationalised industries to advantage in this respect. This is partly a reflection of the difficulty of problem recognition and partly because the problem, once recognised, is extremely complex to solve.

10.6   INVESTMENT PERFORMANCE

INTRODUCTION

It will be recalled from the discussion in section 10.4 that the main decision criterion advocated for investment projects is that they should show a positive net social benefit and that, where funds are limited, priority should be given to those projects showing the greatest net benefits. In order that the benefits and costs of a project occurring over a number of years into the future can be compared meaningfully, some way of discounting future monetary values is needed. The appropriate discount rate to use is the rate of social time preference indicating the strength of society's preference for current consumption *vis-à-vis* future consumption.

The 1967 White Paper proposed the use of discounted cash flow techniques of appraisal using a test discount rate of 8 per cent. This, however, made no pretence of being the social time preference rate; rather it was:

> ... broadly consistent, having regard to different circumstances in relation to tax, investment grants, etc., with the average rate of return in real terms looked for on low-risk projects in the private sector in recent years.[76, 77]

It also advocated the use of social cost–benefit techniques in certain circumstances (paragraphs 14 and 15) 'where comparison cannot be made on financial terms because pricing arrangements in different parts of the sector are not comparable'.[78] Also, it admitted that, because some of the benefits were 'in fields where nationalised industries are not in a position to make estimates', such studies ought to be carried out by the government departments concerned. Thus, provided that all the projects in which the divergence between private and social costs and benefits was significantly large were assessed using these techniques and that the rate of discount used approximated to the government's estimate of the social time preference rate, the 1967 criteria were largely consistent with those set out in section 10.4.

In practice, as already discussed, the criteria were not applied to any marked extent, and replacement investment was effectively exempted from evaluation according to these criteria. The 1978 criteria retain the use of discounting methods in investment appraisal; but as with the pricing criteria, they leave considerably more scope for variations in interpretation by the industries themselves. The conclusion is that the criteria of the 1978 White Paper provide a framework in which it is possible to make investment decisions that are consistent with the criteria for optimal resource allocation.

DEMAND FORECASTING

The first major criticism of actual performance in investment appraisal is the technical one of failures in demand forecasting. The electricity supply industry has probably had the greatest problem in this respect, having both under- and overestimated demand at different times in the past. The blame, however, cannot be laid entirely on its shoulders as the industry itself has often had to rely on erroneous estimates of future demand in the economy as a whole; and because the gestation period between the planning and operation of a power station can be as high as five years, it is clear that some element of forecasting error is unavoidable.

Nevertheless, in the 1950s electricity demand for the early 1960s was underestimated by up to 10 per cent.[79] In the early 1960s, partly as a result of the strictures of the Select Committee on Nationalised Industries and partly because of overoptimistic forecasts of economic growth, overestimates of demand in the late 1960s were made. The 1963 estimate of demand in 1968–9 was 50,000 megawatts, but by 1968 this estimate had been reduced to 38,200.[80] Yet, it was on the 1963 estimate that investment plans were based, although delays in parts of the nuclear programme have had an offsetting effect.

The main result of underinvestment for demand in the early 1960s, besides rationing by power cuts, was that resources were allocated to other uses when the return from investing them in electricity supply could have been higher, and vice versa. Second, there was an effect on the pattern of investment and the vintages of equipment in the electricity supply industry. For instance, overinvestment in the mid to late 1960s meant that investment in equipment in the early 1970s was less than it would otherwise have been. Given that the latter was technically more efficient than the former,[81] the overall efficiency of electricity generation was lower in the 1970s than it would have been with an optimal timing of investment.

In more recent years the impact of overinvestment has been that the suppliers of electricity-generating equipment have faced severe fluctuations in demand from their largest domestic customer – a problem that has also beset the suppliers of telecommunications equipment. As a result the government decided that the Central Electricity Generating Board would order a power station in advance of its commercial requirements and would be compensated accordingly. Such action has only postponed the problems faced by both the industry and its suppliers, but it is significant that the effects on suppliers have been mentioned in the 1978 White Paper as something that the government needs to take into account in determining policy towards nationalised industries. This could possibly develop into another area in which the industries' performance will have to be evaluated in future, probably taking into account the government's 'industrial strategy', discussed in Chapter 9.

THE RELATIONSHIP OF INVESTMENT AND PRICING POLICIES

The situation in the electricity industry also raises the crucial question of the link between pricing and investment policies. If pricing policies are not those associated with an optimal resource allocation, it is very unlikely that optimal investment policies will be formulated, because pricing policies influence both the level of demand and estimates of investment requirements. The point has been made with respect to peak and off-peak demand for electricity by Hawkins,[82] who has argued that so long as differential pricing is not pursued the load factor – a measure of relative peak and off-peak demands – is unlikely to improve, thereby necessitating further investment in meeting peak capacity only. In other words, if the price of peak electricity is less than its long-run marginal cost and if demand is sensitive to price, demand will be above the level that it would be at if price equalled long-run marginal cost. In these circumstances investment in peak generating facilities may yield a lower benefit than the equivalent investment elsewhere in the economy. Events during 1970–5 further illustrate the interaction between price levels in general and investment. Price restraint increased the demand for electricity above what it would have been at prices that would have covered long-run marginal costs. Except for the overcapacity in the generating system, already discussed, it is likely that further investment in generating capacity would have been needed. This would not have been justified but for the price restraint. In the event the effects of the two policy errors were offsetting – a situation that can never be counted on in the future.

USE OF INVESTMENT APPRAISAL

Another disturbing aspect of the investment policies of the nationalised industries, particularly in the pre-1960 period, was the fact that a large proportion of the railway investment provided for in the 1955 modernisation plan was made with only doubtful reference to the financial viability of the projects and with no reference at all to the social costs and benefits associated with its implementation. Rather, it seemed to have modernisation *per se* as its main objective. The report of the Select Committee on Nationalised Industries was particularly enlightening in respect of the railways' modernisation plan.[83] The plan was first published in 1955 when it was given general approval by the Ministry of Transport and the Treasury, although it was apparent that neither party knew the details of the plan. Between 1956 and 1959 a series of reappraisals took place, which eventually resulted in greater ministerial control. It is apparent from the select committee's report, however, that the criterion used by British Railways to justify the investment at that time tended to be the improvement in net receipts that it would bring. It did not, however, seem to be based on an estimation of whether a particular service, modernised or not, was in fact worthwhile.[84] The select committee's doubts on this score led it to study in more detail the London–Manchester electrification scheme, which accounted for more than 10 per cent of the £1,660 million total expenditure under the plan. Its conclusion was:

> The Committee found that no prior calculation had been made of the rate of return to be expected, and *ex post* calculations indicated a rate of return of between 5 and 7 per cent against interest on capital of 5–6 per cent.[85]

It may be added with the benefit of hindsight that the growth in traffic as a result of electrification has been much greater than originally forecast, so that the project is now probably showing a positive return.

In general the select committee was:

> . . . astonished at the way in which the Commission have been able to set in motion great modernisation schemes, without the departments comparing the economics of them with those of possible alternative schemes.[86]

The main conclusions, therefore, seem to be that the degree of sophistication in investment appraisal – certaintly within the railways – was very limited indeed in the financial sphere during this early period and that questions of social costs and benefits were ignored altogether.

The 1967 White Paper[32] at least provided that more satisfactory appraisals would be made of investment projects, although, as previously discussed, this policy has not been widely applied in practice. However, a combination of the select committee's strictures and the introduction of the test discount-rate procedure has had some impact within the transport sector in ensuring that investment proposals are now evaluated more thoroughly.

Appraisals of different investment projects within the nationalised sector have often been made without reference to the wider interdependence of benefits and costs. For example, the calculations of the benefits of the London–Manchester railway electrification scheme were made without allowing for the investment in the motorway system taking place at the same time. Similarly, the cost–benefit study of the London–Birmingham motorway (i.e. the M1) took no account of this railway investment.[87] What the results of a combined appraisal of both projects and each alone or in combination would have been is now a matter of conjecture; but the issue is an important one, given that the combined cost of the two projects was over £190 million. It seems possible that the benefits derived from these projects could have been achieved by a different and less expensive pattern of investment, especially as a large propor- tion of the M1 benefits could have been achieved at a fraction of the costs by bypassing the main towns on the A5.[88]

SOCIAL COST–BENEFIT ANALYSIS

A further criticism of investment practice in the nationalised sector has been the failure to take into account the divergence between private and social costs and benefits, which has been particularly marked in the transport sector. This point has been well illustrated by Foster and Beesley's 1963 study of investment in the Victoria underground line in London.[89]

Foster and Beesley have first stated why a social cost–benefit calculation was necessary. First, the pricing policy pursued by London Transport, which was effectively average-cost pricing, meant that the value to intramarginal users of the system was greater than the price paid by them and that price was less than would have been charged by a commercial enterprise; thus, the revenue did not represent fully the value that passengers placed on their journeys. Second, the fares paid by users took no account of the value of the investment to non-users. Foster and Beesley have in fact argued that, if marginal road charges were related to congestion, sufficient motorists would be diverted to public transport, so that the usage of the line would be higher than it currently was even if a commercial price were charged. Their overall conclusion was that in these circumstances the line could in fact show a positive rate of return on commercial grounds.

Foster and Beesley have attempted to estimate both the private costs and benefits to London Transport for the assumed fifty-year period of operation of the line – together with those occurring over the construction period of five and a half years – and the costs and benefits accruing to others. These included the value of time savings and of comfort and convenience to underground users and to users of British Rail services as a result of traffic diverted to the line. They have also attempted to evaluate the cost and time savings that would accrue to private motorists following the reduction in congestion resulting from the diversion of traffic to the line and to evaluate all these parameters in respect of traffic not diverted to the line.

Several interesting problems came to light in the process of the study – in particular those concerned with the valuation of travel time and of comfort and convenience, which have not yet been settled entirely but are crucial to such studies in this field. The main conclusion of the study was that, while on private cost criteria and assuming a 6 per cent rate of interest the loss on the Victoria line would be about £2·14 million per annum and the overall loss to London Transport £3·12 million,[90] on social cost criteria the net benefit to the community discounted over the $55\frac{1}{2}$ years' construction and operation would be £3·19 million.

It may be concluded from this analysis that there may have been an under-investment in public transport facilities in congested areas because commercial or break-even criteria were used for public transport and because no satisfactory road-pricing system was in operation. More generally, there has been little or no systematic appraisal of investment in urban transport as a whole. Investment in urban roads has tended to be dealt with on a variety of criteria, which have only in recent years incorporated social cost–benefit techniques.[91] One reason for this has been that roads have not been regarded as an 'industry' as such with costs and revenues. Public transport investments, with a few recent exceptions such as the Victoria line, have been considered on commercial grounds, which follows naturally enough from the quasi-commercial break-even objective set to operators. The only attempts at a systematic appraisal of urban transport investments as a whole, rather than individual road building or public transport investments, have been as part of transportation studies where the method of appraisal has tended to be somewhat crude – usually a first-year rate of return. It seems that this is a field where resources may be continually misallocated because of unsatisfactory pricing and investment policies.

Both within the transport sector and more generally within the nationalised industry sector, social cost–benefit analysis has considerable potential as a technique to help in guiding investment decisions. As the example of the Victoria line – one of the first social cost–benefit studies in the United Kingdom – shows, the technique is basically an extension of the type of financial investment-appraisal techniques described in Chapter 7. While a financial evaluation is concerned with costs and benefits – usually receipts – to the party undertaking the investment, a social cost–benefit study includes all costs and benefits, no matter who is affected. Consequently, it can in principle handle situations where resources are unpriced, e.g. road space, where an investment affects other sectors of the economy and where pricing constraints make it impossible for consumer surpluses to be recovered in extra revenue.

Apart from the procedures that are necessary to overcome these problems – for example, methods for measuring consumer surplus in the absence of a market have had to be devised – the basic principles of a social cost–benefit study are similar to those of a financial evaluation except, as already noted, for its wider remit. Thus, the objectives of the evaluations are to compare benefits in relation to costs and to help to determine the most efficient allocation of resources. Various criteria for comparison, e.g. net discounted present values and internal rates of return, are used in the same way as in financial evaluations.

A detailed discussion of the present state of the art in social cost–benefit analysis cannot be given here, but the proceedings of a conference held by the Royal Economic Society in 1974 have summarised many of the outstanding issues in its application to the public sector.[92] In the present context, however, it is relevant to conclude that, as almost all the problems described above that social cost–benefit analysis tries to overcome apply in the nationalised industries, its wider use would be a positive step towards the better allocation of investment resources. This was the thinking behind the recommendation contained in part of the 1976 NEDO study to use it in all parts of the nationalised sector. In addition to the reasons given in that study there is the consideration that, because social cost–benefit analysis covers a much wider spectrum of the effects of an investment, the rates of return obtained from it are not directly comparable with those of financial appraisal; in consequence the partial application of its wider criteria can be very misleading. This is another argument in favour of the wider adoption of social cost–benefit analysis by the nationalised industries.

THE STABILITY OF INVESTMENT

A more recent criticism concerning the government control of the nationalised industries is that public expenditure reductions have seriously affected investment by the nationalised industries. This has meant they have been unable to plan investment on more than a year-to-year basis, with two adverse consequences. First, in some industries, because of long lead times for major projects, there has been a reluctance to undertake such projects, which has resulted in suboptimal decisions being made. This has probably applied most to the railways where decisions on rolling stock replacement have been postponed for some time by uncertainty about future investment levels. Second, there have been effects on suppliers, partly discussed above, which have resulted in an inability to produce capital equipment at minimum cost because of difficulties in establishing optimal production runs or difficulties in maintaining a trained labour force during periods when demand has been low. This has been admitted by the government in the 1978 White Paper, which has proposed giving partial approvals for investment programmes for some years ahead.

CONCLUSION

Summarising the area as a whole, there must be considerable doubt about whether the allocation of investment funds by the nationalised industries has been in the projects that have been most likely to yield the greatest sum of net social benefits. One reason for this has undoubtedly been the lack of clear objectives on the part of the government, resulting in confusion about which criteria should be applied to investment decisions. As well the industries have often failed to apply any systematic evaluation to investment proposals, and some evaluations that have been carried out have been based on poor forecasts. While most of these faults have now been identified it remains to be seen whether they will be remedied and whether other problems will appear.

10.7 CONCLUSION

In summarising the relationship between the government and the nationalised industries it is possible to distinguish four phases between 1945 and the present. The first phase lasted from the mid 1940s until about 1955 with minor changes in emphasis according to the political views of the government. During this period attention was mainly concentrated on the problems of nationalisation itself and on the ultimate size of the nationalised industry sector. Thus, both political administrations promoted various nationalisation Acts, which resulted in changes in the size of the sector. The definition and monitoring of performance, however, were left very much in the hands of those running the industries, and only general objectives were set out in the nationalising Acts themselves. The interpretation of the objectives was largely left to the industries themselves, subject to the financial constraint of 'balancing the books'.

In 1956 the Select Committee on Nationalised Industries began its inquiries into the nationalised industries, and in many cases, e.g. British Rail, it was severely critical both of those running the industry and of the government in the light of what it considered to be inadequate performance. The government's reaction to this mainly took the form of adopting more precise financial targets, as in the 1961 White Paper.

The third policy phase commenced with the publication of the 1967 White Paper, which recognised for the first time that sound performance in the sense of efficient resource allocation could only result from sound pricing and investment policies and that financial criteria, while an important and necessary discipline, were really secondary to such policies.

Finally, there was the period from the early 1970s, when some retreat from the above policies occurred under pressure from the government's counter-inflation policy objectives. This phase ended with the publication of the 1978 White Paper, which in many respects sets a framework in which many of the criticisms of government relationships with the nationalised industries can in theory be overcome. What will be achieved in practice remains to be seen.

In the context of these phases in government policy towards the nationalised industries, what can be said of the role of the government? In the first period the government can be criticised for its largely passive role and in particular for not coming to terms with the problems involved in setting clear objectives. The second phase was characterised by an attempt to set objectives, initially financial, which resulted in the government being faced more clearly with the implications of the nationalised industries behaving in a fully commercial manner. The response to this was the 1967 White Paper, which took a number of significant steps – particularly on pricing and investment criteria and their relationship to financial performance – to create an environment in which the industries could make a larger contribution to the efficiency of their particular sectors of the economy. As a result the industries were working in a framework that was more conducive to efficient pricing and investment performance than ever before. The future, following the 1978 White Paper, is difficult to predict.

This still, however, leaves unanswered many questions on the extent to which the broader objectives of nationalisation set out at the beginning of this chapter have been achieved. On the question of technical efficiency Pryke's evidence[4] seems favourable. There has doubtless been an improvement in working conditions, although whether this has been the result of nationalisation or not is a debatable point. Control over the basic industries in the economy has been achieved and exercised, although to what degree it has furthered economic planning is another point for discussion. Finally, the question of the contribution of nationalisation to the broader socialist objective of creating a more egalitarian and co-operative society cannot be answered in this context as the setting of criteria against which to judge it involves making value judgements beyond the scope of this chapter.

FURTHER READING

Besides references mentioned in the text the following four books may be of more general interest: Thompson and Hunter on the nationalised transport industries;[93] Reid, Allen and Harris on the nationalised fuel industries;[94] Foster on the control of public enterprise;[95] and Turvey on economic analysis and public enterprise.[96]

Readers interested in analysing the role of the government in greater depth are recommended to read the 1961,[31] 1967[32] and 1978[2] White Papers and the 1976 NEDO report.[3] As a result of the 1978 White Paper the annual reports of the individual industries, which are always useful for statistical and financial information, should prove extremely useful in studying objectives and performance as they are to include details of the objectives and performance indicators agreed between the government and the industry.

NOTES AND REFERENCES

1 The British National Oil Corporation holds a substantial interest in British Petroleum, however.
2 *The Nationalised Industries*, Cmnd 7131 (London, HMSO, 1978), para. 52.
3 A thorough, although concise, account of the main features of the nationalised industries can be found in National Economic Development Office (NEDO), *A Study of UK Nationalised Industries*, 2 vols (London, HMSO, 1976), appendix volume, appendix C.
4 The subject of technical efficiency is not dealt with in this chapter. For a further discussion of this subject, see R. W. S. Pryke, 'Are the nationalised industries becoming more efficient?', *Moorgate and Wall Street* (1970); and R. W. S. Pryke; *Public Enterprise in Practice* (London, MacGibbon & Kee, Granada Publishing, 1971). In brief, Pryke has argued that the productivity of both labour and capital of the nationalised industries (with minor exceptions) has increased at a greater rate than that of private industry over the period since nationalisation. Some of Pryke's analysis of the railway industry has been challenged in S. Joy, *The Train that Ran Away* (London, Ian Allen, 1973), which is itself an interesting case study of a nationalised industry.
5 NEDO, op. cit. (n. 3), Vol. 1, chs 2 and 3.
6 For full details, see R. Kelf-Cohen, *Twenty Years of Nationalisation* (London, Macmillan, 1969), pp. 61–5.
7 In consequence the British Transport Commission acquired minority shareholdings in a number of other bus undertakings from the railways and several were acquired indirectly as a result of nationalising electricity undertakings.
8 Besides the organisational changes outlined above both the 1953 and the 1962 Acts took a number of significant steps in other directions, especially in that of freeing the railways from the statutory restrictions on charging policies to which they had been subject since Victorian times. These are further discussed in section 10.5.
9 *Transport Policy*, Cmnd 3057 (London, HMSO, 1966); *Railway Policy*, Cmnd 3439 (London, HMSO, 1967); *The Transport of Freight*, Cmnd 3470 (London, HMSO, 1967); *Public Transport and Traffic*, Cmnd 3481 (London, HMSO, 1967); and *British Waterways Recreation and Amenity*, Cmnd 3401 (London, HMSO, 1967). Also of relevance is *Transport in London*, Cmnd 3686 (London, HMSO, 1968).
10 Space precludes a discussion of the details of the legislation and reorganisation. For a critique of the provisions of the 1968 Act, see N. Lee, 'A review of the Transport Bill', *District Bank Review*, no. 165 (March 1968), pp. 45–62.
11 This is discussed in *Transport Policy: A Consultation Document*, 2 vols (London, HMSO, 1976); and *Transport Policy*, Cmnd 6836 (London, HMSO, 1977).
12 In Scotland the system is different. Originally, the generation and distribution of electricity were both the responsibility in the north of the North of Scotland Hydro-Electricity Board, which existed prior to 1947. In the south two area boards were set up, which operated in the same way as the English boards, including the purchase of supplies from the Central Electricity Authority; in 1955 they were unified and given responsibility for generation too.
13 *Report of the Committee of Enquiry into the Electricity Supply Industry*, Cmnd 9672 (London, HMSO, 1956).

14 For a more detailed account of the provisions of the Acts, see Kelf-Cohen, op. cit. (n. 6), chs 2–6.
15 The 'appropriate ministers' have changed over time as a result of government re-organisations. At present the Departments of Trade, Energy, Industry and Transport together with the Scottish Economic Planning Department are responsible for the major nationalised industries.
16 For a more detailed analysis, see Kelf-Cohen, op. cit. (n. 6), chs 7 and 8; and W. Thornhill, *The Nationalised Industries: An Introduction* (London, Nelson, 1968), chs 1–4.
17 Quoted in Thornhill, op. cit. (n. 16), pp. 56–7.
18 *The Role of British Rail in Public Transport: First Report from the Select Committee on Nationalised Industries, Session 1976–77*, 3 vols, HC 305 (London, HMSO, 1977).
19 NEDO, op. cit. (n. 3), main report, p. 8.
20 Cmnd 7131, op. cit. (n. 2).
21 Gas Act 1948, s. 1(1).
22 Electricity Act 1947, ss 1(1), (2) and (6).
23 Transport Act 1947, s. 3(1).
24 Gas Act 1948, s. 41.
25 Transport Act 1947, s. 3(4).
26 British Transport Commission, *Annual Report and Accounts, 1949* (London, HMSO, 1950), p. 6.
27 Kelf-Cohen, op. cit. (n. 6), pp. 200–1.
28 G. L. Reid and K. E. Allen, *Nationalised Industries* (Harmondsworth, Penguin Books, 1970), p. 115.
29 *British Railways: Report from the Select Committee on Nationalised Industries*, HC 254 (London, HMSO, 1960), paras 413–16.
30 See page 404 above.
31 *The Financial and Economic Objectives of the Nationalised Industries*, Cmnd 1337 (London, HMSO, 1961).
32 *Nationalised Industries: A Review of Economic and Financial Objectives*, Cmnd 3437 (London, HMSO, 1967), para. 3.
33 For details of targets actually set in the period to 1967, see Cmnd 3437, op. cit. (n. 32), table 1. Although agreements between the government and industries about targets are mentioned in some industry annual reports in this period, no discussion is found of the factors taken into account in determining them.
34 Cmnd 3437, op. cit. (n. 32), para. 17.
35 Cmnd 3437, op. cit. (n. 32), paras 17–18.
36 For a fuller discussion, see Cmnd 3437, op. cit. (n. 32), paras 17–26.
37 Cmnd 3057, op. cit. (n. 9); and Cmnd 3439, op. cit. (n. 9).
38 Cmnd 7131, op. cit. (n. 2).
39 NEDO, op. cit. (n. 3), Vol. 2, appendix D.
40 Cmnd 7131, op. cit. (n. 2), para. 56.
41 Cmnd 3437, op. cit. (n. 32), para. 35.
42 As an example of this there is little doubt that restrictions on the supply both of private cars and of petrol kept the demand for public transport at an artificially high level in the late 1940s and early 1950s.
43 For detailed financial performance in the period 1955–6 to 1966–7, see Cmnd 3437, op. cit. (n. 32), tables 3 and 4. The data confirm the assertion in the text.
44 Cmnd 7131, op. cit. (n. 2), para. 5.
45 The latter method is preferable for several reasons. For a fuller·discussion, see W. J. Tyson, 'A critique of road passenger transport subsidy policies', *Manchester School*, vol. 40 (December 1972).
46 Cmnd 7131, op. cit. (n. 2), paras 86–8.

47 Pryke, op. cit. (n. 4, 1971).
48 R. G. Lipsey and K. Lancaster, 'The general theory of the second best', *Review of Economic Studies*, vol. 24 (1956) have expounded the theoretical principle. O. A. Davies and A. Whinston, 'Welfare economics and the theory of the second best', *Review of Economic Studies*, vol. 33 (1965) have discussed some points arising from its application. For a discussion in the context of a pricing policy for a nationalised industry, see R. Turvey, *Optimal Pricing and Investment in Electricity Supply* (London, Allen & Unwin, 1968), ch. 8.
49 R. Millward, *Public Expenditure Economics* (London, McGraw-Hill, 1971), ch. 4, pp. 95–100. The rest of this chapter discusses some other important aspects of the problems raised in this sector and contains a formal analysis of the second best.
50 Millward, op. cit. (n. 49), p. 97.
51 Millward, op. cit. (n. 49), p. 98.
52 Millward, op. cit. (n. 49), p. 99.
53 Millward, op. cit. (n. 49), p. 100.
54 Cmnd 7131, op. cit. (n. 2), paras 59 and 62.
55 The Railway and Canal Act 1854 introduced the concept.
56 For an explanation of the rationale of this argument, see A. C. Pigou, *The Economics of Welfare* (London, Macmillan, 1924), p. 219.
57 See, for example, S. Joy, 'British Railways' track costs', *Journal of Industrial Economics*, vol. 13 (1964).
58 British Railways Board, *The Reshaping of British Railways* (London, HMSO, 1963), table 1.
59 W. J. Tyson, 'The peak in road passenger transport: an empirical study', *Journal of Transport Economics and Policy*, vol. 6 (January 1972); and W. J. Tyson, 'A study of peak cost and pricing in road passenger transport', *Institute of Transport Journal*, vol. 34 (November 1970).
60 Tyson, op. cit. (n. 45).
61 National Board for Prices and Incomes (NBPI), *Gas Prices (Second Report)*, Report No. 102, Cmnd 3924 (London, HMSO, 1968), ch. 4.
62 For papers on this subject by Boiteaux, see J. R. Nelson, *Marginal Cost Pricing in Practice* (Englewood Cliffs, Prentice-Hall, 1964), chs 1, 3–6 and 10.
63 Another feature of the nationalisation Acts was that they imposed the duty to 'meet all reasonable demands' for their products on the boards concerned.
64 See Central Electricity Generating Board, *Annual Report and Accounts, 1965–66* (London, HMSO, 1966), pp. 48–52; and R. L. Meek, 'The new bulk supply tariff for electricity', *Economic Journal*, vol. 78 (1968), pp. 43–66.
65 National Board for Prices and Incomes (NBPI), *The Bulk Supply Tariff of the Central Electricity Generating Board*, Report No. 59, Cmnd 3575 (London, HMSO, 1968), para. 16.
66 For actual details, see Reid and Allen, op. cit. (n. 28), pp. 41–2.
67 NBPI, op. cit. (n. 61), para. 57.
68 Effectively, the gas boards can cut off supplies at peak periods, subject to varying degrees of notice agreed between them and the consumer. This is technically feasible because many appliances burning gas can quite easily be converted to use other fuels, and other fuels can be stored at relatively low cost.
69 NBPI, op. cit. (n. 61), paras 73–8.
70 An account of railway costing and pricing policies can be found in S. Joy, 'Pricing and investment in railway freight services', *Journal of Transport Economics and Policy*, vol. 5 (September 1971). More recent developments are referred to in British Railways Board, *Annual Report and Accounts, 1977* (London, British Railways Board, 1978), pp. 10–14.
71 *Consultation Document*, op. cit. (n. 11).

72 For a further analysis, see Millward, op. cit. (n. 49), pp. 112–18.
73 *Consultation Document,* op. cit. (n. 11); and Cmnd 6836, op. cit. (n. 11).
74 It can be argued that the present system of confining payment to unremunerative services and basing it on the financial deficit is not optimal. See Tyson, op. cit. (n. 45).
75 In cases where average cost is falling and marginal cost is thus below average cost the existence of a required positive financial return will result in an inconsistency of objectives: either a departure from marginal cost pricing, or a deficit. Several solutions have been proposed, of which the most practicable is the two-part tariff with a variable charge that equals marginal cost and a fixed charge set so as to enable the target to be met. For a further discussion, see Millward, op. cit. (n. 49), pp. 242–51, and references cited therein.
76 Cmnd 3437, op. cit. (n. 32), para. 10.
77 It was argued subsequent to the publication of Cmnd 3437, op. cit. (n. 32), that on the criteria adopted a 10 per cent discount rate was appropriate. Later the rate *was* raised to 10 per cent. See A. M. Alfred, 'The correct yardstick for state investment', *District Bank Review,* ed. no. 1966 (June 1968).
78 Cmnd 3437, op. cit. (n. 32), para. 15.
79 NBPI, op. cit. (n. 65), p. 7.
80 NBPI, op. cit. (n. 65), p. 8.
81 Thermal efficiency in the electricity supply industry increased from 21·6 per cent in 1950 to 27·9 per cent in 1967. See Reid and Allen, op. cit. (n. 28), p. 29.
82 E. K. Hawkins, 'Investment and the demand for electricity', *Oxford Economic Papers,* vol. 9 (1957).
83 *British Railways,* op. cit. (n. 29), paras 161–225 and 381–96. References to evidence are given in the report.
84 *British Railways,* op. cit. (n. 29), paras 384–96.
85 Reid and Allen, op. cit. (n. 28), p. 116.
86 *British Railways,* op. cit. (n. 29), para. 222.
87 Road Research Laboratory, *The London–Birmingham Motorway: Traffic and Economics,* Technical Paper No. 46 (London, HMSO, 1960).
88 D. J. Reynolds, 'The economics of rural motorways', *Journal of Industrial Economics,* vol. 10 (November 1961), pp. 10–20; and M. E. Beesley, 'Some aspects of the economics of the M1', *Journal of Industrial Economics,* vol. 10 (July 1962), pp. 204–8.
89 C. D. Foster and M. E. Beesley, 'Estimating the social benefit of constructing an underground railway in London', *Journal of the Royal Statistical Society,* vol. 125 (1963).
90 Because of loss in net revenue on other services.
91 See, for example, Road Research Laboratory, *The Economic Assessment of Road Improvement Schemes,* Technical Paper No. 75 (London, HMSO, 1968).
92 M. V. Posner, *Public Expenditure: Allocating Between Competing Ends* (Cambridge, Cambridge UP, 1977).
93 A. W. J. Thompson and L. C. Hunter, *The Nationalised Transport Industries* (London, Heinemann, 1972).
94 G. L. Reid, K. Allen and D. J. Harris, *The Nationalised Fuel Industries* (London, Heinemann, 1972).
95 C. D. Foster, *Politics, Finance and the Role of Economics: An Essay in the Control of Public Enterprise* (London, Allen & Unwin, 1971).
96 R. Turvey, *Economic Analysis and Public Enterprises* (London, Allen & Unwin, 1971).
97 Cmnd 3437, op. cit. (n. 32), para. 5.

11 Government Policy and the Location of Industry

11.1 INTRODUCTION

This chapter is concerned with the question of 'where' industrial activities take place, the reasons why locations change and the role of government policy in modifying locational influences. Changes occur in the spatial distribution of activities in a variety of different ways, such as by:

(1) the setting up of new firms (births);
(2) the opening of new establishments belonging to existing firms (branches);
(3) the relocation of existing establishments (transfers);
(4) the closure of existing establishments or firms (deaths); and
(5) changes in the distribution of production between existing establishments.

Each of these forms has had an important impact on the location of industry. However, few have been fully investigated; and in most cases until recently, location studies have been mainly restricted to manufacturing activities.

The structure of this chapter is as follows. Section 11.2 provides an overview of the current location pattern of industrial activity in Britain and of the ways in which it has been changing, both inter-regionally and intra-regionally, during the recent past. This is followed by a review of the development of theory relating to the location of the individual firm, leading to the formulation of neoclassical profit-maximising location theory (section 11.3). This is then evaluated by examining empirical studies of the location decision, in the form of both location surveys and correlation analyses (section 11.4).

The extent to which twentieth-century location patterns are associated with the emergence of a regional or urban problem is examined in section 11.5 by analysing the nature of this problem and how its magnitude may be measured. This is followed by a review of the development of the distribution of industry policy in Britain at the central, regional and local levels of government (section 11.6). Three aspects of the impact of central government policies are then examined: their impact on regional employment levels and plant movements, on central government net revenue, and on social costs and benefits (section 11.7). Finally, section 11.8 contains a comparative evaluation of the different instruments of location policy that are available and concludes with advice on further reading.

11.2 INDUSTRIAL LOCATION IN BRITAIN: AN OVERVIEW

In this section the current location pattern of industrial activity in Britain and the manner in which it has been changing during the most recent past is analysed. The basic indicator used is the distribution of employment by region and, for the more recent past, by subregion and urban area.

Table 11.1 Distribution of employment by industry and region: % of total male and female employees in employment, 1975

Region	Total (millions)	Sex	Manufacturing	Distribution and other services	Agriculture	Mining, gas, electricity, water	Construction
North	1·4	M	43	35	2	8	12
		F	24	73	1	1	1
Yorkshire and Humberside	2·2	M	43	38	2	9	9
		F	28	69	1	1	1
East Midlands	1·7	M	43	36	3	10	8
		F	35	60	2	1	1
East Anglia	0·8	M	34	45	8	3	10
		F	22	71	5	1	1
South East	8·2	M	31	57	1	2	8
		F	19	78	1	1	1
South West	1·8	M	34	48	4	4	10
		F	19	77	2	1	1
West Midlands	2·5	M	55	33	2	4	7
		F	33	64	1	1	1
North West	3·0	M	46	42	1	3	8
		F	29	68	1	1	1
Wales	1·2	M	38	40	3	9	10
		F	22	74	2	1	1
Scotland	2·3	M	36	43	3	5	13
		F	23	74	1	1	1
Northern Ireland	0·6	M	34	45	4	4	13
		F	27	70	1	1	1

Source: Central Statistical Office, Regional Statistics, No. 13 (London, HMSO, 1977).
Key: M = males, F = females.

Table 11.2 *Distribution of employment by industry and region: % of male employees in employment, 1975.*

Region	Coal, petroleum, chemical products, metal manufactures	Engineering and allied industries	Textiles, leather and clothing
North	12	20	3
Yorkshire and Humberside	10	17	6
East Midlands	6	19	7
East Anglia	2	16	1
South East	3	17	1
South West	2	19	2
West Midlands	9	36	1
North West	6	21	6
Wales	15	13	2
Scotland	5	18	3
Northern Ireland	1	13	8

Source: Central Statistical Office, *Regional Statistics,* No. 13 (London, HMSO, 1977).

The regional distribution of employment in 1975 is summarised in Tables 11.1 and 11.2, which illustrate the variation in:

(1) the relative importance of the regions as sources of employment (the South East being the most important and Northern Ireland the least important);
(2) the relative importance of the services sector between regions (most important in the South East and least important in the West Midlands);
(3) the relative importance of the manufacturing sector between regions (most important in the West Midlands and least important in the South East); and
(4) the relative importance of industries in the manufacturing sector between regions (e.g. the relative dependence of Wales on basic industries and of the West Midlands on engineering industries).

Table 11.3 summarises the available evidence on variations in the growth rate of total employment between the regions during 1921–76. During the period up to the early/middle 1960s the South East and West Midlands experienced the most rapid growth in employment, followed by a small group of geographically adjacent regions consisting of the South West, East Midlands and East Anglia. By contrast the regions most distant from the two key growth regions – i.e. Scotland, Wales and Northern Ireland – experienced the most modest increases, or actual decreases, in employment.[1] Typically, then, during this period the centre regions grew relative to the peripheral regions. Since the middle 1960s, however, this trend appears to have been interrupted, if not modestly reversed. The total employment statistics for the period 1970–6, for example, record small increases for all the peripheral regions,

Table 11.3   *Rate of growth in regional employment, 1921–76.*

Region	1921–61[a] (% per annum)	1970–6[b] (% change)
South East	0·87	−0·9
West Midlands	0·84	−2·7
South West	0·65	+5·9
East Midlands	0·59	+3·2
East Anglia	0·47	+7·7
North	0·26	+1·7
Yorkshire and Humberside	0·19	−0·1
North West	0·03	−3·5
Scotland	0·02	+0·6
Wales	0·01	+2·9
Northern Ireland	−0·11	+2·9

Source:
(a) C. H. Lee, *Regional Economic Growth in the UK since the 1880s* (London, McGraw-Hill, 1971) p. 213.
(b) Central Statistical Office, *Regional Statistics,* No. 13 (London, HMSO, 1977).

modest decreases in the cases of the South East, West Midlands and North West, but continued employment expansion in the regions adjacent to the South East.

This reversal in regional employment trends has also been identified by Keeble in a study of regional manufacturing employment.[2] He has observed that:

> various evidence agrees that the 1950s witnessed massive absolute and relative manufacturing growth in and around the central industrial conurbations of London and Birmingham . . . Since the early 1960s, and especially the later 1960s, concentration has been replaced by increasing *spatial* dispersion of manufacturing industry, both to relatively unindustrialised subregions and to the peripheral areas.[3]

This is illustrated in Figure 11.1 for the period 1966–71.

Attempts to explain differences in the employment trends between regions have usually involved the use of *shift-and-share* analysis,[2, 4] which attempts to disaggregate the change over time in the employment level of each region into three main components:

(1) *Regional share component* – the amount by which the region's employment would have changed if it had changed at the same rate as national employment.

(2) *Structural (or proportionality) shift component* – the extra amount by which the region's employment has changed through having an industrial structure that is different from the national industrial structure. Regional specialisation in relatively declining industries causes a negative structural-

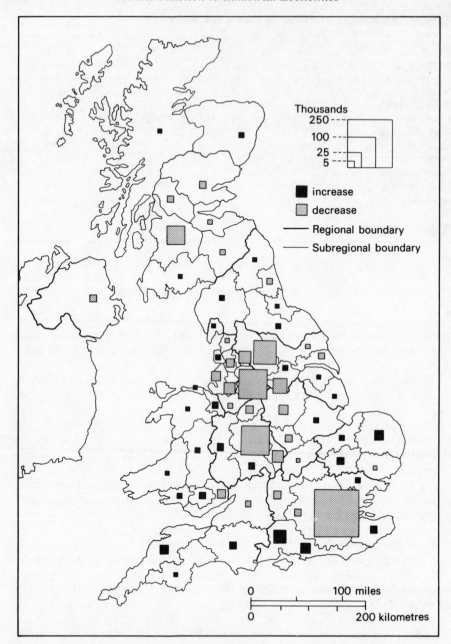

Fig. 11.1   Regional and subregional manufacturing employment change in the United Kingdom, 1966–71.

Source: D. E. Keeble, *Industrial Location and Planning in Britain* (London, Methuen, 1976), p. 18.

shift component; specialisation in relatively fast-growing industries yields a positive component.

(3) *Differential shift component* – the residual change in a region's employment after the deduction of the regional share and proportionality shift components. As such it is supposed to measure the effect of the above or below average growth or decline of particular industries in the region, compared with the national growth rates of those same industries. A positive differential-shift component implies above average growth, and a negative component implies below average growth in the region's industries.

Before presenting the results of the shift-and-share analyses that have been used to interpret regional employment change in Britain, it is necessary to draw attention to its limitations as an analytical tool,[4] which include the following:

(1) The results obtained are sensitive to the degree of industrial disaggregation used when calculating the structural shift component. If broad industrial categories are used, part of the impact of the region's industrial structure may be missed and be incorrectly treated as a residual, i.e. as a differential shift component.
(2) The results are sensitive to the weighting system used in separating the structural and differential shift components.
(3) Structural and differential shift components are not completely independent of each other. For example, a region with a favourable industrial structure may be expected to experience above average growth in a number of its local industries through the effect of the regional multiplier. Therefore, the differential shift component cannot be unambiguously treated as an indicator of the relative competitiveness of a region's industries.

A number of shift-and-share analyses of regional, total and manufacturing employment in Britain covering the period 1920–70 have now been carried out.[2, 5–7] These indicate, first, for the period from 1920 to the early 1960s:

(1) a strong positive structural-shift component in the case of the South East and West Midlands, reflecting the relative importance in these regions of the fast-growing service and engineering industries respectively – an effect supplemented by the more modest positive differential-shift impact in the two regions;
(2) a fairly strong positive differential-shift component in the cases of regions immediately adjacent to the South East; and
(3) negative structural- and differential-shift components in the cases of the main peripheral regions, e.g. Scotland, Wales, Northern Ireland and the North West.

However, corresponding analyses relating to manufacturing employment during the 1960s suggest that:

(1) The positive structural-shift component in the South East continued, although it may have become slightly negative in the West Midlands; but this was accompanied by a substantial negative differential-shift component in these two regions, which in the later 1960s was resulting in negative total shifts in both cases.
(2) The fairly strong positive differential-shift component in regions adjacent to the South East continued.
(3) The negative structural-shift component in the peripheral regions continued to apply, but with the exception of the North West this influence was increasingly offset by positive differential shifts in these regions.

Although these findings are necessarily tentative they lend further support to the view that significant changes in the underlying trend in industrial location in Britain commenced during the 1960s and became more noticeable as the decade advanced. It is also to be noted that the main feature of these changes – i.e. a tendency for the enterprises located in the peripheral regions to gain employment relatively at the expense of enterprises in the same industries located in the South East and West Midlands – coincided with the strengthening of the government's location-of-industry policy from the early 1960s. This is examined more fully in sections 11.6 and 11.7.

The analysis above has highlighted the longer-distance inter-regional changes that have occurred in the spatial distribution of industrial activities, particularly as they have affected the centre and peripheral regions. Equally significant, however, are the shorter-distance, frequently intra-regional, changes in employment patterns that have occurred. These can be most easily detected by urban area analysis.

Employment trends in British urban areas during the period 1951–71 are now examined.[8] For this purpose each urban area is defined in terms of three geographic components:

(1) *urban core* – composed of single or contiguous local authority areas with an employment density of over five workers per acre or a total employment of over 20,000 jobs;
(2) *metropolitan ring* – composed of those contiguous local authorities from which more than 15 per cent of the working population commute to the core; and
(3) *outer metropolitan ring* – composed of all other areas sending more workers to a particular core than to any other core.

The urban core combined with its metropolitan ring is called the standard metropolitan labour area (SMLA); and when the outer metropolitan ring is added the whole is termed the metropolitan economic labour area (MELA).

Table 11.4 highlights the major difference in employment trend between the 1950s and the post 1960 period. Prior to 1960 employment in the urban cores and their metropolitan rings was increasing at a similar overall rate, which exceeded the national growth rate in employment. In other words there was a continued centralisation of employment within urban centres, although a decentralisation in the resident population to suburban areas occurred during

Table 11.4   *Employment change in urban areas, 1951–71* (%).

Urban area	1951–61	1961–71
Urban cores	6·7	−3·1
Metropolitan rings	6·6	15·0
SMLAs	6·7	1·4
Outer metropolitan rings	−0·4	3·9
MELAs	5·6	1·8
Unclassified areas	−5·5	−0·7
Total	5·1	1·7

Source: Department of the Environment, *British Cities: Urban Population and Employment Trends, 1951–71*, Research Report 10 (London, DOE, 1976).

this period. However, since 1960 the decentralisation of employment has accompanied the decentralisation of the population. Employment in urban cores has fallen while it has grown dramatically in the metropolitan rings and, to a lesser degree, in the outer metropolitan rings. The available evidence suggests that this trend has continued during the 1970s.

This tendency to decentralisation has not been uniform in all major urban areas. At the one extreme a group of relatively new towns surrounding the London SMLA were experiencing relative centralisation during this period, whereas older major cities – e.g. Liverpool, Manchester, Newcastle and Glasgow – together with a number of smaller industrial towns in eastern Lancashire and western Yorkshire experienced absolute employment losses in their urban core that were well above the national average.[8]

Most studies show that the manufacturing sector has been one of the leading sectors in the decentralisation of jobs from the urban core, although the effects of this on total employment may have been masked in the early stages by more-than-proportionate increases in service employment.[9-11] More recently, however, decentralisation in service and office employment from the older city areas has also occurred (see Table 11.5).[12]

Table 11.5   *Changes in total and office employment in conurbation centres, 1966–71* (%).

Conurbation centre	Total employment	Office employment
Greater London	−4·1	0·1
Merseyside	−34·7	−19·9
SE Lancashire	−12·1	−11·9
Tyneside	−9·9	−12·7
W. Midlands	−4·2	0·5
C. Clydeside	−12·3	−11·6

Source: P. W. Daniels, 'Office location in the British conurbations: trends and strategies', *Urban Studies*, vol. 14 (1977), pp. 261–74.

The causes of urban core decline are still being investigated and are as yet imperfectly understood. However, it seems that decline could be due to a combination of the following factors:

(1) improved road transport facilities during the present century, which have increased the relative accessibility of the outskirts of urban areas;
(2) the suburbanisation of the resident population seeking a higher-quality living environment, which has resulted in a corresponding decentralisation in certain labour markets;
(3) structural and competitive weaknesses in the economic base of inner city areas, i.e. their dependence on employment in declining industries and in old uncompetitive plants; and
(4) the adverse influence on employment of central and local government land-use controls and other urban policies in inner city areas.[13, 14]

If the first two factors are the dominant causes of urban decentralisation in employment, urban core decline may be the long term consequence of the operation of ordinary economic forces, and it may be inappropriate for government policy to be used to restrain or reverse this trend. On the other hand, if a significant part of the decline is due to correctable weaknesses in the economic base of cities and to the application in the past of inappropriate land use controls, government policy has a more obviously important role to play in influencing the location of industry at urban and subregional levels. This is examined further in section 11.9.

In summary, two types of trend have been identified in the spatial distribution of industry:

(1) *An inter-regional trend.* Prior to 1960 this trend favoured the centre regions at the expense of the peripheral areas. It led to the political recognition of a 'regional' problem and to attempts to deal with this through government policy to modify the geographic distribution of manufacturing industry. During the 1960s this underlying trend was apparently reversed, at least in terms of the differential shift component, and this coincided with a considerable strengthening in government policy towards the distribution of industry.
(2) *An intra-regional trend.* Prior to 1960 the overall trend of centralising employment in the urban cores continued, although there were also corresponding proportionate increases in employment in the metropolitan rings. Since the early 1960s this trend has been reversed to one of decentralisation; that is, total employment in the cores has fallen, but in compensation it has increased very substantially in the metropolitan rings and to a lesser extent in the outer metropolitan rings. In turn this has led to the relatively recent political recognition of an 'inner city' problem for which a range of governmental remedial measures have been launched or are being prepared.

The policy issues raised by the spatial trends summarised above are examined later in this chapter; but first it is intended to examine, at both the theoretical and the empirical levels, the determinants of the location decisions of individual firms in the next two sections.

11.3   DEVELOPMENT OF LOCATION THEORY

TRANSPORT COST MINIMISATION

Early writers on location theory attached prime importance to transport costs as a locational determinant of a new single-plant enterprise.[15] Assume, for example, that a new plant will use two kinds of factor input, X and Y. Factor X is available at a uniform factor price at all possible locations – that is, its supply is ubiquitous – but factor Y can only be supplied from site A. The commodity to be produced by the establishment will be sold in a single market located at site B. The optimal location for this establishment, assuming an objective of profit maximisation, is the site that enables it to minimise its total transport costs for any given level of output and sales. If Y is expensive to transport but loses a great deal of its weight in the production process, e.g. like coal, the establishment will tend to be resource orientated in its location, i.e. near A. On the other hand, if the product is difficult and expensive to transport – e.g. because it is bulky, fragile or highly perishable – its location will tend to be market orientated, i.e. nearer B.

If two or more factor inputs are not ubiquitously available, the optimal location of the establishment is the resultant of the relative strengths of the locational pull of the market and all such factor inputs, which satisfies overall the transport-cost minimisation criterion (see Figure 11.2).

The optimal location, in terms of transport cost minimisation, of an establishment will tend to alter over time due to changes in:

(1)   the location of resource and/or market sites;
(2)   the relative unit transport costs for resources and products; and
(3)   production processes that bring about modifications to the type and combination of factor inputs used.

There are many examples of the location pattern of plants in particular industries responding over long periods of time to changes in these economic forces. For example, the early cotton mills were pulled to the Pennine communities where water power was immediately available, but they later

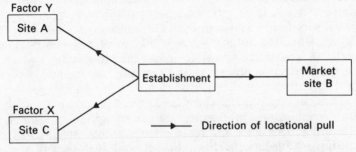

Fig. 11.2   Locational pull of resource and market sites.

moved down into the valleys to be nearer to markets and other resource supplies once steam power had been introduced.[16] Similarly, the steel industry was initially located in the coalfields, but as the dependence on coal diminished the locational pull of iron ore supplies became relatively stronger, causing new steel plants to be located on inland ore sites or at coastal sites that were accessible to imported ore supplies.[17]

PRODUCTION COST MINIMISATION

Particularly during the early stages of economic development when transport systems were both limited in scope and relatively expensive, existing transport facilities were almost certainly a more decisive direct influence on the choice of location for a new establishment than is the case today. However, transport cost remains the most fundamental influence in the sense that, if all resources and customers were perfectly mobile, i.e. transportable at zero cost, all locations would be equally attractive and the location decision would largely cease to be of economic significance.

In fact some resources are effectively non-transportable, e.g. land, and others can only be transported at a cost of both money and time. This means that resources differ in their locational accessibility to those who wish to use them and hence that the price of a resource varies according to its relative accessibility. Land at the centre of a city is more accessible to many markets than land on the urban periphery and thereby commands a higher rental. Wage levels at the centre of a city may be higher than on its outskirts because workers who live in the suburbs have to be compensated for the journey-to-work costs that they incur. In short, the relatively higher land prices in city centres embody the transport costs avoided in central locations, and the higher labour costs in city centres embody the higher transport costs incurred by journey-to-work commuters.

Hence, there are both intra-regional and inter-regional variations in factor prices resulting from the existence of non-transportable factors and of the costs incurred in transporting or transferring the factors that are movable. Therefore, a firm that wishes to minimise its total production costs for any given level of output must take into account the spatial variation in factor prices, after adjusting for any variation in factor quality, as well as the incidence of transport costs at different locations. Therefore, the transport cost-minimising location will not, except by chance, be optimal for the profit-maximising firm where factor prices are not spatially uniform.

The spatial variation in factor prices will simultaneously influence both the optimal location and the optimal factor combination of a new establishment, assuming that it is technically possible to vary the proportion in which factors are used in the production process.[18, 19] Essentially, the method of production selected will be that which economises on the use of the spatially most expensive resource. Thus, in city centres where land prices are relatively high, space-economising methods of production and consumption predominate, e.g. medium- and high-rise office and retail establishments, small-scale specialist manufacturing establishments, town houses and high-density multi-storey apartments. By contrast, on the outskirts of a city are to be found large-scale single-storey industrial establishments, large discount retail outlets with extensive car-parking facilities, and semi-detached and detached housing developments with extensive gardens.

THE SPATIAL DISTRIBUTION OF MARKETS

So far it has been assumed that the new establishment will only serve a single market centre. Where this is the case profits will be maximised if the establishment is located so that for a given output level its production costs, including transport costs, are minimised. However, if the potential market is divided between two or more locations, this no longer provides an adequate explanation of the determinants of the location decision.

Suppose, for example, that there are two distinct market centres, E and F, and that the site of the establishment may be in *either* of these two centres but not, for managerial reasons, in *both*. The unit costs of *production* are identical for both sites ($MC=AC$ in Figure 11.3), but the unit costs of *delivery* ($MC_1=AC_1$) will be higher at one of the market centres because of the need to transport the finished product from the production site in the other market centre.

Does it follow, given these costs assumptions, that both locations are equally attractive as a production site? As illustrated in Figure 11.3, the establishment is able to make a maximum profit in E that is higher if production is sited at E (*abcd*) rather than at F (*efgh*), but it will make a greater maximum profit in F if production is sited at F (*ijkl*) rather than at E (*mnop*). Given the assumption that production cannot be divided between the two locations, it is preferable to site production at E because the gain in profit in so doing (*abcd−efgh*) exceeds the reduction in profit at F (*ijkl−mnop*). Only if demand conditions were identical in both market centres would both centres be equally attractive as a production centre. Hence, demand differences between market centres, as well as production and transport

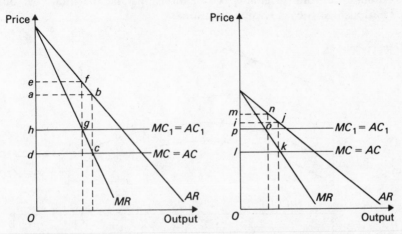

Fig. 11.3 Profit maximisation in multiple markets under alternative locational assumptions.

cost differences between different sites, are relevant to the location decision of the profit-maximising establishment.

THE PROFIT-MAXIMISING MODEL

The analysis contained in the previous subsection can also be used to demonstrate that the sales that a plant is able to make, given its ex-works price, will vary according to its location and that these sales will tend to be largest if it is located closest to the largest market centres.[20] This is shown in the *space revenue function, TR,* in Figure 11.4, which shows, given a constant ex-works price, how total receipts are expected to vary according to the location of the plant at different points on a line between A and B and indicates that two peaks occur in the space revenue function at locations X_1 and X_2. Which of these two locations will yield the higher profit requires consideration also of the *space cost function, TC*. The space cost function describes how the total production cost, including the costs of transporting materials etc. to the plant, varies between one location and another for a given level of output. In Figure 11.4 TC_1 is the space cost function for the output level required to meet sales at X_1, and TC_2 is the corresponding space cost function for the output level required to meet sales at X_2. The expected profit, therefore, is shown at X_1 by the vertical distance at that point between TR and TC_1, and at X_2 by the vertical distance at that point between TR and TC_2. The following points emerge from the example:

(1) The revenue-maximising location (X_1) and cost-minimising location (A) may not coincide.
(2) The profit-maximising location (X_2) may coincide with neither the revenue-maximising location (X_1) nor the cost-minimising location (A).
(3) The location decision may be particularly demanding in its information requirements, since in reaching the decision it is in principle necessary to estimate the total revenue–price relationships and the total cost–output relationships at each feasible location.

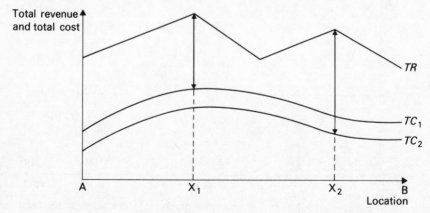

Fig. 11.4 Spatial equilibrium of a profit-maximising enterprise.

The market, production and transport cost variables described above are the basic building blocks of the neoclassical theory of plant location. The analysis has been conducted in relation to the siting of a new single-plant enterprise, i.e. a new operation, but this can be readily extended to the other types of location decision described in section 11.1. For example, in siting a new branch factory the effects of the choice of location on plant costs and revenues that are a function of distance from the other establishments of the parent enterprise have to be incorporated into the analysis. In siting a plant transfer the costs of moving to possible new locations from the existing plant site have to be taken into consideration.

SCALE ECONOMIES

In addition the analysis may be further refined by the inclusion of scale economies as further determinants of location decisions. The influence of three types of scale effect on the plant location decision may be distinguished:

(1) internal economies of plant size;
(2) economies of scale that are external to the firm but internal to the industry; and
(3) agglomeration economies, which are external to both the firm and the industry.

Internal Economies of Scale
Internal economies of scale are relevant to the location decision of an enterprise where it has the alternative of undertaking production within a single large establishment or in a number of smaller units in different locations. Assume for the purposes of simplification that the price of each factor input is uniform at all locations. If supply sources of the raw material are dispersed and if these materials lose a great deal of weight in the production process, there will be some tendency to establish a number of separate production establishments, each located near a raw material source in order to minimise transport costs. Similarly, if markets are dispersed and the products are bulky, fragile or perishable, the optimal transport-cost solution may be to establish separate establishments, each located near a local market. However, neither of these approaches may result in the least *total*-cost solution if important technical economies are obtainable through concentrating production within a single plant.

The literature on internal economies of scale is reviewed in section 2.10 and indicates the following conclusions:

(1) In a considerable number, but not a majority, of manufacturing activities the minimum economic size at which unit production costs are at their lowest point forms a substantial proportion of the total UK market.
(2) When plants are smaller than 50 per cent of their minimum economic size their units costs rise substantially.
(3) For many manufacturing activities the minimum economic size has been increasing through time.

The combined influence of (1) and (2) determines those types of manufacturing activity where the locational influence of internal economies of scale are most likely to over-rule the locational influence of transport cost minimisation. The influence of (3) should be reflected in the increasing range of manufacturing activities to which this situation is applicable. It suggests an increasing degree of locational concentration in manufacturing activities, which is of both urban and regional policy significance.

External and agglomeration economies affect the location decision, in theory, through their impact on the availability and price of factor inputs and transport facilities in those locations where such economies accrue. If, as is commonly the case in the neoclassical model, the market mechanism is assumed to eliminate temporary local shortages or surpluses in factor supply, the impact via factor and transport prices will be the fundamental influence on plant location.

External Economies of Scale

External economies of scale accrue because of the scale of the industry rather than the size of its constituent firms and establishments. Once an industry exceeds a certain size in a given location, it attracts to itself a variety of institutions that enable the constituent establishments in the same locality to obtain their factors of production more reliably and cheaply, and to sell their products more effectively, than would otherwise be the case. Examples of such external economies include:

(1) the development of specialist raw-material markets to service the industry, e.g. cotton and wool exchanges for purchasing the raw materials used in the textile industries;
(2) the availability of local supplies of labour experienced in the techniques and operations of the industry;
(3) the local provision of appropriate training facilities and co-operative research-and-development facilities in technical colleges, industrial research institutes etc.; and
(4) the development of local advertising and marketing organisations to promote the sales of the industry.

Agglomeration Economies

Agglomeration economies accrue as a result of the scale of aggregate economic activity in an area rather than as a result of the scale of one industry. Such economies are most likely to be significant where the economic activities in an area are linked to each other in a complementary manner in the following ways:

(1) They generate the need for similar infrastructure facilities, the provision of which is subject to increasing returns to scale.
(2) They require types of labour that are in joint supply, e.g. heavy industry using male labour and mail order establishments using female labour.
(3) They require workers with basically similar skills, e.g. the engineering industries, and so enlarge the size of the local labour supply that may be

tapped by an individual establishment and stimulate the development of appropriate educational and training facilities.
(4) They have close buyer and seller relationships with each other – in other words, there are strong local interindustry linkings (see section 2.6) – which may result in transport cost savings or in other forms of purchasing and selling economies.

However, the continued growth of an establishment, industry or some broader aggregate of economic activity in an area may eventually result in diseconomies of scale, which will tend to have the opposite influence on location decisions. If a factory grows beyond a certain size, it may become more difficult to manage, and the resulting *internal diseconomies* may cause further production requirements to be met by the creation of a new branch factory at a different location. Similarly, the continued expansion of aggregate economic activity in an area may result in:

(1) materials and labour having to be acquired from greater distance and, therefore, at greater expense to individual establishments; and
(2) increased congestion on the transport network, resulting in increased transport costs to individual establishments.

The *agglomeration diseconomies* that arise, which may be exaggerated by faulty urban and regional policies, encourage the movement of the most seriously affected establishments away from the more central locations. Thus, just as agglomeration economies play an important role in the development and growth of urban areas as centres of economic activity, so the subsequent emergence of agglomeration diseconomies later contributes to their decentralisation.

11.4   EVALUATION OF THE PROFIT-MAXIMISING MODEL

During the post-1945 period there have been a considerable number of empirical studies of the determinants of industrial location in Britain, although these have been mostly restricted to manufacturing establishments.[2, 21, 22] They have been of two broad kinds:

(1) surveys of the location decisions of industrial firms using questionnaires and/or interview techniques of investigation; and
(2) correlation analyses using more aggregate statistical data on plant movements and on the explanatory variables hypothesised to have influenced these.

LOCATION SURVEYS

Surveys have mainly been concerned with transfer and branch decisions within manufacturing industry and, therefore, have been uneven in their coverage of both the types of location decision and the types of economic activity. They have also differed among themselves in the geographic area covered by the survey and the time period in which it was undertaken; and in the minimum size of the transfer or branch move and the minimum distance of moves investigated in the survey. Despite these differences, certain broad characteristics of location decision making have emerged from these studies and similar studies in other countries.

Push and Pull Factors

Branch and transfer moves most commonly result from a stress situation within the firm. According to surveys conducted at the beginning of the 1970s, the major reason for inter-regional movement, in approximately 80 per cent of the cases investigated, was the pressure for space created by the growth of the firm, combined in many instances with such subsidiary reasons as an inadequate supply of local labour or the inadequacy of existing premises (see Table 11.6).[21, 22]

The dominant factors in 'pulling' plants to the particular sites selected were: the availability of a satisfactory labour supply; public policy, e.g. financial inducements, training facilities or government-built factory units; accessibility to markets; and the availability of a fully-serviced site with ample room for

Table 11.6   *Factors in the decision to move by 531 firms, 1964–7 (% of all firms).*

Factor	Major reason	Minor reason	Outstanding single reason
To permit an expansion of output	83	8	20
Inadequate existing premises or site	50	11	8
Unsatisfactory labour supply at existing location	40	11	15
Inducements and facilities made available by official bodies	27	14	2
Opportunity to purchase or rent premises or site at new location	20	8	3
Too far from established or potential markets	19	1	9
Refusal or expected refusal of Industrial Development Certificate	12	4	5
Town-planning difficulties	11	3	4
Lease of former premises fell in, or good offer received	5	2	3
Desire to be in more attractive surroundings	4	8	1
Too far from supplies, actual or prospective, of materials or services	3	2	1
More profitable to operate elsewhere	1	—	1
No one outstanding reason	—	—	28
Total			100

Source: Inquiry into Location Attitudes and Experience: House of Commons Expenditure Committee (Trade and Industry Sub-Committee), Minutes of Evidence (London, HMSO, 1973); summarised in M. Sant, Industrial Movement and Regional Development: The British Case (Oxford, Pergamon, 1975) pp. 54–5.

expansion (see Table 11.7). Of lesser general importance were such factors as the price of the site or accessibility to sources of supplies.

Less is known about the 'push' and 'pull' factors involved in intra-regional movements. Small firms in particular are known to prefer short distance movement and only then where this is forced upon them, e.g. by the expiration of a lease or by central area redevelopment. In addition to the potentially greater influence of personal factors on the relocation decision, it has been suggested that specialist firms are more likely to depend on the interfirm linkages that characterise particular localities, including central urban areas, so that agglomeration economies preclude movement over great distances.[23]

Business Procedures and Evaluation Criteria
The procedures and evaluation criteria used by fifty-nine companies in selecting a new plant site were investigated by Townroe in 1969.[21] The survey revealed the following features:

(1) The sources of information used to identify potential sites were often limited, particularly outside Development Areas:

> Although some companies were very systematic, such as the one who wrote to the town clerk of each local authority in its major sales area, others discovered possibilities almost by accident . . . The opportune arrival of circulars just after the decision to move had been

Table 11.7 *Factors in the location decisions of inter-regional movers, 1964–7 (% of all firms).*

Factor	Major reason	Minor reason	Outstanding single reason
Availability of labour at new location	72	20	20
Knowledge or expectations that Industrial Development Certificate will be obtainable	48	18	2
Accessibility to markets or supplies	39	21	9
Availability of government inducements	39	7	7
Assistance from local authorities or promotional bodies	36	30	3
Accessibility to one of firm's plants or to location from which moving	32	18	7
Access to specified transport facilities	31	20	2
Good amenities and environment	29	41	1
Availability of suitable non-government factory	28	5	6
Special characteristics of site	20	17	3
Other factors	12	2	3
No outstanding single factor	—	—	38
Total			100

Source: As for Table 11.6, p. 57.

taken was of overwhelming importance in three cases – nothing else was considered. And two firms went to Central Wales from the Midlands because the managing directors both spent their weekends on the Welsh coast and passed the sites en-route.[24]

(2) Although a small minority of firms considered only one site, three-fifths of firms considered less than ten sites, and a number of these sites were eliminated fairly quickly to leave three or four possibilities for more detailed examination.

(3) In 76 per cent of firms a set of criteria to work to in the search process was established, although in only half of these cases were the criteria written down:

> At most, this was a tight detailed specification of the new plant with full technical details and data on requirements for labour, local supplies, etc., and with criteria for judging the general area required in terms of maximum transport costs or distance from the present plant. As a minimum, these firms had a check list of key factors to look for at each location.[25]

(4) In 22 per cent of cases no costing or financial evaluation was performed, and in over half of the remaining cases only the final choice was costed. Approximately 35 per cent of all firms, including approximately 60 per cent of all firms employing over 500 employees, used discounted cash-flow techniques in their financial evaluation: 'These results seem to indicate that, for a majority of companies, alternative locations are not evaluated on explicit cost grounds and that the financial assessment comes after the locational choice.'[26]

This is consistent with the earlier findings by Luttrell, based upon location decisions in the 1940s:

> We should have liked to have given an example of a classic case of location choice in which operating cost estimates were made for two or more possible places, all imponderables or non-cost factors assessed and then a way found of comparing the good or bad points of one place with those of the other. Unfortunately we have not been able to find such a case.[27]

Criticisms of the Model

The findings of these studies and of similar studies in the United States have led to the questioning of the neoclassical analysis of location decisions, principally in relation to its assumptions of profit-maximising objectives, rationality and conditions of certainty.

A number of empirical studies have drawn attention to the apparently critical role of personal factors, e.g. the place of birth or residence of the owner, in the location decision, particularly for small firms. However, in these instances the inconsistency with the behavioural assumptions of neo-classical theory may be more apparent than real.[28] Through his superior personal contacts in such locations the business owner may have better access to suppliers, credit sources and competitive markets than would be the case in less well-known locations. Alternatively, if the owner derives psychic income from working and living in a particular locality, the neoclassical model may be reformulated, without undermining its essential features, on the assumption of utility maximisation.

A further criticism, which is more appropriate in the case of larger firms, is that businesses are motivated in their location decisions more by considerations of growth than by profit maximisation. This is in line both with the theoretical expectation, given the divorce of ownership (see section 3.4), and with the empirical finding that the main motivational 'push' from central to plant movement is the pressure generated by the growth of the firm. If this criticism were accepted, a sales maximisation model of location could be developed. The optimal location of a sales maximiser could differ from that of a profit maximiser as illustrated in Figure 11.4, where X_1 is the sales-maximising location and X_2 is the profit-maximising location. This illustrates that sales maximisers will tend to be more market orientated than profit maximisers in their location decisions.

The formulation of a location policy that is consistent with a business goal of growth or profit maximisation presumes a level of rationality in the firm's decision-making process that may not be found in practice. Hamilton has observed an approach to location decision making based upon a more bounded form of business rationality:

> . . . firms do not necessarily, or even usually, recognise that the location aspect is important: for many firms and for many types of business decision, the location aspect is likely to be a byproduct of a particular policy to achieve some non-spatial goal. There appears rarely to be a conscious location policy except among very large or market-dominant corporations.[29]

Thus:

> One management may decide that corporate growth may best be achieved by diversification: the emergent pattern of plant locations within the corporation is likely to differ significantly from a corporation whose management is bent on growth via larger control of the market for a fairly narrow range of products.[29]

Similarly, corporate objectives for growth by acquisition and merger will condition policies towards constructing new branch plants:

> . . . Blackbourn's comparison of the international expansion strategies of American firms into Western Europe shows that corporate managements may have definite policies either for acquisition (notably General Motors) or for internal corporate growth via new branch plant construction (notably Ford). One may hypothesize that a company will never deviate from that policy unless the stress factors are so great that management feels that the survival or current operations of the firm are threatened if they do not yield.[29]

The neoclassical model assumes that the decision maker possesses a certain knowledge of all the relevant variables and the capacity and willingness to evaluate all alternatives in order to identify the action that will maximise his payoff function. By contrast, empirical studies have emphasised the pervasiveness of uncertainty and the bounded rationality of decision makers. The responses of decision makers in these circumstances are similar in many respects to those hypothesised in the behavioural theory of the firm (see section 3.5):

(1) Each business possesses multiple goals, and location decisions are made where necessary in relation to the attainment of such specific lower-order objectives as described above.
(2) The considerable uncertainty associated with a transfer or branch move is avoided by utilising existing premises as long as practicable. Hence, all moves are precipitated by unavoidable pressure of the types outlined in the empirical studies. Where a move is unavoidable there will be some preference to minimise the uncertainty created either by making the move over as short a distance as possible (in the case of transfer) or by acquisition (in the case of plant addition), provided that this does not conflict with the corporate growth strategy.
(3) The search for profitable alternative, or new, sites is not a continuing corporate activity. Search is only activated by the corporate recognition of an unavoidable pressure on existing plant facilities.
(4) Search is not directed to all possible plant locations but only to a subset of these, which are often unsystematically identified in the near vicinity of existing establishments.
(5) Search is for a *satisfactory* site, which meets a range of physical and other requirements, rather than for the *best* site, at which profits or sales may be maximised. Financial evaluation often takes place after the satisfactory site has been identified and is only infrequently used in making a selection between alternative sites.

These criticisms of the neoclassical model of location decision making parallel those made of the neoclassical model in such other areas as pricing and investment, which are also largely based on surveys of decision motives and procedures in individual businesses. In turn they are vulnerable to the same countercriticisms as levelled by Machlup,[30] Friedman[31] and others of empirical findings derived by these methods. The results obtained emphasise the specific components comprising the motives, procedures and criteria of the investment decision; but they are less clear in refuting the view that these reflect, possibly inexactly and incompletely, the economic forces that are treated as the determinants of the location decision in the neoclassical model. For example:

(1) The reluctance to countenance a transfer or a new branch is consistent with there being high costs in the relocation of an existing plant or in the initial setting-up costs of a new plant.
(2) Although (according to Tables 11.6 and 11.7) only 1 per cent of firms

chose to move explicitly to increase profits, the other reasons given may reduce to the demand and cost considerations highlighted in the neo-classical model.

(3) The limited search procedures and crude evaluation criteria used may be consistent with the profit assumptions of the neoclassical model, given the high costs of search and the large element of irreducible uncertainty in financial estimates both for transfer and for branch moves.

If this is at least partially the case, three groups of variables that are likely to influence the level and composition of economic activity in particular areas may be identified:

(1) basic market, cost and agglomeration variables, as identified in the profit-maximising model in section 11.3;

(2) behavioural variables, which cause the market and cost variables to have a modified impact due to the 'filtering effect' of uncertainty and bounded rationality on individual-plant movement decisions;

(3) government policy variables, which through Industrial Development Certificates, information and advisory services etc. modify:
    (a) market and/or cost variables (e.g. by purchasing policies or capital subsidy policies); and
    (b) the site alternatives that firms have available and that they consider.

CORRELATION ANALYSES

In principle these three sets of variables should be statistically discernible influences on:

(1) the locational distribution of establishments (and of the pattern of employ-ment) within an economy at particular points in time; and

(2) the location and pattern of plant movements, both transfer and branch, between the different parts of an economy (and changes in the pattern of employment) both at particular points in time and over time.

However, the attempts to test these two types of relationship, using regression and other forms of correlation analysis, have been handicapped by difficulties in obtaining meaningful measures of many of the variables, particularly the behavioural variables; and by multicollinearity problems such that the influence of one set of variables often cannot be reliably distinguished from the influence of other sets of variables. Additionally, most of the studies have been primarily concerned to isolate the impact of government policy variables; therefore, they have tended to specify the other types of explanatory variables in an incomplete and sometimes crude manner. The main findings of three of the broader-based studies are outlined below, prior to summarising the main conclusions on the main determinants of plant location.

    Latham, in a study of the regional distribution of establishments in American industry,[32] has hypothesised that firms locate their plant according to the following characteristics of their parent industries:

(1) *market orientation* – the proportion of the industry's output sold to final demand sectors;
(2) *labour orientation* – the proportion of wages to the value added in the industry;
(3) *material orientation* – the proportion of inputs purchased from primary resource industries; and
(4) *agglomeration orientation* – measured in terms of the importance of inter-industry flows between pairs of industries or as a general agglomerative factor.

The findings point to the primary importance of agglomeration economies and market attraction as determinants of the regional distribution of establishments. Similar findings have been obtained by Chalmers and Beckhelm in an analysis of the determinants of the shift in location of US manufacturing employment during 1963–7.[33]

Sant has attempted to explain the regional pattern of the origin and destination of manufacturing plant moves in Britain between 1945 and 1971, using regression analysis.[22] The three most significant variables that explained the *generation* of plant movements were found to be:

(1) total employment in the region of origin – a proxy for the total number of establishments in the region;
(2) the industrial composition of the region of origin – taking into consideration the fact that the most rapidly expanding industries tend to generate the most plant movements; and
(3) urban employment density and the proportion of the region of origin having urban status – an indicator of the congestion of the region.

In explaining the regional *destination* of plant movements the most significant variables were identified as:

(1) total numbers unemployed in the region – both a proxy for the size of the destination region and an indicator of general labour availability;
(2) the distance between origin and destination regions – reflecting increased resistance to plant movements over long distances; and
(3) the distribution of industry policy variables.

Keeble,[2] in a parallel study relating to changes in subregional employment in the periods 1959–66 and 1966–71, has identified the following significant variables: the industrial structure of the area (indicating the favourable influence of the presence of fast-growing industries); total manufacturing employment (generally significant with a negative sign, which was interpreted as an indication of the presence of agglomeration diseconomies); residential space preference (an environmental quality variable); and assisted area status (1966–71 only). In a supplementary study[2] of employment created by manufacturing plant movements (1966–71) the same variables, excluding the industrial structure variable but incorporating the distance variable used by Sant, were found to be significant.

It seems, then, that the following six conclusions may be tentatively drawn from these and similar studies. First, the *pressure of demand* is basically important as a determinant of the volume of plant movement.[2, 22, 34, 35] The pressure of demand may be important for two reasons: it stimulates new investment, which to be accommodated may involve a plant move; and it increases the relative attractiveness of those regions in which factor inputs, e.g. labour, are relatively less scarce. The first of these two reasons is consistent with the findings of the empirical surveys. The second relates to supply conditions in the destination regions and, therefore, overlaps the factors mentioned in the second conclusion below. The pressure of demand has been measured as the national male unemployment rate[35] and by an index of spare capacity,[34] both of which have captured the two aspects of this variable.

Second, generally speaking the *regional labour price* has not been established as a significant explanatory variable in those models in which it has been tested.[2, 6, 22] However, as discussed later, there is a measure of dispute concerning the extent to which government policy, by changing the relative price of manufacturing labour between regions through the regional employment premium, has influenced the pattern of plant movement – and more generally of manufacturing employment – between regions. The interpretation of this finding is complicated by the facts that insufficient allowance may have been made for regional differences in labour productivity; and because inadequate account may have been taken of the countervailing locational influence of regional differences in the price and availability of other factor inputs, particularly raw materials, which may have caused some capital-intensive activities to locate in low labour-cost regions. Subject to these qualifications, however, the statistical studies have supported the location surveys in attaching only minor significance to labour price differences as determinants of plant movement.

Third, considerable difficulty has been encountered in finding a suitable measure of *labour availability*, beyond the national unemployment measure mentioned in the first conclusion above.[2, 22, 34] Regional differences in activity rates and unemployment rates are significant in some regression models, but their importance does not match that indicated by the location surveys. The location survey data suggest that, for certain types of activity at least, the *quality* of the available labour in terms of training and experience may be as important as the *quantity* of unemployed labour that is available. Therefore, greater success may be achieved with this variable in the future, once it has been redefined to incorporate a qualitative dimension.[2]

Fourth, market location and agglomeration economies are not included as variables in all regression models, partly because they are not important factors in explaining short term fluctuations in the aggregate total of plant movements. However, where they are included they have usually been shown to be significant,[2, 22, 32, 33] although their importance varies according to the type of industry and, less certainly, to the size of firm involved. The inhibiting role of distance on plant movement[2, 22] may be interpreted as further evidence of the importance of these variables and may reinforce the significance given to them in the empirical surveys.

Fifth, environmental variables have been systematically examined only by Keeble,[2] although they are included in Sant's interpretation of his regression results.[22] These lend support to the view, described in the empirical surveys, that such variables have a subsidiary but significant influence on the regional distribution of plant movements, particularly in favour of the environmentally more attractive regions in the southern part of the country.

Sixth, government policy variables are prominent in the statistical analyses undertaken[2, 22, 34, 35] and have generally been established as significant influences on the distribution of plant movements and on the regional distribution of manufacturing employment since the early 1960s. There is, however, controversy over the magnitude of their influence and their welfare significance, which are examined in sections 11.7 and 11.8.

In summary, the statistical analyses, although not conclusive, appear to reinforce the findings of the location surveys in stressing the importance of the following variables:

(1) market and agglomerative variables in explaining the general location pattern of manufacturing establishments;
(2) demand pressure, particularly in already developed urban areas, in precipitating transfer and branch movements;
(3) behavioural variables not readily accommodated within the neoclassical model, such as environmental variables and variables reflecting the desire to avoid uncertainty (e.g. resistance to movement, particularly over longer distances); and
(4) government policy variables influencing the choice of destination region in transfer and branch movements.

In addition the empirical findings point to the following conclusions, which have significance for government policy:

(1) The success of large economically-viable regions is self-perpetuating, given the locational pull of market and agglomeration economies and the reluctance to transfer existing plant or to establish new branches at great distances from such regions. This suggests the possibility of continuing regional imbalance in the absence of government intervention.
(2) Urban cores in both the prosperous and the less prosperous regions are potentially vulnerable, given:
    (a) the tendency for larger establishments to move to the urban periphery when unable to satisfy their expansion requirements at the core; and
    (b) the dependence of smaller firms and establishments in urban cores on the network of interindustry and market linkages that exists there and that may be disrupted by these outward plant movements to the urban periphery as well as by central area redevelopment.
(3) The determinants of location decisions in an unregulated market situation are likely to be inconsistent with the attainment of a social welfare optimum.

These matters receive further attention in the next section, which examines the rationale of government intervention in the locational distribution of industry.

11.5   INDUSTRIAL LOCATION AND REGIONAL AND URBAN PROBLEMS

The changing pattern of industrial location has since the 1920s been associated with the continued existence of a 'regional problem' in Britain. More recently, during the late 1960s and 1970s it has also been linked to the emergence of an 'urban problem'. In both cases, although commencing at different points in time, this has led to government intervention to influence industrial plant movements and employment at both the inter-regional and the intra-regional level. Before describing and evaluating the government policies used, the extent to which such problems, particularly regional problems, exist in Britain is examined in this section.

INDICATORS OF REGIONAL INEQUALITY

The most commonly used indicators of the regional problem are: regional differences in unemployment rates and in *per capita* income levels; and various measures of regional imbalance, e.g. regional disparities in the growth rate in employment and population or in the rates and direction of migration. Each of these is briefly examined below, drawing attention to particular problems in measuring and interpreting the regional statistics available.

Regional Unemployment Rates
The regional unemployment rate measures the percentage of the insured working population of a region registered as unemployed at particular points in time. Regional differences in these rates may not be an accurate reflection of regional differences in unemployment levels, for two reasons. First, a proportion of those who are employed but who form part of the insured working population may not register themselves as unemployed at employment exchanges, particularly if they expect to become re-employed in the near future. It has been suggested that in the past this may have resulted in a small *overstatement* of regional differences in male unemployment rates.[36]

Second, and more seriously, unemployment levels in higher unemployment regions may be relatively *understated* if those prepared to work cease to form part of the insured working population because of very poor job prospects. This tendency should be reflected in regional differences in economic activity rates, i.e. in the ratios between total insured employees and measures of the size of the adult population in the regions. In turn, however, disparities in regional activity rates require careful interpretation because they are also affected by regional differences in the age structure of the adult population, in the relative importance of self-employment and in industrial structures.

Unemployment rates that are above the national average in the peripheral regions and below the average in the central regions have characterised the British economy for most of the present century. Regional unemployment rates during the more recent past are shown in Table 11.8. This indicates that as the general level of unemployment in the economy has varied, the *absolute* difference in rates between the peripheral regions as a group and the economy as a whole has been more or less maintained, although in *relative* terms the

Table 11.8   *Unemployment rates in the peripheral and central regions, 1960–75 (%).*

Region	1960	1965	1970	1975
North West	1·9	1·6	2·7	5·3
North	2·8	2·6	4·7	5·9
Wales	2·7	2·6	3·9	5·6
Scotland	3·6	3·0	4·2	5·2
Northern Ireland	6·7	6·1	6·8	7·9
South East	1·0	0·9	1·6	2·8
West Midlands	1·0	0·9	2·0	4·1
United Kingdom	1·6	1·5	2·6	4·2
Difference between all peripheral regions (unweighted average) and UK average	1·9	1·7	1·7	1·8

Source: Central Statistical Office, *Regional Statistics*, No. 13 (London, HMSO, 1977).

rate in the peripheral regions has fallen during the 1970s as the general unemployment level in the country has risen.

The analysis of activity rates (see Table 11.9) indicates that these are generally lower in the peripheral regions than in the central regions, particularly in the case of female labour, so that the recorded regional differences in unemployment rates probably understate the full extent of this form of regional disparity.[37] However, regional differences in female activity rates have been falling since the early 1960s, and so the extent of this understatement has probably also been diminishing.[22]

Regional per capita *Income Levels*
The estimation of regional *per capita* income in real terms involves assigning income to its regional base and then making adjustments for taxation, for central government contributions to the regional provision of goods and services, and for the regional cost of living. Because of the empirical difficulties involved the estimates obtained can only be regarded as very approximate.

Table 11.9   *Economic activity rates in the peripheral and central regions, 1971 (%).*

Region	Male	Female
North West	81	44
North	80	40
Wales	79	36
Scotland	81	42
South East	82	45
West Midlands	84	45
Great Britain	81	43

Source: Central Statistical Office, *Abstract of Regional Statistics*, No. 10 (London, HMSO, 1974).

Table 11.10   *Personal disposable income per head (in money terms) in selected regions, 1972 and 1975 (United Kingdom=100).*

Region	1972[a]	1975[a]	Price Index[b]
North West	97	99	99
North	90	96	96
Wales	91	90	98
Scotland	93	98	99
South East	112	110	106
West Midlands	101	97	98

Source:
(a) Central Statistical Office, *Regional Statistics,* No. 13 (London, HMSO, 1977).
(b) A. J. Brown, *The Framework of Regional Economics in the United Kingdom* (Cambridge, Cambridge UP, 1972) p. 79.

After a careful analysis of the available statistics for 1964, Brown has drawn the conclusion that:

> At the end of the story, SE England and W. Midlands stood near together at the top of the range, 10% or 11% lower came Scotland, Wales and all the remaining English regions except the North, with only such gaps between them as are within the margins of error of the estimates, and 4% or 5% lower still comes the Northern region.[38]

Since then official estimates of personal disposable income per head by region have been published for more recent years (Table 11.10). If the regional differences in the cost of living as measured by Brown still apply, a narrowing in disparities between regional *per capita* real-income levels may have occurred during the 1970s.

Regional Imbalance
The substantial differences in the growth rates in regional employment between 1920 and the early 1960s have already been described (section 11.2 and Table 11.3). These imbalances in employment were reflected in regional differences in population growth and in the direction and rate of migration during the same period (Table 11.11). The regional share of the UK population by each peripheral region fell during this period, whereas it rose substantially in the cases of the South East and West Midlands and to a lesser degree in a group of regions adjacent to these. Similarly, prior to 1961 all the peripheral regions were experiencing net outward migration in contrast to the centre regions and their immediate satellite regions, which were net gainers of migrants.

However, as in the case of regional employment (Table 11.3), these trends have been modified during the 1960s and 1970s (Table 11.12). During the latter half of the 1960s both the South East and West Midlands began for the first time to experience a modest level of outward migration, and during the 1970s there has been a modest decline in the total population of the South

Table 11.11 *Distribution of population by region (1921–61) and net migration by region (1956–61).*

Region	Change in % share of UK population, 1921–61[a]	Net migration in 1956–61 as % of total regional population in 1956[b]
North West	−0·8	−0·9
North	−0·7	−0·9
Yorkshire and Humberside	−0·6	−1·3
Wales	−1·0	−0·8
Scotland	−1·3	−2·8
Northern Ireland	−0·1	−6·8[c]
South East	+2·8	+2·2
West Midlands	+1·0	+1·2
East Anglia	+0·1	n.a.
South West	+0·4	+2·8
East Midlands	+0·6	+1·2

Source:
(a) C. H. Lee, *Regional Economic Growth in the UK since the 1880s* (London, McGraw-Hill, 1971), p. 213.
(b) G. McCrone, *Regional Policy in Britain* (London, Allen & Unwin, 1969), p. 156.

Note:
(c) 1951–61.

Table 11.12 *Changes in population by region (1970–6) and in net migration by region (1961–71).*

Region	Population change, 1970–6 (%)	Annual net migration in 1961–71 per 1,000 popuation in 1971
North West	−0·7	−1·7
North	−0·4	−3·3
Yorkshire and Humberside	+0·5	−1·5
Wales	+1·6	−0·1
Scotland	−0·2	−6·2
Northern Ireland	0·0	−4·3
South East	−0·6	−0·2
West Midlands	+0·9	−0·3
East Anglia	+7·0	+7·2
South West	+4·0	+5·9
East Midlands	+2·7	+2·1

Source: Central Statistical Office, *Regional Statistics*, No. 13 (London, HMSO, 1977).

East and an equally modest increase in the West Midlands population. During 1961–71 only the three regions adjacent to these two central regions experienced net inward migration, and these recorded the greatest population increases during the 1970s. All the peripheral regions continued to experience net outward migration during the 1960s, but in a number of cases at reduced rates compared with previous periods. Certain of these regions – i.e. Wales, Scotland and Northern Ireland – have been recording modest increases or very modest decreases in population during the 1970s.

Viewed in its international context the regional problem in Britain, as defined above, exists on a smaller scale than in many other developed and developing countries.[39, 40] At the same time the regional data presented are statistical averages and as such conceal the more substantial spatial changes occurring at subregional and intra-urban levels. Table 11.13, for example, draws attention both to the great differences in the directional extent of migration within regions and to the considerable intra-regional differences in unemployment rates that exist. Even greater differences are to be found within the major conurbations (Table 11.4).[8, 11, 14] In short, the more spatially detailed the analysis, the greater is the range of economic difference observed, and, therefore, the greater is the apparent magnitude of the regional or urban problem identified. However, this highlights the need to examine the implicit assumption in the foregoing analysis: can the economic variables described above be used to indicate the existence of regional and urban problems and the consequent need for government intervention?

Table 11.13   *Intraregional variations in migration (1961–71) and in unemployment rates (1976–7).*

Region	Migration in 1961–71 per 1,000 population in 1971 (range between subdivisions of standard regions)	Unemployment, 1977 (%)	
		Average for region	Development or Special Development Area
North West	−6·7 to +10·5	7·1	10·7
North	−5·6 to +4·6	7·8	8·6
Yorkshire and Humberside	−6·2 to +6·8	5·6	5·6
Wales	−6·8 to +16·4	7·6	9·1
Scotland	−9·1 to +0·9	7·5	8·8
South East	−13·2 to +16·1	4·3	n.a.
West Midlands	−2·4 to +13·4	5·8	7·7
East Anglia	+1·9 to +11·1	5·0	n.a.
South West	+3·8 to +8·7	6·6	9·9
East Midlands	−0·6 to +8·9	4·9	5·3

Source: Central Statistical Office, *Regional Statistics* (London, HMSO, annual); and Department of Industry, *Annual Report on the Industry Act* (London, HMSO, 1978).

IS THERE A REGIONAL PROBLEM?

The nature and extent of the regional problem in Britain, and more particularly the usefulness of the above indicators in assessing its incidence, are a subject of continuing debate. In order to distinguish the issues involved three possible interpretations of the regional adjustment process are presented below. Similar interpretations might also be applied to the urban situation.

First, in a dynamic economy the changes in demand and supply conditions that occur inevitably have a different impact on individual regions because of the differences in their industrial structure. Therefore, a change in the pattern of demand will initially cause some regions to increase their production, employment and income relative to others. However, the regional differences in unemployment and *per capita* income levels which then exist will themselves precipitate adjustment towards a new long-term equilibrium through:

(1) the movement into the weaker regions of labour-intensive plants, attracted by the relatively lower unit wage costs that now exist there; and

(2) the outward migration of surplus labour from the weaker regions to the more prosperous regions where the marginal product of labour is relatively higher.

In other words, in a competitive market situation in which factors of production are perfectly mobile, the existence of regional differences in unemployment and *per capita* real incomes is an indication of short run disequilibrium, which will be self-correcting through the migration of labour, capital and enterprise without the need for government intervention.

Second, the acceptability of the above interpretation depends upon the usefulness of the assumptions that it makes about the nature of existing markets and the smoothness with which they operate. However, in practice:

(1) enterprises do not periodically review the siting of their existing plant, or determine the siting of new plant, with fine regard to changes that may have occurred in the relative economic advantages of different locations (see section 11.4); and

(2) labour may be relatively immobile because of a lack of knowledge of employment opportunities in other regions, because of the specific nature of its skills or because of the high costs of movement.

In these circumstances the self-correcting mechanism may not work or may work too slowly, in terms of both economic and social costs. In turn this may justify government intervention to promote the efficient spatial working of factor markets by such measures as establishing employment exchanges and retraining centres, providing assistance with rehousing costs, and supplying information and consultancy services to industry on site selection.

However, a third view is that the process of adjustment in an already declining region may be self-perpetuating rather than self-correcting,[41] for the following reasons:

(1) An initial decline in employment in an industry will have a regional multiplier effect on employment in the production of consumer goods and services in the same region. It may also have an effect on employment in other local industries with which it has links as supplier or purchaser.
(2) The contraction in employment reduces the size of the regional market and the scope for agglomeration economies, which in turn may reduce the attractiveness of the region to migrant firms.
(3) The labour migrating from a declining region may consist of the younger, more adaptable and skilled component of the regional labour force. The labour that remains may not constitute an attractive labour reserve to new firms contemplating entering the region.
(4) As employment falls the rateable base of the region is also diminished. If the costs of maintaining and renewing public infrastructure cannot be reduced proportionately, the incidence of local rates and taxes falling on the individual business rises, or the quality of public infrastructures and local services falls.

In these circumstances measures to improve the mobility of labour between declining and more prosperous regions may exacerbate the process just described, if unaccompanied by other types of measures. Instead, it has been argued, governmental strategy should be to modify the operation of such short-run disequilibrating forces so that each region can retain its economic and social viability. To achieve this a wider armoury of government measures may be justified – e.g. the use of capital and labour subsidies and selective development controls to stimulate new investment and employment to replace the production and employment that has been lost – provided that the social benefits obtained exceed the social costs of implementation (see section 11.8).

In each of these three interpretations inter-regional disparities in levels of unemployment, *per capita* income and migration are recognised as indicators of inter-regional disequilibrium. *Ceteris paribus,* the greater the differences recorded, the greater is the disequilibrium to be corrected. Where the interpretations differ is in the nature of the responses that they indicate to be justified to resolve the disequilibria. However, it is possible that each interpretation taken by itself is incomplete, whereas taken collectively they may justify a government response that:

(1) takes into account the longer-term economic forces that caused the original disequilibrium and does not attempt to restore regional and urban balance in the form that previously existed;
(2) reduces the spatial imperfections in markets that are responsible for slowness and costliness in the adjustment process; and
(3) uses an array of financial and administrative measures to maintain economically and socially viable regions and cities in declining areas where these can be justified in terms of the benefits and costs involved.

11.6 DEVELOPMENT OF GOVERNMENT POLICY

CENTRAL GOVERNMENT INTERVENTION

The origins of a policy of central government intervention in the location of industry are usually dated from the establishment of the Industrial Transference Board in 1928 and, more particularly, from the passing of the Special Areas Act 1934. The purpose of the Board was to aid the retraining and relocation of the unemployed, whereas the Act was designed to attract establishments in the expanding light industries to specially designated areas of high unemployment by making land and/or factory space available to them. It has generally been agreed that both these measures had a very small influence on unemployment levels in the 1930s.[42, 43] However, the Act was significant because it set the pattern for subsequent policy by designating problem areas for special treatment, promoting additional employment in those areas rather than encouraging the movement of unemployed workers to more prosperous areas, and by restricting assistance to non-service activities.

Following the termination of the Second World War three further measures of importance were enacted. First, the Distribution of Industry Act 1945 redefined the Special Areas and renamed them Development Areas. Within these Development Areas the Board of Trade was empowered to construct factories, to make loans to industrial estate companies, to make provision for basic services, to reclaim derelict land and, under restrictive conditions, to make loans or grants to specific industrial undertakings. Second, the Town and Country Planning Acts 1947 provided that any proposed new industrial development in excess of 5,000 square feet must obtain an Industrial Development Certificate (IDC) from the Board of Trade before planning permission for the development could be granted. This certificate could be withheld at the discretion of the Board of Trade, on the grounds that it would add to or create industrial congestion. In practice this instrument has been used to complement the inducements to set up new factories in Development Areas by adopting a restrictive attitude to the granting of IDCs in the more prosperous regions, notably the South East. Third, the New Towns Act 1946 made provision for the establishment of new towns to reduce congestion and curb the further growth of existing cities, particularly London. These new towns were therefore in competition both with the Development Areas and with major cities for new factories and employment.

A feature of this new legislation was that it left central government with considerable discretion in the degree of firmness with which its location policy was implemented. During the greater part of the 1950s it was enforced with a relatively light hand, partly because of the political philosophy of the government in office but also because unemployment levels, both nationally and regionally, were at historically low levels. From the late 1950s the unemployment situation changed, and the period from then until the early 1960s may be regarded as a transitional period in the switch from a passive to an active policy of government intervention.

The changes in government policy that have subsequently occurred may be summarised in terms of changes in the IDC system, in the geographic areas in which assistance has been given, and in the form and extent of financial assistance that has been available. A number of changes have been made both in the geographic areas in which an IDC is required and in the size of development to which an IDC is applicable; but as mentioned above, of main significance is the degree of severity with which the system has been operated. Moore and Rhodes[35] have attempted to quantify this on the basis of the annual IDC refusal rate, and this supports the view of a tightening of control after 1958, which was relaxed in the early 1970s following a change of government. Additionally, a requirement for office development permits (ODPs) in London and Birmingham was enacted by the Control of Office and Industrial Development Act 1965.

The areas within which assistance has been available have also been redefined on a number of occasions. The Distribution of Industry Act 1958 permitted the Board of Trade to give financial assistance in areas outside Development Areas provided that the local unemployment rate was sufficiently high. The Local Employment Act 1960 abolished the Development Areas and replaced them by smaller Development Districts, which could be scheduled or descheduled according to the level of their unemployment rate. However, the Industrial Development Act 1966 reverted to previous practice in re-establishing the broader-based Development Areas. In 1967 provision was made for the designation of Special Development Areas, the purpose of which was to provide a higher level of assistance in particular problem areas than was available in ordinary Development Areas. Then in 1969, Intermediate Areas were designated, in which certain but not all forms of assistance given to Development Areas were available. Thus, a graduated system of assisted areas has been evolved, as shown in Figure 11.5.

The types of financial assistance that have been available in assisted areas since the early 1960s have related mainly to the acquisition of land, buildings and machinery and to the subsidisation of employment, although considerable assistance has also been given to improving basic infrastructures. Prior to 1960 financial assistance to industry in the acquisition of land, buildings and machinery was limited, discretionary and tied to the creation of additional employment in the assisted areas. In 1960 more generous building grants were introduced, which were standardised in 1963 at 25 per cent of actual construction costs by the Finance Act and Local Employment Act 1963 and later raised to 35 per cent in the case of Special Development Areas. The 1963 legislation also introduced a 10 per cent grant towards the cost of new plant and machinery, to which was added provision for accelerated depreciation on the equipment acquired. This was changed by the Industrial Development Act 1966, which replaced the 1963 arrangements by a system of investment grants on plant and machinery of 40 per cent in Development Areas and of 20 per cent elsewhere. Unlike previous systems these grants were not conditional upon the creation of additional employment. In 1970 this system was briefly abandoned following a change of government, to be later replaced by the more far-reaching Industry Act 1972. This established two types of regional financial assistance:[44]

(1) regional development grants towards new buildings, plant or machinery

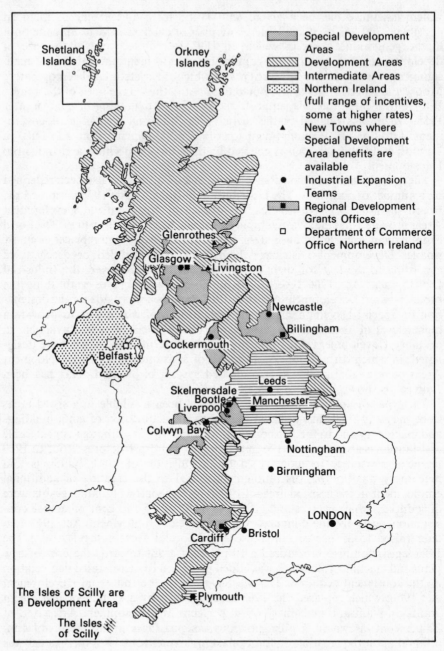

Fig. 11.5 The areas for expansion, 1977.

Source: Department of Industry, *Incentives for Industry in the Areas for Expansion* (London, DOI, 1977) p. 4.

in manufacturing areas located in assisted areas, standardised at 20 per cent in Development Areas and with variations from this level in the other types of assisted area; and

(2) selective financial assistance, not restricted to manufacturing activities, that was conditional upon the creation or protection of employment in the assisted areas.

The extent to which the relative value of the grants that have been available in assisted areas has varied since the early 1960s cannot be easily determined, because account has to be taken of changes in the level of grants in non-assisted areas and in tax allowances and tax rates. However, attempts have been made to estimate the net present value (NPV) of regionally differentiated investment incentives, and these suggest that between 1963 and 1970 this represented 17–20 per cent of new capital expenditure, falling to 10 per cent in 1971 and then rising to approximately 20 per cent immediately following the implementation of the 1972 Act.[45] However, net present value is not necessarily a good indicator of businessmen's assessments of these incentives, given the relative simplicity in the techniques of investment appraisal that many of them use (see Chapter 7). It may be, for example, that the simpler system of incentives introduced in 1966 had a greater impact on investment than the 1963 incentives, even though the latter had a slightly higher net present value.

The financial incentives described so far have been in the form of capital subsidies; provision for labour subsidies only dates from 1967 when the regional employment premium (REP) was introduced as part of the selective employment tax system. Under this scheme each employer engaged in manufacturing in a Development or Special Development Area was eligible to receive a fixed weekly sum for each worker he employed; this was initially approximately £2 in the case of a male adult worker. In 1971 it was announced that REP would be phased out and after a stay of execution it was terminated at the end of 1976.

With the establishment of the Regional Development Fund by the EEC in 1975 grants became available from the European Commission to member states, of up to 30 per cent of public expenditure on eligible projects in the assisted areas. According to the provisions of the Fund a member state may choose either to use Fund assistance to supplement aid granted to the particular capital investment by public authorities or to retain it as a partial repayment of this aid. To date member states have always chosen the second alternative, and to this extent the Fund has simply been used to assist each member state in financing its own distribution of industry policy. However, it is the longer term goal of the European Commission to co-ordinate the regional policies of member states; therefore, it may play a more active role in distribution of industry policy in the future. Additionally, loans are available on favourable terms for eligible projects in the assisted areas from the European Investment Bank and the European Coal and Steel Community.[44]

REGIONAL AND LOCAL GOVERNMENT INTERVENTION

The attempt to broaden location of industry policy into a policy of regional planning is usually dated from the publication in 1963 of two White Papers on employment problem areas in central Scotland and northeastern England.[46] McCrone has described the purpose of these documents in the following terms:

> . . . to create an economic environment conducive to growth in each of their problem areas. To this end the programmes promised to co-ordinate and increase public investment expenditures in their areas. Growth areas were selected . . . and these would be especially favoured by this expenditure on infrastructure and services. These, it was thought, offered the best locations for sound economic expansion.[47]

In 1965 the United Kingdom was divided into a number of regions, and for each a Regional Economic Council and Regional Economic Planning Board was established. The members of each council, who are appointed by central government, represent the industrial and other interests of the region that they serve; the members of each board are civil servants from various government departments, who work in the regions. The main function of the councils is to assist in formulating regional plans and to advise on their implementation, while the boards co-ordinate the work of government departments concerned with regional planning and development.

The councils mainly discharge their planning function by preparing Regional Strategies. These identify the main problems that a region faces, indicate the most suitable future distribution of population and industry, provide for the general improvement of the regional environment and indicate the means by which the strategies may be best achieved. The impact of these strategies, and of the work of the councils and boards more generally, on the location of industry is difficult to assess. Unquestionably, their influence has been restricted since councils are appointed rather than elected, except in the new regional councils in Scotland, and since their powers are advisory. Their influence has largely been indirect and has operated in two main directions: on the regional distribution of public sector investment, and on the plan-making activities of local government authorities.

Under a long-established system of town and country planning all new industrial developments, extensions to existing developments and major changes in the use of premises require planning permission from the local planning authority.[48] In deciding whether or not to grant permission the planning authority will take into consideration whether the proposed development is likely to comply with any existing development plans for the area. The land use plans that are in force at the present are mainly 'old-style' development plans, which are in the process of being superseded by structure plans (prepared by county councils in England and Wales and by elected regional councils in Scotland) and local plans (prepared by district councils) under the provisions of the Town and Country Planning Acts 1971 and 1972. In addition local authorities also possess powers to acquire properties and to redevelop areas. They may also exercise considerable influence on the pattern of development in an area through municipal-housing, school-building and local road schemes.

The powers that are available to local authorities to influence the pattern of land use in their area are, therefore, very considerable; yet, this has received little attention in industrial location analysis because attention has mainly been focused on the inter-regional movement of industrial activities. However, the recent recognition of the decline in employment, particularly manufacturing employment, in the urban cores has kindled an interest in the ways in which these powers are discharged. Central government has supported a programme of research into the causes of inner city decline[11] and has indicated the policies that it will pursue to deal with these in *Policy for the Inner Cities,* published in 1977.[49] Legislation to facilitate the implementation of these policies was enacted during 1978.[50] Local authorities are also preparing their own industrial strategies to revitalise such areas.[14] Consequently, during the 1960s and 1970s government intervention to influence the distribution of industry has increasingly become a multi-level activity.

11.7 IMPACT OF CENTRAL GOVERNMENT POLICY

A considerable number of studies have now been completed on the impact of central government policies concerned with the location of industry, and these have mainly been concerned with three issues:

(1) the impact of policies on the volume of employment or the number of plant movements in the assisted areas;
(2) the impact on central government net revenue; and
(3) broader social cost and benefit impacts.

Each issue is now examined in turn.

THE IMPACT ON EMPLOYMENT AND PLANT MOVEMENTS

In one of the more detailed studies on this subject,[35] Moore and Rhodes have tried to estimate the total impact of the government's distribution of industry policy and the contributory impacts of its main constituents during the period 1960–71, later updated to 1976.[72] Their findings have subsequently been questioned on methodological grounds; therefore, it is necessary to review their method of analysis as well as their results.

In brief, their approach was to assess the *expected* change in manufacturing employment in the Development Areas, in the absence of the policy measures introduced during the 1960s, and to compare this with the *actual* change in manufacturing employment during this decade. This involved taking account of the impact on employment change of the main differences in industrial composition between Development Areas and the United Kingdom as a whole, using a shift-share technique, and of variations in the pressure of demand in the economy as a whole, *before* estimating the impact of regional policy. The differences between expected and actual employment in each year were then related to the particular policy measures in force at the time in order to establish the relative contribution of each measure to the total number of jobs created or saved. Supplementary tests, such as the use of regression analysis to estimate the number of new factory openings in the Development Areas that was attributable to the different policy measures, were also used. The results obtained may be summarised as follows:

(1) The total policy impact on employment in all the manufacturing industries in all the Development Areas during 1960–71 was approximately 250,000, which in turn may have generated additional service employment of 50,000. This is equivalent to approximately 10 per cent of total employment in the Development Areas in 1977.
(2) During the same period regional policy was responsible for the opening of approximately 800 new factories, generating approximately 150,000 jobs, the remaining jobs being generated in existing establishments.
(3) Of the 150,000 jobs created in *new* factories, the distribution between policy instruments was as shown in Table 11.14.
(4) The effect of REP in both existing and new factories may have been to create up to 50,000 jobs, when its impact was at a maximum.
(5) Between 1971 and 1976 the impact of regional policy on employment was smaller than during the second half of the 1960s, and this was partly due to the less stringent application of IDC controls and to reductions in the real value of certain financial incentives – i.e. REP and, for part of the early 1970s, capital subsidies.

Moore and Rhodes have acknowledged that their results are tentative and subject to the usual limitations of statistical studies of this kind. However, they have considered their findings sufficiently well based to conclude that distribution of industry policy during this period had a very considerable impact on manufacturing plant location and employment in the Development Areas and, more particularly, that REP at its peak had a substantial influence on employment levels. However, some writers have criticised these conclusions, as follows:

(1) Ashcroft and Taylor[34] have questioned the use of the unemployment rate, in the Moore–Rhodes model, to measure the pressure of demand. Instead, they have used an index of spare capacity and found the total policy impact on plant movements, although still substantial, to be reduced by between one-third and one-half. They have also found measures

Table 11.14 *Impact on employment of distribution of industry policy, 1960–71.*

Policy instrument	Total jobs, 1960–71	Annual average
Additional impact of IDC policy, 1960–71	75,000	6,250
Investment incentives (8 years)	47,000	5,875
REP (4 years)	14,000–21,000	3,500–5,250
Special Development Area designation (4 years)	0–10,000	0–2,500

Source: B. C. Moore and J. Rhodes, 'A quantitative analysis of the effects of the regional employment premium and other regional policy instruments', in A. Whiting (ed.), *The Economics of Industrial Subsidies* (London, HMSO, 1976), pp. 191–219.

of the relative importance of different policy instruments to be very sensitive to the specification of the model used.

(2) The shift-share correction factor used in the Moore–Rhodes model has been criticised by Buck and Atkins.[51] The use of a finer industrial-classification system in the analysis has caused them to doubt that the policy impact was greater after 1967 when subsidies were no longer conditional on employment creation.

(3) Statistically, it is not possible to distinguish reliably between the impact of REP and of the creation of Special Development Areas since both commenced at the same time. Some writers, e.g. MacKay,[52] have believed that Moore and Rhodes may have overestimated the REP impact through undervaluing the impact of Special Development Area status.

In the case of a number of the disputed points an element of judgement is unavoidable in reaching a conclusion. Therefore, given the political and policy significance of the issues concerned, it is likely that the debate on the impact of these policy instruments will continue.

THE IMPACT ON CENTRAL GOVERNMENT NET REVENUE

A number of studies have attempted to assess the financial implications to the National Exchequer of the implementation of distribution of industry policies.[53–55] Such studies have served the useful purpose of drawing attention to the financial benefits to the Exchequer of saving or creating employment in the assisted areas, since this saves payments of unemployment benefits and national assistance and enables the Exchequer to obtain tax revenues on the extra income created. For example, Needleman and Scott have estimated that during 1960–3 the government received a net financial gain from its distribution of industry policies of £900 for every workless person that it employed.[54] However, such measures of impact need to be treated with a measure of caution. First, they are often sensitive to the estimate of the number of jobs created; and as indicated above, the extent to which jobs have been created is a subject of continuing debate. Second, the financial benefit to the government of these policies is to be distinguished from their net social benefit to the national community, which is the more appropriate criterion by which such policies should eventually be judged.

SOCIAL COST–BENEFIT IMPACT

In view of the conclusion reached above it has been suggested that the impact of distribution-of-industry policy should be evaluated within the framework of social cost–benefit analysis[56] (see section 10.4). This technique was developed for individual project rather than policy or plan assessment, but it may be of use in the present context. The types of impacts that may arise from government policies that cause plant movements into assisted areas are listed in Table 11.15. This table could be extended to include impacts associated with the protection or increase of employment in existing establishments in the assisted areas. The construction of the format of such social 'balance sheets' is a relatively

Table 11.15 *Social benefits and costs of distribution-of-industry policies.*

Benefits	Costs
(1) Labour and capital income directly attributable to the jobs created	(5) Costs of administering distribution-of-industry policies
(2) Multiplier effects: (a) income multiplier effect (b) agglomeration externality effect	(6) Movement costs in relocating plant in assisted areas
(3) Resource costs avoided by forestalling outward migration	(7) Social opportunity cost of additional infrastructure provided in assisted areas
(4) Other social costs avoided by creating employment and forestalling outward migration	(8) Costs of a continuing nature resulting from accepting a higher cost location than would otherwise have been chosen

straightforward exercise, but there are considerable measurement and interpretation problems associated with estimating the particular items included, as illustrated below.

Benefits
(1)   Labour and capital income associated with job creation in the assisted areas can only be fully credited as a social benefit to the extent that the jobs have been created by the distribution-of-industry policy and not some other factor and that no opportunity cost has been incurred in their use, i.e. that those taking the jobs would otherwise have been unemployed. A deficiency in the early estimates of the additional employment due to distribution-of-industry policies was that they failed to distinguish the employment that would have been attracted to the assisted areas in the absence of such policies and the employment that replaced jobs previously existing there. Studies of the Moore–Rhodes kind, described above, are designed to overcome this deficiency; but as already mentioned, their estimates of job creation are also in dispute.
(2)   The reliability of the estimate of the local income-multiplier effect is obviously dependent on the reliability of the estimate of the initial labour- and capital-income injection described above. The agglomerative effect, i.e. the beneficial effect of policy through preserving or strengthening interindustry linkages in the assisted areas, is difficult to measure and, therefore, tends to be ignored.
(3)   The resource costs avoided by forestalling outward migration are dependent on the estimate of the number of jobs saved, discussed above, and of the level of *per capita* personal- and public-resource costs avoided. Estimates of the public resource costs avoided are sensitive to the assumptions made about the existence of spare infrastructure capacity in potential destination areas. Care is also needed to avoid the double

counting of items in this category and category 1 above. If labour were to move to a more prosperous region, incurring the costs described in this section, then it might cease to be unemployed, and *in such circumstances* category 1 income should not also be included as a benefit.

(4) The less tangible and therefore less measurable social costs of unemployment and/or outward migration – such as, in the latter case, impacts on the social structure of the community and on the lifestyles of its members – tend to have been ignored in formal analyses of this kind, although their general importance to policy is acknowledged.

Costs

(5) The costs of administering distribution-of-industry policies may include administrative costs, largely falling on government departments, and the capital costs of the various incentives supplied. The second item should only be included where it involves a social opportunity cost, i.e. if alternative public- or private-sector investment or consumption opportunities are pre-empted as a consequence, and where it does not lead to the double counting of other cost items, listed below.

(6) and (7) Movement costs comprise 'starting-up' costs, e.g. the costs of training labour and moving key personnel, in excess of those which would have been incurred in the absence of government policy. Estimates are available on total movement costs,[56] but there is difficulty in determining the proportion of these that is attributable to distribution-of-industry policy. Similar difficulties arise in establishing the proportion of infrastructure expenditure in assisted areas that is attributable to this policy.

(8) The determination of this social cost item is probably the most contentious of all. If it could be assumed that firms act as if they wish to maximise profits and that this is achieved by locating in least cost sites – a simplified version of the neoclassical model outlined in section 11.3 – then the average increase in costs for plants persuaded to locate in assisted areas might be estimated as 50 per cent of the governmental financial inducements received. Part of the cost increase would be in the form of its 'starting-up' costs, already included. However, this percentage figure could be an underestimate where the IDC system had 'compelled' plant movements, even where these were financially disadvantageous after taking the incentives into account. On the other hand, counterarguments suggest that this percentage figure may be an overestimate. As indicated in sections 11.3 and 11.4, there are both theoretical and empirical objections to the view that, in the absence of these government measures, firms will select sites where their production costs are at a minimum. Indeed, surveys seem to indicate that the cost differences between original and new sites are usually small, once the settling-in period has passed, and that in a number of cases cost levels at the new sites are eventually lower.[22]

Given these various difficulties it is not surprising that the small number of social cost–benefit studies of distribution-of-industry policy that have been attempted have obtained results that are very sensitive to the assumptions made on the contentious issues already described. Therefore, the social cost–benefit approach cannot yet be used to determine unambiguously whether this policy, in its present form, enhances community welfare. Equally, it cannot be used to compare the relative merits of the different instruments used within this policy, in terms of the particular costs and benefits for which they are responsible. Therefore, such a comparative evaluation, which is the subject of the next section, inevitably involves a significant element of personal judgement.

11.8   POLICY INSTRUMENTS: COMPARATIVE EVALUATION

Distribution-of-industry policy, under a variety of different names, has now existed in Britain for half a century. During this period many different policy instruments have been tried, and many others have been advocated. Therefore, in concluding this chapter an attempt is made to review the main policy options and the issues surrounding their possible use. These issues are discussed below in the following order: manufacturing or total activity intervention; labour or plant mobility; stick or carrot policies; capital subsidies; labour subsidies; infrastructure investment; and integrated spatial planning. The chapter ends with guidance on further reading.

POLICY INSTRUMENTS

Manufacturing or Total Activity Intervention
For the greater part of the last half-century, distribution-of-industry policy has been restricted to industrial, principally manufacturing, establishments and employment in respect both to IDC controls and to financial incentive systems in the assisted areas. This has only recently been modified to the extent that ODP controls over office developments were enacted in 1965 and selective financial assistance to certain categories of service activity were made available during the 1970s. The justification for the difference in treatment between manufacturing and service activities appears to lie in the greater likelihood that the former will 'export' their products to other areas and generate further income and employment in the assisted areas. However, some service industries – notably tourism and higher educational establishments – also export their output. Also, the extent to which a new establishment generates additional local income and employment depends less upon whether it engages in manufacturing or service activities than upon its relation to existing inter-industry linkages in the area. Therefore, the recent tendency to broaden the base of distribution-of-industry policy to include service activities may merit reinforcement. This is particularly the case, given that service activities have become the major source of new employment in the economy; and the urban cores in particular, which have been experiencing serious employment problems, are now very dependent on service employment.[12, 14, 59, 60]

Labour or Plant Mobility
One interpretation of the regional problem is that inter-regional inequalities are temporary phenomena that are self-rectifying provided that inter-regional

factor mobility is sufficiently high (section 11.5). This interpretation has been used to justify a series of measures to encourage labour mobility, i.e. 'taking the workers to the work',[57] such as employment information and retraining schemes and financial assistance with travel and removal expenses. This approach has been criticised for failing to take sufficient account of the social congestion created in the labour-receiving areas and of the harmful effect on the viability of the local economy that unemployed workers are encouraged to leave.[41, 58] More recently, mobility instruments have been extended to include assistance with the movement costs[44] incurred by establishments prepared to locate in the assisted areas; this facilitates the mobility of capital and enterprise into areas of above average unemployment.

Stick or Carrot Policies
There has also been considerable debate over the merits of administrative controls (e.g. the IDC system), which can 'force' a different location decision from that which would otherwise have been chosen, relative to financial incentives (e.g. regional investment grants), which 'induce' a change in location decisions. The IDC system has been a major influence on the number of plant moves into the assisted areas, and from the standpoint of the Exchequer it is a financially attractive instrument of government policy (section 11.7). The criticisms of the system concern the hidden costs for which it may be responsible. For example, some plants may not be established anywhere in the country as a result of IDC controls, or they may be established in locations where their long run costs are higher than would otherwise be the case. However, the available evidence seems to indicate that in general these hidden costs have not been very substantial (section 11.7) and that in some cases the control system may have resulted in firms choosing more suitable locations than would otherwise have been the case (section 11.4). Despite this reassurance some doubt remains as to whether the implementation of IDC and ODP controls is sufficiently informed and discriminating.[61] The need for such qualities in the implementation of controls is particularly evident in city cores, including those in the prosperous regions, where the problems of decline in employment coexist with the problems of urban congestion, which such controls have traditionally sought to alleviate.

Capital Subsidies
Direct financial incentives to industry have mainly taken the form of subsidies in the acquisition of industrial buildings, plant and machinery. In some cases the subsidy has taken the form of a tax allowance rather than an investment grant; at times it has been linked to the creation of employment rather than been automatic.[44]

Much of the debate relating to the different forms of capital subsidy has concerned their relative efficiency in creating employment. For example, it has been argued that investment grants are more likely to be effective than equivalent tax allowances because they are more easily understood by businessmen. However, more large companies now take tax allowances into account in investment appraisal (Chapter 7), and econometric evidence indicates that both investment and employment levels are to some extent sensitive to changes in tax allowances.[59, 62] The linking of financial assistance to the condition of employment creation not only increases the administrative complexity of the system but also raises the more basic issue of what constitutes employment creation. To provide financial assistance for the *creation* of new jobs but deny it where it could *safeguard* existing jobs would seem inconsistent. However, the latter is even more difficult to authenticate in practice than the former and adds to the problem of administrative complexity already mentioned.

At a more fundamental level the whole system of capital subsidies has been criticised – in the absence of comparable labour subsidies, discussed below – on the grounds that it introduces a bias in capital intensity in the industrial activities located in the assisted areas. This, it has been suggested, is an undesirable feature in a policy primarily intended to increase labour employment in the assisted areas. The practical importance of this bias has been examined by Moore and Rhodes, who have reached the following conclusion:

> Firstly, there is evidence that a high proportion of capital subsidies are paid to capital intensive firms and that some of these capital intensive plants have been diverted by high capital subsidies into Development Areas. Secondly, it is also argued that capital subsidies promote capital substitution so that all firms are more capital intensive than they would otherwise be. We can find little evidence to support this second contention either at national or regional level.[63]

More speculatively, it has been argued in favour of capital subsidies that, in attracting capital-intensive enterprises from the faster-growing industries, they have introduced progressive and innovative activities into the assisted areas, which should have a demonstration effect on existing enterprises and stimulate these to greater technical progressiveness and efficiency.

Labour Subsidies

The only significant attempt to use labour subsidies as an instrument of distribution-of-industry policy in Britain has been the use of REP during 1967–76. Shortly before it was introduced it was anticipated that it would have a very substantial effect, resulting eventually in halving the disparity in unemployment rates between the Development Areas and the rest of the country.[64] In fact, even if the most optimistic estimates are accepted,[35] it is clear that its impact has fallen well below expectations, although this may be partly due to the reduction in its real value through inflation and to uncertainty about its future continuance. It has been criticised on the grounds that it was available to all manufacturing establishments in the Development Areas 'whether new or old, expanding or contracting, progressive or asleep'.[73] Although this is also a feature of the main capital grants, in these cases there is at least the minimum assurance that firms are sufficiently progressive to contemplate expansion or re-equipment, whereas there was no corresponding assurance in the case of REP.

Notwithstanding the disappointments with REP, the potential weakness of a distribution-of-industry policy that only uses capital subsidies as financial incentives to relieve unemployment and improve the deployment of resources within assisted areas is all too apparent. Some writers have moved to the opposite extreme in arguing for a system of payroll taxes and subsidies as the sole instrument of distribution-of-industry policy. In 1964 Clark and Peters[65] proposed a system whereby the subsidy or tax varied as a percentage of payroll according to the level of urban and regional congestion and of unemployment. This would have resulted in a 21 per cent payroll tax in some London boroughs and a 17 per cent payroll subsidy in the Shetlands. By contrast, Hutton and Hartley's payroll tax system was based upon three variables: the target rate of national unemployment, the local unemployment rate and the ratio of plant labour costs to total costs by plant and by area.[66] In view of the theoretical arguments in its favour it seems that the possibility of a new form of labour subsidy, possibly better tailored to welfare as well as to unemployment objectives in assisted areas, should not be ruled out for the future.

Regional Infrastructure Investment

Since the early 1960s there has been some attempt to alleviate the regional problem by additional investment in public infrastructure in the assisted areas, to remedy deficiencies in their transport facilities and to improve the quality of their social capital. The justification of this strategy lies in the apparent significance of adequate transport facilities and a good environmental quality for the location decisions made by firms (section 11.4). However, because of the difficulty in measuring the size of the regional bias in infrastructure investment and the indirect effect that this has on location decisions, it is not possible to assess its practical importance in present policy. From a welfare standpoint the direction of policy to the once-and-for-all correction of inherited deficiencies in regional infrastructures has a certain attraction when compared with a continuing system of capital subsidies on plant and machinery. However, Brown has suggested that the role of this policy instrument may be as a permissive rather than a sufficient condition of growth.[67] In other words, it may help to create the basic economic conditions in assisted areas in which the more specific capital and other incentives can then become more fully effective.

Integrated Spatial Planning

A recurring criticism of distribution-of-industry policy in Britain has been the failure to develop an integrated strategy involving the different levels of government and the different policy instruments at their disposal. Governmental thinking first moved in this direction in the early 1960s when it was suggested that the problems of the peripheral regions might be resolved by a more systematic attempt to promote the expansion of 'growth centres' in these regions.[68] This notion of a growth centre owed much to the growth pole philosophy developed from work by Perroux. A growth pole is:

... a set of industries capable of generating dynamic growth in the economy, and strongly interrelated to each other via input–output linkages around a leading industry. This industry and its interdependent sectors grow faster than the rest of the economy because of advanced technological practice and high innovation rates, high income elasticities of demand for their products, sale to nation-wide markets, and large spillover and multiplier effects on other segments of the economy.[69]

This approach implies that government authorities should be selective, both in their choice of areas for expansion and in the activities that they attract to the areas. In fact the expectation that an integrated strategy, based upon the growth centre approach, would be prepared and then implemented in Britain has largely been unrealised for the following reasons.

First, international experience in the implementation of growth pole strategies has to date been discouraging. This has been attributed to a variety of factors, such as: the lack of clear policy objectives; the inadequate understanding of the interindustry linkages involved in the strategy; the bluntness of the policy instruments used; political opposition from other areas; and the failure to sustain the strategy over a sufficient length of time.[70] Consequently, the enthusiasm for growth centres has been reduced during the 1970s, although the basic intellectual appeal of such a type of strategy is undiminished.

Second, the required degree of multilevel government co-ordination in the implementation of location strategies has not yet been achieved. This has been noticeable, for example, in the lack of co-ordination between the implementation of the IDC system by the Department of Industry – previously the Board of Trade – and the plan implementation and development control system operated by local planning authorities.

However, factors now operating indicate that a more co-ordinated approach to the spatial planning of industrial activities may emerge in the future. These include:

(1) The emergence of the urban core problem, which has highlighted the need for distribution-of-industry policies that differentiate between areas and activities *within* regions as well as *between* regions;[13, 14, 49]
(2) the development of a new hierarchy of land use plans (i.e. regional strategies, structure plans, local plans), which should provide a multilevel planning framework within which a more systematic approach to the implementation of distribution-of-industry policy may be achieved[48] – this could be further strengthened if the sectoral strategies evolved at national level (see section 9.4) were given a spatial dimension and linked to the above planning framework; and
(3) the increased involvement of local authorities, in partnership with central government agencies, in the implementation of development strategies for local areas, particularly in the inner cities.[14, 49]

While these factors should strengthen the organisational framework within which more integrated spatial planning takes place, the results obtained could be disappointing if this were not accompanied by a clearer expression of the welfare objectives of distribution-of-industry policy[71] and by a better understanding of the structural basis of the urban and subregional areas to be revived[70] and of the contribution that different policy instruments can make to this end.

FURTHER READING

A further examination of many of the locational and policy issues raised in this chapter can be found in Richardson.[4] The main empirical studies of the location decision are reviewed in Keeble[2] and Sant.[22] The nature and extent of the regional problem, together with the policy instruments used to tackle the problem, are examined in: Brown;[5] Brown and Burrows;[40] Hallett, Randall and West;[57] and the House of Commons Expenditure Committee.[61] The changing nature of the regional problem, the emergence of the urban problem and the policy implications of these are discussed in Manners[13] and *Policy for the Inner Cities*.[49] A further appreciation of the controversies involved in assessing the impacts on employment of distribution-of-industry policies may be obtained from the contributions of Moore and Rhodes and of MacKay in Whiting's *The Economics of Industrial Subsidies*,[35] while the difficulties involved in estimating the impact of these policies on community welfare can be studied further in Schofield.[56]

NOTES AND REFERENCES

1 C. H. Lee, *Regional Economic Growth in the UK since the 1880s* (London, McGraw-Hill, 1971).

2 D. E. Keeble, *Industrial Location and Planning in Britain* (London, Methuen, 1976).

3 Keeble, op. cit. (n. 2), pp. 14–15.

4 H. W. Richardson, *Regional and Urban Economics* (Harmondsworth, Penguin Books, 1978), pp. 202*ff*.

5 A. J. Brown, *The Framework of Regional Economics in the United Kingdom* (Cambridge, Cambridge UP, 1972).

6 R. J. Dixon and A. P. Thirlwall, *Regional Growth and Unemployment in the United Kingdom* (London, Macmillan, 1975), ch. 8.

7 F. J. B. Stilwell, 'Regional growth and structural adaptation', *Urban Studies*, vol. 6 (1969), pp. 162–78.

8 Department of the Environment, *British Cities: Urban Population and Employment Trends, 1951–71*, Research Report 10 (London, DOE, 1976).

9 E. S. Mills, *Urban Economics* (Glenview, Ill., Scott, Foresman, 1972), chs 2 and 8.

10 G. C. Cameron and A. W. Evans, 'The British conurbation centres', *Regional Studies*, vol. 7 (1973), pp. 47–55.

11 Department of the Environment, *Inner Area Studies* (London, HMSO, 1977).

12 P. W. Daniels, 'Office location in the British conurbations: trends and strategies', *Urban Studies*, vol. 14 (1977), pp. 261–74.

13 G. Manners, 'Reinterpreting the regional problem', *Three Banks Review*, no. 111 (1976), pp. 33–55.

14 A. R. Townsend, 'The relationship of inner city problems to regional policy', *Regional Studies*, vol. 11 (1977), pp. 225–51.

15 Richardson, op. cit. (n. 4), ch. 3.

16 P. Mathias, *The First Industrial Nation* (London, Methuen, 1969), pp. 132*ff*.

17 D. L. Burn (ed.), *The Structure of British Industry*, 2 vols (Cambridge, Cambridge UP, 1958), Vol. 1, ch. 7.

18 Mills, op. cit. (n. 9), ch. 3.

19 Richardson, op. cit. (n. 4), ch. 11.

20 H. W. Richardson, *Regional Economics: Location Theory, Urban Structure and Regional Change* (London, Weidenfeld & Nicolson, 1969), ch. 4.

21 P. M. Townroe, *Industrial Location Decisions* (Birmingham, University of Birmingham, 1971).

22 M. C. Sant, *Industrial Movement and Regional Development: The British Case* (Oxford, Pergamon, 1975).

23 Sant, op. cit. (n. 22), pp. 40–51.

24 Townroe, op. cit. (n. 21), p. 55.

25 Townroe, op. cit. (n. 21), pp. 64–5.

26 Townroe, op. cit. (n. 21), p. 69.

27 W. F. Luttrell, *Factory Location and Industrial Movement,* Vol. 1 (London, National Institute for Economic and Social Research, 1962), p. 79.

28 M. L. Greenhut, *Plant Location in Theory and Practice* (Chapel Hill, University of North Carolina, 1967), pt 3.

29 F. E. I. Hamilton (ed.), *Spatial Perspectives on Industrial Organisation and Decision-Making* (London, Wiley, 1974), pp. 13–16.

30 F. Machlup, 'Marginal analysis and empirical research', *American Economic Review,* vol. 36 (1946), pp. 519–54.

31 M. Friedman, *Essays in Positive Economics* (Chicago, Chicago UP, 1953), ch. 1.

32 W. R. Latham, *Location Behavior in Manufacturing Industries* (Leiden, Martinus Nijhoff, 1976).

33 J. A. Chalmers and T. L. Beckhelm, 'Shift and share and the theory of industrial location', *Regional Studies,* vol. 10 (1976), pp. 15–23.

34 B. Ashcroft and J. Taylor, 'The movement of manufacturing industry and the effect of regional policy', *Oxford Economic Papers,* vol. 29 (1977), pp. 84–101.

35 B. C. Moore and J. Rhodes, 'A quantitative analysis of the effects of the regional employment premium and other regional policy instruments', in A. Whiting (ed.), *The Economics of Industrial Subsidies* (London, HMSO, 1976), pp. 191–219. See also B. C. Moore and J. Rhodes, 'Regional economic policy and the movement of manufacturing firms to development areas', *Economica,* vol. 43 (1976), pp. 17–31.

36 Brown, op. cit. (n. 5), pp. 215–31.

37 Brown, op. cit. (n. 5), pp. 205–14.

38 Brown, op. cit. (n. 5), p. 81.

39 E. A. G. Robinson (ed.), *Backward Areas in Advanced Countries* (London, Macmillan, 1969).

40 A. J. Brown and E. M. Burrows, *Regional Economic Problems: Comparative Experiences of Some Market Economies* (London, Allen & Unwin, 1977).

41 N. Kaldor, 'The case for regional policies', *Scottish Journal of Political Economy,* vol. 17 (1970), pp. 337–47.

42 Brown, op. cit. (n. 5), pp. 281–7.

43 G. McCrone, *Regional Policy in Britain* (London, Allen & Unwin, 1969), pt 2.

44 Department of Industry, *Incentives for Industry in the Areas for Expansion* (London, DOI, annual).

45 C. L. Melliss and P. W. Richardson, 'Value of investment incentives for manufacturing industry, 1946–74', in Whiting, op. cit. (n. 35).

46 *Central Scotland: A Programme for Development and Growth,* Cmnd 2188 (London, HMSO, 1963); and *The North-East: A Programme for Development and Growth,* Cmnd 2206 (London, HMSO, 1963).

47 McCrone, op. cit. (n. 43), p. 225.

48 J. B. Cullingworth, *Town and Country Planning in the United Kingdom,* 6th edn (London, Allen & Unwin, 1976).

49 *Policy for the Inner Cities,* Cmnd 6845 (London, HMSO, 1977).

50 Inner Urban Areas Act, 1978.

51 T. W. Buck and M. H. Atkins, 'The impact of British regional policies on employment growth', *Oxford Economic Papers*, vol. 28 (1976), pp. 118–32.

52 R. R. MacKay, 'The impact of the regional employment premium', in Whiting, op. cit. (n. 35), pp. 225–44.

53 National Economic Development Council (NEDC), *Conditions Favourable to Economic Growth* (London, HMSO, 1963).

54 L. Needleman and B. Scott, 'Regional problems and location of industry policy in Britain', *Urban Studies*, vol. 1 (1964), pp. 153–73.

55 B. C. Moore and J. Rhodes, *Economic and Exchequer Implications of Regional Policy: House of Commons Expenditure Committee (Trade and Industry Sub-Committee), Minutes of Evidence, Session 1972–3* (London, HMSO, 1973).

56 J. A. Schofield, 'Economic efficiency and regional policy', *Urban Studies*, vol. 13 (1976), pp. 181–92.

57 H. W. Richardson and E. G. West, 'Must we always take work to the workers?', *Lloyds Bank Review*, no. 71 (1964), pp. 21–32; and G. Hallett, P. Randall and E. G. West, *Regional Policy for Ever?*, IEA Readings No. 11 (London, Institute of Economic Affairs, 1973).

58 Richardson, op. cit. (n. 4), pp. 233–7.

59 J. Rhodes and A. Kan, *Office Dispersal and Regional Policy* (Cambridge, Cambridge UP, 1971).

60 J. B. Goddard, *Office Location in Urban and Regional Development* (London, Oxford UP, 1975).

61 House of Commons Expenditure Committee, *Regional Development Incentives Report* (London, HMSO, 1974).

62 A. J. Corner and A. Williams, 'The sensitivity of businesses to initial and investment allowances', *Economica*, vol. 32 (1965), pp. 32–47; R. Agarwala and G. C. Goodson, 'An analysis of the effects of investment incentives on investment behaviour in GB', *Economica*, vol. 36 (1969), pp. 377–88.

63 Moore and Rhodes in Whiting, op. cit. (n. 35), p. 218.

64 Department of Economic Affairs, *The Development Areas: A Proposal for a Regional Employment Premium* (London, HMSO, 1967).

65 C. Clark and G. H. Peters, 'Steering employment by taxes and subsidies', *Town and Country Planning*, vol. 32 (1964), pp. 145–9.

66 J. P. Hutton and K. Hartley, 'A regional payroll tax', *Oxford Economic Papers*, vol. 20 (1968), pp. 417–26.

67 Brown, op. cit. (n. 5), pp. 314–5.

68 McCrone, op. cit. (n. 43), ch. 10.

69 Richardson, op. cit. (n. 4), p. 165.

70 Richardson, op. cit. (n. 4), ch. 7.

71 Richardson, op. cit. (n. 4), pp. 221–33.

72 B. C. Moore, J. Rhodes and P. Tyler, 'The impact of regional policy in the 1970s', *Centre for Environmental Studies Review*, vol. 1 (1977), pp. 67–77.

73 Whiting, op. cit. (n. 35), p. 218.

Index